Distributed Artificial Intelligence, Agent Technology, and Collaborative Applications

Vijayan Sugumaran
Oakland University, USA

INFORMATION SCIENCE REFERENCE

Hershey · New York

Director of Editorial Content: Kristin Klinger
Assistant Development Editor: Deborah Yahnke
Director of Production: Jennifer Neidig
Managing Editor: Jamie Snavely
Assistant Managing Editor: Carole Coulson
Typesetter: Carole Coulson
Cover Design: Lisa Tosheff
Printed at: Yurchak Printing Inc.

Published in the United States of America by
Information Science Reference (an imprint of IGI Global)
701 E. Chocolate Avenue, Suite 200
Hershey PA 17033
Tel: 717-533-8845
Fax: 717-533-8661
E-mail: cust@igi-global.com
Web site: http://www.igi-global.com

and in the United Kingdom by
Information Science Reference (an imprint of IGI Global)
3 Henrietta Street
Covent Garden
London WC2E 8LU
Tel: 44 20 7240 0856
Fax: 44 20 7379 0609
Web site: http://www.eurospanbookstore.com

Library of Congress Cataloging-in-Publication Data

Distributed artificial intelligence : agent technology and collaborative applications / Vijayan Sugumaran, editor.

p. cm. -- (Information science reference)

Includes bibliographical references and index.

Summary: "This book is a catalyst for emerging research in intelligent information, specifically artificial intelligent technologies and applications to assist in improving productivity in many roles such as assistants to human operators and autonomous decision-making components of complex systems"--Provided by publisher.

ISBN 978-1-60566-144-5 (hardcover) -- ISBN 978-1-60566-145-2 (ebook)

1. Distributed artificial intelligence. 2. Artificial intelligence--Industrial applications. I. Sugumaran, Vijayan, 1960-

Q337.D577 2009

006.3--dc22

2008023190

British Cataloguing in Publication Data
A Cataloguing in Publication record for this book is available from the British Library.

Distributed Artificial Intelligence, Agent Technology, and Collaborative Applications is part of the IGI Global series named *Advances in Intelligent Information Technologies (AIIT)* Series, ISBN: 1935-3375

Advances in Intelligent Information Technologies Series (AIIT)

ISBN: 1935-3375

Editor-in-Chief: Vijay Sugumaran, Oakland University, USA

Distributed Artificial Intelligence, Agent Technology, and Collaborative Applications

Information Science Reference • copyright 2008 • 314pp • H/C (ISBN: 978-1-60566-144-5) • US $195.00(our price)

Cutting-edge developments in artificial intelligence are now driving applications that are only hinting at the level of value they will soon contribute to organizations, consumers, and societies across all domains. Distributed Artificial Intelligence, Agent Technology, and Collaborative Applications offers an enriched set of research articles in artificial intelligence (AI), covering significant AI subjects such as information retrieval, conceptual modeling, supply chain demand forecasting, and machine learning algorithms. This comprehensive collection provides libraries with a one-stop resource to equip the academic, industrial, and managerial communities with an in-depth look into the most pertinent AI advances that will lead to the most valuable applications.

Application of Agents and Intelligent Information Technologies

IGI Publishing • copyright 2007 • 377 pp • H/C (ISBN: 1-59904-265-7) • US $89.96 (our price) • E-Book (ISBN: 1-59904-267-3) • US $68.76 (our price)

Intelligent agent technology is emerging as one of the most important and rapidly advancing areas. Researchers are developing a number of agent-based applications and multi-agent systems in a variety of fields, such as: electronic commerce, supply chain management, resource allocation, intelligent manufacturing, mass customization, industrial control, information retrieval and filtering, collaborative work, mobile commerce, decision support, and computer games. Application of Agents and Intelligent Information Technologies presents an outstanding collection of the latest research associated with intelligent agents and information technologies. Application of Agents and Intelligent Information Technologies provides a comprehensive analysis of issues related to agent design, implementation, integration, deployment, evaluation, and business value. This book presents research results and application of agents and other intelligent information technologies in various domains. Application of Agents and Intelligent Information Technologies offers the intelligent information technologies that will potentially revolutionize the work environment as well as social computing.

Intelligent Information Technologies and Applications

IGI Publishing • copyright 2007 • 300+ pp •H/C (ISBN: 978-1-59904-958-8) • US $99.95 (our price)

With the inundation of emergent online- and Web-centered technologies, there has been an increased focus on intelligent information technologies that are designed to enable users to accomplish complex tasks with relative ease. Intelligent Information Technologies and Applications provides cutting-edge research on the modeling; implementation; and financial, environmental, and organizational implications of this dynamic topic to researchers and practitioners in fields such as information systems, intelligent agents, artificial intelligence, and Web engineering.

The Advances in Intelligent Information Technologies (AIIT) Book Series endeavors to bring together researchers in related fields such as information systems, distributed Artificial Intelligence, intelligent agents, and collaborative work, to explore and discuss various aspects of design and development of intelligent technologies. Intelligent information technologies are being used by a large number of organizations for improving productivity in many roles such as assistants to human operators and autonomous decision-making components of complex systems. While a number of intelligent applications have been developed in various domains, there are still a number of research issues that have to be explored in terms of their design, implementation, integration, and deployment over the Internet or a corporate Intranet. The Advances in Intelligent Information Technologies (AIIT) Book Series aims to create a catalyst for emerging research in this field of growing importance through developing and delivering comprehensive publications for the betterment of intelligent information technologies and their applications. Through the availability of high-quality resources, the series hopes to further the development of this field and build upon the foundation of future implications.

Hershey • New York
Order online at www.igi-global.com or call 717-533-8845 x100 –
Mon-Fri 8:30 am - 5:00 pm (est) or fax 24 hours a day 717-533-7115

Table of Contents

Section I
Distributed Agent Applications and Decision Support

Section II
Search and Retrieval

Detailed Table of Contents

Section I
Distributed Agent Applications and Decision Support

Chapter I

In Chapter I a program construction method based on γ-Calculus is proposed. The problem to be solved is specified by first-order predicate logic and a semantic verification program is constructed directly from the specification. We exploit this method in synthesizing the architectural specifications of multi-agent systems (MAS) in γ-Calculus based on the logic specifications of the MAS. By enabling the transformation from the logic specifications to operational specifications of MAS, this method allows the design of the MAS to be focused on the architectural definition level. It benefits the development of MAS by enabling logic deduction on behaviors of the MAS, and a design methodology in an incremental fashion. We present this method by a case study of designing a course information management system.

Chapter II

In Chapter II we present an Architecture for knowledge-based decision support, delivered through a Multi-Agent Architecture. We illustrate how to represent and exchange domain-specific knowledge in XML-format through intelligent agents to create exchange and use knowledge to provide intelligent decision support. We show the integration of knowledge discovery techniques to create knowledge from organizational data; and knowledge repositories (KR) to store, manage and use data by intelligent software agents for effective knowledge-driven decision support. Implementation details of the architecture, its business implications and directions for further research are discussed.

Chapter III

Farid Meziane, University of Salford, UK
Samia Nefti, University of Salford, UK

Many trust models have been developed, however, most are subjective and do not take into account the vagueness and ambiguity of EC trust and the customers' intuitions and experience when conducting online transactions. Chapter III describes the development and implementation of a model using fuzzy reasoning to evaluate EC trust. This trust model is based on the information customers expect to find on an EC Web site and that is shown from many studies to increase customers trust towards online merchants. We argue that fuzzy logic is suitable for trust evaluation as it takes into account the uncertainties within EC data and like human relationships; it is often expressed by linguistic terms rather then numerical values. The evaluation of the proposed model is illustrated using four case studies and a comparison with two other models is conducted to emphasise the benefits of using fuzzy decision system.

Chapter IV

Mehdi Yousfi-Monod, University of Montpellier, France
Violaine Prince, University of Montpellier, France

Chapter IV concentrates on a learning situation where two agents, in a "teacher/student" relationship, exchange information with a learning incentive (on behalf of the student), according to a Socratic dialog. The teacher acts as the reliable knowledge source, and the student is an agent whose goal is to increase its knowledge base in an optimal way. The chapter first defines the nature of the addressed agents, the types of relation they maintain, and the structure and contents of their knowledge base. The chapter describes learning goals and strategies, student and teacher roles within both dialog and knowledge handling. It also provides solutions for problems encountered by agents. A general architecture is then established and a comment on a part of the theory implementation is given. The conclusion is about the achievements carried out and the potential improvement of this work.

Chapter V

Sungchul Hong, Towson University, USA
Barin N. Nag, Towson University, USA
Dong-qing Yao, Towson University, USA

In Chapter V we present a two-tier supply chain composed of multiple buyers and multiple suppliers. We have studied the mechanism to match trading parameter, specifically volume in this study, between buyers and suppliers. The chapter discusses the architecture of the agent and the agent community when there is cooperative matching of volume. We present a Dynamic Programming algorithm to describe the agent's decision process and heuristic algorithms as the practical solution methodology. The results of extensive experiments show the improvement achieved by the cooperation.

Chapter VI

Manoj A. Thomas, Virginia Commonwealth University, USA
Victoria Y. Yoon, University of Maryland, Baltimore County, USA
Richard Redmond, Virginia Commonwealth University, USA

Different FIPA-compliant agent development platforms are available for developing multiagent systems. FIPA compliance ensures interoperability among agents across different platforms. Although most agent implementation platforms provide some form of white- and yellow-page functionalities to advertise and identify agent roles and descriptions, there are no clear architectural standards that define how an agent community can effortlessly adapt to operate in a federated information system (FIS) where new content sources are constantly added or changes are made to existing content sources. Chapter VI presents a framework based on the semantic Web vision to address extensibility in a loosely coupled FIS.

Chapter VII

H. Hamidi, Iran University of Science & Technology, Iran-Tehran
K. Mohammadi, Iran University of Science & Technology, Iran-Tehran

The reliable execution of mobile agents is a very important design issue in building mobile agent systems and many fault-tolerant schemes have been proposed so far. Security is a major problem of mobile agent systems, especially when monetary transactions are concerned. Security for the partners involved is handled by encryption methods based on a public key authentication mechanism and by secret key encryption of the communication. To achieve fault tolerance for the agent system, especially for the agent transfer to a new host, we use distributed transaction processing. In Chapter VII we propose a fault-tolerant approach for mobile agents design which offers a user transparent fault tolerance that can be activated on request, according to the needs of the task. We also discuss how transactional agents with different types of commitment constraints can commit transactions. Furthermore, we present a solution for effective agent deployment using dynamic agent domains.

Section II
Search and Retrieval

Chapter VIII

Xiannong Meng, Bucknell University, USA
Song Xing, California State University—Los Angeles, USA

Chapter VIII reports the results of a project attempting to assess the performance of a few major search engines from various perspectives. The search engines involved in the study include the Microsoft Search Engine (MSE) when it was in its beta test stage, AllTheWeb, and Yahoo. In a few comparisons, other search engines such as Google, Vivisimo are also included. The study collects statistics such as the average user response time, average process time for a query reported by MSE, as well as the number of pages relevant to a query reported by all search engines involved. The project also studies the quality of search results generated by MSE and other search engines using RankPower as the metric. We found MSE performs well in speed and diversity of the query results, while weaker in other statistics, compared to some other leading search engines. The contribution of this chapter is to review the performance evaluation techniques for search engines and use different measures to assess and compare the quality of different search engines, especially MSE.

Information retrieval can take great advantages and improvements considering users' feedbacks. Therefore, the user dimension is a relevant component that must be taken into account while planning and implementing real information retrieval systems. In Chapter IX we first describe several concepts related to relevance feedback methods, and then propose a novel information retrieval technique which uses the relevance feedback concepts in order to improve accuracy in an ontology-based system. In particular, we combine the Semantic information from a general knowledge base with statistical information using relevance feedback. Several experiments and results are presented using a test set constituted of Web pages.

Chapter X presents an efficient algorithm to classify and retrieve images from large databases in the context of rough set theory. Color and texture are two well-known low-level perceptible features to describe an image contents used in this chapter. The features are extracted, normalized, and then the rough set dependency rules are generated directly from the real value attribute vector. Then the rough set reduction technique is applied to find all reducts of the data which contains the minimal subset of attributes that are associated with a class label for classification. We test three different popular distance measures in this work and find that quadratic distance measures provide the most accurate and perceptually relevant retrievals. The retrieval performance is measured using recall-precision measure, as is standard in all retrieval systems.

Text documents stored in information systems usually consist of more information than the pure concatenation of words, i.e., they also contain typographic information. Because conventional text retrieval methods evaluate only the word frequency, they miss the information provided by typography, e.g., regarding the importance of certain terms. In order to overcome this weakness, Chapter XI presents an approach which uses the typographical information of text documents and show how this improves the efficiency of text retrieval methods. Our approach uses weighting of typographic information in addition to term frequencies for separating relevant information in text documents from the noise. We have evaluated our approach on the basis of automated text classification algorithms. The results show that our weighting approach achieves very competitive classification results using at most 30% of the terms used by conventional approaches, which makes our approach significantly more efficient.

Chapter XII

    Ben Choi, Louisiana Tech University, USA
    Zhongmei Yao, Louisiana Tech University, USA

Chapter XII will focus on organizing Web contents. Since a majority of Web contents are stored in the form of Web pages, this chapter will focus on techniques for automatically organizing Web pages into categories. Various artificial intelligence techniques have been used; however the most successful ones are classification and clustering. This chapter will focus on clustering. Clustering is well suited for Web mining by automatically organizing Web pages into categories each of which contain Web pages having similar contents. However, one problem in clustering is the lack of general methods to automatically determine the number of categories or clusters. For the Web domain, until now there is no such a method suitable for Web page clustering. To address this problem, this chapter describes a method to discover a constant factor that characterizes the Web domain and proposes a new method for automatically determining the number of clusters in Web page datasets. This chapter also proposes a new bi-directional hierarchical clustering algorithm, which arranges individual Web pages into clusters and then arranges the clusters into larger clusters and so on until the average inter-cluster similarity approaches the constant factor. Having the constant factor together with the algorithm, this chapter provides a new clustering system suitable for mining the Web.

Chapter XIII

    John Goh, Monash University, Australia
    David Taniar, Monash University, Australia

Mobile user data mining is about extracting knowledge from raw data collected from mobile users. Previously proposed methods share the common drawbacks of costly resources that have to be spent in identifying the location of the mobile node and constant updating of the location information. The proposed method in Chapter XIII aims to address this issue by using the location dependent approach for mobile user data mining. Matrix pattern looks at the mobile nodes from the point of view of a particular fixed location rather than constantly following the mobile node itself. This can be done by using sparse matrix to map the physical location and use the matrix itself for the rest of mining process, rather than identifying the real coordinates of the mobile users. This allows performance efficiency with slight sacrifice in accuracy. As the mobile nodes visit along the mapped physical area, the matrix will be marked and used to perform mobile user data mining. The proposed method further extends itself from a single layer matrix to a multi-layer matrix in order to accommodate mining in different contexts, such as mining the relationship between the theme of food and fashion within a geographical area, thus making it more robust and flexible. The performance and evaluation shows that the proposed method can be used for mobile user data mining.

Section III
Information Systems and Modeling

Chapter XIV

Salvatore T. March, Vanderbilt University, USA
Gove N. Allen, Brigham Young University, USA

Active information systems participate in the operation and management of business organizations. They create conceptual objects that represent social constructions, such as agreements, commitments, transactions, and obligations. They determine and ascribe attributes to both conceptual and concrete objects (things) that are of interest to the organization. Active information system infer conclusions based on the application of socially constructed and mutable rules constituting organizational policies and procedures that govern how conceptual and concrete objects are affected when defined and identified events occur. The ontological foundations for active information systems must include constructs that represent concrete and conceptual objects, their attributes, and the events that affect them. Events are a crucial component of conceptual models that represent active information systems. The representation of events must include ascribed attributes representing data values inherent in the event as well as rules defining how conceptual and concrete objects are affected when the event occurs. The state-history of an object can then be constructed and reconstructed by the sequence of events that have affected it. Alternate state-histories can be generated based on proposed or conjectured rule modifications, enabling a reinterpretation of history. Future states can be predicted based on proposed or conjectured events and event definitions. Such a conceptualization enables a parsimonious mapping between an active information system and the organizational system in which it participates.

Chapter XV

John M. Artz, George Washington University, USA

Earlier work in the philosophical foundations of information modeling identified four key concepts in which philosophical groundwork must be further developed. Chapter XV reviews that earlier work and expands on one key area—the Problem of Universals—which is at the very heart of information modeling.

The motivation for Chapter XVI is the observation that many companies build their strategy upon poorly validated hypotheses about cause and effect of certain business variables. However, the soundness of these cause-and-effect-relations as well as the knowledge of the approximate shape of the functional dependencies underlying these associations turns out to be the biggest issue for the quality of the results of decision supporting procedures. Since it is sufficiently clear that mere correlation of time series is not suitable to prove the causality of two business concepts, there seems to be a rather dogmatic perception of the inadmissibility of empirical validation mechanisms for causal models within the field of strategic management as well as management science. However, one can find proven causality techniques in other sciences like econometrics, mechanics, neuroscience, or philosophy. Therefore this chapter presents an approach which applies a combination of well-established statistical causal proofing methods to strategy models in order to validate them. These validated causal strategy models are then used as the basis for approximating the functional form of causal dependencies by the means of artificial neural networks. This in turn can be employed to build an approximate simulation or forecasting model of the strategic system.

In Chapter XVII we propose to use N-gram models for improving Web navigation for mobile users. N-gram models are built from Web server logs to learn navigation patterns of mobile users. They are used as prediction models in an existing algorithm which improves mobile Web navigation by recommending shortcuts. Our experiments on two real data sets show that N-gram models are as effective as other more complex models in improving mobile Web navigation.

Section IV
Supply Chain Management

Chapter XVIII investigates the applicability of Machine Learning (ML) techniques and compares their performances with the more traditional methods in order to improve demand forecast accuracy in supply chains. To this end we used two data sets from particular companies (chocolate manufacturer and toner cartridge manufacturer), as well as data from the Statistics Canada manufacturing survey. A representative set of traditional and ML-based forecasting techniques have been applied to the demand data and the accuracy of the methods was compared. As a group, Machine Learning techniques outperformed traditional techniques in terms of overall average, but not in terms of overall ranking. We also found that a support vector machine (SVM) trained on multiple demand series produced the most accurate forecasts.

Chapter XIX

The present study in Chapter XIX implements a generic methodology for describing and analyzing demand supply networks (i.e. networks from a company's suppliers through to its customers). There can be many possible demand supply networks with different logistics costs for a product. Therefore, we introduced a Petri Net-based formalism, and a reachability analysis-based algorithm that finds the optimum demand supply network for a user-specified product structure. The method has been implemented and is currently in production use inside all Nokia business groups. It is used in demand supply planning of both network elements and handsets. An example of the method's application to a concrete Nokia product is included.

Preface

According to Torsun, the area of Distributed Artificial Intelligence (DAI) deals with "cooperative problem solving using a federation of collaborating agents." These software agents are intelligent in the sense that they are adaptive, independent, and posses reasoning capability. They can plan and execute tasks in cooperation with other agents in order to satisfy their goals. They also learn in the process and adapt to changes in the environment dynamically. These agents are often heterogeneous. A multi-agent system (MAS) is defined as a loosely coupled network of problem solvers that work together to solve problems that are beyond the individual capabilities or knowledge of each problem solver. The increasing interest in MAS research is due to significant advantages inherent in such systems, including their ability to solve problems that may be too large for a centralized single agent, provide enhanced speed and reliability, and tolerate uncertain data and knowledge. Some of the key research issues related to problem-solving activities of agents in a MAS are in the areas of coordination, negotiation, and communication.

Similar to multi-agent systems, where agents communicate and collaborate with each other to accomplish a goal, in collaborative applications, a set of programs communicate with each other using proprietary protocols to let users collaborate with each other by accessing shared information. This may be accomplished by running the same application on different machines. In such a configuration, these applications are essentially clients that accept user input to drive updates to shared state and propagate the updates to other collaborating clients. With advances in Web technologies, collaborative applications are now server based and the user interface is typically a Web browser. Thus, a collaborative application can be a Web-based solution that runs on a local server that allows people communicate and work together, share information and documents, and talk in real-time over the Internet.

Recently, much research has been conducted in distributed artificial intelligence and collaborative applications. Several interesting methodologies and systems have been developed in areas such as distributed multi-agent systems for decision support, Web search and information retrieval, information systems modeling, and supply chain management. In particular, intelligent agents and multi-agent systems, and a myriad of applications have been built in various domains. This book discusses a number of agent-based applications developed for knowledge-driven decision support, online auctions, federated information systems, and mobile computing. Similarly, in the area of search and retrieval, the book provides current research in search engine performance, user centered approach for information and image retrieval, Web mining, and document clustering. Event and information modeling is an active area of research and this book presents a few chapters highlighting the salient aspects of modeling. Finally, in the area of supply chain management, forecasting demand and supply network optimization are important areas of investigation and the book presents the latest research. The following sections briefly outline the different applications discussed in various chapters of this book.

BOOK ORGANIZATION

Section I
Distributed Agent Applications and Decision Support

This section presents seven chapters that discuss distributed agent applications and decision support. Chapter I by Hong Lin, discusses a program construction method based on γ-Calculus. The problem to be solved is specified by first-order predicate logic and a semantic verification program, which is constructed directly from the specification. This method synthesizes the architectural specifications of multi-agent systems (MAS) in γ-Calculus based on the logic specifications of the MAS. By enabling the transformation from the logic specifications to operational specifications of MAS, this method allows the design of the MAS to be focused on the architectural definition level. It benefits the development of MAS by enabling logic deduction on behaviors of the MAS, and a design methodology in an incremental fashion. This chapter presents a case study of designing a course information management system.

In Chapter II, Rahul Singh presents a "Multi-Agent Architecture for Knowledge-Driven Decision Support". Organizations use knowledge-driven systems to deliver problem-specific knowledge over Internet-based distributed platforms to decision-makers. Increasingly, artificial intelligence (AI) techniques for knowledge representation are being used to deliver knowledge-driven decision support in multiple forms. This chapter illustrates how to represent and exchange domain-specific knowledge in XML-format through intelligent agents to create exchange and use knowledge to provide intelligent decision support. It shows the integration of knowledge discovery techniques to create knowledge from organizational data; and knowledge repositories (KR) to store, manage, and use data by intelligent software agents for effective knowledge-driven decision support. Implementation details of the architecture, its business implications, and directions for further research are discussed.

Chapter III by Farid Meziane and Samia Nefti is titled "A Decision Support System for Trust Formalization," in which the authors point out that trust is widely recognized as an essential factor for the continual development of business-to-customer (B2C) electronic commerce (EC). Many trust models have been developed, however, most are subjective and do not take into account the vagueness and ambiguity of EC trust and the customers' intuitions and experience when conducting online transactions. In this chapter, the authors describe the development and implementation of a model using fuzzy reasoning to evaluate EC trust. This trust model is based on the information customers expect to find on an EC Web site and that is shown from many studies to increase customers trust towards online merchants. They argue that fuzzy logic is suitable for trust evaluation as it takes into account the uncertainties within EC data and like human relationships; it is often expressed by linguistic terms rather then numerical values. The evaluation of the proposed model is illustrated using four case studies and a comparison with two other models is conducted to emphasize the benefits of using fuzzy decision system.

Mehdi Yousifi-Monod and Violaine Prince investigate learning and communication between cognitive artificial agents in Chapter IV. They attempt to answer the question: Is it possible to find an equivalency between a communicative process and a learning process, to model and implement communication and learning as dual aspects of the same cognitive mechanism? The chapter focuses on a learning situation where two agents, in a "teacher/student" relationship, exchange information with a learning incentive (on behalf of the student), according to a socratic dialog. The teacher acts as the reliable knowledge source, and the student is an agent whose goal is to increase its knowledge base in an optimal way. This chapter first defines the nature of the addressed agents, the types of relation they maintain, and the structure and contents of their knowledge base. It emphasizes the symmetry between the interaction and knowledge management, by highlighting knowledge "repair" procedures launched through dialogic means. The chapter describes learning goals and strategies, student and teacher roles within both dialog, and knowledge handling. It also provides solutions for problems encountered by agents. A general architecture is then established.

In Chapter V titled "Improving E-Trade Auction Volume by Consortium," Sungchul Hong, Barin Nag and Dong-qing Yao present a two-tier supply chain composed of multiple buyers and multiple suppliers. They have studied the mechanism to match trading parameter, specifically volume in this study, between buyers and suppliers. The chapter discusses the architecture of the agent, and the agent community when there is cooperative matching of volume. They present a Dynamic Programming algorithm to describe the agent's decision process and heuristic algorithms as the practical solution methodology. The results of extensive experiments show the improvement achieved by the cooperation.

Chapter VI by Manoj A. Thomas, Victoria Yoon, and Richard Redmond is titled "Extending Loosely Coupled Federated Information Systems Using Agent Technology". Different FIPA complaint agent development platforms are available for developing multi-agent systems. FIPA compliance ensures interoperability among agents across different platforms. Although most agent implementation platforms provide some form of white and yellow page functionalities to advertise and identify agent roles and descriptions, there is no clear architectural standard that defines how agent community can effortlessly adapt to operate in Federated Information System (FIS), where new content sources are constantly added or changes are made to existing content sources. This chapter presents a framework based on the Semantic Web vision to address extensibility in a loosely coupled FIS.

In Chapter VII, H. Hamidi and K. Mohammadi discuss "Modeling Fault Tolerant and Secure Mobile Agent Execution in Distributed Systems". The reliable execution of mobile agents is a very important design issue in building mobile agent systems and many fault-tolerant schemes have been proposed so far. Security is a major problem of mobile agent systems, especially when monetary transactions are concerned. Security for the partners involved is handled by encryption methods based on a public key authentication mechanism and by secret key encryption of the communication. To achieve fault tolerance for the agent system, especially for the agent transfer to a new host, they use distributed transaction processing. They propose a fault-tolerant approach for mobile agent design, which offers a user transparent fault tolerance that can be activated on request, according to the needs of the task. They also discuss how transactional agents with different types of commitment constraints can commit transactions. Furthermore, they present a solution for effective agent deployment using dynamic agent domains.

Section II
Search and Retrieval

This section presents six chapters dealing with various aspects of search engines, information retrieval, and Web mining. Xiannong Meng and Song Xing in Chapter VIII, titled "Search Engine Performance Comparisons," present a comparative analysis of Microsoft Search Engine (MSE), AllTheWeb and Yahoo. In a few comparisons, other search engines such as Google, Vivisimo are also included. The study collects statistics such as the average user response time, average process time for a query reported by MSE, as well as the number of pages relevant to a query reported by all search engines involved. The chapter also studies the quality of search results generated by MSE and other search engines using *RankPower* as the metric. They found that MSE performs well in speed and diversity of the query results, while weaker in other statistics, compared to some other leading search engines. The contribution of this chapter is to review the performance evaluation techniques for search engines and use different measures to assess and compare the quality of different search engines, especially MSE.

Antonio Picariello and Antonio Rinaldi, in Chapter IX titled "A User-Centered Approach for Information Retrieval," emphasize that information retrieval can gain great advantages and improvements by considering users' feedback. The user dimension is a relevant component that must be taken into account while planning and implementing real information retrieval systems. In this chapter they first describe several concepts related to relevance feedback methods, and propose a novel information retrieval technique which uses the relevance feedback concepts in order to improve accuracy in an ontology-based system. In particular, they combine the semantic information from a general knowledge base with statistical information using relevance feedback. Several experiments and results are presented using a test set constituted of Web pages.

In Chapter X titled "Classification and Retrieval of Images from Databases Using Rough Set Theory," Jafar Ali and Aboul Ella Hassanien present an efficient algorithm to classify and retrieve images from large databases using rough set theory. Color and texture are two well-known, low-level perceptible features to describe an image contents. The features are extracted, normalized, and then the rough set dependency rules are generated directly from the real value attribute vector. Then the rough set reduction technique is applied to find all reducts of the data which contains the minimal subset of attributes that are associated with a class label for classification. They have tested three different popular distance measures and found that quadratic distance measures provide the most accurate and perceptually relevant retrievals. The retrieval performance is measured using recall-precision measure, as is standard in all retrieval systems.

Chapter XI by Lars Werner and Stefan Böttcher is titled "Supporting Text Retrieval by Typographical Term Weighting". Text documents stored in information systems usually consist of more information than the pure concatenation of words, for instance they also contain typographic information. Because conventional text retrieval methods evaluate only the word frequency, they miss the information provided by typography (e.g., regarding the importance of certain terms). In order to overcome this weakness, the authors present an approach which uses the typographical information of text documents and shows how this improves the efficiency of text retrieval methods. Their approach uses weighting of typographic information in addition to term frequencies for separating relevant information in text documents from the noise. They have evaluated their approach on the basis of automated text classification algorithms. The results show that their weighting approach achieves very competitive classification results using at most 30% of the terms used by conventional approaches, which makes their approach significantly more efficient.

Ben Choi and Xhongmei Yao discuss a Web mining approach in Chapter XII titled "Web Mining by Automatically Organizing Web Pages into Categories". Since the majority of Web content is stored in the form of Web pages, this chapter focuses on techniques for automatically organizing Web pages into categories. Various Artificial Intelligence techniques have been used; however the most successful ones are classification and clustering. Clustering is well suited for Web mining by automatically organizing Web pages into categories each of which contains Web pages having similar contents. However, one problem in clustering is the lack of general methods to automatically determine the number of categories or clusters. For the Web domain, until now there is no such method suitable for Web page clustering. To address this problem, this chapter describes a method to discover a constant factor that characterizes the Web domain and proposes a new method for automatically determining the number of clusters in Web page datasets. This chapter also proposes a new bi-directional hierarchical clustering algorithm, which arranges individual Web pages into clusters and then arranges the clusters into larger clusters and so on until the average inter-cluster similarity approaches the constant factor. Having the constant factor together with the algorithm, this chapter provides a new clustering system suitable for mining the Web.

In Chapter XIII, John Goh, and David Taniar discuss "Mining Matrix Pattern from Mobile Users". Mobile user data mining is about extracting knowledge from raw data collected from mobile users. There have been a few approaches developed, such as frequency pattern, group pattern, parallel pattern, and location dependent mobile user data mining. Previously proposed methods share the common drawbacks of costly resources that have to be spent in identifying the location of the mobile node and constant updating of the location information. The proposed method aims to address this issue by using the location dependent approach for mobile user data mining. Matrix pattern looks at the mobile nodes from the point of view of a particular fixed location rather than constantly following the mobile node itself. This can be done by using sparse matrix to map the physical location and use the matrix itself for the rest of mining process, rather than identifying the real coordinates of the mobile users. This allows performance efficiency with slight sacrifice in accuracy. As the mobile nodes visit along the mapped physical area, the matrix will be marked and used to perform mobile user data mining. The performance and evaluation shows that the proposed method can be used for mobile user data mining.

Section III
Information Systems and Modeling

This section presents four chapters that discuss the use of modeling in information systems, particularly, event and information modeling, predictive modeling, and causal strategy modeling. In Chapter XIV titled "Conceptual Modeling of Events for Active Information Systems," Sal March and Gove Allen argue that the ontological foundations for active information systems must include constructs that represent concrete and conceptual objects, their attributes, and the events that affect them. Events are a crucial component of conceptual models that represent active information systems. The representation of events must include ascribed attributes representing data values inherent in the event as well as rules defining how conceptual and concrete objects are affected when the event occurs. The state-history of an object can then be constructed and reconstructed by the sequence of events that have affected it. Alternate state-histories can be generated based on proposed or conjectured rule modifications, enabling a reinterpretation of history. Future states can be predicted based on proposed or conjectured events and event definitions. Such a conceptualization enables a parsimonious mapping between an active information system and the organizational system in which it participates.

Chapter XV by John Artz discusses "Information Modeling and the Problem of Universals". Earlier work in the philosophical foundations of information modeling identified four key concepts in which philosophical groundwork must be further developed. This chapter reviews that earlier work and expands on one key area – the Problem of Universals – which is at the very heart of information modeling.

In Chapter XVI titled "Empirical Inference of Numerical Information into Causal Strategy Models by Means of Artificial Intelligence," Christian Hillbrand observes that many companies build their strategy upon poorly validated hypotheses about cause and effect of certain business variables. However, the soundness of these cause-and-effect-relations as well as the knowledge of the approximate shape of the functional dependencies underlying these associations turns out to be the biggest issue for the quality of the results of decision supporting procedures. It is sufficiently clear that mere correlation of time series is not suitable to prove the causality of two business concepts. However, one can find proven causality techniques in other sciences like econometrics, mechanics, neuroscience, or philosophy. This chapter presents an approach which applies a combination of well-established statistical causal proofing methods to strategy models in order to validate them. These validated causal strategy models are then used as the basis for approximating the functional form of causal dependencies by the means of Artificial

Neural Networks. This in turn is employed to build an approximate simulation or forecasting model of the strategic system.

Chapter XVII by Yongjian Fu, Hironmoy Paul, and Namita Shetty is titled "Improving Mobile Web Navigation Using N-Grams Prediction Models". This chapter discusses the use of N-gram models for improving Web navigation for mobile users. N-gram models are built from Web server logs to learn navigation patterns of mobile users. They are used as prediction models in an existing algorithm which improves mobile Web navigation by recommending shortcuts. The experiments on two real data sets show that N-gram models are as effective as other more complex models in improving mobile Web navigation.

Section IV
Supply Chain Management

This section contains two chapters that discuss supply chain management using intelligent technologies such as machine learning and petri nets. Chapter XVIII by Réal Carbonneau, Rustam Vahidov, and Kevin Laframboise is titled "Forecasting Supply Chain Demand using Machine Learning Algorithms". In this chapter, the authors point out that demand prediction in a supply chain is aggravated by the fact that communication patterns between participants tend to distort the original consumer's demand and create high levels of noise. Distortion and noise negatively impact forecast quality of the participants. This chapter investigates the applicability of Machine Learning (ML) techniques and compares their performances with the more traditional methods in order to improve demand forecast accuracy in supply chains. The authors use two data sets from particular companies (chocolate manufacturer and toner cartridge manufacturer), as well as data from the Statistics Canada manufacturing survey. A representative set of traditional and ML-based forecasting techniques have been applied to the demand data and the accuracy of the methods was compared. As a group, Machine Learning techniques outperformed traditional techniques in terms of overall average, but not in terms of overall ranking. A Support Vector Machine (SVM) trained on multiple demand series produced the most accurate forecasts.

In Chapter XIX "Supporting Demand Supply Network Optimization with Petri Nets", Teemu Tynjala proposes a generic methodology for describing and analyzing demand supply networks, (i.e. networks from a company's suppliers through to its customers). There can be many possible demand supply networks with different logistics costs for a product. Therefore, a Petri Net-based formalism, and a reachability analysis-based algorithm that finds the optimum demand supply network for a user-specified product structure is introduced. This method has been implemented and is currently in production use inside all Nokia business groups. It is used in demand supply planning of both network elements and handsets. An example of the method's application to a concrete Nokia product is discussed in the chapter.

Effective use of distributed artificial intelligence technologies and collaborative applications is critical for improving productivity. An outstanding collection of latest research associated with artificial intelligence techniques, collaborative applications, agent-based systems, Web search and mining, information systems modelling, and supply chain management is presented in this book. Use of intelligent information technologies will greatly assist in gaining competitive advantage.

Vijayan Sugumaran
Editor-in-Chief
Distributed Artificial Intelligence, Agent Technology, and Collaborative Applications

Section I
Distributed Agent Applications and Decision Support

Chapter I
Designing Multi–Agent Systems from Logic Specifications:
A Case Study

Hong Lin
University of Houston—Downtown, USA

ABSTRACT

In this chapter a program construction method based on γ-Calculus is proposed. The problem to be solved is specified by first-order predicate logic and a semantic verification program is constructed directly from the specification. We exploit this method in synthesizing the architectural specifications of multi-agent systems (MAS) in γ-Calculus based on the logic specifications of the MAS. By enabling the transformation from the logic specifications to operational specifications of MAS, this method allows the design of the MAS to be focused on the architectural definition level. It benefits the development of MAS by enabling logic deduction on behaviors of the MAS, and a design methodology in an incremental fashion. We present this method by a case study of designing a course information management system.

INTRODUCTION

The modeling issue in the abstract computing machine level has been studied in (Banâtre, Fradet, & Radenac, 2004), where the chemical reaction model (CRM) (Banatre & Le Metayer, 1990 & 1993; Banatre, Fradet, & Radenac, 2005a; Le Metayer, 1994) is used to model an autonomic system. Given the dynamic and concurrent nature of multi-agent systems (MAS), we find that the chemical reaction metaphor provides a mechanism for describing the overall architecture of the distributed MAS precisely and concisely, while giving the design of the real system a solid starting point and allowing step-by-step refinement of the system using transformational methods (Lin, 2004; Lin & Yang, 2006).

Although CRM is suitable for modeling MAS, it serves as an operational specification language for MAS and it requires the designers of MAS to have the understanding of chemistry-inspired computational models. As a matter of fact, logic specification of MAS is better suited as a specification method in the current understanding, because logic specification focuses on behavioral properties of the systems without concerns with underlying computational model. We propose a method for generating MAS specifications in γ-Calculus from their logic specifications. We use the "generate-and-test" method to design the re-write process. Generally speaking, this process generates data in the domain of logic specification and creates a verification program in γ-Calculus to verify the logic specification with the generated data.

When applying this method to MASs, there are some problems to solve. The architectural specification of a MAS is different from that of a normal program, because for a MAS, we need to consider a collection of aspects, including distribution, security, performance, etc. This will cause a much more complex synthesizing process. For example, the distribution aspect will cause the communication pattern to be considered in the synthesizing process. In our approach, the communications are defined by the logic specifications of the interfaces of the system in terms of either message passing or shared memory. The practicability of this method is further strengthened by a transformation method we have proposed to implement CRM specifications on realistic computational models (Lin, 2004; Lin & Yang, 2006).

MASs are considered as complex systems whose design issues are difficult to be handled by logic systems. By bridging logic specifications and operational specifications of MASs, our study opens a path to introducing derivative methods in the higher level architectural design of MASs. This work will help formalize the design processes and promote the current research endeavor to end the state of MAS design in case-by-case fashion.

MODELING MULTI-AGENT SYSTEMS BY CHEMICAL REACTION MODELS

Gamma (Banatre & Le Metayer, 1990 & 1993) is a kernel language in which programs are described in terms of multiset transformations. In Gamma programming paradigm, programmers can concentrate on the logic of problem solving based on an abstract machine and are free from considering any particular execution environment. It has seeded follow-up elaborations, such as Chemical Abstract Machine (Cham) (Berry & Boudol, 1992), higher-order Gamma (Le Metayer, 1994), and Structured Gamma (Fradet & Le Metayer, 1998).

While the original Gamma language is a first-order language, higher order extensions have been proposed to enhance the expressiveness of the language. These include higher-order Gamma (Le Metayer, 1994), hmm-calculus (Cohen & Muylaert-Filho, 1996), and others. The recent formalisms, γ-Calculi, of Gamma languages combine reaction rules and the multisets of data and treat reactions as first-class citizens (Banatre, Fradet, & Radenac, 2004, 2005a, & 2005b). Among γ-Calculi, γ_0-Calculus is a minimal basis for the chemical paradigm; γ_c-Calculus extends γ_0-Calculus by adding a condition term into γ-abstractions; and γ_n-Calculus extends γ_0-Calculus by allowing abstractions to atomically capture multiple elements. Finally, γ_{cn}-Calculus combines both γ_c-Calculus and γ_n-Calculus. For notational simplicity, we use γ-Calculus to mean γ_{cn}-Calculus from this point on. Also, we assume that the readers have the basic knowledge about the syntax and semantics of γ-Calculus.

We found that the dynamic nature of distributed agents makes it an ideal object for modeling using the Gamma languages. An agent shows a combination of a number of characteristics, such as autonomy, adaptability, knowledge, mobility, collaboration, and persistence. These features exist in different types of agent systems such as collaborative agents, interface agents, reactive agents, mobile agents, information agents, heterogeneous agents, and economic agents. The concurrency and automation of agents require that the modeling language does not have any sequential bias and global control structure. In addition, the dynamic nature and non-determinism of interaction between an agent and its environment are suited to a computation model with a loose mechanism for specifying the underlying data structure. For example, data, which move around the Internet, can be well modeled by chemical solution; and mobile agents, which are created dynamically and transferred from clients to servers, can be represented as molecules containing γ-abstractions that transfer among solutions. This provides a mechanism for describing inter-agent communications and agent migration in a single framework. It is worthwhile to note that CRM specifications separate architectures from nonessential features of the system effectively. For example, it catches the way program units interact with one another and leaves nonessential specifications, such as the number of program units, connection links for communications, and organizations of data, to the subsequent design phases.

We refer the readers to (Lin, 2004) and (Lin & Yang, 2006) for detailed justifications for the appropriateness of using the CRM to model MAS. Here we give the summary of our findings. The benefits of using the CRM to model MAS include: (1) The architectural design of the system can be separated from the design of individual units that have to deal with proprietary features of the underlying computing resources, because CRM allows us to treat each node in the distributed networking systems as an element of a multi-set data structure, which in-turn can be an active program to be defined in a lower level of the program structure. (2) Parallelism can be easily achieved without extra efforts in designing communication and synchronization mechanism because CRM express them implicitly. (3) Concurrency and dynamic nature of MAS can be easily reflected by CRM's non-determinism feature. (4) Autonomy can be expressed naturally by CRM's locality of reaction feature. (5) It provides a framework for combining different programming technologies because no assumptions are made about the way for implementing each node in the system hierarchy. (6) The reusability of the agent systems can be promoted by higher-order CRM languages because the existing agents can be combined by using higher-order operations defined in those languages.

PROGRAM SYNTHESIS FOR GAMMA

A barrier to make an automatic software design system practical is that there is no a straightforward way to bridge descriptive specifications and operational ones. For example, first-order logic formulas, unless in some elaborately arranged recursive forms (e.g., as those studied in learning systems (Shapiro, 1981)), is hard to be mapped to programs directly.

In Gamma language, the classical method proposed by Banatre and Le Metayer (1990) is to decompose the specification into an invariant and a termination condition. The program is synthesized by deduction to meet the termination condition while keeping the invariant satisfied. The program is designed under the guidance of the invariant and the variant rather than derived out directly from the specification. And much skill is need in figuring out the invariant and variant.

We propose a method for constructing programs from first-order specifications (Lin & Chen, 1998). The method constructs a semantic verification program for a specification. Few syntactic derivations are needed in constructing the program. In addition, the target programs, which are in Gamma language, are parallel programs instead of sequential programs. This distinguishes our method from classical methods for program synthesis, such as those studied in type theory (Martin-Lof, 1980; Aarts et. al., 1992), algebraic specification (Ehrig & Mahr, 1990), program transformation (Bauer et. al., 1985), deductive synthesis (Manna & Waldinger, 1992; Traugott, 1989), term rewriting system (Klop, 1990; Meseguer & Winkler, 1991; Meseguer, 1992), and other methods in automatic software engineering. Comparing to automatic construction of sequential programs, the construction of parallel programs is a much harder issue, because there is not a unified computation model for parallelism and concurrency, and details of parallel architectures have to be considered when efficiency of the programs is to be improved (Paige & Watcher, 1993). This method is based on the original first-order Gamma language, which is a single module language. In this paper, we exploit this method on λ-Calculus, which is a higher-order language fit for describing complex systems such as MAS.

Logical Specification

In general, we shall be dealing with specifications of the form:

$f(a) \Leftarrow$ find z such that $Q(a, z)$

where $Q[a, z]$ is a sentence of the background theory. Function f should be synthesized in a procedure of theorem proving. The theorem corresponding to this specification is

$\forall a{:}T_a.\exists z{:}T_z.Q(a, z)$

In other words, for every input a of type T_a, there exists an output z of type T_z that satisfies the input-output relation $Q[a, z]$. We assume there is a theory TH composed of

- Axioms and theorems on type T_a and T_z;
- Assertions about constrains on input a.

Theory TH can be used as facts in program construction. So the logic specification is:

$spec \equiv \forall a{:}T_a. (TH \rightarrow \exists z{:}T_z.Q(a, z))$

And we define

$goal \equiv \exists z{:}T_z.Q(a, z)$

In the following sections, we call a *input parameter*.

For example, the program verifying Goldbach Conjecture (Richstein, 2001) can be specified as

$spec \equiv \forall n{:}N.(TH \rightarrow \exists m,k{:}N.(prime(m) \wedge prime(k) \wedge n = m{+}k))$

where N is the type of natural numbers;

$TH \equiv N \cup n{>}2 \wedge \text{even}(n)$

where $\mathcal{N}$ is the theory of Peano arithmetic; and

$prime(n) \equiv n{=}2 \vee n{>}2 \wedge \forall m{:}N.(1{<}m{<}n \rightarrow n\%m{\neq}0)$
$goal \equiv \exists m,k{:}N.(prime(m) \wedge prime(k) \wedge n{=}m{+}k)$

In this paper, we use the logical operators: $\forall, \exists, \neg, \wedge, \vee, \rightarrow, \leftrightarrow$, which are listed with the decreasing order of their priorities.

All the variables in the logic specifications are typed. That is to say that each variable has an associated domain of values to test when determining whether the specification is provable. To ensure termination of the verification process, the domains of all variables must be enumerable the domains of universally quantified variables must be bounded. The bounds can be determined from the domain theory *TH* and a recursive deduction on the logic specification. Appendix A discusses the methods for determining the bounds of variables. For non-enumerable domains, we need to establish a sampling function from the domain theory that ensures the coverage of the domain when applied recursively. See (Lin & Chen, 1998) for detailed description of the deduction process.

Constructing the Verification Program

The verification program in γ-Calculus is constructed recursively. For a clause p, the constructed program is a solution, denoted by $<p>$. The recursive process is governed by the following rules:

Rule 1. For clause $q = \forall x{:}N.\ p(x)$, $<q> = <f,\ tt,\ true,\ false,\ N,\ \textbf{true}>$ where
  $true = \gamma(x{:}N)\lfloor<p[x]>{=}<\textbf{true}>\rfloor.\ \textbf{true},\ true$
  $false = \gamma(x{:}N)\lfloor<p[x]>{=}<\textbf{false}>\rfloor.\ \textbf{false},\ false$
  $tt = \gamma(\textbf{true},\ x)\lfloor x{\neq}\textbf{false}\rfloor.\ \textbf{true}$
  $f = \gamma(\textbf{false},\ x)\lfloor\textbf{true}\rfloor.\ \textbf{false}$

Rule 2. For clause $q = \exists x{:}N.\ p(x)$, $<q> = <t,\ ff,\ true,\ false,\ N,\ \textbf{false}>$ where
  $true = \gamma(x{:}N)\lfloor<p[x]>{=}<\textbf{true}>\rfloor.\ \textbf{true},\ true$
  $false = \gamma(x{:}N)\lfloor<p[x]>{=}<\textbf{false}>\rfloor.\ \textbf{false},\ false$
  $ff = \gamma(\textbf{false},\ x)\lfloor x{\neq}\textbf{true}\rfloor.\ \textbf{false}$
  $t = \gamma(\textbf{true},\ x)\lfloor\textbf{true}\rfloor.\ \textbf{true}$

Rule 3. For clause $q = \neg p$, $<q> = <negate,\ <p>>$ where
  $negate = \gamma(<p>)\lfloor\textbf{true}\rfloor.\ <\neg p>$

Rule 4. For clause $r = p \rightarrow q$, $<r> = <imply,\ <p>{:}P,\ <q>{:}Q>$ where
  $imply = \gamma(<p>{:}P,\ <q>{:}Q)\lfloor\textbf{true}\rfloor.\ <p \rightarrow q>$

Rule 5. For clause $r = p \wedge q$, $<r> = <and,\ <p>{:}P,\ <q>{:}Q>$ where
  $and = \gamma(<p>{:}P,\ <q>{:}Q)\lfloor\textbf{true}\rfloor.\ <p \wedge q>$

Rule 6. For clause $r = p \lor q$, $<r> = <or, <p>:P, <q>:Q>$ where
   $or = \gamma(<p>:P, <q>:Q)\lfloor \mathbf{true}\rfloor. <p \lor q>$

Rule 7. For the $goal = \exists z:T_z.Q(a, z)$, $<goal> = <t, f\!f, true, false, T_z, \mathbf{false}, \varnothing:R>$ where
   $true = \gamma(z:T_z)\lfloor <Q[a, z]>=<\mathbf{true}>\rfloor. \mathbf{true}, z:R, true$
   $false = \gamma(z:T_z)\lfloor <Q[a, z]>=<\mathbf{false}>\rfloor. \mathbf{false}, false$
   $f\!f = \gamma(\mathbf{false}, z)\lfloor x\neq\mathbf{true} \land type(z)\neq R\rfloor. \mathbf{false}$
   $t = \gamma(\mathbf{true}, z)\lfloor type(z)\neq R\rfloor. \mathbf{true}$
   where $type(z)$ determines the type of element z.

Rule 1 generates a program that verifies a universally quantified clause. It tests the values in domain N and replaces the values by either true or false according to the results of the verification. This is done by two sub-programs *true* and *false*. Program *tt* then removes redundant **true**'s and *f* removes everything including redundant **false**'s. However, a **false** cannot be removed by a **true**. This is because that once there is a value that causes $p(x)$ to be evaluated to **false**, $\forall x:N. p(x)$ is **false**. Note that $p[x]$ denotes the molecule obtained by replacing the hole by x. The **true** in the initial solution $<f, tt, true, false, N, \mathbf{true}>$ ensures that there is at least a **true** in the multiset if $N = \varnothing$. When the solution $<q>$ becomes inert, it should be either $<\mathbf{true}>$ or $<\mathbf{false}>$.

Similarly, *Rule* 2 generates a program that verifies an existentially quantified clause. Program *ff* removes redundant **false**'s and *t* removes everything including redundant **true**'s. However, a **true** cannot be removed by a **false**. This is because that once there is a value that causes $p(x)$ to be evaluated to **true**, $\exists x:N. p(x)$ is **true**. The **false** in the initial solution $<t, f\!f, true, false, N, \mathbf{false}>$ ensures that there is at least a **false** in the multiset if $N = \varnothing$. Also, when the solution $<q>$ becomes inert, it should be either $<\mathbf{true}>$ or $<\mathbf{false}>$.

Rule 3-6 generate programs that verify clauses based on the results of the sub-programs that verify the sub-clauses.

Rule 7 is similar to *Rule* 2. However, since it generates the program in the top level of the nesting hierarchy of the program tree, it should return the result that satisfies the *goal*. To this end, a multiset R (initially set to $\varnothing$) is added into the solution to store the values in T_z that satisfy $Q(a, z)$. When sub-program *true* finds a value that satisfies $Q(a, z)$, it stores the values in R. *ff* and *t* are modified to keep values in R. The final result of the program, viz., the inert solution $<goal>$, should be either $<\mathbf{true}, R>$ and $R \neq \varnothing$; or $<\mathbf{false}, \varnothing>$. The latter indicates that the no results are found that meet the *goal*.

As an example, let's construct the program that verifies the Goldbach Conjecture (Richstein, 2001). Firstly, let's construct the program that verifies predicate *prime(n)*, which is defined as:

$prime(n) \equiv n{=}2 \lor n{>}2 \land \forall m:N.(1{<}m{<}n \rightarrow n\%m\neq0)$

Based on clause $1{<}m{<}n$, the bounds of domain N is 2 (lower bound) and $n{-}1$ (upper bound). Let $M = [2 .. n{-}1]$, the clause $\forall m:N.(1{<}m{<}n \rightarrow n\%m\neq0)$ can be transformed to $\forall m:M. n\%m\neq0$. The program that verifies $\forall m:M. n\%m\neq0$ can then be written (based on *Rule* 1) as:

$<prime\_m> = <f, tt, true, false, N, \mathbf{true}>$ where
$true = \gamma(m:M)\lfloor n\%m\neq0\rfloor. \mathbf{true}, true$
$false = \gamma(m:M)\lfloor n\%m=0\rfloor. \mathbf{false}, false$

$tt = \gamma(\textbf{true}, m)\lfloor m{\neq}\textbf{false}\rfloor.\ \textbf{true}$
$f = \gamma(\textbf{false}, m)\lfloor \textbf{true}\rfloor.\ \textbf{false}$

The program that verifies $n{>}2 \wedge \forall m{:}N.(1{<}m{<}n \rightarrow n\%m{\neq}0)$ can then be written (*Rule* 5) as:

$<prime\_n> = <and, <n{>}2>{:}P, <prime\_m>{:}Q>$ where
$and = \gamma(<n{>}2>{:}P, <prime\_m>{:}Q)\lfloor \textbf{true}\rfloor.\ <n{>}2 \wedge prime\_m>$

The program that verifies *prime(n)* can then be written (*Rule* 6) as:

$<prime> = <or, <n{=}0>{:}P, <prime\_n>{:}Q>$ where
$or = \gamma(<n{=}2>{:}P, <prime\_n>{:}Q)\lfloor \textbf{true}\rfloor.\ <n{=}2 \vee prime\_n>$

Then, we can construct the program that verifies the *goal*, which is defined as:

$goal \equiv \exists m,k{:}N.(prime(m) \wedge prime(k) \wedge n{=}m{+}k)$

The domain of variable m is [2 .. n-1], as stated above. The domain of k is dependent upon that of m based on the fact that $n = m + k$. The *goal* can be transformed to the following:

$goal \equiv \exists m{:}M.(prime(m) \wedge prime(n{-}m))$

The verification program can be constructed based on *Rule* 7 as follows:

$<goal> = <t, ff, true, false, M, \textbf{false}, \varnothing{:}R>$ where
$true = \gamma(m{:}M)\lfloor prime[m] \wedge prime[n{-}m]\rfloor.\ \textbf{true}, m{:}R, true$
$false = \gamma(m{:}M)\lfloor \neg(prime[m] \wedge prime[n{-}m])\rfloor.\ \textbf{false}, false$
$ff = \gamma(\textbf{false}, m)\lfloor x{\neq}\textbf{true} \wedge type(m){\neq}R\rfloor.\ \textbf{false}$
$t = \gamma(\textbf{true}, m)\lfloor type(m){\neq}R\rfloor.\ \textbf{true}$

The constructed program is a semantic verification program of the given logic specification. The essence of this method is its adaptability to be implemented as an automatic rewrite system. We can design a parser that generates the verification program for a given logic specification. In this process, efficiency of the target program is not taken into consideration. It is well understandable that the target program may have a low efficiency because the verification process involves a brute force testing of samples in the input domain. Although there are methods for improving the efficiency of the program by reducing the size of the domain using logic properties in the domain theory (see (Lin & Chen, 1998) for detailed descriptions), let's highlight that this method is not intended to be used in the construction of concrete programs that directly perform computations on first-class input data. Instead, it aims to transform the logic specifications of system architectures to operational specifications. The architectural specifications of MASs, for example, are composed of entities in the interfaces of program modules instead of first-class data. These entities may include the messages exchanged among program units in a distributed network system as well as meta data used for global control of the overall system. In the following section, we discuss the application of this method in the design of MASs.

DESIGNING MULTI-AGENT SYSTEMS FROM LOGIC SPECIFICATIONS

A special issue in a distributed system is that the system is composed of interacting, but independent program units, each has its own data domain; and the architectural design focuses on the conversation among these units (Bradshaw, 1997). A conversation is a sequence of messages involving two or more agents and centering on a set of pre-designated topics, intended to achieve a particular purpose. To correctly and efficiently engineer software architecture, we can model and specify agent interactions in distributed learning as conversation schemata, in which interaction patterns and task constraints in collaborative agent systems are constructed within class hierarchies of conversation schemata (Lin et. al., 2000). When the agent system is modeled by γ-Calculus, conversation is modeled as solution, which can be constructed automatically when the logic specification is converted into the verification program, if the conversing agents and their input-output are included in the specification. Therefore, for a specification in the form of

$$spec \equiv \forall a{:}T_a.\ (TH \rightarrow \exists z{:}T_z.Q(a, z))$$

when input a and output z are not handled by the same agent, *spec* must be decomposed into a series of sub-specifications:

$$spec_i = \forall x_i{:}\ T_i.\ (TH_i \rightarrow \exists x_{i+1}{:}\ T_{i+1}.\ Q_i(x_i, x_{i+1})) \qquad i = 0, \ldots, n$$

where $x_0 = a$ and $x_{n+1} = z$, and sub-goals

$$goal_i(x_i) = \exists x_{i+1}{:}\ T_{i+1}.\ Q_i(x_i, x_{i+1}) \quad i = 0, \ldots, n$$

to be verifiable, where $Q_i(x_{i-1}, x_i)$ is the specification of an agent with respect of the conversation and TH_i and its ground theory (or constraints). To this end, theory $TH\ (= TH_0 \cup \ldots \cup TH_n)$ may be used to decompose the original specification.

Because the output x_{i+1} of $goal_i$ is the input to $goal_{i+1}$, the verification program of $goal_{i+1}$ must use the result obtained by the verification program of $goal_i$. Referring to Section 3, we know the verification program of a logic expression is a solution. Let $<goal_i>$ be the verification program of $goal_i$, according to the the construction rules, when $<goal_i>$ is inert, it must be either $<x_{i+1}$, **true**$>$ or $<$**false**$>$, where x_{i+1} is the result. Let's define:

extract $= \gamma<x,$ **true**$>\lfloor$**true**$\rfloor.\ x$
fail $= \gamma<$**false**$>\lfloor$**true**$\rfloor.$ **false**
result $= \gamma<x,$ **false**$>\lfloor$**true**$\rfloor.\ x$
then the verification program of $goal_{i+1}$ can be written as:
$<goal_{i+1}[extract, fail, result, <goal_i>]>$

For example, let's consider an online course material maintenance system, which was studied in (Lin, Lin, & Holt, 2003), (Lin, 2004), and (Lin & Yang, 2006). The conversation schema is shown in Figure 1. As we know of e-learning systems, the online course materials are updated often in order to keep them as current as possible, esp. in some rapidly changing fields like "computing and information

Figure 1. The conversation schema of course maintenance

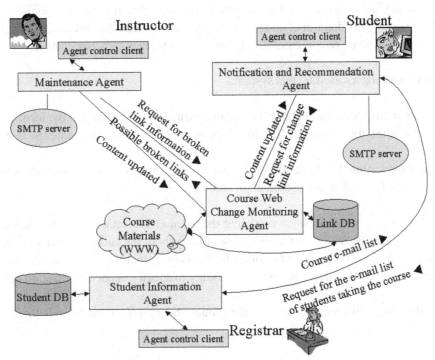

systems". As part of the duty of the course instructor in his/her effort to make the necessary adjustments for the benefit of students, whenever there's a significant change in the content of several designated Web pages of online course materials, he/she should notify by e-mails the students who are taking the course and those who are interested in the topic. The conversation model of the system consists of the following core elements:

- **Student information agent (ST):** A Student Information Agent is designed for providing services about student information, such as providing an e-mail list for a course by automatically maintaining the email list of students taking a course; and maintaining the profile of each student. While student information agent performs various tasks, for our purpose, we use *EM* to denote the email domain and predicate $ST(e, s)$ to denote that an notification email e is sent to student s.

- **Notification agent (NT):** The basic function of the Notification Agent is to send e-mails to students who take the course according to the student profiles stored in a database when the course material has been significantly changed. We use *NF* to denote the domain of notifications and predicate $NT(n, e)$ to denote that email e is to disseminate notification n.

- **Monitoring agent (MT):** This agent maintains the content of the topic tree, a course material URL database, monitors updates and notifies the notification agent when a change is made to the database. The domain handled by the monitoring agent is the topic link database *LK*. We use predicate $MT(l, n)$ to denote that notification n is created in accordance to the change made on topic link l.

- **Maintenance agent (MA):** The maintenance agent provides proxy services to the instructor. It takes updating instructions from the instructor and dispatches them to the monitoring agent. We use *UD* to denote the domain of updates made by the instructor and predicate *MA(u, l)* to denote that an update is made on topic link *l*. We assume that there is only one instructor in the system.

There are two databases used by this system:

- **Topic tree or Link database (LK):** The course material is organized in the form of a topic tree. Each entry in the topic tree is a link to a Web page. We use *LK* to denote the domain of topic links.
- **Student information database (DT):** This database maintains student information and their mail boxes. We use *DT* to denote the domain of students.

Note that although we will focus on modeling the agent conversation in the following discussion, we would like to point out that by no means we are talking about the entire system for e-learning. As a matter of fact, the background system has other functionalities that we do not address here (Lin, Lin, & Holt, 2003). Our point is to describe our methodology to specify agent conversation in a distributed system.

Based on the above conversation schema, the ground theory *TH* should include the following constraints:

A1: $\forall u\colon UD.\ \forall l\colon LK.\ (MA(u, l) \rightarrow \exists n\colon NF.\ MT(l, n))$
A2. $\forall l\colon LK.\ \forall n\colon NF.\ (MT(l, n) \rightarrow \exists e\colon EM.\ NT(n, e))$
A3. $\forall n\colon NF.\ \forall e\colon EM.\ (NT(n, e) \rightarrow \forall s\colon DT.\ ST(e, s))$

A1 means that if the instructor makes any update on any topic link, there exists a notification message that is generated to notify the change made on the topic link. A2 means that for any notification message that is generated to notify a change made on any topic link, there exists an email to deliver the notice. A3 means that for any email that is generated to deliver any notice, the email to sent to all students.

The logic specification of the system is:

$spec \equiv \forall u\colon UD.\ (TH \rightarrow \exists e\colon EM.\ \forall s\colon DT.\ ST(e, s))$

which means that for any update made by the instructor, an email notification is sent to all students.

The input is *u* and the goal is:

$goal \equiv \exists e\colon EM.\ \forall s\colon DT.\ ST(e, s)$

The goal is not verifiable with respect to the given input because the input is not present in the goal, which means that the input and the output are not handled by the same agent. Based on constraint A3, we can infer that:

$\forall n\colon NF.\ \forall e\colon EM.\ (NT(n, e) \rightarrow \forall s\colon DT.\ ST(e, s))$
$\Rightarrow\ \forall n\colon NF.\ \exists e\colon EM.\ (NT(n, e) \rightarrow \forall s\colon DT.\ ST(e, s))$

⇒ ∀*n*: *NF*. ∃*e*: *EM*. *NT*(*n*, *e*) → ∃*e*: *EM*. ∀*s*: *DT*. *ST*(*e*, *s*)

Therefore, we get a sub-goal which leads to the goal:

*goal*2(*n*) ≡ ∃*e*: *EM*. *NT*(*n*, *e*)

with input *n*. However, although *goal*2 checks domain *NF*, it still does not contain input *u*. Using A2, we have the following deduction:

∀*l*: *LK*. ∀*n*: *NF*. (*MT*(*l*, *n*) → ∃*e*: *EM*. *NT*(*n*, *e*))
⇒ ∀*l*: *LK*. ∃*n*: *NF*. (*MT*(*l*, *n*) → ∃*e*: *EM*. *NT*(*n*, *e*))
⇒ ∀*l*: *LK*. ∃*n*: *NF*. *MT*(*l*, *n*) → ∀*n*: *NF*. ∃*e*: *EM*. *NT*(*n*, *e*)

and we obtain another sub-goal:

*goal*1(*l*) ≡ ∃*n*: *NF*. *MT*(*l*, *n*)

with input *l*. With a similar deduction using A1:

∀*u*: *UD*. ∀*l*: *LK*. (*MA*(*u*, *l*) → ∃*n*: *NF*. *MT*(*l*, *n*))
⇒ ∀*u*: *UD*. ∃*l*: *LK*. (*MA*(*u*, *l*) → ∃*n*: *NF*. *MT*(*l*, *n*))
⇒ ∀*u*: *UD*. ∃*l*: *LK*. *MA*(*u*, *l*) → ∃*l*: *LK*. ∃*n*: *NF*. *MT*(*l*, *n*)

we can further obtain:

*goal*0(*u*) ≡ ∃*l*: *LK*. *MA*(*u*, *l*)

which contains input *u*.

Note that the input and output of the sub-goals form a pipelining structure:

$$\xrightarrow{u} goal0 \xrightarrow{l} goal1 \xrightarrow{n} goal2 \xrightarrow{e} goal$$

According to Rule 7 in Section 3, the verification program of *goal*0 can be constructed as:

<*goal*0[*u*]> = <*t*, *ff*, *true*, *false*, *LK*, **false**, ∅:*R*> where
true = γ(*l*:*LK*)⌊<*MA*[*u*, *l*]>=<**true**>⌋. **true**, *l*:*R*, *true*
false = γ(*l*:*LK*)⌊< *MA*[*u*, *l*]>=<**false**>⌋. **false**, *false*
ff = γ(**false**, *l*)⌊*l*≠**true** ∧ *type*(*l*)≠*R*⌋. **false**
t = γ(**true**, *l*)⌊*type*(*l*)≠*R*⌋. **true**

where *MA*[*u*, *l*] denote the molecule constructed to verify specification MA(u, l).

Similarly, <*goal*1> can be constructed as:

<*goal*1[*l*]> = <*t*, *ff*, *true*, *false*, *MT*, **false**, $\varnothing$:*R*> where
true = γ(*n:MT*)$\lfloor$<*MT*[*l*, *n*]>=<**true**>$\rfloor$. **true**, *n:R*, *true*
false = γ(*n:MT*)$\lfloor$< *MT*[*l*, *n*]>=<**false**>$\rfloor$. **false**, *false*
ff = γ(**false**, *n*)$\lfloor n \neq$**true** $\wedge$ *type*(*n*)$\neq R\rfloor$. **false**
t = γ(**true**, *n*)$\lfloor type$(*n*)$\neq R\rfloor$. **true**

Because the input *l* in <*goal*1[*l*]> is computed using expression:

extract, fail, result, <*goal*$_0$>

the verification program should be:

<*goal*$_1$[*extract, fail, result,* <*goal*$_0$[*u*]>]> = <*t*, *ff*, *true*, *false*, *MT*, **false**, $\varnothing$:*R*> where
Let *l* = *extract, fail, result,* <*goal*$_0$[*u*]>
true = γ(*n:MT*)$\lfloor$<*MT*[*l*, *n*]>=<**true**>$\rfloor$. **true**, *n:R*, *true*
false = γ(*n:MT*)$\lfloor$< *MT*[*l*, *n*]>=<**false**>$\rfloor$. **false**, *false*
ff = γ(**false**, *n*)$\lfloor n \neq$**true** $\wedge$ *type*(*n*)$\neq R\rfloor$. **false**
t = γ(**true**, *n*)$\lfloor type$(*n*)$\neq R\rfloor$. **true**

With similar reasoning, we can construct:

<*goal*$_2$[*extract, fail, result,* <*goal*$_1$[*l*]>]> = <*t*, *ff*, *true*, *false*, *EM*, **false**, $\varnothing$:*R*> where
Let *n* = *extract, fail, result,* <*goal*$_1$[*l*]>
true = γ(*e:EM*)$\lfloor$<*NT*[*n*, *e*]>=<**true**>$\rfloor$. **true**, *e:R*, *true*
false = γ(*e:EM*)$\lfloor$< *NT*[*n*, *e*]>=<**false**>$\rfloor$. **false**, *false*
ff = γ(**false**, *e*)$\lfloor e \neq$**true** $\wedge$ *type*(*e*)$\neq R\rfloor$. **false**
t = γ(**true**, *e*)$\lfloor type$(*e*)$\neq R\rfloor$. **true**

To construct the program for

goal $\equiv \exists e$: *EM*. $\forall s$: *DT*. *ST*(*e*, *s*)

we firstly construct the program for

$\forall s$: *DT*. *ST*(*e*, *s*)

Using Rule 1, we get:

<*goal'*[*e*]> = <*f*, *tt*, *true*, *false*, *DT*, **true**> where
true = γ(*s:DT*)$\lfloor$<*ST*[*e*, *s*]>=<**true**>$\rfloor$. **true**, *true*
false = γ(*s:DT*)$\lfloor$<*ST*[*e*, *s*]>=<**false**>$\rfloor$. **false**, *false*
tt = γ(**true**, *s*)$\lfloor s \neq$**false**$\rfloor$. **true**

$f = \gamma(\textbf{false}, s)\lfloor\textbf{true}\rfloor.\ \textbf{false}$

Then we have:

$<goal[extract, fail, result, <goal_2[n]>]> = <t, ff, true, false, EM, \textbf{false}, \varnothing:R>$ where

$\textbf{Let}\ e = extract, fail, result, <goal_2[n]>$

$true = \gamma(e{:}EM)\lfloor< goal'[e]>=<\textbf{true}>\rfloor.\ \textbf{true},\ e{:}R,\ true$

$false = \gamma(e{:}EM)\lfloor< goal'[e]>=<\textbf{false}>\rfloor.\ \textbf{false},\ false$

$ff = \gamma(\textbf{false}, e)\lfloor e{\neq}\textbf{true} \wedge type(e){\neq}R\rfloor.\ \textbf{false}$

$t = \gamma(\textbf{true}, e)\lfloor type(e){\neq}R\rfloor.\ \textbf{true}$

From the depicted process we can see that the conversion from logic specification to operational specification can be done using a small number of rules and we can see that the process can be automated with a parsing program. Let's highlight that this approach allows a large complex system to be design modularly. A complex logic specification can be decomposed into simpler specifications and converted into γ programs separately. With the conceptual model of γ-Calculus, it is very easy to combine verification programs (in the form of solutions) into a compound module by using a compassing solution.

IMPLEMENTATION

The above course material updating system has been implemented and simulated using the Message Passing Interface (MPI). This section details the design of the e-learning agent system, the design and architecture of the agents themselves, and explanation of MPI and how MPI facilitates the simulation.

The System Architecture

In order to provide a comprehensive e-learning environment, the system needs to account for:

- **Changes in the curriculum:** Adding or removing course content
- **Solving problems that occur:** Reporting broken Web links, and fixing them
- **Customizing content presentation:** Displaying course content based on the individual user's needs
- **Matching student models:** Delivering course content based on the specific student's requirements

Using current technology, the implementation of a distributed system, that satisfies these requirements, results in a complex, difficult to administer, and cost prohibitive solution. The complexity of the system is derived from individual components competing for resources and engaging in complex communications in order to deliver data and satisfy their individual goals.

For this project, there are two types of agents to discuss; interface agents and information agents.

Interface Agents: Interface agents are designed to interact directly with the user or other agents. In the e-learning system developed for this project, they are referred to as control agents. They provide a mechanism for accepting commands from a user, processing the command, and delivering the resulting

Figure 2. Hierarchical structure of the agent system

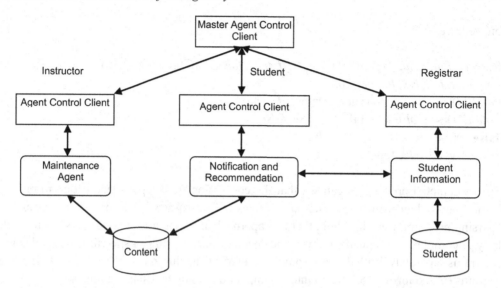

content back to the user. There is an interface agent associated directly with each information agent, and the commands from the user are sent to the information agents to gather the requested data.

Information Agents: Information agents facilitate the mechanisms for data manipulation. They receive command requests from the interface agents and execute the commands. The information agents primarily handle requests relating to adding, updating, and deleting data based on the commands sent by the user to the information agent's corresponding interface agent.

This project implements an agent based e-learning system. Its goal is to simulate the interactions among several agents in an agent based system to facilitate the delivery and manipulation of course content. The e-learning system developed for this project exists in a hierarchical structure. All requests from users are received into a top level agent. The top level agent then process the specific command received and sends the request to a control agent that corresponds to the information agent required to process the command. Once the command is executed, the result of the command is sent back to the top level control agent who then delivers the result to the user. Each information agent has a corresponding control agent that filters the command requested and passes the command on to the information agent. This creates a pairing between a control agent and information agent. The relationship between control agents and information agents is one to many. A single control agent processes requests for all of the information agents it connects to. Figure 2 depicts a high level diagram of the hierarchical structure of the agent system.

Figure 2 also shows the distribution of work based on the user that will be interacting with a specific agent. The Instructor, Student, and Registrar designation help describe the type of processing that will be done by that agent. Also depicted in Figure 2, are 5 types of agents that make up this system. They include the Master Agent Control Client, Agent Control Client, Maintenance Agent, Notification and Recommendation Agent, and Student Information Agent. Communications among the agents occur through the control clients. The system is designed such that, no agent can communicate directly with any agent on the same level in the tree hierarchy. For example, in order for the Maintenance Agent to request information from the Student Information agent, it must pass the request to the Agent Control Client, which then passes the request to the Master Control Client. The request is then sent down to the Student Information Agent. This structure insures an Agent's autonomy by not creating inter-dependencies among the Agents.

Master Control Agent: The Master Control Agent serves multiple purposes. First and foremost, it is the entry point into the system. All user requests are filtered through this Agent and passed along to the appropriate Control Agent to process the request. There are two methods that a request can be sent to the system. The first, to facilitate online courses, is through a network socket used to receive requests from a Web server into the system, and the second method is to pass commands into the system via the command line in the form of a text file. Second, the Master Control Agent is the primary MPI IO process; this is discussed in greater detail in the *Implementing MPI in an Agent System* section. Third, the Master Control Agent receives the result of a command and passes it back to the user. Lastly, the Master Control Agent controls the creation and deletion of the Control Agents.

Control Agent: The Control Agent manages requests to a specific information agent. With respect to the implementation for this project, the Control Agent receives a command from the Master Control Agent. Once the command is received, the Control Agent verifies that the command can be executed by one of its information agents, and then passes the command to the information agent. After the command has been executed, the control agent receives the result from the Information Agent and passes the result to the Master Control Agent. Also, the Control Agent manages the creation and deletion of its information agents.

Maintenance Agent: For this implementation, the maintenance agent corresponds directly with functions executed by an instructor. It processes requests directly relating to the management of course content and class interactivity. In addition, the Maintenance Agent handles the messages sent by students to an instructor and provides the ability for an instructor to send a message to a class or individual student. The Maintenance Agent also has the ability to retrieve a student listing from the Student Information Agent for a specific class.

Notification and Recommendation Agent: The Notification and Recommendation Agent relates to the activities of a student. It delivers the course content to the student as well as any messages sent to the class or from another student. In addition, the Notification and Recommendation allows a student to send messages to the instructor or another student.

Student Information Agent: The Student Information Agent corresponds to the operations of the university registrar. This Agent manages all of the student and class data. The Student Information Agent allows students to be added and removed from a class, retrieve the list of students, retrieve a student's information, and the addition and deletion of a class. This Agent has the highest level responsibility simply because it manages the student information and any changes to a student. In the case of adding a student, the Student Information sends the request to create a Notification and Recommendation agent for the individual student. This operation allows the Notification and Recommendation Agent to begin processing requests on behalf of the student and customizing class content for delivery.

The Master Control Agent and Control Agents both have the responsibility of managing the creation and deletion of agents. This behavior insures the reliability of the system by not allowing a command request to go unprocessed. This behavior is also handled automatically, meaning that specialized code does not be added to additional agents to control agent creation and deletion.

MPI Implementation of the Multi-Agent System

Message passing interface (MPI) is the technology used in this project to simulate the environment that an Agent system would be operated in. Traditionally, MPI is the foundation for distributed parallel communications between running processes on the same machine or on different machines. MPI is primarily used to build applications for problem solving on datasets that would require large amounts of time to calculate using a single a process. However, the versatility of MPI has enabled this technology to be used for this project.

The role of MPI for this project is to facilitate the communication mechanism between the agents. A request sent to the system is packaged into an MPI data structure and sent to the correct information agent using the *MPI_Send* and *MPI_Recv* commands. This communication behavior is common for all of the agents.

The way MPI handles IO also corresponds to the structure of the Agent System developed for this project. MPI allows for a primary IO source that divides the workload and initiate communication with the other process. In the case of this project, the Master Control Client corresponds to this IO source for MPI, thus all job requests originate from the Master Control Client.

The one limitation presented to this project from MPI is the inability for MPI to spawn or create processes. As described earlier, the control agents control the creation and deletion of agents. With the inability to create a new Agent process, a flag was added to each Agent to indicate whether or not an agent existed. In this case that the agent was created, a command was sent to create the agent, thus emulating the procedure required to create a new Agent. Due to the inability to create a new Agent process, the Control Agents have now way maintaining a one-to-many relationship with the corresponding information agents. Instead the MPI limitation keeps the ratio as a one to one relationship.

The E-Learning Agent system was developed exclusively using the C++ programming language. In order to maintain compatibility with MPI, all of the agents are derived from a single program executable. Each Agent's job function is determined by the process ID provided to each process by the MPI

Figure 3. Flowchart of agent startup

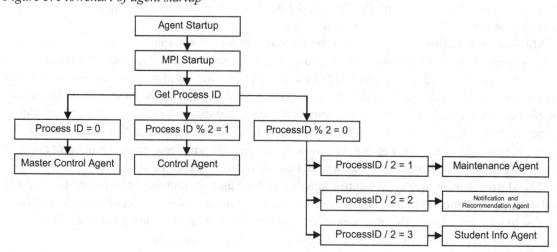

system. The Master Control Agent is assigned process 0. Agents use: `if( process ID % 2 == 1 )` to determine the control agents, and the information Agents for each Control Agent use the result of `process ID / 2` to determine which information agent they will be. Figure 3 illustrates the startup sequence for each agent and the determination of the type of agent.

Web Interface

In order to provide a mechanism for a Web server to communicate with the Agent system, a CGI program was required to gather the data submitted by the user and send the data to the agent system. WEBAGENT.EXE is the program developed to satisfy this requirement.

The Master Control Agent provides a socket interface that can be used to communicate with the agent system. Described below is the process that WEBAGENT.EXE uses to send a request to the Agent system.

- The data from the Web forms are copied from the QUERY_STRING environment variable
- The QUERY_STRING values are translated into an INPUTJOB structure
- The INPUTJOB structure is translated into a string value
- The string value containing the INPUTJOB structure is sent to the Agent system
- WEBAGENT.EXE receives a string from the Agent system containing the result of the command operation
- The string received from the Agent system is translated into a Result Code and Result Message pair
- From the Result code and Result message pair, the Web page is built and sent back to the Web server

WEBAGENT.EXE provides the mechanism for connecting the Web server to the agent system.

FUTURE PLAN

The above example gives us a prototype of applying the method to the design of MASs in large applications. Here we briefly describe an ongoing project of designing an online education system. The task is to design an infrastructure of an educational grid comprised of PC clusters and PCs in networked labs. The barrier in front of us is the integration of various networking technologies into one client/server model to provide a uniform lab environment for different lab activities in the form of grid services. We use the chemical reaction model as a formal language for specifying MASs that implement the grid services.

The system will be developed (the Design Theme) and evaluated (the Application Theme) in a sequence of major steps in a pyramid-shaped model illustrated in Figure 2. A bottom-up strategy will be used in the Design Theme. We will extend our grid and design lab modules using existing toolkits, such as Globus Toolkit 4, Java, and Apache Server. The services provided by the system will be implemented in the client/server architecture. A Java based user interface will deliver the services on the Web. Servers will run on the clusters. Multiple servers interact with one another in the agent based infrastructure. A formal definition of the interfaces of functional units of the system will form

Figure 4. Pyramid model of the educational grid

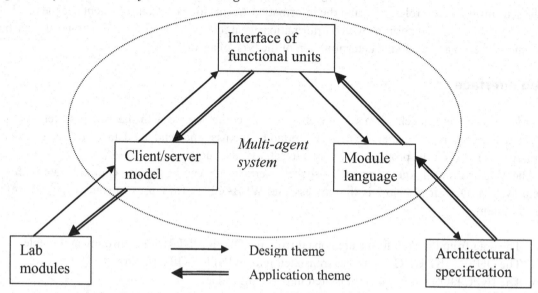

the basis for MAS design. Each agent is then designed in the module language. The overall system is specified in the λ-Calculus. In Figure 4, we can see the MAS is the conceptual model for implementing grid services, and the interfaces of functional units define the interaction among functional units and are the central part of the agent system. The interface also separates the architectural design from the design of individual functional units.

Once the agent system has been designed, adding/deleting services or features in the grid will be done in a top-down strategy (the Application Theme). If a service of a new type is to be added into the system, for example, it is added into the architectural specification. Through an automatic transformation procedure, the specification is re-written into a MAS in the module language. The actual program that encodes the services is then incorporated into the system through the standard interface. Therefore, updating services or lab exercises in the system will not cause any change in other parts of the system and correctness and reliability of the system can be ensured to the maximum extent.

The central component of this architecture is the interfaces of the functional units, to ensure the correctness of the design, the interfaces will be specified logically. Then, λ-Calculus will be derived to give the operational specifications of interfaces and guide the further design of the functional units in the module language.

RELATED WORKS

A number of architecture description languages (ADLs) have recently been proposed to cope with the complexity of architectural engineering. These include Rapide (Luckham et. al., 1995), Darwin (Magee & Kramer, 1996), Aseop (Garlan, Allen, & Ockerbloom, 1994), Unicon (Shaw, et. al., 1995), and ACME (Garlan, Monroe, & Wile, 1997). ADLs provide constructs for specifying architectural abstractions in a formal notation and provide mechanisms for reasoning about the architecture. They focus on defining architectural elements that can be combined to form a configuration. Few research efforts aim at truly defining an ADL for MAS architectures. Nor do they address the design from logic specifications.

There are some formal languages proposed to address design issues of MASs. For example, Skw-yRL-ADL (Faulkner & Kolp, 2002) is proposed as a BDI-MAS language to capture a "core" set of structural and behavioral abstractions, including relationships and constraints that are fundamental to the description of any BDI-MAS architecture. Kokar, Baclawski, and Eracar (1999) developed a control-theory-based architecture for self-controlling software. However, none of them is a complete formal system based on a finished computation model and serve as a language that encourages program design by derivation or transformation.

Back to the classical program derivation area, the deductive-tableau method (Manna & Waldinger, 1992) synthesizes programs in a proof of the specification in the first-order logic. This method requires the use of an intelligent strategy. Instead, the method presented in this paper constructs a program from the process of semantic proving of the specification. RAPTS system is based on the SETL language and derivation techniques have been developed based on ''generate-and-test'' algorithms (Kaldewaij, & Schoenmakers, 1990; Smith & Lowry, 1990; Smith, 1990). In these techniques, parallelism, however, is not addressed. In these methods, the most difficult task is the deductions in the logic level. We believe that the difficulty can be relieved by using a high-level programming language such as γ-Calculus. By bridging the logic specifications and operational specifications, we provide a design method in a multi-phase transformational fashion, and we find that this method is effective in the design of the architectures of multi-agent systems.

We would like to point out that using γ-Calculus to facilitate a system design method in the transformational style is congruent to the current research themes in γ-Calculus. As the inventors of γ-Calculus stated: "Another direction is to propose a realistic higher-order chemical programming language based on γ-Calculus. It would consist in defining the already mentioned syntactic sugar, a type system, as well as expressive pattern and module languages." (Banâtre, Fradet, & Radenac, 2004). In the author's point of view, a realistic chemical programming language must be based on, directly or indirectly, a realistic computational model. If the module language is to express construct details of higher-order chemical programming languages, it should be implementable by a realistic computational model in order to make the chemical programming language realistic. In addition, because the chemical programming languages, including γ-Calculus, are primarily used as specification languages, it would be sensible to address the practicability issue by providing a system that transforms Gamma specifications into specifications in the module language.

Despite the promises this method has made, there are limitations that come from the traditional area of automatic software design, specifically, from the use of logic specifications in MASs. Firstly, program derivation from logic specification requires mastering logic proofing. Secondly, MASs are complex systems with a lot of non-functional facets that cannot be directly captured by a functional programming language such as γ-Calculus. On the theoretical study side, we are planning to apply γ-Calculus to aspect-oriented programming to develop a framework for designing complex systems and use this framework in MAS design. On the practical side, we are continuing to develop the module language and implement it in common network programming environments.

CONCLUSION

We present a program construction method by verifying specifications in first-order logic. In this method, programs in γ-Calculus are constructed directly from logical specifications. The constructed programs are parallel programs, thanks to the inherently parallel nature of the Gamma computational model. We exploited the use of this method in the design of the architectures of multi-agent systems. Starting from logic specification of the architecture, which defines the input/output relationship among the interacting agents, a semantic verification program in γ-Calculus is constructed in a systematic rewriting process by recursively applying a set of rules. The method is effective in the architectural design due to the automation of the process. The method translates the specification from logic level to operational level and this furnishes transformational design of the system in an incremental fashion. We used this method in the design of a course information management system. The derived specification of the system in Gamma language described the architecture of the interacting agent system and guided the correct implementation of the system. The implementation of the system is also presented.

ACKNOWLEDGMENT

This research is supported by the National Science Foundation grant (#0619312) and U.S. Army Research Office award (#W911NF-04-1-0024) through Scholars Academy of University of Houston-Downtown.

REFERENCES

Aarts, C., et. al. (1992). *A relational theory of datatypes*. Technical report. The Netherlands: Utrecht University.

Banatre, J.-P., & Le Metayer, D. (1990). The gamma model and its discipline of programming. *Science of Computer Programming, 15,* 55-77.

Banatre J.-P., & Le Metayer, D. (1993). Programming by multiset transformation. *CACM, 36*(1), 98-111.

Banâtre, J.-P., Fradet, P., & Radenac, Y. (2004, July). Chemical specification of autonomic systems. In *Proceedings of the 13th International Conference on Intelligent and Adaptive Systems and Software Engineering* (IASSE'04).

Banâtre, J.-P., Fradet, P., & Radenac, Y. (2005). Principles of chemical programming. In S. Abdennadher and C. Ringeissen (eds.), *Proceedings of the 5th International Workshop on Rule-Based Programming (RULE'04), 124,* ENTCS, (pp. 133-147).

Banâtre, J.-P., Fradet, P., & Radenac, Y. (2005). Higher-order chemical programming style. In *Proceedings of Unconventional Programming Paradigms.* (LNCS, 3566, 84-98). Springer-Verlag.

Bauer, F.L., et. al. (1985). *The Munich Project CIP, Vol. 1: The wide spectrum language.* CIP-L, (LNCS 183).

Berry, G., & Boudol, G. (1992). The chemical abstract machine. *Theoretical Computer Science, 96,* 217-248.

Bradshaw, J. M. (1997). *Software agents.* Menlo Park, CA: AAAI/MIT Press.

Cohen, D., & Muylaert-Filho, J. (1996). Introducing a calculus for higher-order multiset programming. In *Coordination languages and models.* (LNCS 1061, 124-141).

Creveuil, C. (1991). Implementation of gamma on the connection machine. In *Proceedings of the Workshop on Research Directions in High-Level Parallel Programming Languages*, Mont-Saint Michel, 1991. (LNCS 574, 219-230). Springer-Verlag.

Ehrig, H., & Mahr, B. (1990). Fundamentals of algebraic specification. Brauer, W., Rozenberg, G., & Salomaa, A. (eds.), *EATCS Monographs on Theoretical Computer Science, 21*, Springer-Verlag.

Faulkner, S., & Kolp (Isys), M. (2002). *Towards an agent architectural description language for information systems.* School of Management, the Catholic University of Louvain (UCL), Technical Report, November 2002.

Fradet, P., & Le Metayer, D. (1998). Structured gamma. *Science of Computer Programming, 31*(2-3), 263-289.

Garlan, D., Allen, R., & Ockerbloom, J. (1994, December). Exploiting style in architectural design environments. *In Proceedings of SIGSOFT'94: Foundations of Software Engineering*, New Orleans, Louisiana, (pp. 175-188).

Garlan, D., Monroe, R., & Wile, D. (1997, January). ACME: An architecture description interchange language. In *Proceedings of CASCON 97*, Toronto, (pp. 169-183).

Gladitz, K., & Kuchen, H. (1996). Shared memory implementation of the gamma-operation. *Journal of Symbolic Computation 21*, 577-591.

Griss M., & Pour, G. (2001). Accelerating development with agent components. *Computer, IEEE*, 37-43.

Kaldewaij, A., & Schoenmakers, B. (1990). Searching by elimination. *SCP, 14*, 243-254.

Klop, J. W. (1990). Term rewriting systems. In: Abramsky, S., Gabbay, D., & Maibaum, T. (eds.), *Handbook of logic in computer science, 1.* Oxford University Press.

Kokar, M. M., Baclawski, K., & Eracar, Y. (1999). Control theory-based foundations of self-controlling software. *IEEE Intelligent Systems*, May/June, 37-45.

Le Metayer, D. (1994). Higher-order multiset processing. *DIMACS Series in Discrete Mathematics and Theoretical Computer Science, 18*, 179-200.

Lin, H., Chen, G., & Wang, M. (1997). Program transformation between unity and gamma. *Neural, Parallel & Scientific Computations, 5*(4), 511-534. Atlanta,GA: Dynamic Publishers.

Lin, H., & Chen, G. (1998). Program construction by verifying specification. *Journal of Computer Science and Technology, 13*(6), 597-607.

Lin F., Norrie D. H., Flores, R. A., & Kremer R.C. (2000, June 3-7). Incorporating conversation managers into multi-agent systems. In M. Greaves, F. Dignum, J. Bradshaw & B. Chaib-draa (Eds.), *Proceedings of the Workshop on Agent Communication and Languages, 4th Inter. Conf. on Autonomous Agents (Agents 2000),* Barcelona, Spain, (pp. 1-9).

Lin, F. O., Lin, H., & Holt, P. (2003, May 18-23). A method for implementing distributed learning environments. *Proceedings of 2003 Information Resources Management Association International Conference*, Philadelphia, Pennsylvania, (pp. 484-487).

Lin, H. (2004). A language for specifying agent systems in e-learning environments. In F.O. Lin (ed.), *Designing distributed learning environments with intelligent software agents*, 242-272.

Lin, H., & Yang, C. (2006). Specifying distributed multi-agent systems in chemical reaction metaphor. *The International Journal of Artificial Intelligence, Neural Networks, and Complex Problem-Solving Technologies, 24*(2), 155-168. Springer-Verlag

Luckham, D. C., Kenney, J. J., Augustin, L. M., Vera, J., Bryan, D., & Mann, W. (1995). Specification and analysis of system architecture using Rapide. *IEEE Trans. on Software Engineering*, April, 336-355.

Magee, J., & Kramer, J. (1996, October). Dynamic structure in software architectures. In *Proceedings of the 4th Symposium on the Foundations of Software Engineering (FSE4)*, San Francisco, CA, (pp.3-14).

Manna, Z., & Waldinger, R. (1992). Fundamentals of deductive program synthesis. *IEEE Trans. On Software Engineering, 18*(8), 674-704.

Martin-Lof, P. (1980). Intuitionistic type theory. *Notes by Giovanni Sambin of a series of lectures given in Padua, Bibliopolis.*

Meseguer, J., & Winkler, T. (1991). Parallel programming in Maude. In Banatre, J.P., & Le Metayer, D. (eds.), *Proceedings of the Workshop on Research Directions in High-Level Parallel programming Languages*, Mont Saint-Michel, France, (pp. 253-293). Springer-Verlag.

Meseguer, J. (1992). Conditional rewriting logic as a unified model of concurrency. *Theoretical Computer Science, 96*, 73-155.

Paige, R., Reif, J., & Watcher, R. (eds.) (1993). Parallel aorithm derivation and program transformation. *The Kluwer International Series in Engineering and Computer Science*. Kluwer Academic Publishers.

Richstein, J. (2001). Verifying the Goldbach conjecture up to $4 \cdot 10^{14}$. *Math. Comp., 70*(236), 1745-1749.

Shapiro, E. Y. (1981). Inductive inference of theories from facts. (Report 192). Department of Computer Science, Yale University.

Shaw, M., DeLine, R., Klein, D. V., Ross, T. L., Young, D. M., & Zelesnik, G. (1995). Abstractions for software architecture and tools to support them. *IEEE Trans. On Software Engineering*, April, 314-335.

Smith, D. R., & Lowry, M. R. (1990). Algorithm theories and design tactics. *SCP, 14*, 305-321.

Smith, D.R. (1990). KIDS: A semi-automatic program development system. *IEEE Trans. on Software Engineering, 16*(9), 1024-1043.

Traugott, J. (1989). Deductive synthesis of sorting programs. *Journal of Symbolic Computation, 7*, 533-572.

APPENDIX A. DETERMINING BOUNDS OF QUANTIFIED VARIABLES

Definition (Boundedness of variables) A quantified variable x of type T is

- **Upper bounded,** iff there exists an expression e such that $x \le e$, where $\le$ is a complete ordering on type T;
- **Lower bounded,** iff there exists an expression e such that $x \ge e$;
- **Fully bounded,** iff there exists an expression e_1 and e_2 such that $e_1 \le x \le e_2$.

This is a recursive definition because boundedness of a variable may depend on boundedness of other variables. For example, $x \le 1\text{-}y$ and $y \ge 0$, or $x \le 1\text{-}y$ and $y \le 0$.

Because we will construct a verification program for the specification, we should know the value domain that ought to be checked for a variable. Boundedness of variables ensures termination of the evaluation process.

Bounds of variables are determined based on the following principles:

- For clause $\forall x.p$, if

$$TH \vdash x \ge e \rightarrow p$$

then e is an upper bound of x; otherwise, if

$$TH \vdash x \le e \rightarrow p$$

then e is a lower bound of x. Intuitively, e is regarded as an upper (lower) bound of x if any value greater than e needs not to be checked because $\forall x.p$ cannot be proved false in the domain that $x \ge e\ (\le e)$.

- For clause $\exists x.p$, if

$$TH \vdash x \ge e \rightarrow \neg p$$

then e is an upper bound of x; otherwise, if

$$TH \vdash x \le e \rightarrow \neg p$$

then e is a lower bound of x. Intuitively, e is regarded as an upper (lower) bound of x if any value greater than e needs not to be checked because $\exists x.p$ cannot be proved true in the domain that $x \ge e\ (\le e)$.

We call e the *upper (lower) bound of x deduced from* $\forall x.p$, written $e = \uparrow x(\forall x.p)$ ($e = \downarrow x(\forall x.p)$) (Precisely, it should be written as $e \in \uparrow x(\forall x.p)$ or $e \in \downarrow x(\forall x.p)$), or *from* $\exists x.p$, written $e = \uparrow x(\exists x.p)$ ($e = \downarrow x(\exists x.p)$), in the above cases. If there is no free occurrence of x in p, then we write $\uparrow x(\forall x.p) = \mathbf{irrel}$ or $\uparrow x(\exists x.p) = \mathbf{irrel}$, which means that $\forall x.p$ or $\exists x.p$ is irrelevant to the upper bound of x. Some rules apply to the lower bounds.

Based on the above principles, we can establish some propositions for the deduction of variable bounds. For instances:

1. $(p = q \wedge r) \wedge e = \downarrow x(\exists x.q) \Rightarrow e = \downarrow x(\exists x.p)$
2. $(p = q \rightarrow r) \wedge e = \downarrow x(\exists x.q) \Rightarrow e = \downarrow x(\forall x.p)$
2'. $(p = q \rightarrow r) \wedge e = \uparrow x(\exists x.q) \Rightarrow e = \uparrow x(\forall x.p)$
3. $(p = q \vee r) \wedge e = \downarrow x(\forall x.q) \Rightarrow e = \downarrow x(\forall x.p)$
3'. $(p = q \vee r) \wedge e = \uparrow x(\forall x.q) \Rightarrow e = \uparrow x(\forall x.p)$
4. $(p = q \vee r) \wedge e_1 = \downarrow x(\exists x.q) \wedge e_2 = \downarrow x(\exists x.r) \Rightarrow min(e_1, e_2) = \downarrow x(\exists x.p)$
5. $(p = q \wedge r) \wedge e_1 = \downarrow x(\forall x.q) \wedge e_2 = \downarrow x(\forall x.r) \Rightarrow min(e_1, e_2) = \downarrow x(\forall x.p)$
5'. $(p = q \wedge r) \wedge e_1 = \uparrow x(\forall x.q) \wedge e_2 = \uparrow x(\forall x.r) \Rightarrow max(e_1, e_2) = \uparrow x(\forall x.p)$

When rule (4), (5), and (5') are concerned, we should keep in mind the fact that $min(e, \textbf{irrel}) = e$ and $max(e, \textbf{irrel}) = e$.

For example, the goal of Goldbach Conjecture is:

$\exists m, k: N. (prime(m) \wedge prime(k) \wedge n = m + k)$

where $prime(l)$ is defined as:

$prime(l) \equiv (l = 2 \ \vee l > 2 \wedge \forall i: N. (1 < i < l \rightarrow l\%i \neq 0))$

we can get the following bounds for variables m and k by applying the above rules to the goal.

$2 \leq m \leq n\text{-}2$
$k = n\text{-}m$ (viz., $n\text{-}m \leq k \leq n\text{-}m$)

In fact, because

$2 = \downarrow m(\exists m.m > 2)$

by rule (1), we have

$2 = \downarrow m(\exists m.m > 2 \wedge \forall i: N. (1 < i < m \rightarrow m\%i \neq 0))$

We also have

$2 = \downarrow m(\exists m.m = 2)$

Now by using rule (4), we have

$2 = \downarrow m(\exists m.(m = 2 \vee m > 2 \wedge \forall i: N. (1 < i < m \rightarrow m\%i \neq 0)))$

or

$2 = \downarrow m(\exists m.prime(m))$

By using rule (1) twice, we have

$2 = \downarrow m(\exists m, k: N. (prime(m) \wedge prime(k) \wedge n = m + k))$

In a similar procedure, we can determine that 2 is also the lower bound of k, i.e.,

$2 = \downarrow k(\exists m, k: N. (prime(m) \wedge prime(k) \wedge n = m + k))$

Now using $n = m+k$ and the lower bound of k, we can get the upper bound of m, which is n-2. Thus we have

$2 \leq m \leq n\text{-}2$

Again, using $n = m+k$, we have

$k = n - m$

As for variable i in

$prime(l) \equiv (l = 2 \ \vee l > 2 \wedge \ \forall i: N. (1 < i < l \rightarrow l\%i \neq 0))$

$2 \leq i$ is determined by the fact that

$2 = \downarrow i(\exists i.1 < i < l)$

Using rule (2), we get

$2 = \downarrow i(\forall i: N. (1 < i < l \rightarrow l\%i \neq 0))$

$i \leq m\text{-}1$ is determined by the fact that

$m\text{-}1 = \uparrow i(\exists i.1 < i < l)$

Using rule (2'), we get

$m\text{-}1 = \uparrow i(\forall i: N. (1 < i < l \rightarrow l\%i \neq 0))$

Therefore, we have

$2 \leq i \leq m\text{-}1$

The following propositions provide means for recursively deducing the bounds of variables:

Proposition A.1 (Deduction rules to determine the bounds for $\forall x.\ p$)

1. $(p = \neg q) \wedge e = \uparrow x(\exists x.q) \Rightarrow\ e = \uparrow x(\forall x.p)$
2. $(p = \neg q) \wedge e = \downarrow x(\exists x.q) \Rightarrow\ e = \downarrow x(\forall x.p)$
3. $(p = q \rightarrow r) \wedge e = \uparrow x(\exists x.q) \Rightarrow e = \uparrow x(\forall x.p)$
4. $(p = q \rightarrow r) \wedge e = \downarrow x(\exists x.q) \Rightarrow e = \downarrow x(\forall x.p)$
5. $(p = q \rightarrow r) \wedge e = \uparrow x(\forall x.r) \Rightarrow e = \uparrow x(\forall x.p)$
6. $(p = q \rightarrow r) \wedge e = \downarrow x(\forall x.r) \Rightarrow e = \downarrow x(\forall x.p)$
7. $(p = q \wedge r) \wedge e_1 = \uparrow x(\forall x.q) \wedge e_2 = \uparrow x(\forall x.r) \Rightarrow\ max(e_1, e_2) = \uparrow x(\forall x.p)$
8. $(p = q \wedge r) \wedge e_1 = \downarrow x(\forall x.q) \wedge e_2 = \downarrow x(\forall x.r) \Rightarrow\ min(e_1, e_2) = \downarrow x(\forall x.p)$
9. $(p = q \vee r) \wedge e_1 = \uparrow x(\forall x.q) \wedge e_2 = \uparrow x(\forall x.r) \Rightarrow\ min(e_1, e_2) = \uparrow x(\forall x.p)$
10. $(p = q \vee r) \wedge e_1 = \downarrow x(\forall x.q) \wedge e_2 = \downarrow x(\forall x.r) \Rightarrow\ max(e_1, e_2) = \downarrow x(\forall x.p)$
11. $(p = q \vee r) \wedge e = \uparrow x(\forall x.q) \Rightarrow\ e = \uparrow x(\forall x.p)$
12. $(p = q \vee r) \wedge e = \downarrow x(\forall x.q) \Rightarrow\ e = \downarrow x(\forall x.p)$
13. $(p = q \leftrightarrow r) \wedge e_1 = \uparrow x(\forall x.q) \wedge e_2 = \uparrow x(\forall x.r) \Rightarrow\ max(e_1, e_2) = \uparrow x(\forall x.p)$
14. $(p = q \leftrightarrow r) \wedge e_1 = \downarrow x(\forall x.q) \wedge e_2 = \downarrow x(\forall x.r) \Rightarrow\ min(e_1, e_2) = \downarrow x(\forall x.p)$
15. $(p = q \leftrightarrow r) \wedge e_1 = \uparrow x(\exists x.q) \wedge e_2 = \uparrow x(\exists x.r) \Rightarrow\ max(e_1, e_2) = \uparrow x(\forall x.p)$
16. $(p = q \leftrightarrow r) \wedge e_1 = \downarrow x(\exists x.q) \wedge e_2 = \downarrow x(\exists x.r) \Rightarrow\ min(e_1, e_2) = \downarrow x(\forall x.p)$

Proposition A.2 (Deduction rules to determine the bounds for $\exists x.\ p$)

17. $(p = \neg q) \wedge e = \uparrow x(\forall x.q) \Rightarrow\ e = \uparrow x(\exists x.p)$
18. $(p = \neg q) \wedge e = \downarrow x(\forall x.q) \Rightarrow\ e = \downarrow x(\exists x.p)$
19. $(p = q \rightarrow r) \wedge e_1 = \uparrow x(\forall x.q) \wedge e_2 = \uparrow x(\exists x.r) \Rightarrow\ max(e_1, e_2) = \uparrow x(\exists x.p)$
20. $(p = q \rightarrow r) \wedge e_1 = \downarrow x(\forall x.q) \wedge e_2 = \downarrow x(\exists x.r) \Rightarrow\ min(e_1, e_2) = \downarrow x(\exists x.p)$
21. $(p = q \wedge r) \wedge e = \uparrow x(\exists x.q) \Rightarrow\ e = \uparrow x(\exists x.p)$
22. $(p = q \wedge r) \wedge e = \downarrow x(\exists x.q) \Rightarrow\ e = \downarrow x(\exists x.p)$
23. $(p = q \vee r) \wedge e_1 = \uparrow x(\exists x.q) \wedge e_2 = \uparrow x(\exists x.r) \Rightarrow\ max(e_1, e_2) = \uparrow x(\exists x.p)$
24. $(p = q \vee r) \wedge e_1 = \downarrow x(\exists x.q) \wedge e_2 = \downarrow x(\exists x.r) \Rightarrow\ min(e_1, e_2) = \downarrow x(\exists x.p)$
25. $(p = q \leftrightarrow r) \wedge e_1 = \uparrow x(\forall x.q) \wedge e_2 = \uparrow x(\exists x.r) \Rightarrow\ max(e_1, e_2) = \uparrow x(\exists x.p)$
26. $(p = q \leftrightarrow r) \wedge e_1 = \downarrow x(\forall x.q) \wedge e_2 = \downarrow x(\exists x.r) \Rightarrow\ min(e_1, e_2) = \downarrow x(\exists x.p)$

Chapter II
Multi–Agent Architecture for Knowledge–Driven Decision Support

Rahul Singh
University of North Carolina at Greensboro, USA

ABSTRACT

Organizations use knowledge-driven systems to deliver problem-specific knowledge over Internet-based distributed platforms to decision-makers. Increasingly, artificial intelligence (AI) techniques for knowledge representation are being used to deliver knowledge-driven decision support in multiple forms. In this chapter, we present an Architecture for knowledge-based decision support, delivered through a Multi-Agent Architecture. We illustrate how to represent and exchange domain-specific knowledge in XML-format through intelligent agents to create exchange and use knowledge to provide intelligent decision support. We show the integration of knowledge discovery techniques to create knowledge from organizational data; and knowledge repositories (KR) to store, manage and use data by intelligent software agents for effective knowledge-driven decision support. Implementation details of the architecture, its business implications and directions for further research are discussed.

INTRODUCTION

Knowledge is an organizational asset that contributes to sustainable competitive advantage. This explains the increasing interest organizations take in knowledge management (KM). Many organizations are developing knowledge management systems (KMS), specifically designed to share and integrate knowledge, as opposed to data or information, in decision support activities (Bolloju et al., 2002). Decision support systems (DSS) are computer technology solutions used to support complex decision-making and problem solving (Shim et al., 2002). Organizations are increasingly complex with increased emphasis on decentralized decision-making. Such changes create the need for DSS that focus on supporting problem solving activities on distributed platforms by providing problem specific knowledge, and supporting information, to a decision maker using Internet-based technologies. This trend requires enterprise DSS for effective decision-making with processes and facilities to support the use of knowledge management.

Recent advances in systems support for problem solving and decision-making witness the increased use of artificial intelligence (AI) based techniques for knowledge representation (Whinston, 1997; Goul 2005). Knowledge representation takes multiple forms including the incorporation of business rules, decision analytical models and models generated from the application of machine learning algorithms. Intelligent decision support systems (IDSS) incorporate intelligence in the form of knowledge about the problem domain, with knowledge representation to inform the decision process, facilitate problem solving and reduce the cognitive load of the decision maker. Weber *et. al.* (2003) identified requirements for organizational KMS where the central unit is a repository of knowledge artifacts collected from internal or external organizational sources. These KMS can vary based on the type of knowledge artifact stored, the scope and nature of the topic described and the orientation (Weber et al., 2003). Ba *et. al.* (1997) enumerate the KM principles necessary to achieve intra-organizational knowledge bases as: (i) the use of corporate data to derive and create higher-level information and knowledge, (ii) provision of tools to transform scattered data into meaningful business information. Knowledge repositories play a central and critical role in the storage, distribution and management of knowledge in an organization. Interestingly, Bolloju *et. al.,* (2002) proposed an approach for integrating decision support and KM that facilitates knowledge conversion through suitable automated techniques to:

- Apply knowledge discovery techniques (KDT) for knowledge externalization
- Employ repositories for storing externalized knowledge
- Extend KDT for supporting various types of knowledge conversions

This chapter is motivated by these principles. We present an intelligent knowledge-based multi-agent architecture for knowledge-based decision support using eXtensible Markup Language (XML) related technologies for knowledge representation. This allows for knowledge exchange over distributed and heterogeneous platforms. The proposed architecture integrates DSS and KMS using XML-based technologies as the medium for the representation and exchange of domain specific knowledge. Intelligent agents to facilitate the creation, exchanges and use of the knowledge in decision support activities. This is the primary contribution of this chapter to the existing body of knowledge in DSS, KMS and multi-agent research.

This chapter builds on existing bodies of knowledge in intelligent agents, KM, DSS and XML technology standards. Our research focuses on achieving a transparent translation between XML and Decision Trees through software agents. This creates the foundation for knowledge representation and exchange, through intelligent agents, to support decision-making activity for users of the system. We use a knowledge repository to store knowledge, captured in XML documents, that can used and shared by software agents within the multi-agent architecture. We call this architecture *"an Intelligent Knowledge-based Multi-agent Decision Support Architecture"* (IKMDSA) IKMDSA integrates KDT and knowledge repositories to store externalized knowledge. It uses an intelligent multi-agent system with explanation facility to provide distributed decision support using Internet-based technologies.

The implementation incorporates XML related technologies for knowledge representation, storage and knowledge exchange among participating intelligent agents to deliver decision support to the user. In IKMDSA agents provide distributed intelligent decision support by exchanging their knowledge using XML and its related set of standards. Implementation details of the architecture and implications for further research in this area by academics and practitioners are provided.

In section 2, we review relevant literature in intelligent agents and the role of decision trees in inductive learning and knowledge representation in terms of decision rules. In section 3, we discuss the role of XML in representing and facilitating knowledge exchange for intelligent agents. Section 4 provides a detailed description of the various components of the IKMDSA architecture and their inter-relationships in facilitating the creation, representation, exchange and use of domain specific knowledge for decision support tasks. In section 5, we provide a detailed description of the implementation of the architecture through the use of an illustrative example. Section 6 includes a discussion of the implications of integrating KMS and DSS support in business, and the role of the proposed IKMDSA architecture. Section 7 concludes with limitations and future research directions.

LITERATURE REVIEW

Knowledge is an important organizational asset for sustainable competitive advantage. Organizations are increasingly interested in knowledge-driven decision analytics to improve decision quality and the decision support environment. This requires use of corporate data to develop higher-level knowledge in conjunction with analytical tools to support knowledge-driven analysis of business problems (Ba et al., 1997). Advances in systems support for problem solving and decision-making increasingly use artificial intelligence (AI) based techniques for knowledge representation (KR) (Whinston, 1997; Goul et al., 1992; Goul and Corral, 2005). KR takes multiple forms including business rules, decision analytics and business intelligence generated from various machine learning algorithms and data mining techniques. *Intelligence is the ability to act appropriately in an uncertain environment to increase the probability of success and achieve goals* (Albus, 1991). Intelligent decision support systems (IDSS) incorporate intelligence as problem domain knowledge with knowledge representation that informs and supports the decision process to facilitate problem solving and reduce the cognitive load of the decision maker.

Software Agents and Intelligent Decision Support Systems (IDSS)

An intelligent agent is "a computer system situated in some environment and that is capable of flexible autonomous action in this environment in order to meet its design objectives" (Jennings and Wooldridge, 1998). The terms agents, software agents and intelligent agents are often used interchangeably in the literature. However, all agents do not necessarily have to be intelligent. Jennings and Wooldridge (Jennings and Wooldridge, 1998) observe that agent-based systems are not necessarily intelligent, and require that an agent be flexible to be considered intelligent. Such flexibility in intelligent agent based systems requires that the agents should be: (Bradshaw, 1997; Jennings and Wooldridge, 1998)

- Cognizant of their environment and be *responsive* to changes therein
- Reactive and proactive to opportunities in their environment
- Autonomous in goal-directed behavior

- Collaborative in their ability to interact with other agents in exhibiting the goal-oriented behavior
- Adaptive in their ability to learn with experience

Agent-based systems may consist of a single agent engaged in autonomous goal-oriented behavior, or multiple agents that work together to exhibit granular as well as overall goal directed behavior. In the general multi-agent system, the interoperation of separately developed and self-interested agents provides services beyond the capability of any single agent model. Mutli-agent systems provide a powerful abstraction that can be used to model systems where multiple entities, exhibiting self directed behaviors must coexist in a environment and achieve the system wide objective of the environment.

Intelligent Agents are action-oriented abstractions in electronic systems entrusted to carry out various generic and specific goal-oriented actions on behalf of users. The agent abstraction manifests itself in the system as a representation of the user and performs necessary tasks on behalf of the user. This role may involve taking directions from the user on a need basis and advising and informing the user of alternatives and consequences (Whinston, 1997). The agent paradigm can support a range of decision making activity including information retrieval, generation of alternatives, preference order ranking of options and alternatives and supporting analysis of the alternative-goal relationships. In this respect, intelligent agents have come a long way from being digital scourers and static filters of information to active partners in information processing tasks. Such a shift has significant design implications on the abstractions used to model information systems, objects or agents, and on the architecture of information resources that are available to entities involved in the electronic system. Another implication is that knowledge must be available in formats that are conducive to its representation and manipulation by software applications, including software agents.

Decision Trees and IDSS

Models of decision problem domains provide analytical support to the decision maker, enhance understanding of the problem domain and allow the decision maker to assess the utility of alternative decision paths for the decision problem (Goul and Corral, 2005). Decision Trees are a popular modeling technique with wide applicability to a variety of business problems (Sung et al., 1999). The performance of a particular method in modeling human decisions is dependent on the conformance of the method with the decision makers' mental model of the decision problem (Kim et al., 1997). Simplicity of model representation is particularly relevant if the discovered explicit models are to be internalized by decision makers (Mao and Benbasat, 2000) Decision Trees represent a natural choice for IDSS whose goal is to generate decision paths that are easy to understand, explain and convert to natural language (Sung, et al., 1999). The choice of decision trees as the modeling methodology affords the ability to incorporate inductive learning in the IDSS. Decision trees are among the most commonly used inductive learning techniques used to learn patterns from data (Kudoh and Haraguchi, 2003; Takimoto and Maruoka, 2003). The ID3, C4.5 and SEE5 algorithms provide a formal method to create and model decision rules from categorical and continuous data (Takimoto and Maruoka, 2003; Kudoh and Haraguchi, 2003). Kiang (2003) compared multiple machine learning techniques and found that the decision tree technique had the most interpretive power. They suggest the use of multiple methods in systems for effective intelligent decision support.

The explanatory power afforded by decision trees comes from generation of understandable rules, clear identification of fields that are most important for prediction and classification and the incorporation of explanation facility. Explanation is essential to the interaction between users and knowledge-based systems (KBS) describing what a system does, how it works, and why its actions are appropriate (Mao and Benbasat, 2000). Explanation can make KBS conclusions more acceptable (Ye and Johnson, 1995) and build trust in a system (Swartout, 1983). Decision trees lend themselves to automatic generation of structured queries to extract pertinent data from organizational data repositories making them particularly useful in providing insights and explanations for the non-technical user (Apte and Weiss, 1997). Decision trees are especially suitable for decision problems that require generation of human understandable decision rules based on a mix of classification of categorical and continuous data (Quinlan, 1996). They clearly indicate the importance of individual data fields to the decision problem and reduce the cognitive burden of the decision maker (Mao and Benbasat, 2000). Decision trees represent a powerful and easily interpretable technique for modeling business decisions that can be reduced to a rule-based form.

XML AND DECISION TREES FOR KNOWLEDGE REPRESENTATION AND EXCHANGE

XML and Document Type Definitions (DTDs)

HTML provides a fixed set of tags that are used to markup content (information) primarily for consumption by human beings. Despite its efficiency for presenting information in human readable format, HTML is very limited in extensibility and customization of markup tags and description of the data contained in those tags. This constraint limits the use of HTML by application software for information sharing in a distributed computing environment where application programs, including intelligent agents are expected to work with available data, rules and knowledge without human intervention.

The use of XML and its related set of standards, developed by the World Wide Web Consortium, (W3C http://www.w3c.org), have helped overcome some of these limitations. XML allows for the creation of custom tags that contain data from specific domains. XML is a meta-language that allows for the creation of languages that can be represented by customized XML tags. For example, a company in the furniture industry may develop customized tags for the representation of content to serve its business domain. By creating custom tags, the company can represent the data in a more meaningful and flexible way than it could using HTML. The company may also develop documents that represent business-rules using XML that can shared either with human agents or with software agents. Unambiguous understanding of the content of customized XML tags by interested parties requires description of both the content and structure of XML documents. This description of structures in XML documents is provided by the XML schema which can be written following the set of standards called XML Schema and/or the document type definition (DTD) language as adopted and standardized by the W3C. XML schema describes specific elements, their relationships and specific types of data that can be stored in each tag. XML documents can be validated and parsed by application software provided either the DTD or the XML Schema of the corresponding document is made available. XML parsers written in C, C++ or Java can process and validate XML documents (containing business rules and data) based on XML schemas written based on either the DTD or the XML schema specification. Application software appropriate parser utilities are able to read and/or write to XML documents following the W3C standards and specification. This provides the foundation technology, built upon an agreed and accepted standard from W3C, for the capture, representation, exchange and storage of knowledge represented by business rules and related data in XML format that can be potentially used and shared by software agents.

Recent initiatives to develop technologies for the "Semantic Web" (Berners Lee et al., 2001) make the content of the Web unambiguously computer-interpretable, thus making it amenable to agent interoperability and automatic reasoning techniques (McIllraith, et al., 2001). Two important technologies for developing Semantic Web are already in place - XML and the resource description framework (RDF). The W3C developed the RDF as a standard for metadata to add a formal semantics to the Web, defined on top of XML, to provide a data model and syntax convention for representing the semantics of data in standardized interoperable manner (McIllraith, et al., 2001). The RDF working group also developed RDF schema (RDFS), an object-oriented type system that can be effectively thought of as a minimal ontology modeling language. Recently, there have been several efforts to build on RDF and RDFS with more AI-inspired knowledge representation languages such as SHOE, DAML-ONT, OIL and DAML+OIL (Fensel, 1997). While these initiatives are extremely promising for agent interoperability and reasoning, they are at their early stages of development. In this chapter, we focus on the use of more mature and widely used and available standardized technologies such as XML and DTDs to represent knowledge. This approach, along with other initiatives, should allow researchers to develop intelligent agent-based systems that are both practical and viable for providing intelligent decision support to users in a business environment.

XML and Decision Trees for Knowledge Representation

The W3C XML specification allows for the creation of customized tags for content modeling. Customized tags are used to create data-centric content models and rule-based content models. Data-centric content models imply XML documents that have XML tags that contain data, for example from a database, and can be parsed by application software for processing in distributed computing environments. XML documents containing rule-based content models can be used for knowledge representation. XML tags can be created to represent rules and corresponding parameters. Software agents can then parse and read the rules in these XML documents for use in making intelligent decisions. Before making intelligent decisions, the software agents should be able to codify or represent their knowledge. Decision Trees and inductive learning algorithms such as ID3, C4.5 can be used by agents to develop the rule-based decision tree. This learned decision tree can be converted into an XML document with the corresponding use of a DTD. This XML document, containing the learned decision tree, forms the basis for knowledge representation and sharing with other software agents in the community. We demonstrate architecture for agent-based intelligent information systems to accomplish this.

XML and Decision Trees for Knowledge Representation and Exchange

Software agents for knowledge exchange and sharing in the agent community can exchange decision trees represented in XML documents. For example, a new agent can learn from the knowledge of the existing agents in the community by using the decision tree available in XML format in a knowledge repository. The existence of this knowledge repository allows knowledge to be stored and retrieved as needed basis by the agents and updated to reflect the new knowledge from various agents in the community. The explanatory power of decision trees from their ability to generate understandable rules and the provide clear indication of important fields for classification allows the incorporation of explanation facility, similar to expert systems, among the agents in this type of architecture (Sung et al., 1999). Moreover, explanation is essential to the interaction between users and knowledge-based systems (KBS), describing what a system does, how it works, and why its actions are appropriate (Mao and Benbasat, 2000). Among 87 KBS shell capabilities, users rated explanation facilities and the capability to customize explanations as the fourth and fifth most important factors, respectively (Stylianou et al., 1992). Explanation can make KBS conclusions more acceptable (Ye and Johnson, 1995) and builds trust in a system. The ability of the agents to explain the decision rules used in the decision making process makes agents powerful tools to aid human agents in complex decision tasks. Such intelligent agent architecture, built around well-grounded and well-researched decision models along with standards-based widely available technologies (such as XML, DTDs), is a significant contribution to furthering research on agent-based distributed computing and DSS. In the following section, we present the details of IKMDSA and discuss its knowledge externalization, knowledge representation, knowledge management and knowledge delivery mechanism for decision support.

INTELLIGENT KNOWLEDGE-BASED DECISION SUPPORT ARCHITECTURE (IKMDSA)

A KMS has facilities to create, exchange, store and retrieve knowledge in an exchangeable and usable formatfor decision-making activity. IKMDSA utilizes ID3 algorithms to create knowledge from raw data to a decision tree representational form. A domain knowledge object represents information about a specific problem domain in IKMDSA. The domain knowledge object contains information about the characteristics of the various domain attributes important to the problem domain. The domain knowledge object describes the problem context and provides rules for making decisions in the problem context. The domain knowledge object represents the abstraction used for creating, exchanging and using modular knowledge objects in IKMDSA. IKMDSA uses intelligent software agents as the mechanism for encapsulation and exchange of knowledge between agents at the site of knowledge creation and the

Figure 1. Agents have access to Domain Knowledge objects that abstract domain specific knowledge

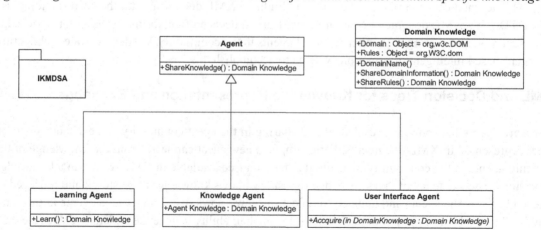

Figure 2. A schematic showing the generation, exchange, storage, retrieval and use of knowledge in IKMDSA

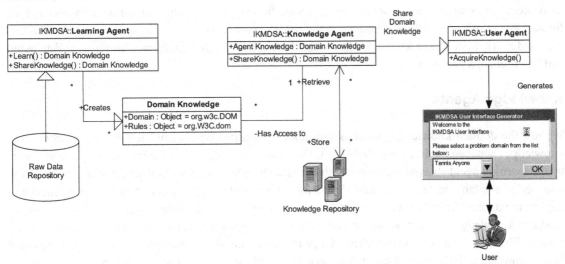

site of knowledge storage. Intelligent agents deliver knowledge to the user interface to support intelligent decision-making activity. The agent abstraction is built upon basic objects that take on additional behaviors, as required by its function (Shoham, 1993). Knowledge exchange and delivery in IKMDSA is facilitated through the exchange of the domain knowledge objects among intelligent agents. Figure 1 illustrates this basic building block of IKMDSA, where an agent has a composition relationship with the domain knowledge object, and thereby has access to knowledge in the form of standard XML document object model (DOM) objects.

Every agent can share its knowledge through the domain knowledge component by invoking its ShareKnowledge behavior. The domain knowledge object contains behaviors to inform agents of the name of the problem domain, share information about the various domain attributes that are pertinent to the specific knowledge context, and share rules about making decisions for their specific problem domain. These core components are used to develop the functionality of IKMDSA to learn rules and domain attributes from raw data, create domain specific knowledge, share it with other agents and apply this knowledge in solving domain specific problems with a user. Once the attributes and domain rules are captured in the domain knowledge object, using standard XML DOM format, they can be exchanged between agents. Figure 2 provides a schematic of this activity sequence where knowledge is created from raw data and ultimately delivered in usable form to the decision maker.

Learning Agents

Learning agents interact with a raw data repository and extract raw data used to generate domain specific knowledge. Our model does not specify the storage representation and the data contained in the repository may be of multiple representation formats including flat files, data stored as relational tables that can be extracted using multiple queries into a recordset, or raw data represented using XML documents. The learning agent extracts the raw data and applies machine learning algorithms to generate decision rules for the problem domain. The repository contains information about the context and syntactical representation of the information. This information provides the domain attributes pertinent to the decision problem. This generates domain specific knowledge in the form of domain attribute information and rules for making decisions in the specific problem context. The system ensures that this knowledge is generated in a format conducive for sharing and use of the information across a distributed and heterogonous platform.

Knowledge Agents

We use the domain knowledge object as the modular abstraction for knowledge representation and knowledge exchange facilitation in IKMDSA. Domain knowledge objects are made available to agents by the learning agent sharing the object with the knowledge agent. The knowledge agent manages the knowledge available in IKMDSA and allows for other agents in the system to know of, request and receive the domain knowledge in the system. The system utilizes the domain knowledge object as the modular knowledge abstraction for communication of knowledge across the multiple agents of the system. Therefore, when the domain knowledge object is shared with an agent of the system, the agent becomes aware of the problem context descriptions, in addition to the rules that govern decision-making in the specific problem context. The knowledge agent is also responsible for the maintaining the collection of domain knowledge available in the system through interactions with a knowledge repository. The knowledge agent contains methods to generate rules to support ad-hoc queries by the user agent. This is supported through the interactions of the knowledge agent with the knowledge repository of the system that is implemented as a set of XML documents that can be stored in a repository that is capable of storing XML documents such as the Oracle 9i family of information management products. This knowledge repository allows for the easy storage and retrieval of the knowledge contained in a domain knowledge object. Thus, the knowledge is available to all the agents in the system through the activities of the KM behaviors of the knowledge agent object. In this respect, the interactions among the agents in this system are modeled as collaborative interactions, where the agents in the multi-agent community work together to provide decision support and knowledge-based explanations of the decision problem domain to the user.

As shown in Figure 2, users of IKMDSA interact with the system through user agents that are constantly aware of all domain knowledge contexts available to the system, through a list of names of the domain knowledge objects that is published and managed by the knowledge agent. This allows every user agent, and hence every user, to be aware of the entire problem space covered by the system. The user agent requests and receives the knowledge available for a specific problem domain by making a request to the knowledge agent, at the behest of the user. The knowledge agent, upon receiving this request, shares a domain knowledge object with the user agent, thereby making problem domain information and decision rules available to the user agent. The knowledge agents also serve as the means to service any ad-hoc queries that cannot be answered by the user interface agents, such as queries regarding knowledge parameters that are not available to the user interface agents. In such cases, the Knowledge agent, with direct access to the knowledge repository can provide such knowledge to the user agents, for the benefit of the user. This information is shared in the form of two W3C compliant XML document object model (DOM) objects, domain and rules, which represent an enumeration and explanation of the domain attributes that are pertinent to the problem context and the rules for making decisions in the specified problem context. Once the domain knowledge object is available to the user agent, the user agent becomes problem domain aware and is ready to assist the user through a decision making process in the specific problem domain.

User Agents

The user agent contains methods to generate a user-friendly interface to inform the user about problem domain attributes that are pertinent to the decision problem under consideration. The user interface offers explanations about each domain attribute and provides the user with contextual information on the different values that each domain attribute may take. This serves the purpose of informing the user and increasing their knowledge about the various factors that affect a decision in the problem domain under consideration. The user agent also contains methods to generate a decision making interface that allows a decision maker to consider and choose values for pertinent attributes. This selection process creates an instance of an observation that can be compared against the rules available to the user agent through the domain knowledge. The user interacts with the User Interface agent by asking question about the decision problem and receives responses containing decision alternatives and explanation of

Figure 3. The intelligent knowledge-based multi-agent decision support architecture (IKMDSA).

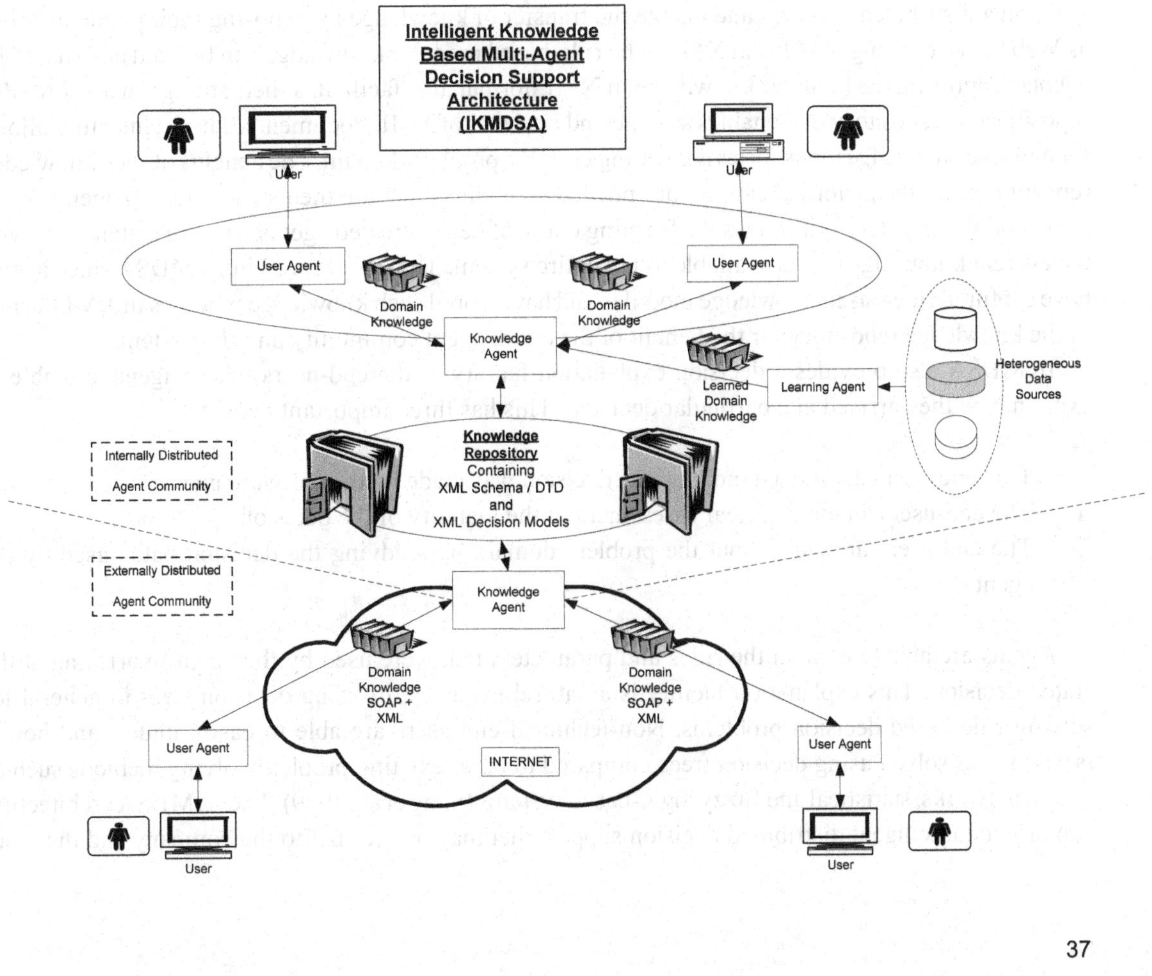

the choices made by the agent. This is achieved through parsing the decision rules based on the parameters supplied by the user. The agent compares the users' selections with the known rules and decides on the rule(s) that are fired for the given instance. These rules are formatted in a user-friendly format and made available to the user. This provides the user with a decision, given their selection of domain attributes and provides the user with explanations of the decisions made, given the selections made by the users.

The above sections provide a complete description of the process of knowledge creation, knowledge representation, knowledge exchange, KM and the use of the knowledge for decision making employed by IKMDSA. Figure 3 provides a schematic of this overall process. As shown in figure 3, IKMDSA is designed for a distributed platform where the knowledge available to the agents in the system can be made available on an intranet and an Internet based platform by enclosing the domain knowledge objects in SOAP wrappers that enables the knowledge broker functions of the knowledge agent by making its knowledge available as a Web service.

IKMDSA consists of intelligent agents as discussed above that are able to provide intelligent decision support to the end-users. All of the agents in the architecture are FIPA compliant in terms of their requirements and behavior. The learning agents create knowledge from the raw data in a data repository, knowledge agents primarily acquire this knowledge from learning agents and manage this knowledge through a knowledge repository, while user agents help the users make decisions on specific problems using the knowledge contained in the decision trees. The exchange of knowledge between agents and between users and agents is achieved through sharing of content information using XML. The agents work on a distributed platform and enable the transfer of knowledge by exposing their public methods as Web Services using SOAP and XML. The rule-based modular knowledge can be used and shared by agents. Capturing the modular knowledge in XML format also facilitates their storage in a knowledge repository - a repository that enables storage and retrieval of XML documents. The architecture allows for multiple knowledge repositories depending upon the problem domain. The benefits of such knowledge repositories are the historical capture of knowledge modules that are then shared among agents in the agent community. This minimizes the learning curve of newly created agents who are instantiated with the current knowledge that is available to the entire system. This is achieved in IKMDSA since agents have captured rule-based knowledge modules and have stored such knowledge modules in XML format in the knowledge repository for the benefit of the entire agent community and the system.

IKMDSA also provides a decision explanation facility to the end-users where agents are able to explain how they arrived at a particular decision. This has three important benefits:

i.   Tthe end-user can understand how the decision was made by the software agent
ii.   The end-user can make a clear assessment of the viability of the decision
iii. The end-user can learn about the problem domain by studying the decision paths used by the agent

Agents are able to explain the rules and parameters that were used by the agent in arriving at the stated decision. This explanation facility is a natural extension of using decision trees in general for solving rule-based decision problems. Non-technical end-users are able to easily understand how a problem was solved using decision trees compared to other existing problem-solving methods such as neural networks, statistical and fuzzy logic-based systems (Sung et al., 1999). The IKMDSA architecture can provide intelligent distributed decision support that may be internal to the company and the other focusing on providing intelligent distributed decision support that may be external to the company. In the second case, the proposed architecture incorporates the W3C Web Services architecture that uses the simple object access protocol (SOAP) and XML. The incorporation of this architecture creates a flexible means of exposing the services of the agents using the Web Services architecture by a company to its potential or existing global population of customers and suppliers.

IMPLEMENTATION OF THE IKMDSA ARCHITECTURE AND ILLUSTRATIVE EXAMPLE

The problem domain selected for the initial proof of concept is the play tennis decision problem (Mitchell, 1997) using the ID3 decision tree method. The selection of the problem domain was due to it being widely adopted (Mitchell, 1997) to represent decision problems in the ID3 decision tree research and also for its simplicity in illustrating the proposed architecture. The decision problem for this problem domain is to decide whether, or not, to play tennis on a particular day based on climatic conditions such as the day's weather outlook, the level of humidity, the temperature, and the wind conditions. Figure 4 shows a schematic of the decision solutions under consideration. The leaf nodes of the decision tree represent the final outcome of the decision of whether to play tennis on a certain day, based on what the weather is like. The problem is simple to understand; yet it illustrates the fundamental requirements of the system and provides an elegant way to test the various features of the agents and the architecture.

The end-user provides the existing weather condition to the user agent as input and the agent makes a decision and presents the decision to the end-user whether or not tennis can be played that particular

Figure 4. Decision tree representation of the Play Tennis Problem (Adapted from Mitchell, 1997)

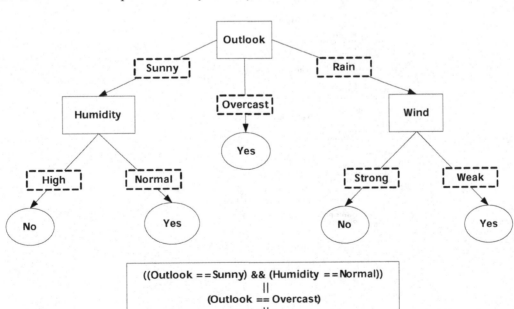

Figure 5. DTD for the representation of domain attribute in the Play Tennis problem

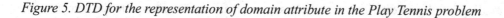

Figure 6. XML document showing domain attributes for the Play Tennis problem

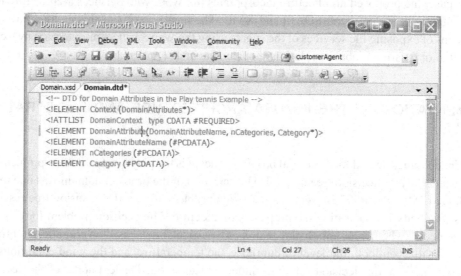

Figure 7. The User interface presented to a user by the IKMDSA user agent

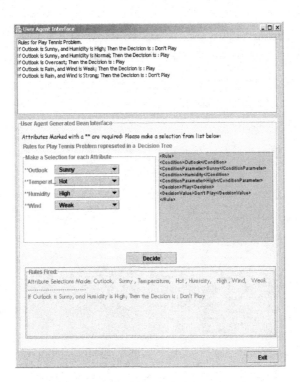

Figure 8. DTD representation of the structure of rules

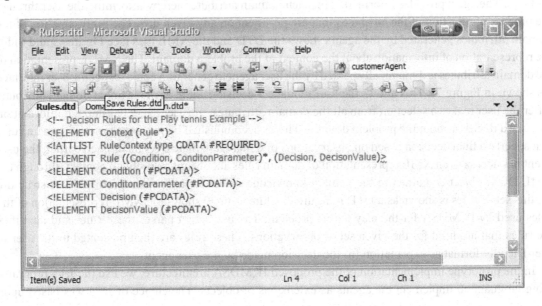

Figure 9. Decision tree representation of the rule-based knowledge module for the Play Tennis Problem in XML format

day given the conditions entered by the user. The user is given information about each of the atmospheric conditions and their categories. These atmospheric conditions form the domain attributes for the play tennis problem and define the context specific information that is pertinent to this decision problem. The agent provides information on each domain attribute thereby informing the user through the process of selection of the attributes that are pertinent on any given day. The representation of the domain attributes generated by the agents shows the DTD and the XML files (see Figures 5 and 6) for the representation of information about the context of the problem domain. The XML representation of the domain attributes is dynamically parsed by the user agent to generate a context specific user interface (as shown in Figure 7). This allows the user to make a decision about each pertinent domain attribute. After the user makes a selection from all the domain attributes, the user agent has enough information to make a decision about the problem domain. This is accomplished by parsing the set of domain rules that specify a final decision based on observations of domain attributes. As mentioned earlier, the user agent has access to an XML representation of domain rules about a given problem context, through the XML DOM object contained in the domain knowledge object for a decision problem. The structure for this set of rules is shown as a DTD in figure 8, while figure 9 shows the XML representation of the rules used by IKMDSA for the play tennis problem. The user agent parses these rules and identifies the rules that are fired for the given set of observations. These rules are then presented to the user in user-friendly format as explanation fro the decision made by the user agent.

In the prototype implementation of the proposed IKMDSA architecture, we use the Java programming language to implement the agents as extensions of objects. The choice of Java was based upon the widely accepted advantage of Java providing portable code and XML providing portable data. In addition, we use Oracle 9i Database and Application Server platforms (http://www.oracle.com) to implement the knowledge repository and use the Sun Microsystems Java XML API toolkit to interface the agents with the XML repository. The decision tree implementation consists of tree nodes with branches for every category of the node variable. Each traversal from the root node of the decision tree to a leaf node leads to a separate decision path as illustrated in figure 4. The agents contain methods to traverse the decision tree and obtain a decision path that can then be translated into an XML object and an XML document using a DTD file. These form the basis for the generation of decision alternatives and for the explanations of decisions by the agents. The agents are implemented as java beans and their explanations are available to the user through calls made to their public methods that are exposed as services, and presented to the user as dynamically generated Web content by using Java Server Pages technology (http://java.sun.com/products/jsp/index.html).

BUSINESS APPLICATION

Organizations use data mining techniques to leverage the vast amount of data to make better business decisions (Padmanabhan, et al., 1999; Fan, et al., 2002). Data mining is used for customer profiling in CRM and customer service support (Hui and Jha, 2000), credit card application approval, fraud detection, telecommunications network monitoring, market-based analysis (Fayyad et al., 1996), healthcare quality assurance (Tsechansky et al., 1999) and many other decision-making areas (Brachman et al., 1996). There is a growing need to not only mine data for decision support, but also to externalize knowledge from enterprise data warehouses and data marts, to share such knowledge among end users through automated knowledge discovery and distribution system for effective decision support. In other words, there is an increasing need for the integration of KMS and DSS systems to meet the needs of the complex business decision situations. According to Bolloju *et. al.,* "Such integration is expected to enhance the quality of support provided by the system to decision makers and also to help in building up organizational memory and knowledge bases. The integration will result in decision support environments for the next generation," (Bollojou, 2002, pg. 164). The proposed IKMDSA architecture illustrates such a next generation integrated KMS and DSS system. The detailed presentation of the implementation of the architecture is intended to further the research that combines multiple but related set of research streams such as data mining, automated knowledge discovery, knowledge representation and storage using XML, knowledge exchange among participating intelligent agents using knowledge context, and explanation facility (from expert systems research). The authors are currently extending the architecture in various business domains such as credit approval processing, bankruptcy prediction, electronic commerce and consumer behavior and Web mining.

Emergent Internet technologies have significant impact on business processes of organizations operating in the digital economy. Realizing the potential benefits of emergent technologies is dependent on the effective sharing and use of business intelligence and process knowledge among business partners to provide accurate, relevant and timely information and knowledge. This requires system models to support and enable information integration, knowledge exchange and improved collaboration among business partners. Such systems must provide collaborating partners with intelligent knowledge management (KM) capabilities for seamless and transparent exchange of dynamic supply and demand information. Implementing and managing such integration over distributed and heterogeneous information platforms, such as the Internet, is a challenging task; yet, realizing this task can have significant benefits for organizations embracing such collaborations. An application of the IKMDSA for Collaborative Commerce to enable collaborative work in B2B e-Marketplaces would have significant benefits in developing information partnerships by creating the foundation for knowledge representation and exchange by intelligent agents that support collaborative work between business partners.

CONCLUSION, LIMITATIONS AND FUTURE DIRECTION FOR RESEARCH

In this chapter we have presented a methodology to represent modular, rule-based knowledge using the extensible markup language (XML) and the document type definition (DTD) standards from the World Wide Web Consortium (W3C). Using this methodology, we have shown how such an approach can be used to create problem-specific knowledge modules that can easily be distributed over the Internet to support distributed IDSS design. Such an approach will facilitate intelligent decision support by providing the required knowledge representation and the decision analytical support. We had presented the conceptual architecture of such a distributed IDSS, and have provided details of the components of the architecture, including the agents involved and their interactions, the details of the knowledge representation and implementation of knowledge exchange through a distributed interface. We also provided indication of how such architecture might be used to support the user and how it might assume the role of an expert and provide explanations to the user, while retaining the benefits of an active DSS through extensible knowledge generation by incorporating machine learning algorithms. The example used in this chapter is simple, intuitive and elegantly achieves its purpose of illustrating the use of the architecture while minimizing complications inherent to a more complex problem domain. We continue to do research on elaborating this architecture for a variety of problems that lend themselves to rule-based, inductive decision making with a need for user interactions and which benefit from greater understanding of the problem domain by the user.

The limitations of this research derive from the use of decision trees and inductive learning algorithms and techniques. The limitations inherent to decision trees and such techniques are also the limitation of this architecture. Therefore, further research needs to be conducted to understand how this architecture can be expanded to incorporate other types of learning and rule induction or rule creation to be shared and used by software agents. Despite this limitation, this chapter contributes significantly to the advancement of our understanding of how emerging technologies can be incorporated into intelligent agent-based architecture to enhance the value of such systems in distributed intelligent DSS that incorporates knowledge.

REFERENCES

Adriaans, P., & Zantinge, D. (1996). *Data mining.* Harlow, UK: Addison-Wesley.

Apte, C., & Weiss, S. (1997). Data mining with decision trees and decision rules. *Future Generation Computer Systems,* (13), 197-210.

Ba, S., Lang, K. R., & Whinston, A. B. (1997). Enterprise decision support using Intranet technology. *Decision Support Systems, 2*(20), 99-134.

Berners-Lee, T., Hendler, J., & Lassila, O. (2001). The Sematic Web. *Scientific American*, 34-43.

Bolloju, N., Khalifa, M., & Turban, E. (2002). Integrating knowledge management into enterprise environments for the next generation decision support. *Decision Support Systems*, (33), 163-176.

Brachman, R., Khabaza, T., Kloesgen, W., Piatetsky-Shapiro, G., & Simoudis, E., (1996). Mining business databases. *Communications of ACM, 39*(11), 42-48.

Bradshaw, J. M., (1997). *Software agent*s. Boston: MIT Press.

Fan, W., Lu, H., Madnick, S. E., & Cheung, D. (2002). DIRECT: A system for mining data value conversion rules from disparate data sources. *Decision Support Systems*, (34), 19-39.

Fayyad, U., Piatetsky-Shapiro, G., & Smyth, P. (1996). From data mining to knowledge discovery: an overview. In: U. Fayyad, G. Piatetsky-Shapiro, P. Smyth and R. Uthurusamy, (Eds.), *Advances in knowledge discovery and data mining*, (pp. 1-36). Cambridge, MA: AAAI/MIT Press.

Fensel, D., (2000). The Semantic Web and its languages. *IEEE Intelligent Systems*, Nov./Dec., 67.

Goul, M., & Corral, K. (2005). Enterprise model management and next generation decision support *Decision Support Systems*. (In Press), Corrected Proof, Available online 12 July 2005.

Holsapple, C., & Singh, M., (2000,July/September). Toward a unified view of electronic commerce, electronic business, and collaborative commerce: A knowledge management approach. *Knowledge and Process Management*, 7(3), 159.

Hui, S., & Jha, G. (2000). Data mining for customer service support. *Information and Management, 38*(1), 1-14.

Jennings, N. R., & Wooldridge, M. (1998). *Agent technology: Foundations, applications, and markets.* London: Springer.

Kiang, M. Y. (2003, July). A comparative assessment of classification methods. *Decision Support Systems, 35*(4), 441-454.

Kim, C. N., Chung, H. M., & Paradice, D. B. (1997). Inductive modeling of expert decision making in loan evaluation: A decision strategy perspective. *Decision Support Systems, 21*(2), 83-98.

Kudoh, Y., Haraguchi, M., & Okubo, Y. (2003, January 27). Data abstractions for decision tree induction. *Theoretical Computer Science, 292*(2), 387-416.

Mao, J., & Benbasat, I. (2000, Fall). The use of explanations in knowledge-based systems: Cognitive perspectives and a process-tracing analysis. *Journal of Management Information Systems, 17*(2), 153-179.

McIlraith, S., Son, T. C., & Zeng, H. (2001). Semantic Web Services. *IEEE Intelligent Systems*, March/April,46-53.

Mitchell, T. M. (1997). *Machine learning.* McGraw-Hill.

Padmanabhan, B., & Tuzhilin A. (1999). Unexpectedness as a measure of interestingness in knowledge discovery. *Decision Support Systems,* (27), 303-318.

Quinlan, J. R. (1996). Improved use of continuous attributes in C4.5. *Journal of Artificial Intelligence Research,* (4) 77-90.

Quinlan, J. R. (1996). Learning first-order definitions of functions. *Journal of Artificial Intelligence Research,* (5) 139-161.

Shim, J. P., Warkentin, M., Courtney, J. F., Power, D. J., Sharda, R., & Carlsson, C. (2002). Past, present, and future of decision support technology. *Decision Support Systems,* (33) 111-126.

Singh, R. (2007). A multi-agent decision support architecture for knowledge representation and exchange. *International Journal of Intelligent Information Technologies, 3*(1), 37-59,

Stylianou, A. C. Madey, G. R., & Smith, R. D. (1992). Selection criteria for expert systems shells: A socio-technical framework. *Communications of the ACM, 10*(35), 30-48.

Sung, T., Chang, N., & Lee, G. (1999). Dynamics of modeling in data mining: Interpretive approach to bankruptcy prediction. *Journal of Management Information Systems, 16*(1), Summer, 63-85.

Shoham, Y. (1993). Agent oriented programming. *Journal of Artificial Intelligence, 1*(60), 51-92.

Takimoto, E., & Maruoka, A. (2003). Top-Down decision tree learning as information based booting. *Theoretical Computer Science, 292*(2), 447-464.

Tsechansky, M., Pliskin, N., Rabinowitz, G., & Porath, A. (1999). Mining relational patterns from multiple relational tables. *Decision Support Systems, 27*(1999), 177-195.

Whinston, A. B. (1997). Intelligent agents as a basis for decision support systems. *Decision Support Systems, 20*(1).

Weber, R. O., & Aha, D. W. (2003). Intelligent delivery of military lessons learned. *Decision Support Systems, 3*(34), 287-304.

Ye, L. R., & Johnson, P. E. (1995). The impact of explanation facilities on user acceptance of expert systems advice. *MIS Quarterly, 2*(19), 157-172.

Chapter III
A Decision Support System for Trust Formalization

Farid Meziane
University of Salford, UK

Samia Nefti
University of Salford, UK

ABSTRACT

Trust is widely recognized as an essential factor for the continual development of business-to-customer (B2C) electronic commerce (EC). Many trust models have been developed, however, most are subjective and do not take into account the vagueness and ambiguity of EC trust and the customers' intuitions and experience when conducting online transactions. In this chapter, we describe the development and implementation of a model using fuzzy reasoning to evaluate EC trust. This trust model is based on the information customers expect to find on an EC Web site and that is shown from many studies to increase customers trust towards online merchants. We argue that fuzzy logic is suitable for trust evaluation as it takes into account the uncertainties within EC data and like human relationships; it is often expressed by linguistic terms rather then numerical values. The evaluation of the proposed model is illustrated using four case studies and a comparison with two other models is conducted to emphasise the benefits of using fuzzy decision system.

INTRODUCTION

Business to consumer (B2C) electronic commerce (EC) has seen a phenomenal growth since the development of the Internet, and there is a growing interest from many organizations to use it as a way to improve their competitiveness and reach a wider customer base. According to eMarketer, the total business of B2C EC has increased from $30 billions in 2002 to $90.1 billions in 2003 and continued increasing to around $133 billions in 2005 (Grau, 2006). Similar figures were also predicted by Jupiter Research, which estimated an increase from $85.7 billion in 2003 to $132.2 billion in 2005 (Naraine, 2003). This growth is usually attributed to the increasing number of online users over the 2000-2005 period and this is expected to continue (Naraine, 2003). Although for the 2005-2009 period the growth is expected at a lower rate of 18.6 %, the expansion of EC can still be considered as strong (Grau, 2006).

Though the expansion and development in EC is encouraging, this growth may not be achieved if the prevailing obstacles for a greater acceptance of EC as a transaction medium are not addressed carefully. Among the obstacles that hinder the development of EC, consumers lack of trust has often been identified as one of the main reasons (Luo, 2002; Merrilees & Fry, 2003; Corbitt, Thanasankit, & Yi, 2003; Cazier, Shao & Louis, 2006) and other factors include: consumer dissatisfaction of the unstable EC systems, a low level of personal data security, disappointments with purchases such as non-delivery of goods, hidden charges, difficulties in getting a refund, unwillingness to provide personal details and fraud (Han & Noh, 1999; Lewicki & Bunker, 1996; Matthew & Turban, 2001; Mayer, Davis, & Schoorman, 1995; Patton and Jøsang, 2004; Shapiro, Sheppard, & Cheraskin, 1992). In B2C EC, the concept of trust is crucial because it affects a number of factors essential to online transactions.

Kasiran and Meziane (2002) developed a trust model for B2C EC that is based on the kind of information customers are looking for on a vendor's Website to help them decide whether to engage in a transaction or not. The model identified four major factors that need to be present on a merchant's Website to increase customers' trust when shopping online. These factors are: existence, affiliation, policy, and fulfilment. The information customers need to know to satisfy the existence factor include physical existence, such as the merchant's telephone number, fax number, postal address, mandatory registration, and peoples' existence. These are known as variables. The affiliation factor looks at third-party endorsement, membership and portal and the policy factor looks at information with regards to customer satisfaction policy, privacy statement, and warranty policy. Finally, the fulfilment factor looks at delivery methods, methods of payment and the community comments. Hence, a total of 12 variables have been identified for the trust model as summarized in Figure 1.

Given the large amount of information the model requires, an information extraction system has been developed to automate the data collection process (Meziane & Kasiran, 2003, Meziane & Kasiran,

Figure 1. The trust model (Kasiran & Meziane, 2002)

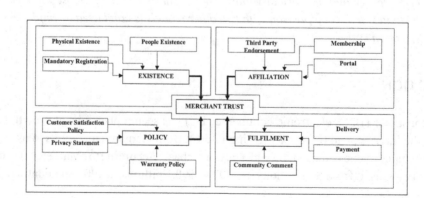

2005). Indeed it has been reported that users are finding it difficult to identify specific information on Websites (Center for the Digital Future, 2004). In addition, we do recognize that users may not be able to make proper use of the collected information. For this purpose, we developed tools to evaluate the trustworthiness of an EC Website based on the collected information. Two models have been developed in (Meziane & Kasiran, 2005, Meziane & Kasiran, 2008) for evaluating the trust factor; the linear model and the parameterized model. More details about these two models will be provided in the comparison section.

However, for both models, we do recognize that this is not the natural way customers use to evaluate their trust towards online merchants or make the decision to buy or not to buy. As with any other business transaction, customers develop in their mind some sort of ambiguity and uncertainties when purchasing online (Mohanty & Bhasker, 2005). Customers may wish to classify merchants using different preferences or take into account other parameters such as the cost or the brand of a product. The decision to complete an online transaction is often based on the customer's human intuitions, common sense, and experience rather than on the availability of clear, concise, and accurate data (Akhter, Hobbs, & Maamar, 2005). In this article, we develop a new trust evaluation model using fuzzy reasoning to evaluate the trust factor as it allows the encoding of the information available on the merchant's Website in a form that can be used to reflect the way customers reach the decision to engage in an EC transaction.

The remaining of the article is organized as follows. In the second section we review some related work on trust and trust modelling in EC. In the third section, we describe the fuzzy inference and fuzzy logic system, we justify the use of fuzzy logic in the fourth section and we construct the rules base in the fifth section. We evaluate the newly developed fuzzy model in the sixth section and we compare it with the linear and parameterized models and underline the advantages of our fuzzy system in the seventh section. We conclude in the final section.

RELATED WORK

New technologies have deeply modified traditional forms of social relations and communications, in particular norms, social rules, hierarchies, familiarity, reputation, delegation and trust (Castelfranchi & Pedone, 2003). This is certainly true for B2C EC, one of the areas that benefited the most from the development of the Internet and the WWW. EC applications have created a new global market (Cohan, 2000) where businesses and consumers are no longer restricted by physical boundaries such as geographical or time differences (Guo & Sun, 2004). Today, EC influences business in a major way and shapes the future of the B2C segment (Li, Kuo, & Russell, 1999; Schmitz & Latzerb, 2002). In reality, EC has redefined several business processes (Hoffman, Novak, & Chatterjee, 1995) such as marketing (Hoffman, Novak, & Peralta, 1997), customer services (Romano, Nicholas, & Fjermestad, 2003), payment (Ranganathan & Ganapathy, 2002) and fulfilment (Bayles, 2001).

Most people have an understanding of EC based on their experience as shoppers and buyers in a traditional brick and mortar environment, and they bring this experience with them when they start shopping online. EC sites play their role of seller by trying to broadcast two messages to potential buyers: "buy from us" and "trust us". The impact of these explicit messages, though, is often corrupted by contradictory or distracting messages implicit in the site's implementation of the navigation flow, page layout, visual continuity and information space (Nah & Davis, 2002). In the next subsection, we introduce the concept of trust in the context of EC and than review works on attempts to model trust in general and using fuzzy logic in particular.

Trust

The widespread of EC websites and their adoption by many customers has created challenging problems of trust. Indeed, Klang (2001) states that "the size and the anonymity of the Internet make it more difficult for the parties entering into the transaction to judge the trustworthiness of his or her counterpart". It is also generally perceived that it is relatively easy to set up a company in the digital world that appears legitimate but is actually a fraud (Ngai and Wat, 2002). Hence, the fundamental question in EC is "whether consumers trust sellers and products they cannot see or touch and electronic systems with which they have no previous experience" (Matthew & Turban, 2001).

Trust is studied and defined in several areas such as psychology, sociology, political science, economics, history and socio-biology (Lewicki & Bunker, 1996; Castelfranchi & Pedone, 2003). In the context of EC, trust is "the confidence that participants in commerce have on the business activities involved (transactions and other exchanges of information, goods, and services) which will be protected and conducted as intended" (Steinauer, Wakid, & Rasberry, 2000) and can be measured based on reliability and predictability (Keen, et al. 2000). The most widely used definition of trust in EC is that provided by (Mayer, Davis & Schoorman, 1995), "the willingness of a party to be vulnerable to the action of the other party based on the expectation that the other party will perform a particular action important to the trustor, irrespective of the ability to monitor or control that other party". Once the concept of trust in EC is agreed upon the next step is about understanding the factors that influence the development of trust and than attempt to model trust; a more challenging problem!

Trust Modelling

Trust is a very complex concept and can be analysed from different angles using various parameters. The development of trust can be modelled as a function of time and is built based on experience (Cheskin/Studio Archetype, 1999). Within the business context, an initial trust is created based on external factors such as the strength of a particular brand or recommendation from others. Naturally, if the initial trust warrants a purchase, this will allow customers to personally experience dealing with this particular merchant. Consequently, the foundation of trust starts to change from the external factors to inside information such as own experience with the product or merchandise. The experience and trust will further develop with future purchases. McCullagh, (1998) suggests that the development of trust usually starts by recommended trust to direct trust. Furthermore, he also suggests that trust is not generally transitive but can be conditionally transitive particularly during the early stage of trust relations.

Trust is very often linked with risk as it is widely recognised that the placement of trust is closely related with the element of risk (Konrad, Fuchs, & Barthel, 2000; Mayer, Davis, & Schoorman, 1995). The higher the risk, the higher the level of trust is needed. It is suggested by Tan and Theon (2000) that to enhance trust, more control should be given to the trustor. Hence, establishing trust is establishing the acceptances of risk. Since EC is strongly linked to Internet technology development, then creating trust in EC is a process of taking risks in believing that the Internet technology is able to function as expected for the purpose of EC transactions. In addition, creating trust in EC is also accepting the risk that everybody involved in this faceless business environment will perform his duties as expected.

Araujo and Araujo (2003) classified risks taken in EC transactions into two categories. Technology related risk that includes security, privacy, and integrity and business related risk that include misuse of personal information and incorrect fulfilment of transactions. Interface web design and usability and ease of navigation have also been found to influence user behaviour and trust towards EC websites (Basso et al, 2001; Hu et al, 2004; Riegelsberger & Sasse, 2001). Web retailers use eye-catching graphics not only to grab a user's attention but also to convey competence and professionalism. A model developed by Matthew and Turban (2001) acknowledges the importance of both network technology and other parameters such as merchant factor and third party certification factor. Meanwhile, Cheung, Lee and Matthew (2000) recognize the legal framework role in creating a trusted environment in the EC setting. They also recognize the role of individual trust propensity in determining the level of trust required before someone is ready to commit in a trust relationship. This trust propensity is influenced by individual personality traits, culture and experience (Jarvenpaa, Tranctinsky, & Vitale, 2000). Fuzzy logic is used to model and evaluate trust in EC and some systems will be summarised in the following subsection.

Fuzzy Logic in Electronic Commerce

Akhter et al. (2005) developed a fuzzy logic based system for assessing the level of trust in B2C EC. In their model, trust (T) is composed of three variables which are security (S), familiarity (F) and the Website's design layout (D) hence T = f(S, F, D). In addition, they have also used competitiveness (C) in the evaluation of the business transaction. Hence the business transaction is a function of trust and competitiveness and formulated as $L_{B2C}=g(T, C)$. However, in their model they are not clear on what factors they use to evaluate each of the three variables S, F and D. They assume that users by just using a Website can decide if the trust is high, average or low with regards to these three variables. Studies on the use of Websites design for example to convey trust are well documented and the characteristics well defined (Basso et al., 2001; Hu et al., 2004; Riegelsberg & Sasse, 2001).

Manchala (2000) proposes a model for the measurement of trust variables and the fuzzy verification of EC. He highlights the fact that trust can be determined by evaluating the factors that influence it, namely risk. He defines cost of transaction, transaction history, customer loyalty, indemnity, and spending patterns as the trust variables. Each variable is measured using semantic labels. His notation is focused on defining when two trust variables are related by an EC trust relationship (ECTR). Using this ECTR, a trust matrix is constructed between the two variables and a trust zone is established. He also describes a method for trust propagation and the construction of a single trust matrix between vendor and customer that governs the transaction. The problem with Manchala's model is that it is (1) unclear, which variables should be used by default for the best results; (2) if it is actually possible for a computer to automatically establish that two variables are related by an ECTR. In his definition, he mentions a semantic relationship between the variables, but neglects to mention how this fact will be specified to the computer so that evaluation can be automated; and (3) if ECTR merging will scale in the face of large trust matrices. These concerns are all related to the viability of implementing his model. These models do not support a theoretic approach to trust and they are not suitable for e-commerce (Tyrone, 2003).

Fuzzy logic was also used for product classification in EC (Mohanty & Bhasker, 2005). When faced with a choice of many products, users need to make a decision on which product to purchase. Taking the case of a car purchase, the authors used five variables which are the cost, re-sale value, mileage, comfort, and maintenance cost. A typical statement would then be to purchase a car with a price around a particular value, a high resale price, with a mileage around certain mileage, comfortable and a low maintenance cost. Such systems would work only on a specific type of products (cars in this case) if one wishes to purchase a personal computer for example, the variables would change as is the fuzzy logic system.

THE FUZZY INFERENCE SYSTEM

There are two concepts within fuzzy systems that play a central role in our application domain. The first one is a linguistic variable, that is, a variable whose values are words or sentences in a natural or synthetic language. Fuzzy set theory, which is based on such paradigm, deals with the ambiguity found in semantics (Zadeh, 1965). The second concept is that of a fuzzy IF-THEN rules, in which the antecedent and the consequent parts are propositions containing linguistic variables (Mamdani, 1994). These two concepts are effectively used in the fuzzy logic controller paradigm as shown in Figure 2. The numerical values of the inputs $x_i \in U_i$ with $(i = 1, ..., n)$ are fuzzified into linguistic values $F_1, F_2, ..., F_n$ where F_j's are defined as fuzzy sets in the input universe of discourse $U = U_1 \times U_2 \times \cdots \times U_n \subset \Re^n$.

A fuzzy inference engine judges and evaluates several linguistic values $G_1, G_2, ..., G_n$ in the output universe of discourse V by using fuzzy IF-THEN rules which are defined in the rule base:

$$R^{(j)} : IF \quad x_i \in F_1^j \; and...and \quad x_n \in F_n^j \; Then \; y \in G^j \tag{1}$$

where $(j = 1, ... M)$ and M is the number of rules in the principle base. Each fuzzy IF-THEN rule in the form of (1) defines a fuzzy set $F_1^j \times F_2^j \times ... \times F_n^j \to G^j$ in the product space $U \times V$. Let A' be an arbitrary input fuzzy set in U. A fuzzy set B^m in V can be calculated as:

$$\mu_{A' \circ R^m}(y) = \oplus (x_1, ..., x_n)^T \in U \left[\mu_{A'}(x_1, ..., x_n) \otimes \mu_{F_1^m \times ... \times F_n^m \to G_n^m}(x_1, ..., x_n, y) \right] \tag{2}$$

Figure 2. The fuzzy logic controller

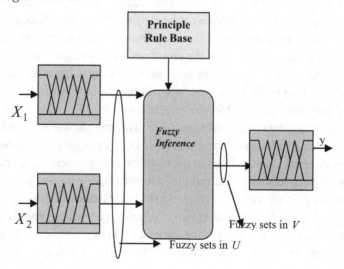

where t-norm $\otimes$ and s-norm $\oplus$ are used for the intersection and the union operations respectively. The final output is a fuzzy set in V, which is a combination of the M fuzzy sets, $A' \circ (R^{(1)},...,R^{(M)})$. The membership function of this inferred fuzzy set will be:

$$\mu_{A' \circ (R^{(1)},...,R^{(M)})}(y) = \mu_{A' \circ R^{(1)} \oplus ... \oplus} \mu_{A' \circ R^{(M)}}(y) \tag{3}$$

The above membership function defines the fuzzy value of the output action $\mu_B(y)$. The crisp value of the output action can be obtained, say, by using the Centre of Gravity (COG) defuzzification method, where the shape of membership function, $\mu_{A' \circ (R^{(1)},...,R^{(M)})}(y)$, is considered to determine the crisp value of the output action

$$y' = \frac{\sum y \mu_B}{\sum \mu_B}.$$

JUSTIFICATION OF THE USE OF FUZZY LOGIC TO EVALUATE TRUST

Trust relationships among customers and vendors are hard to assess due to the uncertainties and ambiguities involved in evaluating trust in EC. For example, in the proposed trust model, the community comments variable in the fulfilment factor has a wide range of values as we may have a small or a large number of customers providing positive or negative feedback to the vendor. Hence, the number of comments and their nature will affect the decision made by the associated evaluation module. In addition, in the trust model used, there are dependencies between some variables. For example the mandatory registration variable in the existence factor is dependent on the membership and third-party endorsements variables in the affiliation factor. Indeed, if an organization is a member of an association or endorsed by a third party, we assume that this organization is fully registered with the required authorities even though the mandatory registration was not extracted by the information extraction system.

Thus, the use of fuzzy reasoning is justified as an adequate approach to deal with evaluating trust in EC as it has the ability to quantify imprecise data and quantify uncertainties in measuring the trust

Figure 3. The ecommerce fuzzy trust model

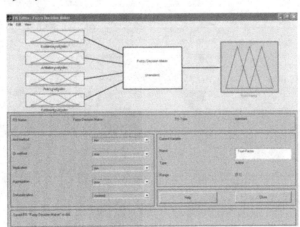

factor of the vendors and to deal with variable dependencies in the system by decoupling them using human expertise in the form of linguistics rules (Oussalah, Nefti, & Eltigani, 2007).

The general trust model proposed in this section is composed of five modules. Four modules will be used to quantify the trust measure of the four factors identified in our trust model (existence, affiliation, policy, and fulfilment) and the fifth module will be the final decision maker to quantify the trust factor as illustrated in Figure 3.

The inputs of the existence module are the physical existence, people existence, mandatory registration variable, and the output of the affiliation module. Indeed, as explained earlier in this section, the mandatory registration variable is dependent on the third party endorsement and membership variables of the affiliation module. We also note here that the physical existence variable is composed of three sub-variables, which are the telephone number, the fax number, and the physical address. For the affiliation module, the inputs are the third-party endorsement, membership, and portal variables. For the policy module, the inputs are the customer satisfaction, privacy, and warranty variables. Finally, the fulfilment module has as inputs the delivery, payment methods, and community comments variables. The decision maker has as inputs the outputs of the four modules which are Existence_Trust_Index, Fulfilment_Trust_Index, Policy_Trust_Index and the Affiliation_Trust_Index. The output of this module is the trust factor of the merchant's Website. In our model, this trust factor will be determined by the aggregations of the trust indices of all modules.

In the fuzzification phase, two membership functions described by the labels "Low" and "High" will be used for each variable related to each module. However, we introduce a third membership function "Average" for the outputs. For the decision maker module, we use all three membership functions for the inputs and output corresponding to Low, Average, and High degree of trustworthiness of the Website. These membership functions are represented by Gaussians defined by the centre and the standard deviation parameters. The output values are normalized within the interval (0, 1), with 1 for full trust

Figure 4. Output of the finale decision maker module

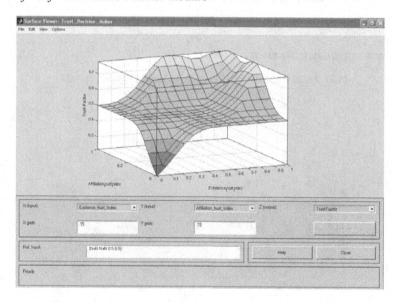

Figure 5. The final decision maker module rules

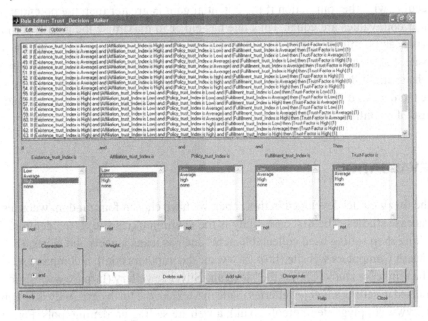

and 0 for no trust. For example a vendor's Website with 0.75 trust factor is considered high and should be trusted.

The inference rules are subject to the user's choice based on criteria of the risk and the gain as defined by Tao and Thoen (2001). Fuzzy inference is a process to assess the trust index in five steps: (1) register the initial values of each variable as defined by the information extraction system, (2) use the membership functions to generate membership degrees for each variable related to each module, (3) apply the fuzzy rule set defined for each module onto the output space (trust index) through fuzzy 'and' and 'or' operations, (4) aggregate the outputs from each rules related to each module, and (5) derive the trust index through a defuzzification process using the centroid method. These same steps will also be used for the decision maker module to generate the trust factor. From Figure 4, we can see that the trust index increases with the increase of the contributing attribute of all trust indices values and decrease when the decrease of all the attribute. Figure 5 shows a sample of the IF-THEN rules for the final decision maker module.

THE CONSTRUCTION OF THE RULES BASE

The decision to trust or not to trust EC as a shopping medium is up to consumers' evaluation, which can be based on many factors such as price, convenience, selection of choice, and the information available on the merchant's Website like those defined in our model. It is widely accepted that if the economic gain is greater than the risk involved then the transaction is reasonably viable. Based on this assumption, Tao and Thoen (2001) formalized the process as: $G_b = P_b L_b$ where G_b is the gain entering the EC transaction, P_b is the risk that the consumer takes for trusting the EC merchants and L_b is the loss the consumer has to bear when the transaction does not produce the result as expected. Consumers are usually proceeding with the transaction if the potential gain is greater than the potential lost and will be indifferent if both values are equal. Thus one has either to maximise the gain G_b or minimise the risk P_b. The risk can be minimised by providing all the information required by the customer on the vendor's website. Based on this model, we assume that if a large amount of information is available on a vendor's website and if this information is valid then the vendor can be trusted. However, the importance of these factors can differ from one user to another. To validate our rules we conducted a survey through the use of an online questionnaire.

SYSTEM EVALUATION

To evaluate the fuzzy model developed in this paper, we have chosen four random websites selling different items as case studies. The first case study is the Denimjunkies site (http://denimjunkies.com/), a vintage clothing shop selling used collectable items such as jeans jackets and shirts; the second case study is the Mesh Computers website (http://www.meshcomputers.com), a company selling PCs and peripherals; the third case study (CS3) is the Mexicana Silver Jewellery (http://www.mexicana.co.uk), a website specialised in selling silver jewelleries made in Mexico; the forth case study is simply gardening website (http://www.simplygardeningtools.co.uk), a website selling gardening tools. For each factor, a set of three variables is considered giving a total of 13 variables (including the output of the affiliation module which is used as an input to the existence module). Thus combining all variables yield to a total of 12,288 possible combinations for each Website. We use two membership functions for all the inputs, except the output from the affiliation module, which has three membership functions. Given the complexity of the problem, it becomes apparent why we grouped our variables into four factors which

Table 1. The extracted information for the case studies

	Variables	Case Study 1	Case Study 2	Case Study 3	Case Study 4
Existence Module	Physical Existence	P/A	P/F/A	P/F/A	P/F/A
	People Existence	yes	yes	yes	no
	Registration	yes	yes	no	yes
Affiliation Module	Endorsement	no	yes	yes	no
	Membership	yes	yes	no	no
	Portal	no	yes	yes	yes
Policy Module	Customer Satisfaction	yes	yes	yes	yes
	Privacy Statement	yes	no	yes	yes
	Warranty Policy	no	2 years	30 days	30 days
Fulfilment Module	Delivery	immediately	delayed	immediately	immediately
	Payment	Credit C/Debit C/ Cheque	Credit C/Debit C/ Cheque	Credit C/ Debit C	Credit C/ Debit C
	Community Comments	no	no	no	yes

are processed by separate modules as defined in (Nefti, 2002; Nefti & Djouadi, 2002). This allows us to consider only eight possible combinations per module except the existence module which has 24 combinations. For the final decision support module, three membership functions are used *Low*, *Average* and *High* and this gives a possible total of 81 combinations. Table 1 summarizes the information extracted from the two case studies.

Table 2 shows the fuzzification of the extracted values related to each variable. In the first case study, the information extraction system found two sub-variables (phone number and address) out of a possible three; hence a value of 0.6 is assigned to the physical existence variable, thus after the fuzzification step the degree of membership function of this value is 0.4 for Low and 0.6 for High. The remaining two variables (people existence and mandatory registration) in the existence factor were assigned the membership functions 1 (or High) In the remaining case studies, all information related to the existence factor were found; thus the degree of membership function of all three existence variables is 1. After all the selected rules were inferred in parallel, the fuzzy operator 'and' is applied to determine the support degree of the rules. The 'and' results are aggregated and the final trust factor for the case studies were is generated by defuzzifying the aggregation using the centroid method as shown in Figure 6.

Example of rules used to process the policy_trust_index for the case study 1 is as follows:

IF customer_satisfaction is Low and privacy_statement is High and warranty_policy is low THEN Policy_trust_index is Low .
IF customer_satisfaction is High and privacy_statement is High and warranty_policy is low THEN Policy_trust_index is Average.

Table 2. the fuzzification of the extracted information for the case studies

	Variables	Case Study 1	Case Study 2	Case Study 3	Case Study 4
Existence Module 1	Physical Existence	{0.4/L; 0.6/H}	H	H	H
	People Existence	H	H	H	L
	Registration	H	H	L	H
	Affiliation_trust_index	L	H	L	H
	Existence_trust_index	H	H	L	H
Affiliation Module 2	Endorsement	L	H	H	L
	Membership	H	H	L	L
	Portal	L	H	H	H
	Affiliation_trust_index	L	H	A	L
Policy Module	Customer Satisfaction	{0.2/L;0.8/H}	H	H	H
	Privacy Statement	H	L	H	H
	Warranty Policy	L	H	A	A
	Policy_trust_index	H	A	A	A
Fulfilment Module	Delivery	L	H	H	H
	Payment	H	H	H	H
	Community Comments	L	L	L	H
	Fulfilment_trust_index	L	A	A	H

Figure 6. Case study4: Rules aggregations and outputs

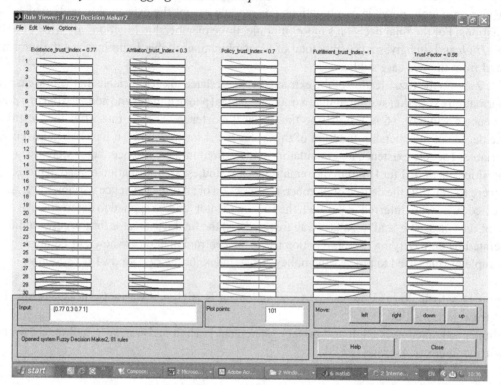

Table 3.The trust factor of the case studies

Outputs	Case Study 1	Case Study 2	Case Study 3	Case Study 4
Existence_trust_index	High	High	Low	High
Affiliation_trust_index	Low	High	Average	Low
Policy_trust_index	High	Average	Average	High
Fulfilment_trust_index	Low	Average	Average	High
Trust_factor	Average (0.62)	High (0.765)	Average(0.5)	Average(0.58)

The rules used for the aggregation of the final results for the case studies 1 and 2 and the outputs of the decision maker module are summarised in Table 3.

COMPARISON OF THE FUZZY MODEL WITH OTHER MODELS

Meziane and Kasiran (2005 & 2008) developed two models to evaluate EC trust using the same model shown in Fig 1, the linear model and the parameterised model. Both models were based on the presence or not of the variables on the EC website. The linear model is used for new or inexperienced users. The system automatically assigns the value of 1 when a variable is found and 0 otherwise. The total is then divided by the number of variables (12) and a trust factor with a value in the interval [0,1] is calculated using equation (4) were T is the trust factor and v_i .represents one of the 12 variables of the trust model.

$$T = \frac{1}{12}\left(\sum_{i=1}^{12} v_i\right) \tag{4}$$

The parameterised model is used with more experiences users which are asked to evaluate the importance (according to their perception) of each variable by assigning the value 1 if the variable is judged important, 0.5 if the variable is fairly important and 0 if it is not important. These values are used as weights to the linear model variables and again a trust factor T in the interval [0,1] is calculated using equation (5).

$$T = \frac{1}{4}\left(\frac{\sum_{i=1}^{3} E_i w_i}{\sum_{i=1}^{3} w_i} + \frac{\sum_{j=1}^{3} A_i w_i}{\sum_{j=1}^{3} w_i} + \frac{\sum_{k=1}^{3} P_i w_i}{\sum_{k=1}^{3} w_i} + \frac{\sum_{l=1}^{3} F_i w_i}{\sum_{l=1}^{3} w_i}\right) \tag{5}$$

In both cases, the closer to 1 the trust factor is the higher the trust is towards the merchant's website. We have compared the results obtained by the Fuzzy model with those obtained by the linear and parameterised model and the results are shown in Table 4. The weights used for the parameterised model used in this experiment, chosen by the authors, are as follows: Physical existence (1), People existence (0), Mandatory registration (1), Third Party endorsement (1), Membership (0.5), Portal (0.5), Customer Satisfaction (1), Privacy statement (1),Warranty (1), Delivery (0.5), Payment (0), Community comments (0.5).

The results obtained by the linear model, which are those provided for a new or inexperienced user, are high compared to those obtained by the other two models. The linear model results are only based on the existence or non existence of the variables on the merchant's Website and this may be misleading as not all variables are of the same importance. The results of the fuzzy and parameterized models are close because in this particular experiment, those who choose the weights for the parameterized model, namely the authors, are themselves experts and have experience in EC transactions. Hence, the results are similar to those produced by the fuzzy systems where experts have produced the IF-THEN rules.

The small differences can be justified as the aggregation method used in the parameterised model given in equation 5, do not capture the notion of uncertainty as the weights are only limited to three

Table 4. Trust models comparison

	Fuzzy Model	Linear Model	Parameterised Model
Case study 1	0.62	0.66	0.60
Case study 2	0.76	0.83	0.79
Case study 3	0.5	0.75	0.5
Case study 4	0.58	0.75	0.54

values (0, 0.5, 1) this would certainly affect the precision of the results of the trust factor compared to those obtained by the fuzzy model

By developing the fuzzy model, there is now no need for the use of the parameterized model as the expertise, on a general scale rather then chosen by individual users, is incorporated in the evaluation process. Users experience is also subjective and the use of the fuzzy model will provide a stronger and a more objective tool to all users regardless of their expertise and experience. It is clear from this experiment that the linear model should be discarded as the results produced do not reflect the true evaluation of trust in EC.

CONCLUSION AND FUTURE WORK

In this article, we presented a system based on fuzzy logic to support the evaluation and the quantification of trust in EC. Although, the system has addressed many issues that other systems did not such as taking into account the fuzzy nature of trust and using a substantial number of variables, we believe that the system can be improved in many ways. As stated in many trust models, there are other aspects that contribute to the completion of online transactions. This include the price, the rarity of the item and the experience of the customer. In order to develop an effective decision support system, future development should include some if not all of these aspects. The price of the item is certainly an important variable as it is shown in many studies that if the price is reasonably low, customers are ready to take the highest risk to purchase the item. Online transactions also depend on customer's experience and personality. Some customers may value some variables more then others. Hence we believe that future systems should allow customers to rank trust variables according to their own perception and experience.

REFERENCES

Akhter, F., Hobbs, D., & Maamar, Z. (2005). A fuzzy logic-based system for assessing the level of business-to-consumer (B2C) trust in electronic commerce. *Expert Systems with Applications, 28*, 623–628.

Araujo, I., & Araujo I. (2003). Developing trust in internet commerce. *In proceedings of the IBM conference of the Centre for Advanced Studies on Collaborative Research*, (pp. 1-15). Toronto, Canada.

Basso, A., Goldberg, D., Greenspan, S., & Weimer, D. (2001). First impressions: Emotional and cognitive factors underlying judgments of trust E-Commerce. *In Proceedings of the 3rd ACM conference on Electronic Commerce,* (pp.137-143). Tampa, FL.

Bayles, D. L. (2001). E-commerce logistics and fulfillment: Delivering the goods. New Jersey:Prentice Hall.

Castelfranchi, C., & Pedone, R. (2003). *A review of trust in information technology.* The ALFEBIITE Project, http://alfebiite.ee.ic.ac.uk/docs/papers/D1/ab-d1-cas+ped-trust.pdf

Cazier, J. A., Shao, B. B. M., & Louis, R. D. St. (2006). E-business differentiation through value-based trust. *Information & Management, 43*(6), 718-727.

Center for the Digital Future (2004). *USC Annenberg School, The digital future report.* Retrieved from http://www.digitalcenter.org/downloads/DigitalFutureReport-Year4-2004.pdf

Cheskin Research group (1999). *E-commerce study trust.* Retrieved from http://www.studioarchetype. com/cheskin/assets/images/etrust.pdf

Cheung, C. & Lee, Matthew, K. O. (2000). Trust in Internet shopping: A proposed model and measurement instrument. In *Proceeding of the Americas Conference on Information System (AMCIS 2000),* Long Beach, California.

Cohan, P. S. (2000). E-profit: High-payoff strategies for capturing the e-commerce edge. New York: American Management Association.

Corbitt B. J., Thanasankit T., & Yi H.(2003). Trust and e-commerce: A study of consumer perceptions. *Electronic Commerce Research and Applications,* (2), 203-215.

Grau, J. (2006). Retail e-commerce: Future trends. Retrieved from http://www.ecominfocenter.com/index.html?page=/infossources/websites/ststistics.html

Guo, J., & Sun, C. (2004). Global electronic markets and global traditional darkets. *Electronic Markets 14*(1), 4-12.

Han, K. S., & Noh, M. H. (1999). Critical failure factors that discourage the growth of electronic commerce. *International Journal of Electronic Commerce, 4*(2), 25-43.

Hoffman, D. L., Novak, T. P., & Chatterjee, P. (1995). Commercial scenario for the Web: Opportunities and challenges. *Journal of Computer-Mediated Communication, Special Issues on Electronic Commerce, 1*(3). [Electronic version available online at http://jcmc.indiana.edu/vol1/issue3/hoffman.html].

Hoffman, D. L., Novak, T. P., & Peralta, M. (1999). Building consumer trust online. *CACM, 42*(4), 80-85.

Hu, J., Shima, K., Oehlmann, R., Zhao, J., Takemura, Y., & Matsumoto, K. (2004). An empirical study of audience impressions of B2C Web pages in Japan, China and the UK. *Electronic Commerce Research and Applications,* (3), 176-189.

Jarvenpaa, S. L, Tranctinsky, N., & Vitale, M. (2000). Consumer trust in an Internet store. *Information Technology and Management Journal, 1*(1-2), 45-71.

Jøsang, A. (1998). Modelling trust in information society. Unpublished doctoral thesis, Department of Telematics, Norwegian University of Science and Technology, Trondheim, Norway.

Kasiran, M. K., & Meziane, F. (2002). An information framework for a merchant trust agent in electronic commerce. In H. Yin, N. Allinson, R. Freeman, J. Keane, & Hubbard S. (Eds), *Intelligent data engineering and automated learning,* (pp. 243-248). Springer.

Kasiran, M. K., & Meziane, F. (2004). The usage of third party endorsement in ecommerce websites. *In proceedings of the 7th International Conference on Work with Computing Systems (WWCS2004),* (pp.794-798). Kuala Lumpur, Malaysia.

Keen, P., Balance, C., Chan, S., & Schrump, S. (2000). Electronic commerce relationship: Trust by design. New Jearsey: Prentice Hall.

Klang, M. (2001). Who do you trust: Beyond encryption, secure e-business. *Decision Support System, 31*(3), 293-301.

Konrad, K., Fuchs, G., & Barthel, J. (1999). Trust and electronic commerce – More than a technical problem. In *Proceeding of the 18th IEEE Symposium on Reliable Distributed Systems,*, (pp 360-365). Lausanne, Switzerland.

Lewicki, R. J., & Bunker, B. B. (1996). Developing and maintaining trust in working relationships. In R.M. Kramer & T. Tyler (Eds.), *Trust in organizations,* (pp.114–139). Thousand Oaks, CA: Sage.

Li, H., Kuo, C., & Russell, M. G. (1999, December). The impact of perceived channel utilities, shopping orientation, and demographics on the consumer's online buying behaviour. *Journal of Computer-Mediated Communication, 5*(2).

Luo, X. (2002). Trust production and privacy concerns on the Internet: A framework based on relationship marketing and social exchange theory. *Industrial Marketing Management, 31*(2), 111-118.

Mamdani, E. (1994). Application of fuzzy algorithms of simple dynamic plants. In *Proceedings of IEEE, 121*, (pp. 585-588).

Manchala, D. W. (2000). E-commerce trust metrics and models. *IEEE Internet Computing, March-April,* 36-44.

Matthew, K. O., & Turban, E. (2001). A trust model for consumer internet shopping. *International Journal of Electronic Commerce, 6*(1), 75-91.

Mayer, R. C., Davis, J. H., & Schoorman, F. D. (1995). An integrative model of organizational trust. *Academy of Management Review, 20*(3), 709-734.

McCullagh, A. (1998, November 7). The establishment of trust in the electronic commerce environment. *Proceedings of The 1998 Information Industry Outlook Conference.* Retrieved from http://www.acs. org.au/president/1998/past/io98/mccullgh.htm

Merrilees, B. & Fry, M. (2003). E-Trust: The influence of perceived interactivity on e-tailing users. *Marketing Intelligence and Planning, 21*(2),123-128.

Meziane, F., & Kasiran, M. K. (2003). Extracting unstructured information from the WWW to support merchant existence in e-commerce. In A. Dusterhoft & B. Thalheim (Eds.), *Lecture Notes in Informatics, Natural Language Processing and Information Systems*, GI-Edition (pp.175-185). Bonn, Germany.

Meziane, F., & Kasiran, M. K. (2005, June). Strategizing consumer logistic requirements in e-commerce transactions: Evaluation of current implementations. In *Proceedings of the 3rd European Conference on Intelligent Management Systems in Operations*, (pp.116-125). Salford, Manchester, UK: The Operational Research Society.

Meziane, F., & Kasiran, M. K. (2008). Evaluating trust in electronic commerce: A study based on the information provided on merchants' Web sites. *Journal of the Operational Research Society, 59*(4), 464-472.

Mohanty, B. K., & Bhasker, B. (2005), Product classification in the Internet business: A fuzzy approach. *Journal of Decision Support Systems, 38*, 611-619.

Nah, F., & Davis, S. (2002). HCI research issues in e-commerce. *Journal of Electronic Commerce Research, 3*(3), 98-113.

Naraine, R. (2003). B2C e-commerce market will reach $90 billion in 2003. Retrieved from http://gcis.ca/cdne-497-apr-26-2003.html

National Fraud InformationCentre (no date). *Fraud information centre.* Retrieved from http://www.fraud.org/2002intstats.htm

Nefti, S., & Djouani, K. (2002, October). Fuzzy modeling of MIMO non linear system: Complexity reduction. *IEEE International Conference on Systems, Man and Cybernetics, 2*, 185-189.

Nefti, S. (2002, October 6-9). New algorithm for simplification of rule base generated by automated fuzzy modeling. *IEEE International Conference on Systems, Man and Cybernetics, 2*, 190-195.

Ngai, E. W. T., & Wat, F. K. T. (2002). A literature review and classification of electronic commerce research. *Information & Management*, (39), 415-429.

Ranganathan, C., & Ganapathy, S. (2002). Key dimension of business-to- consumer Web sites. *Journal of Information & Management, 39*, 457-465.

Oussalah, S., Nefti, S., & Eltigani, A. (2007) Personalized information retrieval system in the framework of fuzzy logic. *Expert systems with applications.* Elsevier.

Patton, M. A., & Jøsang, A. (2004). Technologies for trust in electronic commerce. *Electronic Commerce Research*, (4), 9-21.

Riegelsberger, J., & Sasse, M. A. (2001). Trustbuilders and trustbusters: The role of trust cues in interfaces to e-commerce applications. In *Proceedings of the 1st IFIP Conference on E-Commerce, E-Business, E-Government,* (pp. 17-30). Kluwer.

Romano, J., Nicholas C., & Fjermestad, J. (2003). Electronic commerce customer relationship management: A research agenda. *Information Technology and Management, 4*(2-3), 233-258.

Shapiro, D., Sheppard, B. H., & Cheraskin, L. (1992, October). Business on a handshake. *The Negotiation Journal*, 365-378.

Schmitz, S.W., & Latzerb, M. (2000). Competition in B2C e-commerce: Analytical issues and empirical evidence. *Electronic Markets, 12*(3), 163-174.

Steinauer, D. D., Wakid, S. A., & Rasberry, S. (1999, September). Trust and traceability in electronic commerce. Retrieved from http://nii.nist. gov/pubs/trust-1.html

Tao-Huan, T., & Theon, W. (2001). Towards a generic model of trust in electronic commerce. *International Journal of Electronic Commerce, 5*(2), 61-74.

Tyrone, W. A., Grandison (2003). *Trust management for Internet applications.* Unpublished doctoral thesis, Imperial College of Science, Technology and Medicine University of London, Department of Computing.

Zadeh, L. (1965). Fuzzy sets. *Information and Control, 8,* 338-353.

Chapter IV
Using Misunderstanding and Discussion in Dialog as a Knowledge Acquisition or Enhancement Procecss

Mehdi Yousfi-Monod
University of Montpellier, France

Violaine Prince
University of Montpellier, France

ABSTRACT

The work described in this chapter tackles learning and communication between cognitive artificial agents and trying to meet the following issue: Is it possible to find an equivalency between a communicative process and a learning process, to model and implement communication and learning as dual aspects of the same cognitive mechanism? Therefore, focus is on dialog as the only way for agents to acquire and revise knowledge, as it often happens in natural situations. This particular chapter concentrates on a learning situation where two agents, in a "teacher/student" relationship, exchange information with a learning incentive (on behalf of the student), according to a Socratic dialog. The teacher acts as the reliable knowledge source, and the student is an agent whose goal is to increase its knowledge base in an optimal way. The chapter first defines the nature of the addressed agents, the types of relation they maintain, and the structure and contents of their knowledge base. It emphasizes the symmetry between the interaction and knowledge management, by highlighting knowledge "repair" procedures launched through dialogic means. These procedures deal with misunderstanding, as a situation in which the student is unable to integrate new knowledge directly, and discussion, related to paradoxical information handling. The chapter describes learning goals and strategies, student and teacher roles within both dialog and knowledge handling. It also provides solutions for problems encountered by agents. A general architecture is then established and a comment on a part of the theory implementation is given. The conclusion is about the achievements carried out and the potential improvement of this work.

INTRODUCTION

Recent research in artificial intelligence (AI) focusing on intelligent software agents has acknowledged the fact that communication has to be seen as an intrinsic cognitive process instead of a plain external data exchange protocol. Communication, and more specifically dialog, is an active process, which modifies the agents internal state. It could be directly or indirectly related to a change in agents environment, as any action does when performed. This is why the Speech Acts Theory (Searle, 1969), formerly defended in philosophy, has emigrated toward computational linguistics and cognitive science, to finally provide a proper frame for a new communication language between artificial agents (Smith & Cohen, 1996), especially within agents societies (Pedersen, 2002). However, even though communication has changed status, it has not been totally exploited by those who have promoted Speech Acts based enhancements to agents design. Communication has been examined as a constraints systems preceding action (Mataric, 1997), a set of actions (mostly with performative communication, where any utterance is equivalent to an action (Cerri & Jonquet, 2003)), a set of heuristics for negotiation strategies (Parsons, Sierra, & Jennings, 1998), (Wooldridge & Parsons, 2000). But, seldom its feedback on the agent knowledge base has been considered as a main issue. Some advances have been attempted to tackle it: Negotiation has been recognized as tied to a process of belief revision by (Amgoud & Prade, 2003) (Zhang, Foo, Meyer, & Kwok, 2004), thus acknowledging the role of communication as a part of knowledge processing in artificial agents, mostly as a back up.

On the other hand, a complementary field of AI has been addressing communication issues: Several Human-Machine Interaction researches have fostered interesting models of an 'intelligent' communication, i.e, an information exchange in which actions related with knowledge acquisition and update are involved. (Draper & Anderson, 1991) and (Baker, 1994) model dialogs as fundamental elements in human learning, and try to import them into automated tutoring systems (ITS). (Asoh et al., 1996), (Cook, 2000) and (Ravenscroft & Pilkington, 2000), among several others, relate dialog to cognitive actions such as mapping, problem-seeking and investigation by design. All authors tend to emphasize the same point: Dialog supports cognition in human activity, and thus might support it if modeled in an ITS. Cognition is seen in AI as the sum of belief and knowledge acquisition or change, and reasoning. Supporting it in human learning process could be also done in machine learning: The idea that a learning process could be triggered or handled through queries, which are an element of the query-answer basic pattern in dialog, has been long defended by (Angluin, 1987). Strangely, descriptions of cognition do not directly include communication as an intrinsic cognitive process, although this has been pointed out in the more 'human' part of cognitive science (i.e. in cognitive psychology) and despite the fact that some twenty years ago, researchers in AI did emphasize the deep relationship between knowledge and its communicative substrate in very famous publications such as (Allen & Perrault, 1980) or (Cohen & Levesque, 1992).

In our opinion, there was a gap that was not filled: When considering artificial agents, especially those which are qualified as cognitive, is it possible to find an equivalency between a communicative process and a learning process, to model and implement communication and learning as dual aspects of the same cognitive mechanism? This was a research issue for which all the mentioned work seemed hinting at, but without directly focusing on it. A previous publication (Prince, 2006) has described an implemented agent model in which communication is a native property, and messages could be exchanged as 'knowledge chunks', following theoretical specifications first presented in (Prince, 1996). The present research is broader, and aims at making artificial agents acquire knowledge through dialog, but mostly implement dialog materializations of their knowledge revision process. A feasibility study has been presented in (Yousfi-Monod & Prince, 2005), extended in (Yousfi-Monod & Prince, 2007) to include knowledge conflict management. However, this point has been tackled only from the reasoning point of view. But knowledge gathering has its discrepancies: Misunderstandings, conflict between captured knowledge and inner knowledge base are usual situations. Some authors (Beun & Eijk, 2003) have tackled the issue. They have also recognized the important 'repair role' devoted to interaction (Beun & Eijk, 2005). Therefore, misunderstandings and discussion, external forms of an internal knowledge process, and dialog counterparts of knowledge revision through an external help, have been here thoroughly analyzed. Their originality could be summarized by two items. First, conflict in a knowledge base is 'uttered' and therefore triggers an external and no more an internal revision process: The agent is no more 'alone' and knowledge revision is no more a solitary action. Second, the response of the other agent is a fresh contribution of new facts or knowledge and therefore cannot be anticipated. This creates a very interesting situation in which misunderstandings can pile up, and where discussion might create unanticipated reasoning tracks.

This chapter tries to provide a possible instantiation of this issue, highlighting the deep interaction between the knowledge acquisition and revision process on one hand, and the dialog strategy and model on the other.

BACKGROUND

Several notions have to be explained and grounded before proceeding further. In this section, a survey on cognitive artificial agents basic properties is provided. Since learning is a typical task of knowledge acquisition and revision, we focus here on learning related to communication, and the way it has been dealt with in the literature.

Cognitive Artificial Agents

By *cognitive agents* we mean entities able to acquire, store and process knowledge therefore able of "understanding, inferencing, planning and learning" (Lycan, 1999). Notice that communication, and its basic tool, language, are not mentioned here, although they appear as such in cognitivists' works. (Nelson, 1996) specifically states that: "language is a catalyst for cognitive change". A catalyst does not enter the reaction and is not modified by it. In this chapter, we will show that if 'language', as a tool, is not modified, dialog, as a language and communication process, gets a feedback when knowledge is revised.

When cognitive agents are programs or robots, they are called *artificial cognitive agents*. In AI and knowledge representation terminology, this can be translated into systems possessing knowledge bases, making them evolve either by environment observation (reactivity) or by derivation modes (inductive, deductive and abductive reasoning). *Deduction* is the natural mode of knowledge derivation in a propositional logic, or in first order logic with Modus Ponens as a basic axiom. It relies on the implication transitivity. *Induction* is a more advanced process, that can be represented by the term 'inferencing' used here above. It is multifaceted and might as well include *generalization* and some *syllogisms*, predictive reasoning and bayesian (statistical) induction (Holland, Holyoak, Nisbett, & P.Thagard, 1989). As a whole induction is a process that tries to augment the knowledge base by extending the truth value from an assumption to another by other means than transitivity. In this chapter, we will use inductive reasoning as a set of axioms defined in (Manna, 1974). It represents generalization and predictive reasoning. *Abduction* is the process through which similarity could be assessed or falsified: Does a fact belong to a given law (general knowledge)? This simple question triggers the abductive process, which is an inferential process (Josephson & Josephson, 1994), thus making abduction a possible 'subcase' of induction, seen as a large set of different types of reasoning. *Unification* is a simple successful abduction. However, in most of the cases abduction is associated to conflict: A given knowledge is often either contradicted by an incoming fact, of this incoming fact cannot be attached to the current knowledge base. How does the agent restore the broken chain or extend it to include the next fact? It needs to create a new knowledge item (abductive induction) or to relax constraint to attach the fact to a broader knowledge. All these issues are tackled in this chapter.

Cognitive Agents are considered as able of planning and decision making. Therefore, one has to include goals and intentions as elements of cognition (Pollack, 1998). Reaching a goal needs reasoning. Strategies, which are procedures derived through reasoning, consider the goal as a consequence and the possible set of actions (the plan) as a part of the knowledge base.

Learning is a process that tackles both acquisition (capturing inputs) and reasoning (including those inputs into the agent knowledge base, and deriving further knowledge out of them). Therefore learning seems to be a very representative process of cognition. In AI literature, learning is not much associated to communication. One may find several types of learning methods for symbolic agents like reinforcement learning, supervised learning, neural networks and bayesian learning models that are very far from our domain. This type of learning prepares agents for typical situations, whereas, a natural situation in which dialog influences knowledge acquisition, has a great chance to be unique and not very predictable (Ravenscroft & Pilkington, 2000).

Learning Through Communication

Human beings as natural cognitive agents favor dialog as their main source knowledge revision. Each agent tends to consider any fellow agent as a possible knowledge source. The source is 'triggered' through questioning, and information is acquired, from the answer. This question-answer process is launched to meet a given goal, proper to the asking agent, and for which he/she has planned a set of actions (Pollack, 1998). There are several possible cases. Either the asking agent is looking for a very precise information, and therefore, its locutor agent might not possibly provide information, therefore he/she will undertake a research in order to find the appropriate interlocutor. Thus the plan is not tightly associated to dialog which stabilizes a given pair of agents, but to the proper interlocutor recognition through a very brief question-answer session. The other case is when the agent needs knowledge. (Williams, 2004) has described an application in which agents augment a common ontology, as well as their own by sharing knowledge and learning from each other. The author has sketched an overall communication framework to do so. It is not properly a dialog situation, since several agents may communicate simultaneously however, its interest relies in the fact that it designates communication as a mean of cognitive change.

This, naturally is the anchor of a revision based process, where the a given concept, playing the role of an assumption, is subject to confrontation with the inner knowledge source of the requiring agent. Thus, it drives the latter to proceed to derivation (by reasoning).

However, here appears the question of evaluation: Is the provided knowledge reliable? In a general situation, one will tend to implicitly accept Grice's recommendations about information quality: Agents must not utter something unless they believe it to be true. But are their beliefs equivalent to a certain knowledge? Is any interlocutor a reliable knowledge source?

Some authors try to meet this issue by assuming that a consensus about knowledge is what could be the closer to truth. It is what happens in negotiation-based models for knowledge revision. Mutual belief revision, defended by (Zhang et al., 2004), reaches an equilibrium assumed to be a clue for the quality of shared knowledge. But negotiating knowledge among several agents might tend to favor group attitudes instead of a search for truth. Several agents sharing the same wrong belief might weigh more than one proposing a good but individual solution. Therefore, these questions have led some authors focus on dialog between two agents, one playing the role of a reliable source (and being acknowledged as one), and the second, playing the role of the learning agent (Beun & Eijk, 2003). However, these dialog situation are assimilated to game strategies in the cited paper. It is also the case in (Amgoud & Prade, 2003). Therefore, sometimes dialog is more an interaction process than a real 'logos' (the Greek root in the word dialog, i.e. related to discourse and language) process.

Dialog in Learning

Human learning with human teachers relies on language and communication. A classroom learning in which a teacher talks, and students sometimes ask questions is not a dialog situation, and obviously it is a personal teacher, with a true dialog between teacher and student, that gets the best results in knowledge transfer. The situation could be rapidly described as: A teacher provides knowledge when asked, or as a lecture. The feedback commonly observed in natural dialog is that the teacher, playing the role of the knowledge source could be addressed by the learner, in order to test whether the acquisition process has succeeded. This is called *tutored learning*.

Human learning with machines has tried to emulate this privileged interaction. Authors in the domain have repeatedly insisted on the importance of dialog as an acquisition and evaluation process for the human learner (VanLehn, Siler, & C.Murray, 1998), (Muansuwan, Sirinaovakul, & Thepruangchai, 2004). Literature is truly abundant on the subject and we cannot but grossly summarize the main tendencies of the state-of-the-art. The main achievements could be described as:

- Dialog models in computer science are based on *intentions* (Cohen & Levesque, 1992), and define dialog instances as a succession of planned communicative actions modifying implicated agents' mental state.
- Thus a dialog-based ITS has a dialog model implemented in it. The ITS is in a knowledge transfer situation, and as a goal, needs to teach a set of knowledge items. On the other hand, the human partner also has a goal: He/she needs to learn these very items. The ITS must check that the human has effectively acquired knowledge.
- Several researches have shown that a predetermined plan does not work, because the human's actions and/or answer cannot be predicted. Therefore, ITSs react *step by step*, according to the

interlocutor's answer. This is why an *opportunistic* model of linguistic actions is better than a planning model.

Since tutoring learning seems to be a good framework for knowledge transfer, we have chosen a particular tutoring action, the *socratic dialog*. It is a simple conversation structure in which transfer as well as checking is done in the way of questions on behalf of the teaching agent. For instance, a socratic dialog might begin with: *What do you know about X?* and then answer, and then *Why is Y related to X?* where Y was present in the answer, etc.

Some Features Of Tutored Learning Situations

Dialog Peculiarities. Even reduced to socratic dialog, a tutored learning situation implies a *finalized* dialog (aiming at carrying out a task) as well as *secondary* exchanges (precision, explanation, confirmation and reformulation requests can take place to validate a question or an answer). Therefore, speech acts appear as crucial elements in the interaction process. We have chosen to assign functional roles (FR) to speech acts since this method, described in (Sabah et al., 1998), helps unpredictable situations modeling, whereas the Speech Act Theory (i) assigns multiple illocutionary values to the same speech act thus maintaining ambiguity ; (ii) is more efficient *a posteriori* than *a priori* ; (iii) relies on verbs interpretation by human-based pragmatics, and therefore is difficult to transform into a reliable computational model. The FR theory is closer to an adaptive computational model since it tries to compute an exchange as an adjustment between locutors mental states. We have adapted this method, originally designed for human-machine dialog, to artificial agents.

Reasoning. Reasoning, from a learning point of view, is a knowledge derivation mode, included in agent functionalities, or offered by the 'teacher' agent. Reasoning modifies the recipient agent state, through a set of reasoning steps. In such a frame, *learning* is the process that takes as an input the result of a reasoning procedure over new facts or predicates, and ends up in engulfing them in the agent knowledge base. Thus, inspired from human behavior, the described model includes the three types of reasoning described in the preceding section: Deduction, induction and abduction. Currently, our system is based on axioms which are abstractions of inductive and deductive mechanisms. Abduction is investigated in some knowledge discovery strategies, and in repair after misunderstanding strategies, that are an original contribution of this chapter. Abduction implicitly plays a very crucial role. We consider *dialog as an abductive bootstrap technique* which, by presenting new knowledge, enables knowledge addition or retraction and therefore leads to knowledge revision (Josephson & Josephson, 1994, Pagnucco, 1996). So, its explicit mechanisms, related to 'explanation' in the dialog features, are definitely contributing to the system task.

Simplification Due To Artificial Agents

Transposing a human learner model to an artificial cognitive agent must not be done without acknowledging the particularities of artificial agents. So, although our system is heavily inspired from dialog between humans and from human-machine dialog systems, it differs from them with respect to the following items:

- Natural language is not used as such and a formal-based language is preferred, in the tradition of languages such as KIF, that are thoroughly employed in artificial agents communication. These formal languages prevent problems that rise from the ambiguity intrinsic to natural language.
- When one of the agents is human, then his/her knowledge is opaque not only to his/her interlocutor (here, the system) but also to the designer of the system. Therefore, the designer must build, in his system, a series of 'guessing' strategies, that do not necessarily fathom the interlocutor's state of mind, and might lead to failure in dialog. Whereas, when both agents are artificial, they are both transparent to the designer, if not to each other. Thus, the designer embeds, in both, tools for communication that are adapted to their knowledge level. The designer might check, at any moment, the state variables of both agents, a thing he or she cannot do with a human.

These two restrictions tend to simplify the problem, and more, to stick to the real core of the task, i.e. controlling acquisition through interaction.

THE THEORETICAL FRAMEWORK

Agents Frame

Our environment focuses on a situation where two cognitive artificial agents are present, and their sole interaction is through dialog. During this relationship, an agent will play the role of a teacher and the other will momentarily act as a student. We assume they will keep this status during the dialog session. Nevertheless, role assignation is temporary because it depends on the task to achieve and on each agent's skills. The 'teacher' agent must have the required skill to teach to the 'student' agent, i.e. *to offer unknown and true knowledge, necessary for the 'student' to perform a given task*. Conventionally, 'student' and 'teacher' terms will be used to refer, respectively, to the agents acting as such. The 'teacher' aims at 'freely' offering a set of predetermined knowledge to the 'student'. This, naturally subsumes that agents cooperate. Thereby, no erroneous data will be exchanged and agents will attempt, using all means they can, to satisfy their interlocutor's expectancy. Nevertheless, as in a natural situation, the 'student' could be not really self-motivated and by this way making harder the 'teacher's task. For instance, the 'student' could provide indefinite data to the 'teacher'.

Knowledge Base Properties

First-Order Logic. Each agent owns a knowledge base (KB), structured in first-order logic, with functions, so the knowledge unit is a *formula*.

First-order logic has been preferred to propositional logic, or description logic, because of the expressive power of predicates, and the existence of functions was necessary to the nature of our first test corpus, which was in physics (teaching laws of mechanics). However, functions have been abandoned because of intrinsic difficulties, and we changed the corpus into a basic science corpus. Since quantifiers not being tested, the traps related to them in first-order logic have been avoided. So, first-order logic here mostly appears because FR modeling, introducing particular predicates (functional roles), has driven us to use this level of expressivity.

Basic Assumptions About True And False. The 'student' can make mistakes, i.e. possess *wrong* knowledge. From an axiomatic point of view, if an agent acts as a 'teacher' in relation to a given knowledge set, then the 'student' will consider as true every item provided by the 'teacher'.

Conventions. Each KB is manually initiated, however, its update will be automatic, thanks to 'learning' and reasoning abilities. In order to simplify modeling, we only use formulas such as (P), $(P \rightarrow Q)$ and $(P \leftrightarrow Q)$. (P) and (Q) are predicates conjunctions (or their negation) of type $(p(A))$ or $(p(X))$ (or $(\neg(p(A)))$ or $(\neg(p(X))))$, where $A = \{a_1, a_2, ..., a_n\}$ is a set of terms and $X = \{x_1, x_2, ..., x_n\}$ a set of variables. For simplification sake, we note P and Q such predicates conjunctions. Universal quantification is implicit for each formula having at least one variable. We consider that, to initiate learning (from the 'student' position), the 'teacher' has to rely on the 'student's' previous knowledge. This constraint imitates humans' learning methods. Therefore, before performing a tutored learning dialog, agents must have a part of their knowledge identical (called *basic common knowledge*). The 'teacher' will be able to teach new knowledge by using the 'student''s already known one. However, our agents do not 'physically' share any knowledge (their KBs are independent).

Connexity As A KB Fundamental Property. During learning, each agent will attempt to make its KB as 'connex' as possible.

Definition 1. A KB is *connex* when its associated graph G_Γ is connex. A graph is associated to a KB Γ as such:

Each formula is a node. An edge is created between each couple of formulas having the same premise or the same conclusion or when the premise of one equals the conclusion of the other. For the moment, variables and terms are not taken into account in premise or conclusion comparison (An abductive reasoning mechanism is contemplated as a possible mean to compare a constant fact $q(a)$ with a predicate with a variable $q(y)$. We only consider the result of a succeeding abduction.) Thus, in a connex KB, every knowledge element is linked to every other, the path between them being more or less long. As the dialogic situation must be as close as possible to a natural situation, *agents' KBs are not totally connex:* A human agent can often, but not always, link two items of knowledge, haphazardly taken.

Examples:

A connex KB: $\Gamma_1 = \{t(z) \wedge p(x) \rightarrow q(y), r(x) \rightarrow q(y), s(x) \rightarrow r(y), q(a), r(b)\}$
A non connex KB: $\Gamma_2 = \{t(z) \wedge p(x) \rightarrow q(y), r(x) \rightarrow q(y), s(x) \rightarrow u(y), q(a), u(b)\}$
Figures 1(a) and 1(b) respectively represent graphs associated to Γ_1 and Γ_2.

Definition 2. A connex component (or just component) is a connex subset of formulas in a KB.

Theorem 1. Let A, B and C be three connex formulas sets. If $A \cup B$ and $B \cup C$ are connex then $A \cup B \cup C$ is connex.

Proof. Let us assume that $A \cup B$ and $B \cup C$ is connex and G_A, G_B and G_C are graphs respectively associated to A, B and C. According to definition 1: $A \cup B$ connex is equivalent to $G_A \cup G_B$ connex. Also, $B \cup C$ con-

Figure 1. KB associated graphs

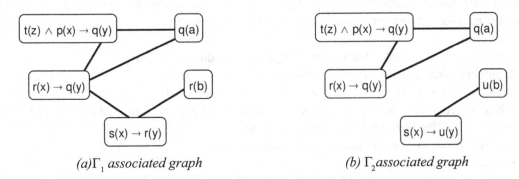

(a)Γ_1 *associated graph*   (b) Γ_2 *associated graph*

nex is equivalent to *BC* connex. And according to connex graph properties: $G_A \cup G_B$ connex and $G_B \cup G_C$ connex implies $G_A \cup G_B \cup G_C$ connex. So $A \cup B \cup C$ is connex.

The agent situation we envisage is such that agents will not attempt to increase the number of their connex components. However, there will be some cases where the 'student' will be forced to do so. Fortunately, in some other cases, learning new knowledge may link two connex components into a new larger one, decreasing the components total number (according to Theorem 1).

Dialog: Using Functional Roles (FR)

A dialog session is the image of a *lesson*. A lesson is performed either because the presumed 'student' has been asking for an important piece of information (not limited to a simple yes-or-no question or "where do I find something..." questions), or because the 'teacher' finds him/herself in a situation where he/she has to transmit his/her knowledge. Transposed to artificial agents situation, both cases are available. In those, the assigned 'teacher' must know what knowledge to teach to the 'student': Therefore a lesson has to be planed. It is then composed of several elements, each of them contained, in our framework, in a logic formula. In our model for artificial agents, the teaching agent provides each formula to the 'student'. However, before that, the 'teacher' waits for the 'student''s understanding (or misunderstanding) message of the last formula. If the 'student' doesn't understand or is not at ease, it can just inform its interlocutor of the misunderstanding or, requests a particular information bit.

The FR theory, that models exchanges in this dialog, provides a role attachment to each utterance. Both agents, when receiving a message, know its role and come up with an adequate answer. In our framework, knowledge about roles is possible, because opacity, natural to human situation, is absent. A particular clause is expressed and conveyed to the interlocutor. This clause denotes the *dialogic role* of the formula to be transmitted. At the same time, this clause provides an indication about the *formula evaluation*. We assign the type *knowledge* to universal or existential general logical formulas. This type is neutral from the evaluation point of view, that is, knowledge might either be true or false, as a formula. Whereas, we assign the type *information* to constant-uttering answer (or question), i.e. which value is 'true', 'false', or 'unknown'. Knowledge and Information, when exchanged, might be stamped as 'inevitably true' or 'possibly false' or, and this takes us out of the first-order logic language, 'unknown', i.e. not evaluable to both locutors. What makes the evaluation possible, is a complex result of three components: The dialog situation, the agent role, and the conveyed functional role.

To illustrate this, let us detail the main FR types used in the our tutored learning dialog. Our convention for FR naming is: 'VERBAL PREDICATE'-'OBJECT TYPE'('*argument*').

1. GIVE-KNOWLEDGE(): Used to teach a knowledge and introduce an exchange.
    Argument's general form: $(P{\rightarrow}Q)$ or $(P{\leftrightarrow}Q)$.
    Example: GIVE-KNOWLEDGE($CAT(X){\rightarrow}MORTAL(X)$); "Cats are mortal."
    When uttered by the 'teacher', a GIVE-KNOWLEDGE() argument has to be evaluated as true by the 'student' (see 'FR Interpretation Axioms' section).

2. ASKFOR/GIVE-INFORMATION() (boolean evaluation case):
    *   ASKFOR-INFORMATION().
        Argument's general form: Either (P), or $(P{\rightarrow}Q)$, or $(P{\leftrightarrow}Q)$, with or without variable.
        Examples:
        ASKFOR-INFORMATION($CAT(FOLLEY)$); "Is Folley a cat?"
        ASKFOR-INFORMATION($CAT(X){\rightarrow}MORTAL(X)$); "Are cats mortal?"
    When conveyed to the interlocutor this function bids him/her to answer. In a very cooperative framework as the one we need to install between artificial agents, the 'teacher' agent is compelled to answer with a GIVE-INFORMATION() utterance, which gives the interpretation of the formula $(cat(x){\rightarrow} mortal(x))$ according to the 'teacher'.
    *   GIVE-INFORMATION().
    Argument's general form: Either $(True)$, or $(False)$, or $(Unknown)$.
    Example: GIVE-INFORMATION($True$): "Yes."

3. GIVE-EXPLANATION() (predicate case).
    Argument's general form: Either $(p(x){\leftrightarrow}P)$, or $(Unknown)$.
    Example: GIVE-EXPLANATION($CAT(X){\leftrightarrow}(ANIMAL(X){\wedge}PET(X))$): "A cat is a pet animal."
    A GIVE-EXPLANATION() formula is provided as an answer to a question of the type: "what is X?" or "Why/how is X related to Y?". In other words, when a 'student' has no value to a predicate, or cannot relate it to another, the 'student' asks the 'teacher' to provide the links between the unknown element and other possibly known predicates. The situation can be triggered by an ASKFOR-EXPLANATION() clause taking as an argument the unknown predicate or formula. The 'student' expects the 'teacher' to provide a formula in which known predicates are related to the unknown one. By this process, the 'student' might augment its KB while increasing its connexity. A "Why/how is X related to Y?" question is about connexity, and a "what is X?" question increases KB elements through KB connexity.

4. SAY-DIS/SATISFACTION: Tells the other agent that the last provided data has (has not) been well understood. This is a meta-evaluation clause, since it has no direct argument, but leads to the evaluation of the interaction (and not of the formula). SAY-DIS/SATISFACTION is particular to dialog modeling (most linguistic and psycholinguistic theories account for interaction evaluation), and is very useful in checking dialog feedback.

There are some FR we do not detail here (ASKFOR-KNOWLEDGE, ASKFOR/GIVE-EXAMPLE, ASKFOR/GIVE-PRECISION, ASKFOR/GIVE-REFORMULATION) likewise some specific uses like the type ASKFOR/GIVE-INFORMATION in the case of an evaluation by a function. So FR are dialogic clauses leading to the interpretation of exchanged formulas. A functional role of the 'ASKFOR' kind implies one or a series of clauses of the

'GIVE' type, with the possibility of using another 'ASKFOR' type if there is a misunderstanding. This case will bring about a clause without argument: 'SAY-SATISFACTION'. Only 'ASKFOR' type roles will lead to interpretative axioms. Other ones are behavioral startings.

Tutored Learning

The learning mechanism lays on a set of axioms, depends on the learning situation and is motivated by the teacher's and student's goals. This section describes these different aspects for our tutored learning.

Axioms. Our reasoning system is hypothetical-deductive, so it allows belief revision and dialog is the mean by which this revision is performed. Two groups of axioms are defined: Fundamental axioms of the system and those corresponding to the FR interpretation in the system. Each knowledge chunk of each agent is seen as an assumption.

Fundamental axioms. Our system revision axioms include the hypothetisation axiom, hypothesis addition and retraction, implication addition, implication retraction or modus ponens and the *reductio ad absurdum rule*.

Let Γ be the 'student's' assumptions finite set. The knowledge acquisition mode is represented by addition or substraction 'deducted' by the fraction bar symbol. Generalized to the ensemblist implication, this symbol means that in premise (numerator) there is an ensemblist implication and in conclusion (denominator) there is another ensemblist implication, deductible from the previous one, whose objective is to make the knowledge set evolving. System revision axioms (taken from (Manna, 1974)):

- The hypothetisation axiom:

$$\Gamma, A \Rightarrow A \tag{1}$$

if the agent knows an assumption A, then it can deduce it from its own system.

- The assumption addition:

$$\frac{\Gamma \Rightarrow B; \Gamma}{A \Rightarrow B} \tag{2}$$

if the agent can deduce B, then it will be able to deduce it from any superset of its own system.

- The assumption retraction:

ERROR -Please resubmit formula (3)

if the validity of an assumption A of the system doesn't influence on the assumptions B deductible from this system, A must be removed. To allow A influencing on B, the assumptions set Γ and A must be (but this is not sufficient) connex.

- The implication addition:

$$\frac{\Gamma}{A \Rightarrow B; \Gamma \Rightarrow A \supset B} \tag{4}$$

if B is deductible from an assumptions set and from an assumption A, then the rule $A \supset B$ is deductible from the system. The connexity notion is present here as we need the fact that B is deductible from A to be able to add the rule $A \supset B$, which means that a path between A and B must be present.

- The implication retraction or modus ponens:

ERROR -Please resubmit formula (5)

if A is deductible from the system and if A is the premise of a system deductible rule, then the conclusion of this rule is directly deductible from the system.

- The rule called *reductio ad absurdum*:

ERROR -Please resubmit formula (6)

if B can be deductible AND falsifiable from the system including A, then A is falsified. This axiom introduce the conflict management dealt lately.

FR interpretation axioms. Interpretation axioms are not in the first order since they introduce clauses and multiple values (like the 'unknown' one). Our syntax will be in the first order, but the interpretation is not monotonous.

- GIVE–KNOWLEDGE$(A) \Rightarrow A \vdash True$;
  any knowledge supplied by the 'teacher' is considered as true.
- GIVE–INFORMATION$(A) \equiv A \varepsilon [True, False, Unknown]$;
  any supplied information is a formula interpretable in a multi-valued space.
- GIVE–EXPLANATION$(A) \equiv ($GIVE-INFORMATION$(\text{P}), A \leftrightarrow \text{P})$;
  any explanation consists in supplying a right formula, equivalent to the formula A that has to be explained.

Tutored Learning Situations And Goals. Our learning situation brings into play two characters: A 'teacher' and a 'student'. The learning initiative may come from either the 'teacher' or the 'student'.

Teacher's initiative. In this case, we'll speak about a lesson, i.e. the 'teacher' will try to make the 'student' understanding a set of unknown knowledge.

For our artificial agents, we transpose this situation in the following goal:

1. Enriching the student's KB with new data

Data here may be facts, implications or equivalences.

So the first teacher's goal is to teach a lesson and the first student's goal is to learn this lesson. In our course position, this goal is essential for retaining the taught lesson. This is the commonest and the most natural goal, the one that seems to appear most frequently.

Student's initiative. In this second case we face another type of learning scheme we'll designate by 'the curious student case' as we have here an enterprising entity, who has its own motivations for getting new knowledge from the 'teacher'. Indeed, our agents can be curious, as natural agents are sometimes, and can wish to deepen their learning beyond the basic lesson.

We have identified three student's main goals for this case:

2. Increasing the KB connexity
3. Widening the predicates base
4. Understanding why some formulas imply others

Human goals vs. artificial goals. Each of these four goals (1-4) may just be considered in terms of adjunction of new formulas, however we have defined them accordingly to human-like learning goals, in order to be as close as possible to a natural situation. Each goal respectively corresponds to the accomplishment of the following human-like goals:

1. Teaching/learning pieces of knowledge through a lesson
2. Making more links between pieces of knowledge the 'student' already knows
3. Knowing new entities which check properties the 'student' already knows
4. Understanding why some properties are deductible from others, i.e. is there another way to understand them?

KB connexity preservation goal. Each of these goals should fulfill a common goal: Preserving the connexity property of the KB. This is a student's typical goal. We estimate this goal important as it aims at preserving the KB consistency, in a human meaning: A human cannot use a new piece of knowledge that is not linked to his/her own ones, so when s/he faces such a new data, s/he'll usually try to get data that makes the junction between the new one and the already known.

For example, a human 'student' who ears about the concept of rectangle for the first time cannot do anything with it and so should ask the 'teacher' what a rectangle is. Let us assume the 'student' knows what a quadrilateral is and what the properties 'diagonals intersect in their middle' and 'diagonals length are equals' means. The 'teacher' could then explain a rectangle by a quadrilateral which fulfills these two properties. After this explanation, the rectangle should make sense to the 'student' as s/he can understand this concept with his/her own ones: There is a link between them. We'll detail this example in the next section.

In other words, by *understanding*, we mean 'not increasing the KB components number': The 'student' understands a data that is linked to at least one component of its KB. By definition, we consider that a 'student' agent *knows* a formula if it owns it. If the taught data is not linked to any component, the 'student' have to inform the 'teacher' of its misunderstanding as we'll see in the next section.

KB consistency preservation goal. Here is another student's typical common goal. The 'student' has to keep its KB consistent in order to prevent reasoning conflicts. For example, it cannot own the two next formulas at the same time: $(P{\rightarrow}Q)$ and $(P{\rightarrow}\neg(Q))$. When learning new data, it will then have to check if the new knowledge doesn't generate a conflict in its KB. If this happens, it will have to use a conflict management strategy.

Dialogue Strategy

Each learning situation requires a strategy to guide the dialog. Moreover, interaction may lead up to misunderstanding and conflicts during the dialog, each one requiring a specific strategy. We begin by describing the basic strategy for the lesson, then we deal with the 'curious student' strategies, and finally with the problem resolution strategies.

Lesson Strategy. Our strategy is based on the socratic dialog principle: The 'teacher' will provide each piece of knowledge (formulas in our case) to the 'student' and will wait for its satisfaction or dissatisfaction before continuing the lesson. By this way, *each teacher's message is at the same time a knowledge gift and a question about its understanding, thanks to the FR*. As long as the 'student' is satisfied, the 'teacher' continues providing each formula until the end of the lesson. If the 'student' expresses its misunderstanding, then the 'teacher' will have to use a misunderstanding strategy, which we describe later in this section.

KB Connexity Increasing Strategy. At any time, the 'student' can ask itself whether there could be a direct link between two pieces of data of its KB which are currently not linked (belonging to two distinct KB components) or indirectly (by a long path).

Let's take the example of predicates it learns: For instance, the 'teacher' teaches the two next formulas: $human(x) \rightarrow mortal(x)$ and $human(x) \rightarrow animal(x)$, the 'student' will be able to ask itself about a possible direct link between $mortal(x)$ and $animal(x)$. The dialog will be then used to ask to the 'teacher' if it own such a relationship.

The 'student' can then proceed to the two following questions, each one addressing a possible link between predicates:

- ASKFOR-INFORMATION($MORTAL(X) \rightarrow ANIMAL(X)$)
- ASKFOR-INFORMATION($ANIMAL(X) \rightarrow MORTAL(X)$)

The 'teacher' could, for example, confirm the second relationship to the 'student'. The student's KB has then been enriched with a new relationship.

Predicate Base Widening Strategy. Each time the 'student' integrates a piece of data it can use it to generate new knowledge. Thus, if it learns a formula of type $p(a)$ where p is new but a already known in another formula of type $q(a)$, then it can ask itself whether there is a link between predicates p and q. It can then question the 'teacher' about the validity of $q(x) \rightarrow p(x)$.

It's a kind of induction since, from facts having one thing in common (the constant), the 'student' wonders if there is a rule linking them. If the formula is true, then the 'student' will be able to deduce that every constant which satisfies q will now also satisfy p, i.e. increasing the base of the predicate p.

The dialog of the Figure 2 illustrates the use of this strategy. The KB evolution can be followed, step by step, in the Figure 3. We can note that the curiosity of the 'student' has also enabled it to preserve its KB connexity by adding the implication (Step 3).

Figure 2. Dialogue using a strategy for widening a predicate base

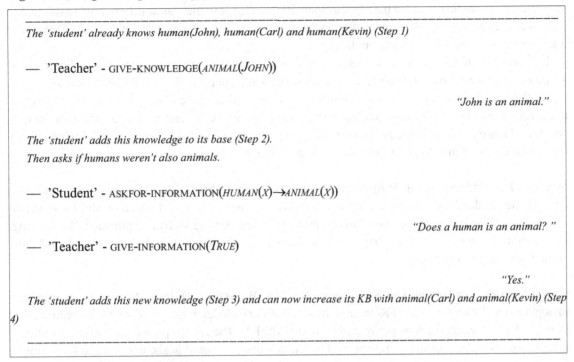

The 'student' already knows human(John), human(Carl) and human(Kevin) (Step 1)

— 'Teacher' - GIVE-KNOWLEDGE(ANIMAL(JOHN))

"John is an animal."

The 'student' adds this knowledge to its base (Step 2).
Then asks if humans weren't also animals.

— 'Student' - ASKFOR-INFORMATION(HUMAN(X)→ANIMAL(X))

"Does a human is an animal? "

— 'Teacher' - GIVE-INFORMATION(TRUE)

"Yes."

The 'student' adds this new knowledge (Step 3) and can now increase its KB with animal(Carl) and animal(Kevin) (Step 4)

Figure 3. KB evolution while widening a predicate base

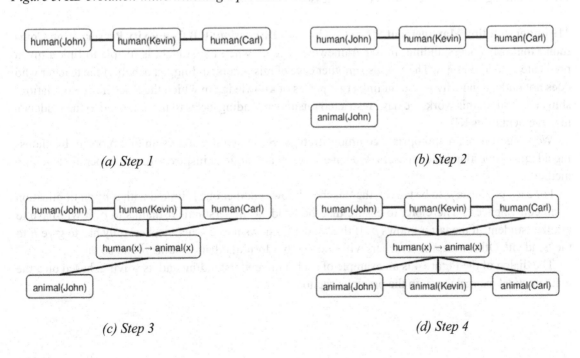

(a) Step 1

(b) Step 2

(c) Step 3

(d) Step 4

New Constants Learning Strategy. Learning predicates remains theoretical, however, learning constants satisfying these predicates allow the agent to apply its knowledge to the real world wherein it evolves. So a curious 'student' agent will be able, after having learned new predicates, to ask the 'teacher' whether it knows constants satisfying these predicates.

For example, if the 'student' learns that it should keep away from hostile agents (*hostile*(*x*)→ *keepaway*(*x*)), then it should be useful for it to know such agents. For example, *hostile*(*Carl*), *hostile*(*Kevin*), … By the way, it should be useful to know values associated to some constants. For example, if the agent learns that the gravity value on Earth is *g*, then it should be interested to know the value of this constant. Thus by proceeding to precision inquiry regarding this value, the 'student' will be able, using the required processing skills, to use it for solving gravity problems.

Strategy For Understanding Why Some Formulas Imply Others. After learning any implication (*P*→*Q*), the 'student' may wonder whether (*P*) directly implies (*Q*) or if it was a result of a series of implications. This is the typical case of an explanation request dealing with an implication. By realizing such a request to the 'teacher', the 'student' gets the opportunity to increase the amount of its KB data while increasing its connexity.

Symmetry Between Dialog And KB Management In Discussions Without Issues. As one can see, dialog, modeled with Functional Roles and the student's knowledge base, present an harmonious relationship. Dialog reflects actions performed to modify the KB. The KB graph denotes the result of these actions and its state, controlled and checked by the student's personal goals, may lead to launching a new utterance/inquiry and therefore increasing the dialog by one step. This complete symmetry can nevertheless be broken by a conflicting piece of information introduced by the dialog. Discrepancies in updating the KB occur, and the two next sections handle the way dialog can be used in order to repair such a dammage and proceed further in the lesson.

Misunderstanding Management Strategy Through Discussion: KB Connexity Preservation Common Goal. Misunderstanding, in our framework, occurs when the student is unable to link a given predicate to its KB graph. There is also another case of misunderstanding, on behalf of the teacher who does not understand why a student links two pieces of knowledge in which the teacher see no relationship at all. But in this work, we have restricted misunderstanding cases to those related to the student's management of its KB.

We suggest here an appropriate common strategy: Solving a misunderstanding problem by choosing adequate questions and answers. We have adopted a technique inspired from the socratic teaching method.

For each predicate p_i to be taught, the 'teacher' knows another one p_j linked with p_i by an implication or an equivalence F. Therefore, to ensure that the 'student' understands p_i thanks to p_j, it will have to ask the 'student' if the latter knows p_j. If the 'student' knows it, then the 'teacher' only has to give F to the 'student'. Otherwise, the 'teacher' will find another formula that explains p_j and so on.

The dialog of the Figure 4 is an example of such a misunderstanding and its solving, based on a the mathematical example seen in the previous section.

Figure 4. Dialogue using a strategy for misunderstanding resolution

_____

— 'Teacher' - GIVE-KNOWLEDGE($RECTANGLE(X) \rightarrow PARALLELOGRAM(X)$)

"A rectangle is a parallelogram."

The 'Student' doesn't know these two predicates, nevertheless it knows the following predicates quad(x) (quadrilateral), DITM(x) (Diagonals Intersect on Their Middle) and DLE(x) (Diagonals Length are Equals).

— 'Student' - SAY-DISSATISFACTION

"I don't understand."

Then the 'Teacher' tries to explain to the 'student' the formula's premise:
What is a rectangle.

— 'Teacher' - ASKFOR-INFORMATION($QUAD(X)$)

"Do you know what a quadrilateral is? "

— 'Student' - GIVE-INFORMATION($TRUE$)

"Yes."

— 'Teacher' - ASKFOR-INFORMATION($DITM(X)$)

"Do you know what 'diagonals intersect in their middle' means? "

— 'Student' - GIVE-INFORMATION($TRUE$)

"Yes."

— 'Teacher' - ASKFOR-INFORMATION($DLE(X)$)

"Do you know what 'diagonals length are equals' means? "

— 'Student' - GIVE-INFORMATION($TRUE$)

"Yes."

— 'Teacher' - GIVE-EXPLANATION($QUAD(X) \wedge DITM(X) DLE(X) \leftrightarrow RECTANGLE(X)$)

"A rectangle is a parallelogram which has its diagonals intersecting in their middle, and the diagonals length are equal."

— 'Student' - SAY-SATISFACTION

"I understand."

As the 'student' has understood what is a rectangle, it can know learn the knowledge (rectangle(x)→parallelogram(x)) by just adding it to its KB, the connexity is preserved.

_____

Conflict Management Strategies Through Discussion: KB Consistency Preservation Common Goal. We have studied several types of conflict, those related to implications as well as those related to facts.

Implication conflicts. These conflicts typically take place when the 'student' has a formula $(P{\rightarrow}Q)$ and attempts to learn a formula $(P{\rightarrow}\neg(Q))$. The solution, for the 'student', is to remove $(P{\rightarrow}Q)$ from its KB and add $(P{\rightarrow}\neg(Q))$. It acts so because this is **'teacher''s knowledge** (thus true) and so it gets the upper hand on the 'student' one (first axiom). However, the conflict could be hidden if the 'student' has the next formulas: $(P_1 {\rightarrow} P_2)$, $(P_2 {\rightarrow} P_3)$, ..., $(P_{n-1} {\rightarrow} P_n)$ and attempts to learn $(P_1 {\rightarrow} P_n)$: The 'student' has an equivalent to the formula 1n. Instead of using a baseline solution consisting in removing all the series of implications, we opted for a more flexible one which attempts to look for a wrong implication and only removes this very one. Indeed, deleting one implication is sufficient to solve the conflict. The 'student' will then attempt to validate each implication with the 'teacher' through an 'ASKFOR-INFORMATION' request. As soon as a wrong implication is found, the 'student' removes it and safely adds the new one. However, if none of the implications is neither validated nor rejected by the 'teacher', the 'student' will be forced to remove all the series before adding the new one to be sure to end up the conflict.

We present now an example of a solvable conflict, inspired from the following sophism:

All that is cheap is rare.
All that is rare is expensive.
Therefore, all that is cheap is expensive.

The dialog of the Figure 5 is an example of dialog our agents should use when facing such a conflict. The KB evolution can be followed, step by step, in the Figure 6.

Figure 5. Dialogue using a discussion strategy for implication conflict resolution

---

The 'student' owns the following knowledge (Step 1):

$cheap(x){\rightarrow}rare(x)$

$rare(x){\rightarrow}expensive(x)$

— 'Teacher' - GIVE-KNOWLEDGE($CHEAP(x){\rightarrow}\neg(EXPENSIVE(x))$)

"All that is cheap is not expensive."

The 'student's' adds this knowledge to its KB (Step 2), however the implication comes into contradiction with the student's base.

The 'student' will then try to locate the wrong implication(s).

— 'Student' - ASKFOR-INFORMATION($CHEAP(x){\rightarrow}RARE(x)$)

"Does all that is cheap is rare? "

— 'Teacher' - GIVE-INFORMATION($TRUE$)

"Yes"

— 'Student' - ASKFOR-INFORMATION($RARE(x){\rightarrow}EXPENSIVE(x)$)

continued on following page

Figure 5. continued

"Does all that is rare is expensive? "

— 'Teacher' - GIVE-INFORMATION(*FALSE*)

"No"

— 'Student' - SAY-SATISFACTION

"I understand"

The 'student' understands then where the conflict comes from (Step 3) and revises its base in consequence. The student's knowledge is now (Step 4):

cheap(x)→rare(x)

cheap(x)→¬(expensive(x))

_____

Figure 6. KB evolution while solving an implication conflict

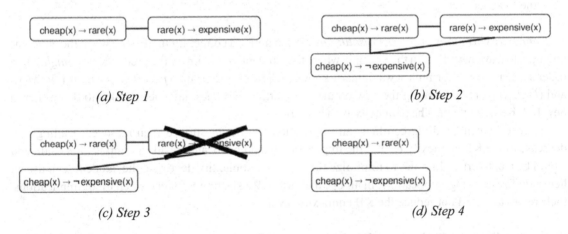

(a) Step 1   (b) Step 2

(c) Step 3   (d) Step 4

Two other implication types of conflict, harder to detect, may also happen:

• Let's assume the 'student' owns the two following series of implication Θ and Λ:

$\Theta = ((P_1 \rightarrow Q_2), (Q_2 \rightarrow Q_3), ..., (Q_{i-1} \rightarrow Q_i)$,

$\Lambda = (Q_{i+1} \rightarrow Q_{i+2}), ..., (Q_{n-1} \rightarrow \neg(P_1)))$.

If the 'teacher' gives the knowledge $(Q_i \rightarrow Q_{i+1})$ then a conflict arises as from Θ, $(Q_i \rightarrow Q_{i+1})$ and Λ we can deduce $\neg(P_1))$ from P_1.

• Let's assume now the 'student' owns the three following series of implication Δ, Θ and Λ:

$\Delta = ((P_1 \rightarrow P_2), (P_2 \rightarrow P_3), ..., (P_{n-1} \rightarrow P_n))$,

$\Theta = ((P_1 \rightarrow Q_2), (Q_2 \rightarrow Q_3), ..., (Q_{i-1} \rightarrow Q_i)$,

$\Lambda = (Q_{i+1} \rightarrow Q_{i+2}), \ldots, (Q_{n-1} \rightarrow \neg(P_n)))$.

If the 'teacher' gives the knowledge $(Q_i \rightarrow Q_{i+1})$ then a conflict arises as from Δ as we can deduce P_n from P_1 and now from Θ, $(Q_i \rightarrow Q_{i+1})$ and Λ as we can deduce $\neg(P_n)$) from P_1.

These two types of conflicts are hard to detect as we have to locate the two or three series of implication being involved. The conflict elimination is done in the same way as the previous case: The 'student' will have to check with the 'teacher' the validity of each implication from Δ and Θ until having found one which is wrong in order to remove it.

Fact conflicts. This case appears when the 'student' thinks a fact true $(p(A))$ and the 'teacher' tells it the fact is false $(\neg(p(A)))$ or the 'teacher' gives it a knowledge which allows the 'student' to deduce that its fact is false. The conflict management is close to the implication conflict one and several cases can occur (the 'student' here thinks $(p(A))$):

- If the 'teacher' tells it $(\neg(p(A)))$, then the 'student' removes $(p(A))$ from its KB;
- If the 'student' thinks, $(p(X) \rightarrow p_2(X))$, $(p_2(X) \rightarrow p_3(X))$, ..., $(p_{n-1}(X) \rightarrow p_n(X))$ and the 'teacher' tells it $(\neg(p_n(A)))$ the a conflict arises as the 'student' can deduce $(p_n(A))$ from $(p(A))$ and the series of implications, which is contradictory with $(\neg(p_n(A)))$. The 'student' will have then to remove $(p(A))$ or one of the previous implications. It will then perform a series of information requests to the 'teacher'.

Connexity variations in conflict resolution. We can notice a connexity increasing when the 'student' attempts to learn new data. In the example where the 'student' has to know the predicate $(rectangle(x))$ in order to learn the new formula, it was already knowing the three predicates $(parallelogram(x))$, $(DITM(x))$ and $(DLE(x))$, and by learning the new predicate, the three old ones have been added to themselves a new link between them. The connexity is then increased.

However, when handling conflicts, an implication can be questioned then removed, leading to a decrease of the KB connexity level if the implication would be located inside an implication chain and would be a cut-vertex. In order to minimize the risks of a connexity decrease, the 'student' can use an heuristic for selecting implications in an optimal order: By starting with end of chain of implications, their removal would not reduce the KB connexity level.

Symmetry Between Dialog And KB Management In Discussions With Issues. When an issue (misunderstanding or KB conflict) arises within the discussion, it breaks the symmetry of the current discussion and opens a new one, bound to solve the issue. This new discussion will install a new symmetry with a repair process headed by one of the agents, depending on the type of the issue.

Tables 1 and 2 describe the different steps of our repair common scheme, for respectively a misunderstanding and a conflict situations. 'S' means a 'student's' intervention and 'T' a 'teacher's' one.

In Table 1, a SAY-DISSATISFACTIONmessage informs the 'teacher' of the 'student's' misunderstanding. Let us assume the 'student' don't understand a predicate P. The 'teacher' will head the dialog and use a misunderstanding strategy to solve the issue. Each GIVE-INFORMATION() message conduces the 'student' to check into its KB the presence of the provided implication. Once the 'teacher' deems the student have the knowledge required to understand P, it will assert the knowledge link by giving an explanation, the formula F. The 'student' ends this repair discussion by informing its interlocutor with a SAY-SATISFACTIONmessage.

Table 1. Misunderstanding repair common scheme

Step	Dialog	KB management
Trigger	S:SAY-DISSATISFACTION	*P* unknown
Launching repair	T:ASKFOR-INFORMATION()	Checking known KB implications
	...	
Asserting knowledge links	T:GIVE-EXPLANATION($F(P,...)$)	Increasing KB with $F(P,...)$
Evaluating repair	S:SAY-SATISFACTION	

Table 2. KB conflict repair common scheme

Step	Dialog	KB management
Trigger & Launching repair	S:ASKFOR-INFORMATION()	Checking involved KB implications
	...	
Asserting wrongness	T:GIVE-INFORMATION(*FALSE*)	Implication removal
Evaluating repair	S:SAY-SATISFACTION	

In Table 2, a ASKFOR-INFORMATION() message informs the 'teacher' of the 'student's' KB conflict, and triggers a dialog headed, *this time*, by the 'student'. The latter will use a conflict management strategy to solve the issue. Each 'student' ASKFOR-INFORMATION() message comes from an introspection on its KB according to the strategy. The 'teacher' task here is just to give the validity value of the provided information. Once the 'student' learns which implication is wrong, it updates its KB by removing this knowledge and thus solving the conflict. It finally ends this discussion with a SAY-SATISFACTIONmessage.

In both situations, each 'teacher's' message conduces the 'student' to analyze and possibly to revise its KB, the result of this process being then used to answer its interlocutor. This symmetry between dialog and KB management continues until the issue solving. This end of the discussion allows the agents to go back to the previous discussion (usually the lesson) and to restore its symmetry.

SYSTEM ARCHITECTURE AND IMPLEMENTATION

The theoretical approach of the previous section has been specified and partially implemented.

Architecture

The Figure 7 displays the main architecture elements of our tutored learning system. It is composed of five main structures: The 'teacher', the 'student', the FR, the strategies and the 'World'. 'Teacher' and 'Student' are agents.

The FR are a shared knowledge base about dialogic clauses, to which both agents have access. The strategies are meta-rules of behavior that help both 'teacher' and 'student' to achieve satisfaction (positive meta-evaluation) and thus to end the dialog with success (an ending with failure is possible, since a repeated negative meta-evaluation might appear. Then, the 'teacher' ends up the dialog, because

Figure 7. The tutored learning system through dialog between artificial cognitive agents

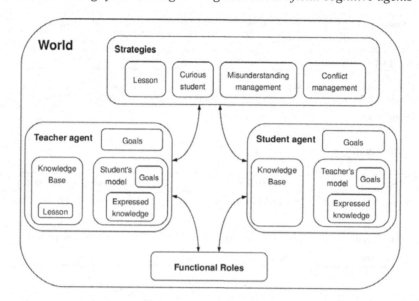

not correct evolution of the situation is observed). The 'World' is a sharable knowledge base, a pool of predicates available to agents.

Each agent has goals, a KB and model of its interlocutor. A model of the interlocutor is what the agent knows that its interlocutor knows. The 'teacher' agent mostly checks its interlocutor's model and updates it, by asking the 'student' questions, when it (the 'teacher') needs to explain something to the 'student'. The 'teacher' also knows what the 'student's' goals are in order to be prepared to any discussion shift. For instance, when the 'student' tries to fulfill its curiosity by asking some knowledge and thus breaking the lesson flow, the 'teacher' will be able to understand the 'student's' intervention and satisfy its request before continuing the lesson. The model the 'student' has of its 'teacher' is that all what the 'teacher' says is true, and thus a GIVE-KNOWLEDGE(P) clause is equivalent to P is *True*(first axiom). It also have an idea of the goals and some knowledge of its 'teacher'.

Naturally, each agent when shifting from a role to another, in a different situation, modifies its interlocutor's model according to its present role. It can freely update them in order to make them evolve. Each agent action is motivated by its own goals, which lead the agent to use the adequate strategies and FR rules.

Implementation

We have implemented a Java program to test conflict solving. This program is a basic prototype aiming at getting experimental results of a part of our theory. We describe this prototype in (Yousfi-Monod & Prince, 2007). The running of our prototype program has shown that the 'student' has been able to detect a conflict between its KB and a new data provided by the 'teacher' and then ask the 'teacher' to validate some potentially conflictual knowledge and finally remove the wrong implication.

CONCLUSION

This work was an extension of previous studies in which the rationale is the following: Sole communication could be a knowledge acquisition process as efficient (if not more) than other gathering mechanisms, for artificial cognitive agents. This communication needs here to be directed and controlled by goals, and it can be instantiated into the sophisticated shape of a dialog. Therefore, we have centered our research on studying equivalency relationships between dialogic structures and knowledge acquisition and revision process. Doing this have led us to restrict the study to the typical case of a socratic lesson, in which two agents, one playing the role of a teacher and the other the role of a student, interact by exchanging messages related to a set of knowledge to be taught. This case has been qualified as a representative tutored learning method. It advantages are:

- Learning is a major incentive for one of the agents, and teaching is symmetrically the teacher's one. In this case, student agents are naturally willing to undertake the acquisition process, and teachers are also willing to provide true and reliable information (highly cooperative situation).
- Since the teacher must deliver true information, this restricts its offer to its skill domain, that is, information for which it is able to design a lesson. At the same time, this makes it a reliable knowledge source for the student, which will accept any statement from the teacher as true.
- Knowledge transfer (and acquisition) is the main goal of both agents, and uses 'discourse' only. By avoiding mixing actions and messages, we isolate the dialogic aspect and therefore may examine its impact much better than in any other situation.
- Lessons are very interesting situations in which several cases of knowledge management appear: Enhancement of facts (predicates instantiated with constants), of concepts (predicates) of laws (implications); Creation of new implications (inductive process); Implications retraction; Facts associations to predicates which do not contain them in their validity domain (abduction).
- At the same time, lessons allow conversational structures to reflect and handle all these cases may occur. This allows us to follow through dialog the track of knowledge management and thus refines our assumption about a possible symmetry (if not exactly an equivalence) between dialog and reasoning.

The study of such a constrained situation has led us to define a notion of *connexity* for a knowledge base (KB), allowing to assess the connection level between each element of knowledge of an agent and so to give it two new goals: Increasing its KB connexity, as well as optimizing its content. As the dialog situation in highly unpredictable and may follow no previous plan, we have adopted the functional role (FR) theory to easily model dialogical exchanges. Agents use strategies to learn new knowledge and solve conflicts between external and internal data. (Angluin, 1987) tackles the problem of identifying an unknown subset of hypothesis among a set by queries to an oracle. Our work differs mainly in:

- **The communication mean:** We use imbricated dialogs instead of queries
- **The learning's aim:** Our agents aim at learning new formulas and increasing their KB connexity instead of identifying assumptions

Moreover, it seems that the FR theory has possible patterns for typical communication occurrences: Misunderstanding and Discussion. As developed in the paper, misunderstanding, limited to the student in our work, appears when the student cannot attach the teacher's knowledge to is KB, because it lacks concepts, or it lacks implications. Discussion appears with two types of profiles: Students with wrong knowledge, and curious students (those who want to learn more than what is in their lesson). We have presented an example of misunderstanding as well as a discussion sample dealing with knowledge conflict management. While scrutinizing both situations we noticed a symmetry between the dialogic structure and the KB management process. Since they were seen as repair procedures through which the teacher helps the student restore its KB integrity and connexity and proceed further in the lesson, they were both subsumed into a generic pattern containing four items: A *trigger* (which causes the need for repair), a *repair process* launched either by the teacher (in misunderstanding) or by the student (in discussion) in which the main actor directs the dialog, a *repairing action* (with a given FR: GIVE-EXPLANATION() in the case of misunderstanding, and GIVE-INFORMATION(*FALSE*) in the case of a knowledge falsification needing discussion), and last *an evaluation of the repair,* uttered by the student.

As much satisfying as it can been, the socratic lesson is a particular case of a wide range of knowledge acquisition and revision using communication. This is why we think that some of our results, here isolated in a sort of *in vitro* state, could be, in turn, experimented in more flexible environments. For instance, agents might learn from each other (symmetrical role) after acknowledging each other's skills, which will require a serious enhancement of our simple 'other agent's model' embedded in the system architecture. Agents might also check knowledge with another knowledge source, which will provide contradiction, and possibly an interesting set of discussion procedures, that might involve more than a pair, and so forth. Nevertheless, we think that this study has shown that the assumption of symmetry between dialog and knowledge management is a plausible one, and most of all, an implementable solution, and nothing for the moment prevents its extension to more complex situations.

REFERENCES

Allen, J., & Perrault, R. (1980). Analyzing intention in utterances. *Artificial Intelligence, 15(3)*, 11-18.

Amgoud, L., & Prade, H. (2003). A possibilistic logic modeling of autonomous agents negotiation. In *Epia* (p. 360-365).

Angluin, D. (1987). Queries and concept learning. *Machine Learning, 2*(4), 319-342.

Asoh, H., Motomura, Y., Hara, I., Akaho, S., Hayamizu, S., & Matsui, T. (1996). Acquiring a probabilistic map with dialogue-based learning. In H. Hexmoor and L. Meeden (Eds.), *ROBOLEARN '96: An International Workshop on Learning for Autonomous Robots,* (pp. 11-18).

Baker, M. (1994). A model for negotiation in teaching-learning dialogues. *Journal of Artificial Intelligence in Education, 5*(2), 199-254.

Beun, R.-J., & van Eijk, R. M. (2003). A cooperative dialogue game for resolving ontological discrepancies. In *Workshop on agent communication languages.* (Lecture notes in computer science, pp. 349-363).

Beun, R.-J., & van Eijk, R. M. (2005). Conceptual mismatches and repair in human-computer interaction. In *Proceedings of the Seventh Belgium-Netherlands Conference on Artificial Intelligence, BNAIC,* (pp. 315-316).

Cerri, S. A., & Jonquet, C. (2003). Apprentissage issu de la communication pour des agents cognitifs. *Technique et Science Informatiques*, *22*(4), 83-87.

Cohen, P., & Levesque, H. (1992). *Intentions in communication*. Bradford: Rational Interaction as the Basis for Communication. Bradford Books, MIT Press, seconde Ã©dition, chap. 12.

Cook, J. (2000, June). Cooperative problem-seeking dialogues in learning. In G. Gauthier, C. Frasson and K. VanLehn (Eds.), *Intelligent Tutoring Systems: 5th International Conference, ITS 2000 Montreal, Canada, 1839*, (pp. 615-624).

Draper, S., & Anderson, A. (1991). The significance of dialogue in learning and observing learning. *Computers and Education*, *17*(1), 93-107.

Holland, J., Holyoak, K., Nisbett, R., & Thagard, P. (1989). *Induction: Processes of inference, learning, and discovery*. Cambridge, MA: The MIT Press.

Josephson, J., & Josephson, S. (1994). *Abductive inference, computation, philosophy, technology*. New York: Cambridge University Press.

Lycan, W. (1999). *Mind and cognition: An anthology*. Madden, MA: Blackwell Publishers, Inc.

Manna, Z. (1974). *Mathematical theory of computation*. International Student Edition. McGraw Hill Computer Science Series.

Mataric, M. (1997). Using communication to reduce locality in multi-robot learning. In *AAAI-97* (pp. 643-648). Menlo Park: CA: AAAI Press.

Muansuwan, N., Sirinaovakul, B., & Thepruangchai, P. (2004). Intelligent tutoring and knowledge base creation for the subject of computer programming. In *Proceedings of tencon 2004* (p. 353-356). IEEE.

Nelson, K. (1996). *Language in cognitive development: Emergence of the mediated mind*. Cambridge University Press.

Pagnucco, M. (1996). *The role of abductive reasoning within the process of belief revision*. Unpublished doctoral dissertation, University of Sydney.

Parsons, S., Sierra, C., & Jennings, N. (1998). Agents that reason and negotiate by arguing. *Journal of Logic and Computation*, *8*(3), 261-292.

Pedersen, H. (2002). *Speech acts and agents: A semantic analysis*. Unpublished master's thesis, Informatics and Mathematical Modelling, Technical University of Denmark, DTU.

Pollack, M. E. (1998, July). Plan generation, plan management, and the design of computational agents. In *Proceedings of the 3rd International Conference on Multi-Agent Systems* (pp. 643-648). Paris, France.

Prince, V. (1996). *Vers une informatique cognitive dans les organisations, le role central du langage*. Paris: Editions Masson.

Prince, V. (2006). Modelling and managing knowledge through dialogue: A model of communication-based knowledge management. In *ICSOFT 2006, First International Conference on Software and Data Technologies* (p. 266-271).

Ravenscroft, A., & Pilkington, R. (2000). Investigation by design: Developing dialogue models to support reasoning and conceptual change. *International Journal of Artificial Intelligence in Education, 11*(1), 273-298.

Sabah, G., Ferret, O., Prince, V., Vilnat, A., Vosniadou, S., Dimitrakopoulo, A., (1998). What dialogue analysis can tell about teacher strategies related to representational change. In *Modelling changes in understanding: Case studies in physical reasoning.* Oxford: Cambridge University Press.

Searle, J. (1969). *Speech acts: An essay in the philosophy of language.* Cambridge: Cambridge University Press.

Smith, I. A., & Cohen, P. R. (1996). Toward a semantics for an agent communication language based on speech acts. In H. Shrobe & T. Senator (Eds.), *Proceedings of the Thirteenth National Conference on Artificial Intelligence and the Eighth Innovative Applications of Artificial Intelligence Conference,* vol. 2, (pp. 24-31). Menlo Park, California: AAAI Press.

VanLehn, K., Siler, S., & C.Murray. (1998). What makes a tutorial event effective? In *Proceedings of the Twenty-Frst Annual Conference of the Cognitive Science Society.*

Williams, A. B. (2004). Learning to share meaning in a multi-agent system. *Autonomous Agents and Multi-Agent Systems, 8*(2), 165-193.

Wooldridge, M., & Parsons, S. (2000). Languages for negotiation. In *Proceedings of ECAI2000* (pp. 393-400).

Yousfi-Monod, M., & Prince, V. (2005). Knowledge acquisition modeling through dialogue between cognitive agents. In *ICEIS 2005, Proceedings of the Seventh International Conference on Enterprise Information Systems,* (pp. 201-206).

Yousfi-Monod, M., & Prince, V. (2007). Knowledge acquisition modeling through dialogue between cognitive agents. *International Journal of Intelligent Information Technologies, 3,* 60-78.

Zhang, D., Foo, N., Meyer, T., & Kwok, R. (2004). Negotiation as mutual belief revision. In *Proceedings of AAAI 2004.*

Chapter V
Improving E–Trade Auction Volume by Consortium

Sungchul Hong
Towson University, USA

Barin N. Nag
Towson University, USA

Dong-qing Yao
Towson University, USA

ABSTRACT

In this chapter, we present a two-tier supply chain composed of multiple buyers and multiple suppliers. We have studied the mechanism to match trading parameter, specifically volume in this study, between buyers and suppliers. The chapter discusses the architecture of the agent and the agent community when there is cooperative matching of volume. We present a Dynamic Programming algorithm to describe the agent's decision process and heuristic algorithms as the practical solution methodology. The results of extensive experiments show the improvement achieved by the cooperation.

INTRODUCTION

Agent-based auction trading plays an important role in the electronic acquisition of products/service for organization or e-procurement, especially for MRO materials. Effective agent-based trading has multiple benefits, such as reducing inventory levels, and a dual impact of centralizing strategic procurement objectives while decentralizing the operational procurement processes (Puschmann and Alt, 2005).

The environment of agent-based auction trading involves online auctions with Web-based buyers and Web-based sellers, typically multiple buyers and multiple suppliers. Therefore how to improve the performance of agent-based auction, specifically match buyers and suppliers, is a challenge for both academia and practitioners. In practice, there are two major parameters of a proposed trade, the price and the volume. This is equally true for a seller's offer or for a buyer's bid. Typically, volumes larger than certain lower levels go with lower prices. Thus, a match between a seller's offer and a buyer's bid that would lead to a transaction is a combination of matches with volume and price. In this research, we only consider the match of volume, since MRO products usually have a prevailing marketing price, and thus price is automatically matched. Volume is subject to individual agent's bids and offers in a buyer and seller context, and when a direct match is not possible, a match may still be obtained by cooperation/consortium between buyers and sellers, respectively. The focus of this chapter is on the effectiveness of cooperation in making the match and completing the trade.

In this chapter, we propose a two-tier e-procurement auction agent structure made up of multiple suppliers and multiple buyers. Trading begins with a buyer proposing a trading amount. A seller may match the trading amount, or may propose a different trading amount. The buyer then seeks to match the trading amount with cooperation from other buyers. Alternately, the seller seeks to suit the buyer, or hold the order for a future offer that matches. The purpose of this approach is to provide better matches with offers, while reducing wait periods by means of cooperative trading. Thus, the efficiency of trading is increased.

When agents work together within a community, collaborating to achieve individual goals, it becomes a *multi-agent system* (MAS), where the interactions between the agents become as important as the decision-oriented actions of the individual agents. At this time, some research has been done on agent cooperation in multi-agent systems. For example, Binbasioglu (1999) proposed an approach to identify problem components, which supports the progress of understanding and structuring for multi-agent cooperative decision making environment. Fox et al. (2000) presented a solution to construct agent-oriented software architecture to manage supply chain at tactical and operational levels. In their framework, they used multiple agents, such as order acquisition agents, logistics agents, transportation agents, scheduling agents, resources agents, etc. One important capability of their agents, related to the present work, is the coordination. The authors developed a generic application-independent language to implement the multi-agent coordination issue. Kosakaya et al. (2001) developed a new cooperation and negotiation algorithm to improve cooperation in a system using multi-agent system. Zhao et al. (2001) developed the agent-based CLOVER platform that can improve system interoperability among agents, and furthermore support dynamic and flexible cooperation. Aknine et al. (2004) proposed two methods of agents' coalition formation for both cooperative and non-cooperative multi-agent systems, and cooperative agents can exchange information/preferences among them. Based on the *virtual enterprise* (VE) paradigm and the concept of multi-agent, Roy et al. (2004) proposed a new way to manage supply chains. They defined tiered supply chain architecture, where a virtual enterprise node (VEN) only interacts with an adjacent VEN. The objective is to coordinate the decentralized VEN decisions in real time, and each VEN needs to make a tradeoff between local benefits and global benefits. Anussornnitisarn et al. (2005) developed a model of distributed network for distributed resource allocation, and they investigated if multi-agent system, as a whole, can achieve efficient resource allocation in a collaborative environment. Hill et al. (2005) designed a cooperative multi-agent approach for decentralized decision-making environment in free flight, which provides effective results for different scenarios. Zho et al. (2006) applied intelligent multi-agent technology in manufacturing systems, where agents can be cooperative with each other for multi-tasks performed in a plant. They proposed a modeling framework to ease the design of autonomous agents for large-scale production systems. Different from the applications of cooperative multi-agents in other industries, the focus of our work and contribution is to develop a trading cooperative multi-agent system to increase trading efficiencies in matching volumes in an auction environment, at a competitive price.

Collaboration between buyer agents and seller agents, respectively, is the basis of the mechanism of matching trading parameters to close a trade where no trade would be possible because of the mismatch between the buyer's and seller's trading volume. Each buyer and each seller desire to achieve a trade consistent with the quantity of the buyer's bid, or the seller's offer. There is a cost associated with non-completion, necessitating a carry-over to the next period. This chapter presents the impact of consortiums formed by the cooperation between buyer agents, and seller agents, respectively, to increase volume by combining bids and offers, as needed, as a means of matching and closing a trade. Thus, trading volumes may be increased, with the associated reduction of trading inventory and carry-overs of trading volumes to succeeding periods.

The remainder of the chapter is organized as follows. A mathematical programming model using dynamic programming is described to model the decision problem of volume matching by consortium. An analytical solution to the dynamic programming model is difficult to achieve in real time, and is impractical in a real world auction environment. To circumvent this situation, heuristic rules of modeling to quickly analyze and solve the problem are developed and presented. Also shown in this section are experimental results of auction trades by consortium from randomly generated trade offers. The conclusions of the study are stated, together with ideas and directions for future research.

MODEL FOR AGENT TRANSACTIONS

We consider a two-tier supply chain composed of m suppliers and n buyers with k types of products. The two tiers consist of sellers and buyers. Buyers buy directly from sellers, with no intermediaries, negotiators, or other traders. It is a simple construct of suppliers and buyers, respectively, bidding for the goods directly to one another. The construct has been kept simple to emphasize the complexity of the decision process and trading actions, and to focus on the best practices of decision-making in this trading environment.

An agent makes decisions and performs actions in trading in a difficult environment of uncertainty where nothing is known about the future. A seller agent has no information about the future needs of buyer agents, *i.e.* about the quantities that might be asked for and the future possibility of a better match with the seller agent's offer. A buyer agent has no information about future offers by a seller agent, and the future possibility of a better match of the buyer agent's quantity requirement with the quantity offered by a future seller agent's offer. The only information available is the present set of conditions. These are described as follows:

1. A buyer agent is aware of the selling bids placed by seller agents.
2. A seller agent is aware of the buying bids placed by buyer agents.
3. A buyer agent is aware of the community of buyer agents and the quantities requested by each buyer agent.

4.   A seller agent is aware of other seller agents and the quantities offered by each seller agent.

The decisions to buy or sell, and the trading actions to implement the decision, must proceed in this environment. The objective is still to minimize trading costs and to achieve a best match with the trading requirements. The community knowledge, on the part of buyers and sellers respectively, is what enables the formation of consortiums that help to match trading offers that would otherwise not be resolved.

The end result of the decision is to buy, or to sell, involving a decision to accept, or reject, an existing offer. This result may also be achieved by modifying an existing offer by partnering with other agents. The seller agent's offered quantity may exceed the quantity requested by a buyer agent, or the quantity required by a buyer agent may exceed the quantity offered by a seller agent. There are four possible decisions or actions as listed below:

1.   **Seller agent offers quantity larger than the requirement of a single buyer**
   o   Buyer agent proposes part sale that is accepted or rejected by seller agent.
   o   Buyer agent looks for (and finds) partner buyer agents to complete the quantity.
2.   **Seller agent offers quantity smaller than the requirement of a single buyer**
   o   Seller agent looks for a partner seller agent to match the required quantity
   o   Buyer agent rejects the offer and waits for a better match
   o   Buyer agent accepts the offer and waits for a part offer from another seller agent to complete the quantity
3.   **Buyer agent requests quantity larger than the offer of a single seller**
   o   Seller agent looks for a partner seller agent to match the required quantity
   o   Buyer agent rejects the offer and waits for a better match
   o   Buyer agent accepts the offer and waits for a part offer from another seller agent to complete the quantity
4.   **Buyer agent requests quantity smaller than the offer of a single seller**
   o   Buyer agent proposes part sale that is accepted or rejected by seller agent.
   o   Buyer agent looks for (and finds) partner buyer agents to complete the quantity.

Figure 1. Information flows in an agent

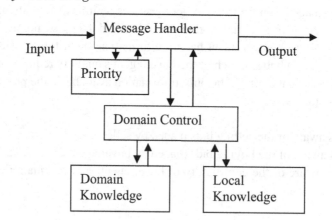

In short, the actions and sales performed by the seller and buyer agents are dynamic in nature, and for optimization are best represented as a Dynamic Programming formulation.

In a typical application of this nature, the preferred system architecture is a *Blackboard*, with open information about all offered trades in a given period available to all participating agents, for possible matching individually or by consortium, for a particular commodity (Nag, 2007). The internal agent architecture, preferably common to all participating agents, includes *domain knowledge* as an understanding of the trading task in terms of the tasked trading volume and the commodity to be traded. Another part of the internal agent architecture is the *communication capability* that enables an agent to process the community information versus the trading volumes and seek for help from other interested agents in forming consortiums.

The implementation of an agent is an algorithmic software representation of a set of priorities and working rules. The basic internal architecture is shown in Figure 1. A simplified set of rules and actions is shown in Figure 2, in which, local and domain knowledge are both included. For reasons of simplicity, the domain knowledge does not show details of trading parameters, such as product characteristics used to find a trade, or knowledge of agent's objectives in making a trade. To implement the consortium, an additional part of the domain knowledge of an agent is a map that has information about surrounding agents. Without a supervising authority, the map information with each agent is incomplete, but information overlaps exist between adjacent agents extending the available information.

In agent trading, the consortium effect is implemented as a combination of the map and message passing. The algorithms for map determination and for messaging are shown in Figure 3. There are two methods of message passing, broadcast and point-to-point. When an agent needs to find a potential trading partner, it is best to broadcast trade requirements and conditions to many agents. To identify

Figure 2. Agentdomain algorithms

A_i: represents agent i.

$T(A_i)$:   represents a set of tasks of A_i

$t_j(A_i)$:   represents a sub-task j of A_i

$I(A_i)$:   represents Input of A_i

$O(A_i)$:   represents Output of A_i

$P(I(A_i))$:   priority of Input of A_i

$P(O(A_i))$: priority of Output of A_i

$D(T(A_i))$: set of domain for specific task of A_i

$L(T(A_i))$: local knowledge of A_i

$T(A_i) = \cup_j t_j(A_i)$

{*Begin Trade*}

   Select Input $(I(A_i), P(I(A_i))$: select input according to the priority

   Send Output$(O(A_i), P(O(A_i))$: send out output with a priority.

   Apply (Select Input $(I(A_i), P(I(A_i)))$, $D(T(A_i))$, $L(T(A_i))$, Send Output $(O(A_i), P(O(A_i))))$: select input, apply domain knowledge.

{*End Trade*}

Figure 3. Algorithms for map and messaging

```
Map
I: Address index set for entire agents.
aᵢ has mᵢ such that ∪mᵢ ⊆ M
M: Map information for I
Size_of(M): unknown
If there are mᵢ in aᵢ and mⱼ in aⱼ then mᵢ ∩mⱼ ≠ ∅ because of the memory overlap.


Messaging
M_{i,D} = (s, Message_content, D), i could be the source or intermediate agent
  If |D| > 1 then it is a broadcast
  If |D| = 1 then it is a point-to-point connection
  S: message sender
  D: a set of message destinations
Message_content = (Objective, rule, attributes, priority)
```

and confirm a potential trading partner, and to continue the negotiation process, the agent switches the messaging method to point-to-point.

The issues in the decision problem as described above are stated as follows. A seller agent that has to split an offer, and sell a smaller quantity than originally offered, has a remainder quantity to sell that is relatively small. It may become difficult to find a buyer for this small quantity. Although there is a cost associated with waiting, there is an incentive for the seller agent in this position to wait for a buyer ready to buy the full quantity. A similar situation arises for a buyer agent when the seller agent's offered quantity is smaller that that required by the buyer. The buyer agent then has to look for a relatively small quantity offered by another seller agent to complete the transaction. Whether an agent is selling or buying, there is an inevitable decision problem based on the match, or mismatch, of selling and buying quantities.

Without a central control, there is no concern over scalability. Agents form a community where the size of the community can vary over a wide range from small to large. The domain information varies according to the size of the community. Agents exchange information within a community, and perform trading based on the available information. As it is not necessary for an agent to know all members of the community, in a condition of ideal communication the size of the community can be very large.

The architecture of the agent community is designed in a way that overcomes the problems of mismatched quantities. The mechanism of overcoming is cooperation between buyer agents and seller agents. Thus, a buyer agent can seek the help of another buyer agent in matching a sale quantity and closing the transaction. In the same way, a seller agent can seek the help of another seller agent in matching the quantity of a larger bid by the buyer agent. The Dynamic Programming (*DP*) formulation of the problem, as given below, describes optimum policies of accepting an offer, or waiting for a better offer, with the understanding that there is a cost associated with rejecting an offer and waiting and an associated build-up of cost in waiting until the next offer simply has to be accepted, leading to a termination (Bertsekas, 2000). The equations that define the decision are given as follows.

Let us suppose that the buyer agent's requirement quantity is v°. Then, at each stage k of time t, the buyer agent can accept the seller agent's quantity on hand v_k, or wait till the next time period $(k + 1)$ for another offer. However, at the end of bidding time $(t = N)$, the buyer agent has to accept the open offer, or lose everything.

Let us assume that the seller agent's quantity, v_k, is a random number. The buyer agent has knowledge only of the probability distribution of the quantity, but no future knowledge of exactly how much the seller agent will have available in the following stage, or time period.

We define $L_k(v_k) = \alpha(v^\circ - v_k)^2$, as a loss function of the buyer agent if the buyer agent accepts the offer from the seller agent at stage k, where α is a constant. In the case of an exact match, where the seller agent's quantity $q^\circ = v_k$, it becomes evident that the loss, $L_k(v_k) = 0$, *i.e.* there is no loss. Therefore, the buyer agent has to decide if he/she will accept the loss associated with the transaction, $L_k(v_k)$, or wait till the next stage.

The traditional objective in operations research is the minimization of loss, with an implicit understanding that is loss is more definite than profit, and if loss is minimized profit will be increased. The algorithm of DP as formulated to minimize loss, is stated as follows:

$$J_N(q_N) = \alpha(v^0 - v_k)^2 \tag{1}$$

$$J_k(q_k) = \min[\alpha(v^\circ - v_k)^2, E\{J_{k+1}(v_{k+1})\}] \tag{2}$$

The Dynamic Programming algorithm given above defines the decision problem. Thus, the algorithm defines when to accept an offer and when to reject the offer, subject to minimizing the costs of acceptance and rejection. An optimal solution to the algorithm is an optimal strategy for minimizing cost in the transaction, and a transaction is completed when the cost is minimal to both the seller and buyer agents involved in the transaction.

There has to be a stopping point in the transaction, when the cost of waiting exceeds the cost of completing the transaction. As defined in the DP formulation, the optimal stopping strategy is given as follows:

Buy: if $\alpha(v^\circ - v_k)^2 < E\{J_{k+1}(v_{k+1})\}$ (3)

Wait: if $\alpha(v^\circ - v_k)^2 > E\{J_{k+1}(v_{k+1})\}$ (4)

Thus, the buyer agent will wait if there is a net gain in waiting, or accept the seller agent's offer if there is no further gain, or if this is the end of the waiting period.

The formulation can be repeated in reverse order for the seller agent. Matching quantities is a decision in reverse order for a seller agent, as it is for a buyer agent, because a part quantity left behind from a transaction is a higher cost transaction from a selling perspective. Again, the transaction has to be completed at the end of the time period, or the seller agent is left holding a quantity that has to be disposed of. A DP formulation describes an excellent set of decision rules that exactly describe a problem that is dynamic in nature, where little is known about future states. The essential characteristic of a DP formulation is that, while it is exact in describing the decision problem, it is difficult to implement in practice because so little is known about the future, and even the next state of the decision problem.

Figure 4. Agent trading diagram

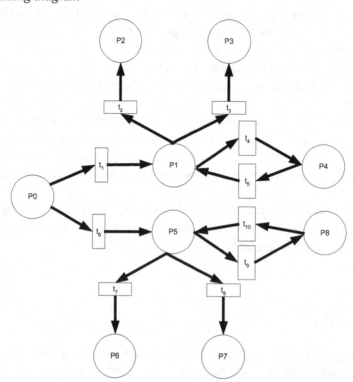

It is a tradition that DP formulations are treated as elegant descriptions of the decision problem, which is then solved by *heuristic* methods. A *heuristic* method is a reasonable and logical method of solving the problem in a manner similar to the mathematical approach, but not necessarily using the mathematical approach, or even producing the optimal solution as given by the mathematical approach. Described below are heuristic solution approaches as a proposed *agent based transaction system* (ABTS) to the trading problem.

The *agent based transaction system* (ABTS) goes beyond the basic DP decision process by using cooperative actions within the community to maximize transaction volume and utility for both buyer and seller agents. Actions within the community, such as message passing and cooperation between agents in matching an offer in buying or selling to maximize the volume, are not specified in the DP formulation. In this approach, heuristic algorithms are described that include message passing between agents to match an offer by using part quantities from cooperating agents.

In the real world of supply-chain transactions, split quantities represent higher costs. A seller agent stuck with a small remaining quantity may be stuck with it for a long time with no buyer available. It means increasing administrative costs and increasing inventory costs, until a buyer agent is found. There is also the uncertainty that a buyer agent will be found, and the remaining inventory will not go into salvage. For a buyer agent, a split quantity implies a small quantity to be purchased at a higher price, if a seller agent can be found to sell such a small quantity. This work does not consider negotiations of prices and costs. Instead, the issues of match and mismatch of quantities have been made issues of feasibilities of the transactions, and cost considerations associated with remainder quantities which have to be sold at lower prices with higher transaction costs leading to higher prices for a buyer agent.

PROCEDURES OF AGENT TRADING

As described above, the *Dynamic Programming* algorithm is an elegant and correct representation of the trading conditions, but is difficult to solve and apply in practice. We describe below a *heuristic* approach to solving the decision problem in agent trading. In this process, we describe the architecture of the agent community involved in trading and the interactions between the agents involved in the transactions. Presented in Figure 4 is a *Petri Net* representation of the agent-trading model. The representations correspond to the conventions of a *Petri Net* representation, with a circle designated "P_n" representing a decision state in the trading actions performed by an agent, and a box designated "t_n" representing an action, such as an offer, an acceptance or rejection of an offer, or a request for help from other members of the community. The arrows represent transitions between decision states, or actions, induced by the occurrences of events. The complete diagram is a representation of all possible states and transitions encountered in the environment of auction trading by agents.

The agent structure described in Figure 1 leads to the decision states and events of auction transactions in Figure 4. A more specific set of definitions of the decision states, and the events that lead to transitions to other decision states is given below:

$P0$: Start
$P1$: Buyer's trading decision state
$P2$: Buyer's no trading state
$P3$: Buyer's trading state
$P4$: Sellers' consortium state
$P5$: Seller's trading decision state
$P6$: Seller's no trading state
$P7$: Seller's trading state
$P8$: Buyers' consortium state

t_1: Buyer offer & seller ask
t_2: Buyer rejects the seller's offer
t_3: Buyer accepts the seller's offer
t_4: Buyers form a buyer's consortium
t_5: Buyers offer jointly
t_6: Seller ask & buyer offer
t_7: Seller rejects the buyer's offer
t_8: Seller accepts the buyer's offer
t_9: Seller forms a seller's consortium
t_{10}: Sellers offer jointly

With these definitions, and with the understanding that arrows represent times to an event and a state transition, the diagram in Figure 4 explains itself. However, the dynamic programming model in

Section 2 is not solvable in a theoretical sense, and can only be explained by means of action scenarios, as is done later.

Some scenarios of agent trading are described below. The focus is on *reverse auctions*, where a buyer agent places an order that is matched by a seller agent, or by the community of seller agents, in a situation where help is sought from the community in matching an order. Three cases are proposed where a seller agent can meet the buyer agent's demand, or a seller agent can decline to meet that demand, or the seller agent does not have enough quantity to meet the demand. This work is based entirely upon volume, rather than upon price or profitability. The objective is always to maximize the volume of transaction equally for the buyer agent, as it is for the seller agent. The decisions and actions are intended to facilitate transactions by means of co-operation, as needed, to maximize volume of transaction in either direction of buying and selling as performed by the agents.

Reverse Auction (Tendering)

There are *n* suppliers and *one* buyer. During fixed time duration of Δ*t,* *i.e.* during the time the offer is open, there is a need to maximize the buyer's utility. The buyer's utility is a function of trading volume, and profit. During the auction of this tendering the following auction cases can happen:

1. **Auction case 1**. Supplier can supply the demand, *i.e.* there is a match between the buyer's demand and the seller's quantity.
2. **Auction case 2**. Supplier has volume larger than the buyer's required quantity, but does not want to sell a split quantity corresponding to the buyer's requirement, because of the characteristics of the goods.
3. **Auction case 3**. Supplier does not have enough goods for a buyer's demand, *i.e.* seller's quantity is short of the buyer's requirements.

In *Auction case 1*, there is no difference between traditional trading and the **ABTS,** *i.e. Agent Based Trading System*. This is the simple case, with a volume match between the buyer and the seller, and the volume is maximized in the given circumstance.

Thus, the utility functions of both the buyer and the seller are defined in terms of increasing volume, or, in terms of completing the volume of the sale. The *Auction cases 2 and 3* are designed with stated conditions that enable the *ABTS* to improve the seller and buyer's utility with respect to volume. Let *V* be the volume of transaction in question, with respect to either buyer or seller, in the given time space Δ*t*, which is a fixed time duration. The transaction volumes within the fixed time period are maximized by volume matching by agents. The corresponding matching results are described below.

The achieved transaction volumes are described in a fixed time period. The assumption is that of a steady state, *i.e.* whatever gains are observed in this time period will also be true in an extended period. Thus, for the fixed time duration of Δ*t*, the volume of transaction is given as described below:

$$V = \sum_i v_{ti} \tag{5}$$

Where, v_{ti} is the volume of transaction *i* with traditional matching in Δ*t*, and

$$V' = \sum_i v'_{ti} \tag{6}$$

Where, v'_{ti} is the volume of traction in ABTS in Δt. We also note that

$$\mathbf{V'} \geq \mathbf{V} \tag{7}$$

Thus, *Auction case 1* is the simple case where there is a direct match in volume between the buyer's order and the seller's offer. In this case, $V' = V$, and there is no special contribution from ABTS. In contrast, *Auction cases 2 and 3*, serve to actively increase volume and utility on the parts of buyer and seller. This is why $\mathbf{V'} \geq \mathbf{V}$. The contribution of this chapter is in using ABTS to maximizing $\mathbf{V'}$, *i.e.* to increase the respective transaction volumes, and utilities, of both the buyer and seller agents, by efficient matching of the requirements and capacities of the buyer and seller agents.

Reverse Auction Functions

In our model of Reverse Auction Functions, there are several different trading situations. One buyer (i) posts his product requirements including the product quantity Q_i^b, and its price p_i^b in t_1. The product quantity is variable but the price is fixed in the proposed model. Thus, trading negotiations and matching of trades relates to product quantity rather than product price. Similarly, trading utility is treated as a function of product volume, and not the product price.

We describe below a number of scenarios. The base conditions of the trading transaction are described as follows. Each seller (j) will offer its product with the available quantity q_j^s at state P1. At this point, there are tree possible actions: (1) Q_i^b and q_j^s are not matched and the deal will be over (t_1 and P2), 2) Q_i^b and q_j^s are matched and the transaction will be occurred (t_3 and P3), and 3) the seller gathers other seller's offer to match the buyer's requested quantity (t_4, t_5 and P4). At P4 the seller j collects other sellers' offer and present the joined offer to the buyer i (t_5). If the joined offer

$$\sum_{j=1}^{J} q_j^s \neq Q_i^b \; ,$$

and the buyer does not accept the offer, then either the deal is over (t_2 and P2) or the seller tries collecting new seller's group again (P4 and t_5). If the joined offer

$$\sum_{j=1}^{J} q_j^s = Q_i^b$$

then the transaction will be occurred (t_3 and P3).

Similarly, each seller (j) will offer its product to a buyer (i) with the buyer's needed quantity Q_i^b at state P5. At this point, there are tree possible actions: (1) Q_i^b and q_j^s are not matched and the deal will be over (t_7 and P6); (2) Q_i^b and q_j^s are matched and the transaction will take place (t_8 and P7); and (3) the buyer gathers other buyer's offer to match the seller's requested quantity (t_9, t_{10} and P8). At P8 the seller (j) collects other buyers' offer and presents the joined offer to the seller j (t_{10}). If the joined offer

$$\sum_{i=1}^{I} Q_i^b \neq q_j^s$$

and the seller does not accept the offer then either the deal is over (t_7 and P6), or the seller tries collecting new seller's group again (P8 and t_{10}). If the joined offer

Figure 5. Algorithm 1: Buyers collected offer

```
IF Sell.amount > Buy.amount
    { Get friend (|Buy.amount – Sell.amount|, Buyer) // form a buyer's consortium
      IF ( Σ (amount_from_friends) + Buy.amount = Sell.amount)
              DO transaction
      }
ELSE DO transaction
```

Figure 6. Algorithm 2: Sellers collected offer

```
IF Sell.amount < Buy.amount
    { Get friend (|Buy.amount – Sell.amount|, Seller) //form a seller's consortium
      IF (Sell.amount +Σ (amount_from_friends) = Buy.amount)
              DO transaction
      }
ELSE DO transaction
```

$$\sum_{i=1}^{I} Q_i^b = q_j^s$$

then the transaction will be considered to have occurred (t_8 and P7).

For buyers' and sellers' consortium offers, each trading agent must evaluate joined volumes and evaluation algorithms are described in Figure 5 and Figure 6.

There are six scenarios that describe the trading transactions, summarized for the purpose of action, in two algorithms:

- **Scenario 1:** In case of buyer's intended buying volume is equal to the seller's selling volume, the seller can do transaction without the help of the consortium. (Auction case 1)
- **Scenario 2:** In case of buyer's intended buying volume is not meet the seller's selling volume and there is no possibility of forming neither seller's consortium nor the buyer's consortium. (Auction case 1)
- **Scenario 3:** In case of seller's intended selling volume is smaller than a buyer's intended buying volume, the sellers could form a consortium and their collected volume meets the buyer's required volume. (Auction case 2)
- **Scenario 4:** In case of seller's intended selling volume is greater than a buyer's intended buying volume, the seller tried to form a consortium but fail to meet the buyer's required volume. (Auction case 2)

- **Scenario 5:** In case of buyer's intended buying volume is smaller than the seller's selling volume, the buyer can form a consortium with the combined volume meeting the seller's volume. (Auction case 3)
- **Scenario 6:** Incase of buyer's intended buying volume is smaller than the seller's selling volume, the buyer tried to form a consortium but fail to meet the seller's volume. (Auction case 3)

The details of state transitions associated with the trading transaction scenarios are shown in Tables 1 to 6.

Table 1. Scenario 1

Situation Point	Condition	Outcome
P0	A buyer (*i*) wants product A, 100 (Q_i^b) units for p dollars each. And there is a seller wants to sell the product A. The seller has 100 units.	Move to t_1
t_1	The buyer offers 100 units of product A for p dollars each.	Move to P1
P1	Q_i^b = 100 and it matches the sum of the seller's volumes.	It goes to t_3.
t_3	The buyer *i* and the seller do transaction.	Move to P3
P3	Buyer and seller's trading volume is met and the buyer accepts the seller's offer.	Terminate with transaction.

Table 2. Scenario 2

Situation Point	Condition	Outcome
P0	A buyer (*i*) wants product A, 100 (Q_i^b) units for p dollars each. And there is a seller wants to sell the product A. And there is only one seller who has 40 units of the product A.	Move to t_1
t_1	buyer offer product A, 100 units for p dollars each.	Move to P1
P1	Q_i^b = 100 and it does not match the seller's volumes. It goes to t_2.	Move to t_2
t_2	Seller rejects the offer. It goes to P2	Move to P2
P2	Match is failed	Terminate with no transaction

Table 3. Scenario 3

Situation Point	Condition	Outcome
P0	A buyer (i) wants product A, 100 (Q_i^b) units for p dollars each. And there are 4 sellers want to sell the product A: seller 1 has 20 units, seller 2 has 40 units seller 3 has 30 units and seller 4 has 10 units	The process t_1 will be tried.
t_1	A buyer offers 100 units of product A for p dollars each.	Move to P1
P1	None of the sellers has the required volume of the buyer.	The process t_4 will be tried
t_4	Run algorithm 2. As a result of the algorithm, agents of all four sellers combine their volumes of the product A and offer to buyer i again.	Move to P4
P4	$Q_i^b = 100$ and it matches with the sum of all four seller's volumes.	It goes to t_5.
t_5	4 sellers jointly offer to buyer i	Move to P1
P1	Seller (i) consider the joint offer	It goes to t_3
t_3	Seller (i) accepts the joint offer	Move to P3
P3	Buyer and seller's trading volume is met and the transaction is occurred.	Terminate with transaction

Table 4. Scenario 4

Situation Point	Condition	Outcome
P0	A buyer (i) wants product A, 100 (Q_i^b) units for p dollars each. And there are 4 sellers want to sell the product A: seller 1 has 20 units, seller 2 has 20 units seller 3 has 20 units and seller 4 has 10 units.	Move to t_1
t_1	buyer offer product A, 100 units for p dollars each.	Move to P1
P1	None of the sellers has the required volume of the buyer.	It goes to t_4
t_4	run algorithm 2. Agents of all four sellers combine their volumes of the product A and offer to buyer i. It goes to P4.	Move to P4
P4	Sellers form a consortium	Move to t_5
t_5	4 sellers jointly offer to buyer i	Move to P1
P1	$Q_i^b = 100 >$ the sum of the seller's volumes = 70.	It goes to t_2
t_2	Seller rejects the combined offer.	Move to P2
P2	Match is failed	Terminate without any transaction.

Table 5. Scenario 5

Situation Point	Condition	Outcome
P0	A buyer (i) wants product A, 20 (Q_i^b) units for p dollars each. And there is only one seller wants to sell the product A: the seller has 100 units and do not want to break the volume. There are other buyers want same product A too (30, 40, 10).	The process t_6 will be tried.
t_6	A buyer offers 20 units of product A for p dollars each.	Move to P5
P5	None of the sellers has the required volume of the buyer.	The process t_9 will be tried
t_9	Run algorithm 1. As a result of the algorithm, agents of all four buyers combine their volumes of the product.	Move to P8
P8	Buyer's consortium state	It goes to t_{10}.
t_{10}	4 buyers jointly offer to seller j	Move to P5
P5	$$\sum_{i=1}^{I} Q_i^b = q_j^s = 100$$ and it matches with the sum of all four buyers' volume.	It goes to t_8
t_8	Seller (j) accepts the joint offer	Move to P7
P7	Buyer and seller's trading volume is met and the transaction is occurred.	Terminate with transaction

Table 6. Scenario 6

Situation Point	Condition	Outcome
P0	A buyer (i) wants product A, 20 (Q_i^b) units for p dollars each. And there is only one seller wants to sell the product A: the seller has 100 units and do not want to break the volume. There are other buyers want same product A too (30, 20, 10).	The process t_6 will be tried.
t_6	A buyer offers 20 units of product A for p dollars each.	Move to P5
P5	None of the sellers has the required volume of the buyer.	The process t_9 will be tried
t_9	Run algorithm 1. As a result of the algorithm, agents of all four buyers combine their volumes of the product.	Move to P8
P8	Buyer's consortium state	It goes to t_{10}.
t_{10}	4 buyers jointly offer to seller j	Move to P5
P5	$$\sum_{i=1}^{I} Q_i^b \neq q_j^s = 100$$ and it does not match with the sum of all four buyer's volumes.	It goes to t_7
t_7	Seller (j) rejects the joint offer	Move to P6
P6	Buyer and seller's trading volume is not met and no transaction is occurred.	Terminate without transaction

A simple simulation experiment shows the impact of consortium on volume matching. This is not a complete simulation with agent generation using agent technologies, but a simple spreadsheet example using trading matches. The trading volume offers of ten sellers and ten buyers are randomly generated in Excel using the random number generators provided by Excel. Trading volumes are generated in multiples of 10 for simplicity. The trading offers are matched first by a direct match of trading volumes. The remaining offers are matched by a consortium, either of sellers to match a buyer, or of buyers to match a seller, or of both. The uncertainty of a result using random number generation is resolved by repeating the process 10 times, in 10 cases. The results are shown in Table 7, with the summary results in Table 8. It may be seen that consortium is never less than direct matching in generating trading volume. There is only one case of the 10 in which consortium does no better than direct matching. In every other case, consortium is an improvement in volume ranging from small to substantial. This is a clear indication of the benefits of the proposed consortium approach.

Table 7. Experimental results for trading volumes with and without consortium

Case 1.

Price is fixed

Seller ID	Volume	Buyer ID	Volume
S1	50	B1	20
S2	150	B2	30
S3	100	B3	50
S4	50	B4	40
S5	100	B5	10
S6	150	B6	70
S7	50	B7	50
S8	130	B8	30
S9	100	B9	300
S10	50	B10	200

Matching without Consortium			Matching with Consortium		
Seller	Buyer	Trading Volume	Seller	Buyer	Trading Volume
S1	B3	50	S1	B3	50
S4	B7	50	S4	B7	50
			{S2,S6}	B9	300
			S3	{B1,B2,B4,B6}	100
			S5	{B6,B8}	100
			{S7,S9,S10}	B10	200
Total Volume		100	Total Volume		800

Case 2.

Seller ID	Volume	Buyer ID	Volume
S1	50	B1	10
S2	80	B2	10
S3	90	B3	10
S4	60	B4	10
S5	70	B5	90
S6	10	B6	70
S7	70	B7	10
S8	60	B8	10
S9	70	B9	40
S10	20	B10	90

Matching without Consortium			**Matching with Consortium**		
Seller	Buyer	Trading Volume	Seller	Buyer	Trading Volume
S3	B5	90	S3	B5	90
S5	B6	70	S5	B6	70
S6	B1	10	S6	B1	10
			S1	{B2,B9}	50
			S10	{B3,B4}	20
Total Volume		170	Total Volume		240

Case 3.

Seller ID	Volume	Buyer ID	Volume
S1	40	B1	10
S2	90	B2	60
S3	40	B3	50
S4	10	B4	90
S5	90	B5	100
S6	70	B6	40
S7	40	B7	20
S8	30	B8	80
S9	100	B9	50
S10	20	B10	10

continued on following page

Case 3. continued

Matching without Consortium			Matching with Consortium		
Seller	Buyer	Trading Volume	Seller	Buyer	Trading Volume
S1	B6	40	S1	B6	40
S2	B4	90	S2	B4	90
S4	B1	10	S4	B1	10
S9	B5	100	S9	B5	100
S10	B7	20	S10	B7	20
			S5	{B8,B10}	90
Total Volume		260	Total Volume		350

Case 4.

Seller ID	Volume	Buyer ID	Volume
S1	100	B1	100
S2	100	B2	40
S3	20	B3	70
S4	100	B4	80
S5	90	B5	40
S6	100	B6	50
S7	20	B7	70
S8	20	B8	40
S9	40	B9	10
S10	100	B10	40

Matching without Consortium			Matching with Consortium		
Seller	Buyer	Trading Volume	Seller	Buyer	Trading Volume
S1	B1	100	S1	B1	100
S9	B2	40	S9	B2	40
			S2	{B5,B6,B9}	100
			{S7,S8}	B8	40
Total Volume		140	Total Volume		280

Case 5.

Seller ID	Volume	Buyer ID	Volume
S1	90	B1	50
S2	50	B2	90
S3	80	B3	90
S4	80	B4	100
S5	30	B5	80
S6	60	B6	40
S7	90	B7	30
S8	60	B8	30
S9	40	B9	90
S10	30	B10	70

Matching without Consortium			**Matching with Consortium**		
Seller	Buyer	Trading Volume	Seller	Buyer	Trading Volume
S1	B2	90	S1	B2	90
S2	B1	50	S2	B1	50
S3	B5	80	S3	B5	80
S5	B8	30	S5	B8	30
S7	B3	90	S7	B3	90
S9	B6	40	S9	B6	40
S10	B7	30	S10	B7	30
Total Volume		410	Total Volume		410

Case 6.

Seller ID	Volume	Buyer ID	Volume
S1	50	B1	60
S2	90	B2	80
S3	100	B3	70
S4	50	B4	20
S5	100	B5	20
S6	60	B6	40
S7	100	B7	50
S8	40	B8	90
S9	30	B9	60
S10	100	B10	100

continued on following page

Case 6. continued

Matching without Consortium			Matching with Consortium		
Seller	Buyer	Trading Volume	Seller	Buyer	Trading Volume
S1	B7	50	S1	B7	50
S2	B8	90	S2	B8	90
S3	B10	100	S3	B10	100
S6	B1	60	S6	B1	60
S8	B6	40	S8	B6	40
			S5	{B4,B5,B9}	100
			{S4,S9}	B2	80
Total Volume		340	Total Volume		520

Case 7.

Seller ID	Volume	Buyer ID	Volume
S1	10	B1	80
S2	40	B2	10
S3	60	B3	100
S4	80	B4	40
S5	40	B5	90
S6	80	B6	20
S7	90	B7	60
S8	50	B8	40
S9	10	B9	80
S10	20	B10	30

Matching without Consortium			Matching with Consortium		
Seller	Buyer	Trading Volume	Seller	Buyer	Trading Volume
S1	B2	10	S1	B2	10
S2	B4	40	S2	B4	40
S3	B7	60	S3	B7	60
S4	B9	80	S4	B9	80
S5	B8	40	S5	B8	40
S6	B1	80	S6	B1	80
S7	B5	90	S7	B5	90
			S8	{B6,B10}	50
Total Volume		400	Total Volume		450

Case 8.

Seller ID	Volume	Buyer ID	Volume
S1	20	B1	70
S2	50	B2	40
S3	50	B3	70
S4	70	B4	40
S5	100	B5	40
S6	40	B6	80
S7	50	B7	50
S8	60	B8	90
S9	60	B9	80
S10	20	B10	20

Matching without Consortium			Matching with Consortium		
Seller	Buyer	Trading Volume	Seller	Buyer	Trading Volume
S1	B10	20	S1	B10	20
S2	B7	50	S2	B7	50
S4	B1	70	S4	B1	70
S6	B2	40	S6	B2	40
			{S8,S9}	{B4,B6}	120
			{S5,S7,S10}	{B8,B9}	170
Total Volume		180	Total Volume		470

Case 9.

Seller ID	Volume	Buyer ID	Volume
S1	90	B1	10
S2	70	B2	60
S3	20	B3	10
S4	10	B4	60
S5	70	B5	30
S6	90	B6	70
S7	10	B7	80
S8	50	B8	20
S9	20	B9	10
S10	30	B10	10

continued on following page

Case 9. continued

Matching without Consortium			Matching with Consortium		
Seller	Buyer	Trading Volume	Seller	Buyer	Trading Volume
S2	B6	70	S2	B6	70
S3	B8	20	S3	B8	20
S4	B9	10	S4	B9	10
S7	B1	10	S7	B1	10
S10	B5	30	S10	B5	30
			S1	{B7,B10}	90
			S2	{B2,B3}	70
Total Volume		140	Total Volume		300

Case 10.

Seller ID	Volume	Buyer ID	Volume
S1	10	B1	70
S2	80	B2	30
S3	80	B3	50
S4	80	B4	60
S5	70	B5	20
S6	80	B6	40
S7	10	B7	100
S8	60	B8	60
S9	40	B9	40
S10	60	B10	40

Matching without Consortium			Matching with Consortium		
Seller	Buyer	Trading Volume	Seller	Buyer	Trading Volume
S5	B1	70	S5	B1	70
S8	B4	60	S8	B4	70
S9	B6	40	S9	B6	40
S10	B8	60	S10	B8	60
			{S1,S2,S7}	B7	100
			S3	{B2,B3}	80
			S4	{B9,B10}	80
Total Volume		230	Total Volume		490

Table 8. Summary results for trading volumes with and without consortium

Method \ Case	Matched Volumes									
	Case 1	Case 2	Case 3	Case 4	Case 5	Case 6	Case 7	Case 8	Case 9	Case 10
Direct Match	100	170	260	140	410	340	400	180	140	230
Consortium	800	240	350	280	410	520	450	470	300	490

CONCLUDING REMARKS

This chapter considers a two-tier online auction supply chain system in which buyer agents propose transactions that are matched by seller agents, or are otherwise referred to a community of seller agents, who will match the buyer demand in terms of volume. Price is fixed and is not a consideration in the matching process. Alternately, the seller agent proposes a volume that is matched individually by a buyer, or by the community of buyer agents by means of collaboration. It is also possible to have trades matched and completed by a consortium of seller agents matching the volume of a consortium of buyer agents, or vice versa. The hypothesis is that collaboration between the same class of agents, and the formation of consortiums within the respective agent communities, offers greater opportunities for matching trading volumes and increases the total trading volume. Experimental results with random generation of individual trading volumes for buyers and sellers, and volume matching of trades irrespective of price, shows that collaboration and consortium formation is usually an improvement in trading volumes, with a major improvement in some cases of the volume of trade, over the traditional model of non-cooperation and competition.

An implementation is possible with *JADE (Java Agent Development Framework)*[1]. JADE is implemented in Java, and can be controlled by a remote GUI. It is compliant with FIPA[2] specifications, and can be implemented on multiple machines on multiple operating systems. The current JADE version is 3.4 (released March 14, 2006). JADE is free software from Telecom Italia, as a FIPA compliant agent platform with a reduced footprint, and with compatibility with a mobile Java environment. An alternate modeling and implementation framework is *MADKIT (Multi-Agent Development Kit*[3]*)* available as a free download. This is a modular and scalable multi-agent platform in Java, built on the AGR (Agent/Group/Role) organizational model, *i.e.* agents are situated in groups and play roles. MADKIT allows simulations of agent performance, heterogeneity in agent architectures and communication languages, as well as a number of customizations. Like JADE, MADKIT is a peer-to-peer mechanism with full facilities full facilities for launching, displaying, developing, and monitoring agents and agent organizations.

The real direction of future work consists of extending the model to include other considerations important in modeling auction trades by agents. The patterns of agent trading follow the patterns of auction trading in general. In auction trading practice, one of the primary considerations is price. A seller agent makes an offer at a certain price. If the offer is not matched at the quantity and price it must be carried over to the next period at a cost to the seller agent. The seller agent may have to dispose of the offer at a reduced price in a future period to avoid carryover costs. Similar conditions apply to buyer agents and their offers with reversed conditions. An extended model will study this behavior in a multi-period environment. A mathematical model is often an elegant representation of the problem. The development of heuristic solution approaches is the real solution methodology applicable to real problems. This is part of the direction of future research.

REFERENCES

Aknine, S., Pinson, S., & Shakun, M. F. (2004). A multi-agent coalition formation method based on preference models. *Group Decision and Negotiation, 13*, 513-538.

Anussornnitisarn, P., Nof, S. Y., & Etzion, O. (2005). Decentralized control of cooperative and autonomous agents for solving the distributed resource allocation problem. *International Journal of Production Economics, 98*, 114-128.

Bertsekas, D. P. (2000). *Dynamic programming and optimal control, 1.* Belmont, MA: Athena Scientific.

Binbasioglu, M. (1999). Problem structuring support for collaboration and problem solving. *Journal of Computer Information Systems, 40*(2), 54-63.

Fox, M., *Barbuceanu, M., & Teigen, R.* (2000). Agent-oriented supply chain management. *International Journal of Flexible Manufacturing Systems, 12*(2/3), 165-188.

Hill, J. C., Johnson, F. R., Archibald, J. K., Frost, R. L., & Stirling, W. C. (2005). A cooperative multi-agent approach to free flight. In *Proceedings of the Fourth International Joint Conference on Autonomous Agents and Multiagent Systems AAMAS '05*, (pp. 1083-1090).

Kosakaya, J., & Yamaoka, K. (2001). Cooperative multi-agent intelligent field terminals. In *Proceedings of the Fifth International Conference on Autonomous Agents*, (pp. 348-354).

Nag, B. (2007). A Blackboard agent community architecture in a supply chain environment. *Design Principles and Practices, 1*(1), 91-104.

Puschmann, T., & Alt, R. (2005). Successful Use of E-procurement in Supply Chains. *Supply Chain Management: An International Journal, 10*(2), 122-133.

Roy, D., Anciaux, D., Monteiro, T., & Ouzizi, L. (2004). Multi-agent architecture for supply chain management. *Journal of Manufacturing Technology Management, 15*(8), 745-755.

Zhao, G., Deng, J., & Shen, W. (2001). CLOVER: An agent-based approach to systems interoperability in cooperative design systems. *Computers in Industry, 45*, 261-276.

Zho, S. C., Ramirez-Serrano, A., & Brennan, R. W. (2006). Cooperative multi-agent reconfigurable manufacturing environments. *International Journal of Manufacturing Technology and Management, 8*, 283-303.

ENDNOTES

[1]   **Source:** htttp://jade.tilab.com/*Telecom Italia*
[2]   Federation of International Physical Agents
[3]   **Source:** htttp://www.madkit.org/

Chapter VI
Extending Loosely Coupled Federated Information Systems Using Agent Technology

Manoj A. Thomas
Virginia Commonwealth University, USA

Victoria Y. Yoon
University of Maryland, Baltimore County, USA

Richard Redmond
Virginia Commonwealth University, USA

ABSTRACT

Different FIPA-compliant agent development platforms are available for developing multiagent systems. FIPA compliance ensures interoperability among agents across different platforms. Although most agent implementation platforms provide some form of white- and yellow-page functionalities to advertise and identify agent roles and descriptions, there are no clear architectural standards that define how an agent community can effortlessly adapt to operate in a federated information system (FIS) where new content sources are constantly added or changes are made to existing content sources. This chapter presents a framework based on the semantic Web vision to address extensibility in a loosely coupled FIS.

INTRODUCTION

The process of automating the interorganizational information exchange between trading partners has been an ongoing challenge. In recent years, information exchange in business-to-business (B2B) work-flow models have started migrating to Internet-based technological solutions such as Web services and service-oriented architectures (SOAs) over older systems based on electronic data interchange (EDI) and object request brokerage (ORB). UDDI (universal description, discovery, and integration) business registries allow businesses to list themselves on the Internet and be discovered by others while offering the benefits of platform independence and minimal implementation costs to the trading partners. In a federated environment where a finite set of partner institutions collaborate and exchange information, federated information systems (FISs) have evolved as a fertile area of research seeking new methods and tools to help provide integrated access to a finite, predefined set of autonomous and heterogeneous databases. Busse, Kutsche, Leser, and Weber (1999) define an FIS as a set of distinct and autonomous information system components: the participants of this federation. The participants operate independently, but negotiate some levels of autonomy among themselves in order to participate in the federated environment (Busse et al.). Conceptually, an FIS can be characterized by the presence of an integration layer that allows a degree of autonomy, heterogeneity, and interoperability among the underlying legacy applications and databases (Busse et al.; Sheth & Larson, 1990).

The success of an FIS is strongly dependent on the generation of federated schemas from the participating source database schemas. A federated schema allows business analysts to accomplish complex goals such as generating data-mining reports, perform computations along multiple dimensions of data stored in different sources, and help developers by providing incremental views for quick access to information along with data warehouses' capabilities (Jarke, Jeusfeld, Quix, & Vassiliadis, 1999). It is a common practice in FIS to view an organization's business model as conceptual perspectives based on shared information and build a higher level schema representation as a logical model (Busse et al., 1999; Jarke et al.). Defining higher level representations in the form of federated schemas offers a convenient logical perspective to store and find data linked to the disparate local schemas. As the source of information changes due to the insertion of new data sources or deletion of existing data sources, timely changes are necessitated on the federated schema. Prior research has made significant strides in addressing many problems related to the communications and interoperation issues covering data sources as well as nondatabase information sources (Hasselbring, Heuvel, & Roantree, 2000). Unfortunately, little research addressed issues related to dynamic updates to a loosely coupled federated schema as data sources are added and/or removed.

The objective of this chapter is to develop a framework that provides extensibility in a loosely coupled FIS. This study proposes to integrate semantic Web and multiagent systems to enhance the extensibility of loosely coupled federated schemas derived from heterogeneous database components within an FIS architecture. The semantic Web architecture can provide a common framework for semantics and data to be shared and reused across applications and enterprise boundaries (Berners-Lee, Hendler, & Lassila, 2001; Thomas, Redmond, Yoon, & Singh, 2005). A goal-based agent community can be overlaid on an FIS model (Jennings, Sycara, & Wooldridge, 1998; Zou, Finin, Ding, Chen, & Pan, 2003). By integrating the semantic Web and an agent community, the chapter aims to develop an extensibility model in which ontological documents describe the semantic structure of the data sources in an agent-enriched FIS environment. The next section presents a high-level overview of FIS and the necessity for the extensibility of a loosely coupled FIS. This section also presents the use of the ontology Web language (OWL) to generate ontology documents and an agent-based architecture to interpret the ontology documents. The following section elucidates a real-world scenario to demonstrate the need for FIS to adjust to the changes in data sources. We use this running example as a supporting disposition to provide a detailed explanation of the agent-based framework for semantic extensibility proposed in this chapter. Finally, we conclude with a summary section that identifies immediate benefits of the framework and suggests future directions of research and development to address the limitations in this model.

BACKGROUND

Conceptually, a federated information system can be treated as a three-tier architecture (adapted representation from Busse et al., 1999) as shown in Figure 1. The data sources in the foundation layer can be heterogeneous, autonomous, or distributed. The form of schema management in the federation layer defines whether the FIS is tightly federated or loosely federated (Sheth & Larson, 1990). A tight federation creates a unified schema through the semantic integration of component schemas (Busse et al.). The users in the presentation layer therefore need to have little knowledge about the individual component schemas. However, tracking changes in the component schemas and correspondingly making changes to the unified federated schema can be intractable and may be performed only by a domain expert. To address this limitation, a loose federation adopts an approach where reliance on a central federated schema is eliminated. This becomes a viable option only if a uniform query language is available to

Figure 1. Three-tier representation of a federated information system with Web service support

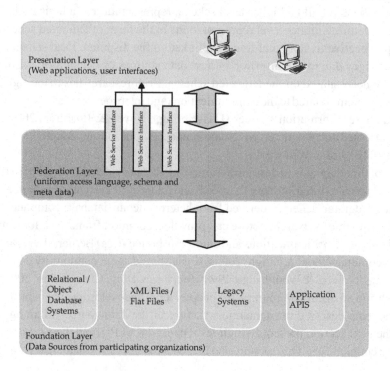

hide the heterogeneity of the component data sources in the federation. Uniform query languages such as MDBQL (multidatabase query language) have evolved to create the requisite binding between the presentation layer and the federation layer (Busse et al.). MDBQL can be used to create specific custom-defined global views from the participating schema in order to reduce the overhead on the users trying to interact with the foundation layer. With the increasing prominence of Web services and service composition models for quick and easy information interchange, loosely coupled federations are evolving as the sensible alternative compared to tightly coupled federations (Zimmermann, Krogdahl, & Gee, 2004). However, the dynamics of the Internet environment poses formidable integration challenges, especially if the FIS is to allow organizations to join or leave the federation with a certain desired level of trust, ease, freedom, and security.

The importance of generating a correspondence between the logical schema and federated layer for conducting queries in an FIS is very evident (Busse et al., 1999). One meaningful way to express correspondence is through the use of ontological descriptions defined by humans or semiautomatically generated by computer systems using newer standards of ontology description languages like OWL, OWL-S (OWL for semantic Web services), or BPEL (business process execution language; *OWL-S*, n.d.). Grounded in robust theoretical foundations based on description logic (DL; Baader, Calvanese, McGuinness, Nardi, & Patel-Schneider, 2003), OWL has evolved as the W3C (World Wide Web Consortium) standard for semantic knowledge representation (Thomas et al., 2005). In conjunction with XML (extensible markup language), which is widely supported in almost all database management systems, interoperability challenges between schema definitions are significantly lowered since DL-based XML schema can be generated with relative ease (*OWL-S*). The inclusion of semantic support in common query languages also offers software applications and agents the ability to execute KQML (knowledge query and manipulation language) performatives with a strong semantic focus (Labrou & Finin, 1997). Many commercial tools are now available on the market (Protégé, http://protege.stanford.edu; Racer, http://www.racer-systems.com) that can generate domain ontology from DL and verify its consistency and conformance against schema models. OWL-S-based ontology documents can store all service properties of a data source and advertise service capabilities that can be used for automatic service discovery and composition in alignment with the fundamental concepts of service composition architectures (SCA, 2005).

The growing popularity of semantic Web models has drawn a stronger impetus toward the use of intelligent agents to discover, invoke, compose, and monitor services using ontology documents in an automated or semiautomated way (Thomas et al., 2005; Zou et al., 2003). Agent technology has evolved as critical middleware in a variety of distributed systems, both peer to peer as well as client-server, and in numerous other software component architectures that use the agent paradigm (FIPA, n.d.; JADE Project, n.d.). The FIPA agent interoperability specifications are designed to facilitate end-to-end internetworking of intelligent agents and lays down standards for a variety of implementation-specific stipulations such as agent communication languages, the message transport protocol for IIOP, quality of service, and ontology specifications (FIPA; Open Financial Exchange [OFX], 2006). Almost all popular agent development environments (such as MadKit, JADE, etc.) allow extensive and flexible agent configuration and development capabilities and are compliant with the FIPA interoperability standards.

In an FIS, the objective of semantic integration is undertaken at the federation layer. The different steps in the semantic integration process include collection, fusion, abstraction, and supplementation (Busse et al., 1999). In a tightly coupled FIS, this is rigid and fixed since changes to local data sources are least probable or not allowed. Given the dynamic environment of the Internet, a tightly coupled

FIS is limiting and inadequate. There is a compelling demand for flexibility that allows data sources to join and leave an FIS. The work presented in this chapter rides on a stern belief that the need for flexibility can be accomplished by extending the loosely coupled FIS model to include concepts from the semantic Web model. The beliefs are validated by a detailed discussion of the proposed model and how the model adds value in a real-world loosely coupled FIS setting. Whereas current FIS models function efficiently in a tightly coupled federation, a loosely coupled federation poses formidable integration challenges. Interweaving the fundamental FIS model with the semantic Web model (Berners-Lee et al., 2001) consisting of documents based on ontology description languages and a multiagent system could be a viable solution to liberate the loosely coupled federation from the clutches of prior concerns that limited their practical adoption.

A MOTIVATING EXAMPLE

The role of federating schemas in an FIS can be best explained using a running example. Consider the case of a home buyer requesting prequalifying for a loan prior to the loan application process. To the potential home owner, this is where the rubber meets the road. The prequalifying process essentially determines the amount that the borrower will qualify for. To the loan officer, it is a critical process that can identify red flags before the loan approval and sanction. In reviewing the preloan request application, the loan officer interacts with numerous sources of information in an attempt to paint the most accurate picture of the borrower. For the sake of contextualization, assume that the loan officer operates in a federated environment where he or she constantly accesses specific data sources pertaining to the following four categories of information: employment history, financial stability, credit check, and property valuation. The information from these sources will help the loan officer to determine the correct loan amount based on an applicant's unique credit and employment history, income and debt, and property investment goals. The employment history provides pertinent information regarding employment dates, addresses, and salary data, while financial stability is shown through multiple other data sources to validate information regarding investment accounts, stocks and bonds, checking and savings account balances, retirement plans, and life insurance policies. In addition, the final loan amount is also dependent upon the applicant's residential history (real estate rented, owned, or sold) and the credit-rating scores from one or many credit-reporting agencies. The loan officer interacts with the finite set of data sources in the foundation layer via the federation layer using the presentation layer. This is represented in Figure 2.

As organizations evolve and grow over time, new information becomes available, and changes to the federation become inevitable. New data sources may be added to the federation while some data sources are no longer retained or undergo structural and semantic changes. If the federation layer is incapable of adjusting to changes in the foundation layer, the federated schema is no longer in correspondence with the local data sources, thereby severely falling short in meeting the levels of expectations of the presentation layer. For example, the FIS for an online loan-approval system may decide to include additional insurance companies in their listing or may terminate partnership with a specific credit-reporting agency. Irrespective of whether the federated schema is tightly coupled or loosely coupled, changes in the foundation layer have to be reflected in the overlying architectural layers of the FIS to reduce inconveniences to the loan officer and to reduce the time lost during the approval process. Deficiencies of this nature commonly experienced when working with multiple heterogeneous data sources can be

Figure 2. The extended FIS model

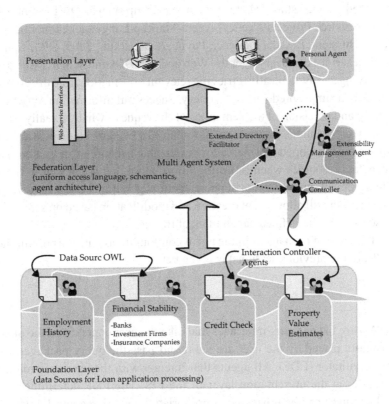

addressed by overlaying a multiagent architecture in conjunction with a set of ontological documents that specify the semantic structure of the underlying data sources. The multiagent architecture can interpret these ontological documents to discover changes and semiautomatically help with the extensibility of the federated schema in the FIS by drawing semantic inferences from the ontological documents.

Figure 2 shows the OWL-S-based DL knowledge representation required for an agent system to interact with the data source schemas. OWL-S provides the structured knowledge representation and maintains abstraction from the underlying data models (*OWL-S*, n.d.). OWL-S also provides the software agents with a global knowledge of the federation's data model, including the subcomponents of the federated schema and the service components offered by the different participating organizations.

The Semantic Web (Berners-Lee et al., 2001) portrays an architecture where agents can collect content from diverse sources and exchange data enriched with semantics, facilitated by ontology documents. Agents can further assist in automated reasoning from the knowledge representations by applying inference rules on the structured collection of information represented in the ontology documents. The model proposed in the next section mainly focuses on extending loosely coupled FISs using agent technology.

An Agent-Based Framework for Semantic Extensibility

Semantic brokering models over dynamic heterogeneous data sources that use agents for subquery processing and service discovery have been proposed in the past (Nodine, Bohrer, & Ngu, 1999). As loosely coupled FISs are becoming the preferred mode for information exchange over the Web, the benefits of languages based on open standards for semantic markup such as OWL-S and DAML (DARPA [Defense Advanced Research Projects Agency] Agent Markup Language) cannot be ignored (MadKit Project, n.d.; Martin, Burstein, Lassila, Paolucci, Payne, & McIlraith, 2003; *OWL-S*, n.d.). In addition, the importance of data service discovery over the Web (using UDDI and WSDL [Web service definition language]) for identifying and dynamically retrieving relevant information from different content sources is no longer the result of a simple predetermined query. Successful information retrieval is thus a direct function of the clarity and precision of the semantics of the request: what we really want from a query. As flexibility to allow data sources to come and go in an FIS becomes indispensable, it is imperative that new mechanisms are developed that will allow extensible agent (new or existing) architectures to exploit all available data resources when returning information that is relevant to the user. Currently available agent development environments support agent negotiations and task delegations, but lack architectural templates that will allow agent creation and modification based on semantic matchmaking between the data source and the defined capabilities of the agent.

A description of the role of each agent in the agent community and its purpose in the context of the running example (from the previous sections) is given below.

Personal Agent

Personal agents (PAs) are the end-user interfaces that take the user context and the query clause. They ensure that the requests placed by the user are valid and pass the query packaged in KQML to the extended directory facilitator (EDF). All agents that interact with the user are grouped into an agent community that resides at the presentation layer of the FIS. The EDF determines the relevant data source on which the request can be processed. Appropriate interaction controller (IC) agents are also identified based on agent capability (ask all, ask specific), agent functionalities (O-O [object-oriented] query processing), restrictions imposed, supported ontologies (finance), ontological language capacities (BPEL, OWL-S), and adaptivity (able to be cloned, replicable; Nodine et al., 1999). The PA acts as a gateway between the EDF and the end user with the authority to query, update, or modify data from the data sources in an FIS.

Table 1. Sequence of communication and OWL-S profile descriptions for the multiagent architecture

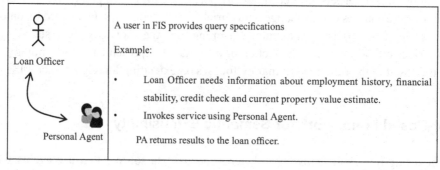

continued on following page

Table 1. continued

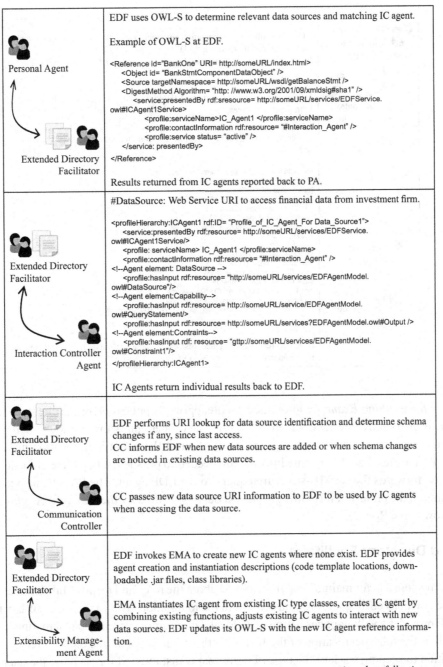

	EDF uses OWL-S to determine relevant data sources and matching IC agent.
Personal Agent ↕ **Extended Directory Facilitator**	Example of OWL-S at EDF. ```<Reference Id="BankOne" URI= http://someURL/index.html> <Object id= "BankStmtComponentDataObject" /> <Source targetNamespace= http://someURL/wsdl/getBalanceStmt /> <DigestMethod Algorithm= "http://www.w3.org/2001/09/xmldsig#sha1" /> <service:presentedBy rdf:sresource= http://someURL/services/EDFService. owl#ICAgent1Service> <profile:serviceName>IC_Agent1 </profile:serviceName> <profile:contactInformation rdf:resource= "#Interaction_Agent" /> <profile:service status= "active" /> </service: presentedBy> </Reference>``` Results returned from IC agents reported back to PA.
Extended Directory Facilitator ↕ **Interaction Controller Agent**	#DataSource: Web Service URI to access financial data from investment firm. ```<profileHierarchy:ICAgent1 rdf:ID= "Profile_of_IC_Agent_For Data_Source1"> <service:presentedBy rdf:resource= http://someURL/services/EDFService. owl#ICAgent1Service/> <profile: serviceName> IC_Agent1 </profile:serviceName> <profile:contactInformation rdf:resource= "#Interaction_Agent" /> <!--Agent element: DataSource --> <profile:hasInput rdf:resource= "http://someURL/services/EDFAgentModel. owl#DataSource"/> <!--Agent element:Capability--> <profile:hasInput rdf:resource= http://someURL/service/EDFAgentModel. owl#QueryStatement/> <profile:hasInput rdf:resource= http://someURL/services?EDFAgentModel.owl#Output /> <!--Agent element:Contraints--> <profile:hasInput rdf: resource= "gttp://someURL/services/EDFAgentModel. owl#Constraint1"/> </profileHierarchy:ICAgent1>``` IC Agents return individual results back to EDF.
Extended Directory Facilitator ↕ **Communication Controller**	EDF performs URI lookup for data source identification and determine schema changes if any, since last access. CC informs EDF when new data sources are added or when schema changes are noticed in existing data sources. CC passes new data source URI information to EDF to be used by IC agents when accessing the data source.
Extended Directory Facilitator ↕ **Extensibility Management Agent**	EDF invokes EMA to create new IC agents where none exist. EDF provides agent creation and instantiation descriptions (code template locations, downloadable .jar files, class libraries). EMA instantiates IC agent from existing IC type classes, creates IC agent by combining existing functions, adjusts existing IC agents to interact with new data sources. EDF updates its OWL-S with the new IC agent reference information.

continued on following page

Table 1. continued

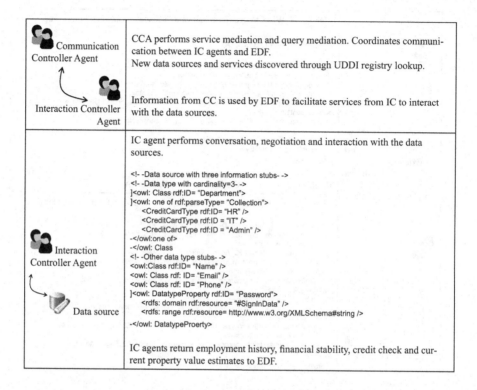

Communication Controller Agent Interaction Controller Agent	CCA performs service mediation and query mediation. Coordinates communication between IC agents and EDF. New data sources and services discovered through UDDI registry lookup. Information from CC is used by EDF to facilitate services from IC to interact with the data sources.
Interaction Controller Agent Data source	IC agent performs conversation, negotiation and interaction with the data sources. <pre><!- -Data source with three information stubs- ->\n<!- -Data type with cardinality=3- ->\n]<owl: Class rdf:ID= "Department">\n]<owl: one of rdf:parseType= "Collection">\n <CreditCardType rdf:ID = "HR" />\n <CreditCardType rdf:ID = "IT" />\n <CreditCardType rdf:ID = "Admin" />\n-</owl:one of>\n-</owl: Class\n<!- -Other data type stubs- ->\n<owl:Class rdf:ID= "Name" />\n<owl: Class rdf: ID= "Email" />\n<owl: Class rdf: ID= "Phone" />\n]<owl: DatatypeProperty rdf:ID= "Password">\n <rdfs: domain rdf:resource= "#SignInData" />\n <rdfs: range rdf:resource= http://www.w3.org/XMLSchema#string />\n-</owl: DatatypeProerty></pre>IC agents return employment history, financial stability, credit check and current property value estimates to EDF.

Utility in the Running Example: From the loan preapproval application of the client, the loan officer invokes the user-friendly interface screen of the PA. The officer enters the employment details and the banking and stock information, and requests verification of the client identification number and address. The PA ensures that all requisite information needed to pursue the objective of the loan officer is available and forwards the KQML-structured query to the EDF agent. The PA returns with the results of the finding in the preferred formatting style and detail specified by the loan officer. This is shown in Table 1 (Row 1 and Row 2).

Extended Directory Facilitator

The EDF is responsible for maintaining information about the roles and responsibilities of each IC agent that interacts with its corresponding data sources in the foundation layer of the FIS. OWL-S maintained by the EDF provides a yellow-pages listing of all local data sources currently participating in the federation as well as the role specification of the IC agents that interface with the data sources.

In addition to keeping track of the type of agent that is instantiated for each unique data source, the EDF will have the reasoning capability to determine whether an existing instance of an IC agent will be compliant to interface with a new data source that might become available in the foundation layer. The reasoning ability of the EDF agent is grounded in the semantic abstractions summarized from the OWL-S document at the data source and the agent-specific information maintained by the EDF in its own OWL-S document. The ontology document used by the EDF agent will store the syntactic and semantic information about the agents and the localized URI (uniform resource identifier) needed to access the OWL-S document at the data source. The OWL-S document at the EDF includes the following information:

- Data sources registered with the FIS
- The URI for accessing the ontology document at each individual data source
- Active IC agent addresses, locations, and templates deployed for each known data source

Data-source updates (addition, changes, deletion) at the foundation layer of the FIS are conveyed to the EDF by the communication controller (CC) agent. The URI to access the ontology document of the new data source is registered in the OWL-S document maintained by the EDF. As soon as a new data source enters the FIS, the CC agent passes the URI to access the ontology document of the new data source to the EDF, which in turn updates its own OWL-S document. This mechanism provides a means to maintain a data-source access list that is current and in correspondence with the structure of the foundation layer. If new data sources enter the federation that are similar to existing data sources, then active IC agents can be deployed to interface with the new sources. If a new IC agent has to be created or changes have to be made, all requisite information needed to implement the changes is passed on to the extensibility management agent (EMA). It is the role of the EMA to provide the appropriate code templates needed to create or modify the IC agents. Schema changes, if any, which may occur at an existing data source, are also conveyed to the EDF by the CC agent by referring to the last updated tag of the source URI. The scope of the change can then be determined by accessing the ontology document of the data source via the URI before an IC agent is called into service. In the same manner, data sources that are no longer valid are removed from the EDF's listing once the CC agent informs the EDF about the deletion of the data source.

Utility in the Running Example: The loan officer requests an employment check and verification of bank accounts and stock investments of the client. Assuming that an IC agent is already active and deployed to query the employment information data source, all relevant data pertaining to the client will be returned by the IC agent to the EDF. Banks that are in partnership with the loan office are already part of the federation, and IC agents can be called into service to review the bank history of the application. However, if the stock investment firm is newly added to the federation, the EDF can invoke the services of the EMA to create a new IC agent that can interact with the new data source. The results from the IC agents are assimilated by the EDF and presented to the PA. A snippet of the sample OWL document maintained by the EDF is shown in Table 1 (Row 3).

Extensibility Management Agent

The role of the EMA is to help with the actual creation or modification of the IC agents that interact with the data sources. The EMA plays an active role under the following circumstances:

- Creation of new agents to interact with a new data source
  - Instantiation of an IC agent, which maybe derivable from an existing IC type if the new data source is similar to one that already exists
  - Creation of a new IC agent by combining functions from existing agent templates

- o   Instantiation of a new IC agent that is unlike any other exiting IC agent
- Adjustments to existing IC agents to interact with a new data source without having to create a new IC agent
- Provision of agent creation and instantiation mechanisms (downloadable .jar files, .zip files, or .xml files defining the agent-creating criteria) and code templates. If it is determined that there exists no IC agent that can interact with the new data source, EMA will initiate a dialog with the user informing the need to create a new IC template programmatically. The EMA can assist the user in this process by providing the skeletal templates needed to create the new IC agent.

It is the EDF that informs the EMA whether existing IC agents can be modified or a new IC agent has to be created. The EDF uses inference mechanisms by exploiting the ontology information from the OWL-S document to make this decision. If the EDF determines that an existing IC agent can be adjusted, it communicates all necessary reconfiguration information to the EMA, which in turn executes the necessary changes. The EDF will use the OWL-S document to infer the threshold at which dynamic reconfiguration of an existing IC agent will no longer be able to cater to the changes made to the data source (Figure 3).

Since the location of the templates and the source-code archives will also be stored in the OWL-S document managed by the EDF, all necessary files can be made available to the EMA using Java Web-start technology or compressed and archived file formats (such as .gz, .tar, etc.) downloadable from a secure URI location.

Utility in the Running Example: In the FIS environment where the loan officer is currently operating, two IC agents are already active. Let IC_{edb} represent the agent interacting with the employment data source, and IC_{eb} be the agent for the bank. The IC agents can query the local data sources using their corresponding domain ontologies. For example, financial institutions can use any of the open Web financial standards (OFX, XBRL, FIXML, SwiftML, FpML, etc.) for semantic markup that can be interpreted by the IC agent. For a stock investment firm that newly joined the federation, the EDF uses inference drawn from the firm's service-definition URI to determine if an existing IC agent can accomplish the task or a clone has to be instantiated to interface with the data source. The service definition may show that the financial institution uses standard financial markup tags for data description and therefore informs the EMA to create an additional agent, IC_{finvst}, similar to IC_{eb}. In cases where the EDF finds no IC agents with matching roles and no templates are available to invoke the creation of a new IC agent instance, the loan officer will be informed of the exception condition. It is evident that all new IC agents with roles similar to an existing agent, IC_p can be created with minimal human intervention. This is shown in Table 1 (Row 5).

Figure 3.

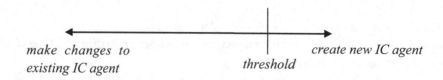

make changes to   create new IC agent
existing IC agent   threshold

Communication Controller

The role of the CC agent is to facilitate communication between the different agent communities and monitor any agent malfunction and inactivity. Changes to the foundation layer through newly added, edited, or deleted local schemas are made known to the EDF by the CC agent. New data sources and services offered by participating organizations are discovered by the CC based on UDDI registry queries. Most multiagent development environments (like the JADE Project and the MadKit Project) are sophisticated enough to recognize agents that join the community as well as to search and discover other agents using some form of white- or yellow-page mechanism. The agent-monitoring and -facilitator mechanism offers advanced functions such as tracking agents using unique names and addresses, discovering services offered by the agents, and searching for agents providing specific services (JADE Project, n.d.). The role of the CC is to capitalize on this core agent-monitoring operative and act as a coordinator to manage the communication between the different IC agents and the EDF. The communication controller traces the addition or deletion of data sources from the FIS and tracks the status modes (active, sleep, inactive, defunct) of all IC agents at the foundation layer. The communication controller works in conjunction with the EDF to handle exceptions during subquery executions on a data source and determine how results from multiple data-source subqueries can be filtered and combined before the results are returned to the end user. The communication controller orchestrates this process through service mediation and query mediation (JADE Project; MadKit Project, n.d.). Service mediation allows agents to identify service components from the participating organizations and combine them to handle specific client requests. After the service components are identified, the query mediator will carry out the query execution on specific views or local schemas. Query mediation breaks down a user query into subqueries against the local schemas. IC agents can execute the subqueries while being aware of the schema restrictions, semantic differences, and structural limitations (Busse et al., 1999) by analyzing the OWL-S document at the local data source.

Utility in the Running Example: As the new stock investment firm decides to join the FIS for providing applicant information to the loan officer, the CC conducts service mediation to identify the URI that describes all services offered by the investment firm. The URI reference is passed to the EDF, which updates its OWL-S document with the new data source reference. The CC plays a vital role in ensuring that the OWL-S document at the EDF stays in congruence with the data sources present in the foundation layer. Query-mediation services allow the CC to designate and structure the subqueries for the newly created IC agent and handle known exceptions in a manner that reduces the need for human intervention. The results are returned to the CC, which then forwards this to the EDF for final verification and compilation. This is shown in Table 1 (Row 4).

Interaction Controller

The architecture presented here involves the cooperative activity of multiple agent communities in conjunction with ontology documents such as OWL-S that describe the semantic structure of the content sources as well as the roles and responsibilities of the agent community. Figure 2 shows the multiagent system that interacts with the data sources in an FIS. The IC agents can perform operations on the data sources by drawing ontological inferences from semantic documents maintained at the data sources. Semantic-based information abstraction has several real-world applications such as constructing summary indexes of available information from the data source, obtaining intensional repositories for data description and localization, deriving support structure for query optimization and view maintenance, and even giving compression schemes that are semantics based (Rosaci, Terracina, & Ursino, 2004). Tools to generate domain ontology from data sources are publicly available and are also provided by popular database software vendors. Ontology maintenance at the data source is the responsibility of the individual organization that participates in the federation. This can be accommodated as part of standard operating procedures undertaken by the personnel in charge of maintaining the local schema. The OWL-S documents will extensively describe the information stubs to access the data sources (data reference ID, connection configuration data, database connectivity driver details, etc.) and allow cardinal values for input subquery conditions, query preconditions, and result output-message formatting syntax (SOAP [simple object access protocol] standards and other programming language support such as API [application programming interface]). It is the IC agent that performs conversation, negotiation, and interaction with the data sources. The OWL-S documents help the IC agents to provide the EDF with subquery results, semantically consolidated views of the data source, specific data descriptions, and other localized information that was requested. Any local data source that maintains OWL-S documents can expose information to the agents via service components that can be discovered and accessed dynamically over the Web using Web services.

Utility in the Running Example: To fulfill the requirements of the loan officer, the agent community at the federation layer (EDF, EMA, and CC) works as a coalition to invoke the appropriate IC agents. The IC agents that are called into service use the OWL-S document at the local data source for executing the subquery operatives. Ontological knowledge of the local schema allows the IC agents to perform the correct operative and return the results to CC. The subquery results are validated for error by the CC

Table 2. Checklist of items to implement the proposed model

Presentation Layer:

> 1. Develop and deploy FIPA compliant Personal Agents (PA) hosted on client systems.
> 2. Customize user interface to allow end user interaction (query, update or modify FIS schema) with the PA.
> 3. PA hosted on single or multiple client systems.

Federation Layer:

> 1. Develop and deploy FIPA compliant agent architecture to support EMA, EDF and CC agents.
> 2. Agent environment can be on single system or distributed systems.
> 3. OWL-S ontology document accessible from reference URI maintains list of participating data sources and IC agent role specifications.

Foundation Layer:

> 1. Local schema managers develop OWL-S ontology documents that are accessible from reference URI.
> 3. Configure web services to expose OWL-S ontology document to the IC agents.
> 2. Deploy and develop FIPA compliant Interaction Controller (IC) agents at the local schema host systems.

and forwarded to the EDF, which in turn passes the final outcomes to the PA. This is shown in Table 1 (Row 6 and Row 7).

The different steps involved in implementing the proposed model are shown in Table 2. Any FIPA-compliant agent environment is used to support the agent architecture at the presentation, federation, and foundation layers. At the presentation layer, personal agents with customized user interfaces are deployed on a single or multiple hosts. The agent environment at the federation layer supports EMA, EDF, and CC agents on a single system or across a distributed architecture. Schema managers are responsible for developing the OWL-S ontology documents at the foundation layer, and Web services are configured at this layer to expose the OWL-S documents to the IC agents using reference URIs. The agent architecture at this layer enables direct binding between the IC agents and the local schemas at the individual host systems.

CONCLUSION

Although FIS models operate efficiently in a tightly coupled federation, the evolution pattern of the Web is forcing a switch toward using loosely coupled federations of information sources. Loosely coupled FISs pose immediate formidable integration challenges, especially when flexibility to allow organizations to join or leave the federation is highly desired. This chapter presents an extensibility model with sumptuous bargaining power over traditional models of loose coupling. By integrating the fundamental concepts borrowed from the semantic Web model (Berners-Lee et al., 2001) with the FIS architecture, we inherit a solution model that is natural and semantically eliminates reliance on permanent structures. The use of the multiagent system and documents based on ontology Web languages helps to construe an extensible FIS model that is not simply adaptable to changes, but can also encourage organizations to create mutually beneficial federations that is void of physical or geographical rigidity.

The major contribution of this work is the demonstration that FIPA-compliant agents within a semantic Web framework can offer support for extensibility in a loosely coupled FIS. This is increasingly important as the semantic Web framework becomes widely adopted in the future. The research also demonstrates how the use of ontology markup (OWL-S) allows semantic heterogeneity irrespective of the structural heterogeneity in the data model at the participating organizations. The model provides implementation details regarding the ability to publish and access the OWL-S documents as URI references. This allows independence between the agent framework and the information sources while allowing the agent architecture to reconfigure and adjust based on the individual data-source profile. The chapter demonstrates this using a real-world example.

This research assumes that agents have direct access to ontology documents stored at the local data sources. Although this may be viewed as a limitation of the model, it was necessary in order to clearly present how an agent community can effortlessly adapt and operate in an FIS where new content sources are added constantly or changes are made to existing content sources. For the same reason, we did not address data quality explicitly, but recognize that it is an important issue in FISs. Both data-quality and access-control issues are heavily researched areas, and there is no discernable reason why outcomes from existing research cannot be included into the proposed model. Left for future research is the task of performance testing and evaluation. Although the implementation and testing of the framework may not be an easy task, it will be a worthwhile effort since simplistic forms of loosely coupled semantic Web infrastructures are making inroads into personal and commercial computing environments.

REFERENCES

Baader, F., Calvanese, D., McGuinness, D., Nardi, D., & Patel-Schneider, P.F. (Eds.). (2003). *The description logic handbook: Theory, implementation and applications.* Cambridge: Cambridge University Press.

Berners-Lee, T., Hendler, J., & Lassila, O. (2001). The Semantic Web. *Scientific American*, 36-43.

Busse, S., Kutsche, R., Leser, U., & Weber, H. (1999). Federated information systems: Concepts, terminology, and architectures. *Federated information systems.* Retrieved from http://citeseer.ist.psu. edu/cache/papers/cs/8150/http:zSzzSzcis.cs.tu-berlin

FIPA2000 compliant agent development environment. (n.d.). Retrieved March 27, 2006, from http://jade. tilab.com

Foundation for Intelligent Physical Agents (FIPA). (n.d.). Retrieved March 27, 2006, from http://www. fipa.org

Hasselbring, W., Heuvel, W., & Roantree, M. (2000). Research and practice in federated information systems: Report of the EFIS 2000 International Workshop. *SIGMOD Record, 29*(4), 16-18.

JADE Project. (n.d.). *Jade white paper.* Retrieved March 27, 2006, from http://jade.cselt.it/

Jarke, M., Jeusfeld, M., Quix, C., & Vassiliadis, P. (1999). Architecture and quality in data warehouses: An extended repository approach. *Information Systems, 24*(3), 229-253.

Jennings, N., Sycara, K., & Wooldridge, M. (1998). A roadmap of agent research and development. *International Journal of Autonomous Agents and Multi-Agent Systems, 1*(1), 7-38.

Labrou, Y., & Finin, T. (1997). Semantics and conversations for an agent communication language. In *Readings in agents* (pp. 235-242). Morgan Kaufmann Publishers Inc.

MadKit Project. (n.d.). *MadKit documentation.* Retrieved March 27, 2006 from http://www.madkit. org/madkit/doc/index.php3

Martin, D., Burstein, M., Lassila, O., Paolucci, M., Payne, T., & McIlraith, S. (2003). Retrieved from http://www.daml.org/services/owl-s/1.0/owl-s-wsdl.html

Nodine, M., Bohrer, W., & Ngu, A. (1999). Semantic brokering over dynamic heterogeneous data sources in InfoSleuth. *15th International Conference on Data Engineering*, 358-365.

Open Financial Exchange (OFX). (2006). *Open Financial Exchange home page.* Retrieved from March 27, 2006, from http://www.ofx.net/ofx/default.asp

OWL-S. (n.d.). Retrieved March 10, 2006, from http://www.daml.org/services/owl-s/1.0/

Rosaci, D., Terracina, G., & Ursino, D. (2004). A framework for abstracting data sources having heterogeneous representation formats. *Data & Knowledge Engineering, 48*(1), 1-38.

Service Component Architecture (SCA). (2005). *Service component architecture and service data objects.* Retrieved March 27, 2006, from http://www.128.ibm.com/developerworks/webservices/library/ specification/ws-scasdosumm/

Sheth, A. P., & Larson, J. A. (1990). Federated database systems for managing distributed, heterogeneous, and autonomous databases. *ACM Computing Surveys, 22*(3), 183-236.

Thomas, M., Redmond, R., Yoon, V., & Singh, R. (2005). A semantic approach to monitor business process performance. *Communications of the ACM, 48,* 55-59.

Zimmermann, O., Krogdahl, P., & Gee, C. (2004). *Elements of service-oriented analysis and design.* Retrieved from http://www-128.ibm.com/developerworks/webservices/library/ws-soad1/

Zou, Y., Finin, T., Ding, L., Chen, H., & Pan, R. (2003). Using semantic Web technology in multi-agent systems: A case study in the TAGA trading agent environment. *Proceedings of the 5th International Conference on Electronic Commerce* (pp. 95-101).

This work was previously published in International Journal of Intelligent Information Technologies, Vol. 3, Issue 3, edited by V. Sugumaran, pp. 1-20, copyright 2007 by IGI Publishing, formerly known as Idea Group Publishing (an imprint of IGI Global).

Chapter VII
Modeling Fault Tolerant and Secure Mobile Agent Execution in Distributed Systems

H. Hamidi
Iran University of Science & Technology, Iran-Tehran

K. Mohammadi
Iran University of Science & Technology, Iran-Tehran

ABSTRACT

The reliable execution of mobile agents is a very important design issue in building mobile agent systems and many fault-tolerant schemes have been proposed so far. Security is a major problem of mobile agent systems, especially when monetary transactions are concerned. Security for the partners involved is handled by encryption methods based on a public key authentication mechanism and by secret key encryption of the communication. To achieve fault tolerance for the agent system, especially for the agent transfer to a new host, we use distributed transaction processing. We propose a fault-tolerant approach for mobile agents design which offers a user transparent fault tolerance that can be activated on request, according to the needs of the task. We also discuss how transactional agents with different types of commitment constraints can commit transactions. Furthermore, we present a solution for effective agent deployment using dynamic agent domains.

INTRODUCTION

A mobile agent is a software program which migrates from a site to another site to perform tasks assigned by a user. For the mobile agent system to support agents in various application areas, the issues regarding reliable agent execution, as well as compatibility between two different agent systems or secure agent migration, have been considered. Some of the proposed schemes are either replicating the agents (Hamidi & Mohammadi, 2005) or check-pointing the agents (Park, Byun, Kim, & Yeom, 2002; Pleisch & Schiper, 2001;) For a single agent environment without considering inter-agent communication, the performance of the replication scheme and the check-pointing scheme is compared in Park et al. (2002) and Silva, Batista, and Silva (2000). In the area of mobile agents, only few works can be found relating to fault tolerance. Most of them refer to special agent systems or cover only some special aspects relating to mobile agents, such as the communication subsystem. Nevertheless, most people working with mobile agents consider fault tolerance to be an important issue (Izatt, Chan, & Brecht, 1999; Shiraishi, Enokido, & Takzawa, 2003). Mobile agents are becoming a major trend for designing distributed systems and applications in the last few years and foreseeable future. It can bring benefits such as reduced network load and overcoming of network latency (Chan, Won, & Lyu, 1993). Nevertheless, security is one of the limiting factors of the development of these systems. The main unsolved security problem lies in the possible existence of malicious hosts that can manipulate the execution and data of agents (Defago, Schiper, & Sergent, 1998). Most distributed applications we see today are deploying the *client/server paradigm*. There are certain problems with the client/server paradigm, such as the requirement of a high network bandwidth, and continuous user-computer interactivity.

In view of the deficiencies of the client/server paradigm, the *mobile code paradigm* has been developed as an alternative approach for distributed application design. In the client/server paradigm, programs cannot move across different machines and must run on the machines they reside on. The mobile code paradigm, on the other hand, allows programs to be transferred among and executed on different computers. By allowing code to move between hosts, programs can interact on the same computer instead of over the network. Therefore, communication cost can be reduced. Besides, *mobile agent* (Fischer, Lynch, & Paterson, 1983) programs can be designed to work on behalf of users autonomously. This autonomy allows users to delegate their tasks to the mobile agents, and not to stay continuously in front of the computer terminal. The promises of the mobile code paradigm bring about active research in its realization. Most researchers, however, agree that security concerns are a hurdle (Greenberg, Byington, & Harper, 1998).

In this chapter, we investigate these concerns. First, we review some of the foundation materials of the mobile code paradigm. We elaborate Ghezzi and Vigna's classification of mobile code paradigms (Ghezzi & Vigna, 1997), which is a collection of the *remote evaluation, code on demand,* and *mobile agent* approaches. In the next section, we address the current status of mobile code security. The following section presents the model for fault-tolerant mobile agent. In the next section, security issues of the mobile agent are discussed, and we discuss security modeling and evaluation for the mobile agent in the section after. In the following section, simulation results and influence of the size of agent are discussed. We then conclude the chapter.

THE MOBILE CODE PARADIGM

The mobile code paradigm is essentially a collective term, applicable wherever there is mobility of code. While different classes of code mobility have been identified, Ghezzi and Vigna proposed three of them, namely *remote evaluation, code on demand,* and *mobile agent* (1997). This classification, together with the client/server paradigm, is summarized in Table 1.

Table 1. Ghezzi and Vigna's (1997) classification of mobile code paradigms

Paradigm		Local side	Remote side	Computation takes place at
Client/server		--	Know-how	Remote side
			Processor	
			Resources	
Mobile code	Remote evaluation	Know-how ----------	→	Remote side
Mobile code			Processor	
Mobile code			Resources	
......	Code on demand		←	... Know-how	Local side
......		Processor		
......		Resources		
......	Mobile agent	Know-how	→	Remote side
......		Processor ----------	→	
......			Resources	

In particular, the "know-how" in Table 1 represents the code that is to be executed for the specific task. In the mobile code paradigms (*remote evaluation, code on demand,* and *mobile agent*), the *know-how* moves from one side to another side regarding where the computation takes place; while in the client/server paradigm, the *know-how* is stationary on the remote (server) side. *Resources* are the input and output for the code, whereas *processor* is the abstract machine that carries out and holds the state of the computation. The arrows represent the directions in which the specific item should move before the required task is carried out. Ghezzi and Vigna's classification is found to be comprehensive and representative of most existing mobile code paradigms (such as the rsh utility, Java applets and mobile agent systems), and we will base our discussion on this classification.

SECURITY CONCERNS OF MOBILE CODE PARADIGMS

In this section, we discuss some possible security attacks to different mobile code paradigms, and possible mechanisms against these attacks.

Security Attacks

A security attack is an action that compromises the security requirements of an application. Applications developed using different paradigms are subject to different attacks. In the conventional client/server model, the local computer is usually assumed to be a secure premise ("*information fortress*") for code and data. This effectively limits the source of security attacks to outsiders of the local machine. Therefore, the main possible attacks are *masquerading* (pretending to be the server or the client), *eavesdropping* on the communication channel, and *forging messages* to the client or the server.

While the security fortress model is usually assumed in the client/server paradigm, it also applies to the *remote evaluation* and *code-on-demand* approaches, with the additional concern that the code receiving side must make sure the code is not harmful to run. In remote evaluation, the code receiving side is the remote side, while it is the local side in code-on-demand.

Mobile agent, on the other hand, is the most challenging area of mobile code security, due to the autonomy of agents. Mobile agent security is usually divided into two aspects: *host security* and *agent security*. Host security deals with the protection of hosts against malicious agents or other hosts, while agent security deals with the protection of agents against malicious hosts or other agents. For host security, the security fortress model can still apply. However, it hardly applies to agent security, due to the lack of trusted hardware with which to anchor security (Tschudin, 1999). There are two branches of new possible attacks to agents:

1.   **Data tampering:** A host or another agent may modify the data or execution state being carried by an agent for malicious purpose.
2.   **Execution tampering:** A host may change the code executed by an agent, or rearrange the code execution sequence for malicious purpose.

Security Mechanisms

Security mechanisms are mechanisms designed to prevent, detect or recover from security attacks. We see from the previous section that the main security challenges of the client/server paradigm are the mutual trust building between clients and servers, plus the protection of messages in transit. These problems can be satisfactorily solved by cryptographic techniques such as *security protocols* and *message encryption*. These mechanisms are already extensively employed in existing client/server applications. A lot of details can be found in Schneier (1996) and Stallings (1999).

As there are more possible attacks to mobile code paradigms, more mechanisms are required to secure mobile code applications. We see from a previous section that the main additional challenge to security of mobile code paradigms is the verification of the received code. One significant approach to this problem is the *sandbox model*. In the sandbox model, the code or agent received from a remote side can only access a dedicated portion of system resources. Therefore, even if the received code or agent is malicious, damage would be confined to the resources dedicated to that code or agent.

While the sandbox technique is well known and generally accepted for host security, there is yet no good mechanism for agent security. Some approaches have been proposed, and they can be classified into two categories. The first category is agent-tampering detection. These techniques aim at detecting whether an agent's execution or data have been tampered with along the journey. Some possible approaches are *range verification, timing information, addition of dummy data items and code,* and *cryptographic watermarks* (Tschudin, 1999). Another category is agent-tampering prevention. These techniques aim at preventing agent code or data being tampered with. Two representative approaches are the *execution of encrypted functions* (Sander & Tschudin, 1998) and *time-limited black-boxes* (Hohl, 1998). These approaches are enlightening in the way they open new areas in computer security. Yet they provide limited protection to agents for the time being. Agent protection is still in its early stage, compared with the maturity of protection for hosts and client/servers, and efforts should be spent on improving the already-proposed mechanisms, or developing new protection mechanisms.

MODEL

We assume an asynchronous distributed system, that is, there are no bounds on transmission delays of messages or on relative process speeds. An example of an asynchronous system is the Internet. Processes communicate via message passing over a fully connected network.

Mobile Agent Model

A mobile agent executes on a sequence of machines, where a place $P_i (0 \leq i \leq n)$ provides the logical execution environment for the agent. Each place runs a set of services, which together compose the state of the place. For simplicity, we say that the agent "accesses the state of the place," although access occurs through a service running on the place. Executing the agent at a place P_i is called a stage S_i of the agent execution. We call the places where the first and last stages of an agent execute (i.e., P_i and P_n) the agent source and destination, respectively. The sequence of places between the agent source and destination (i.e., $P_0, P_1, \dots P_n$) is called the itinerary of a mobile agent. Whereas a static itinerary is entirely defined at the agent source and does not change during the agent execution, a dynamic itinerary is subject to modifications by the agent itself.

Logically, a mobile agent executes in a sequence of stage actions (Figure 1). Each stage action consists of potentially a multiple set of operations $op_0, op_1, \dots op_n$. Agent $A_i (0 \leq i \leq n)$ at the corresponding stage S_i represents the agent that has executed the stage action on places $P_j (j < i)$ and is about to execute on place P_i. The execution of A_i at place P_i results in a new internal state of the agent as well as potentially a new state of the place (if the operations of an agent have side effects, i.e., are non idempotent). We denote the resulting agent A_{i+1}. Place P_i forwards to P_{i+1} (for $i < n$).

Fault Model

Several types of faults can occur in agent environments. Here, we first describe a general fault model, and focus on those types, which are important in agent environments due to high occurrence probability, and those that have been addressed in related work insufficiently.

- **Node failures:** The complete failure of a compute node implies the failure of all agent places and agents located on it. Node failures can be temporary or permanent.

Figure 1. Model of mobile agent execution with three stages

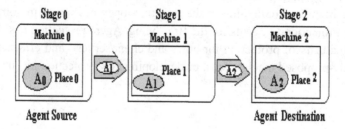

- **Failures of components of the agent system:** Failures of agent places, or components of agent places become faulty, for example, faulty communication units or incomplete agent directory. These faults can result in agent failures, or in reduced or wrong functionality of agents.
- **Failures of mobile agents:** Mobile agents can become faulty due to faulty computation, or other faults (e.g., node or network failures).
- **Network failures:** Failures of the entire communication network or of single links can lead to isolation of single nodes, or to network partitions.
- **Falsification or loss of messages:** These are usually caused by failures in the network or in the communication units of the agent systems, or the underlying operating systems. Also, faulty transmission of agents during migration belongs to this type.

Especially in the intended scenario of parallel applications, node failures and their consequences are important. Such consequences are loss of agents, and loss of node specific resources. In general, each agent has to fulfill a specific task to contribute to the parallel application, and thus, agent failures must be treated with care. In contrast, in applications where a large number of agents are sent out to search and process information in a network, the loss of one or several mobile agents might be acceptable (Pleisch & Schiper, 2000, 2001).

Model Failures

Machines, places, or agents can fail and recover later. A component that has failed but not yet recovered is called down; otherwise, it is up. If it is eventually permanently up, it is called good (Aguilera, 2000). In this chapter, we focus on crash failures (i.e., processes prematurely halted). Benign and malicious failures (i.e., Byzantine failures) are not discussed. A failing place causes the failure of all agents running on it. Similarly, a failing machine causes all places and agents on this machine to fail as well. We do not consider deterministic, repetitive programming errors (i.e., programming errors that occur on all agent replicas or places) in the code or the place as relevant failures in this context. Finally a link failure causes the loss of messages or agents currently in transmission on this link and may lead to network partitioning. We assume that link failures (and network partitions) are not permanent. The failure of a component (i.e., agent, place, machine, or communication link) can lead to blocking in the mobile agent execution.

Figure 2. The redundant places mask the place failure

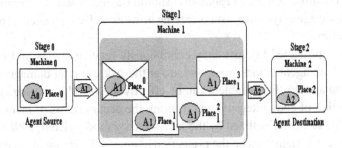

Assume, for instance that place P_1 fails while executing A_1 (Figure 2). While P_1 is down, the execution of the mobile agent cannot proceed, that is, it is blocked. Blocking occurs if a single failure prevents the execution from proceeding. In contrast, an execution is non-blocking if it can proceed despite a single failure, the blocked mobile agent execution can only continue when the failed component recovers. This requires that recovery mechanism be in place, which allows the failed component to be recovered. If no recovery mechanism exists, then the agent's state and potentially its code may be lost. In the following, we assume that such a recovery mechanism exists (e.g., based on logging [Ghezzi & Vigna, 1997]). Replication prevents blocking. Instead of sending the agent to one place at the next stage, agent replicas are sent to a set of M_i places P_i^0, P_i^1,.., P_i^n (Figure 2). We denote by A_i^j the agent replica of A_i executing on place P_i^j, but will omit the superscripted index if the meaning is clear from the context. Although a place may crash (i.e., Stage 1 in Figure 2), the agent execution does not block. Indeed, P_2^1 can take over the execution of a1 and thus prevent blocking. Note that the execution at stages S_0 and S_2 is not replicated as the agent is under the control of the user. Moreover, the agent is only configured at the agent source and presents the results to the agent owner at the agent destination. Hence, replication is not needed at these stages.

Despite agent replication, network partitions can still prevent the progress of the agent. Indeed, if the network is partitioned such that all places currently executing the agent at stage S_i are in one partition and the places of stage S_{i+1} are in another partition, the agent cannot proceed with its execution. Generally (especially on the Internet), multiple routing paths are possible for a message to arrive at its destination. Therefore, a link failure may not always lead to network partitioning. In the following, we assume that a single link failure merely partitions one place from the rest of the network. Clearly, this is a simplification, but it allows us to define blocking concisely. Indeed, in the approach presented in this chapter, progress in the agent execution is possible in a network partition that contains a majority of places. If no such partition exists, the execution is temporally interrupted until a majority partition is established again. Moreover, catastrophic failures may still cause the loss of the entire agent. A failure of all places in M_i (Figure 2), for instance, is such a catastrophic failure (assuming no recovery mechanism is in place). As no copy of A_i is available any more, the agent A_i is lost and, obviously, the agent execution can no longer proceed. In other words, replication does not solve all problems. The definition of non-blocking merely addresses single failures per stage as they cover most of the failures that occur in a realistic environment.

SECURITY ISSUES OF THE MOBILE AGENT

Any distributed system is subject to security threats, so is a mobile agent system. Issues such as encryption, authorization, authentication, non-repudiation should be addressed in a mobile agent system. In addition, a secure mobile agent system must protect the hosts as well as the agents from being tampered with by malicious parties.

First, hosts must be protected because they continuously receive agents and execute them. They may not be sure where an agent comes from, and are at the risk of being damaged by malicious code or agents (Trojan horse attack). This problem can be effectively solved by strong authentication of the code sources, verification of code integrity, and limiting the access rights of incoming agents to local resources of hosts. This is mostly realized by the Java security model (Hohl, 1998). The main security challenge of mobile agent systems lies on the protection of agents. When an agent executes on a remote host, the host is likely to have access to all the data and code carried by the agent. If by chance a host is malicious and abuses the code or data of an agent, the privacy and secrecy of the agent and its owner would be at risk.

Seven types of attack by malicious hosts (Defago, Schiper, & Sergent, 1998) can be identified:

1. Spying out and manipulation of code;
2. Spying out and manipulation of data;
3. Spying out and manipulation of control flow;
4. Incorrect execution of code;
5. Masquerading of the host;
6. Spying out and manipulation of interaction with other agents; and
7. Returning wrong results of system calls to agents.

There are a number of solutions proposed to protect agents against malicious hosts (Chan et al., 1993), which can be divided into three streams:

- Establishing a closed network: Limiting the set of hosts among which agents travel such that agents travel only to hosts that are trusted.
- Agent tampering detection: Using specially designed state-appraisal functions to detect whether agent states have been changed maliciously during its travel.
- Agent tampering prevention: Hiding from hosts the data possessed by agents and the functions to be computed by agents, by messing up code and data of agents, or using cryptographic techniques.

None of the proposed solutions solve the problem completely. They either limit the capabilities of mobile agents, or are not restrictive enough. A better solution is being sought, and there is no general methodology suggested to protect agents. In the mean time, developers of mobile agent systems have to develop their own methodologies according to their own needs. Apart from attacks by malicious hosts, it is also possible that an agent attacks another agent. However, this problem, when compared with the problem of malicious hosts, is less important, because the actions of a (malicious) agent to another agent can be effectively monitored and controlled by the host on which the agent runs, if the host is not malicious.

Table 2. Analogy between reliability and security

Security	Reliability
Vulnerabilities	Faults
Breach	Failure
Fail upon attack effort spent	Fail upon usage time elapsed

SECURITY MODELING AND EVALUATION FOR THE MOBILE AGENT

There is no well-established model for mobile agent security. One of the few attempts so far is given in Hohl (1998). Software reliability modeling is a successful attempt to give quantitative measures of software systems. In the broadest sense, security is one of the aspects of reliability. A system is likely to be more reliable if it is more secure. One of the pioneering efforts to integrate security and reliability is (Brocklehurst, Littlewood, Olovsoon, & Jonsson, 1994). In this chapter, the following similarities between security and reliability were observed.

Thus, we have *security function, effort to next breach distribution,* and *security hazard rate* similar to the *reliability function, time to next failure distribution,* and *reliability hazard rate* respectively as in reliability theory. One of the works to incorporate system security into a mathematical model is (Jonsson, 1997), which presents an experiment to model the attacker behavior. The results show that during the "standard attack phase," assuming breaches are independent and stochastically identical, the period of working time of a single attacker between successive breaches is found to be exponentially distributed.

Now, let us consider a mobile agent traveling through n hosts on the network, as illustrated in Figure 3. Each host, and the agent itself, is modeled as an abstract machine as in Hohl (1998). We consider only the standard attack phase described in Jonsson (1997)) by malicious hosts. On arrival at a malicious host, the mobile agent is subject to an attack effort from the host. Because the host is modeled as a machine, it is reasonable to estimate the attack effort by the number of instructions for the attack to carry out, which would be linearly increasing with time. On arrival at a non-malicious host, the effort would be constant zero. Let the agent arrive at host i at time T_i, for $i = 1, 2, ..., n$. Then the effort of host i at total time t would be described by the *time-to-effort function*:

$E_i(t) = k_i(t - T_i)$, where k is a constant

We may call the constant k_i the *coefficient of malice*. The larger the k_i, the more malicious host i is $(ki = 0$ if host i is non-malicious). Furthermore, let the agent stay on host i for an amount of time t_i, then there would be breach to the agent if and only if the following breach condition holds:

$E_i(t_i + T_i) >$ effort to next breach by host i

that is, $k_i t_i >$ effort to next breach by host i

Figure 3. A mobile agent traveling on a network

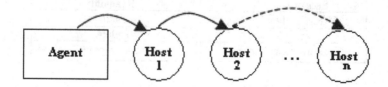

As seen from Brocklehurst et al. (1994) and Jonsson (1997), it is reasonable to assume exponential distribution of the effort to next breach, so we have the *probability of breach at host i,*

P(breach at host i)

$\quad$ = P(breach at time $t_i + T_i$)

$\quad$ = P(breach at effort $k_i t_i$)

$\quad$ = $1 - exp(-vk_i t_i)$, v is a constant

$\quad$ = $1 - exp(-\lambda_i t_i)$, $\lambda_i = vk_i$

We may call v the *coefficient of vulnerability* of the agent. The higher the v, the higher is the probability of breach to the agent. Therefore, the *agent security E* would be the probability of no breach at all hosts, that is,

$$E = \prod_{i=1}^{n} e^{-\lambda_i t_i} = e^{-\sum_{i=1}^{n} \lambda_i t_i}$$

Suppose that we can estimate the coefficients of malice k_i's for hosts based on trust records of hosts, and also estimate the coefficient of vulnerability v of the agent based on testing and experiments, then we can calculate the desired time limits T_i's to achieve a certain level of security E. Conversely, if users specify some task must be carried out on a particular host for a fixed period of time, we can calculate the agent security E for the users based on the coefficients of malice and vulnerability estimates.

EVALUATION RESULTS AND INFLUENCE OF THE SIZE OF THE AGENT

We evaluate transactional agents in terms of access time compared with client-server model. The computation of mobile agents is composed of moving, class loading, manipulation of objects, creation of clone, and commitment steps. In the client-server model, there are computation steps of program initialization, class loading to client, manipulation of objects, and two-phase commitment.

Access time from the time when the application program starts to the time when the application program ends is measured for agents and the client-server model. Figure 4 shows the access time for a number of object servers. The non-fault tolerant and secure mobile agents show that mobile agent classes are not loaded when an agent A_i arrives at an object server. Here, the agent can be executed after Aglets classes are loaded. On the other hand, the fault tolerant and secure mobile agents mean that an agent manipulates objects in each object server where mobile agent classes are already loaded, that is, the agent comes to the object server after other agents have visited on the object server. As shown in Figure 4, the client-server model is faster than the transactional agent. However, the transactional agent is faster than the client-server model if object servers are frequently manipulated, that is, fault tolerant and secure mobile agent classes are a priori loaded.

A simulator was designed to evaluate the algorithm. The system was tested in several simulated network conditions and numerous parameters were introduced to control the behavior of the agents. We also investigated the dynamic functioning of the algorithm. Comparing to the previous case, the parameter configuration has a larger effect on the behavior of the system. The most vital parameter was the frequency of the trading process and the pre-defined critical workload values.

Figure 4. Access time for number of object servers

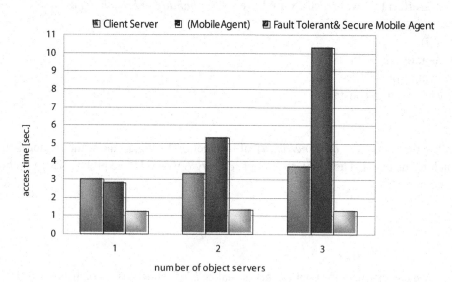

Figure 5. The size of the agent population under changing network conditions

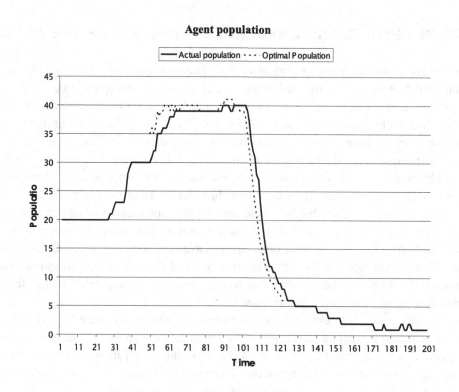

Figure 6. Costs of single and replicated agent execution increasing agent size

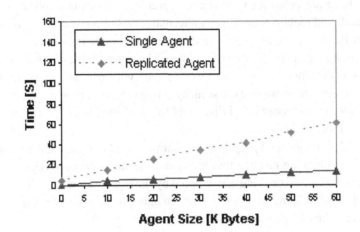

Figure 5 shows the number of agents on the network in a dynamic network situation. The optimal agent population is calculated by dividing the workload on the whole network with the optimal workload of the agent. Simulation results show that by choosing the correct agent parameters the workload of agents is within ten percent of the predefined visiting frequency on a stable network. In a simulated network the population overload dynamically grows to meet the increased requirements and smoothly returns back to normal when the congestion is over.

To measure the performance of fault tolerant mobile agent system our test consists of sequentially sending a number of agents that increment the value of the counter at each stage of the execution. Each agent starts at the agent source and returns to the agent destination, which allows us to measure its round–trip time. Between two agents, the places are not restarted. Consequently, the first agent needs considerably longer for its execution, as all classes need to be loaded into the cache of the virtual machines. Consecutive agents benefit from already cached classes and thus execute much faster. We do not consider the first agent execution in our measurement results. For a fair comparison, we used the same approach for the single agent case (no replication). Moreover, we assume that the Java class files are locally available in each place. Clearly, this is a simplification, as the class files do not need to be transported with the agent. Remote class loading adds additional costs because the classes have to be transported with the agent and then loaded into the virtual machine. However, once the classes are loaded into the class loader, other agents can take advantage of them and do not need to load these classes again.

The size of the agent has a considerable impact on the performance of the fault-tolerant mobile agent execution. To measure this impact, the agent carries a Byte array of variable length used to increase the size of the agent. As the results in Figure 6 show, the execution time of the agent increases linearly with increasing size of the agent. Compared to the single agent, the slope of the curve for the replicated agent is steeper.

CONCLUSION

In this chapter, we have presented the mobile code paradigm, which is a collection of remote evaluation, code on demand, and mobile agents, as an alternative to the conventional client/server paradigm. We examine security concerns of the mobile code paradigm, and survey existing security attacks and mechanisms to evaluate the current status of mobile code security. We conclude that the mobile code paradigm is still to be developed with respect to its security aspects and that mobile agent protection needs particular attention. To investigate the security threats to mobile agents, we implemented a simple Traveling Information Agent System, and discussed the possible attacks to the agents in this system, based on the attack model in [26].

We have identified two important properties for fault-tolerant mobile agent execution: non-blocking and exactly-once. Non-blocking ensures that the agent execution proceeds despite a single failure of either agent, place, or machine. Blocking is prevented by the use of replication. This chapter discussed a mobile agent model for processing transactions, which manipulate object servers. An agent first moves to an object server and then manipulates objects.

General possibilities for achieving fault tolerance in such cases were discussed and the respective advantages and disadvantages for mobile agent environments and the intended parallel and distributed application scenarios were shown. This leads to an approach based on warm standby and receiver side message logging. We have used dynamically changing agent domains to provide flexible, adaptive and robust operation. The performance measurement of Fault-Tolerant Mobile Agent System shows the overhead introduced by the replication mechanisms with respect to a non-replicated agent. Not surprisingly, it also shows that this overhead increases with the number of stages and the size of the agent.

REFERENCES

Aguilera, M. K., Chen, W. & Toueg, S. (2000). Failure detection and consensus in the crash-recovery model. *Distributed Computing, 13*(2), 99-125.

Brocklehurst, S., Littlewood, B., Olovsson, T., & Jonsson, E. (1994). On measurement of operational security. In *Proceedings of the Ninth Conference on Computer Assurance (COMPASS'94): Safety, Reliability, Fault Tolerance and Real Time, Security* (pp. 257-266).

Chan, H. W., Wong, K. M., & Lyu, R. (1993). Design ,implementation ,and experimentation on mobile agent security for electronic commerce application. In S. Mullender (Ed.), *Distributed systems* (2nd ed.) (pp. 199-216), Reading, MA: Addison-Wesley.

Chess, D., Harrison, C. G., & Kershenbaum, A. (1998). Mobile agents: Are they a good idea? In G. Vigna (Ed.), *Mobile agents and security* (pp. 25-47). Springer-Verlag.

Defago, X., Schiper, A. & Sergent, N. (1998, October). Semi-passive replication. In *Proceedings of the 17th IEEE Symposium on Reliable Distributed System (SRDS'98)* (pp. 43-50).

Fischer, M. J., Lynch, N. A. & Paterson, M. S. (1983, March). Impossibility of distributed consensus with one faulty process. In *Proceedings of the second ACM SIGACT-SIGMOD Symposium: Principles of Database System* (p. 17).

Ghezzi, C. & Vigna, G. (1997, April). Mobile code paradigms and technologies: A case study. In K. Rothermet, R. Popescu-Zeletin (Eds.), *Mobile Agents, First International Workshop, MA'97, Proceedings, LNCS 1219* (pp. 39-49), Berlin, Germany. Springer.

Greenberg, M. S., Byington, J. C., & Harper, D. G. (1998). Mobile agents and security. *IEEE Communications Magazine, 367.*

Hamidi, H. & Mohammadi, K. (2005, March). Modeling and evaluation of fault tolerant mobile agents in distributed systems. In *Proceedings of the 2nd IEEE Conference on Wireless & Optical Communications Networks (WOCN2005)* (pp. 91-95).

Hohl, F. (1998a) Time limited Blackbox security: Protecting mobile agents from malicious hosts. In G. Vigna (Ed.), *Mobile agents and security, LNCS 1419* (pp. 92-113). Springer.

Hohl, F. (1998b). A model of attacks of malicious hosts against mobile agents. In *Fourth Workshop on Mobile Object Systems (MOS'98): Secure Internet Mobile Computations.* Retrieved from http://cuiwww. unige.ch/~ecoopws/ws98/papers/hohl.ps

Hohl, F. (1998c). A model of attacks of malicious hosts against mobile agents. In *Proceedings of the ECOOP Workshop on Distributed Object Security and 4th Workshop on Object Systems: Secure Internet mobile computations* (pp. 105-120), Inria, France.

Izatt, M., Chan, P., & Brecht, T. (1999, June). Agents: Towards an environment for parallel, distributed and mobile Java applications. In *Proceedings of the 1999 ACM Conference on Java Grande* (pp. 15-24).

Jonsson, E. (1997). A quantitative model of the security intrusion process based on attacker behavior. *IEEE Transactions on Software Engineering, 23*(4).

Park, T., Byun, I., Kim, H. & Yeom, H. Y. (2002). The performance of checkpointing and replication schemes for fault tolerant mobile agent systems. In *Proceedings of the 21st IEEE Symposium on Reliable Distributed Systems.*

Pleisch, S. & Schiper, A. (2000). Modeling fault: Tolerant mobile agent execution as a sequence of agree problems. In *Proceedings of the 19th IEEE Symposium on Reliable Distributed Systems* (pp. 11-20).

Pleisch, S. & Schiper, A. (2001, July). FATOMAS — A Fault-Tolerant Mobile Agent System based on the agent-dependent approach. In *Proceedings of the 2001 International Conference on Dependable Systems and Networks* (pp. 215-224).

Pleisch, S. & Schiper, A. (2003). Fault-tolerant mobile agent execution. *IEEE Transactions on Computers, 52*(2).

Sander, T. & Tschudin, C. F. (1998). Protecting mobile agents against malicious hosts. In G. Vigna (Ed.), *Mobile agents and security, LNCS 1419* (pp. 44-60). Springer.

Schneier, B. (1996). *Applied cryptography.* Wiley.

Shiraishi, M., Enokido, T. & Takizawa, M. (2003). Fault-tolerant mobile agents in distributed objects systems. In *Proceedings of the Ninth IEEE Workshop on Future Trends of Distributed Computer Systems (FTDCS, 03)* (pp. 11-20).

Silva, L. Batista, V., & Silva, L.G. (2000). Fault-tolerant execution of mobile agents. In *Proceedings of the International Conference on Dependable Systems and IIIenvorks.*

Stallings, W. (1999). *Cryptography and network security, principles and practice.* Prentice Hall.

Strasser, M. & Rothermel, K. (2000). System mechanism for partial rollback of mobile agent execution. In *Proceedings of the 20th International Conference on Distributed Computing Systems.*

Tschudin, C. F. (1999). Mobile agent security. In M. Klusch (Ed.), *Intelligent information agents* [Forthcoming *LNCS*]. Retrieved from http://www.docs.uu.se/~tschudin/pub/cft-1999-iia.ps.gz

This work was previously published inInternational Journal of Intelligent Information Technologies, Vol. 2, Issue 1, edited by V. Sugumaran, pp. 21-36, copyright 2006 by IGI Publishing, formerly known as Idea Group Publishing (an imprint of IGI Global).

Section II
Search and Retrieval

Chapter VIII
Search Engine Performance Comparisons

Xiannong Meng
Bucknell University, USA

Song Xing
California State University—Los Angeles, USA

ABSTRACT

This chapter reports the results of a project attempting to assess the performance of a few major search engines from various perspectives. The search engines involved in the study include the Microsoft Search Engine (MSE) when it was in its beta test stage, AllTheWeb, and Yahoo. In a few comparisons, other search engines such as Google, Vivisimo are also included. The study collects statistics such as the average user response time, average process time for a query reported by MSE, as well as the number of pages relevant to a query reported by all search engines involved. The project also studies the quality of search results generated by MSE and other search engines using RankPower as the metric. We found MSE performs well in speed and diversity of the query results, while weaker in other statistics, compared to some other leading search engines. The contribution of this chapter is to review the performance evaluation techniques for search engines and use different measures to assess and compare the quality of different search engines, especially MSE.

INTRODUCTION

Search engines, since their inception in the early to mid-1990, have gone through many stages of development. Early search engines were derived from the work of two different, but related fronts. One is to retrieve, organize, and make searchable the widely available, loosely formatted HTML documents over the Web. The other is then-existing information access tools such as Archie (Emtage, 1992), Gopher (Anklesaria *et.al.* 1993), and WAIS (Kahle, 1991) (Wide Area Information Servers). Archie collects information about numerous FTP sites and provides a searchable interface so users can easily retrieve files through different FTP sites. Gopher provides search tools to large number of Gopher servers on the Internet. WAIS has similar functionality to that of Archie, except that it concentrated on wide variety of information on the Internet, not just FTP sites. With the fast development of Web, search engines designed just for the Web started to emerge. Some of the examples include WWWW (World Wide Web Worm), then-most-powerful search engine AltaVista, NorthernLight, WebCrawler, Excite, InforSeek, HotBot, AskJeeves, AlltheWeb, MSNSearch, and of course, Google. Some of these search engines disappeared in history; others were re-tooled, re-designed, or simply merged; yet others have been able to stay at the front against all the competition. Google since its inception in 1998 has been the most popular search engine mostly because of its early success in its core algorithm for search, the *PageRank* algorithm (Brin & Page, 1998). Search engines today are generally capable of searching not only free text, but also structured information such as databases, as well as multi-media such as audio and video. Some of the representative work can be found in (Datta *et.al.*, 2008) and (Kherfi *et.al.*, 2004), More recently some academic search engines start to focus on indexing *deeper* Web and producing *knowledge* based on the information available on the Web, e.g., the *KnowItAll* project by Etzioni and his team, see for example (Banko *et.al*,. 2007). In a relatively short history, many aspects of search engines including software, hardware, management, investment and others have been researched and advanced. Microsoft, though a later comer in the Web search business, tried very hard to compete with Google and other leading search engines. As a result, Microsoft unveiled its own search engine on November 11th, 2004 with its Web site at http://beta.search.msn.com (Sherman, 2005). We refer to it as MSN in this discussion. The beta version of the search has since evolved to what is now called *Live* search engine (http://www.live.com). This chapter reports the results of a project attempting to assess the performance of the Microsoft search engine when it was in its beta version from various perspectives. Specifically the study collects statistics such as the average user response time, average process time for a query reported by MSE itself, the number of pages relevant to a query, the quality of the search in terms of *RankPower*, and comparisons with its competitors. The rest of the chapter is organized as follows: Section 2 provides an overview of search engine performance metrics. The goals and the metrics of this study are described in Section 3. Section 4 discusses the method of study and the experimental settings, followed by the results and their analysis in Section 5. Our thoughts and conclusions about the study are presented in Section 6.

PERFORMANCE METRICS FOR WEB SEARCH ENGINES

While user perception is important in measuring the retrieval performance of search engines, quantitative analyses provide more "scientific evidence" that a particular search engine is "better" than the other. Traditional measures of *recall* and *precision* (Baeza-Yates 1999) work well for laboratory studies of information retrieval systems. However, they do not capture the performance essence of today's Web information systems for three basic reasons. One reason for this problem lies in the importance of the rank of retrieved documents in Web search systems. A user of Web search engines would not go through the list of hundreds and thousands of results. A user typically goes through a few pages of a few tens of results. The *recall* and precision *measures* do not explicitly present the ranks of retrieved documents. A relevant document could be listed as the first or the last in the collection. They mean the same as far as recall and precision are concerned at a given recall value. The second reason that recall and precision measures do not work well is that Web search systems cannot practically identify and retrieve all the documents that are relevant to a search query in the whole collection of documents. This is required by the *recall/precision* measure. The third reason is that these *recall/precision* measures are a pair of numbers. It is not easy to read and interpret quickly what the measure means for ordinary users. Researchers (see a summary in (Korfhage 1997)) have proposed many *single-value* measures such as estimated search length *ESL* (Cooper 1968), averaged search length *ASL* (Losee 1998), *F harmonic mean*, *E-measure* and others to tackle the third problem.

(Meng 2006) compares through a set of real-life Web search data the effectiveness of various single-value measures. The use and the results of *ASL*, *ESL*, average precision, F-measure, E-measure, and the *RankPower*, applied against a set of Web search results. The experiment data was collected by sending 72 randomly chosen queries to *AltaVista* (AltaVista, 2005) and *MARS* (Chen & Meng 2002, Meng & Chen 2005).

The classic measures of user-oriented performance of an IR system are precision and recall which can be traced back to the time frame of 1960's (Cleverdon *et.al.* 1966, Treu 1967). Assume a collection of N documents, of which N_r are relevant to the search query. When a query is issued, the IR system returns a list of L results where $L <= N$, of which L_r are relevant to the query. Precision P and recall R are defined as follows:

$$P = \frac{L_r}{L} \text{ and } R = \frac{L_r}{N_r} \tag{1}$$

Note that $0 <= P <= 1$ and $0 <= R <= 1$. Essentially the precision measures the portion of the retrieved results that are relevant to the query and recall measures the percentage of relevant results are retrieved out of the total number of relevant results in the document set. A typical way of measuring precision and recall is to compute the precision at each recall level. A common method is to set the recall level to be of 10 intervals with 11 points ranging from 0.0 to 1.0. The precision is calculated for each of the recall level. The goal is to have a high precision rate, as well as a high recall rate. Several other measures are related to the measure of precision and recall. *Average precision and recall* (Korfhage 1997) computes the average of recall and precision over a set of queries. The *average precision at seen relevant documents* (Baeza-Yates 1999) takes the average of precision values after each new relevant document is observed. The *R-precision* (Baeza-Yates 1999) measure assumes the knowledge of total number of relevant documents R in the document collection. It computes the precision at R-th retrieved documents. The *E measure*

$$E = 1 - \frac{1 + \beta^2}{\frac{\beta^2}{R} + \frac{1}{P}} \tag{2}$$

was proposed in (Van Rijsbergen 1974) which can vary the weight of precision and recall by adjusting the parameter β between 0 and 1. In the extreme cases when β is 0, $E = 1 - P$, where recall has the least effect, and when β is 1,

$$E = 1 - \frac{2}{\frac{1}{R} + \frac{1}{P}} \qquad\qquad\qquad\qquad (3)$$

where recall has the most effect. The *harmonic F measure* (Shaw 1986) is essentially a complement of the *E measure*,

$$F = \frac{2}{\frac{1}{R} + \frac{1}{P}}. \qquad\qquad\qquad\qquad (4)$$

The precision-recall measure and its variants are effective measures of performance of information retrieval systems in the environment where the total document collection is known and the sub-set of documents that are relevant to a given query is also known.

The drawbacks of the precision-recall based measures are multi-fold. Most noticeably, as Cooper pointed in his seminal paper (Cooper 1968), it does not provide a single measure; it assumes a binary relevant or irrelevant set of documents, failing to provide some gradual order of relevance; it does not have built-in capability for comparison of system performance with purely random retrieval; and it does not take into account a crucial variable: the amount of material relevant to the query which the user actually needs. The *expected search length* (*ESL*) (Cooper 1968, Korfhage 1997) is a proposed measure to counter these problems. ESL is the average number of irrelevant documents that must be examined to retrieve a given number i of relevant documents. The weighted average of the individual expected search lengths then can be defined as follows,

$$ESL = \frac{\sum_{i=1}^{N} i * e_i}{\sum_{i=1}^{N} i} \qquad\qquad\qquad\qquad (5)$$

where N is the maximum number of relevant documents, and e_i the expected search length for i relevant documents.

The *average search length* (*ASL*) (Losee 1998, Losee 1999, Losee 2000) is the expected position of a relevant document in the ordered list of all documents. For a binary judgment system (i.e. the document is either relevant or irrelevant), the average search length is represented by the following relation,

$$ASL = N[QA + (1-Q)(1-A)] \qquad\qquad\qquad\qquad (6)$$

where N is the total number of documents, Q is the probability that ranking is optimal, and A is the expected proportion of documents examined in an optimal raking if one examines all the documents up to the document in the average position of a relevant document. The key idea of *ASL* is that one can *compute* the quality of an IR system without actually measuring it if certain parameters can be learned in advance. On the other hand, if one examines the retrieved documents, the value A can be determined experimentally, which is the total number of retrieved relevant documents divided by the total number of retrieved documents, thus the quality indicator Q can be computed.

Except the basic *precision* and *recall* measures, the rest of the afore-mentioned measures are single-value measures. They have the advantage of representing the system performance in a single value, thus it is easier to understand and compare the performance of different systems. However these single-value measures share weakness in one of the two areas. Either they do not consider explicitly the positions of the relevant documents, or they do not explicitly consider the count of relevant documents. This makes the measures non-intuitive and difficult for users of interactive IR systems such as Web search engines to capture the meanings of the measures.

To alleviate the problems using other single-value measures for Web search, Meng & Chen proposed a single-value measure called *RankPower* (Meng & Chen 2004) that combines the precision and the placements of the returned relevant documents. The measure is based on the concept of *average ranks* and the *count* of returned relevant documents. A closed-form expression of the optimal *RankPower* can be found such that comparisons of different Web information retrieval systems can be easily made. The *RankPower* measure reaches its optimal value when all returned documents are relevant.

RankPower is defined as follows:

$$RankPower(N) = \frac{R_{avg}(N)}{n} = \frac{\sum_{i=1}^{n} S_i}{n^2} \tag{7}$$

where N is the total number of documents retrieved, n is the number of relevant documents among N, S_i is the place (or the position) of the ith relevant document.

While the physical meaning of *RankPower* as defined above is clear -- average rank divided by the count of relevant documents, the domain in which its values can reach is difficult to interpret. The optimal value (the minimum) is 0.5 when all returned documents are relevant. It is not clear how to interpret this value in an intuitive way, i.e. why 0.5. The other issue is that *RankPower* is not bounded above. A single relevant document listed as the last in a list of m documents assures a *RankPower* value of m. If the list size increases, this value increases. In their recent work, (Tang et.al. 2007) proposed a revised *RankPower* measure defined as follows:

$$RankPower(N) = \frac{\frac{n(n+1)}{2}}{\sum_{i=1}^{n} S_i} = \frac{n(n+1)}{2\sum_{i=1}^{n} S_i} \tag{8}$$

where N is the total number of documents retrieved, n is the number of relevant documents among the retrieved ones, and S_i is the rank of each of the retrieved, relevant document. The beauty of this revision is that it now constrains the values of the *RankPower* to be between 0 and 1 with 1 being the most favorite and 0 being the least favorite. A minor drawback of this definition is that it loses the intuition of the original definition that is the average rank divided by the count of relevant documents.

The experiment and data analysis reported in (Meng 2006) compared *RankPower* measure with a number of other measures. While the exact numerical results may not be much relevant any more because they are dated, the data do show the effectiveness of *RankPower* measure. The results show that

Table 1. Average recall and precision at the first 20 returned results

Recall	0.00	0.10	0.20	0.30	0.40	0.50	0.60	0.70	0.80	0.90	1.00	sum	Avg
0.00	4	0	0	0	0	0	0	0	0	0	0	4	0.00
0.10	0	2	1	1	3	0	0	1	1	1	1	11	0.48
0.20	0	6	4	1	1	4	2	5	0	3	4	30	0.52
0.30	0	0	1	2	8	4	1	1	0	0	0	17	0.43
0.40	0	1	0	0	2	1	0	0	1	1	0	6	0.52
0.50	0	0	0	0	0	0	1	0	0	0	0	1	0.60
0.60	0	0	0	0	0	0	0	0	0	0	0	0	0.00
0.70	0	1	0	1	0	0	0	0	0	0	0	2	0.20
0.80	0	0	0	0	0	0	0	0	0	0	0	0	0.00
0.90	0	0	0	0	0	0	0	0	0	0	0	0	0.00
1.00	0	1	0	0	0	0	0	0	0	0	0	1	0.10
sum	4	11	6	5	14	9	4	7	2	5	5	72	
avg	0.00	0.32	0.20	0.32	0.26	0.27	0.30	0.20	0.25	0.22	0.18		Precision

the *RankPower* measure was effective and easy to interpret. A similar approach to that was discussed in (Korfhage 1997) was used in the study. A set of 72 randomly chosen queries are sent to the chosen search engines (AltaVista, (AltaVista, 2005) and MARS (Chen & Meng, 2002)). The first 200 returned documents for each query are used as the document set. Each of the 200 documents for each of the query is examined to determine the collection of relevant document set. This process continues for all 72 queries. The average recall and precision are computed at each of the recall intervals. The results are listed in Table 1.

Shown in Table 2 are the numerical values of the various single-value measures collected from the same data set. Following (Cooper 1968)'s discussion, five different types of ESL measures were studied. These five types are listed as follows:

1. **Type-1:** A user may just want the answer to a very specific factual question or a single statistics. Only one relevant document is needed to satisfy the search request.
2. **Type-2:** A user may actually want only a fixed number, for example, *six* of relevant documents to a query.
3. **Type-3:** A user may wish to see *all* documents relevant to the topic.
4. **Type-4:** A user may want to sample a subject area as in 2, but wish to specify the ideal size for the sample as some proportion, say *one-tenth*, of the relevant documents.
5. **Type-5:** A user may wish to read *all* relevant documents in case there should be less than five, and exactly *five* in case there exist more than five.

Notice that various ESL measures are the number of irrelevant documents that must be examined in order to find a fixed number of relevant documents; ASL, on the other hand, is the average position of the relevant documents; *RankPower* is a measure of average rank divided by the number of relevant documents with a lower bound of 0.5. In all cases, the smaller the values are, the better the performance

Table 2. Various single-value measures applied to the experiment data

		AV	MARS
ESL	Type 1	3.78	0.014
	Type 2	32.7	25.7
	Type 3	124	113
	Type 4	7.56	0.708
	Type 5	25.7	17.3
ASL	Measured	82.2	77.6
	Estimate	29.8	29.8
RankPower		3.29	2.53
Revised Rank Power		0.34	0.36

is. Revised *RankPower* has values between 0 and 1 with 0 being the least favorite and 1 being the most favorite.

We can draw the following observations from the data shown in Table 2. Note that these observations demonstrate the effectiveness of single-value measures, especially, the *RankPower*. The focus was not on the comparison of the actual search engines since the experimental data is a few years old.

1. In ESL Type 1 comparison, AltaVista has a value of 3.78 which means on the average, one needs to go through 3.78 irrelevant documents before finding a relevant document. In contrast, ESL Type 1 value for MARS is only 0.014 which means a relevant document can almost always be found at the beginning of the list. MARS performs much better in this comparison because of its relevance feedback feature.

2. ESL Type 2 counts the number of irrelevant documents that a user has to go through if she wants to find *six* relevant documents. AltaVista has a value of 32.7 while MARS has a value of 25.7. Again because of the relevance feedback feature of MARS, it performs better than AltaVista.

3. It is very interesting to analyze the results for ESL Type 3 request. ESL Type 3 request measures the number of irrelevant documents a user has to go through if she wants to find all relevant documents in a fixed document set. In our experiments, the document set is the 200 returned documents for a given query and the result is averaged over the 72 queries used in the study. Although the average *number* of relevant documents is the same between AltaVista and MARS (see the values of estimated ASL) because of the way MARS works, the positions of these relevant documents are different. This results in different values of ESL Type 3. In order to find all relevant documents in the return set which the average value is 29.8 documents, AltaVista would have to examine a total of 124 irrelevant documents while MARS would examine 113 irrelevant documents because MARS have arranged more relevant documents to the beginning of the set.

4. ESL Type 4 requests indicate that the user wants to examine one-tenth of all relevant documents and how many irrelevant documents the user has to examine in order to achieve this goal. In this case, all relevant documents in the returned set of 200 have to be identified before the 10 percent can be counted. On average AlatVista would have to examine about 8 irrelevant documents before reaching the goal, while it only takes MARS fewer than one irrelevant documents.

5. ESL Type 5 requests examine up to a certain number of relevant documents. The example quoted in Cooper's paper (Cooper 1968) was five. For AltaVista, it takes about 26 irrelevant documents to find five relevant documents, while MARS requires only about 17.

GOALS AND METRICS OF THE STUDY

Since the early days of search engines in early 1990s, relatively few performance studies about search engines have been available to the public. Researchers and engineers at Google published a few papers about their systems with some mention of the performance (Ghemawat *et.al.*, 1999; Barroso *et.al.*, 2003). Most other performance comparisons come as news reports from users' perceptions, that is, how satisfied the users *feel* about a particular search engine. The goal of this study is to assess the performance of MSE from a user's point of view with collected statistics. The study is trying to answer the following questions. How long would it take for a search engine to respond to a user query? How many total relevant results are there from a search engine's point of view? Given that a typical user cannot examine all returned results, which is typically in the order of millions, how many of the top-20 results returned by a search engine are actually relevant to the query from a user's point of view? We also compare the performance of search engines in these respects. The search engines involved in the study include Microsoft Search Engine (beta version) (MSE, 2005), AlltheWeb (ATW, 2008), Google (Google, 2008), Vivisimo (Vivisimo, 2008), and Yahoo! (Yahoo, 2008).

A number of performance metrics were measured in this study. The average response time is a measure of duration between the time when a query is issued and the time when the response is received, as seen by the user's computer. Since a query typically retrieves hundreds and thousands of pages, we simply measure, separately, the response time for the first page of URLs (typically 10 URLs), and then the following four pages of URLs. The reason for the separation between the first and the rest of the pages comes from the fact that it takes much more time to generate the first page than the rest of the pages. The second piece of statistics collected is the number of relevant URLs per query posted by the search engines. Although this is not necessarily a measure of how accurate the search results are, nor a measure of how large the collected data for the search engines is, it is an interesting indication of the data set kept by a search engine. The third measurement is a user-perceived relevance measure for the queries. The authors sent 27 randomly chosen queries to MSE and the other peer search engines, the relevance of the first 20 returned results from each of the search engines is examined manually. The single value measurement *RankPower* (see discussion in Section previous section) is used to compare the performance of the selected search engines from an end-user point of view.

EXPERIMENT METHODS

Two separate sets of experiments were conducted to study the performance of MSE and the other chosen peer search engines. The first set of experiments collects the statistics about search quality such as the relevance of the returned search results. A list of 27 randomly chosen queries is sent to the five search engines. The first 20 returned URLs (typically in two pages) are examined manually by the authors. The authors determine, before sending each query to the search engine, what types of URLs are deemed relevant. Hence, when the results are returned, only those URLs that are relevant to the pre-determined interpretation of the query are considered as relevant. For example, when querying "thread", we wanted to see the Web pages relating to the thread programming commonly seen in computer science, not "thread" seen as in textile industry. The number of relevant URLs and their places in the returned list (ranks) are recorded. The *average rank* and *RankPower* are computed. This experiment took place between November and December of 2004 for AlltheWeb, Google, Vivisimo, and Yahoo!. The data collection for MSE took place in December of 2004 and January of 2005.

The second set of experiments examined some "hard" statistics, which include the average response time and the number of relevant URLs from the search engine's point of view. To obtain these statistics, a set of client programs are developed in Java, one for each of the search engines. The client program can send queries to a search engine automatically. The duration between the time when query is sent and the time when the responses are received from a search engine is recorded using Java's *System.current-TimeMillis()* method which reports the wall-clock time in milli-second resolution. The client program runs three times a day for a few days. Each time when a client program is running, four queries are sent to a search engine in sequence. The average response times for the first five pages are computed. Because it typically takes longer for a search engine to respond to the query the first time (the first page return), the statistics for the first returned page is collected separated from the rest pages. We ran this set of experiments with three of the five studied search engines, AlltheWeb, MSE, and Yahoo!. We did not run the experiment for Google because it does not respond to programmed queries through the browser interface. Although Google provides a nice set of APIs (Google API, 2005) to query its data collection directly, the information provided through the API is not exactly the same as that through the browser

Figure 1. Yahoo! returning page showing 36,500,000 relevant results to the query "thread" and a processing time of 0.10 seconds

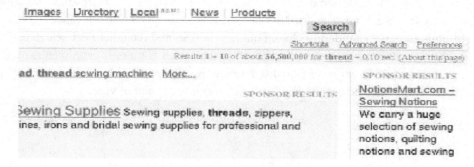

interface as a common Web user would see. Thus the authors decided not to use Google as a comparison. The data from Vivisimo was also not collected because of Vivisimo's relatively small data sets.

Also collected in this set of experiments are the total number of relevant pages that each search engine claims to have for a given query, and the processing time that the search engine takes to service the query. The processing time is typically listed on each page, that is, search engines process and return each page separately. Figure 1 illustrates this point, showing that there are a total of about 36,500,000 pages related to the query "thread", and it took Yahoo! 0.1 seconds to process the first page. Other search engines including MSE have the similar features.

RESULTS AND ANALYSIS

In this section, we present the results from the experiments and some observations about the results. The first set of results reported here is the search quality. This is measured by the average number of relevant URLs among the first 20 returned URLs, the average rank, and the *RankPower*. Notice that the *RankPower* measure has a theoretical lower bound of 0.5. The closer to that value, the better the search quality. Table 3 shows the results from the five search engines we tested.

From the table one can tell that Google has the most favored *RankPower* measure because it contains the highest average number of relevant URLs (13.52) in the results AND these relevant URLs are placed relatively high on the returned list (average 10.33). On the other hand, MSE doesn't seem to be doing well in the measure of *RankPower*. However, Microsoft's new search engine seemed to have included a very diverse array of results for the queries that we sent to it, while Google's results seemed to be more focused. For example, when the "basketball" query was given to Microsoft, the results included scouting/recruitment and high school basketball. Google focused on the more popular NBA and collegiate levels of basketball. This seems fairly self-evident: Google became the search leader because of its high rate of return for more popular results based on its *PageRank* algorithm (Brin & Page, 1998). MSE seems to return more diverged results with "high novelty". This observation is supported by the results from a number of queries. If the number of relevant URLs does not reveal intuitively the significance, the percentage of pages that are relevant among the total number of returned pages gives us more information. The average ranks from different search engines don't differ greatly, ranging from 10.32 to 10.56. Thus a measurement of their "deviation" becomes important. The *RankPower* measure captures some sense of the deviation of a set of values. The *RankPower* value of Google for example

Table 3. Average number of relevant URLs, average rank, and rankpower for the 27 queries measured from the first 20 return results

Search Engine	AlltheWeb	Google	MSE	Vivisimo	Yahoo
Avg. No. Relevant URLs	13.33	13.52	10.81	13.15	12.19
Pcnt. Of Relevant URLs	67%	68%	54%	66%	61%
Avg. Rank	10.56	10.33	10.32	10.32	10.39
RankPower	0.79	0.76	0.95	0.78	0.85
Revised RankPower	0.68	0.70	0.57	0.69	0.63

Table 4. Average number of relevant URLs from search engines' view for the 27 queries

Search Engine	AlltheWeb	Google	MSE	Yahoo
Avg. No. of Relevant Pages	47,693,444	69,380,370	66,047,923	57,423,667

Table 5. Time needed to generate a return page reprted by the search engines (seconds)

Search Engine	Google	MSE	Yahoo
Avg. Page 1	0.20	0.25	0.13
Std. Dev. Page 1	0.11	0.09	0.07
Avg. Pages 2-5	0.16	0.22	0.10
Std. Dev. Pages 2-5	0.07	0.12	0.02
Avg. Overall	0.17	0.23	0.11

is 0.76, the smallest among the five. Because the theoretical value of *RankPower* can be any value that is greater than 0.5, the direct measured values shown in the table do not indicate how sensitive these values are, the revised *RankPower*, as described in Section 2, does give a direct comparison because its values vary from 0 to 1, the larger the values are, the better the results. The table indicates the revised *RankPower* values for Google, AlltheWeb, and Vivisimo are 0.70, 0.68, and 0.69, respectively, notably better than that of MSE and Yahoo!.

The second set of results presented is the average number of relevant URLs for a given query from search engine's point of view. Four out of the five search engines presented this piece of information somewhere in their returned pages with the exception of Vivisimo. See Figure 1 for an example from Yahoo! where it shows that 36,500,000 pages were relevant to the query "thread". Table 4 lists the average of relevant URLs over the 27 testing queries reported by the search engines. One should note that it is not necessarily true that a higher average number of results implies larger overall data sets. One also should keep in mind that Google declared to have indexed about eight billion Web pages (Google, 2005) while MSE is said to have indexed about five billion Web pages (MSE, 2005).

The next set of statistics to be reported is the average time a search engine takes to generate a return page for a given query. This information is reported on each of the returning pages generated by Google, MSE, and Yahoo!. To determine if there is a difference between the response time for the first page of a search engine and that of the rest of the pages, we collected the statistics separately for the first and the rest of the pages. The results in Table 5 include the average time for the first returning page, its standard deviation, the average time for the returning pages 2 through 5, and their standard deviation.

As can be seen from the table, Yahoo! has overall the shortest time to generate a response page and the smallest standard deviation. Also the difference of average response time between the first page and the rest pages is relatively small for Yahoo!, indicating that it has an overall smooth response time. For both Google and MSE there is a visible difference between the response time for the first page (0.20 seconds and 0.25 seconds) and the rest pages (0.16 seconds and 0.22 seconds).

The last set of statistics to be reported here is the measured response time from three of the five search engines, namely, AlltheWeb, MSE, and Yahoo!. In this collection of statistics, the actual wall-clock timing between the time when the query is sent and the time when the return page is received is recorded and averaged over a number of runs. In our client programs, we used the following logic to collect data for each of the three aforementioned search engines.

```
Connect to the search engine;
Start timing for first page response;
Send the query;
Read the first page response;
Stop timing for first page response;
Start timing for rest of the pages;
Loop
  Send the query;
  Read next page response;
End loop
Stop timing for rest of the pages.
```

In order to study the perceived user response time, the data is collected from two places, a desk-top computer on the campus of California State University at Los Angeles from the west coast, and a desk-top computer on the campus of Bucknell University from the east coast. As we will see, the data presents some interesting results. The data collected from Bucknell is shown in Table 6, the ones collected from Cal State LA is shown in Table 7. Note that in both tables, the information from AlltheWeb is used instead of that of Google for the reasons explained in section Experiment Methods.

Table 6. Wall-clock time for a return page seen from Bucknell University (in milli-seconds)

Search Engine	AlltheWeb	MSE	Yahoo
Avg. Page 1	695	607	720
Std. Dev. Page 1	253	316	320
Avg. Pages 2-5	519	354	533
Std. Dev. Pages 2-5	157	54	252
Avg. Overall	606	480	627

Table 7. Wall-.clock time for a return page seen from Cal. State at Los Angeles (in milli-seconds)

Search Engine	AlltheWeb	MSE	Yahoo
Avg. Page 1	733	428	619
Std. Dev. Page 1	330	170	272
Avg. Pages 2-5	539	282	527
Std. Dev. Pages 2-5	109	116	200
Avg. Overall	636	355	573

A few facts emerged from the tables. Both Yahoo! and AlltheWeb have similar access timing from the east coast and from the west coast. For AlltheWeb it was an average of 636 milli-seconds from the west compared to 606 milli-seconds from the east (less than 5 percent difference). For Yahoo! it was 573 milli-seconds from the west compared to 627 from the east (about 10 percent difference). For MSE, it was 355 milli-seconds from the west compared to 480 milli-seconds from the east (about 35 percent difference). This is an indication that MSE has not replicated its service evenly throughout the country, as some other search engines do (e.g. Google). The second observation is that there is a clear difference in time needed to serve the first page and the rest of the pages. This can be explained by the reason that when the search engine receives the query, it has to retrieve relevant pages from vast amount data. Once retrieved, the subsequent pages can be cached, which speeds up the service time. The third fact is that MSE has overall the fastest average service time.

Since the timing statistics were taken from two different computers, one from Bucknell University on the east coast and the other one from California State University at Los Angeles on the west coast. The hardware and software systems on both computers also have an effect on these timing. In order to minimize this side effect, a baseline timing is collected. Each of the two computers was instructed to access a local Web server installed on the host computer. The local Web server generates a random page for each given query, simulating the behavior of a real search engine. The same number of Web pages was requested as if it were accessing a chosen search engine on the Internet. The baseline timing statistics are presented here in Table 8.

As can be seen from Table 8 that the two desk-top systems used in the measurement have quite different timing statistics, indicating two quite different computer systems used in the experiments. It is not practical to have the exact, completely un-biased comparison from the two sites because of the differences in hardware and software used on the desk-top computers and in the network environment on the two campuses. We attempted to minimize the discrepancy by subtracting the local access time from the overall statistics and compare the results.

measured timing = overall timing − local access timing

Table 8. Baseline wall-clock time (in milli-seconds)

Search Engine	Local host (east)	Local host (west)
Avg. Page 1	108	45.4
Std. Dev. Page 1	7.34	9.82
Avg. Pages 2-5	13.7	5.41
Std. Dev. Pages 2-5	0.36	1.39
Avg. Overall	60.7	25.3

Table 9. Adjusted wall-clock timing for a page seen from Bucknell University (in milli-seconds)

Search Engine	AlltheWeb	MSE	Yahoo
Avg. Page 1	587	499	612
Avg. Pages 2-5	505	341	520
Avg. Overall	545	419	566

Table 10. Adjusted wall-clock timing for a page seen from Cal State University at Los Angeles (in milliseconds).

Search Engine	AlltheWeb	MSE	Yahoo
Avg. Page 1	688	383	574
Avg. Pages 2-5	534	277	521
Avg. Overall	611	330	547

For example, for MSE, the overall average first page timing from Cal State LA is 428 milli-seconds (Table 7), the average local access timing for a randomly generated first page is 45.4 milli-seconds, then we consider the measured timing for MSE from Cal State LA to be 428 – 45.4 = 383 milli-seconds. The adjusted results after removing the local access timing component are presented in Table 9 for Bucknell University and Table 10 for California State University at Los Angeles, respectively.

By comparing the data in Table 9 with that in Table 6, and the data in Table 10 with that in Table 7, the relative relations in performance among these search engines do not change. The MSE has the fastest response time on both campuses; the one on the west coast is visibly faster even after removing the differences in host computers. This suggests that the MSE at the time of this measurement was located somewhere on the west coast. Yahoo! has the longest response time on the east coast which may suggest that the Yahoo! servers are close to the west coast, while AlltheWeb has the longest one on the west coast.

CONCLUSION

We reviewed the theory and practices of search engine performance analysis. A performance study of a few popular search engines is conducted including AlltheWeb, Google, Microsoft Search Engine, and Yahoo!. The quality of the search results is examined manually by marking relevant pages returned from the search engines in response to a set of randomly chosen queries and computing the *RankPower*. The average response time is computed by constructing a client program for each of the search engines and collecting the actual average wall-clock time between the time when a query is sent and the time when the search is complete with the first five pages received by the client. Other statistics such as the average time needed to generate a page and the number of relevant pages to a given query both of which are claimed by the search engine are extracted from the returning pages sent by the search engines.

By comparing the empirical results, it is shown that the Microsoft search engine (beta) performs well in terms of speed to deliver the results and the diversity of the results. It does not do very well in terms of the quality of the search measured by *RankPower*, compared to other search engines such as Google and Yahoo!.

REFERENCES

AltaVista (2005). *AltaVista search engine.* Retrieved November, 2005, from http://www.altavista. com/

Anklesaria, F., McCahill, M., Lindner, P., Johnson, D., Torrey, D., & Alberti, B. (1993). *The Internet Gopher Protocol (A distributed document search and retrieval protocol).* RFC 1436, University of Minnesota, March 1993.

ATW (2008). *AlltheWeb search engine.* Retrieved March 1, 2008, from http://www.AlltheWeb.com/

Baeza-Yates, R., & Ribeiro-Neto, B. (1999). *Modern information retrieval.* Addison Wesley.

Banko, M., Cafarella, M. J., Soderland, S., Broadhead, M., & Etzioni, O. (2007, January 6-12). Open information extraction from the Web. In *Proceedings of the 20th International Joint Conference on Artificial Intelligence (IJCAI 2007)*, Hyderabad, India.

Barroso, L. A., Dean, J., & Holzle, U. (2003). Web search for a planet: The Google cluster architecture. *IEEE Micro, 23*(2), 22-28.

Brin, S., & Page, L. (1998). The anatomy of a large-scale hypertextual Web search engine. In *Proceedings of the Seventh World Wide Web Conference*, April 1998. Brisbane, Australia.

Chen, Z., & Meng, X. (2002). MARS: Applying multiplicative adaptive user preference retrieval to Web search. In *Proceedings of the International Conference on Internet Computing 2002*, (pp. 643-648).

Cleverdon, C. W., Mills, J., & Keen, E. M. (1966). *Factors determining the performance of indexing systems, Volume 1— Design.* Cranfield, England: Aslib Cranfield Research Project.

Cooper, W. S. (1968). Expected search length: A single measure of retrieval effectiveness based on weak ordering action of retrieval systems. *Journal of the American Society for Information Science, 19*(1), 30-41.

Datta, R., Dhiraj, J., D., Li, J., & Wang, J. Z. (in press). Image retrieval: Ideas, influences, and trends of the New Age. *ACM Computing Surveys.*

Emtage, A., & Deutsch, P. (1992). Archie: An electronic directory service for the Internet. In *Proceedings of the USENIX Association Winter Conference*, (pp. 93-110). San Francisco.

Ghemawat, S., Gobioff, H., & Leung, S.T., (1999). The Google file system. In *Proceedings of the 19th ACM Symposium on Operating Systems Principles*, vol. 400, (pp. 107-109).

Google (2008). Google search engine: http://www.google.com/ last accessed March 1, 2008.

GoogleAPI (2008). Google Web APIs: http://www.google.com/apis/ last accessed March 1, 2008.

Kahle, B., & Medlar. A. (1991). An information system for corporate users: Wide area information servers. *ConneXions—The Interoperability Report, 5*(11), 2-9.

Kherfi, M. L., Ziou, D., & Bernardi, A. (2004). Image retrieval from the World Wide Web: Issues, techniques, and systems. *ACM Computing Survey, 36*(1), 35-67.

Korfhage, R. R. (1997). *Information storage and retrieval.* New York: John Wiley & Sons.

Live (2008). *Microsoft Live search engine.* Retrieved March 1, 2008, from http://www.live.com/

Losee, R. M. (1998). *Text retrieval and filtering: Analytic models of performance.* Boston:Kluwer Publisher.

Losee, R. M. (1999). Measuring search engine quality and query difficulty: Ranking with target and freestyle. *Journal of the American Society for Information Science, 50*(10), 882-889.

Losee, R. M. (2000). When information retrieval measures agree about the relative quality of document rankings. *Journal of the American Society for Information Science, 51*(9), 834-840.

Meng, X. & Chen, Z. (2004, June 21-24). On user-oriented measurements of effectiveness of Web information retrieval systems. In *Proceedings of the 2004 International Conference on Internet Computing,* Las Vegas, NV, (pp. 527-533).

Meng, X., & Chen, Z. (2005). *On single-value performance measures of search engines from users' perspective.* Manuscript, submitted for publication. September 2005.

Meng, X., & Clark, T. (2005, April 4-6). An empirical user rating of popular search engines using *RankPower.* In *Proceedings of the 2005 International Conference on Information Technology,* Las Vegas, (pp. 521-525).

Meng, X. (2006, April 10-12). A Comparative Study of Performance Measures for Information Retrieval Systems. Poster presentation, in the *Proceedings of the Third International Conference on Information Technology: New Generations,* Las Vegas, NV, (pp. 578-579).

MSE (2005). *Microsoft Search Engine, Beta.* Retrieved January 23, 2005, from http://beta.search.msn.com

Rijsbergen, van C. (1974). Foundation of evaluation. *Journal of Documentation, 30*(4), 365-373.

Sherman, C. (2005). *Microsoft unveils its new search engine—At last.* SearchEngineWatch.com, published November 11, 2004, quoted January 20, 2005, http://searchenginewatch.com/searchday/article.php/3434261

Salton, S. (1989). *Automatic text processing.* Addison Wesley.

Shaw Jr., W. M. (1986). On the foundation of evaluation. *Journal of the American Society for Information Science, 37*(5), 346-348.

Spink, A., Wolfram, D., Jansen, B. J., & Saracevic, T. (2001). Searching the Web: The public and their queries. *Journal of the American Society for Information Science and Technology, 52*(3), 226-234.

Tang, J., Chen, Z., Fu, A. W., & Cheung, D. W. (2007). Capabilities of outlier detection schemes in large databases, framework and methodologies. *Knowledge and Information Systems. 11*(1), 45-84. New York: Springer.

Treu, S. (1967). Testing and evaluation— Literature review. In A. Kent, O.E. Taulbee, J. Belzer, & G.D. Goldstein (Eds.), *Electronic handling of information: Testing and evaluation* (pp. 71-88). Washington, D.C.:Thompson Book Co.

Vivisimo (2008). *Vivisimo search engine.* Retrieved March 1, 2008, from http://www.vivisimo.com/

Yahoo (2008). *Yahoo! search engine.* Retrieved March 1, 2008, from http://www.yahoo.com/

Chapter IX
A User–Centered Approach for Information Retrieval

Antonio Picariello
Università di Napoli Federico II, Italy

Antonio M. Rinaldi
Università di Napoli Federico II, Italy

ABSTRACT

Information retrieval can take great advantages and improvements considering users' feedbacks. Therefore, the user dimension is a relevant component that must be taken into account while planning and implementing real information retrieval systems. In this chapter, we first describe several concepts related to relevance feedback methods, and then propose a novel information retrieval technique which uses the relevance feedback concepts in order to improve accuracy in an ontology-based system. In particular, we combine the Semantic information from a general knowledge base with statistical information using relevance feedback. Several experiments and results are presented using a test set constituted of Web pages.

INTRODUCTION

One of the most important components of a real information retrieval (IR) system is the user: in this framework, the goal of an information retrieval system is to satisfy a user's information needs. In several contexts, such as the Web, it can be very hard to satisfy completely the request of a user, given the great amount of information and the high heterogeneity in the information structure. On the other hand, users find it difficult to define their information needs, either because of the inability to express information need or just insufficient knowledge about the domain of interest, hence they use just few keywords.

In this context, it is very useful to define the concept of relevance information. We can divide relevance into two main classes (Harter, 1992; Saracevic, 1975; Swanson, 1986) called objective (system-based) and subjective (human (user)-based) relevance respectively. The objective relevance can be viewed as a topicality measure, i.e. a direct match of the topic of the retrieved document and the one defined by the query. Several studies on the human relevance show that many other criteria are involved in the evaluation of the IR process output (Barry, 1998; Park, 1993; Vakkari & Hakala, 2000). In particular the subjective relevance refers to the intellectual interpretations carried out by users and it is related to the concepts of aboutness and appropriateness of retrieved information. According to Saracevic (1996) five types of relevance exist: an algorithmic relevance between the query and the set of retrieved information objects; a topicality-like type, associated with the concept of aboutness; cognitive relevance, related to the user information need; situational relevance, depending on the task interpretation; and motivational and affective relevance, which is goal-oriented. Furthermore, we can say that relevance has two main features defined at a general level: multidimensional relevance, which refers to how relevance can be perceived and assessed differently by different users; dynamic relevance, which instead refers to how this perception can change over time for the same user. These features have great impact on information retrieval systems which generally have not a user model and are not adaptive to individual users.

It is generally acknowledged that some techniques can help the user in information retrieval tasks with more awareness, such as relevance feedback (RF). Relevance feedback is a means of providing additional information to an information retrieval system by using a set of results provided by a classical system by means of a query (Salton & Buckley, 1990). In the RF context, the user feeds some judgment back to the system to improve the initial search results. The system can use this information to retrieve other documents similar to the relevant ones or ranks the documents on the basis of user clues. In this chapter we describe a system which uses the second approach. A user may provide the system with relevance information in several ways. He may perform an explicit feedback task, directly selecting documents from list results, or an implicit feedback task, where the system tries to estimate the user interests using the relevant documents in the collection. Another well known technique is the blind (or pseudo) relevance feedback where the system chooses the top-ranked documents as the relevant ones.

LITERATURE OVERVIEW

Relevance feedback techniques have been investigated for more then 30 years (Spink & Losee, 1996) and several papers show that they are effective for improving retrieval performance (Harman, 1992; Rocchio, 1971). From a general point of view RF techniques refer to the measure of relevance. In this context an end-user bases his judgment on the expected contribution of the analyzed document to his task. Resnick et al., (1994) presents GroupLens, a collaborative filter-based system which ranks the documents on the basis of numeric ratings explicitly assigned by the user. The basic idea is that people who agreed with the evaluation of past articles are likely to agree again in the future. Moreover the system tries to predict user's agreement using the ratings from similar users. SIFT (Yan & Garcia-Molina, 1995) approach requires the user to explicitly submit his profile and update it using relevance feedback. The SIFT engine uses profiles to filter documents and notifies them according to user-specified parameters. AntWorld (Kantor et al., 2000) pursues the ant metaphor allowing Internet users to get information about other users' quests. The users have to give a judgment about the visited pages. The judgment is expressed using textual annotation and numeric value. The quests are stored in the system and the similarity between them and the documents is computed as the sum of a tf/idf (term frequency/inverse document frequency) score and user relevance feedbacks. Powerize Server (Kim, Oard & Romanik, 2000) is a content-based system which builds a model to take into account user's information needs. This model is constructed explicitly by the user or implicitly inferring user behaviour. The proposed system is based on parameters to define the user behaviour and starting from them and their correlations the user model. In White, Ruthven & Jose (2002) a system for relevance feedback in Web retrieval is presented. The authors follow two types of approaches based on explicit and implicit feedback. They investigate on the degree of substitution between the two types of evidence. Using relevance feedback the system displays new documents and in particular documents that have been retrieved but not yet considered. The paper (Tan et al., 2007) studies the use of term-based feedback for interactive information retrieval in the language modelling approach. The authors propose a cluster-based method for selecting terms to present to the user for judgment, as well as effective algorithms for constructing refined query language models from user term feedback. The authors (Lad & Yang, 2007) propose news ways of generalizing from relevance feedback through a pattern-based approach to adaptive filtering. The patterns are wildcards that are anchored to their context which allows generalization beyond specific words, while contextual restrictions limit the wildcard-matching to entities related to the user's query. In (Chang & Chen, 2006) the authors present a method for query re-weighting to deal with document retrieval. The proposed method uses genetic algorithms to re-weight a user's query vector, based on the user's relevance feedback, to improve the performance of document retrieval systems. It encodes a user's query vector into chromosomes and searches for the optimal weights of query terms for retrieving documents by genetic algorithms. After the best chromosome is found, the proposed method decodes the chromosome into the user's query vector for dealing with document retrieval. The proposed query re-weighting method can find the best weights of query terms in the user's query vector, based on the user's relevance feedback. In Russ et al. (2007) a relevance feedback technique for association rules which is based on a fuzzy notion of relevance is proposed. The used approach transforms association rules into a vector-based representation using some inspiration from document vectors in information retrieval. These vectors are used as the basis for a relevance feedback approach which builds a knowledge base of rules previously rated as (un)interesting by a user. Given an association rule the vector representation is used to obtain a fuzzy score of how much this rule contradicts a rule in the knowledge base. This yields a set of relevance scores for each assessed rule which still need to be aggregated. Rather than relying on a certain aggregation measure the authors utilize OWA operators for score aggregation to gain a high degree of flexibility and understandability.

Relevance feedback techniques are also used in other contexts, such as multimedia retrieval; e.g., in Zhang, Chai & Jin (2005) a text-based image retrieval system is described, Djordjevic & Izquierdo (2007) introduce a framework for object-based semi-automatic indexing of natural images and Grigorova et al. (2007) proposes an adaptive retrieval approach based on the concept of relevance-feedback, which establishes a link between high-level concepts and low-level features.

Ontologies

In past years, the ontological aspects of information have acquired a strategic value. These aspects are intrinsically independent from information codification, so the information itself may be isolated, recovered, organized, and integrated with respect to its content.

A formal definition of ontology is proposed in Gruber (1993) according to whom "an ontology is an explicit specification of a conceptualization;" conceptualization is referred to as an abstract model of a specified domain in which the component concepts are identified; explicit means that the type of concepts used and the constraints on them are well defined; formal is referred to as the ontology propriety of being "machine-readable", shared is about the propriety that an ontology captures consensual knowledge, accepted by a group of person, not only by individuals.

We also consider other definitions of ontology; in Neches et al., (1991) "an ontology defines the basic terms and relations comprising the vocabulary of a topic area, as well as the rules for combining terms and relations to define extensions to the vocabulary." This definition indicates the way to proceed in order to build an ontology: (i) identification of the basic terms and their relations; (ii) agreeing on the rules that arrange them; (iii) definition of terms and relations among concepts.

From this perspective, an ontology does not include just the terms that explicitly are defined in it, but also those that can be derived by means of well defined rules and properties. In our work, the ontology can be seen as the set of "terms" and "relations" among them, denoting the concepts that are used in a domain. We use ontologies to represent the user interest domain.

Semantic Relatedness

The concept of "Semantic relatedness" refers to the perceived relations between words and concepts. Several metrics have been defined in the literature in order to measure the Semantic relatedness of two words.

These metrics can be grouped in the following categories:

- **Dictionary-based:** Dictionaries are a natural linguistic information source for people knowledge about the world; they form a knowledge base in which the headwords are defined by other headwords and/or their derivatives;
- **Thesaurus-based:** These metrics use a thesaurus in which words are related to concepts; each word is related to a category by means of an index structure;
- **Semantic network-based:** These metrics use Semantic networks, i.e. graphs in which the nodes are the concepts and the arcs represent relations between concepts;
- **Integrated approach:** This approach takes into account additional knowledge sources to enrich the information already present in the network.

An exhaustive overview of the metrics based on these approaches can be found in Budanitsky (1999) and a new approach for measuring Semantic similarity is proposed in Li, Bandar & Mclean (2003).

SYSTEM ARCHITECTURE

We propose a Web search engine that takes into account relevance feedback to improve the precision of an information retrieval system based on general ontologies. The information used to build the domain ontology is dynamically extracted from WordNet (Miller, 1995). For this reason the query structure is constituted as a list of terms to retrieve (i.e., subject keywords) and a domain of interest (i.e., domain keyword) provided by the user using the system interface. For example, if a user wants to get information about the famous jazzman Miles Davis, we have: Subject keywords:="Davis," and domain keyword:="music." We want to be able to retrieve the interesting pages from the user perspective, without considering the ones related to tennis Davis Cup, that pertains to the sport domain. Our system must be able to retrieve and rank results, taking into account the Semantics of the pages and the interaction with the user. In other words, this system performs the following tasks:

- **Fetching:** Fetching consists of searching Web documents containing the keywords specified in the query. This task can be accomplished using traditional search engines.
- **Preprocessing:** This task is needed to remove from Web documents all those elements that do not represent useful information (HTML tags, scripts, applets, etc.).
- **Mining:** Mining consists of analyzing the content of the documents from a Semantic point of view, assigning them a score with respect to the query.
- **Reporting:** This task consists in ranking and returning the documents relevant to the query allowing some functionality for relevance feedback.

We use external search engines in the fetching step.

The system implementation is based on several services. In this context each software module performs one of the actions previously described.

Figure 1 presents a complete architectural view of the proposed system.

Figure 1. System architecture

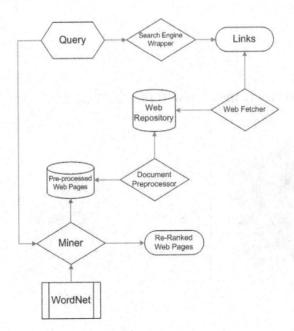

The Dynamic Semantic Network

In the proposed system, the implementation of the ontology is obtained by means of a Semantic network (i.e., DSN), dynamically built using a dictionary based on WordNet. WordNet organizes several terms using their linguistic proprieties. Moreover, every domain keyword may have various meanings (senses) due to the polysemy property, so a user can choose its proper sense of interest. In WordNet these senses are organized in synsets composed of synonyms; therefore, once the sense is chosen (i.e., the appropriate synset), it is possible to take into account all the possible terms (synonyms) that are in the synset. Beyond the synonymy, we consider other linguistic properties applied to typology of the considered terms in order to have a strongly connected network. The DSN is built starting from the domain keyword that represents the context of interest for the user. We then consider all the component synsets and construct a hierarchy based on the hyponymy property; the last level of our hierarchy corresponds to the last level of WordNet's hierarchy. After this first step, we enrich our hierarchy by exploiting all the other kinds of relationships in WordNet. Based on these relations we can add other terms to the hierarchy obtaining a highly connected Semantic network.

Figure 2 shows an example of DSN. Figure 2 (A) represents the music domain; we can see the high complexity of the network, due to the generality of the chosen term. On the other hand, Figure 2 (B) shows a Semantic network about the concept car; in this figure we can see better the network structure organized around the hyperonymy/hyponymy hierarchy.

The arcs between the nodes of the DSN are assigned a weight σ_i, in order to express the strength of the relation. The weights are real numbers in the [0,1] interval and their values are defined experimentally. To calculate the relevance of a term in a given domain we assign a weight to each element in the DSN considering the polysemy property (that can be considered as a measure of the ambiguity in the use of a word, when it can assume several senses). Thus we define the centrality of the term i as:

$$\varpi(i) = \frac{1}{poly(i)} \qquad\qquad (1)$$

Figure 2. An example of DSN: (A) Music, sense 1; (B) Car, Sense 1

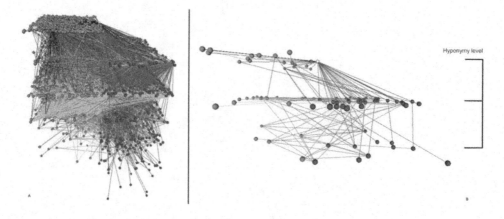

where poly(i) is the polysemy (number of senses) of i. For example, the word music has five senses in WordNet, so the probability that it is used to express a specific meaning is equal to 1/5.

Therefore, we build a representation of the retrieved Web pages using the DSN; each word in the page which matches any of the terms in the DSN is a component of the document representation and the links between them are the relations in the DSN.

SYMILARITY METRIC

Given a conceptual domain, in order to individuate the interesting pages by using a DSN, it is necessary to define a grading system to assign a vote to the documents on the basis of their Syntactic and Semantic content. Therefore, to measure the relevance of a given document we consider the Semantic relatedness between terms and, using relevance feedback techniques, statistical information about them.

The proposed measure considers two types of information; one concerning syntactic information based on the concepts of word frequency and term centrality and another one concerning the Semantic component calculated on each set of words in the document. The relevance feedback techniques we used take into account two types of feedback: explicit and blind feedback.

The first one is performed after the first results presentation. In fact, the system, using the metric for ranking described below, presents to the user a result list and shows for each result the top 2 ranked sentences from the related page. The top sentences are detected using the system metric on each sentence in the document and ordering them. With this information the user can manually choose relevant documents or he can open the whole page.

With the blind approach the user can allow the system to automatically perform the relevance feedback on a defined number of documents.

The first metric contribution is called the Syntactic-Semantic grade (SSG). In this chapter we propose a new approach to calculate the SSG and compare it with the one proposed in Albanese, Picariello & Rinaldi (2004); the metric proposed there represents our standard metric. We can define the relevance of a word in a given conceptual domain and, if the feedback functions are chosen, in the set of selected documents. Therefore we use a hybrid approach exploiting both statistical and Semantic information. The statistical information is obtained by applying the relevance feedback technique described in Weiss, Vélez & Sheldon (1996), and it is enriched with the Semantic information provided by computing the centrality of the terms (Equation 1). In this way we divide the terms into classes, on the basis of their centrality:

$$SSG_{i,k} = \frac{\left(0.5 + 0.5\left(TF_{i,k}\middle/TF_{max,k}\right)\right)\varpi_i}{\sqrt{\sum_{i \in k}\left(0.5 + 0.5\left(TF_{i,k}\middle/TF_{max,k}\right)\right)^2 (\varpi_i)^2}} \tag{2}$$

where k is the k-th document, i is the i-th term, $TF_{i,k}$ is the term frequency of i in k, $TF_{max,k}$ is the maximum term frequency in k, ϖ_i is the centrality of i.

We use this approach to improve the precision of the model of the domain of interest and to overcome the lack of very specific terms in Wordnet (e.g. computer science specific terminology). Thus, the use of relevance feedback re-weights and expands the Semantic network by adding new terms -not present in the DSN- from relevant documents. After the relevance feedback step, the system assigns a $\varpi_i = 1$ to the new terms thus considering them as important in the context.

The other contribution is based on a combination of the path length (l) between pairs of terms and the depth (d) of their subsumer (i.e. the first common ancestor), expressed as the number of hops. The correlation between terms constitutes the Semantic relatedness and it is computed through a nonlinear function. The choice of a nonlinear function to express the Semantic relatedness between terms derives from several considerations. The value of the length and the depth of a path, based on how they are defined, may vary from 0 to infinity, while relatedness between two terms should be expressed as a number in the [0,1] interval. In particular, when the path length decreases to 0 the relatedness should monotonically increase to 1, while it should monotonically decrease to 0 when path length goes to infinity. Also we need a scaling effect on the depth, because words in the upper levels of a Semantic hierarchy express more general concepts than the words in a lower level. We use a non linear function for scaling down the contribution of subsumers in an upper level and scaling up those in a lower one.

Given two words w_1 and w_2, the length l of the path between w_1 and w_2 is computed using the DSN and it is defined as:

$$l(w_1, w_2) = \min_j \sum_{i=1}^{h_j(w_1, w_2)} \frac{1}{\sigma_i} \qquad (3)$$

where j spans over all the paths between w_1 and w_2, $h_j(w_1, w_2)$ is the number of hops in the j-th path and σ_i is the weight assigned to the i-th hop in the j-th path in respect to the hop linguistic property. As an example, let us consider three concepts X, Y and Z and some possible *f* paths between them. The paths, represented by arcs, are labelled with their linguistic properties σ and the concepts have a common subsumer S having a distance of 8 levels from the WordNet root. Now suppose that $\sigma_i = \sigma_j = 0.8$ and $\sigma_t = 0.3$, where σ_i is the path between X and Z, σ_j is the one between Y and Z and σ_t is the path between X and Y. In this case the best path is the one traversing Z with a value of l=1.58. The depth d of the subsumer of w_1 and w_2 is also computed using WordNet. To this aim only the hyponymy and hyperonymy relations (i.e. the IS-A hierarchy) are considered; $d(w_1, w_2)$ is computed as the number of hops from the subsumer of w_1 and w_2 to the root of the hierarchy.

Given the above considerations, we selected an exponential function that satisfies the previously discussed constraints; our choice is also supported by the studies of Shepard (1987), who demonstrated that exponential-decay functions are a universal law in psychological science.

We can now introduce the definition of Semantic Grade (SeG), which extends a metric proposed in Li, Bandar & Mclean (2003):

$$SeG(v) = \sum_{(w_i, w_j)} e^{-\alpha \cdot l(w_i, w_j)} \frac{e^{\beta \cdot d(w_i, w_j)} - e^{-\beta \cdot d(w_i, w_j)}}{e^{\beta \cdot d(w_i, w_j)} + e^{-\beta \cdot d(w_i, w_j)}} \qquad (4)$$

where v is the considered document, (w_i, w_j) are the pairs of words in pre-processed document and $\alpha \geq 0$ and $\beta > 0$ are two scaling parameters whose values are experimentally defined.

This formula has been used in our previous work (Albanese, Picariello & Rinaldi, 2004) with good results and its fine performance is highlighted in Varelas et al. (2005).

Figure 3. An example of sense selection

	Choose a sense and click on the send button
Home Page	○ Sense 1 a strong belief in a supernatural power or powers that control human destiny
New Query	
Results	○ Sense 2 institution to express belief in a divine power
Configuration	Send

Figure 4. Search page and results

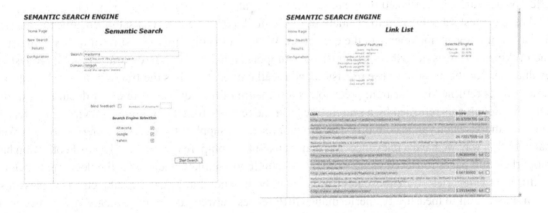

Both grades are computed for each Web page element considering them as composed of four elementary document elements, namely the title, the keywords, the description and the body and all metric components are computed for each of these elements.

USING EXAMPLE

Let us consider the case of a user interested in finding some pages about the Madonna, in the religion domain. The user can submit a query specifying "Madonna" as the subject keyword and "religion" as the domain keyword (see Figure 4). If the domain keyword has more than a single sense, the user is asked to choose one of them; in this case the system shows the WordNet the descriptions of all the senses related to the word religion as shown in Figure 3.

The user can perform three different types of search:

- **Standard searching:** The system ranks the results without relevance feedback;
- **Explicit feedback:** The results interface allows choosing relevance documents as feedback;
- **Blind feedback:** The search interface allows choosing relevance documents by the system.

The user interface allows the insertion of keywords and it also enables the setting of a certain number of parameters, namely: the search engines used in to fetch Web pages; the number of links to be returned by the underlying search engines, the relative weights of title, description, keywords and body tags, the relative weights of Syntactic-Semantic grade and Semantic grade.

EXPERIMENTAL RESULTS

The need for a suitable evaluation of information retrieval systems imposes the adoption of methodologies to give answers about why, what and how-to evaluate. Several authors give answers to these questions (Cleverdon, Mills & Keen, 1996; Vakkari & Hakala, 2000). The techniques used to measure the effectiveness are often affected by the used retrieval strategy and the results presentation.

We use a test set collection to evaluate our system. A test collection is a set of documents, queries and a list of relevant documents in the collection. We use it to compare the results of our system using the ranking strategies described previously. It is important to have standard parameters for IR system evaluation. For this reason we use precision and recall curves. Recall is the fraction of all relevant material that is returned by a search; precision is a measure of the number of relevant documents in the set of all documents returned by a search. We built the test set from the directory service of the search engine yahoo (search.yahoo.com/dir). The directory service supplies the category referred to each Web page. In this way we have a relevance assessment useful to compare our results. The test collection has more then 800 pages retrieved using words with a high polysemic value so that the documents belong to different categories. We choose keywords about both general and specific subjects. This class distinction is useful to measure the performance differences between the rank strategies using a general knowledge base and adding relevance feedback.

In Ruthven and Lalmas (2003) there are some important considerations derived from the analysis of references, criticising the use of the precision-recall measure for RF (Borlund & Ingwersen, 1997; Chang, Cirillo & Razon, 1971; Frei, Meienberg & Schauble, 1991). In fact, using relevance feedback the documents marked as relevant are pushed to the top of the result list improving artificially the recall-precision curve (ranking effect) rather then taking into account the feedback effect, that is liable to push to the top of the ranked list the unseen relevant documents.

The proposed alternatives to consider the feedback on the unseen relevant documents are:

- **Residual ranking:** This strategy removes from the collection those items which were assessed for relevance for feedback purposes, and it evaluates two runs (with or without feedback) on the reduced collection.
- **Freezing:** The documents, examined for relevance before feedback, are retained as the top-ranking documents in the feedback run.
- **Test and control groups:** The collection is randomly split into two collections: The test group and the control group. Relevance feedback information is taken from the test group but the recall-precision is performed only on the control group, so there is no ranking effect.

Figure 5. Experimental results

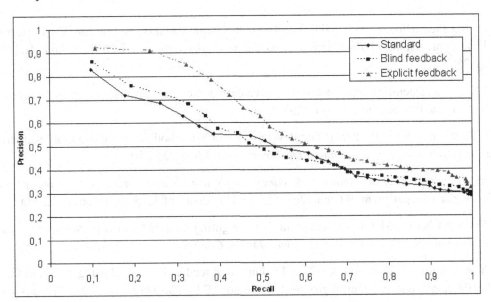

In our approach we use the last strategy to perform our experiments. The document collection is split randomly in order to consider documents from all topics. The random function is calculated on each single category. The used test set simulates a "real" search on the Web because we analyze the pages that are fetched from a standard search engine and we consider also problems such as "page not found," "redirecting" and so on.

In Figure 5 the trend of the experimental results is shown: For low recall values, the precision is high with all strategies. This is a suitable effect in IR retrieval systems because the real relevant documents are immediately presented to the user moreover RF techniques improve the results accuracy with respect our standard strategy (without RF) because by increasing the recall the precision also improves. We note that the blind RF strategy gives an initial improvement but it is lower than the standard one because the system considers false positives in the feedback step.

CONCLUSION

We have described a system and a novel metric to improve ranking accuracy in IR on the Web, using relevance feedback techniques, discussing a hybrid approach that takes into account both syntactic, Semantic and statistical information; we also described a general knowledge base used to dynamically extract a Semantic network for representing user information needs.

Many other topics could be further investigated such as: (1) Using implicit feedback and user characteristics; (2) adding relevance terms to user query refinement to consider new documents after the first interaction; (3) considering multimedia information to perform RF on other features different to textual ones; (4) inferring relevant documents and related terms in order to have specialized ontologies merged with the proposed DSN.

REFERENCES

Albanese, M., Picariello, A., & Rinaldi A. (2004). A Semantic search engine for WEB information retrieval: An approach based on Dynamic Semantic Networks. *Semantic Web Workshop, ACM SIGIR 2004,* (pp. 25-29).

Barry, C. L. (1998). Document representations and clues to document relevance. *Journal of the American Society for Information Science, 49*(14), 1293-1303.

Borlund, P., & Ingwersen, P. (1997). The development of a method for the evaluation of interactive information retrieval systems. *Journal of Documentation. 53*(3), 225-250.

Budanitsky, A. (1999). *Lexical Semantic relatedness and its application in natural language processing.* (Technical report). Department of Computer Science, University of Toronto, Toronto, Canada.

Chang, Y. C., & Chen, S. M. (2006). A new query reweighting method for document retrieval based on genetic algorithms. *IEEE Transactions on Evolutionary Computation, 10*(5), 617-622.

Chang, Y. K., Cirillo, C., & Razon, J. (1971). Evaluation of feedback retrieval using modified freezing, residual collection & test and control groups. In G. Salton (Ed.), *The SMART retrieval system—experiments in automatic document processing,* (pp. 355-370).

Cleverdon, C., Mills, J., & Keen, M. (1966). *Factors determining the performance of indexing systems.* (Technical report). ASLIB Cranfield Research Project, Cranfield.

Djordjevic, D., & Izquierdo, E. (2007). An object- and user-driven system for Semantic-based image annotation and retrieval. *IEEE Transactions on Circuits and Systems for Video Technology, 17*(3), 313-323.

Frei, H. P., Meienberg, S., & Schauble, P. (1991). The perils of interpreting recall and precision values. In *Proceedings of GI/GMD-Workshop Information Retrieval*, (pp. 1-10).

Grigorova, A., De Natale, F. G. B., Dagli, C., & Huang, T. S. (2007). Content-based image retrieval by feature adaptation and relevance feedback. *IEEE Transactions on Multimedia, 9*(6), 1183-1192.

Gruber, T. R. (1993). A translation approach to portable ontology specifications. *Knowledge Acquisition, 5*(2), 199-220.

Harman, D. (1992) Relevance feedback revisited. In *Proceedings of the 15th Annual International ACM SIGIR Conference on Research and Development in Information,* (pp. 1-10).

Harter, S. P. (1992). Psychological relevance and information science. *Journal of the American Society for Information Science, 43*(9), 602-615.

Kantor, P., Boros, E., Melamed, B., Menkov, V., Shapira, B., & Neu, D. (2000). Capturing human intelligence in the Net. *Communications of the ACM, 43*(8), 112-115.

Kim, J., Oard, D., & Romanik, K. (2000). *Using implicit feedback for user modelling in Internet and Intranet searching.* (Technical Report). College of Library and In- formation Services, University of Maryland at College Park, MD

Lad, A., & Yang, Y. (2007). Generalizing from relevance feedback using named entity wildcards. In *Proceedings of the Sixteenth ACM Conference on Conference on information and Knowledge Management - CIKM '07*, (pp. 721-730).

Li, Y., Bandar Z. A., & Mclean, D. (2003). An approach for measuring Semantic similarity between words using multiple information sources. *IEEE Transactions on Knowledge and Data Engineering, 15*(4), 871-882.

Miller, G. (1995). WordNet: A lexical database for English. *Communication of the ACM, 38*(11), 39-41.

Neches, R., Fikes R., Finin, T., Gruber, T., Patil, R., Senator, T., & Swartout, W. R. (1991). Enabling technology for knowledge sharing. *AI Magazine, 12*(3), 36-56.

Park, T. (1993).The nature of relevance in information retrieval: An empirical study. *Library Quarterly, 63*, 318-351.

Russ, G., Bottcher, M., & Kruse, R. (2007). Relevance feedback for association rules using fuzzy score aggregation. In P*roceedings of the Annual Meeting of the North American Fuzzy Information Processing Society-NAFIPS'07*, (pp. 54-59).

Resnick, P., Iacovou, N., Suchak, M., Bergstrom, P., & Riedl, J. (1994). GroupLens: An open architecture for collaborative filtering of net- news. In *Proceedings of the 1994 ACM Conference on Computer Supported Cooperative Work*, (pp. 175-186).

Rocchio, J. (1971). Relevance feedback in information retrieval. *The SMART Retrieval System*, (pp. 313–323).

Ruthven, I., & Lalmas, M. (2003). A survey on the use of relevance feedback for information access systems. *Knowledge Engineering Review, 18*(2), 95-145.

Salton, G., & Buckley, C. (1990). Improving retrieval performance by relevance feedback. *Journal of the American Society for Information Science, 41*(4), 288-97.

Saracevic, T. (1975). Relevance: A review of and framework for the thinking n the notion in information science. *Journal of the American Society for Information Science, 26*(6), 321-343.

Saracevic, T. (1996). Relevance reconsidered. In P*roceedings of the Second Conference on Conceptions of Library and Information Science (CoLIS 2)*, (pp. 201-218).

Shepard, R. N. (1987). Towards a universal law of generalisation for psychological science. *Science, 237*, 1317-1323.

Spink, A., & Losee, R. (1996). Feedback in information retrieval. *Review of Information Science and Technology, 31*, 33-78.

Swanson, D. (1986). Subjective versus objective relevance in bibliographic retrieval systems. *Library Quarterly, 56*(4), 389-398

Tan, B., Velivelli, A., Fang, H., & Zhai, C. (2007). Term feedback for information retrieval with language models. In *Proceedings of the 30th Annual international ACM SIGIR Conference on Research and Development in information Retrieval*, (pp. 263-270).

Vakkari, P., & Hakala, N. (2000). Changes in relevance criteria and problem stages in task performance. *Journal of Documentation, 56*(5), 540-562.

Varelas, G., Voutsakis, E., Raftopoulou, P., Petrakis, E. G., & Milios, E. E. (2005). Semantic similarity methods in WordNet and their application to information retrieval on the web. In *Proceedings of the 7th Annual ACM international Workshop on Web information and Data Management - WIDM'05*, (pp. 10-16).

VanRijsbergen, C. J. (1979). *Information retrieval.* Newton, MA: Butterworth-Heinemann.

Weiss, R., Vélez, B., & Sheldon, M. A. (1996). HyPursuit: A hierarchical network search engine that exploits content-link hypertext clustering. In *Proceedings of the Seventh ACM Conference on Hypertext*, (pp. 180-193).

White, R. W., Ruthven, I., & Jose, J. M. (2002). The use of implicit evidence for relevance feedback in web retrieval. In *Proceedings of 24th BCS-IRSG European Colloquium on IR Research. Lecture notes in Computer Science 2291*, (pp. 93-109).

Yan, T., & Garcia-Molina, H. (1995). SIFT—A tool for wide-area information dissemination. In *Proceedings of USENIX Winter 1995 Technical Conference*, (pp. 177-186)

Zhang, C., Chai, J. Y., & Jin, R. (200%). User term feedback in interactive text-based image retrieval. In *Proceedings of the 28th Annual international ACM SIGIR Conference on Research and Development in Information Retrieval*, (pp. 51-58).

Chapter x
Classification and Retrieval of Images from Databases Using Rough Set Theory

Aboul Ella Hassanien
Cairo University, Egypt

Jafar M. Ali
Kuwait University, Kuwait

ABSTRACT

This chapter presents an efficient algorithm to classify and retrieve images from large databases in the context of rough set theory. Color and texture are two well-known low-level perceptible features to describe an image contents used in this chapter. The features are extracted, normalized, and then the rough set dependency rules are generated directly from the real value attribute vector. Then the rough set reduction technique is applied to find all reducts of the data which contains the minimal subset of attributes that are associated with a class label for classification. We test three different popular distance measures in this work and find that quadratic distance measures provide the most accurate and perceptually relevant retrievals. The retrieval performance is measured using recall-precision measure, as is standard in all retrieval systems.

INTRODUCTION

The growth of the size of data and number of existing databases far exceeds the ability of humans to analyze this data, which creates both a need and an opportunity to extract knowledge from databases. There is a pressing need for efficient information management and mining of the huge quantities of image data that are routinely being used in databases (Cios, Pedrycz, & Swiniarski, 1998; Laudon, &

Laudon, 2006; Starzyk, Dale, & Sturtz, 2000). These data are potentially an extremely valuable source of information, but their value is limited unless they can be effectively explored and retrieved, and it is becoming increasingly clear that in order to be efficient, data mining must be based on Semantics. However, the extraction of Semantically rich meta-data from computationally accessible low-level features poses tremendous scientific challenges (Laudon & Laudon, 2006; Mehta, Agrawal, & Rissanen, 1996; Mitra, Pal, & Mitra, 2002).

Content-based image classify and retrieval (CBICR) systems are needed to effectively and efficiently use the information that is intrinsically stored in these image databases. This image retrieval system has gained considerable attention, especially during the last decade. Image retrieval based on content is extremely useful in many applications (Smith, 1998; Molinier, Laaksonen, Ahola, & Häme, 2005; Yang & Laaksonen, 2005; Koskela, Laaksonen, & Oja, 2004; Viitaniemi & Laaksonen, 2006; Huang, Tan, & Loew, 2003; Smeulders, Worring, Santini, Gupta., & Jain, 2000; Ma & Manjunath, 1999; Carson, Thomas, Belongie, Hellerstein, & Malik, 1999) such as crime prevention, the military, intellectual property, architectural and engineering design, fashion and interior design, journalism and advertising, medical diagnosis, geographic information and remote sensing systems, cultural heritage, education and training, home entertainment, and Web searching. In a typical CBIR system, quires are normally formulated either by query by example or similarity retrieval, selecting from a color, shape, skelton, and texture features or a combination of two or more features. The system then compares the query with a database representing the stored images. The output from a CBIR system is usually a ranked list of images in order of their similarity to the query.

Image classification (Hassanien & Dominik 2007) is an important data mining task which can be defined as a task of finding a function that maps items into one of several discrete classes. The most commonly used techniques in classification are neural network [Dominik et. al. 2004, Hassanien & Dominik 2007], genetic algorithms [Satchidananda et. al., 2008], decision trees [Yang et. al., 2003], fuzzy theory [Ashish G., Saroj K. Meher, & Uma B. Shankar 2008], multi-resolution wavelet [Uma et. al., 2007] and rough set theory [Hassanien & Ali, 2004]. Rough set concept was introduced by Polish logician, Professor Zdzisław Pawlak in early eighties [Pawlak, Z. 1982]. This theory become very popular among scientists around the world and the rough set is now one of the most developing intelligent data analysis [Slowinski, 1995, Pawlak, 1995, Pawlak, 1991]. Rough sets data analysis was used for the discovery of data dependencies, data reduction, approximate set classification, and rule induction from databases. The generated rules represent the underlying Semantic content of the images in the database. A classification mechanism is developed by which the images are classified according to the generated rules.

Image searching (Graham, 2004) is one of the most important services that need to be supported by such systems. In general, two different approaches have been applied to allow searching on image collections: one based on image textual metadata and another based on image content information. The first retrieval approach is based on attaching textual metadata to each image and uses traditional database query techniques to retrieve them by keyword. However, these systems require a previous annotation of the database images, which is a very laborious and time-consuming task. Furthermore, the annotation process is usually inefficient because users, generally, do not make the annotation in a systematic way. In fact, different users tend to use different words to describe the same image characteristic. The lack of systematization in the annotation process decreases the performance of the keyword-based image search. These shortcomings have been addressed by so-called content-based image classification and retrieval. In CBICR systems, image processing algorithms are used to extract feature vectors that represent image properties such as color, texture, and shape (Hassanien & Ali, 2004; Viitaniemi & Laaksonen, 2006; Ma & Manjunath, 1999, Hassanien & Ajith 2008). In this approach, it is possible to retrieve images similar to one chosen by the user (i.e., query-by-example). One of the main advantages of this approach is the possibility of an automatic retrieval process, contrasting to the effort needed to annotate images.

The work introduced in this chapter is based on the second retrieval approach. Image similarity is typically defined using a metric on a feature space. Numerous similarity metrics have been proposed so far. The search results are combined with existing textual information and collections of other features via intelligent decision support systems. In this paper, we use a new similarity function based on the rough set theory (Grzymala-Busse, Pawlak, Slowinski, & Ziarko, 1999; Kent, 1994; Pawlak, 1991; Pawlak, 1982; Pawlak, Grzymala-Busse, Slowinski, & Ziarko, 1995, Jafar M. Ali, 2007). This theory has become very popular among scientists around the world. Rough sets data analysis was used for the discovery of data dependencies, data reduction, approximate set classification, and rule induction from databases. The generated rules represent the underlying Semantic content of the images in the database. A classification mechanism is developed by which the images are classified according to the generated rules.

RELATED WORK AND PROBLEM DEFINITION

Image classification and retrieval methods aim to classify and retrieve relevant images from an image database that are similar to the query image. The ability to effectively retrieve nonalphanumeric data is a complex issue (Jafar M. Ali, 2007). The problem becomes even more difficult due to the high dimension of the variable space associated with the images. Image classification is a very active and promising research domain in the area of image management and retrieval. A representative example is presented by (Lienhart & Hartmann, 2002)) who implemented and evaluated a system that performs a two-stage classification of images: first, photo-like images are distinguished from nonphotographic ones, followed by a second round in which actual photos are separated from artificial, photo-like images, and nonphotographic images are differentiated into presentation slides, scientific posters, and comics. This scheme is neither exclusive nor exhaustive; many images fall into multiple categories. Some systems have used edge and shape information that is either supplied by the user or extracted from training samples (Saber & Tekalp, 1998). However, such systems require detailed region segmentation. Segmentation has been used to extract region-based descriptions of an image by NeTra, Blobworld, and SIMPLIcity (Ma & Manjunath, 1999; Carson, Thomas, Belongie, Hellerstein, & Malik, 1999; Wang, Li, & Wiederhold, 2001). NeTra and Blobworld present a user with the segmented regions of an image. The user selects regions to be matched, together with attributes such as color and texture. SIMPLIcity is able to match all segmented regions automatically. However, a user's Semantic understanding of an image is at a higher level than the region representation. Often it is difficult for a user to select a representative region for the entire image; coupled with the inaccuracy of automatic segmentation, the retrieved results do not match the user's intuition, or understanding of the images. An object is typically composed of multiple segments with varying color and texture patterns. One or more segmented regions are usually not sufficient to address Semantic object representation.

A key feature of our approach is that segmentation and detailed object representation are not required. Our approach is a texture-color-based image retrieval system using a similarity approach on the basis of the matching of selected texture-color features. Image texture features are generated via a gray level co-occurrence matrix, and color features are generated via an image histogram. Since they are computed over gray levels, color images of the database are first converted to 256 gray levels. For each image of the database, a set of texture-color features is extracted. They are derived from a modified form of the gray level co-occurrence matrix over several angles and distances from the image histogram. Five texture features and one color feature are extracted from the co-occurrence matrix and image histogram. These features are represented and normalized in attribute vector, then the rough set dependency rules are generated directly from the real value attribute vector. Then the rough set reduction technique is applied to find all reducts of the data that contain the minimal subset of attributes associated with a class label for classification. To measure the similarity between two images, a new distance measure between two feature vectors based on rough sets is calculated and evaluated.

Problem Definition: Assume that we have an image database that contains a collection of images IDB = $\{I_1, I_2, ... I_n\}$. Let Q be a query image and be a real inter-image distance between y two images I_i and I_j. The user can specify a query to retrieve a number of relevant images. Let m be the number of images that are closed to the query Q that the user wants to retrieve such that $m < n$. This image retrieval problem can be defined as the efficient retrieval of the best of m images based on IDB from a database on n images.

ROUGH SET THEORY: THEORETICAL BACKGROUND

Basically, rough set theory (Hassanien & Ali, 2004; Pawlak, 1991; Pawlak, 1982; Pawlak, Grzymala-Busse, Slowinski, & Ziarko, 1995; Slowinski, 1995) deals with the approximation of sets that are difficult to describe with the available information. In a medical application, a set of interest could be the set of patients with a certain disease or outcome. In rough set theory, the data are collected in a table, called a decision table. Rows of the decision table correspond to objects, and columns correspond to attributes. In the dataset, we assume we are given a set of examples with a class label to indicate the class to which each example belongs. We call the class label the decision attributes, the rest of the attributes the condition attributes. Rough set theory defines three regions based on the equivalent classes induced by the attribute values: lower approximation, upper approximation, and boundary. Lower approximation contains all the objects that are definitely classified based on the data collected, and upper approximation contains all the objects that can probably be classified. The boundary is the difference between the upper approximation and the lower approximation. So, we can define a rough set as any set defined through its lower and upper approximations.

On the other hand, the notion of indiscernibility is fundamental to rough set theory. Informally, two objects in a decision table are indiscernible if one cannot distinguish between them on the basis of a given set of attributes. Hence, indiscernibility is a function of the set of attributes under consideration. For each set of attributes, we can thus define a binary indiscernibility relation, which is a collection of pairs of objects that are indiscernible to each other. An indiscernibility relation partitions the set of cases or objects into a number of equivalence classes. An equivalence class of a particular object is simply the collection of objects that are indiscernible to the object in question. Some formal definitions of the rough sets are given as follows:

Information Systems

Knowledge representation in rough sets is done via information systems, which are a tabular form of an OBJECT→ATTRIBUTE VALUE relationship. More precisely, an information system, $\Gamma = <U, \Omega, V_q, f_q>_{q \in \Omega}$, where U is a finite set of objects, $U = \{x_1, x_2, x_3, ..., x_n\}$, and Ω is a finite set of attributes (features). The attributes in Ω are further classified into disjoint condition attributes A and decision attributes D, $\Omega = A \cup D$. For each q $\in \Omega$, V_q is a set of attribute values for q, each $f_{q:}U \rightarrow V_q$ is an information function that assigns particular values from domains of attributes to objects such that $f_q(x_i) \in V_q$ for all $x_i \in U$ and $q \in \Omega$.. With respect to a given q, the functions partitions the universe into a set of pairwise disjoints subsets of U:

$$R_q = \{x : x \in U \wedge f(x,q) = f(x_0,q) \; \forall x_0 \in U \tag{1}$$

Assume a subset of the set of attributes, $P \subseteq A$ Two samples, x and y in U, are indiscernible with respect to P if and only if $f(x,q) = f(y,q) \forall q \in P$. The indiscernibility relation for all $P \subseteq A$ is written as $IND(P)$. $U / IND(P)$ is used to denote the partition of U given $IND(P)$ and is calculated as follows:

$$U / IND(P) = \otimes \{q \in P : U / IND(P)(\{q\})\}, \tag{2}$$

$$A \otimes B = \{X \cap Y : \forall q \in A, \forall Y \in B, X \cap Y \neq \{\}\}. \tag{3}$$

Approximation Spaces

A rough set approximates traditional sets using a pair of sets named the lower and upper approximations of the set. The lower and upper approximations of a set $P \subseteq U$, are defined by equations (4) and (5), respectively.

$$\underline{P}Y = \bigcup \{X : X \in U / IND(P), X \subseteq Y\} \tag{4}$$

$$\overline{P}Y = \bigcup \{X : X \in U / IND(P), X \cup Y \neq \{\}\} \tag{5}$$

Assuming P and Q are equivalence relationships in U, the important concept positive region $POS_P(Q)$ is defined as:

$$POS_P(Q) = \bigcup_{X \in Q} \underline{P}X \tag{6}$$

A positive region contains all patterns in U that can be classified in attribute set Q using the information in attribute set P.

Degree of Dependency

The degree of dependency $\gamma(P,Q)$ of a set P of attributes with respect to a set Q of class labeling is defined as:

$$\gamma(P,Q) = \frac{|POS_P(Q)|}{|U|} \tag{7}$$

where $|S|$ denotes the cardinality of set S.

The degree of dependency provides a measure of how important P is in mapping the dataset examples into Q. If $\gamma(P,Q) = 0$, then classification Q is independent of the attributes in P, hence the decision attributes are of no use to this classification. If $\gamma(P,Q) = 1$, then Q is completely dependent on P, hence the attributes are indispensable. Values $0 < \gamma(P,Q) < 1$ denote partial dependency, which shows that only some of the attributes in P may be useful, or that the dataset was flawed to begin with. In addition, the complement of $\gamma(P,Q)$ gives a measure of the contradictions in the selected subset of the dataset.

A RULE-BASED SYSTEM FOR IMAGE CLASSIFICATION

Figure 1 shows a typical architecture of a content-based image retrieval system. It contains two main subsystems. The first one is concerned with the data insertion that is responsible for extracting appropriate features from images and storing them in the image database. This process is usually performed offline. The second subsystem is concerned with the query processing, which is organized as follows: the interface allows a user to specify a query by means of a query pattern and to visualize the retrieved similar images. The query-processing module extracts a feature and rule vector from a query pattern and applies a metric distance function to evaluate the similarity between the query image and the database images. Next, the module ranks the database images in a decreasing order of similarity to the query image and forwards the most similar images to the interface module.

Texture and Color Feature Extraction

Texture is one of the most important defining characteristics of an image. Texture is characterized by the spatial distribution of gray levels in a neighborhood (Kundu & Chen, 1992; Mari, Bogdan, Moncef & Ari, 2002). In order to capture the spatial dependence of gray-level values that contribute to the perception of texture, a two-dimensional dependence texture analysis matrix is discussed for texture consideration. In the literature, different kinds of textural features have been proposed, such as multi-channel filtering features, fractal-based features, and co-occurrence features (Haralick, 1979; Li, Gray & Olshen, 2000; Zhang, H. Gong, Y. Low, C.Y. & Smoliar S.W , 1995). For our classification purposes, the co-occurrence features are selected as the basic texture feature detectors due to their good performance in many pattern recognition applications, including medical image processing, remote sensing, and content-based retrieval. In the following paragraph, we describe the co-occurrence matrices and the features we computed from them.

A co-occurrence matrix is the two-dimensional matrix of joint probabilities $P_{d,r}(i,j)$ between pairs of pixels, separated by a distance d in a given direction r.

Figure 1. Content-based image classification and retrieval architecture

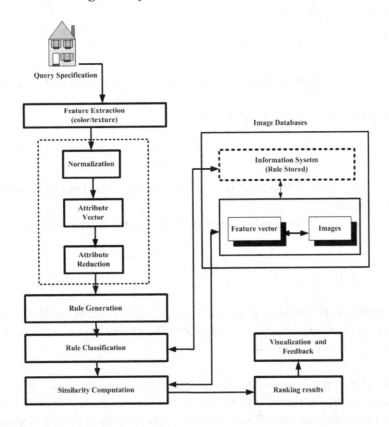

Definition 1 (Descriptor). Using a co-occurrence matrix, different properties of the pixel distribution can be obtained by applying mathematical operations to the matrix values. These operations are called descriptors. Each descriptor is related to a particular visual feature about the texture.

Haralick et al. proposed a set of 14 descriptors (Haralick, 1979) derived from the co-occurrence matrix. In this paper, five features (descriptors) were selected for further study: maximum probability (*MP*), contrast (*Cont*), inverse different moment (*IM*), angular second moment (*AM*), and entropy (*Entro*). Where:

- Maximum probability (*MP*) is defined as follows:

$$MP = \max \sum_{i,j} P(i,j),$$ (8)

- Contrast feature is a measure of the image contrast or the number of local variations is present in an image. It takes the following form:

$$Cont = \sum_{i,j} (i-j)^2 P(i,j),$$ (9)

- Inverse different moment (*IM*) is a measure of the image contrast or the amount of local variations present in an image. It takes the following form:

$$IM = \sum_{i,j} \frac{1}{1+(i-j)^2} P(i,j) \qquad (10)$$

This descriptor has large values in cases in which the largest elements in *P* are along the principal diagonal.

- Angular second moment (*AM*) takes the form:

$$AM = \sum_{i,j} P(i,j)^2, \qquad (11)$$

For homogeneous textures value of angular second moment turns out to be small compared to nonhomogeneous ones.

- Entropy is a measure of information content. It measures the randomness of intensity distribution.

$$Entro = \sum_{i,j} P(i,j) \log(P(i,j)) \qquad (12)$$

Where $P(i,j)$ refers to the normalized entry of the co-occurrence matrices. That is, $P(i,j) = P_d(i,j)/R$ where R is the total number of pixel pairs (i, j) for a displacement vector $d = (dx, dy)$ and image of size *NxM*, R is given by $(N - dx)(M - dy)$.

In order to obtain better retrieval results, the image texture features can be combined with the color features to form a powerful discriminating feature vector for each image. Various color identification schemes have been proposed and used. The RGB (Red, Green, Blue) model has been widely adopted because of its implementation simplicity (Ahuja & Rosefeld, 1978; Yining & Manjuncth, 1999 ; Zhang, H. Gong, Y. Low, C.Y. & Smoliar S.W , 1995). Despite this, the RGB model has proved unable to separate the luminance and chromatic components; furthermore, it results in perceptually nonuniform, i.e., perceptual changes in color, which are not linear with numerical changes. The HVC (Hue, Value, Chroma) color model completely separates the luminance and chromatic components with Hue representing the color type, Value representing the luminance, and Chroma representing the color purity. The transformation from the RGB model to the HVC model can be performed in several ways; in this work, the transformation is obtained through the CIE L*a*b* model. Assuming a 24-bit-per-pixel context, the RGB components are transformed into the CIE XYZ components using the following equations:

$$\begin{cases} X = 0.607*R + 0.17*G + 0.210*B \\ Y = 0.299*R + 0.587*G + 0.114*B \\ Z = 0.066*G + 1.117*B \end{cases}$$

Then the HVC values are finally obtained as follows:

$$H = \arctan\left[\frac{200*\left[\left(\frac{Y}{Y_0}\right)^{\frac{1}{3}} - \left(\frac{Z}{Z_0}\right)^{\frac{1}{3}}\right]}{500*\left[\left(\frac{X}{X_0}\right)^{\frac{1}{3}} - \left(\frac{Y}{Y_0}\right)^{\frac{1}{3}}\right]}\right]$$

$$V = 116*\left(\frac{Y}{Y_0}\right)^{\frac{1}{3}} - 16$$

$$C = \sqrt{\left(500x\left[\left(\frac{X}{X_0}\right)^{\frac{1}{3}} - \left(\frac{Y}{Y_0}\right)^{\frac{1}{3}}\right]\right)^2 + \left(200x\left[\left(\frac{Y}{Y_0}\right)^{\frac{1}{3}} - \left(\frac{Z}{Z_0}\right)^{\frac{1}{3}}\right]\right)^2}$$

where X_0, Y_0, Z_0 are the values for pure white.

Rough Set Attribute Reduction

In an information system, there often exist some condition attributes that do not provide any additional information about the objects in U. So, we should remove those attributes since the complexity and cost of the decision process can be reduced if those condition attributes are eliminated (Bazan, Skowron, & Synak, , 1994; Kryszkiewicz & Rybinski, 1994; Stefanowski, 1993; Zhong & Skowron, 2000).

Definition 2 (Reduct). Given a classification task mapping a set of variables C to a set of labeling D, a reduct is defined as any $R \subseteq C$, such that $\gamma(C,D) = \gamma(R,D)$.

Definition 3 (Reduct Set). Given a classification task mapping a set of variables C to a set of labeling D, a reduct set is defined with respect to the power set $\mathbf{P}(C)$ as the set $R \subseteq \mathbf{P}(C)$ such that $R = \{A \in \mathbf{P}(C) : \gamma(A,D) = \gamma(C,D)\}$. That is, the reduct set is the set of all possible reducts of the equivalence relationship denoted by C and D.

Definition 4 (Significance). Given $P, Q,$ and an object $x \in P$, the significant $\sigma_x(P,Q)$ of x in the equivalence relation denoted by P and Q is $\sigma_x(P,Q) = \gamma(P,Q) - \gamma(P - \{x\}, Q)$.

Definition 5 (Minimal Reduct). Given a classification task mapping a set of variables C to a set of labeling D, and R, the reduct set for this problem space, a minimal reduct is defined as any reduct R such that $|R| \leq |A|, \forall A \in R$. That is, the minimal reduct is the reduct of least cardinality for the equivalence relationship denoted by C and D.

Algorithm-1: Reduct (Minimal number of attributes)

Input: A decision table $DT(C, D)$, where C: the set of all conditional attributes;
    and D: the set of decisional attributes;

Processing:

$\quad$ Red←{}

$\quad\quad$ Do

DT←Red

$\quad$ Loop $x \in (C - \text{Red})$

$\quad\quad\quad$ if $\gamma_{R \cup \{x\}}(D) > \gamma_T(D)$
$\quad\quad\quad DT = \text{Red} \cup \{x\}$

$\quad\quad\quad$ Red ← DT

$\quad$ Until $(\gamma_R(D) = \gamma_C(D))$

$\quad$ Return Red

Output: Red: A set of minimum attribute subset ; Red $\subseteq C$

A dataset has at least one reduct in its reduct set—the trivial reduct (i.e., the dataset itself). It also has one or more minimal reducts.

Rule Generation and Building the Classifier

The main task of the rule generation method is to compute reducts relative to a particular kind of information system. The process by which the maximum number of condition attribute values is removed without losing essential information is called value reduction, and the resulting rule is called maximally general or minimal length. Computing maximally general rules is of particular importance in knowledge discovery since they represent general patterns existing in the data. In this subsection, we discuss a method to simplify the generated decision rules by dropping some condition attributes. The rule generation algorithm is described as follows: (Refer to Algorithm-2).

Algorithm-2: Rule Generation Algorithm

Input: A set of specific decision rules RULE
Processing:

GRULE ←Φ

N ←|RULE|

For i=0 to N-1 do

$\quad\quad$ $r \leftarrow r_i$

$\quad\quad$ $M \leftarrow |r|$

$\quad\quad$ For j = 0 to M-1 do

$\quad\quad$ Remove the jth condition attribute a_j in rule r

$\quad\quad$ If r inconsistent with any rule $r_n \in$ RULE then restore the dropped condition a_j

$\quad\quad$ End if

$\quad\quad$ End for

$\quad\quad$ Remove any rule $r' \in$ GRULE that is logically included in rule r

$\quad\quad$ If rule r is not logically included in a rule $r' \in$ GRULE then

$\quad\quad$ GRULE ← $r \cup$ GRULE

   End if
End for
Output: A set of general rules GRULE

   The rule generation algorithm initializes general rules GRULE to an empty set and copies one rule $r_i \in$ RULE to rule r. A condition is dropped from rule r, and then rule r is checked for decision consistency with every rule $r_j \in$ RULE. If rule r is inconsistent, then the dropped condition is restored. This step is repeated until every condition of the rule has been dropped once. The resulting rule is the generalized rule. Before rule r is added to GRULE, the rule is checked for rule redundancy. If rule r is logically included in any rule $r_a \in$ GRULE, rule r is discarded. If any rules in GRULE are logically included in rule r, these rules are removed from GRULE. After all rules in RULE have been processed, GRULE contains a set of general rules.

   The goal of classification is to assign a new object to a class from a given set of classes based on the attribute values of this object. To classify objects, which has never been seen before, rules generated from a training set will be used (Refer to Algorithm-3). The classification algorithm is based on the method for decision rules generation from decision tables. The nearest matching rule is determined as the one whose condition part differs from the attribute vector of re-image by the minimum number of attributes.

Algorithm-3: Classification of a new object.
Input: A new image to be classified, the attribute vector of the new image, and the set of rules
Processing:
   Begin
   For each rule in Rule set Do
         If match (rule, new object) Then
         Measure = |Objects|, K→|Classes|;
   For i=1 to K Do
         Collect the set of objects defining the concept X^i
         Extract Mrule(X^i, u^t) = {r ∈ Rule}
   For any rule r ∈ Mrule(X^i, u^t) Do
               T=Match $_A$ (r) $\cap$ X^i and LL=LL $\cup$ T ;
               Strength =Card(LL)/Card(X^i)
               Vote = Measure* Strength
               Give Vote(Class(Rule),Vote)
               Return Class with highest Vote
   End
Output: The final classification

   A similarity measure is required to calculate the distance between a new object with each object in the reduced decision table and classify the object to the corresponding decision class.

   In this chapter, three different distance functions are used. They are Euclidean, Histogram and quadratic distance functions, which are defined below. The h_e and h_p are M-dimensional histograms. The $h_e[m]$ and $h_p[m]$ are the frequencies of an element in bin m of histogram h_e and h_p, respectively.

$$d^2_{Eculidean}(e,p) = \left[\sum_{m=0}^{M-1}\left|h_e[m]-h_p[m]\right|^2\right]^2 \qquad (8)$$

$$d_{H-intersection}(e,p) = 1 - \frac{\min(h_e[m,]h_p[m])}{\min(\sum_{m=0}^{M-1}h_e[m],\sum_{m=0}^{M-1}h_p[m])} \qquad (9)$$

$$d^2_{Quadratic}(e,p) = (h_e-h_p)^T A(h_e-h_p) \qquad (10)$$

Where A is a matrix of similarity weights, $A=[a_{ij}]$, $0 \le a_{ij} < 1$, $a_{ii}=1$ and

$$a_{i,j} = \begin{cases} 1-d_{i,j}/d_{max} & d_{i,j} \le T_d \\ 0 & di\ j > T_d \end{cases} \qquad (11)$$

d_{ij} is the Euclidean distance between colors i and j, and d_{max} is the greater distance between colors on the normalized HSV/I space. That is, coefficients a_{ij} for two colors are defined by: $m_0 = (h_e, s_e, v_e)$ and $m_1 = (h_p, s_p, v_p)$.

New Similarity Measure in Rough Sets

In this section, we adopt a new similarity measure in rough sets. Let $U = \{x_1, x_2, ... x_n\}$ be the features sets, the similarity between two values is defined as follow:

$$SM(x_i,x_j) = \sum^n Similar(x_i,x_j) = \begin{cases} 1, \text{ if } ([x]_R) \text{ contains } x_i \text{ and } x_j \\ 0, \text{ otherwise} \end{cases}$$

A category in equivalence relationship R containing an object $x\varepsilon\ U$

EXPERIMENTAL RESULTS AND DISCUSSION

In our experiment, we used two image databases. The first one consists of 521 images of size adjusted to 512x512 acquired from the ground level using the Sony Digital Mavica camera. The second one consists of 630 images of size adjusted to 1024x1024 - 24 bit color images (http://www.visualdelights.net). We convert the images from RGB to HVC space. The transformation from RGB to HVC has been obtained through the CIE L*a*b* model. The weight vector is set to be 1/3.

Once the feature values associated with the images have been computed and stored, queries may be done. Various models have been proposed for similarity analysis in image retrieval systems (Swets & Weng, 1999; Wu & Huang, 2000). In this work, we use the vector space model, which is widely used in textual document retrieval systems. A new similarity distance function was adopted to measure the similarity in the classification results. The query was performed by providing a query image from a dataset that contains visual features (i.e., color) and five texture features (maximum probability [MP], contrast [Cont], inverse difference moment [IM], angular second moment [AM], and entropy [Entro]) calculated from each occurrence matrix. Their values were saved in the feature vector of the corresponding image. Then the rules were generated and ordered. The similarity between the images was estimated by summing up the distance between the corresponding features in their feature vectors. Images having feature vectors closest to the feature vector of the query image were returned as best matches. The results were then numerically sorted, and the best images were displayed along with the query image.

All inputs to the rough set classifier (the image mixed textual and color vectors) were normalized, and a set containing a minimal number of features (attributes) was contracted based on the rough set criteria. Then we trained the model to have a mean of zero and variance of 1.

Our visual system then analyzed the sample images associated with each subtask. If the query image was deemed to be a color image by the system, the set of top 50 textual images was processed and those that were deemed to be color were moved to the top of the list. Within that list, the ranking was based on the ranking of the textual results. The introduced image classification system was created using MATLAB and ROSETTA software Figure 2 shows an example of the retrieved results.

Precision-recall measure is the conventional information retrieval performance measure. Precision is defined as the number of relevant images retrieved relative to the total number of retrieved images,

Figure 2. Images retrieved

Table 1, Retrieval by image classification, where T, R, and C are the Total, Retrieved, and Correct number of images in structure class

Distance measure	T,R,C	Re=C/T%	Pr=C/R%	Fm=(2*Pr*Re)/ (Re+Pr)
Rough distance	305,262,235	77.00%	89.697%	82.86%
Histogram intersection	305,189,152	49.83%	80.42%	61.73%
Euclidean distance	305,155,96	31.47%	42.58%	36.19%

Figure 3. A comparative between similarities measures

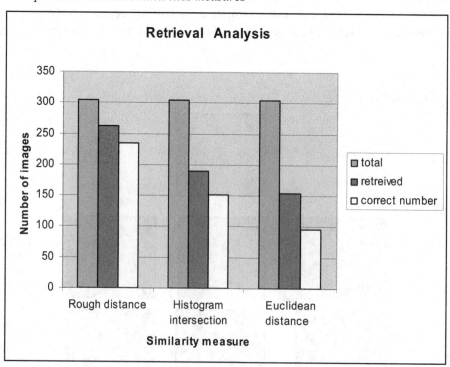

while recall measures the number of relevant images retrieved, relative to the total number of relevant images in the database. Table 1 displays the results for retrieval rates measured in terms of recall (Re), precision (Pr), and F-measure (Fm) for the above-mentioned distance measures. We have partitioned the databases into two classes: structure and non-structure. These two partitioned classes based upon the measure of structure present in an image.

Figure 3 shows the comparative analysis between the three different similarity measures used in this chapter plus the proposed one. We observe that the rough-based similarity measure is better in terms of the number of retrieved and correct number of images in class.

It has been shown that a rough distance measure can lead to perceptually more desirable results than Euclidean distance and histogram intersection methods as a rough distance measure considers the cross similarity between features.

Figure 4 and 5 illustrate the overall classification accuracy in terms of total, retrieved, and correct number of images in structure class compared with Decision tree, Discriminant analysis, Rough-neural and rough set. Empirical results reveal that the proposed rough approach performs better than the other classifiers. The number of generated rules before pruning was very large, which make the classification slow. Therefore, it is necessary to prune the generated rules as we have done, and then the number of rules has been reduced. Moreover, in the neural networks classifier, more robust features are required to improve the performance of the neural networks classifier.

Figure 4. The overall classification accuracy

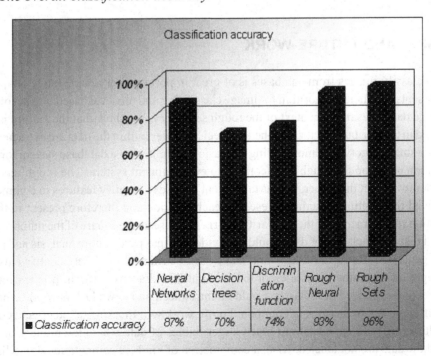

	Neural Networks	Decision trees	Discrimination function	Rough Neural	Rough Sets
■ Classification accuracy	87%	70%	74%	93%	96%

Figure 5. Numbers of generated rules before and after pruning

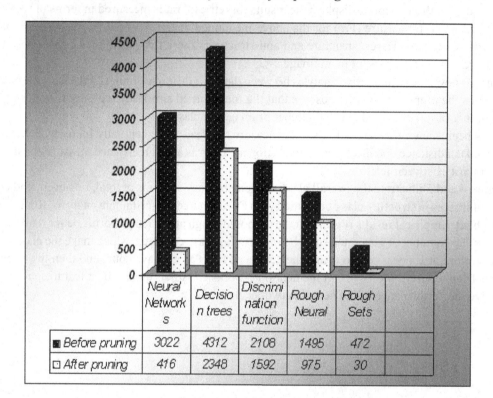

	Neural Networks	Decision trees	Discrimination function	Rough Neural	Rough Sets	
■ Before pruning	3022	4312	2108	1495	472	
□ After pruning	416	2348	1592	975	30	

CONCLUSION AND FUTURE WORK

The ability to classify images from databases is of great importance for a wide range of applications. This paper presents an efficient algorithm for image classifying and retrieval based on a set of generated rules from large databases in the context of the rough set theory. We show that the feature is extracted and represented in the attribute vector, and then the decision rules within the data are extracted. The current system is a small prototype demonstrating the basic capabilities of a database system for retrieving and classification based on the rough set theory as a new intelligent system. The rough sets similarity measure is not proven, yet this paper, to a certain extent, is able to identify features in common that are probably derived from actual structures present in each location and therefore present in the images. The computation requirements for the similarity matrix increase as the square of the number of images. It is envisaged that larger classes of data would be divided up into parts before analysis and a hierarchy of exemplars generated. Retrieval tasks would make use of such a hierarchy to identify clusters likely to contain target images rather than attempt to carry out an exhaustive search. It is expected that as an image collection expanded new classes would be introduced and new clusters would emerge based on entirely different sets of features in common. Future work will investigate the effectiveness of unsupervised clustering with application to much larger bodies of data where the number of clusters is unknown and the data are not labeled. Also, a combination of kinds of computational intelligence (CI) techniques in application area of multimedia processing, in particular image classification and retrieval has become one of the most important ways of research of intelligent information processing. Neural network shows us its strong ability to solve complex problems for many multimedia processing. From the perspective of the specific rough sets approaches that need to be applied, explorations into possible applications of hybridize rough sets with other intelligent systems like neural networks, genetic algorithms, fuzzy approaches, etc., to multimedia processing and content-based information system, in particulars in multimedia computing problems could lead to new and interesting avenues of research and it is always a challenge for the CI researchers.

NOTE

This work was supported by Kuwait university, Research Grant No.[IQ01/03].

REFERENCES

Ahuja, N., & Rosefeld, A. (1978). A note on the use of second-order gray-level statistics for threshold selection. *IEEE Trans. Systems, Man, and Cybernatics, SMC (8)*, 895-898.

Ashish G., Saroj, K., Meher, & Uma, B. S. (2008). A novel fuzzy classifier based on product aggregation operator. *Pattern Recognition, 41*(3), 961-971.

Bazan, J., Skowron, A., & Synak, P. (1994). Dynamic reducts as a tool for extracting laws from decision tables. In *Proceedings of the Symposium On Methodologies for Intelligent Systems* (pp. 346-355). Berlin: Springer-Verlag.

Carson, C., Thomas, M., Belongie, S., Hellerstein, J. M., & Malik, J. (1999). Blobworld: A system for region-based image indexing and retrieval. *Third International Conference on Visual Information Systems*, Amsterdam, Netherland, pp. 509-516.

Cios, K., Pedrycz, W., & Swiniarski, R. (1998). *Data mining methods for knowledge discovery.* City: Norwell, MA, USA, Kluwer Academic Publishers.

Graham, M. E. (2004). Enhancing visual resources for searching and retrieval - Is content based image retrieval solution? *Literary and Linguistic Computing, 19*(3), 321-333.

Dominik, S., Marcin, S., Szczuka & Jakub, W. (2004) Harnessing classifier networks: Towards hierarchical concept construction. *Rough Sets and Current Trends in Computing 2004,* (pp. 554-560).

Grzymala-Busse, J., Pawlak, Z., Slowinski, R., & Ziarko, W. (1999). Rough Sets. *Communications of the ACM, 38*(11), 88-95.

Haralick, R. M. (1979). Statistical and structural approaches to texture. *Proceeding of the IEEE, 67*(5), 786-804.

Hassanien, A., & Ali, J. (2004). Enhanced rough sets rule reduction algorithm for classification digital mammography. *Intelligent System Journal, 13*(2), 117-151.

Hassanien, A. & Ajith, A. (in press). Rough morphology hybrid approach for mammography image classification and prediction. *International Journal of Computational Intelligence and Application.* \

Hassanien, A., & Dominik, S. (2007). Rough neural intelligent approach for image classification: A case of patients with suspected breast cancer. *International Journal of Hybrid Intelligent Systems, 3*(4), 205-218.

Huang, W., Tan, C. L., & Loew, W. K. (2003). Model-based chart image recognition. In *Proceedings of the International Workshop on Graphics Recognition (GREC),* (pp. 87-99).

Jafar, M. A. (2007). Content-based image classification and retrieval: A rule-based system using rough sets framework. *International Journal of Intelligent Information Technologies, 3*(3), 41-58.

Kent, R. E. (1994). Rough concept analysis, rough sets, fuzzy sets knowledge discovery. In W. P. Ziarko (Ed.), *Proceedings of the International Workshop on Rough Sets, Knowledge, Discovery* (pp. 248-255). Banff, AB, Canada: Springer-Verlag.

Koskela, M., Laaksonen, J., & Oja, E. (2004). Entropy-based measures for clustering and SOM topology preservation applied to content-based image indexing and retrieval. In *Proceedings of 17th International Conference on Pattern Recognition (ICPR 2004),* (pp. 1005-1009).

Kryszkiewicz, M., & Rybinski, H. (1994). Finding reducts in composed information systems, rough sets, fuzzy sets knowledge discovery. In W. P. Ziarko (Ed.), *Proceedings of the International Workshop on Rough Sets, Knowledge* (pp. 261-273). Banff, AB, Canada: Springer-Verlag.

Kundu, A., & Chen, J. L. (1992). Texture classification using QMF Bank-based subband decomposition. *CVGIP: Graphical Models and Image Processing, 54,* 369-384.

Laudon, K. C., & Laudon, J. P. (2006). *Management information system: Managing the digital FIRM* (9th ed.). New Jersey, Prentice Hall.

Li, J., Gray, R. M., & Olshen, R. A. (2000). Multiresolution image classification by hierarchical modeling with two-dimensional hidden Markov models. *IEEE Trans. on Information Theory, 46*(5), 1826-1841.

Lienhart, R., & Hartmann, A. (2002). Classifying images on the Web automatically. *Journal of Electronic Imaging, 11,* 31-40.

Ma, W. Y., & Manjunath, B. S. (1999). NeTra: A toolbox for navigating large image databases. *Multimedia Systems, 7*(3), 184-198.

Mari, P., Bogdan, C., Moncef, G., & Ari, V. (2002, October). *Rock texture retrieval using gray level co-occurrence matrix.* Paper presented at the NORSIG-2002, 5th NORDIC Signal Processing Symposium, Hurtigruten from Tromsø to Trondheim , Norway.

Mehta, M., Agrawal, R., & Rissanen, J. (1996). SLIQ: A fast scalable classifier for data mining.In *Proceedings of the 5th International Conference on Extending Database Technology*, Avignon, France

Mitra, S., Pal, S. K., & Mitra, P. (2002). Data mining in soft computing framework: A survey. *IEEE Trans. Neural Networks, 13*(1), 3-14.

Molinier, M., Laaksonen, J., Ahola, J., & Häme, T. (2005, October 5-7). Self-organizing map application for retrieval of man-made structures in remote sensing data. In *Proceedings of ESA-EUSC 2005: Image Information Mining - Theory and Application to Earth Observation,* ESRIN, Frascati ,Italy.

Parekh, R. Yang, J., & Honavar, V. (2000). Constructive neural network learning algorithms for pattern classification. *IEEE Trans. Neural Networks, 11*(2), 436-451.

Pawlak, Z. (1982). Rough sets. *International Journal of Computer and Information Science, 11,* 341-356.

Pawlak, Z. (1991). *Rough sets-theoretical aspect of reasoning about data.* Norwell, MA, Kluwer Academic Publishers.

Pawlak, Z., Grzymala-Busse, J., Slowinski, R., & Ziarko, W. (1995). Rough sets. *Communications of the ACM, 38*(11), 89-95.

Saber, E., & Tekalp, A. M. (1998). Integration of color, edge, shape and texture features for automatic region-based image annotation and retrieval. *Electronic Imaging, 7,* 684-700.

Satchidananda D.i, Patnaik, S., Ashish G. & Rajib M. (2008) Application of elitist multi-objective genetic algorithm for classification rule generation. *Appl. Soft Comput. 8*(1), 477-487.

Slowinski, R. (1995). Rough set approach to decision analysis. *AI Expert Magazine, 10*(3), 18-25.

Smeulders, A., Worring, M., Santini, S., Gupta, A., & Jain, R. (2000). Content-based image retrieval at the end of the early years. *IEEE Transactions on Pattern Analysis and Machine Intelligence, 22,* 1349-1380.

Smith, J. R. (1998, June 21). Image retrieval evaluation. In *Proceedings Of IEEE Workshop on Content-based Access of Images and Video Libraries,* (pp. 112-113). Santa Barbara, California.

Starzyk, J. A., Dale, N., & Sturtz, K. (2000). A mathematical foundation for improved reduct generation in information systems. *Knowledge and Information Systems Journal, 2,* 131-147.

Stefanowski, J. (1993). Classification support based on the rough sets. *Foundations of Computing and Decision Sciences, 18,* 371-380.

Swets, D., & Weng, J. (1999). Hierarchical discriminant analysis for image retrieval. *IEEE Trans. PAMI, 21*(5), 386-401.

Viitaniemi, V., & Laaksonen, J. (2006). Techniques for still image scene classification and object detection. In *Proceedings of 16th International Conference on Artificial Neural Networks* (ICANN 2006).

Uma, B. Shankar, S. K., Meher, A. G. (2007). Neuro-wavelet classifier for remote sensing image classification. *ICCTA 2007,* (pp. 711-715).

Wang, J. Z. , Li, J., & Wiederhold, G. (2001). SIMPLIcity: Semantics-sensitive integrated matching for picture libraries. *IEEE Transactions on Pattern Analysis and Machine Intelligence, 23,* 947-963.

Wu, Q. T., & Huang T. (2000). Discriminant algorithm with application to image retrieval. In *Proceedings to the IEEE Conference on Computer Vision and Pattern Recognition, 1,* (pp. 222-227).

Yang, Z., & Laaksonen, J. (2005). Partial relevance in interactive facial image retrieval. In *Proceedings of 3rd International Conference on Advances in Pattern Recognition (ICAPR 2005),* (pp. 216-225).

Yang , C. C., Prasher, S. O., Enright P., Madramootoo C., Burgess M. Goel, Pradeep K. & Callum I. (2003, June) Application of decision tree technology for image classification using remote sensing data. *Agricultural Systems, 76*(3), 1101-1117.

Yining, D., & Manjuncth, B. S. (1999). An efficient low-dimensional color indexing scheme for region-based image retrieval. In *Proceedgins Of IEEE International. Conference on Acoustics, Speech, and Signal Processing (ICASSP),* (pp. 3017-3020).

Zhang, H., Gong, Y., Low, C. Y., & Smoliar, S. W. (1995). Image retrieval based on color feature: An evaluation study. In *Proceedings Of SPIE, 2606,* (pp. 212-220).

Zhong, N., & Skowron, A. (2000). Rough sets in KDD: Tutorial notes. *Bulletin of International Rough Set Society, 4*(1/2), 9-30.

Zhou, Z. H., Jiang, Y., & Chen, S. F. (2000). A general neural framework for classification rule mining. *International Journal of Computers, Systems, and Signals, 1*(2), 154-168.

ENDNOTE

[1]   ROSETTA is a general C++ rough sets toolkit offering the most common rough sets structure and operations.

Chapter XI

Supporting Text Retrieval by Typographical Term Weighting

Lars Werner
University of Paderborn, Germany

Stefan Böttcher
University of Paderborn, Germany

ABSTRACT

Text documents stored in information systems usually consist of more information than the pure concatenation of words, i.e., they also contain typographic information. Because conventional text retrieval methods evaluate only the word frequency, they miss the information provided by typography, e.g., regarding the importance of certain terms. In order to overcome this weakness, we present an approach which uses the typographical information of text documents and show how this improves the efficiency of text retrieval methods. Our approach uses weighting of typographic information in addition to term frequencies for separating relevant information in text documents from the noise. We have evaluated our approach on the basis of automated text classification algorithms. The results show that our weighting approach achieves very competitive classification results using at most 30% of the terms used by conventional approaches, which makes our approach significantly more efficient.

INTRODUCTION

Text documents combine textual and typographical information. However, since Luhn (1958), information retrieval (IR) algorithms use only term frequency in text documents for measuring the text significance, i.e., typographic information also contained in the texts is not considered by most of the common IR methods. Typographic information includes the employment of different character fonts, character sizes and styles, the choice of line length, text alignment and the type-area within the paper format.

Authors use typographical information in their texts to make them more readable. Therefore, we follow the arguments of Apté et al. (1994), Cutler et al. (1997), Kim and Zhang (2000), and Kwon and Lee (2000) that typographical information may help to classify or to better understand the meaning of texts, which results in the following hypothesis that can be regarded as an extension to Luhn's thesis:

The justification of measuring word significance by typography is based on the fact that a writer normally uses certain typographic styles to clarify his argumentation and the description of certain facts.

In order to verify our hypothesis, we have implemented our ideas within the VKC[1] document management system. For an evaluation of the classification quality of our approach, we have used two public data sets of the World Wide Knowledge Base (Web-Kb) project[2], which contains HTML documents with typographical information and our own selection of publications in PDF format from the ACM Digital Library[3]. The evaluation result is that classification algorithms that consider typography information allow reducing the considered term set, thereby significantly improving the efficiency of the automated document classification.

The remainder of the article is organized as follows. The second section describes some related works. The third section outlines our previous HTML tag-based typographical weighting approach and the fourth section describes our catalogue evaluation scenario and summarizes the performance results of the tag based approach. Within the fifth section we describe our new general typography-based weighting approach, which we evaluate in the sixth section. The seventh section outlines a summary and the conclusions.

RELATED WORKS

Apté, Damerau and Weiss (1994) presented the first typographic term weighting approach for text classification. They measured the classification quality of the "Reuters-21578 text categorization test collection"[4] and demonstrated that by counting the terms of the news titles twice, an improvement of nearly 2% (precision recall break even point) could be achieved.

Cutler, Shih and Meng (1997), for the first time, suggested an absolute weighting scheme for HTML tags. By weighting words enclosed in tags depending on the tag weight (c.f. Table 1) the average preci-

Table 1. Absolute term weighting table by Cutler, Shih and Meng

HTML Tag	Tag Weight
<a>	1
<h1>, <h2>	8
<h3>, <h4>, <h5>, <h6>	1
<strong>, <b>, <em>, <i>, <u>, <dl>, <ol>, <ul>	1
<title>	0
Remaining tags and normal text	1

Table 2. Absolute term weighting table by Kim and Zhang

HTML Tag	Tag Weight
\<a\>	1.7634
\<h1\>, \<h2\>, \<h3\>, \<h4\>, \<h5\>, \<h6\>	2.3425
\<b\>	0.7060
\<i\>	1.0192
\<title\>	0.5584

Table 3. Absolute term weighting table by Kwon and Lee

HTML Tag	Tag Weight
\<title\>, \<h1\>, \<meta „keyword"\>, \<meta „description"\>	4
\<b\>, \<blink\>, \<h2-7\>, \<strong\>, \<u\>, \<i\>, \<big\>, \<dt\>, \<dfn\>, \<caption\>, \<abstract\>, \<ul\>, \<alt\>, \<a\>, \<strike\>, \<note\>, \<q\>, \<footnote\>, \<cite\>, \<era\>, \<ol\>, \<option\>, \<role\>	3
remaining tags and normal text	1

sion of their IR system was increased by nearly 7%.

By using a genetic algorithm for learning the tag weights Kim and Zhang (2000) determined a similar weighting table (Table 2).

By measurements of a kNN classifier, Kwon and Lee (2000) determined a weighting table (Table 3) for HTML tags. In combination with feature selection, they determined an improvement of the precision recall break even point of 14.7%. However, the exclusive employment of the tag weighting did not yield an improvement of classification quality. The authors justify this with too strong a weighting of noise terms.

Common to all related works concerning typographic term weighting is that they weight HTML tags absolutely and use this as an additional factor in frequency based term weighting. The tag weighting is based on measurements with test documents and maps HTML tags into a few weighted groups. A larger character font size used for text enclosed in HTML tags leads to a stronger weighting of the enclosed text in all these approaches. The disadvantage of these approaches is that the tag weighting is only based on statistic measurements and not on typographic research, and that thereby these approaches are highly depend on the used training documents. In contrast, we have suggested an absolute weighting approach (Werner et al., 2005), which considers the weighting of HTML tags in the way which was intended by the author of the HTML document.

WEIGHTING OF HTML TAGS

Relevant Information within HTML Tags

HTML tags within a document control the way in which the document will be displayed by a browser. There are in principle three classes of tags: Logical, physical and meta-tags. So HTML allows words to be enclosed either within physical tags (e.g., the tags <i> and </i> require that they are to be displayed in italics) or within logical tags (e.g., <em> and </em> specify that the content is to be emphasized). Meta-tags describe the HTML document and its contents.

Due to this diversity, it is necessary to develop an approach which correctly weights logical and physical tags regarding in a manner consistent with their semantic relevance. For the definition of a suitable evaluation basis, we have examined different criteria to evaluate emphasizing text, with the purpose of finding the greatest possible approximation between objectively measured values and the subjective impression of the weighted emphasis of text passages. Among these criteria, the subjective impression of different font styles depends on the medium used (monitor, paper, etc.) and turned out to be too difficult to weight. Similar difficulties arise in weighting the subjective impression of different colors, which may depend on the medium used, the background color etc. Even worse, weighting colors depending on contrast returns wrong results for signal colors, e.g., a red word among black words on white background.

As a result, we found out that the number of pixels on a typical screen resolution is a much more important relevance criterion than the previously mentioned criteria. The number of pixels is even more important than text height or text width, because this criterion regards not only font size but also bold faced printing. This has motivated us to develop an approach which evaluates the relevance of a text passage based on the number of foreground pixels set.

In addition to the logical and physical HTML tags, which have direct influence on text representation in the Web browser, there are still some tags which have only a describing function. For example, meta-tags can contain recapitulating or supplementing information to the HTML document. Therefore, it is generally advantageous to consult meta-tags for the weighting process. However, if a Web author abuses a meta-tag in such a way that it has no semantic relationship to the context of a Web page, these meta-tags do not help us, e.g., in document classification. As many Web pages contain unrelated key words, which are often required by the users of search engines (Davison, 2000), we use meta-tags for classification only if the words enclosed in the meta-tags are also contained in the document body text.

Computation of Weights

We have used a simple "nearest neighbor classifier" to show the performance of our tag weighting approach. Because of the lack of typographic research mentioned already in Hartley (1986), we have set up the following rules of thumb for the computation of term weights. Within a parser run through the document, all HTML tags are replaced with numeric weighting tags, which correspond to the weight values of Table 4. Column one of Table 4 lists the HTML tags considered. Column two contains the character font size corresponding to the respective HTML tag. The third column contains the square root of the set foreground pixels of an example sentence that uses the respective tag style. Column four and five contain the absolute and relative weights derived from the third column. The relative weight (column five) for bold faced text is derived from the average weight difference between the font size

Table 4. HTML weights used for our evaluation

HTML Tag	Font Size	$\sqrt{\text{Foreground Pixel}}$	Absolute Weight	Relative Weight
default (<font size=3>)	12 pt	36	36	
<font size=1>	8 pt	27	27	
<font size=2>	10 pt	32	32	
<font size=3>	12 pt	36	36	
<font size=4>	14 pt	53	53	
<font size=5>	18 pt	62	62	
<font size=6>	24 pt	87	87	
<font size=7>	36 pt	128	128	
Headline Step 1 <h1>	24 pt <b>	97	97	
Headline Step 2 <h2>	18 pt <b>	74	74	
Headline Step 3 <h3>	14 pt <b>	61	61	
Headline Step 4 <h4>	12 pt <b>	51	51	
Headline Step 5 <h5>	10 pt <b>	41	41	
Headline Step 6 <h6>	8 pt <b>	28	28	
bold <b>		51		+9
italics <i>		36		+9
monospaced text <tt>		33		-9
underlined <u>		43		+9
strikethrough <strike>		41		-26
image text <img alt=...>				+10
meta-tag "description"			50	
meta-tag "keywords"			50	

tags and the headlines, which are normally typed bold faced. The same relevance is assumed for italic and underlined text, thus we use the same weight as for bold faced text. The weights of the remaining tags are selected by rules of thumb.

Weight assignment begins initially with the weighting of the tag for normal script and changes the current weight depending upon the type of HTML tags found. The weight changes either relatively, for instance, if the tags are nested (e.g., <b> or <i>), or absolutely, for instance, if the scope of absolute markup (as e.g., <h3>) is completed (e.g., by </h3>). When set, each weight applies to all following text, until a new tag that changes the assignment of weights occurs.

TAG-BASED EXPERIMENTS

The Catalogue Data used for the Tag Based Experiments

For the evaluation of our HTML tag based approach, we followed Chakrabarti et al. (1998) and used the Yahoo! catalogue because it is accessible for free, well known, and widely used. Since the Yahoo! catalogue is well structured and organized by human experts, we get the additional advantage that we have a highly reliable classification database for the comparison of our approach to document classification with the approach using text only.

The Evaluation Scenario

In order to evaluate the improvement achieved by our approach, we have to compare both our classification extension including HTML tags, and a classification without the use of HTML tags, to an established and widely used classification. We imported 436 categories and 4735 documents from the document class "Finanzen und Wirtschaft" (Business and Economy) of the German Yahoo! catalogue into our database. In order to obtain a reasonable basis for classification, we decided to aggregate all categories with less than six subcategories or documents into their parent category in order to avoid classes that are too small. Thus, we have obtained 191 categories, each of which has six or more documents or sub-categories.

The category vectors in the evaluation database have been set up with the following steps. First, we used the TreeTagger tool (Schmid, 1994) and a Porter stemmer algorithm modified for the German language (Porter, 1980) for extracting more than 100,000 German key phrases and sub key phrases from all the documents, according to the following regular expression:

key phrase = adjective noun$^+$.*

Following this, we propagated all key phrases of a category with a weight limit beyond a predefined threshold towards the root category. For weighting a propagated key phrase, we used the average weight of the phrase in all subcategories. Thus, it is not only possible to classify documents in categories with similar documents, but also to classify documents that fit into several categories, according to a common parent category.

A cross validation method, called the leave-one-out method (Weiss & Kulikowski, 1991), has been used for performance evaluation. This leave-one-out method removes an arbitrary document from the database, renews the classification rules and classifies this document into the structure again. We have performed this for 600 documents. In order to get a comparison to a text-only approach which does not use the knowledge of the HTML tags, we took the same documents without HTML tagging information and applied the same classification steps to these documents.

Results of the Tag-Based Experiments

Our experiments have shown that the information contained in HTML tags improves the accuracy of the classification results from 28.2% to 38.3%. This corresponds to a relative improvement of 35.8%. More details of these results can be found in Werner et al. (2005).

Relative Weighting of HTML Tags

The approach described previously, for the first time, tries to weight typography information from text documents in the way that was intended by the author. The weighting in Table 4 however makes some general assumptions about the design of HTML documents which can easily lead to a false estimation of the relevance weights of HTML tags. For example, the weighting in Table 4 assumes that body texts are always represented in normal script. This may not be true. Some authors may use italic style in the body text for design reasons and make emphases by using normal script. The same principle applies also for the usage of other typefaces.

In order to solve this problem, it was necessary to develop a weighting approach based on a few generally valid typography rules. These weight the text passages contained in a document relative to the document design. Such a relative weighting approach, as described in the following for common text documents, is also possible for HTML documents, but was not evaluated by us.

TYPOGRAPHIC TERM WEIGHTING

All of the approaches described above, obtain typography information from HTML tags and are thereby are directly applicable only to HTML documents. Theoretically, it would be possible to convert different document formats into the HTML format and weight them afterwards as described. However, such a conversion into HTML format is time consuming and a source of errors. Therefore, we present a general approach to typographic term weighting which is applicable to ordinary text documents in the following sections.

Typography in Text Documents

Typographic techniques have been used since the invention of letters for emphasizing certain text fragments and for the design of texts, and are used naturally today in the design process of text documents. Templates of modern word processors and publication guidelines issued by publishers lead to similar typography in text documents. In Table 5, excerpts from the author guidelines of the "Lecture Notes in Informatics (LNI)" of the German Society for Computer Science (GI) are compared with excerpts from the author guidelines of the "Association for Computing Machinery" (ACM).

Approaches to Typographic Term Weighting

Common to all author guidelines is that text paragraphs are more important if they are typographically emphasized. Table 5 shows that font size is significant for the weighting of text passages: The larger the character font, the more relevant is the passage to the text. The abstract is an exception to this rule because it uses smaller character size than continuous text. However, we consider this not to be a source of failure because the abstract usually uses terms that are repeated in the continuous text. The remaining typographic styles are not uniformly used and are highly design dependent. Therefore, different approaches to automated term weighting based on typography information are possible:

Table 5. Comparison of author guidelines of GI and ACM

GI Guidelines	ACM Guidelines
Title: Times, 14 p, bold	Title: Helvetica, 16 p
Abstract: Times, 9 p	Abstract: Times, 8 pt
Section: Times, 12 p, bold	SECTION: Helvetica, 10 p, up-perc.
Subsection: Times, 10 p, bold	Subsection: Helvetica, 10 p
Continuous Text: Times, 10 p	Continuous Text: Times, 10 p
Footnotes: Times, 8 p	Footnotes: Times, 8 p
References: Times, 9 p	References: Times, 8 p

1. *The absolute approach to typographical weighting* was already introduced in Section 3 using HTML tags as an example. Similar to Table 4, a weighting table can also be set up for the general typographical weighting of text passages in other document formats like PDF. Whenever a common style guideline exists, this approach has the advantage that typographical weighting can be adapted to the common style guideline.

2. *Global relative approaches to typographical weighting* of documents were introduced in the second section, again using HTML documents as an example. All of these approaches evaluate each combination of styles based on quality improvement with respect to a weighing function. They are applicable only if the evaluated documents are based on a common style guideline. Nevertheless, they are not limited to HTML, but can be used for PDF documents and other formats as well.

3. *The document-relative approach* evaluates each style combination occurring in a document based on frequency. Less frequent style combinations get stronger weights than more frequent style combinations. This is motivated by the assumption that the most frequently used style combination, i.e., normally the continuous text, has the smallest weight. This approach is appropriate mainly for heterogeneous document collections, but in some cases leads to an overestimation of text passages like footnotes.

4. *The mixed approach* is based on a combination of the document-relative approach with the observation that character size plays an important role in the weighting of text passages. We favor the mixed approach in the following, since it appears to be most appropriate for heterogeneous document collections which typically can be found in document management systems.

The favored weighting procedure considering a combination of absolute character size and relative weighting of the remaining style characteristics is performed in two steps. In the first step, an absolute weight is assigned to each text passage based on its character size. This weight can be assigned proportional or in addition to its character size, in levels of the character sizes actually used. In the second weighting step, the frequency of the remaining style combinations is counted separately for each used character size. Depending on these combination frequencies, an offset is added to the weight previously computed based on character size. To prioritize character size, this offset must be smaller than the difference to the next higher character size weight. In our experiments, we used half of the difference to the next higher character size weight as the maximum for this offset. Thus, it is always guaranteed that a larger character size weights more than all other style combinations together. Instead of increasing typographical weight linearly on character size, a different weighting function could be used. We could achieve the best results in our measurements with a weighting function that increases weighting proportional to the square of the character size, which confirms our pixel-based weighting approach, described in the Relevant Information within HTML Tags section.

The typographic term weighting can be done with a weighting table (see Table 6). During parsing of the texts, the table entry, which corresponds to the typographic style of a parsed term, is incremented for the parsed term. After the parsing process, a weighting table can be computed and numeric typographical weights can be assigned to the text passages in the document based on the collected statistical information and the procedure described previously.

Figure 1 shows the typographical weighting of the author guidelines of Table 5 as a function of character sizes which are normalized according to the highest assigned typographical weight. Note that the sections of both author guidelines are weighted very differently. Due to the standardization, the sections and subsections of the ACM author guidelines are not significantly stronger weighted than continuous text.

The character sizes used in a document are also a design element, that is, they depend on document design. Thereby, the semantic weight of a character size also depends on the design of the document. Therefore, a weighting in the form of size levels, which are based on actually used character sizes, is better than an absolute weighting of font sizes. For this purpose, all used character sizes are determined, sorted ascending according to their size, and then assigned to, e.g., a weight which is linearly increased

Table 6. Typographical weighting table for the mixed approach

Style Size: / Typeface:	1 p	...	9 p	10 p	...	64 p
normal						
bold						
italic						
bold + italic						
underlined						
...						
bold + italic + underlined						
...						

Figure 1. *Typographical weighting similar to character size*

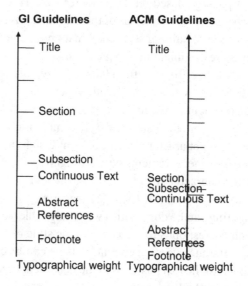

Figure 2. *Typographical weighting in levels of used character sizes*

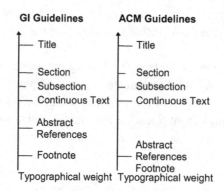

by 100 steps. Figure 2 also shows the typographical weighting of the author guidelines of Table 5, but this time in levels of really used character sizes. Note that this approach assigns similar typographical weights to comparable sections. Only the missing typographic difference between literature and footnote sections and the abstract within the ACM guidelines leads to a different weighting.

EVALUATION

We have evaluated our new typographic term weighting approach by using the widely accepted k nearest neighbor (kNN) classifier as follows. We combined the classical cosine measure with the matching factor described by Kwon and Lee (2000) as the similarity measure. The weighting of the document terms results from the product of our typographical weighting approach described before and the classical inverse document frequency (IDF).

In order to make our results more comparable to other publications, we have considered no information about document hierarchy. Furthermore, we have slightly modified the statistic feature selection methods "mutual information" (MI) and "chi square" (Yang & Pedersen, 1997), both of which are based on the binary decision as to whether a document contains a term or not, as follows. We have replaced the binary probabilities in the feature selection methods with the numeric term probabilities because these methods do not evaluate the real relevance of a term in a document and our typographical weights would not affect the feature evaluation process.

Due to the lack of freely available test collections with typographically enriched text documents, we have evaluated our approach using the freely available HTML test collections "4 Universities Data Set" and "7sectors Data Set" from the "CMU World Wide Knowledge Base" (Web-KB) project and our own selection of publications from the "ACM Digital Library" in PDF format. In order to get the typographic values of the documents of the HTML test collections, the HTML code was rendered by the JEditorPane of the J2SE 5.0[5], before the beginning of the typographic evaluation. This guarantees that HTML documents are evaluated in the same way as PDF or other document formats.

Following the setup in Nigam et al. (1998), we only used the classes "course," "faculty," "project," and "student" for the evaluation of the "4 Universities Data Set," and we used the pages from Cornell University for testing, while all other pages were used as training base.

We have evaluated the "7sectors Data Set" by randomly selecting 80% of the documents for the classification tests and using the remaining 20% as the training base.

For the ACM test collection, we used retrieval queries to the "ACM Digital Library" with labels from the "CCS classification tree"[6] in order to index at most 20 PDF documents for each class. Of these documents, 25% were used for the classification tests.

In our evaluation, we want to show the improvement which is possible by the usage of typographic information contained in text documents. So we have removed documents without typographic information from all test collections, since they would have led to false results otherwise. In all tests, we only considered categories containing at least six documents after the removal of the documents for classification tests and the deletion of the documents without typographic information. Details of the resulting test collections can be inferred from Table 7.

The global MI evaluation proved to be the best method for the selection of the features of the "4 Universities Data Set," however, the local chi square evaluation was better for the other two test collections. Unlike other approaches, we did not select a constant number of features per category. Instead, we selected the number of features depending on the sum of the best feature weights of the current category. The higher the best weights of a category, the fewer terms of this category used for classification.

We used the micro averaged precision recall break even point (Lewis, 1992), a usual performance measure for text classification, for evaluating the classification tests. This measure is shown depending on the number of selected features in the following Figures, 3 to 5, each of which contains three curves. The thin curve shows the classification quality of a conventional purely frequency-based kNN classifier. The dashed curve shows the quality of a frequency-based kNN classifier with relative feature selection, and the relative selection of the features per category for the chi square feature selection, described before. The bold curve shows the quality of this kNN classifier with additional consideration of our typographical weights.

Table 7. Details of the measured test collections

	4 Univ. Data Set	7sectors Data Set	ACM Test Collection
Categories	4	47	149
Training Documents	3,680	725	1,636
Training Terms	36,932	12,986	110,908
Tests	200	2,942	454

Figure 3. Evaluation of the "4 universities data set"

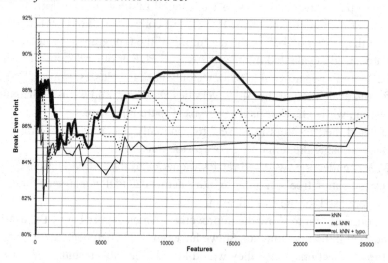

Figure 4. Evaluation of the "7sectors data set"

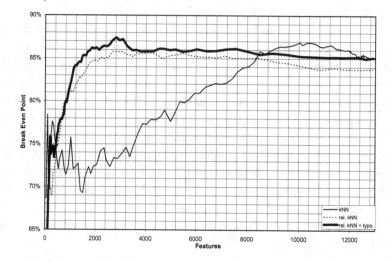

Figure 5. Evaluation of the "ACM data set"

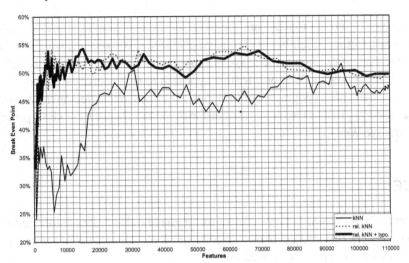

The total improvement of our approach can be seen by comparing the bold curve and the thin curve of the Figures 3, 4, and 5. The classification quality of our typography-weighted kNN classifier is up to 6% better than a purely frequency-based kNN classifier within all test collections. A further interesting improvement can be seen in Figure 4: The bold curve shows that our typography-weighted kNN classifier reaches its saturation substantially earlier than the purely frequency-based kNN classifier represented by the thin plotted line. That is, our approach achieves the same classification quality as the purely frequency-based kNN classifier with at most 30% of the features. We regard this significant performance improvement as one of the major advantages of our improved typography-sensitive term weighting.

Additionally, the dashed curve shows the improvement, which is reached by the described relative feature selection and the relative selection of the features per category alone. Figures 3 and 4 however show that these approaches lead to a better total result when combined with typographical weighting. Figure 5 also shows that typographical weighting does not always achieve an improvement. In case of the ACM publications, this is caused by the fact that ACM publications contain only sparse typographic information. For example, often only the title and the section headings are emphasized, some of which are filtered by the feature selection because of their frequent occurrence, e.g., "abstract," "introduction," "related work," "summary," "conclusion," "references," etc.

SUMMARY AND CONCLUSION

Content-based classification of text documents is essential for intelligent document management systems. The crucial aspect of different classification algorithms for text documents is the classification quality, which can be improved if the textual content is enriched with further information. However, for the majority of text documents, enriched XML versions of the documents are not available. Therefore, typographic information is the only additional information that these text documents offer beyond the text itself. We have presented two typographical weighting approaches, and we have implemented and evaluated classification systems that have been enhanced and improved by our typographical weighting approaches.

The main aspects of our approaches are the usage of the typographical information contained in text documents and a higher weighting of certain emphasized text passages, which differ from plainly typed text. As the evaluation shows, the usage of typographic information significantly improves the classification of text documents. We consider this approach to be a useful extension to all information retrieval processes. Using the typographic information contained in text documents also improves other information retrieval approaches such as text clustering or the focused crawling process which was described in (Gräfe & Werner, 2004).

REFERENCES

Apté, C., Damerau, F., & Weiss, S. (1994). Towards language independent automated learning of text categorization models. In *Proceedings of the 17th ACM SIGIR Conference on Research and Development in Information Retrieval (SIGIR '94)* (pp. 23-30).

Chakrabarti, S., Dom, B. E., & Indyk, P. (1998). Enhanced hypertext categorization using hyperlinks. In L. M. Haas & A. Tiwary, (Eds.), *Proceedings of SIGMOD-98, ACM International Conference on Management of Data* (pp.307-318). New York: ACM Press,

Cutler, M., Shih, Y., & Meng, W. (1997). Using the structure of HTML documents to improve retrieval. In *USENIX Symposium on Internet Technologies and Systems*.

Davison, B. (2000). Topical locality in the Web. In *Research and Development in Information Retrieval (SIGIR)* (pp. 272-279).

Gräfe, G. & Werner, L. (2004). Context-based information retrieval for improved information quality in decision-making processes. In K. Tochtermann & H. Maurer, (Eds.), *Proceedings of the 4th International Conference on Knowledge Management* (pp. 379-387). Graz, Austria.

Hartley, J. (1986). Planning the typographical structure of instructional text. *Educational Psychologist, 21*(4),315–332.

Kim, S. & Zhang, B.-T. (2000). Web-document retrieval by genetic learning of importance factors for HTML tags. In *PRICAI Workshop on Text and Web Mining* (pp. 13-23).

Kwon, O.-W. & Lee, J.-H. (2000). Web page classification based on k-nearest neighbor approach. In *IRAL '00: Proceedings of the fifth international workshop on Information retrieval with Asian languages* (pp. 9-15). New York: ACM Press.

Lewis, D. (1992). An evaluation of phrasal and clustered representations on a text categorization task. In *SIGIR '92: Proceedings of the 15th annual international ACM SIGIR conference on Research and development in information retrieval* (pp. 37-50). ACM Press.

Luhn, H. (1958). The automatic creation of literature abstracts. *IBM Journal of Research and Development, 2*,159–165.

Nigam, K., McCallum, A. K., Thrun, S., and Mitchell, T. M. (1998). Learning to classify text from labeled and unlabeled documents. In *Proceedings of AAAI-98, 15th Conference of the American Association for Artificial Intelligence* (pp.792-799). Madison: AAAI Press.

Porter, M. (1980). An algorithm for suffix stripping. *Program, 14*(3),130-137.

Schmid, H. (1994). Probabilistic part-of-speech tagging using decision trees. In *International Conference on New Methods in Language Processing*, Manchester, UK.

Weiss, S. & Kulikowski, C. A. (1991). *Computer systems that learn: classification and prediction methods from statistics, neural nets, machine learning, and expert systems.*San Francisco: Morgan Kaufmann Publishers Inc.

Werner, L., Böttcher, S., & Beckmann, R. (2005). Enhanced information retrieval by using HTML tags. In H. R. Arabnia & A. Scime (Eds.), *Proceedings of the 2005 International Conference on Data Mining*, (pp. 24-29). CSREA Press.

Yang, Y. & Pedersen, J. O. (1997). A comparative study on feature selection in text categorization. In D. H. Fisher (Ed), *Proceedings of ICML-97, 14th International Conference on Machine Learning*, Nashville (pp. 412-420). San Francisco: Morgan Kaufmann Publishers.

ENDNOTES

[1]   http://www.vkc.info

[2]   http://www.cs.cmu.edu/afs/cs.cmu.edu/project
      /theo-11/www/wwkb/index.html

[3]   http://www.acm.org/

[4]   http://www.daviddlewis.com/resources
      /testcollections/reuters21578/

[5]   http://java.sun.com/

[6]   http://www.acm.org/class/1998/

This work was previously published in International Journal of Intelligent Information Technologies, Vol. 3, Issue 2, edited by V. Sugumaran, pp. 1-16, copyright 2007 by IGI Publishing, formerly known as Idea Group Publishing (an imprint of IGI Global).

Chapter XII
Web Mining by Automatically Organizing Web Pages into Categories

Ben Choi
Louisiana Tech University, USA

Zhongmei Yao
Louisiana Tech University, USA

ABSTRACT

Web mining aims for searching, organizing, and extracting information on the Web and search engines focus on searching. The next stage of Web mining is the organization of Web contents, which will then facilitate the extraction of useful information from the Web. This chapter will focus on organizing Web contents. Since a majority of Web contents are stored in the form of Web pages, this chapter will focus on techniques for automatically organizing Web pages into categories. Various artificial intelligence techniques have been used; however the most successful ones are classification and clustering. This chapter will focus on clustering. Clustering is well suited for Web mining by automatically organizing Web pages into categories each of which contain Web pages having similar contents. However, one problem in clustering is the lack of general methods to automatically determine the number of categories or clusters. For the Web domain, until now there is no such a method suitable for Web page clustering. To address this problem, this chapter describes a method to discover a constant factor that characterizes the Web domain and proposes a new method for automatically determining the number of clusters in Web page datasets. This chapter also proposes a new bi-directional hierarchical clustering algorithm, which arranges individual Web pages into clusters and then arranges the clusters into larger clusters and so on until the average inter-cluster similarity approaches the constant factor. Having the constant factor together with the algorithm, this chapter provides a new clustering system suitable for mining the Web.

INTRODUCTION

Web mining aims for finding useful information on the Web (Scime & Sugumaran, 2007; Linoff & Berry, 2001; Mena, 1999). The first stage of Web mining is searching. **search engines**, such as Google, focus on searching (Berry & Browne, 1999). Search engines first try to find as many Web pages as possible on the Internet. This is done by **Web crawlers**, which go from Web pages to Web pages to retrieve as many addresses (URLs) of Web pages as possible. Since current search engines use keyword search, keywords on each Web page found by the Web crawler are stored on databases for fast retrieval (Baberwal & Choi, 2004).

The next stage of Web mining is the organization of Web contents, which is the objective of this chapter. Since majority of Web contents are stored in the form of Web pages, current search engines and most current researches focus on organizing Web pages (Choi, 2001). Search engines, such as Google, focus of ordering Web pages based on the relevance of the Web pages in relating to the search keywords. Some search engines, such as Yahoo, also try to organize Web pages into categories. Yahoo tries to classify Web pages manually by having people read the contents of the Web pages and assign them to categories. Since the number of Web pages on the Internet has grown to the order of several billions, the manual method of classifying Web pages has been proved to be impractical. Thus, most current researches in Web mining focus on automatically organizing Web pages into categories (Choi & Yao, 2005; Yao & Choi 2007).

Various Artificial Intelligence techniques have been used to facilitate the process of automatically organizing Web pages into categories. Two of the most successful techniques are automatic classification and clustering. **Web page classification** assigns Web pages to pre-defined categories (Choi & Yao, 2005). Since defining a category is not an easy task, machining learning methods have been used to automatically create the definition from a set of sample Web pages (Choi & Peng, 2004). **Web page clustering** does not require pre-defined categories. It is a self-organization method based solely on measuring whether a Web page is similar to others. It groups Web pages having similar contents into clusters. This chapter will focus on automatic clustering of Web pages.

The organization of Web contents will then facilitate the final stage of Web mining, which is the extraction of useful information from the Web. Nowadays the extraction of useful information from the Web is usually done by search engine users, who have to scan Web pages after Web pages in hope of finding the useful information and often give up without getting the needed information. The results of organizing Web pages into categories or clusters will allow the users to focus on the groups of Web pages that are relevant to their needs.

The future of Web mining is moving toward **Semantic Web**, which aims for automatically extracting useful information from the Web (Antoniou & van Harmelen, 2004). For a computer to automatically extract useful information from the Web, the computer first needs to understand the contents of Web pages. This is done with the help of natural language understanding and with the help of assigning meaningful tags to strings of characters. For instance, a string of digits may be assigned as phone number or a string of digits and letters may be assigned as address. Understanding of Web contents will also help organizing Web pages into categories and on the other hand the organization of Web contents can facilitate the understanding (Choi & Guo, 2003; Peng & Choi, 2005).

In this chapter, we are interested in **cluster analysis** that can be used to organize Web pages into clusters based on their contents (Choi & Yao, 2005; Yao & Choi, 2007). Clustering is an unsupervised discovery process for partitioning a set of data into clusters such that data in the same cluster is more similar to one another than data in other clusters (Berkhin, 2002; Everitt et al., 2001; Jain & Dubes, 1998; Jain et al., 1999). Typical application areas for clustering include artificial intelligence, biology, data mining, information retrieval, image processing, marketing, pattern recognition, statistics, and Web mining (Berkhin, 2002; Everitt et al., 2001; Jain et al., 1999). Compared to classification methods, cluster analysis has the advantage that it does not require any training data (i.e., the labeled data), but can achieve the same goal in that it can arrange similar Web pages into groups.

The major aspects of the clustering problem for organizing Web pages are: To find the number of clusters k in a Web page dataset, and to assign Web pages accurately to their clusters. Much work (Agrawal et al., 1998; Dhillon et al., 2001; Ester et al., 1996; Guha et al., 1998a; Guha et al., 1998b; Hinneburg & Keim, 1999; Karypis & Kumar, 1999; Ng & Han, 1994; Rajaraman & Pan, 2000; Sander et al., 1998; Tantrum et al., 2002; Yao & Karypis, 2001; Zhang et al., 1996; Zhao & Karypis, 1999) has been done to improve the accuracy of assigning data to clusters in different domains, whereas no satisfactory method has been found to estimate k in a dataset (Dudoit & Fridlyand, 2002; Strehl, 2002) though many methods were proposed (Davies & Bouldin, 1979; Dudoit & Fridland, 2002; Milligan & Cooper, 1985). As a matter of fact, finding k in a dataset is still a challenge in cluster analysis (Strehl, 2002). Almost all existing work in this area assumes that k is known for clustering a dataset (e.g., Karypis et al., 1999; Zhao & Karypis, 1999). However in many applications, this is not true because there is little prior knowledge available for cluster analysis except the feature space or the similarity space of a dataset.

This chapter addresses the problem of estimating k for Web page datasets. By testing many existing methods for estimating k for datasets, we find that only the average inter-cluster similarity (*avgInter*) need to be used as the criterion to discover k for a Web page dataset. Our experiments show that when the *avgInter* for a Web page dataset reaches a constant threshold, the clustering solutions for different datasets from the Yahoo directory are measured to be the best. Compared to other criterion, e.g., the maximal or minimal inter-cluster similarity among clusters, *avgInter* implies a characteristic for Web page datasets.

This chapter also describes our new **clustering algorithm** called bi-directional hierarchical clustering. The new clustering algorithm arranges individual Web pages into clusters and then arranges the clusters into larger clusters and so on until the average inter-cluster similarity approaches a constant threshold. It produces a hierarchy of categories (see for example Figure 1), in which larger and more general categories locate at the top while smaller and more specific categories locate at the bottom of the hierarchy. Figure 1 shows the result of one of our experiments for clustering 766 Web pages to produce a hierarchy of categories. The top (left-most) category contains all the Web pages (Dataset 1). The next level consists of two categories, one of which has 94 Web pages and the other has 672 Web pages. Then, each of the two categories has sub-categories and so on, as shown in the figure. This example shows that our new clustering algorithm is able to handle categories of widely different sizes (such as 94 comparing to 672 pages). By using two measures, purity and entropy, this example also shows that more general categories (which have lower purity but higher entropy) locate at the top, while more specific categories (which have higher purity but lower entropy) locate at the bottom of the hierarchy.

The rest of this chapter is organized as follows. The second section gives background and an overview of related methods. Our new bi-directional hierarchical clustering algorithm is presented in the third section. The fourth section describes the Web page datasets used in our experiments. The fifth section provides the experimental details for the discovery of a constant factor that characterizes the Web domain. The sixth section shows how the constant factor is used for automatically discovering the number of clusters. The seventh section provides the conclusion and future research.

Figure 1. The hierarchical structure produced for dataset DS1. Each box in this figure represents a cluster. The format of the description of a cluster is: its top three descriptive terms followed by (no. of docs, purity, entropy). Only the descriptions of clusters at the top level contain the F_1 scores.

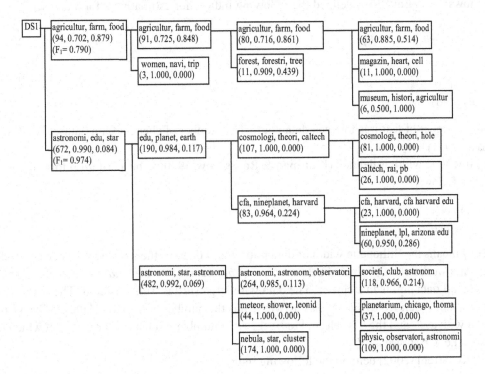

BACKGROUND AND RELATED METHODS

In this section we first give the necessary background of cluster analysis and then briefly review existing methods for estimating the number of clusters in a dataset.

The task of clustering can be expressed as follows (Berkhin, 2002; Everitt et al., 2001; Jain et al., 1999). Let n be the number of objects, data points, or samples in a dataset, m the number of features for each data point d_i with $i \in \{1,...,n\}$, and k be the desired number of clusters to be recovered. Let $l \in \{1,...,k\}$ denote the unknown cluster label and C_l be the set of all data points in the l cluster. Given a set of m-dimensional data points, the goal is to estimate the number of clusters k and to estimate the cluster label l of each data point such that similar data points have the same label. Hard clustering assigns a label to each data point while soft clustering assigns the probabilities of being a member of each cluster to each data point. In the following we present an overview of several common methods for estimating k for a dataset.

Calinski and Harabasz (1974) defined an index, *CH(k)*, to be:

$$CH(k) = \frac{trB(k) / (k-1)}{trW(k) / (n-k)} \qquad (1)$$

where *tr* represents the trace of a matrix, *B(k)* is the between cluster sum of squares with *k* clusters and *W(k)* is the within cluster sum of squares with *k* clusters (Mardia et al., 1979). The number of clusters for a dataset is given by $\arg\max_{k \geq 2} CH(k)$.

Krzanowski and Lai (1985) defined the following indices for estimating *k* for a dataset:

$$diff(k) = (k-1)^{2/m} tr W_{k-1} - k^{2/m} tr W_k \tag{2}$$

$$KL(k) = \frac{|diff(k)|}{|diff(k+1)|} \tag{3}$$

where *m* is number of features for each data point. The number of clusters for a dataset is estimated to be $\arg\max_{k \geq 2} KL(k)$.

The Silhouette width is defined (Kaufman & Rousseeuw, 1990) to be a criterion for estimating *k* in a dataset as follows:

$$sil(i) = \frac{b(i) - a(i)}{\max(a(i), b(i))} \tag{4}$$

where *sil(i)* means the Silhouette width of data point *i*, *a(i)* denotes the average distance between *i* and all other data in the cluster which *i* belongs to, and *b(i)* represents the *smallest* average distance between *i* and all data points in a cluster. The data with large *sil(i)* is well clustered. The overall average silhouette width is defined by $\overline{sil} = \sum_i sil_i / n$ (where *n* is the number of data in a dataset). Each *k* ($k \geq 2$) is associated with a $\overline{sil_k}$ and the *k* is selected to be the right number of clusters for a dataset which has the largest $\overline{sil_k}$ (i.e. $k = \arg\max_{k \geq 2} \overline{sil_k}$).

Similarly, Strehl (2002) defined the following indices:

$$avgInter(k) = \sum_{i=1}^{k} \frac{n_i}{n - n_i} \sum_{j \in \{1, \dots, i-1, i+1, \dots, k\}} n_j \cdot Inter(C_i, C_j) \tag{5}$$

$$avgIntra(k) = \sum_{i=1}^{k} n_i Intra(C_i) \tag{6}$$

$$\varphi(k) = 1 - \frac{avgInter(k)}{avgIntra(k)} \tag{7}$$

where *avgInter(k)* denotes the weighted average inter-cluster similarity, *avgIntra(k)* denotes the weighted average intra-cluster similarity, *Inter(Ci,Cj)* means the inter-cluster similarity between cluster *Ci* with *ni* data points and cluster *Cj* with *nj* data points, *Intra(Ci)* means the intra-cluster similarity within cluster *Ci*, and *φ(k)* is the criterion designed to measure the quality of clustering solution. The *Inter(Ci,Cj)* and *Intra(Ci)* are given by (Strehl, 2002)

$$Inter(C_i, C_j) = \frac{1}{n_i n_j} \sum_{d_a \in C_i, d_b \in C_j} sim(d_a, d_b) \tag{8}$$

$$Intra(C_i) = \frac{2}{(n_i - 1)n_i} \sum_{d_a, d_b \in C_i} sim(d_a, d_b) \tag{9}$$

where *da* and *db* represent data points. To obtain high quality with small number of clusters, Strehl (2002) also designed a penalized quality $\varphi^T(k)$ which is defined as

$$\varphi^T(k) = (1 - \frac{2k}{n})\varphi(k). \tag{10}$$

The number of clusters in a dataset is estimated to be $\arg\max_{k \geq 2} \varphi^T(k)$.

It can be noticed that the above methods cannot be used for estimating $k=1$ for a dataset. Some other methods, e.g., Clest (Dudoit & Fridlyand, 2002), Hartigan (1985), and gap (Tibshirani et al., 2000) were also found in literature.

In summary, most existing methods make use of the distance (or similarity) of inter-cluster and (or) intra-cluster of a dataset. The problem is that none of them is satisfactory for all kinds of cluster analysis (Dudoit & Fridlyand, 2002; Stehl, 2002). One reason may be that people have different opinions about the granularity of clusters and there may be several right answers to k with respect to different desired granularity. Unlike partitional (flat) clustering algorithms, hierarchical clustering algorithms may have different k's by cutting the dendrogram at different levels, hence providing flexibility for clustering results.

In the next section we will present our new clustering algorithm which is used to cluster Web pages and to estimate k for Web page datasets. Throughout this chapter, we use term "documents" or "Web pages" to denote Web pages, the term "true class" to mean a class of Web pages which contains Web pages labeled with the same class label, and the term "cluster" to denote a group of Web pages in which Web pages may have different class labels.

BI-DIRECTIONAL HIERARCHICAL CLUSTERING ALGORITHM

We present our new bi-directional hierarchical clustering (BHC) system (Yao & Choi, 2003, 2007) in this section. The BHC system consists of three major steps:

1. Generating an initial sparse graph
2. Bottom-up cluster-merging phase
3. Top-down refining phase

These major steps are described in detail in the following subsections. Here we outline the workings of the entire system. In the first phase, the BHC system takes a given dataset and generates an initial sparse graph (e.g., Figure 2), where a node represents a cluster, and is connected to its k-nearest neighbors by similarity-weighted edges. The BHC system then creates a hierarchical structure of clusters in the two phases, the bottom-up cluster-merging phase and the top-down refinement phase. During the bottom-up cluster-merging phase, two or more nodes (clusters) are merged together to form a larger cluster. Then, again two or more clusters are merged and so on until a stopping condition is met. During the top-down refinement phase, the BHC system eliminates the early errors that may occur in the greedy bottom-up cluster-merging phase. It moves some nodes between clusters to minimize the inter-cluster similarities. Thus, these two phases make items in a cluster more similar and make clusters more distinct from each other. The key features of the BHC system are that it produces a hierarchical structure of clusters much faster than the existing hierarchical clustering algorithms, and it improves clustering results using a refinement process, as detailed in the following.

Figure 2. The initial all-k-nearest-neighbor (Aknn) graph G₀ with n nodes (n=8 in this case). Each node in this graph contains a single Web page (e.g., node v₁ contains Web page d₁) and is connected to its k-nearest neighbors (k is 3 in this case). The edge connecting two nodes is weighted by the similarity between the two nodes.

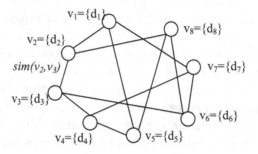

Generating an Initial Sparse Graph

In this subsection we describe how to arrange a set of Web pages to form a weighted graph (e.g., Figure 2) based on the similarities of Web pages. A Web page is first converted to a vector of terms:

$$d_i = (w_{i1}, ..., w_{ij}, ..., w_{im})$$ (11)

where Web page d_i has m terms (also called features), and the weights of the features are indexed from w_{i1} to w_{im}. Usually a feature consists of one to three words, and its weight is the number of occurrences of the feature in a Web page. Common methods to determine w_{ij} are the term frequency-inverse document frequency (tf-idf) method (Salton & Buckley, 1988) or the structure-oriented term weighting method (Peng, 2002; Riboni, 2002). Many approaches (e.g., Rijsbergen, 1979; Strehl et al., 2000) are then used to measure the similarity between two Web pages by comparing their vectors. We choose the cosine (Rijsbergen, 1979) as the metric for measuring the similarity, i.e., $cos(d_i, d_j)$ is the cosine similarity between Web pages d_i and d_j. We then define the similarity between two clusters u and v as:

$$sim(u,v) = \frac{\sum_{d_i \in u, d_j \in v} cos(d_i, d_j)}{|u||v|}$$ (12)

where d_i is a Web page within cluster u, d_j is a Web page within cluster v, $|u|$ is the number of Web pages in cluster u.

An initial sparse graph is generated by using the $sim(u, v)$ to weight the edge between two nodes u and v. Figure 2 shows an example. Initially each node in the graph contains only one Web page. Each node does not connected to all other nodes, but only to k most similar nodes. By choosing k small in comparison to the total number of nodes, we can reduce the computation time in later clustering processes.

Bottom-Up Cluster-Merging Phase

In the bottom-up cluster-merging phase we aim at maximizing the intra-similarities of clusters by merging the most similar clusters together (see Figure 3 for example). To achieve this goal, we transform the

Figure 3. Illustration of the bottom-up cluster-merging procedure. The nodes at the same level are nodes in a same graph. Some nodes at the lower level are merged to form a single node at the higher level. The two nodes at the top level represent the two final clusters in this example.

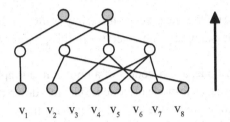

$$V_1 \quad V_2 \quad V_3 \quad V_4 \quad V_5 \quad V_6 \quad V_7 \quad V_8$$

initial sparse graph G_0 into a sequence of smaller graphs G_1, G_2, ..., G_t such that the number of nodes $|V_0|>|V_1|>|V_2|> ... >|V_t|$, where a stopping criteria is met at G_t. The nodes in the smallest graph G_t represent the final clusters for a dataset.

We first define the most similar neighborhood of a node v, $N_v(\delta)$, to be a set of nodes fulfilling the following condition:

$$N_v(\delta_i) = \{u \mid sim(v,u) > \delta_i \} \tag{13}$$

where $sim(v, u)$ is the similarity between node v and node u (see Equation 12), and δ_i is an adaptive threshold (e.g., $\delta_i =0.543$) and is associated with graph G_i. The nodes within $N_v(\delta_i)$ of node v in G_i are merged together to become a new node in the smaller graph G_{i+1} (illustrated in Figure 3). The number of nodes and the number of edges in the smaller graph are reduced, and the number of Web pages in a node in the smaller graph G_{i+1} is increased, resulting in grouping similar Web pages into nodes (or clusters).

After new nodes in the smaller graph G_{i+1} are formed, the edges between nodes are built under two conditions: (1) similarity between two nodes is greater than zero and (2) a new node is connected to at most k most similar nodes. Furthermore, since $N_v(\delta_i) \subseteq N_v(\delta_{i+1})$ whenever $\delta_i \geq \delta_{i+1}$, we design

$$\delta_{i+1} = \delta_i / \beta \tag{14}$$

where $\beta > 1$ is a decay factor (Rajaraman & Pan, 2000), which defines a weaker neighborhood for the smaller graph G_{i+1} in order to continue to transfer G_{i+1} into another smaller graph. Therefore this is an iterative procedure to transfer the initial graph G_0 to the sequence of smaller graph G_1, G_2, ..., G_t such that $|V_0|>|V_1|>|V_2|> ... >|V_t|$. The decay factor β controls the speed of reducing the value of threshold δ in a way that $\delta_0 =1/ \beta$, $\delta_1 = \delta_0/ \beta$, ..., $\delta_t = \delta_{t-1}/ \beta$. The faster the value of δ is reduced, the more nodes in the current graph G_i may be grouped to be a new node in the next smaller graph G_{i+1}, producing less new nodes in G_{i+1}. Therefore the decay factor β determines the speed of reducing the number of the sequence of smaller graphs. A larger β will result in a fewer number of levels in the hierarchical structure.

A stopping factor is required to terminate this bottom-up cluster-merging procedure. The details for the discovery of a stopping factor for Web page datasets are provided in the fifth section. This bottom-up cluster-merging phase is a greedy procedure, which may contain errors or fall into local minima. To address this problem, we apply a top-down refinement procedure.

Top-Down Refinement Phase

The top-down refinement phase refines the greedy clustering results produced by the bottom-up cluster-merging phase (see Figure 4 for example). The objective in this phase is to make clusters more distinct from each other.

We first define the term sub-node: a sub-node s of a node u in a graph G_{i+1} is a node s in graph G_i. For instance in Figure 5, node x is a sub-node of node u. The top-down refinement procedure operates on the following rule: If a sub-node x of a node u is moved into another node v and this movement results in reduction of the inter-similarity between the two nodes, then the sub-node x should be moved into the node v. The reduction of the inter-similarity between two nodes, u and v, by moving a sub-node x from node u to node v can be expressed by a gain function which is defined as:

$$gain_x(u,v) = sim(u,v) - sim((u-x),(v+x)) \tag{15}$$

where u-x means the node after removing sub-node x out of u, and v+x means the node after adding sub-node x into v. Although a sub-node is considered to be moved into any of its connected nodes, it is moved only to its connected node that results in the greatest positive gain. To keep track of the gains, a gain list is used and its implementation can be found in, e.g., Fiduccia and Mattheyses (1982).

Our refinement procedure refines clustering solution from the smallest graph, G_t, at the top level to the initial graph, G_0, at the lowest level (see Figure 4). Sub-nodes are moved until no more positive gain will is obtained. For the example shown in Figure 4, two sub-nodes are moved to different clusters.

This refinement procedure is very effective in climbing out of local minima (Hendrickson & Leland, 1993; Karypis & Kumar, 1999). It not only finds early errors produced by the greedy cluster-merging procedure, but also can move groups of Web pages of different sizes from one cluster into another cluster so that the inter-cluster similarity is reduced.

The nodes in graph G_t at the top level in the hierarchical structure (see Figure 4) generated after the top-down refinement procedure represent final clusters for a dataset. The resultant hierarchical structure

Figure 4. Illustration of top-down refinement procedure. (a) Shows the bottom-up clustering solution, which is used to compare the improvement produced by the top-down refinement procedure. (b) Shows the final clustering solution after the top-down refinement procedure. The dashed lines in (b) indicate the error correction. The hierarchical structure in (b) can be used for users to browse Web pages.

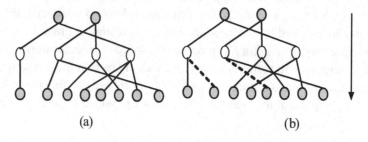

(a)　　　　　　　　　　　　　(b)

Figure 5. Moving a sub-node x into its connected node with the greatest gain

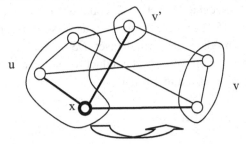

Table 1. Compositions of four representative Web page datasets

DS1: true classes = 2, the number of Web pages= 766, dimension= 1327

true class (the number of Web pages):
agriculture(73) astronomy(693)

DS2: true classes = 4, the number of Web pages=664, dimension=1362

astronomy(169) biology(234) alternative(119) mathematics(142)

DS3: true classes = 12, the number of Web pages = 1215, dimension= 1543

agriculture(108) astronomy(92) evolution(74) genetics(108) health(127) music(103) taxes(80) religion(113) sociology(110) jewelry(108) network (101) sports(91)

DS4: true classes = 24, the number of Web pages = 2524,dimension= 2699

agriculture(87) astronomy(96) anatomy(85) evolution(76) plants(124) genetics(106) mathematics(106) health(128) hardware(127) forestry(68) radio(115) music(104) automotive(109) taxes(82) government(147) religion(114) education(124) art(101) sociology(108) archaeology(105) jewelry(106) banking(72) network (88) sports(146)

can be used for Web browsing, with larger and more general clusters at higher levels while smaller and more specific clusters are at lower levels.

Web Page Datasets for Experiments

For testing our bi-directional hierarchical clustering algorithm and for discovering a new constant stopping factor, we conducted a number of experiments on Web page datasets. Here we report four Web page datasets taken from Yahoo.com (see Table 1) representing datasets with different sizes and different granularity and we skip other datasets for brevity since their experimental results were found to have similar quality. The first dataset, *DS1*, contains 766 Web pages which are randomly selected from two true classes: *agriculture* and *astronomy*. This dataset is designed to show our method of estimating the number of clusters k in a dataset which consists of clusters of widely different sizes: The number of Web pages from the *astronomy* true class is about ten times the number of Web pages from the *agriculture* true class. The second dataset, *DS2*, contains 664 Web pages from 4 true classes. The third dataset, *DS3*, includes 1215 Web pages from 12 true classes. In order to show the performance on a more diverse dataset, we produce the forth dataset, *DS4*, which consists of 2524 Web pages from 24 true classes. After we remove stop words and conduct reduction of dimensionality (Yao, 2004), the final dimension for each dataset is listed in Table 1.

Discovery of a Constant Factor

In this section, we outline our experiments for the discovery of a constant factor that characterizes the Web domain and makes our clustering algorithm applicable for clustering Web pages. For all experi-

Figure 6. The impact of avgInter on clustering performances for four representative Web page datasets

For dataset DS1 (the number of true classes is 2):

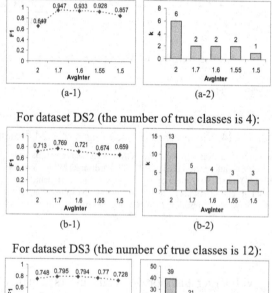

For dataset DS2 (the number of true classes is 4):

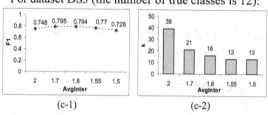

For dataset DS3 (the number of true classes is 12):

For dataset DS4 (the number of true classes is 24):

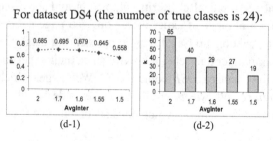

ments, we use the metric, F_1 measure (Larsen & Aone, 1999; Zhao & Karypis, 1999), which makes use of true class labels of Web pages, to measure the quality of clusters in a Web page dataset. The F_1 measure indicates how well a cluster solution matches the true classes in the real world (e.g., the Yahoo directory). In general, the greater F_1 score, the better clustering solution.

In our experiments we test the existing methods $CH(k)$, $KL(k)$, $\overline{sil}_k$, $\varphi(k)$ and $\varphi^T(k)$ (see the second section) to discover the number of clusters k for Web page datasets. These five metrics are computed for different k's for a Web page dataset. However, none of them works well. Our tests results showed that for any dataset in Table 1 their estimated k is more than 5 times different from the true number of classes in the Web page datasets and the corresponding cluster solutions have a lower than 0.3 F_1 score.

After many trials, we find that $avgInter(k)$ for any dataset in Table 1 reaches a common threshold of 1.7, when the F_1 measure of the cluster solution for a dataset is greatest. The relation between the thresholds of $avgInter(k)$ and the F_1 scores of a cluster solution, and the relation between the thresholds of $avgInter(k)$ and k's for the four Web page datasets are illustrated in Figure 6.

In Figure 6 (a-1), (b-1), (c-1) and (d-1), the F_1 scores of cluster performances for the four datasets reach the maximal values when the threshold of $avgInter$ is 1.7, and further increasing or reducing the threshold of $avgInter$ would only worsen the F_1 scores for the datasets $DS1$, $DS2$, $DS3$ and $DS4$. In other words, once the weighted average inter-cluster similarity ($avgInter$) reaches the common threshold, 1.7, the cluster solution is found to be best for a Web page dataset. This shows that, unlike other metric such as $CH(k)$, $KL(k)$, $\overline{sil}_k$, or $\varphi^T(k)$, $avgInter$ implies a common characteristic in different Web page datasets.

Figure 6 (a-2), (b-2), (c-2) and (d-2) show the k's for four Web page datasets produced by setting different thresholds for $avgInter$. In Figure 6 (a-2) it is shown that the $avgInter$ method is able to find $k=1$ while many existing methods are unable to do so. As shown in the figure, when $avgInter$ reaches 1.7, the best estimated values for k is found to be 2 for $DS1$, 5 for $DS2$, 21 for $DS3$ and 40 for $DS4$.

The estimated k is usually greater than the number of true classes in a Web page dataset because outliers are found and clustered into some small clusters, and a few true classes are partitioned into more than one cluster with finer granularity. This situation is exactly shown in Table 2, which shows the clustering solution for the most diverse dataset, $DS4$, obtained when the threshold of $avgInter$ is 1.7. The naming for a newly formed cluster is by selecting the top three descriptive terms. The ranking of descriptive terms for a cluster is conducted by sorting the tf_{ij}'/df_j values of terms in the cluster (tf_{ij}' is defined to be the number of Web pages containing term t_j in cluster C_l and df_j is the document frequency (Yang & Pedersen, 1997) of t_j). It can be noted that for most true classes, a true class has a dominant cluster in Table 2. For instance, the dominant clusters for true class *astronomy*, *anatomy* and *evolution* are cluster C_1, C_4 and C_5, respectively. We can see several true classes have been partitioned more precisely into more than one cluster; e.g., true class *automotive* has been separated into cluster C_{17} which is more related to *car* and *auto*, and cluster C_{18} more related *motorcycle* and *bike*, as indicated by their top descriptive terms. Similar situation happens to true class *agriculture*, *health*, *education* and *archaeology*, each of which has been partitioned into two clusters. As shown in Table 2, outliers, which have low purity scores, can be found as cluster C_{32}, C_{33}, ..., and C_{40}.

Discovering the Number of Clusters

The constant factor described in the last section can be used to estimate the number of clusters in a clustering process. The number of clusters k for a Web page dataset is estimated to be:

Table 2. The clustering solution for dataset DS4

Cluster	The number of web pages	The majority's true class label	Purity	F_1	Top 3 descriptive terms
C_1	106	Astronomy	0.840	0.881	moon, mar, orbit
C_2	29	Agriculture	0.793	0.397	pest, weed, pesticid
C_3	24	Agriculture	0.917		crop, wheat, agronomi
C_4	64	Anatomy	0.906	0.779	anatomi, muscl, blood
C_5	64	Evolution	0.750	0.686	evolut, darwin, erectu
C_6	116	Plants	0.776	0.750	plant, flower, garden
C_7	161	Genetics	0.565	0.682	genom, genet, clone
C_8	101	Mathematics	0.782	0.763	mathemat, math, algebra
C_9	94	Health	0.649	0.550	mental, therapi, health
C_{10}	32	Health	0.875		grief, bereav, heal
C_{11}	115	Hardware	0.452	0.430	font, px, motherboard
C_{12}	21	Hardware	0.857		keyboard, pc, user
C_{13}	83	Forestry	0.675	0.742	forest, forestri, tree
C_{14}	86	Radio	0.709	0.607	radio, broadcast, fm
C_{15}	70	Music	0.800	0.644	guitar, music, instrum
C_{16}	13	Music	1.000		drum, rhythm, indian
C_{17}	86	Automotive	0.849	0.749	car, auto, automot
C_{18}	20	Automotive	0.800		motorcycl, bike, palm
C_{19}	120	Taxes	0.633	0.752	tax, incom, revenu
C_{20}	155	Government	0.806	0.828	congressman, hous, district
C_{21}	108	Religion	0.824	0.802	christian, bibl, church
C_{22}	92	Education	0.761	0.648	montessori, school, educ
C_{23}	43	Education	0.767		homeschool, home school, curriculum
C_{24}	60	Art	0.833	0.621	paint, canva, artist
C_{25}	89	Sociology	0.831	0.751	sociologi, social, sociolog
C_{26}	59	Archaeology	0.864	0.622	archaeologi, archaeolog, excav
C_{27}	18	Archaeology	0.722		egypt, egyptian, tomb
C_{28}	120	Jewelry	0.817	0.867	jewelri, bead, necklac
C_{29}	91	Banking	0.659	0.736	bank, banker, central bank
C_{30}	92	Network	0.565	0.578	network, dsl, storag
C_{31}	159	Sports	0.824	0.859	soccer, footbal, leagu
C_{32}	1	Religion	1.000		struggl, sex, topic
C_{33}	8	Religion	0.250		domain, registr, regist
C_{34}	10	Plants	0.300		florida, loui, ga, part, pioneer,
C_{35}	1	Archaeology	1.000		guestbook, summari, screen
C_{36}	3	Genetics	0.333		pub, patch, demo

continued on following page

Table 2. continued

C_{37}	3	Music	0.333		bell, slide, serial
C_{38}	1	Sociology	1.000		relief, portrait, davi
C_{39}	2	Music	0.500		ontario, predict, archaeolog
C_{40}	4	Music	0.250		unix, php, headlin
overall	2524		0.740	0.698	

(F1 scores are given only for 24 clusters because those clusters represent true classes in dataset DS4. The purity (Strehl et al., 2000) and the top three descriptive terms are given for each cluster.)

$$\arg\max_{k}(avgInter(k) \leq 1.7) \text{ where } 1 \leq k \leq n. \tag{16}$$

The $avgInter(k)$ is computed for different k's. The k that results in $avgInter(k)$ as close to (but less than) the threshold 1.7 is selected to be the final k for a Web page dataset.

For our bi-directional hierarchical clustering system, we determine the number of clusters by using the constant as the stopping factor in the clustering process. Our hierarchical clustering process starts by arranging individual Web pages into clusters and then arranging the clusters into larger clusters and so on until the average inter-cluster similarity $avgInter(k)$ approaches the constant. As clusters are grouped to form larger clusters the value of $avgInter(k)$ is reduced. This grouping process (bottom-up cluster-merging phase) is stopped when $avgInter(k)$ approaches 1.7. The final number of clusters is automatically obtained as the result.

CONCLUSION AND FUTURE RESEARCH

Since the Web contains vast amount of information, Web mining has been proved to be am important area of research. In this chapter, we focused on automatically organizing Web pages into categories by clustering. Although many methods of finding the number of clusters for a dataset have been proposed, none of them is satisfactory for clustering Web page datasets. Finding the number of clusters for a dataset is often treated as an ill-defined question because it is still questionable how well a cluster should be defined. By recognizing this status, we preferred hierarchical clustering methods, which allow us to view clusters at different levels with coarser granularity at the higher level and finer granularity at the lower level. For Web mining in particular, our bi-directional hierarchical clustering method is able to arrange Web pages into a hierarchy of categories that allows users to browse the results in different levels of granularities.

Besides proposing the new bi-directional hierarchical clustering algorithm, we investigated the problem of estimating the number of clusters, k, for Web page datasets. We discovered that the average inter-cluster similarity ($avgInter$) can be used as a criterion to estimate k for Web page datasets. Our experiments showed that when the $avgInter$ for a Web page dataset reaches a threshold of 1.7, the clustering solutions achieve the best results. Compared to other criteria, $avgInter$ implies a characteristic for Web page datasets. We then use the threshold as a stopping factor in our clustering process to automatically discover the number of clusters in Web page datasets.

Having the new stopping factor for the Web domain together with the new bi-directional hierarchical clustering algorithm, we have developed a clustering system suitable for mining the Web. We are working to incorporate the new clustering system into our information classification and search engine (Baberwal & Choi, 2004; Choi, 2001; Choi & Dhawan, 2004; Choi & Guo, 2003; Choi & Peng 2004; Yao & Choi, 2003, 2005, 2007; Chen & Choi, 2008).

The future of Web mining is moving toward Semantic Web. Future works include developing new systems for automatically extracting useful information from the Web and creating new systems to use the vast amount of information contained on the Web.

ACKNOWLEDGMENT

This research was funded in part by a grant from the Center for Entrepreneurship and Information Technology (CEnIT), Louisiana Tech University.

REFERENCES

Agrawal, R., Gehrke, J., Gunopulos, D., & Raghavan, P. (1998, June). Automatic subspace clustering for high dimensional data for data mining applications. In *Proceedings of the 1998 ACM SIGMOD Conference on Management of Data*, Seattle, WA.

Antoniou, G., & van Harmelen, F. (2004). *A Semantic Web Primer*. Cambridge, MA: The MIT Press.

Baberwal, S., & Choi, B. (2004, November). Speeding up keyword search for search engines. *The 3rd IASTED International Conference on Communications, Internet, and Information Technology.* St.Thomas, VI.

Berkhin, P. (2002). *Survey of clustering data mining techniques*. (Tech. Rep.). San Jose, CA: Accrue Software.

Berry, M. W., & Browne, M. (1999). Understanding Search Engines. Philadelphia: SIAM.

Calinski, T., & Harabasz, J. (1974). A dendrite method for cluster analysis. *Communications in Statistics, 3*(1), 1-27.

Chen, G., & Choi, B. (2008, March). Web page genre classification. *The 23rd Annual ACM Symposium on Applied Computing*, Ceará, Brazil.

Choi, B. (2001, October). Making sense of search results by automatic Webpage classifications. *WebNet 2001 World Conference on the WWW and Internet*, Orlando, FL.

Choi, B., & Dhawan, R. (2004, September). Agent space architecture for search engines. *The 2004 IEEE/WIC/ACM International Conference on Intelligent Agent Technology*, Beijing, China.

Choi, B., & Guo, Q. (2003). Applying semantic links for classifying Web pages. *Developments in Applied Artificial Intelligence, IEA/AIE 2003.* (Lecture Notes in Artificial Intelligence, 2718, pp.148-153).

Choi, B., & Peng, X. (2004). Dynamic and hierarchical classification of Web pages. *Online Information Review, 28*(2), 139-147.

Choi, B., & Yao, Z. (2005). Web page classification. In W. Chu & T. Lin (Eds.), *Foundations and Advances in Data Mining* (pp. 221- 274). Springer-Verag.

Davies, D., & Bouldin D. (1979). A cluster separation measure. *IEEE Transactions on Pattern Analysis and Machine Intelligence, 1*(4), 224-227.

Dhillon, I., Fan J., & Guan, Y. (2001). Efficient clustering of very large document collections. In R. Grossman, C. Kamath, P. Kegelmeyer, V. Kumar, & R. Namburu, (Eds.), *Data Mining for Scientific and Engineering Applications* (357-381). Kluwer Academic Publisher.

Dudoit, S., & Fridlyand, J. (2002). A prediction-based resampling method to estimate the number of clusters in a dataset. *Genome Biology, 3*(7), 1-21.

Ester, M., Kriegel, H. P., Sander, J., & Xu, X. (1996). A density based algorithm for discovering clusters in large spatial database with noise. *International Conference on Knowledge Discovery in Databases and Data Mining*, Portland, OR.

Everitt, B. S., Landua, S., & Leese, M. (2001). *Cluster analysis.* London: Arnold.

Fiduccia, C. M., & Mattheyses, R. M. (1982, June). A Linear Time Heuristic for Improving Network Partitions. In *Proceedings 19th IEEE Design Automation Conference.* Las Vegas, NV.

Guha, S., Rastogi, R. & Shim, K. (1998, June). CURE: A Clustering Algorithm for Large Databases. In *Proceedings of the 1998 ACM SIGMOD Conference on Management of Data.* Seattle.

Guha, S., Rastogi, R. & Shim, K. (1999b, March). ROCK: A Robust Clustering Algorithm for Categorical Attributes. In *Proceedings of the 15th International Conference on Data Engineering*, Sydney.

Hartigan, J. (1985). Statistical theory in clustering. *Journal of Classification, 2*, 63-76.

Hendrickson, B., & Leland, R. (1993). *A multilevel algorithm for partitioning graphs.* (Tech. Rep. No. SAND93-1301). California: Sandia National Laboratories.

Hinneburg, A., & Keim, D. (1999, September). An optimal gridclustering: Towards breaking the curse of dimensionality in high-dimensional clustering. In *Proceedings of 25th International Conference on Very Large Data Bases.* Scotland, UK.

Jain, A. K., & Dubes, R. C. (1988). *Algorithms for clustering data.* Englewood Cliffs, NJ: Prentice-Hall.

Jain, A.,Murty, M., & Flynn, P. (1999). Data clustering: A review. *ACM Computing Surveys, 31*(3), 255- 323.

Karypis, G., & Kumar, V. (1999). A fast and high quality multilevel scheme for partitioning rrregular graphs. *SIAM Journal of Scientific Computing, 20*(1), 359-392.

Karypis, G., Han, E.-H., & Kumar, V. (1999). CHAMELEON: A hierarchical clustering algorithm using dynamic modeling. *IEEE Computer, 32*(8), 68-75.

Kaufman, L., & Rousseeuw, P. J. (1990). *Finding groups in data: An introduction to cluster analysis.* New York: Wiley.

Krzanowski, W., & Lai, Y. (1985). A criterion for determining the number of groups in a dataset using sum of squares clustering. *Biometrics, 44*, 23-34.

Larsen, B., & Aone, C. (1999, August). Fast and effective text mining using linear-time document clustering. In *Proceedings of the 5th ACM SIGKDD International Conference on Knowledge Discovery and Data Mining.* San Diego.

Linoff, G.S., & Berry, M.J.A. (2001). *Mining the Web.* New York: Wiley Computer Publishing.

Mardia, K.V., Kent, J. T., & Bibby, J. M. (1979). *Multivariate analysis.* New York: Academic Press.

Mena, J. (1999). *Data Mining Your Website.* Boston: Digital Press.

Milligan, G., & Cooper, M. (1985). An examination of procedures for determining the number of clusters in a data set. *Psychometrika, 50*, 159-179.

Ng, R., & Han, J. (1994). Efficient and effective clustering methods for spatial data mining. In *Proceedings of the 20th International Conference on Very Large Data Bases.* Santiago, Chile.

Peng, X. (2002). *Automatic Web page classification in a dynamic and hierarchical way.* Master thesis, Louisiana Tech University.

Peng, X. & Choi, B. (2005). Document Classifications Based On Word Semantic Hierarchies. *The IASTED International Conference on Artificial Intelligence and Applications*, pp.362-367, Innsbruck, Austria.

Rajaraman, K., & Pan, H. (2000). Document clustering using 3-tuples. *Pacific Rim International Conference on Artificial Intelligence Workshop on Text and Web Mining*, Melbourne.

Riboni, D. (2002). Feature selection for Web page classification. In *Proceedings of the Workshop of EURASIA-ICT.* Austrian Computer Society.

Rijsbergen, C. J. (1979). *Information retrieval.* London: Butterworths. Salton, G., & Buckley, C. (1988). Term weighting approaches in automatic text retrieval. *Information Processing and Management, 24*, 513-523.

Sander, J., Ester, M., Kriegel, H. P., & Xu X., (1998). Density-based clustering in spatial databases: The algorithm GDBSCAN and its applications. *Data Mining and Knowledge Discovery 2*(2), 169-194.

Scime, A., & Sugumaran, V., (Eds.) (2007, April). Special Issue on Web Mining, *International Journal of Intelligent Information Technologies.*

Strehl, A. (2002). *Relationship-based clustering and cluster ensembles for high-dimensional data mining.* Dissertation, The University of Texas at Austin.

Strehl, A. Ghosh, J., & Mooney, R. (2000, July). Impact of similarity measures on Web-page clustering. *AAAI-2000: Workshop of Artificial Intelligence for Web Search,* Austin, TX.

Tantrum, J., Murua, A., & Stuetzle, W. (2002, July). Hierarchical model-based clustering of large datasets through fractionation and refractionation. *The 8th ACM SIGKDD International Conference on Knowledge and Discovery and Data Mining Location.* Edmonton, Canada.

Tibshirani R., Walther, G., & Hastie, T. (2000). *Estimating the number of clusters in a dataset via the gap statistic.* (Tech. Rep.) Palo Alto, California: Stanford University, Department of Bio-statistics.

Yang, Y., & Pedersen, J.(1997, July). A Comparative study on feature selection in text categorization. In *Proceedings of the 14th International Conference on Machine Learning.* Nashville, TN.

Yao Y., & Karypis, G. (2001). *Criterion functions for document clustering: Experiments and analysis* (Tech. Rep.) Minneapolis, MN: University of Minnesota, Department of Computer Science.

Yao, Z. (2004). *Bidirectional hierarchical clustering for Web browsing.* Master thesis, Louisiana Tech University, Ruston.

Yao, Z., & Choi, B. (2003, October). Bidirectional hierarchical clustering for Web mining. *IEEE/WIC International Conference on Web Intelligence.* Halifax, Canada.

Yao, Z., & Choi, B. (2005, June). Automatically discovering the number of clusters in Web page datasets. *The 2005 International Conference on Data Mining,* Las Vegas, NV.

Yao, Z., & Choi, B. (2007, April). Clustering Web Pages into Hierarchical Categories. *International Journal of Intelligent Information Technologies,* 3(2), 17-35.

Zhang, T., Ramakrishnan, R., & Linvy, M. (1996, May). BIRCH: An efficient data clustering method for very large databases. In *Proceedings of the ACM SIGMOD Conference on Management of Data.* Montreal.

Zhao, Y., & Karypis, G. (1999). Evaluation of hierarchical clustering algorithm for document datasets. *Computing Surveys, 31*(3), 264-323.

Chapter XIII
Mining Matrix Pattern from Mobile Users

John Goh
Monash University, Australia

David Taniar
Monash University, Australia

ABSTRACT

Mobile user data mining is about extracting knowledge from raw data collected from mobile users. There have been a few approaches developed, such as frequency pattern (Goh & Taniar, 2004), group pattern (Lim, Wang, Ong, et al., 2003; Wang, Lim, & Hwang, 2003), parallel pattern (Goh & Taniar, 2005) and location dependent mobile user data mining (Goh & Taniar, 2004). Previously proposed methods share the common drawbacks of costly resources that have to be spent in identifying the location of the mobile node and constant updating of the location information. The proposed method aims to address this issue by using the location dependent approach for mobile user data mining. Matrix pattern looks at the mobile nodes from the point of view of a particular fixed location rather than constantly following the mobile node itself. This can be done by using sparse matrix to map the physical location and use the matrix itself for the rest of mining process, rather than identifying the real coordinates of the mobile users. This allows performance efficiency with slight sacrifice in accuracy. As the mobile nodes visit along the mapped physical area, the matrix will be marked and used to perform mobile user data mining. The proposed method further extends itself from a single layer matrix to a multi-layer matrix in order to accommodate mining in different contexts, such as mining the relationship between the theme of food and fashion within a geographical area, thus making it more robust and flexible. The performance and evaluation shows that the proposed method can be used for mobile user data mining.

INTRODUCTION

Data mining (Agrawal & Srikant, 1994, 1995; Chen & Liu, 2005; Xiao, Yao, & Yang, 2005) is the field of research which aims to extract useful and interesting patterns out from source datasets supplied to the algorithm. Data mining is an emerging field which allows organisations such as business and government who have a huge amount of datasets stored in very large database to be able to benefit from the algorithms by converting datasets into patterns and eventually studied and becomes useful knowledge. Data mining is still an ongoing research, and previously available outcomes from data mining include association rules, sequential patterns which derives useful patterns by analysing market basket (Agrawal & Srikant, 1994, 1995), which is the list of items customers buy in a supermarket. Other previously proposed methods in data mining includes time series analysis (Barbar'a, Chen, & Nazeri, 2004; Han, Dong, & Yin, 1999; Han, Gong, & Yin 1998), brain analysis (Claude, Daire, & Sebag, 2004), Web log pattern analysis (Christophides, Karvounarakis, & Plexousakis, 2003; Eirinaki & Vazirgaiannis, 2003; Wilson & Matthews, 2004), increasing overall efficiency of data mining in very large databases (Han, Pei, & Yin, 2000; Li, Tang, & Cercone, 2004; Thiruvady & Webb, 2004), data mining on data warehouses (Tjioe & Taniar, 2005), security of private data in data mining (Oliveira, Zaiane, & Saygin, 2004) and spatial, location dependent data mining (Hakkila & Mantyjarvi, 2005; Koperski & Han, 1995; Lee, Xu, Zheng, & Lee, 2002; Tse, Lam, Ng, & Chan, 2005).

Mobile user data mining (Goh & Tanair, 2004a, 2004b, 2005; Lee, Xu, Zheng, & Lee, 2002; Lim, Wang, Ong, et al., 2003) is an extension of data mining which specializes in looking at how useful patterns can be derived from the raw datasets collected from mobile users. In a mobile environment, two types of entities can usually be found: static nodes, which are fixed entities such as the wireless access points, and mobile nodes, which are the mobile entities which have the flexibility to move along in the environment, such as the personal digital assistant, mobile phones, and laptop computers. The raw datasets from mobile users comes from the physical movement logs of mobile users, the items that mobile users purchased over time, the location of static nodes and their properties and the context in which the mobile users went into over a timeframe.

This chapter aims to propose a new method for finding relationships among two locations in a mobile environment in order to determine the nature of how mobile users visit them. This mobile user data mining method could reduce the consumption of resources for mobile user data mining by using the strategy of gathering data only to the extent that is relevant for the desired accuracy. In this proposed method, the covered area for mobile user data mining is first surveyed and mapped into a matrix, which could be a dense or sparse matrix depending on the amount of items marked into the matrix. Once this mapping is done, the matrix is used when the mobile user starts visiting the physical locations and the visiting behaviours are recorded based on the position in the matrix which the mobile users have contacted. This data is then used for data mining purposes, thus reducing the requirement for constantly identifying and gathering of the latest position information of the mobile users. The elimination of the need to constantly identify the mobile nodes reduces the performance cost required to gather the source data. By using a matrix to identify the mobile users, the behaviours are then totally marked on the matrix itself using simple markers. The chapter also further extends the proposed method by using a multi-layered matrix, which is required to accommodate mining the relationships among two contexts.

The motivation for matrix pattern evolves from mobile user data mining (Goh & Taniar, 2004a; Lee, Xu, Zheng, & Lee, 2002; Lim, Wang, Ong, et al., 2003). First, frequency pattern (Goh & Taniar, 2004a) is developed which finds out the group characteristics among mobile users based on their frequency of communication, in contrast to group pattern (Wang, Lim, & Hwang, 2003) which uses the geographical distance to determine group characteristics behaviour. Later, it was found that the location itself represents another dimension of mobile user data mining instead of the mobile user view. It then leads to place the subject matter to the location, and the location dependent mobile data mining technique (Goh & Taniar, 2004b) was developed. Matrix pattern further enhances the method by drawing the grid lines in the mobile environment in order to improve the performance of mobile user data mining in the location dependent mode.

The rest of the chapter is organised as follows. The second section provides background for concepts that need to be understood for better understanding of the proposed method. The next section gives an overview of the previously proposed method and compares against the proposed method and distinguishes the strength of the proposed method against the weaknesses of the previously proposed method. The section following details the proposed method, including the algorithms. The subsequent section provides the performance evaluations for the proposed method and the final section provides the conclusion for this project.

BACKGROUND

This section will describe three concepts that are required to understand this chapter. First, how the mobile environment works, such as the interaction between mobile nodes and static nodes within the mobile network. Then it further describes how the mobile nodes can be identified by using static nodes or another identification mechanism in a mobile environment. Finally, this section describes the difference between the sparse and dense matrix, and how the matrix pattern will fit into the dense or sparse matrix.

The Mobile Environment

Generally, a mobile environment (Goh & Taniar, 2004a; Lim, Wang, Ong, et al., 2003; Wang, Lim, & Hwang, 2003) consists of a set of static nodes $\{s_1, s_2, s_3, s_4\}$ and mobile nodes $\{m_1, m_2, m_3, m_4\}$. A node refers to machines and often to an individual component of a network. Static nodes (Goh & Taniar, 2004a) refer to devices which remain static in the mobile environment over time. Mobile nodes (Goh & Taniar, 2004a) refer to devices which move along the mobile environment over time. All nodes in the mobile environment run on a network and comply with a pre-agreed protocol in order to remain to be able to communicate with each other.

Figure 1 shows an example of a mobile environment (Goh & Taniar, 2004a; Lim, Wang, Ong, et al., 2003; Wang, Lim, & Hwang, 2003). The dotted line represents the connectivity between the mobile node and the static node. It is a dotted line because the connection can change from time to time depending on the traffic and also depending on the current location of the mobile node (Goh & Taniar, 2004a). It usually consists of more mobile nodes than static nodes. This is because static nodes are usually placed in the mobile environment in order to provide support, such as storage resources, memory, and processing power to the mobile nodes because mobile nodes are often low in power and lack resources as items have to be removed in order to make it more mobile. Each mobile node (Goh & Taniar, 2004a) in the mobile environment (Goh & Taniar, 2004a; Lim, Wang, Ong, et al., 2003; Wang et al., 2003) often is

Figure 1. Mobile environment

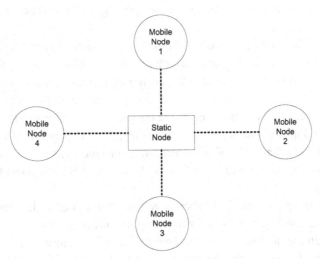

associated with at least one static node in order to remain in the network and be able to communicate with other mobile nodes by means of using the static node as the proxy for communication.

Identification of Mobile Nodes

The identification of mobile nodes (Goh & Taniar, 2004a) in the mobile environment (Goh & Taniar, 2004a, 2004b; Wang et al., 2003) can be classified into two categories, namely the identification of the mobile node itself and the identification of the mobile node in relation to the physical location in the mobile environment. The identification of the mobile node itself can be done by sharing the pre-existing feature of the network system, such as the IEEE 802.11b wireless network system (Wang et al., 2003). The network runs by using ethernet protocol in the data link layer, and the TCP/IP protocol in the network and transport layer.

In the ethernet protocol (Wang et al., 2003), each and every single node in the network must have identification. This identification is formatted as a sequence of hexadecimal digits, such as *00-0F-20-AC-FF-AF*. This number is unique globally. The second identification method in the network is to use IP address, such as *192.128.1.1*. However, this may pose a problem in a complex network which the network can be segmented to many different parts and different parts of the network can have machines of the same IP address (Goh & Taniar, 2005).

The best means of identification of mobile nodes is at the application layer which uses username and domain names to identify the mobile nodes, such as john@science.university.edu. This not only identifies the machine but also identifies the person using the machine and can eliminate the problem which arises from multiple users sharing a single machine.

Matrices in Mobile Environment

Matrices will be used in this chapter as a means to draw grid lines in the mobile environment. Through the use of matrices (Goh & Taniar, 2004b), each individual spot in the mobile environment can be better represented in a discrete form by using x axis and y axis. The benefit of this enhances the pinpoint of location in the mobile environment (Goh & Taniar, 2004b), and it will be used to find the hot spots where a mobile user frequents.

Matrix (Ashcraft & Liu, 1998) is a concept from discrete mathematics. It is a list of items, such as numbers, arranged in a pre-defined sequence which has the width (m) and length (n) specified (Goh & Taniar, 2004b). The number of items available for storing into a matrix is equal to the product of m and n. For example, if $m = 10$, and $n = 10$, the number of storage space available in this *10*10* matrix is *100*. A matrix (Ashcraft & Liu, 1998) can be categorized into dense matrix or sparse matrix. The dense and sparse categorisation is done by looking at how dense the dataset appears in a matrix. If the matrix has meaningful data filled more than 50% of the matrix, it is referred to as dense matrix (Ashcraft & Liu, 1998), and if the matrix has meaningful data filled at less than 50%, it is considered as sparse matrix (Ashcraft & Liu, 1998).

The issue of dense or sparse matrix (Ashcraft & Liu, 1998) is of little concern in this proposed method, as the matrix is used as a method for mapping the physical location map to itself, and serves as a physical location divider and numbering system provider. Therefore, in this proposed method, the matrix (Ashcraft & Liu, 1998) can either be dense or sparse. However, it would be a sparse matrix most of the time, as items of interest to the data miner and related to the problem to be solved should be at a distance from each others, otherwise, if they are very near, they should be considered as one single unit rather than two separate units.

PROPOSED METHOD: MATRIX PATTERN

A matrix is a storage component which contains multiple storage areas across the horizontal and vertical paths in a two dimensional plane (Ashcraft & Liu, 1998). The position of each storage location in the matrix is fixed, and all location must have a value stored. The size of the matrix that is the length of the horizontal and vertical plane can be adjusted depending on the nature of problem to be solved. It is important to note that matrix consists of multiple storage areas and the purpose of doing so will greatly enhance the efficiency of problem solving.

In this paper, we propose a method for using matrix to solve the problem of mobile user data mining. The problem of mobile user data mining is to address the challenges of using source data obtained from mobile users in order to find out useful patterns. These patterns can then be translated into knowledge, whenever the format of the pattern is disclosed. In order to meet the challenge, matrix pattern is proposed.

Matrix pattern is represented as a single matrix or multiple matrices in which each storage area in the matrix is representing a single static node. An example of static node is the wireless network access point, which provides the bandwidth to the mobile users. In order to provide the pattern of the behaviour of mobile users, the relationships in between each storage areas of the matrix is defined. The relationship between two storage areas in the matrix is defined as: $X \rightarrow Y = \{0\% \rightarrow 100\%\}$. The relationship is directional, which translates to $X \rightarrow Y \neq Y \rightarrow X$. Each relationship comes with a magnitude of deepness of the relationship, which is represented as a percentage with lowest value of *0%* and highest value of *100%*.

Each of the storage area in the matrix represents a single static node in the mobile environment. Static nodes are widely available, and their positions are often accurately documented. Due to the fact that it does not move around throughout the lifetime of the network, fewer resources need to be dedicated into identifying each single mobile node and its current location in relation to the time series.

The motivation of the proposed method is that matrix, due to the fixed structure could fit into the mobile environment perfectly by using static nodes. By using static nodes, the behaviour of the mobile users can still be analysed by using location dependent method and merely identifying the mobile users without any tracking system. This allows great performance improvements and cost savings and easy deployment of mobile user data mining systems.

The matrix pattern based mobile user data mining methodology can be divided into two categories, single layer matrix and multi-layer matrix.

A *single layer matrix* uses a two dimensional, single layer matrix for mobile user data mining.

Example 1:

In a shopping centre, retailers of fashion wish to find out how their stores are frequented by mobile users. Fashion is the single layer domain. Consider that there are Retailers *A*, *B*, and *C* in the shopping centre and participate in this mining exercise. The mining exercise is based on the frequency of contact that a mobile user has on a particular point in the matrix. A possible outcome would be:

Relationship 1: $A - B = 70\%$
Relationship 2: $B - C = 80\%$
Relationship 3: $A - C = 30\%$

The above relationships indicate that mobile users frequent both *A* and *B* at the same time, or *B* and *C* at the same time, but not *A* and *C* at the same time. This suggests that *A* may be a total replacement of *C* as mobile users may see no point to visit *C*.

A *multi-layer matrix* uses a three-dimensional matrix for mobile user data mining and is an extension of the single layer matrix to accommodate for robustness and flexibility.

Example 2:

In a shopping centre, retailers of fashion and retailers of leisure wish to find out how their stores are frequented by mobile users. Knowing the reason why could improve their business performance. Fashion and leisure are the two domains in this context. Here, a multi-layer matrix pattern is used.

The mining exercise first performs the single layer operation of fashion and leisure. After this has been done, fashion and leisure domain are analysed together. Consider that there are two retailers of fashion and two retailers of leisure namely *F*1, *F*2, *L*1, *L*2 respectively.

Relationship 1: $F1, L1 = 70\%$
Relationship 2: $F2, L1 = 90\%$
Relationship 3: $F1, L2 = 30\%$

The aobve relationships indicate that there is a strong relationship among *F*1 and *L*1 and among *F*2 and *L*1 but not among *F*1 and *L*2. This suggests that there consists among *F*1, *L*1 or *F*2, *L*1 a good combination of service for mobile users which attracted them to frequent them together one after the other. The weak relationship among *F*1 and *L*2 suggests that *F*1 and *L*2 are lacking of attributes that could attract mobile customers.

Single Layer Matrix

The single layer matrix depicts the relationships between the static nodes within a specified domain. A domain is a context in which the data miner wishes to solve. If the data miner wishes to find out the behaviour of mobile users in relation to shoe buying, the domain here is shoe. Each layer of matrix is focused on the relationship of a specific domain, although the layer can also be configured to analyse the relationships of a set of domains. For the discussion in this chapter, it is assumed that each layer will only represent a single domain, as using one domain per layer of matrix will lead to better categorisation and more meaningful result in the future research.

Figure 2 shows the single layer matrix of a single domain. The number in each box represents the frequency of occurrence of a particular logical event within the area of the static node. That particular

Figure 2. Single layer matrix of a single domain

	0	1	2	3	4	5	6	7	8	9	10
0	90								80		
1											
2											
3									5		
4				30							
5											
6											
7											
8		70						40			
9					20						
10											

Figure 3. Single layer matrix pattern result

	0	1	2	3	4	5	6	7	8	9	10
0	90								80		
1											
2											
3											
4											
5											
6											
7											
8		70									
9											
10											

logical event must be related to the domain, also known as theme of that layer. For instance, the single layer matrix in Figure 2 shows the frequency of occurrence of designer clothing. The designer clothing serves as the domain for the layer of matrix layer. A confidence threshold is determined, depending on the size of the matrix and the size of the population in order to determine which values can be considered relevant for problem solving and which are not. The confidence threshold determines the sensitivity of the result of mobile user data mining. For instance, the confidence threshold for the matrix in Figure 2 is 40%, and therefore only static nodes with logical event confidence occurrence for designer clothing of equal or greater than 40% (X axis = 7; Y axis = 8) are taken into consideration.

A window size, which is a specified timeframe for which the source data from mobile users are gathered, is also required in order to define the scope of the time series that the decision maker wishes to take into consideration. The data collected within the window size timeframe limits the amount of source data to be gathered and this could be based on particular time of the day and can be adjusted by the data miner. By having a window size, it serves as the base number for the calculation of confidence, as *confidence = frequency / window size*. The result of this process is a presentation of all physical locations that contains high activity of the particular logical event.

Figure 3 illustrates the result for single layer matrix pattern. There are three relationships. Relationships are connected from one unit to another. The list of relationships are: (0,0 – 8,0) = 85, (0,0 – 1,8) = 80, (8,0 – 1,8) = 75. It can be seen that low confidence values are all removed and the relationship in between each static nodes are calculated and sorted according to highest confidence first. It shows that there is a significant relationship between these static nodes.

The following steps represent the important phases in the process of generating a single layer matrix pattern. It is important that these steps are followed closely in the sequential order in order to preserve the overall meaning of single layer matrix. The outcome of this algorithm is the single layer matrix, which shows the relationship in between different static nodes with reference to single logical domain.

Step 1: Define Single Layer Matrix

Figure 4 shows the first step in the single layer matrix based mobile user data mining, which involves the definition of the single layer matrix. A single layer matrix is a two-dimensional matrix within the same level of plane. This single layer matrix provides the physical mapping of the positions of static nodes in the mobile environment. The size of the single layer matrix can be defined by using two variables, x and y, that represent the horizontal axis and vertical axis respectively.

It is important to note that the horizontal length and the vertical length need not to be the same, as long as the single layer matrix covers the geographical area in which the decision maker is interested. The definition of single layer matrix must be as one single matrix, that is, when two locations are required, they have to be defined within the same matrix in order to achieve the effect of comparisons.

Figure 4. Algorithm for defining single layer matrix

```
Matrix Create_Matrix(Single Layer, Hsize, Vsize) {
    Array = Create_Array(Hsize, Vsize);
    Initialize_Array(0);
    Return *Array;
}
```

Step 2: Select Window Size

The second step in the process involves selecting the window size. The decision maker can select the size of the window. It is important to note that the size of the window determines the duration in a time series that the mobile user data mining method will take into consideration. It also directly affects the accuracy of the result of the mobile user data mining method. The selection of the window size is dependent on the number of mobile users, the nature of the environment and the nature of the problem to be solved.

The decision maker needs to adjust the window size based on past experience or trial and error. Extra components can be installed into order to dynamically select the size of the window, by looking at the accuracy or expected accuracy of the result compared against the actual result. If they differ, the component can start adjusting the window size to make the result to be similar to the expected result.

Step 3: Collect Frequency Counts

Figure 5 shows that after the window size is selected, the collection of the frequency counts will start. The collection of the frequency counts is based on the window size. The window size represents the duration of time series that the frequency counts will occur. The frequency count is measured by looking at how many mobile users have visited the particular static node within the duration of the specified window size. The frequency counts are collected and the value of frequency is stored in the static node location for the next step.

Figure 5. Algorithm for collecting frequency counts

```
Void Collect_Freq_Counts(Position X, Position Y) {
  If Event().Status=True Then {
    Single_Layer_Array(X, Y)++;
    Nconfidence = Frequency(X,Y) / Window Size;
    Single_Layer_Array(X,Y).Value = Nconfidence;
  }
}
```

Step 6. Calculate Relationship Confidence

```
Confidence Calc_Confidence (Frequency, Window Size)
  Frequency_Valid = (Frequency > Min && Frequency < Max);
  Window_Valid = (Window > Min && Window < Max);
  If (Frequency_Valid && Window_Valid) Then {
    Confidence = Frequency / Window Size;
    If (Confidence < Confidence_Threshold) {
      Confidence = 0;
    }
    Else {
      Location.Mark();
      Return Confidence;
    }

  }
}
```

Step 4: Calculate Confidence

After the frequency counts have been obtained, the confidence of each static node needs to be calculated. The confidence of each static node is: *confidence = frequency / window size.* The result is the ratio between the number of events that mobile users have visited the particular static node vs. the size of the window. The higher the number for confidence, the greater the intensity of visits for mobile users into a particular static node. This confidence value will significantly affect the result of the system and must be calculated according to standard formula.

Step 5: Select Confidence Threshold

Figure 6 shows that after the confidences have been calculated, there is a confidence threshold that needs to be selected. The selection of confidence threshold enables the removal of static nodes with confidence lower than the confidence threshold. This reduces the amount of inaccurate data and the decision maker must take the adjustment of the confidence threshold into account with factors such as the mobile datamining environment, the population size and the level of sensitivity required.

After calculation of confidence threshold, it is time now to calculate the relationship confidence. The relationship confidence is the confidence of two static nodes. The relationship confidence of two static nodes will be: relationship *confidence = (confidence1 + confidence2) / 2.* It is the average of the confidences of two static nodes. It is also important to note that there can only be two static nodes involved in a single relationship. Furthermore, it is important to keep in mind that these relationship confidences will already have passed through the confidence threshold test and are already significant static nodes to the decision makers.

Step 7: Select Relationship Confidence Threshold

Figure 7 show that after the calculation of relationship confidence, it is time now to determine the relationship confidence threshold. It is important that the decision maker determine the relationship confidence threshold. It also is interesting to note that the relationship confidence threshold is actually

Figure 7. Algorithm for calculation of relationship confidence

```
Confidence Calc_Relationship_Conf (Conf1, Conf2)
   C1OK = Conf1.validate();
   C2OK = Conf2.validate();
   If (C1OK && C2OK) {
      Confidence = Average(Conf1, Conf2);
      If (Confidence < Confidence_Threshold) {
         Confidence = 0;
         Return Confidence;
      } Else {
         Conf1.Location.Mark();
         Conf2.Location.Mark();
         Conf_Table.Set(Conf1, Conf2, Confidence);
      }
   }
}
```

Figure 8. Algorithm for generation of single layer matrix pattern

```
Void FindPattern (Single Layer Matrix M) {
  For (I = 0, M.Size(), M++) {
    If M.I.Significance = True {
      Display M.I;
      Display M.I.Confidence();
    }
  }
}
```

less important than the original confidence threshold because at this stage, only highly significant static nodes are taken into consideration. Those low significant static nodes have been taken out of consideration and adjusting a higher relationship confidence threshold than the confidence threshold will filter out the minor inaccuracies.

Step 8: Generate Single Layer Matrix Pattern

Figure 8 shows that the final stage of this mobile user data mining process is the generation of single layer matrix pattern. The generation of this piece of knowledge contains two parts. The first part consists of the generation of knowledge based on the confidence alone, that is, a list of static nodes in a matrix structure that contains high confidence threshold. This can be generated by means of a single layer matrix with the static nodes with high confidence identified with some marker. This piece of knowledge shows the static nodes that are highly significant and the relative positions of them.

The second part of the creation of single layer matrix pattern is the generation of the relationship. Each relationship consists of two static nodes and the strength of the relationship in percentage. The stronger the relationship confidence between two static nodes, the stronger their significance. It is important to group the order of patterns according to relationship confidence. The highest relationship confidence should be displayed first then goes down to the lowest relationship confidence. Finally, the matrix is also displayed and lines are drawn across two static nodes that have highly significant relationship confidence.

Multi-Layer Matrix

A *multi-layer matrix*, as the name suggests, contains multiple layers of matrices. Each layer is associated with a particular domain, that is, a logical theme. A domain or logical theme is the context of the problem which the data miner wishes to solve. For example, two very common logical themes are entertainment and shopping, when the data miner wishes to find out the relationship of mobile user behaviours between an entertainment question and a shopping question. In a multi-layer matrix, each layer will be representing different single logical domain. The advantage of a multi-layer matrix is that it provides a good structure for mobile user data mining by having the ability to analyse the behaviour of mobile users across several logical domains.

In a multi-layer matrix, each layer must have been assigned with a confidence threshold. Each layer can share the same value for the confidence threshold, or they can share different levels of confidence

Figure 9. Sample input and output of multi-layer relationship pattern

	0	1	2	3	4	5	6	7	8	9	10	
0	90								80			
1												
2												
3												
4												
5												
6												
7												
8		70										
9												
10												

	0	1	2	3	4	5	6	7	8	9	10	
0	70								75			
1												
2												
3												
4												
5												
6												
7												
8		85										
9												
10												

threshold. The advantage of doing so is that by using different value of confidence threshold in each layer, decision makers can adjust the confidence thresholds in each layer in order to suit their decision needs. For decisions that need to have a very strong confidence, the confidence threshold can be increased, while for decisions that need to have moderate level of confidence, the confidence threshold could be adjusted down.

Once the confidence threshold for each layer of matrices is obtained, the relationship between static nodes can be compared. Within the same layer, the relationships between the static nodes are defined as the addition of both confidences divided by two. Relationship between static nodes within the same matrix layer: Relationship = [*Confidence* (0,0) + *Confidence* (8,8)] / 2.

Figure 9 shows the result of multi-layer matrix based mining method with a matrix size of *10*10*7* matrix spaces. The upper matrix is fashion domain and the bottom matrix is leisure domain. It measures the confidence between two domains that is fashion and leisure. In the upper matrix, three relationships can be found under the fashion domain. They are: (0,0 – 8,0) = 85, (0,0 – 1,8) = 80, (8,0 – 1,8) = 75. In the lower matrix, three relationships can be found under the leisure domain. They are: (8,0 – 1,8) = 80,

$(0,0 - 1,8) = 77.5$, $(0,0 - 8,0) = 72.5$. The combined relationship between fashion and leisure domain is: $(0,0 - 8,0) = (85 + 72.5) / 2 = 78.75\%$; $(0,0 - 1,8) = (80 + 77.5) / 2 = 78.75\%$; $(8,0 - 1,8) = (75 + 80) / 2 = 77.5\%$.

The inter-domain relationships are calculated based on the average between the two confidences found in the same particular space in different layers. In some instances when the original single layer confidence threshold is set too low, it is possible for the relationship confidence returned low as well. Therefore, a relationship confidence threshold has to be set in order to limit the amount of significant relationships to avoid pattern overloading. All relationships with the relationship confidence lesser than the relationship threshold will be discarded and not taken into consideration.

The relationship confidence within the same layer will only help the decision maker in making a decision which requires single factor related to the specific logical domain. Often, the case is that multiple factors need to be considered. For instance, when setting up a shop that sells designer clothing, one must take into consideration factors such as the income level of the surrounding, the presence of other fashion design domains in the area, the presence of any artistic domains in the area, and finally, the presence of any potential customers in the area.

In order to take multiple factors into consideration, multiple layers of the matrix can be selected. After the list of layers is selected, the multi-domain relationship confidence is calculated. The formula for evaluating the multi-domain relationship confidence is: *Multi-Domain Relationship Confidence = (Layer[1].Relationship_Confidence + Layer[2].Relationship_Confidence + ... + Layer[n].Relationship_Confidence) / n*. It is the average of the combination of all relationships in the multiple layers.

Finally, a multi-domain relationship confidence threshold is set in order to adjust the sensitivity of the pattern found. In order to achieve this, the multi-domain relationship confidence is compared against the multi-domain relationship confidence threshold. For all multi-domain relationship confidence lesser than the multi-domain relationship threshold, they are discarded to ensure the accuracy of the result.

The result of the multi-layer matrix provides a clear examination of the relationships between static nodes, not just within the same layer, but also between multiple layers. By performing analysis into multiple layers in which each layer represents a logical domain, this methodology provides an innovative approach in finding out useful knowledge from mobile users and mobile stations which takes both the physical and logical considerations into account at the same time.

The following steps represent the essential parts of the process of using multi-layer matrix in order to perform mobile user data mining. It is important to note that in a multi-layer matrix, another dimension is added and therefore, three threshold values are required.

Step 1: Define Multi-Layer Matrix

The first step in this mobile user data mining exercise is to define the multi-layer matrix. A multi-layer matrix contains three dimensions. It is essential to note that there is no need to have all three variables the same size. Although they can be configured to be the same size, the decision rests on the decision maker and the problem that needs to be solved. A multi-layer matrix contains multiple layers of single layer matrix. The two-dimensional single layer matrix has to be first defined by defining the horizontal and vertical length of the single layer matrix.

After the size of the single layer matrix, the number of layers in the multi-layer matrix is dependent on how many independent logical domains are present in the mobile data-mining environment. The user can decide this by looking at how many logical domains or themes are present and also how many

Figure 10. Algorithm for defining multi-layer matrix

```
Matrix Create_Multi_Layer_Matrix(size1, size2, size3) {
    s1 = size1;
    s2 = size2;
    s3 = size3;
    M = Matrix.Generate(s1,s2,s3);
    M.Initialize(0);
    Return M;
}
```

Figure 11. Algorithm for collecting frequency counts

```
Void Collect_Freq_Counts(Position X, Position Y, Position Z) {
    If Event().Status=True Then {
        Single_Layer_Array(X, Y, Z)++;
        Nconfidence = Frequency(X, Y, Z) / Window Size;
        Single_Layer_Array(X, Y, Z).Value = Nconfidence;
    }
}
```

logical domains are of interest to the mobile users. After the three variables are defined, the structure of the multi-layer matrix is created. Figure 10 shows how the multi-layer matrix is created.

Step 2: Select Window Size for Each Layer

After the multi-layer matrix structure is defined, the next step is to select a window size for each layer. It is possible for each window size in each layer to be different or to be of equal values. The onus rests on the decision maker in terms of the amount of resources such as memory capacity and processing power that they are ready to invest and the amount of accuracy or sensitivity the results needs to be. The window size for each layer is then defined in relation to the reference of each layer that is the logical domain of each layer.

Step 3: Collect Frequency Counts for Each Layer

Figure 11 shows that after the window size is defined, the frequency count can start to be collected. It is important to keep the frequency counts within the window size to prevent any waste of resources. It is also essential for the data collection to be executed for a suitable timeframe of interest to the decision maker. There is no point in gathering data during a wrong timeframe, such as gathering workplace activity at midnight when workplace activities are well known to be minimal. Each frequency count will contribute to the particular storage area of the matrix for later mobile user data mining purposes.

Step 4: Calculate Confidence for Each Layer

Figure 12 shows that after the window size is defined and the frequencies are properly collected, the initial requirement to calculate confidence is established. Confidence can now be calculated using the formula: *confidence = frequency / window size*. The confidence is the ratio between frequency and

Figure 12. Algorithm for calculating confidence

```
Confidence Calc_Confidence (Frequency, Window Size)
   Frequency_Valid = (Frequency > Min && Frequency < Max);
   Window_Valid = (Window > Min && Window < Max);
   If (Frequency_Valid && Window_Valid) Then {
      Confidence = Frequency / Window Size;
      If (Confidence < Confidence_Threshold) {
         Confidence = 0;
      }
      Else {
         Location.Mark();
         Return Confidence;
      }

   }
}
```

Figure 13. Algorithm for calculation of relationship confidence

```
Confidence Calc_Relationship_Conf (Conf1, Conf2)
   C1OK = Conf1.validate();
   C2OK = Conf2.validate();
   If (C1OK && C2OK) {
      Confidence = Average(Conf1, Conf2);
      If (Confidence < Confidence_Threshold) {
         Confidence = 0;
         Return Confidence;
      } Else {
         Conf1.Location.Mark();
         Conf2.Location.Mark();
         Conf_Table.Set(Conf1, Conf2, Confidence);
      }
   }
}
```

window size. Therefore, both frequency and window size will affect confidence and only window size is under the control of the decision maker. Therefore the adjustment of window size will have a direct effect toward the confidence value.

Step 5: Select Confidence Threshold for Each Layer

After the confidences of all the layers are determined, it is now time to filter out the non-significant confidence static nodes. To start with, the confidence threshold from each layer is determined, obtained, and compared against each storage area of the matrix in every single layer. The confidence threshold can be different in each layer, and all those storage areas with the confidence lower than the confidence threshold will be marked insignificant and will not be taken into future considerations. The rest, which are highly significant confidence static nodes will be identified and used in the next step.

Step 6: Calculate Relationship Confidence for Each Single Layer

Figure 13 shows that after significant confidence is calculated, the time has come to calculate the relationship in between the confidence for each single layer. The relationship in between each static node in each layer must involve two and only two static nodes due to the nature of relationship. The nature of the relationship is the association behaviour, or association characteristics in between two entities, and in this case, the static nodes. The formula to calculate relationship confidence is: *relationship confidence = (static node confidence 1 + static node confidence 2) / 2.*

Step 7: Select Relationship Confidence Threshold for Each Single Layer

After the relationship confidences are calculated, those relationship confidences that are insignificant must be screened out. At this level, the decision maker can be quite confident that the confidence relationships obtained are highly significant and the use of threshold values to screen out relationship confidence may be limited to *confidence threshold* + 10%. After the relationship confidence threshold is determined, all relationships with relationship confidence lesser than the relationship confidence threshold will be marked insignificant, while all relationship confidence greater than the threshold will be marked as significant.

Step 8: Calculate Multi-Layer Relationship Confidence

After both the confidence and relationship confidence have been calculated, it is now necessary to calculate the multi-layer relationship confidence. This is the core of the multi-layer matrix pattern in which it provides a systematic way for decision makers to select multiple layers of the matrix depending on the areas of logical domains that the decision makers wish to take account into. The different selection of logical domain areas leading to different results will further allow the decision maker to compare the results of the tests.

Figure 14. Algorithm for calculation of multi-layer matrix confidence

```
Confidence Calc_Relationship_Conf (Conf1, Conf2)
   C1OK = Conf1.validate();
   C2OK = Conf2.validate();
   If (C1OK && C2OK) {
      Confidence = Average(Conf1, Conf2);
      If (Confidence < Confidence_Threshold) {
         Confidence = 0;
         Return Confidence;
      } Else {
         Conf1.Location.Mark();
         Conf2.Location.Mark();
         Conf_Table3D.Set(Conf1, Conf2, Confidence);
      }
   }
}
```

Figure 14 shows that multi-layer relationship confidence can be calculated by using the formula: *multi-layer relationship confidence = (Relationship Confidence Layer 1 + Relationship Confidence Layer 2 + ... + Relationship Confidence Layer N) / N.* It is essential to note that the number of domains that can be selected is limited to the number of layers, while it can be at least one per size of the layers. It is the average of the relationship confidence in a particular static node over different layers of logical domain.

Step 9: Select Multi-Layer Relationship Confidence Threshold

After the multi-layer relationship confidence is obtained, it is now time to test whether the multi-layer relationships are significant or not. The decision maker can test it by means of determining a multi-layer relationship confidence threshold. By a careful selection of a multi-layer relationship confidence threshold, all non-significant multi-layer relationships can be discarded. This is determined by the multi-layer relationship confidence lesser than the multi-layer relationship threshold.

It is essential that the decision maker be aware that for the multi-layer relationship confidence to come to this stage, it has to pass two previous tests for two different stages. Therefore, these multi-layer relationships are most likely highly significant and only very few are discarded with a population sample of very large size.

Step 10: Generate Multi-Layer Matrix Pattern

Figure 15 shows that after all the confidences, the individual static node confidence, the inter-static node relationship confidence, the multi-layer relationship confidence calculated and screened, it is time to display the result to the users. The system should be adjusted in such a manner that by this stage, the amount of knowledge found must be of high quality and the volume of knowledge must be within an acceptable level that does not overload the decision maker. The ability for information loading is dependent on the decision maker and is another area of research.

PERFORMANCE EVALUATIONS

The purpose of matrix pattern is to provide an efficient way for obtaining useful knowledge from mobile users. By using static nodes as the main domain for mining, it will be more cost efficient compared

Figure 15. Algorithm for generation of multi-layer matrix pattern

```
Void FindPattern (Multi Layer Matrix M) {
  For (I = 0, M.Size(), M++) {
    If M.I.Significance = True {
      Display M.I;
      Display M.I.Confidence();
    }
  }
}
```

to mining by using mobile nodes because of the extra processing power required to track the mobile nodes and gather data from them. Static nodes, being well equipped with processing power and storage resources keep track of mobile nodes at all times by providing resources to them. These static nodes are in the best position to find out knowledge from mobile users as it stays in touch with the mobile nodes at all times.

However, the benefit of using the matrix pattern to be cost efficient comes with a price depending on interpretation. The matrix pattern, a location-dependent data mining method, generates knowledge that represents the pattern among static nodes. Therefore, it will provide a physical location based kind of knowledge. To enhance this, the static nodes in the matrix pattern are named with their logical themes. These logical themes will then be able to be used to judge the relationship among the static nodes better.

The performance evaluation is done on a Pentium IV machine with 384MB of RAM and 10GB of hard disk space. The datasets used in the performance evaluation are derived from synthetic data generator. Three datasets were used, namely *equal*, *double* and *triple*. *Equal*, *double* and *triple* have different sizes

Figure 16. Comparison among single, double, and triple y coordinates

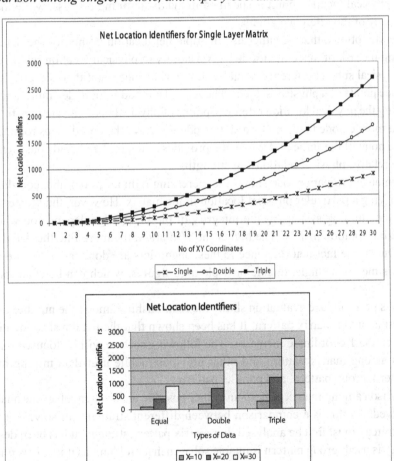

in the *y* axis. The content of the matrix is generated through the random number generator function in Matlab. Performance evaluation is charted using Matlab, Microsoft Excel and SPSS.

Performance of Single Layer Matrix

Figure 16 shows the overall comparison among the different configuration in terms of *Y* coordinates in single layer matrix. It can be seen that the gradients are different, and they are increasing at a different rate. A fine tuning of the total number of *X* and *Y* coordinates is required depending on the physical environment, such as the geographical largeness of the area concerned. Generally, the higher the resolution, the better the identification process and the coordinates can further be rounded back to specific reference point of physical subjects for mobile user data mining. The second chart shows the graphical comparison among the net location identifiers for different configurations of single layer matrix at *X* = 30. The dataset named Equal refers to *X* = *Y*, Double refers to *Y* = 2*X*, and Triple refers to *Y* = 3*X*.

It appears that there exists a trade-off between the greater resolution (greater net location identifiers) and the ability to accurately reference the physical location points. As the resolution increases, that is, the increase of the number of either *X* or *Y* coordinates, it will return higher net location identifiers. The resulting increase of the net location identifiers increases the ambiguity of physical location reference, as a very fine physical location point is specified in the data mining process, while the actual subjects may occupy many of the reference points.

There are two options, that is, either use multiple net location points for the data mining system, while accepting the risk of inaccuracies due to variability of physical location reference point, or use a single fixed physical subject reference point, such as a reference point that is centre, and nearest to all border reference points of a physical subject. The second method is more desirable, and can be achieved by first rounding the physical location reference points of physical visit transactions from mobile nodes. For instance, a mobile node that pass by a static node will have the coordinates rounded to the average fixed reference point of the static node, so that it provides a standardized, and consistent reference point for measuring relative physical relationship strengths.

The performance evaluation also shows the increasing number of possible coordinates that can be used for identifying a particular physical location in the matrix. However, the greater this number, the better for the data mining system, as the integrity of the knowledge depends on whether the system can deliver high resolution matrix. The higher the resolution, the more fine the details that the matrix can support. Due to the fact that reference to these identifiers are done by using integer variables, the consideration is merely a single, double or triple digit figures, which can be considered negligible in todays terms.

The previous performance evaluation shows the relationships among the number of *XY* coordinates and the resolution of the matrix pattern. It has been shown that the net physical identifier increases at a gradual rate as the *Y* coordinate increases. The following section will be focused on the comparison of capabilities among matrix pattern and other previous mobile user data mining methods, such as frequency pattern, group pattern, and parallel pattern.

The comparison among matrix pattern and other possible methods involves the analysis on how the problem is solved. As this is a comparison between different strategies of solving a problem, the efficiency of a strategy must first be analysed. For matrix pattern strategy, it has been described. If group pattern strategy is used, group pattern is unable solve such a problem, as it involves finding knowledge by forming a group of mobile users. For frequency pattern, it also cannot solve this problem, as frequency pattern is frequency of communication oriented.

If parallel pattern is used, parallel pattern, being a method that it finds the similarities of movements by detecting the similarity of change of states among mobile users. It aims to find the trend of movements among mobile users from one state to another. For physical parallel pattern, the frequency of occurrence of mobile nodes moving from B to A will then reveal the knowledge. Although both methods can reveal the same knowledge, matrix pattern has the advantage of being able to fine tune the system, as it utilizes the resolution method. The main disadvantage of physical parallel pattern is that, it must use a fixed location identifier for mobile user data mining. This fixed location identifier is often the static node itself, or the wireless access point. However, it cannot fine tune the system, by detecting patterns that occur *within* the wireless access point area itself.

Therefore, the main advantage of matrix pattern is the ability to use the existing infrastructure, and provide fine tuned data mining system, by providing coordinates based reference points for identifiers in mobile user data mining. This extends identifications beyond the restrictions of the internal boundaries of the wireless access points. For algorithm aspects, both methods use similar steps in arriving at the same knowledge, that is, by using frequency as the primary unit of measurement to generate knowledge by means of percentage of confidence.

Performance of Multi-Layered Matrix

Figure 17 highlights the comparisons for net location identifiers between the three configurations in the multi-layer matrix pattern data mining exercise. It has been found that the increase in the resolution

Figure 17. Net location identifiers for XYZ, Z = 2Y, Z = 3Y datasets

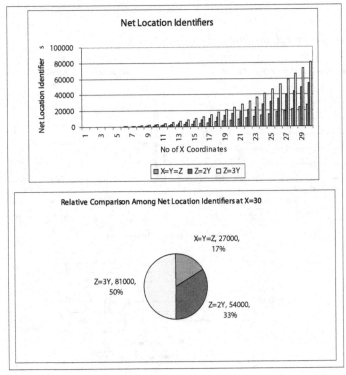

between the different configurations is at a non-equal rate. In other words, the magnitude of increase from the Equal dataset to the Double dataset is different from the magnitude of increase from the Double dataset to the Triple dataset. Figure 17 shows a pie chart that gives the different relative magnitude of net location identifiers at $X = 30$ for the three different configurations in multi-layer matrix pattern mobile user data mining.

Single vs. Multi-Layer Matrix

Multi-layer matrix is an extension of single layer matrix. Multi-layer is a combination of single layer matrix that is closely related to each other in terms of the context of the problem to be solved. However, unrelated independent multiple single layer matrices are not considered a multi-layer matrix. They are simply considered as different instances of single layer matrix structures.

Each of the single layer and multi-layer matrix pattern have their benefits. For instance, single layer matrix pattern is useful for performing exercises that is simple and for single domain problem. Multi-layer matrix pattern is suitable when the problem to be solved requires multi-domain criteria, for example, examining the physical location relationships among multiple domains such as food supplies and mobile phone shops. It can be extended to multiple domains; each layer represents a single domain that is related to a single problem to be solved.

The comparison among the single layer matrix and multi-layer matrix patterns provides an appreciation of the different amount of net location identifiers (resolution). The main goal here is to understand the potential resolution that multiple layer matrix could offer and their huge differences between single layer and multi-layer matrix. Their main differences can be found by the performance charts in Figure 18 that aim to highlight their differences.

Figure 18. Comparison for equal, double and triple datasets

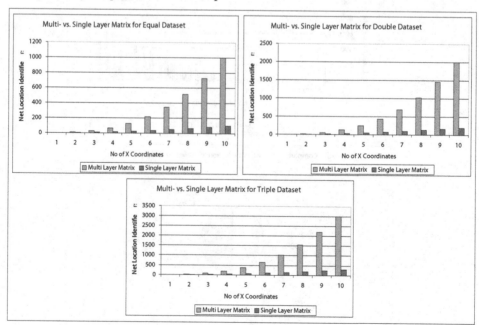

Figure 19. Systematic setup performance evaluation

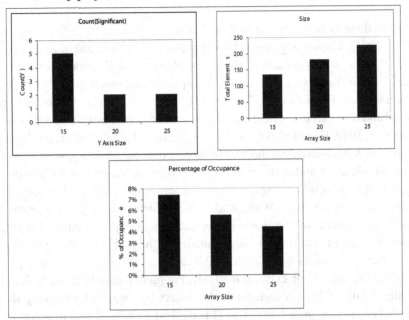

Figure 18 shows the comparisons among the single layer and multi-layer matrix patterns, each graph represents different datasets, namely, Equal, Double and Triple respectively. It can be observed that the relative differences among the net location identifiers were great, and the greater the resolution, the better the capability for fine tuning the system. However, if the net location identifiers were too small, it would mean that each location identifier is for a relatively large amount of geographical space, and it becomes harder to differentiate among the individual physical locations.

Figure 19 shows charts produced from performance evaluation through the systematic setup of test drawn from data of real life in order to generate a non random scenario. Figure 19 shows the chart representing the count of significant elements in a single layer matrix of size 15 * 15, 20 * 20 and 25 * 25. During this test, the number of significant elements, which are elements having frequency of higher than the frequency threshold is high at 15 * 15, but gradually reduced to constant at 20 * 20 and 25 * 25.

The second chart shows the total elements in the array of 15 * 15, 20 * 20 and 25 * 25. The purpose of this chart is to produce a representation of their differences in size, and their rate of increase for each test case. An appreciation of the size of array is essential for the interpretation of data in performance evaluation. It tells how much possible empty spaces are there to be filled up to become significant element through non random process.

The third chart is a comparison chart for the percentage of occupancy of the significant elements in the array. A higher percentage of occupancy represents that there are more significant elements than empty elements. Note that the chart shows different rate of decreasing percentage of occupancy. Although the general trend is decreasing, but the rate of decrease is higher between X = 15 to X = 20, than X = 20 to X = 25.

RELATED WORK

Recent related work done by others in the field of data mining includes the dense region finding (Yip, Wu, Ng, & Chan, 2004), finding negative rules (Thiruvady & Webb, 2004), secure association rules sharing (Oliveira, Zaiane, & Saygin, 2004), discovery of maximally frequent pattern tree (Miyahara, Suzuki, Shoudai, Uchida, Takahashi, & Uedal, 2004), spatial association rules (Koperski & Han, 1995) and time association rules (Barbar'a et al., 2004). It can be observed that data mining (Fayyad, 2004) is widely recognised and research in the field has tried to extend data mining into different areas, such as time series (Han et al, 1999; Han et al., 1998) and geographical (Goh & Taniar, 2004; Koperski & Han, 1995). In our case, we have focused on the area of mobile user data mining, which involves gathering source data from mobile users and perform data mining (Goh & Taniar, 2004a, 2004b, 2005). Mobile user data mining is still at an infant stage, with only a few works having been done. One significant work done by others is group pattern (Wang et al., 2003) which aims to find the group characteristics of mobile users. Group pattern contains some inefficiency, including high amount of processing power required, and weaknesses, such as only physical domains of the problem is being observed. Our previous work in frequency patterns (Goh & Tanair, 2004a) aims to solve this shortcoming.

Frequency pattern is one of our existing methods. Frequency pattern (Goh & Tanair, 2004a) is a method for finding relationships between the mobile users by means of observing the frequency of communication in between these mobile users. This method was developed to enhance group pattern (Lim, Wang, Ong, et al., 2003), that examines the group relationships of mobile users by using physical distance which does not address the fundamental challenge of mobile environment, that is to stay in touch without distance barrier. Frequency pattern (Goh & Tanair, 2004a) solves this problem by using frequency of communication instead of physical distance to calculate closeness of each individual mobile user.

Parallel pattern (Goh & Taniar, 2005) is another one of our existing methods. Parallel pattern aims to find out similarities of decision among mobile users. The similarities of decision can be separated into physical decision and logical decision (Goh & Taniar, 2005). Parallel pattern enables the ability to find out the trends of the movement pattern of mobile users (Goh & Taniar, 2005), by examining either how they move from one location to another, or through examining how they move from one context to another.

Frequency Pattern

Frequency pattern (Goh & Taniar, 2004a) is designed to use frequency of communication between each mobile user, coupled with the pre-specified criteria (Goh & Taniar, 2004a) in order to further enhance the accuracy of frequency pattern. The pre-specified criteria (Goh & Taniar, 2004a) configure the method in order to allow the decision maker to place different amount of emphasis on different parts of time zone concerned. For instance, in the business environment, mobile communications that occur most recently serve as the strongest indication of relationship. This is realised by having the pre-specified criteria to configure high emphasis on the most recent communications.

Frequency pattern (Goh & Taniar, 2004a), therefore, uses pre-specified criteria in order for the decision maker to place different emphasis on different time zones of the window size. Sometimes, it not the recent communications that need to be taken into consideration but somewhere just before the recent communication. The ability to adjust and place different emphasis at different parts of the time

Figure 20. Frequency pattern

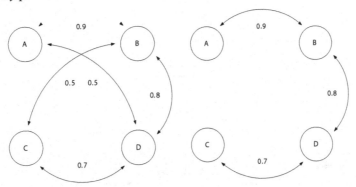

series allows better control for the decision maker. The use of frequency in calculating the confidence of group characteristics of mobile users allows better representation of group formations of mobile users regardless of their physical location. In this way, a family group that spread throughout different parts of the world but remain constant in touch with each other will be detected as a group.

Figure 20 illustrates the frequency pattern with A, B, C, and D represented as mobile nodes. It can be observed that each mobile node has a specific relationship confidence calculated based on the frequency of communication between them. Each arrow represents the logical relationship (Goh & Taniar, 2004a) among two mobile nodes. A, B, C, and D are a set of mobile nodes in the mobile environment that have been determined by the algorithm as logically close to each other. The pre-specified criteria (Goh & Taniar, 2004a) allow different emphasis on different parts of the time series. The diagram on the left in Figure 20 shows the calculated confidences between nodes. When the confidence threshold of *0.6* is set, those relationships which have less confidence are discarded and the right diagram represents the final outcome of frequency pattern that is a list of group of mobile users that are frequently staying in touch with each other (Goh & Taniar, 2004a).

Parallel Pattern

Figure 21 shows the fundamental concept of parallel pattern, which is to find the similarities of arrows, that move in similar directions. The goal of parallel pattern is to find out the similarities in decisions, such as similarities in decisions to move or similarities of decision to change taste from one starting point to another among many mobile users. The result of this exercise is a better understanding of the behaviour of mobile users.

Our related work aims to address different parts of the nature of the problem faced in finding useful knowledge from mobile users. Frequency pattern addresses the issue of using frequency rather than physical distance in order to determine relative closeness. Parallel pattern on the other hand, addresses the interesting issue of movement decisions of mobile users and is a method, which proactively seeks and determines the behaviour of mobile users. All previously proposed methods are resource consuming as there is a requirement to constantly identify the mobile nodes as they move from one location to another. Matrix pattern aims to solve this problem by eliminating the need to precisely identifying the coordinates of the mobile nodes by using a simplified matrix method to identify and mark them, and perform mining on the matrix itself for the rest of the mining process.

Figure 21. Concept of parallel pattern

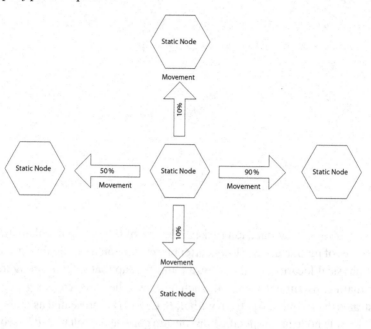

Figure 22. Frequency pattern vs. matrix pattern

Capabilities	Single Layer	Multi-Layer	Frequency Pattern
Ability to Incorporate Multi-Domain Mining	Yes	Yes	No
Requires User Tracking	No	No	Yes
Requires User Identification	No	No	Yes
Uses Existing Infrastructure	Yes	Yes	Yes

Figure 23. Comparison among possible paths for mobile user data mining

Capabilities	Single Layer	Multi-Layer	Group Pattern
Can Perform Physical Data Mining?	Yes	Yes	Yes
Can Perform Logical Data Mining?	No	Yes	No
Ability to Find Relationship Among Interdomain Entities	No	Yes	No
Cost Saving — Requires gathering of Mobile Transactions	No	No	Yes
Using Existing Infrastructures	Yes	Yes	No

Comparison with Previous Related Works

Figures 22 and 23 show the comparison between the capabilities of frequency pattern and matrix pattern (both single layer and multi-layer). Figure 22 shows that matrix pattern has the advantage over other methods in terms of having minimal overhead requirements. Figure 23 shows the comparison among the different possible paths for mobile user data mining that are using single layer matrix pattern, multiple layer matrix pattern, or group pattern. It shows that, in order to fully utilize the resources available, it must be decided with caution whether to use a single layer matrix or multi-layer matrix. Single layer matrix is sufficient for decisions that involve only one domain of activity, such as shoe producers. However, if a decision needs to be made that involves multiple domains, such as the relationship among shoe makers and socks makers, then the multi-layer matrix pattern would be suitable to perform the job.

CONCLUSION AND FUTURE WORK

In conclusion, it is found that matrix pattern is able to provide mobile user data mining in a cost efficient way, by changing the fundamental method by which knowledge is mined. By doing so, the knowledge found previously will be mobile user dependent, but for matrix pattern it will be location dependent. The fact that the knowledge is location dependent does not necessarily mean that the knowledge is only related to the particular physical location. As physical locations can be named with logical themes, the patterns essentially signify the relationships among the logical themes.

Future work in the mobile user data mining area includes the development of cost models to be used for the evaluation of each mobile user data mining model. Different cost models have to be developed in order to cater to different organisational view of costing, including economic costing, accounting costing, and technical costing. Furthermore, a behavioural model of mobile users is also necessary for the better implementation of algorithms in order to seek knowledge about behaviour of mobile users.

REFERENCES

Agrawal, R., & Srikant, R. (1994). Fast algorithms for mining association rules. In *Proceedings of the 20th International Conference on Very Large Data Bases* (pp. 487-499).

Agrawal, R., & Srikant, R. (1995). Mining sequential patterns. In *Proceedings of the 11th International Conference on Data Engineering* (pp. 3-14).

Ashcraft, C., & Liu, J. (1998). Robust ordering of sparse matrices using Multisection. *SIAM Journal on Matrix Analysis and Applications, 19*(3), 816-832.

Barbar'a, D., Chen, P., & Nazeri, Z. (2004). Self-similar mining of time association rules. In *8th Pacific Asia Conference on Knowledge Discovery and Data Mining,* (Lecture Notes in Artificial Intelligence, 3056, pp. 86-95).

Chen, S. Y. & Liu, X. (2005). Data mining from 1994 to 2004: An application-oriented review. *International Journal of Business Intelligence and Data Mining, 1*(1), 4-21.

Christophides, V. Karvounarakis, G., & Plexousakis, D. (2003). Optimizing taxanomic Semantic Web queries using labelling schemes. *Journal of Web Semantics, 1*(2), 207-228.

Claude, I., Daire, J. L., & Sebag, G. (2004). Fetal brain MRI: Segmentation and biometric analysis of the posterior fossa. *IEEE Transactions on Biomedical Engineering, 51*(4), 617-626.

Eirinaki, M. & Vazirgaiannis, M. (2003). Web mining for Web personalization. *ACM Transactions on Internet Technology, 3*(1), 1-27.

Fayyad, U. (2004). Data mining grand challenges. In *8th Pacific Asia Conference on Knowledge Discovery and Data Mining, LNAI, 3056* (p. 2).

Goh, J. & Taniar, D. (2004a). Mining frequency pattern from mobile users. *Knowledge-Based Intelligent Information & Engineering and Systems.* (Lecture Notes in Computer Science Part III, 3215, pp. 795-801).

Goh, J. & Taniar, D. (2004b). Mobile user data mining by location dependencies. In *5th International Conference on Intelligent Data Engineering and Automated Learning,* (Lecture Notes in Computer Science, 3177, pp. 225-231).

Goh, J. & Taniar, D. (2005). Mining parallel pattern from mobile users. *International Journal of Business Data Communications and Networking, 1*(1), 50-76.

Häkkilä, J. & Mäntyjärvi, J. (2005). Combining location-aware mobile phone applications and multimedia messaging. *Journal of Mobile Multimedia, 1*(1), 18-32.

Han, J. Dong, G., & Yin, Y. (1999). Efficient mining of partial periodic patterns in time series database. In *Proceedings of the International Conference on Data Engineering* (pp. 106-115).

Han, J., Gong, W., & Yin, Y. (1998). Mining segment-wise periodic patterns in time related databases. In *Proceedings of the 4th International Conference on Knowledge Discovery and Data Mining* (pp. 214-218).

Han, J., Pei, J., & Yin, Y. (2000). Mining frequent patterns without candidate generation. In *Proceedings of the International Conference on Special Interest Group of Management of Data* (pp. 1-12).

Koperski, K. & Han, J. (1995). Discovery of spatial association rules in geographical information databases. In *Proceedings of the 4th International Symposium on Advances in Spatial Databases* (pp. 47-66).

Lee, D. L., Xu, J., Zheng, B., & Lee, W. C. (2002). Data management in location-dependent information services. *Pervasive Computing, IEEE, 1*(3), 65-72.

Li, J., Tang, B., & Cercone, N. (2004). Applying association rules for interesting recommendations using rule templates. In *8th Pacific-Asia Conference on Knowledge Discovery and Data Mining 2004,* (Lecture Notes in Artificial Intelligence, 3056, pp. 166-170).

Lim, E. P., Wang, Y., Ong, K. L., et al. (2003). Search of knowledge about mobile users. *ERCIM News, 1*(54), 10.

Miyahara, T. Suzuki, Y., Shoudai, T. Uchida, T. Takahashi, K., & Uedal, H. (2004). Discovery of maximally frequent tag tree patterns with contractible variables from semistructured documents. In *8th Pacific-Asia Conference on Knowledge Discovery and Data Mining 2004,* (Lecture Notes in Artificial Intelligence, 3056, 133-144).

Oliveira, S. R. M., Zaiane, O. R., & Saygin, Y. (2004). Secure association rule sharing. In *8th Pacific-Asia Conference on Knowledge Discovery and Data Mining 2004,* (Lecture Notes in Artificial Intelligence, 3056, pp. 74-85).

Thiruvady, D. R. & Webb, G. I. (2004). Mining negative rules using GRD. In *8th Pacific-Asia Conference on Knowledge Discovery and Data Mining 2004.* (Lecture Notes in Artificial Intelligence, 3056, pp. 161-165).

Tjioe, H. C., & Taniar, D. (2005). Mining association rules in data warehouses. *International Journal of Data Warehousing and Mining, 1*(3), 28-62.

Tse, P. K. C., Lam, W. K., Ng, K. W., & Chan, C. (2005). An implementation of location-aware multimedia information download to mobile system. *Journal of Mobile Multimedia, 1*(1), 33-46.

Wang, Y., Lim, E. P., & Hwang, S. Y. (2003). On mining group patterns of mobile users. In *Database and Expert System Applications.* (Lecture Notes in Computer Science, 2736, pp. 287-296).

Wilson, M. & Matthews, B. (2004). The future of the World Wide Web? In *21st Annual British National Conference on Databases 2004.* (Lecture Notes in Computer Science, 3112, pp. 4-15).

Xiao, Y., Yao, J. F., & Yang, G. (2005). Discovering frequent embedded subtree patterns from large databases of unordered labelled trees. *International Journal of Data Warehousing and Mining, 1*(2), 70-92.

Yip, A. M., Wu, E. H., Ng, M. K., & Chan, T. F. (2004). An efficient algorithm for dense regions discovery from large-scale data streams. In *8th Pacific-Asia Conference on Knowledge Discovery and Data Mining 2004, Lecture Notes in Artificial Intelligence, 3056* (pp. 116-120).

This work was previously published in International Journal of Intelligent Information Technologies, Vol. 2, Issue 1, edited by V. Sugumaran, pp. 37-67, copyright 2006 by IGI Publishing, formerly known as Idea Group Publishing (an imprint of IGI Global).

Section III
Information Systems and Modeling

Chapter XIV
Conceptual Modeling of Events for Active Information Systems

Salvatore T. March
Vanderbilt University, USA

Gove N. Allen
Brigham Young University, USA

ABSTRACT

Active information systems participate in the operation and management of business organizations. They create conceptual objects that represent social constructions, such as agreements, commitments, transactions, and obligations. They determine and ascribe attributes to both conceptual and concrete objects (things) that are of interest to the organization. Active information system infer conclusions based on the application of socially constructed and mutable rules constituting organizational policies and procedures that govern how conceptual and concrete objects are affected when defined and identified events occur. The ontological foundations for active information systems must include constructs that represent concrete and conceptual objects, their attributes, and the events that affect them. Events are a crucial component of conceptual models that represent active information systems. The representation of events must include ascribed attributes representing data values inherent in the event as well as rules defining how conceptual and concrete objects are affected when the event occurs. The state-history of an object can then be constructed and reconstructed by the sequence of events that have affected it. Alternate state-histories can be generated based on proposed or conjectured rule modifications, enabling a reinterpretation of history. Future states can be predicted based on proposed or conjectured events and event definitions. Such a conceptualization enables a parsimonious mapping between an active information system and the organizational system in which it participates.

INTRODUCTION

Organizations and the information systems that support them are artificial and intentionally designed artifacts. Policies and procedures created by an organization determine how specifically defined and identified events affect the organization. Active information systems are designed to participate in the operation and management of organizations by implementing such policies and procedures. Events play a crucial role in such organizational processes. They are defined and identified for the purpose of initiating organizational processes among interacting participants.

The event commonly described as "the placement of a purchase order," for example, is an intentional agreement between a customer and a vendor. It is artificially identified and used by each participant to initiate organizational processes. For instance, the vendor may create a conceptual object referred to as a sales order—which is identified by a sales order number—and described by the particulars of the agreement (e.g., payment terms, promised delivery date, FOB point, quantities and prices of products sold, sales tax rate, freight charges). The sales order may also initiate production, shipping, and billing processes. The customer, on the other hand, may create a conceptual object referred to as a purchase order, identified by a purchase order number and described by the particulars of the agreement. The purchase order may also initiate production and sales processes that depend on the receipt of the products on that purchase order. It may also initiate processes to reserve cash required to pay for the purchase.

The ontological definition of an "event" as a state-transition (Bunge 1977) has been widely used in conceptual modeling research (Wand and Weber 1990; Shanks, Tansley, and Weber 2003). This definition has resulted in the premise that an information system is fundamentally a state-tracking mechanism (Wand and Weber 1990). It proscribes the representation of events as entities (Wand, Story, and Weber 1999). A conceptual model based on such a premise can appropriately represent a passive information system (March and Allen 2007a), but it is inadequate in representing an active information system. Effective analysis and design of active information systems requires a more substantive ontological definition of an "event" as an identified causal occurrence (Geerts and McCarthy 2002; Davidson 1980; Casati and Varzi 1996; March and Allen 2007b). Such a definition results in the premise that an information system is fundamentally an event-processing mechanism (Allen and March 2003; March and Allen 2007a). It requires the representation of events as entities for those events in which the information system actively participates. The descriptions of such entities include (a) the organizational rules governing the event processing and (b) the data that describe the event. We contend that it is appropriate to represent events as entities at the conceptual level and argue that doing so is fundamental to the conceptual modeling of information systems that actively participate in organizational work systems (Alter 2003; Alter 2006).

Objects are described by functions that map to values. Such functions may represent properties that objects naturally possess, or they may represent attributes that are artificially ascribed to them. The set of values for the functions of an object at a point in time defines its state at that point in time. A person, for example, possesses the properties height and weight and is ascribed the artificial attribute's name and Social Security number. The mapping functions for a particular person may map that person to the vector (height: 6 feet; weight: 230 lbs; name: Fredrick J. Smith; Social Security number: 001-01-0001) on March 15, 2006. Note that the values of height and weight are each observable: they can be measured at a point in time and they change according to natural laws (possibly influenced by behavior but ultimately outside of human control). The values of name and Social Security number are not observable: they cannot be measured per se and they are ascribed to the person and can be changed according to the rules (laws, regulations, or mores) of a society. These definitions are common in the ontology and data-modeling literatures (Wand et al. 1999; Sowa 1999; Guarino and Welty 2002).

There is a duality between events and states. Events cause states to change (including the event that brings an object into existence), and states reflect the effects of events. Conceptually, it is possible to derive the state of an object at time t1 from its state at time t0 and the events that have occurred between t0 and t1 by the application of event rules and data. However, it is not always possible to derive the event, the rules, and data from the states of an object at times t0 and t1. If the sole purpose of an information system is to record and report on states that have been observed or proposed in some domain, then deriving and tracking events may not be important. We term such state-tracking information systems "passive" because they do not participate in the organizational system. They do not calculate, infer, or predict the states of objects; they simply report on observations or proposed states.

Information systems that exhibit intelligence typically go beyond the recording of states. They ascribe state to objects by applying rules associated with defined and identified events (Geerts and McCarthy 2002). Events and their rules are a significant focus in such information systems. We term such event-processing information systems "active" because they participate in the determination of states rather then simply record observations or determinations of state made outside their scope. Passive information systems are most appropriate for dealing with natural systems, where the interest is in tracking the changes in properties of physical objects. Bunge (1977) uses the terms concrete object or thing for such physical objects. Immutable natural laws govern the way the properties of physical objects change. Active information systems are most appropriate for artificial systems, where the interest is in taking action. Organizationally or socially constructed (Searle 1995, 2006) rules govern the actions that result in changes to conceptual (socially constructed) and concrete objects (Hirschheim, Klein, and Lyytinen 1996).

Active information systems need not implement the state-change rules for all events in the domain they are intended to model. The causal rules that govern state transitions when an event occurs may be unknown, or they may not be of concern to the stakeholders (Ramesh and Browne 1999). For such events, the "rule" may be null. Its description may simply specify new or incremental values that define the subsequent states of the affected objects. In that sense the active, event-processing conceptualization of an information system subsumes the passive, state-tracking conceptualization. Furthermore, it allows for flexibility to later extend an information system by adding intelligence to events as needed.

Ontology of Events

The ontological definition of event has been the source of much philosophical debate, as described below:

Broadly understood, events are things that happen—things such as births and deaths, thunder and lightening, explosions, weddings, hiccups and hand-waves, dances, smiles, walks. Whether such things form a genuine metaphysical category is a question that has attracted the sustained interest of philosophers, especially in the second half of the 20th century. But there is little question that human perception, action, language, and thought manifest at least a prima facie commitment to entities of this sort . . .

Although not undisputed, some standard differences between events and physical objects are commonplace in the philosophical literature. First, there is a difference in mode of being: material objects such as stones and chairs are said to exist; events are said to occur or happen or take place (Hacker 1982a). Second, there are differences in the way objects and events are said to relate to space and time. Ordinary objects have relatively clear spatial boundaries and unclear temporal boundaries; events have relatively unclear spatial boundaries and clear temporal boundaries. Objects are invidiously located in space—they occupy their spatial location; events tolerate co-location (Quinton 1979, Hacker 1982b). Objects can move; events cannot (Dretske 1967). Objects are continuants—they are in time and they persist through time by being wholly present at every time at which they exist; events are occurrents—they take up time and they persist by having different parts (or "stages") at different times (Mellor 1980).

The last distinction is particularly controversial, as there are philosophers who conceive of objects as four-dimensional entities that extend across time just as they extend across space. Some such philosophers would in fact draw no metaphysically significant distinction between objects and events (Quine 1960). Rather, they would regard the relevant distinction as one of degree: both objects and events would be species of the same "material inhabitant of space-time" genus (as opposed to the genus "immaterial inhabitant", such as the Equator); but whereas events appear to develop quickly in time, objects are relatively "firm and internally coherent" (Quine 1970). (http://plato.stanford.edu/entries/events/ accessed 2/10/06)

While we do not deny the existence of such controversy in the philosophy literature, we contend that choosing to represent events as entities at the conceptual level (Chen 1976) naturally supports the requirements of causality needed to implement active information systems. The parsimony of such a representation is even more pronounced when the real-world domain modeled by the information system is artificial rather than natural. While artificial systems such as business organizations have no special dispensation from natural laws, they often define (1) what events are important, (2) how such events are identified and characterized, and (3) the rules (or policies) that govern state transitions when an event occurs. They are concerned not with tracking the effects of natural causes but with ascribing characteristics (i.e., attribute values) to the affected objects when specified events occur.

Events in Natural and Artificial Systems

Events may be conceived at multiple levels of abstraction and granularity. In natural (physical) systems, the processes of nature can be conceived as a series of instantaneous events resulting in incremental and perhaps unperceivable changes in the states of concrete objects. More usefully, an event can be conceived as a perceived or intentional occurrence that causes the states of objects to change in predictable ways, i.e., according to rules. The goal of science is to determine such rules for events that occur in the physical world. Newtonian mechanics, for example, can be viewed as (approximate) rules that govern the changes in the states of physical objects as forces are exerted upon them. Clearly, these rules are useful at a particular level of abstraction and granularity. For human purposes, the event of interest may be the application of a force to an object at a point in time and for a specified duration. The states of interest may be the position of the object or its velocity at other points in time.

An active information system that models a natural domain must include a representation of the natural laws that govern it. An air-traffic control system, for example, must represent the natural laws that enable it to predict the positions of the aircraft it is intended to control. However, the events and associated laws governing state transitions in organizational and societal systems are often artificial, designed by organizations and societies for their intended purposes (Brooks 1987). Generally Accepted Accounting Principles, or GAAP (see http://www.fasab.gov/accepted.html), and Sarbanes Oxley (Green

2004), for example, define business and accounting events (transactions) and the rules that govern how those events appropriately affect the state of the business.

The definition, categorization, and description of events are at the heart of business and other societal systems. Business work systems and processes define business events and the rules by which those events affect the state of the business (Alter 2006). The state of the business is the set values associated with the substantial and invented attributes of objects that are of interest to the organization (March and Allen 2007a). Substantial attributes correspond to properties that are intrinsic to concrete objects; the values of individual properties can, in principle, be measured (Wand and Weber 1995; Wand, Storey, and Weber 1999). Invented attributes are socially constructed and ascribed to objects for intentional purposes (Searle 1995, 2006). The value of an invented attribute cannot be measured, but once ascribed it can be displayed. For example, physical items held in inventory are "objects" in which a business is interested. They have both substantial and invented attributes. The substantial attributes of an inventory item include its weight, size, and location. Categorization of inventory items into product types is by ascription (Parsons and Wand 2000; Lakoff 1987), as are their other invented descriptors. Thus, the invented attributes of a product include its product type, product number, name, unit of sale, and price. These descriptors are not intrinsic to inventory items, as are weight, size, and location, but are ascribed to them by the organization to enable business operations.

In a natural system, rules governing how events affect the states of concrete objects are enacted by nature. While science seeks to discover the rules (natural laws) that govern state transitions, they occur whether the rules are known or not. That is, natural systems consist of concrete objects that are described by intrinsic (naturally occurring) properties. Events (naturally occurring or induced by human intention) in such systems change the values of properties in ways that are fundamentally outside human control. People may intentionally cause an event to occur, but the transition from initial to final state is governed by nature. For example, a person may ignite an explosive device with the intention of causing human injury and property damage. The extent of the injury and damage (changes in states of affected objects), however, are governed by natural laws and are outside of human control.

In an artificial system, such as business organizations, markets, economies, or societies, rules governing how events affect the states of objects are at least partially defined by people, organizations, governments, or other agencies for their own purposes and intentions. Such rules are "malleable" (Simon 1996) and may change, depending on human intention or understanding (Brooks 1987). The enactment of new rules or modifications of existing rules enable the interpretation and reinterpretation of past events.

In other words, artificial systems consist of conceptual and concrete objects that have ascribed attributes (although they may also have intrinsic properties). Events change the values of attributes in ways that are defined by human intention (although changes in property values are still subject to natural laws). Continuing the example of a person who ignites an explosive device, laws enacted by governments control the consequences of such acts. Depending on the extent of the injury and damage, law enforcement agencies may attribute a value of "criminal" or "public enemy" or "terrorist" to that person. The change in value of that attribute is strictly a function of human intention. Furthermore, other people may impose a different set of rules to that event. If, for example, the act was committed during a state of war, then the value ascribed to the person may be "hero" by the group to which the person belongs and "enemy" by the group against which the act was perpetrated. Subsequent analysis of the event may result in a different ascription by an international court as history is written and rewritten over time.

A less dramatic but similar example can be found in the 2005 class-action lawsuit brought against Federal Express by drivers of delivery trucks concerning their classification as "employees" or as "independent contractors" (see http://www.fedexdriverslawsuit.com/). There is no observable, intrinsic characteristic of drivers that enables an objective classification. Federal Express has classified drivers as independent contractors, and as a result, the company has not paid benefits or the employer's portion of FICA taxes for the drivers. However, the concept of "employment" is socially constructed (Searle 2006) and subject to the laws (policies and rules) enacted by the government and interpreted by the court system. If the judicial system decides in favor of the drivers, then all of the transactions (events) in which the drivers and Federal Express participated must be recast from "contractor transactions" to "employee transactions." As a result, Federal Express could be required to pay over $1 billion in back taxes. Complicating matters further, the laws governing the definition of employee are defined by different state legislatures and interpreted by the courts within those states. It is conceivable that drivers in some states could be deemed contractors by those courts while drivers in other states could be deemed employees, even if the relationship between the drivers and Federal Express is exactly the same.

Information System Conceptualizations

Conceptualizing an information system as a state-tracking mechanism and an event as the transition from an initial to a subsequent state is insufficient for this type of analysis. For such analysis, an information system must be conceptualized as an event-processing mechanism and an event as the cause of the transition from an initial state to a subsequent state via the application of its rules.

Business events are frequently artificial and intentional—agreed upon occurrences initiated by agents within the business system. To the extent that an information system must calculate the appropriate state with respect to business work systems and processes, the rules for the attribution of state must be represented within it. Placement of a customer order, for example, is an artificial, agreed-upon, and intentional business event. In a job-shop manufacturing organization, the "place order" event may be described by the prices and quantities of products ordered and the order due date (all agreed-upon and ascribed attributes). It affects the customer, the salesperson, the procurement of raw materials, production schedules, employee assignments, and so forth in prescribed ways, i.e., according to the rules (policies) of the business. Presented with a "place order" event, an active information system applies the rules of the business to calculate the resultant states of affected objects. An information system may be designed to store the event or it may be designed to store the resultant state. This decision is made for reasons of both efficiency and flexibility. However, at the conceptual level, these events and rules are important elements of the representation.

When the business rules associated with an event are subjective, ill defined, or too complex for effective automation, or when an organization chooses to do so, the rules can be applied and the resultant states determined outside the information system. In that case, the role of the information system is not to actively participate in that event but to simply (and passively) record the results. Consider, for example, inventory management. An organization typically determines a set of attributes that it ascribes to its products, such as product name, SKU, description, unit of sale, price, and warehouse location. It then determines a value for each attribute of each product and ascribes them appropriately. This is an event initiated by the marketing department of an organization. The rules by which the marketing department determines these attributes and values are typically considered to be outside the scope of the information system. Hence, marketing information systems are typically designed to passively capture the values of such attributes when these events occur without any representation of the rules by which they are determined.

Conversely, there are numerous applications where information systems actively participate in determining and ascribing attribute values to objects when specified events occur. For example, a business may define the rule that a person "becomes a customer" when that person initiates the "registers at our Web site" event. That is, when the person fills out the registration form at the Web site and presses the "submit" button. The event's properties include its temporal and spatial characteristics, i.e., when and where it occurred. Its attributes include those data items entered on the Web site. Its rules specify that the person who initiated the event is to be ascribed (1) the type "customer" and (2) the set of attributes common to all customers. The set of attributes ascribed to customers may include those associated with the data values entered at the Web site (e.g., name, address, phone number, and email address) as well as attributes whose values are generated according to the event rules, e.g., customer number (sequentially or hash generated), customer status (initialized at "provisionary"), and credit limit (initialized to $1,000). It is noted that some attributes may represent properties intrinsic to the person rather than ascribed to the person (e.g., height, weight, and shoe size). However, even when this is the case, the values are self-reported or measured at a point in time and captured by the information system as a result of an event.

Rules for events represented in an information system may be partial, defining conditions under which the information system will infer a conclusion and conditions under which judgment from outside the information system is required. Furthermore, they may be descriptive or prescriptive. Descriptive conclusions posit the resultant state based on the initial state and the description of the event (its causal rules and data values). Prescriptive conclusions propose the initiation of other events intended to have specific effects.

For example, the rules for the "change credit limit" event may simply ascribe a new value to the credit limit attribute based on the event's "amount" attribute (descriptive). On the other hand, the "request credit limit increase" event may specify evaluation criteria for payment history relative to the amount of the current credit limit and the requested increase. If the requested increase (an attribute of the event) is within the prescribed acceptance criteria, a "change credit limit" event is initiated with the amount requested as its attribute (prescriptive). If it is within the prescribed rejection criteria, no events are prescribed (and no state changes occur). Otherwise, a "request judgment from the finance department" event is initiated (prescriptive).

Critical to this discussion is that the events "request credit limit increase" and "change credit limit" are captured by the information system. In a state-tracking conceptualization, it is awkward to track requests for credit limit increases that are not approved because they do not result in state transitions (conceivably the state of a customer could be defined to include attributes that track the date, amount, and resolution of such requests). Furthermore, if the business decides to change the rules for the event "request credit limit increase," prior requests can be reassessed only if a record of the events is maintained. The application of the new rule to the historical record of events may result in new attributions of credit limit.

Research Challenges

Active information systems are intended to model and represent causality in the real world. They infer conclusions based on the application of rules that govern how objects in the real world transition from state to state when various occurrences (events) happen. We contend that such an information system is most effectively conceptualized as an event-processing mechanism. This conceptualization is based on the ontological definition of an event as an identified causal occurrence that produces state changes according to rules and data that describe the event. Conceptualizing an event in this way is consistent with the definition of an "entity" in conceptual modeling. It provides a parsimonious representation for active information systems not available in a state-tracking conceptualization.

A number of research challenges remain. These challenges involve the development and evaluation of constructs, models, methods, and instantiations by which this ontological definition of event can be effectively represented in the conceptual modeling of active information systems. First, constructs are needed to conceptually represent (1) the rules that govern state transitions inherent in an event and (2) the data used by such rules to determine state transitions when the event occurs (Ramesh and Browne 1999). Such rules are likely to be most appropriately represented at the event-type level. Therefore, a mechanism for categorizing events is also necessary.

Second, such constructs demonstrate effectiveness in enabling the conceptual representation (modeling) of information systems and also lead to effective designs and implementations (methods). Current conceptual modeling formalisms (grammars—such as the Entity-Relationship model—have no such constructs (Chen 1976; Silberschatz and Korth 1996). They must be developed and evaluated (Hevner et al. 2004). The parsimony and understandability of models built using these constructs must be assessed, and methods to guide their construction and evaluation must be developed (March and Smith 1995; Gemino and Wand 2005).

Such work will enable the formalization of an ontology of artificial systems (Simon 1996; Sowa 1999; Geerts and McCarthy 2002; Allen and March 2007a). Such an ontology is needed if we are to represent and build information systems that provide traceability to lessons learned through the instantiation of new or modified rules that allow past events to be reanalyzed and different state-histories to be generated, including proposed future states. The concept of Active Conceptual Modeling (Chen and Wong 2005) is a step in this direction. This effort focuses on enhancing our fundamental understanding of how to model continual learning from past experiences and how to capture knowledge (i.e., causal event rules) from state transitions (Robinson and Hawpe 1986). The conceptualization of an information system as an event-processing mechanism provides the basis for ontological constructs to gain this understanding. It provides a theoretical framework for the representation of episodic and semantic memory (Tulving 1983; Pillemer 1998) within the existing Entity-Relationship formalism (grammar). Future research should investigate how this conceptualization can be used to develop intelligent learning-based applications in areas such as homeland security, global situation monitoring, intelligence, surveillance, and reconnaissance.

Such applications require the capability to analyze and reanalyze interrelated events in order to form conclusions that ascribe attributes to extant objects in the real-world domain. These applications require the capability to predict future states based on prior states and posited events. They must be capable of reporting not only state history as it was believed at a prior point in time, but also as it is currently believed based on events that occurred but were not known to have occurred at that point in time. Such capability requires not only the differentiation of the valid time (when the event occurred) from transaction time (when it was recorded in the systems) (Snodgrass 2000), but it may require the definition of "determination time" (when it was determined that the event occurred).

The Department of Homeland Security may, for example, be concerned about interpreting events to ascribe a "likelihood of terrorist activity" (an artificial attribute) to individuals, groups, and organizations based on events they have initiated. However, the initiation of an event may not be known until a point in time much later than the time at which it occurred. Rules for ascribing the likelihood of terrorist activity may depend not only on the event under consideration but also on other events, and possibly on temporal and relational aspects of those events.

Consider, for example, a person who has purchased a large quantity of ammonium nitrate fertilizer (initiated a "purchase fertilizer" event). If the person has no prior terrorist engagements (no "terrorist engagement" events) and regularly purchases fertilizer (has a number of prior "purchase fertilizer" events), then the rule may specify that this event has no effect on the likelihood of terrorist activity for that person. Conversely, if this is the first time the person has purchased fertilizer and the person has recently purchased other materials related to the production of explosives or is associated with a group that has other members who have recently purchased these materials, then the rule may specify a significant increase in the probability of terrorist activity. Data and rules of this type are consistent with the development of "probable cause" required for a law enforcement agency to take action. However, if we do not find out about the other purchases (events) until a later time, we must reanalyze the historical event stream and develop a new state history, possibly leading to a different conclusion and different actions.

Finally, we observe that an ontology is an artifact, developed by human intention for specific purposes (Gemino and Wand 2005). Philosophically, an ontology can be evaluated by "how well" its constructs enable the description and representation of the natural (physical) world. Within the scope of information systems, however, the purpose of ontology is to enable the development of more effective information systems (Bodart et al. 2001; Bowen et al. 2004; Allen and March 2006). We believe that ontologies constructed to represent natural or physical systems are insufficient to represent artificial systems because they lack constructs by which to represent conceptual objects, invented (meaningful) attributes, intentionality, and causal rules that govern state transitions. We have presented the "event as entity" construct and the conceptualization of an information system as an event-processing mechanism as foundational to such an ontology.

REFERENCES

Allen, G. N., & March, S. T. (2003). Modeling temporal dynamics for business systems. *Journal of Database Management, 14,* 21-36.

Allen, G. N., & March, S. T. (2006). The effect of state-based and event-based data representations on user performance in query formulation tasks. *MIS Quarterly 30,* 269-290.

Alter, S. (2003). 18 reasons why IT-reliant work systems should replace 'The IT Artifact' as the core subject matter of the IS field. *Communications of the AIS, 12,* 365-394.

Alter, S. (2006). *The work system method: Connecting people, processes, and IT for business results.* Work System Press.

Bodart, F., Patel, A., Sim, M., & Weber, R. (2001). Should the optional property construct be used in conceptual modeling? A theory and three empirical tests. *Information Systems Research, 12,* 384-405.

Bowen, P. L., O'Farrell, R. A., & Rohde, F. H. (2004). How does your model grow? An empirical investigation of the effects of ontological clarity and application domain size on query performance.

In *Proceedings of the International Conference on Information Systems,* Association for Information Systems, 77-90.

Brooks Jr., F. P. (1987). No silver bullet: Essence and accidents of software engineering. *IEEE Computer, 20,* 10-19.

Bunge, M. (1977). Ontology I: The furniture of the world, volume 3 of *Treatise on basic philosophy.* Boston: D. Reidel Publishing Company.

Casati, R., & Varzi, A. C. (1996). *Events.* Dartmouth Publishing Group (Ashgate).

Chen, P. P. S. (1976). The entity-relationship model-toward a unified view. *ACM Transactions on Database Systems, 1,* 9-36.

Chen, P. P. S., & Wong, L. (2005). A proposed preliminary framework for conceptual modeling of learning from surprises. *International Conference on Artificial Intelligence*, CSREA Press, 905-910.

Davidson, D. (1980). *Essays on actions and events.* Oxford University Press.

Dretske, F. (1967). Can events move? *Mind, 76,* 479-92.

Geerts, G. L., & McCarthy, W. E. (2002). An ontological analysis of the economic primitives of the extended-REA enterprise information architecture. *International Journal of Accounting Information Systems, 3*, March, 1-16.

Gemino, A. & Wand, Y. (2005). Complexity and clarity in conceptual modeling: Comparison of mandatory and optional properties. *Data and Knowledge Engineering, 55,* 301-326.

Green, S. (2004). *Manager's guide to the Sarbanes-Oxley Act: Improving internal controls to prevent fraud.* Wiley Press.

Hacker, P. M. S. (1982a). Events, ontology and grammar. *Philosophy, 57,* 477-486.

Hacker, P. M. S. (1982b). Events and objects in space and time. *Mind, 91,* 1-19.

Hevner, A., March, S. T., Park, J., & Ram, S. (2004). Design science research in information systems. *MIS Quarterly, 28,* 75-105.

Hirschheim, R., Klein, H. K., & Lyytinen, K. (1996). Exploring the intellectual structures of information systems development: A social action theoretic analysis. *Accounting, Management and Information Technologies, 6,* 1-64.

Lakoff, G. (1987). *Women, fire and dangerous things: What categories reveal about the mind.* Chicago: University of Chicago Press.

March, S. T., & Allen, G. N. (2007a, June 3-6). Challenges in requirements engineering: A research agenda for conceptual modeling. *NSF Science of Design – Design Requirements Workshop*, Cleveland, OH.

March, S. T., & Allen, G. N. (2007b). Ontological foundations for active information systems. *International Journal of Intelligent Information Technologies, 3,* 1-13.

March, S. T. and Smith, G. F. (1995). Design and natural science research on information technology. *Decision Support Systems, 15,* 251-266.

McCarthy, W. E. (1982). The REA accounting model: A general framework for accounting systems in a shared data environment. *The Accounting Review, 57,* 554-578.

Mellor, D. H. (1980). Things and causes in spacetime. *British Journal for the Philosophy of Science, 31,* 282-88.

Parsons, J., & Wand, Y. (2000). Emancipating instances from the tyranny of classes in information modeling. *ACM Transactions on Database Systems, 25,* 228-268.

Pillemer, D. B. (1998). *Momentous events, Vivid memories.* Cambridge, MA: Harvard University Press.

Quine, W. V. O. (1960). *Word and object.* Cambridge (MA): MIT Press.

Quine, W. V. O. (1970). *Philosophy of logic.* Englewood Cliffs, NJ: Prentice-Hall.

Quinton, A. (1979). Objects and events. *Mind, 88,* 197-214.

Ramesh, V., & Browne, G. (1999). Expressing casual relationships in conceptual database schema. *The Journal of Systems and Software, 45,* 225-232.

Robinson, J. A., & Hawpe, L. (1986). Narrative thinking as a heuristic process. In T. R. Sarvin (ed.) *Narrative psychology: The storied nature of human conduct.* New York: Prager Publishers.

Searle, J. R. (1995). *The construction of social reality.* New York: Free Press.

Searle, J. R. (2006). Social ontology: Some basic principles. *Anthropological Theory, 6* 12-29.

Shanks, G., Tansley, E., & Weber, R. (2003). Using ontology to validate conceptual models. *Communications of the ACM, 46,* 85-89.

Silberschatz, A., & Korth, H. F. (1996). Data models. *ACM Computing Surveys, 28,* 105-108.

Simon, H. A. (1996). The sciences of the artificial, 3rd Edition. Cambridge, MA: MIT Press.

Sowa, J. F. (1999). *Knowledge representation: Logical, philosophical, and computational foundations.* Pacific Grove, CA: Brooks/Cole Publishing.

Snodgrass, R. (2000). *Developing time-oriented database applications in SQL.* San Francisco: Morgan Kaufmann,.

Tulving, E. (1983). *Elements of episodic memory.* New York: Oxford University Press.

Wand, Y., Storey, V. C., & Weber, R. (1999). An ontological analysis of the relationship construct in conceptual modeling. *ACM Transactions on Database Systems, 24,* 494-528.

Wand, Y., & Weber, R. (1990). Towards a theory of the deep structure of informationsystems. *International Conference on Information Systems,* Association For Information Systems, 61-71.

Wand, Y., & Weber, R. (1995). On the deep structure of information systems. *Information Systems Journal, 5*, 203-233.

Wand, Y., & Weber, R. (2002). Research commentary: Information systems and conceptual modeling — A research agenda. *Information Systems Research, 13,* 363-376.

Chapter XV
Information Modeling and the Problem of Universals

John M. Artz
George Washington University, USA

ABSTRACT

Earlier work in the philosophical foundations of information modeling identified four key concepts in which philosophical groundwork must be further developed. This chapter reviews that earlier work and expands on one key area—the Problem of Universals—which is at the very heart of information modeling.

INTRODUCTION

For several decades now, articles have been appearing periodically, in the Information Systems research literature, criticizing the field for (1) a lack of theory, (2) no core set of concepts, and (3) no accepted paradigm. All of these criticisms point to a lack of philosophical grounding which would help provide a common basis from which researchers could work, a collection of central problems, and a collection of agreed upon methods for advancing knowledge in the field. It is difficult to tell exactly when this self flagellating critical self-examination first began. But a reasonable point at which to establish the basis of this critical self-examination would be an article by Peter Keen at the 1st International Conference on Information Systems which begins with the observation that "At present, MIS research is a theme rather than a substantive field." (Keen, 1980, pg. 9) Keen goes on to criticize MIS research for a lack of a cumulative tradition and other factors that are key requirements for a scientific discipline.

This idea was elaborated upon several years later by Culnan who cited Keen's remarks, and embarked upon an analysis of the Information Systems research literature looking for common themes and potentially competing paradigms. Culnan points out that "As a field matures, new theories are proposed and compete until paradigms emerge." (Culnan, 1986, pg. 156) Or, at least, that is the way it is supposed to work. Culnan concludes that the Information Systems research literature consists of "research themes rather than paradigms or even well defined subfields" (Culnan, 1986, pg. 167) but excuses the field for its shortcomings with the observation that "MIS is very much a young academic field." (pg. 167)

Culnan's approach was empirical in that she analyzed existing journal articles. Weber, on the other hand, took a theoretical approach sketching out what we should be looking for from a conceptual perspective. Weber observes "If a science progresses only when it has a paradigm, it behooves the members of a field to seek paradigms and to articulate paradigms via normal science as their primary research activities." (Weber 1987, pg. 9) He also remarked, with regard to referent disciplines, that "the IS discipline must develop its own paradigm rather than rely on other disciplines' paradigms if it is to survive in the long run as a distinct discipline." (Weber, 1987, pg. 4)

Orlikowski and Iacono coalesced the concepts of paradigm, cumulative tradition, and core concepts in the "IT Artifact" which may be one of the most important concepts in all of information systems theory and research.

We believe that the lack of theories about IT artifacts, the ways in which they emerge and evolve over time, and how they become independent with socio-economic contexts and practices, are key unresolved issues for our field and ones that will become even more problematic in these dynamic and innovative times. (Orlikowski and Iacono, 2001, Pg. 133.)

This is an important observation and certainly sharpens the focus of the investigation, but doesn't answer the question - What is the "IT Artifact"? Weber (1987) attempts to answer that question. He cites E.F. Codd's (Codd, 1970) paper as one of the most cited articles in Information Systems and one that could be considered a candidate as a paradigm suggesting that the IT Artifact is some kind of a data model. In a later editorial in MIS Quarterly, Weber points out, "After a long period of discernment, we found we could identify only one class of phenomena, for which theories sourced from other disciplines seemed deficient— namely, phenomena associated with building conceptual models and designing databases." (Weber, 2003, pg viii) So maybe the IT Artifact has something to do with information models or information modeling. This is possible since data modeling and information modeling are, perhaps, the only intellectual developments that are unique to information systems. Yet the theories in these areas are sketchy at best.

The field of information systems is in desperate need of some core theory that both defines the field and provides a basis from which researchers can work to develop further theory. But theory must be developed. It doesn't not just appear spontaneously. One way in which theory can be developed is to look at phenomena in the field and attempt to develop explanatory categories. This is a problem for information systems since we are unsure exactly what constitutes phenomena in the field and are less sure about which phenomena belongs uniquely to the field and which belong to a referent field. Another way in which theory can be developed is to take general theories from other areas, apply them to phenomena in Information Systems, and then advance them by making them more specific to Information Systems. An earlier paper did exactly that. Artz [2007] introduced four concepts from metaphysics that are highly relevant to the practice of and research in information modeling. These four concepts were 1) the Concept of Identity, 2) the Problem of Universals, 3) Teleology, and 4) Correspondence versus Coherence views of truth. The purpose of this chapter is to follow that introduction with a discussion of the second of these concepts: The Problem of Universals. The Problem of Universals is, at an arcane level, a central problem in metaphysics and at a practical level the central problem in information modeling. This chapter will review the practice of information modeling, discuss some earlier work related to the Problem of Universals and then more fully explore the Problem of Universals and the key metaphysical problems at the heart of information modeling and the heart of information systems.

Information Modeling

Information modeling, sometimes referred to as conceptual database design, is the first step in the database design process. In this initial step, the information modeler studies the domain of interest and determines the classes of entities that will be represented in the database and the relationship between those classes. In a university database, for example, one entity class may be *Students* while another entity class may be *Courses*. The relationship between *Students* and *Courses* is that *Students Take Courses*. As the modeler continues, attributes of interest are identified for each entity class. These attributes represent facts that are common to all instances of a class. If a particular student has additional facts, those facts are overlooked in order to have a set of facts common to all students. Eventually, the conceptual database design is represented in an information model which contains entity class descriptions, attributes of the entity class, relationships between entity classes, and possibly, additional information about the nature of those relationships such as cardinality and optionality. In the process of constructing the information model, a variety of philosophical assumptions are made that address which classes should be represented in the model, where those classes come from, and whether those classes are discovered or constructed.

A First Pass at The Problem of Universals

When we use the word 'same' to refer to 'same kind' we are organizing the things of the world into categories. Categories are useful because they help us organize our knowledge efficiently. When I point to a tree and call it a tree, I am assigning it to a category. By doing this, I can apply my general knowledge of trees to the specific tree at which I am pointing. The thing at which I am pointing is actually an instance of a tree, but we do not make that distinction in normal speech. Yet, philosophically, we do make that distinction. The instance at which I am pointing is called a particular and the category to which I assign it is called a universal.

The Problem of Universals attempts to address the question – Where do universals come from? Is a tree a tree because it is a member of the set of trees or is it a member of the set of trees because it is a tree? This enigmatic question goes to the heart of universal construction. Is a grouping formed from things of the same kind or are things of the same kind because they are part of the same grouping? There really isn't an easy answer to this question and philosophers have provided a variety of answers over the centuries. (Artz, 1997) A less enigmatic view of the Problem of Universals is to ask -- when we create categories to organize our knowledge where do those categories come from? Are the categories real and hence discovered, or are categories constructed and if so according to what criteria? The Problem of Universals is fundamental to information modeling because the process of constructing entity classes is no more or less than the Problem of Universals. That bears repeating because the central problem in information modeling is the Problem of Universals. And understanding what has been said about the Problem of Universals provides great insight into the process of information modeling. The assumptions one makes on the issue of whether universals are discovered or constructed are called ontological assumptions. And a survey of the literature on information modeling reveals that the ontological assumptions made by information modelers are often confused and conflicting (Artz, 2006).

EARLIER WORK

Earlier attempts have been made to provide some metaphysical grounding for information modeling. The most notable attempts, to date, include William Kent's *Data and Reality*, and *Information Systems Development and Data Modeling: Conceptual and Philosophical Foundations* by Hirschheim, Klein and Lyytinen. *Data and Reality* is a truly astonishing work that is an arcane classic among a far too limited set of readers but is likely destined to become one of the first classics of information systems. That is to say that a century from now readers will still be referring to the concepts in this book whereas little else of what we say today will be remembered. Kent (1978) touches on most of the key points in this paper. He asserts:

There are a few basic concepts we have to deal with here:
- *Oneness*
- *Sameness. When do we say two things are the same or the same thing? How does change affect identity?*
- *What is it? In what categories do we perceive the thing to be? What categories do we acknowledge? How well defined are they? (pg. 3-4)*

The first two bullets refer to the Concept of Identity and the third bullet refers to the Problem of Universals. The problem with Kent's book, despite is enormous insight for the time, is the fact that important questions are raised with insufficient conceptual structure surrounding them. Thus, the book is likely to leave one more confused than enlightened. If one were to read the book, go off and study metaphysics for a while, then come back and read the book again, it would make a great deal more sense. Yet few people do that and *Data and Reality* is unfortunately relegated to a cult classic.

Hirschheim, Klein & Lyytinen (1995) take a different approach, attempting to ground information systems in social philosophy. They criticize prevailing views of information systems because of the prevailing assumption that information systems are "technical systems with social consequences." In opposition to this view they assert that, "In recent years, however, there has been a growing interest in viewing IS as social systems that are technically implemented. They serve as the agent for significant social interactions." Reconceptualizing the phenomenon of information systems they assert, "Hence items of information are meanings that are intended to influence people in some way." (pg. 14)

This is to say that information systems are not benign representations of reality. They are instead constructed realities and those constructions serve some purpose. The intentional nature of information systems development is brought into clear focus when they say "Intentions in systems development are expressed by *objectives*." (pg. 17) This notion that information systems are constructed for a purpose is discussed in more detail in Artz (2007). The teleological approach to information systems development relies on the identification of systems development objectives. Despite their strength in social philosophy and teleology, Hirschhiem, et. al. are a little weak in the metaphysics. They nod toward the Problem of Universals with a brief mention of nominalism (pg. 21) but focus on the social aspects of information systems and their potential for social change.

It is interesting to observe that in juxtaposing the work of Kent with the work of Hirschheim, et. al. we see a tension in philosophy that goes all the way back to the pre Socratic philosophers (Gottlieb). This tension is between the view that reality is in a constant state of change versus the view that reality must be stabilized in order to be understood. The pre Socratic philosopher Heraclites is best know for his assertion that you cannot step in the same river twice and viewed reality as being in a constant state of flux. Parmenides rejected the views of Heraclites on the basis that knowledge is not possible if you accept change as fundamental. We must impose order on reality in order to understanding it and Parmenides viewed the philosophy of Heraclites as destructive to project of knowledge (Roochnik). While this comparison may be over reaching a bit it is an apt comparison to point out that this tension between views of reality has a long history and cannot be resolved in this paper. The views provided here are consistent with Kent and Parmenides and must be considered within that framework.

AN INTUITIVE INTRODUCTION TO THE PROBLEM OF UNIVERSALS

The Problem of Universals is one of the central problems in metaphysics and attempts to address questions about how we organize our experiences about the world into meaningful categories for the purposes of intellectual economy. This is a bit of a mouthful and requires some elaboration, especially for those who have never encountered this concept. The elaboration occurs in the next section. Once the problem is clarified, it is useful to survey some of the commentary on this problem from some of the great minds in Western Philosophy. That will be provided in the following section. After that we address the question of what this has to do with information modeling and show that this is also the central problem in information modeling and that it can be extended to provide some insights into information modeling. The final section address the implications for the future of information modeling.

When we look around us we see objects everywhere: tables, chairs, lamps, trees, fences, birds and so on. Imagine, for a second that you are looking out you window at a tree. You might point at the tree and say, "That is a tree." What you mean more precisely is "That object is a tree." Or even more precisely, "That object is an object of type tree," or "That object is an instance of the class of trees." What we are talking about here is the difference between things and kinds. The object we are looking at is a thing. When we call it a tree we are assigning it to a kind. There are may kinds to which this thing may be assigned. We could call it a home for squirrels, a source of shade, or a source of fire wood instead. Somehow the category tree seems more real than the others, but this is likely to be because it is a basic level category or a category with which we have first hand physical experience (Rosch, 1978B). Nonetheless, a thing can be assigned to any number of kinds. Although we have introduced these notions intuitively here, the difference between things and kinds is difficult to explain without using technical language. So let's introduce some mildly technical language for the purpose of clarifying this discussion.

The thing you are looking at through your window in the previous discussion is an instance, or in metaphysical terminology a particular. The label "tree" is not the name of the object. It is the name of a class to which the object belongs, or once again in metaphysical terminology a universal. Particulars exist in the world and universals are the categories into which we organize them. We do this for the purpose of intellectual economy. We cannot possibly remember all the attributes of every object that we encounter nor could we extent our knowledge from objects we have encountered to objects we haven't encountered without universals. But universals pose a vexing problem and that is – where do universals come from? How do we get from the particulars in the world to the classes into which we organize those particulars? And this, along with some lesser problems constitutes what is referred to metaphysics as the Problem of Universals. Ordinary language often overlooks this problem entirely. When you point to an object and call it a tree, you do not ask yourself how you know it is a tree. Nor do you ask where the quality of treeness came from, nor why it could not be called something else. Mark Twain deals with this problem in a very humorous fashion in the diary of Adam and Eve.

Entry in Adam's diary:

Tuesday: Been examining the great waterfall. It is the finest thing on the estate, I think. The new creature [Eve] calls it Niagara Falls – why, I am sure I do not know. [She] Says it looks like Niagara falls. That is not a reason, it is mere waywardness and imbecility.

Robert Pirsig also addresses this problem at length in his bestseller Lila. So the deep metaphysical nature of this problem does not keep it out of popular culture. Nor does it keep it out of information modeling and database design. Yet, people who have never encountered this problem often find it perplexing in the extreme. Consider the enigmatic question posed earlier – Is a tree a tree because it is a member of the set of trees? Or is it a member of the set of trees because it is a tree? In more straightforward terms these questions are an attempt to find out if kind is determined by category membership or if category membership is determined by kind.

One is tempted to just leave this tricky problem up to philosophers and go on with one's life. However, the many practical implications of this metaphysical problem force us to confront it. For example, when an information modeler looks at an application domain he or she sees particulars which are referred to as entities. These entities are organized into classes called entity classes which are then represented in the information model. Entity classes are universals. And the problem of getting from specific entity occurrences to the entity classes represented in the information model is no more or less than the Problem of Universals. Let's say that we have an information model of university registration. Let's say further that we have an entity class called Student. We can ask – Is a student a student because he or she is a member of the set of students? Or is a student a member of the set of students because he or she is a student? And we are right back to the problem as stated earlier. One would think that people in a university environment would know what a student is. But a few simple questions expose that fallacy very quickly. Is a part time student the same kind of thing as a full time student? Is a student who has not signed up for any classes still a student? Is somebody who sits in class and learns but does not pay tuition still a student? Are alumni auditors considered students? If somebody pays their tuition using loans that they later default on, does that mean they never were a student? How we get from the particulars in the world to the groups into which we organize our knowledge is a foundational problem in information modeling as well as in metaphysics. The next section will explore the opinions of a number of western philosophers as they tried to grapple with this difficult problem.

A BRIEF HISTORY OF PROBLEM OF UNIVERSALS

Plato was the first western philosopher to seriously consider the Problem of Universals. His concern was that a person could recognize an object, such as a tree, for example, even though there is so much variation between individual trees. Some trees are very tall and majestic while others are short and bushy. Some have leaves on their branches while others have needles. And yet, with all this variation, a person can still recognize an object as a tree. In attempting to answer to this problem, Plato took a cue from geometry. There is also a great deal of variation between mathematical objects like triangles, for example. They differ in size, width of the lines making up the sides and angles. But there is also a template definition that covers all triangles regardless of their differences. They are three sided geometric objects with three angles the sum of which is 180 degrees. So, for trees there must be something similar. Plato believed that there was some essential concept of *treeness* against which one compares individual objects and decides whether or not the individual in question qualifies as a tree. But where did this concept of *treeness* come from ? Here Plato offered a unique, if somewhat bizarre, answer. He postulated the existence of a nonmaterial world which he call the World of Forms. The World of Forms contains the eternal unchanging essence of things from the material realm. So that the Form *tree* that describes the eternal unchanging essence of *treeness* exists in this world and this world can only be perceived by the intellect. Plato used the term *Form* in much the same way that an information modeler would use the term entity class. It is the template or general definition of the object type independent of variations between individual entities.

Plato is seen as a realist. He believed that the World of Forms actually existed independent of minds to perceive the Forms. Further, he believed that the World of Forms was more real than the physical world as perceived by the senses because the physical world was unstable and filled with variations and imperfections. The World of Forms, on the other hand, was a world of timeless perfection. While the existence of this World of Forms that is somehow more real than the world perceived by the senses causes one to raise a skeptical eyebrow, it does answer some difficult questions that are not effectively addressed by later views. For example, how can you have a Form without instances ? And how can you derive a perfect Form from widely varying imperfect instances.

Plato's goal, in his theory of universals, was to define concepts with the same precision and perfection that mathematical objects such as a triangle or a square are defined. This is why he had to postulate the existence of an unchanging World of Forms in which mathematically precise definitions did exist. Aristotle, Plato's most famous student, rejected the World of Forms based on the obvious problems of postulating a world that could not be perceived by the senses. Where Plato was interested in ideals, Aristotle was much more interested in the real world of sense perception. Aristotle's goal, in his theory of universals, was to classify natural objects into the natural kinds to which they belong and to organize those kinds into natural hierarchies.

Aristotle saw things a little differently. He did not believe in the independent existence of pure Forms. The only real entities to him were the particular objects of the world. And yet, Aristotle did not believe that the construction of universals was purely arbitrary. Trees have properties that are fundamentally different than the properties of chairs or rocks and these properties are inherent in the individual objects. They are a part of the physical world and can be known through the senses. Not only do these properties exist, but they can be articulated and used to organize particulars into kinds. Those kinds can, in turn, be organized into hierarchies of kinds which Aristotle called genus and species. Hence, universals, according to Aristotle, exist as collections of properties, and these properties, in turn, do exist in the real world. Plato and Aristotle were realists, believing that universals have an existence in the world independent of any minds to perceive them. And this view held throughout the middle ages. However, the British empiricists, beginning with John Locke, began to recognize the role of the mind in creating universals and turned the corner from realism to a new view of universals called conceptualism.

According to Locke, a universal is formed through the cognitive process of abstraction. In this process we view particular instances and abstract from those particulars certain properties that they hold in common. Thus, a universal is one collection of common properties held by a set of particulars. At first glance this sounds like Aristotle's view of universals. And, yet, Locke rejected the Aristotelian view that the classes exist in the world. We do not, according to Locke, find objects and their features neatly divided by nature into objectively delimited classes. Instead, limitless similarities and differences are there for us to perceive but how we perceive them, how we select them, how we use that information to form classes, and how we place objects in different classes is up to us to decide. Locke disagreed with Aristotle by saying that we select the features we use to frame a universal rather than simply taking what is there. Yet, he still believed that universals were explicitly defined. That is, the abstraction process, according to Locke, was rational and could be explained objectively. David Hume went a step beyond Locke and said that the construction of universals was not only done in the mind of the observer, but, according to Hume, this abstraction process occurs below the level of rationality.

According to Hume, universals are constructed by noticing similarities and differences between objects, just as Locke had asserted. However, this process is not guided by abstraction objectives as Locke had claimed. Instead, according to Hume, it is a result of organizing our experience at a preconscious level. Any explicit definition of what constitutes a given universal is done after the universal is defined in our minds and incorporated into our language. If the meaning of universals is constructed at a preconscious level, then an obvious question is raised - is it always possible to explicitly define the characteristics of universals that exist both in the minds of people and in common everyday language ? Wittgenstein didn't think so !

Wittgenstein took an extreme position with regard to universals. To him, universals not only exist solely as concepts in the mind, but they exist in the mind as poorly formed concepts. According to Wittgenstein, explicit definition of certain classes is not possible. In fact, many classes that we use are so poorly formed, that the only thing that the particulars in them have in common is that they are all members of the same class. He illustrates the point by comparing class membership with family resemblances. Members of a family may look like each other, yet it may be difficult to define a set of features that they all share. Some have the same nose. Some the same chin. Some the same eyes. But there is no set of features common to them all. Classes that are held together by family resemblances defy any attempts to construct well defined classes categories or universals.

THE PROBLEM OF UNIVERSAL AND INFORMATION MODELING

The philosophical positions we just discussed represent a range of assumptions that information modeler may hold. It is unlikely that these assumptions are explicit. Yet they can be seen in various approaches to modeling. For example, naïve information modelers often adopt the Platonic approach. They study the domain until the entity classes emerge from some intuitive process as though they had apprehended the World of Forms with their intellects. Platonic modelers cannot tell you how they derived the classes although they seem fairly certain, intellectually, that the classes are correct. They are likely to be naïve realists believing that the classes exist in the domain and that they have discovered them. However, the existence of the World of Forms was even difficult for Plato to justify and the Platonic information modeler is on similarly shaky ground.

Aristotle's position provides much of the philosophical basis for the more disciplined approaches to modern information modeling. The information modeler observes entities in the real world and then identifies their attributes. Next, based on the commonality of attributes, these entities are grouped into entity classes and the common attributes become the class attributes. In object-oriented analysis the commonality of class attributes can be used to define class hierarchies which follow Aristotle's concept of genus and species. However, one must remember that Aristotle was classifying physical objects that had been shaped over millennia by the forces of nature and evolution. Yet, the domain of the information modeler is the artificial world of the organization where conceptual entities such as Customer, Account, Part and Employee are useful constructs not shaped over millennia by the forces of nature. A customer is not a customer because of some set of physical characteristics. A person is a customer because of a relationship that exists between the organization and the person. Another person may be an employee based on a different relationship to the organization. A person may take on different roles at different times or have multiple roles at any one time. Further, the customer need not be a person, the customer may be another organization. Hence, it is not possible to define these classes based on physical characteristics. These classes are defined by the changing needs of the organization to organize its information about the world. Thus, although the scientific realism of Aristotle provides a convenience basis for information modeling, it makes assumptions about the domain of investigation that are probably not valid.

Locke's view of universals provides quite a different perspective for information modeling. Instead of forming classes based on common attributes, the modeler needs to define a set of modeling objectives to guide the abstraction process. From Locke's perspective, there are many ways to model an application domain depending on what the modeler is trying to achieve. Most database applications in organizations fall into this category. Entity classes such as Customer, Part, Employee, or Account are defined in terms of attributes that are important to the problem at hand while vast numbers of attributes are simply ignored as unimportant. This creates problems for the information modeler because it suggests that universals such as Student or Customer may exist in the minds of users and in the language, but may not have any explicit definition. Further, any appropriate and explicit definition may lie in the domain in the future but not the present.

Thus, if Hume's view is correct then the process of information modeling becomes the process of language refinement. Database users employ terms like customer, part or account without a precise understanding of what they mean. The modeler must talk with users and construct useful definitions. Further, these definitions must be agreed upon so that information modeling also becomes the process of achieving a social consensus. Finally, if Wittgenstein is correct, then a domain cannot be modeled without a serious semantic revision to superimpose semantic order upon it.

EXTENDING THE PROBLEM OF UNIVERSALS TO INFORMATION MODELING

Thus far we have discussed the Problem of Universals, some philosophical responses to the problem, and some ways in which these responses can be seen in the practice of information modeling. Next we turn to the task of refining our discussion of the Problem of Universals to begin providing a foundation for the practice of information modeling. From this foundation we will begin making observations about how the practice of information modeling should be refined. In doing so we define four philosophical positions that apply directly to the construction of information models. These are: class realism, class conceptualism, attribute realism, and attribute conceptualism.

Class realism. The class realist believes that classes actually exist in the world for anyone to discover. The class realist attempts to discover the set of classes that exist in a domain by examining the domain; and the validation criteria for a model created by a class realist is that it represent the classes as they exist in the real world. There is no possibility that class formation is influenced at all by the cognition of the observer, because the classes can be discovered and verified objectively. If class realism holds, then there can only be one correct information model for any given domain - the one that accurately models the real world. Although this metaphysical position is quite prevalent among information modelers, there is little philosophical support for it. It is a modern day version of Platonic idealism in which classes exist in some nonmaterial world waiting to be apprehended by the intellect. Even Plato, who originated the position, had quite a bit of trouble with it.

Class conceptualism. The class conceptualist believes that classes are constructed in the mind of the observer through some cognitive process of abstraction based on cues derived from the real world. If class conceptualism is correct, then class formation may be influenced by a wide variety of social and cognitive factors that may influence the abstraction process. Further, validation becomes very difficult. Since the model is the result of an abstraction process it is necessary to validate the resulting model using some criteria other than conformance to the real world. Philosophically, this position is more likely to be correct. However, it brings a host of new problems into the practice of information modeling.

Attribute realism. The attribute realist believes that attributes or properties of individual entities exist in the world independent of the cognition of the observer. Classes can then be formed by grouping entities with like attributes. More rigorous approaches to information modeling adopt this position and there is some justification for it under a limited set of circumstances. There are two forms of attribute realism, limited and extended. Limited attribute realism suggests that entities have a limited set of properties and like entities can be grouped according to the commonality of those limited properties. Extended attribute realism suggests that entities have a virtually unlimited set of properties and groupings are formed based on common subsets of properties. If extended attribute realism holds, then an abstraction process occurs when a small set of like attributes are selected for the grouping process. Once again, social and cognitive factors may influence the grouping process. And attribute selection must be guided by modeling objectives.

Attribute conceptualism. The attribute conceptualist believes that attributes or properties of individual entities are constructed, once again, through a cognitive process of abstraction guided by cues form the real world. It may be reasonable to assume attribute realism in the case of physical properties of entities. However, attributes of entities that are functional in nature or define relationships between entities are almost certainly constructs. If attribute conceptualism holds, then attribute construction may also be influenced by a wide variety of social and cognitive factors that may influence the abstraction process. Once again, attribute construction, like class construction, would have to be guided by modeling objectives. Attribute conceptualism can be constructivist or re-constructivist. The constructivist defines attributes based on cues from the environment largely based on the usage of terms in the language of the domain. The re-constructivist has to redefine the set of attributes in order to make sense out of conflicting usages.

AN ILLUSTRATIVE EXAMPLE: WHAT IS A STUDENT?

Sometimes it appears that we are playing word games when we discuss the semantic complexities of information modeling. For example, when we ask - 'What does it mean to be a student?' - practically minded people often think that we are just engaging in so much philosophical double talk. The purpose of this section is to show how this question is crucial to designing a database that will deliver accurate information. First we will show how it is not at all obvious what we mean by the designation student. And second we will follow with a discussion of the realist versus conceptualist assumptions in terms of this example.

A degree program has 200 students that break down into the following categories: 70 are full time students taking three classes; 20 of the full time students are on full scholarship; 30 are part time students taking two classes; 20 are part time students taking one class; 10 students are on leave of absence taking no classes; 40 students are doing internships taking no classes; 20 are alumni auditors getting continuing education credits; 10 students are sitting in on classes with the permission of the instructor.

There are three courses offered each semester: a two credit course (five sections); a three credit course (three sections); and a four credit course (two sections). The two-credit course has a two-hour lab that is staffed by a teaching assistant or a doctoral student.

Fees are $500 per credit hour. Students on scholarships get a 50% discount. Alumni auditors pay $100 per credit hour.

There are two full time faculty members teaching two sections each and five adjuncts teaching the other sections. There is another full time faculty member who only teaches one class and administers the program.

We have the following potential definitions of student:

1. A student is a person enrolled in the program
2. A student is a person attending classes
3. A student is s person paying tuition
4. A full time equivalent student is taking three classes and paying full tuition

We have the following potential definitions of class:

1. A class is a course
2. A class is a course offering
3. A class equivalent is twenty students taking three credits

We have the following potential definitions for a faculty member:

1. A faculty member is a full time member of the faculty
2. A faculty member is anyone who teaches a class
3. A faculty full time equivalent (FTE) is three covered classes

Now consider the following questions:

1. How many students are there with each of the potential definitions?
2. How many classes are there with each definition?
3. How many faculty members are there with each definition?
4. How many faculty-to-student ratios are there? What are they? Which is the most meaningful?
5. How many class size measures are there? What are they? Which is the most meaningful?
6. In questions 4 and 5 above how would the question of which answer is the most meaningful vary for 1) the university admissions department; 2) the class scheduling office; or 3) the Dean's office that tracks faculty productivity?

Consider how differently this database would be designed given the following potential statements of purpose:

1. The purpose of this database is to track program revenues and compare them again program costs.
2. The purpose of this database is to track program viability in terms of demand for the program and demand for the courses.
3. The purpose of this database is to schedule class meetings and ensure that the appropriate space will be available in the classroom.

Consider how differently this database would be designed given the following problems:

1. An increase in the number of part time students has caused course offerings to be under utilized. Admitting 25 full time students produces 75 enrollments and $37,500 in tuition revenue, whereas 25 part time students taking one class produces 25 enrollments and $12,500 in tuition revenue. Admissions targets must be carefully regulated in order to maintain program quality and program profitability.
2. An important metric of program quality is the faculty to student ratio. As the program expands, it must maintain an adequate ratio in order to maintain accreditation and attractiveness. However, full time faculty are a major long term commitment so increases in full time faculty must be made on strong predictions of program growth.
3. The university financial aid policy allows an average discount of 20%. This includes scholarships and alumni audits. Further, non-enrolled students are encouraged to sit in because it increases the good will of the program and provides some marketing benefit. Unfortunately, the number of chairs in a classroom restricts class sizes and these seats must be allocated in such a way that tuition targets are achieved along with the quality and goodwill of the program.

The purpose of this example was to show that even though we may think that the definitions of categories such as student, faculty and course are beyond question, they actually do raise a large number of questions. Further, when they categories are in question then any data derived from these categories such as student to faculty ratio or faculty course load also become questionable. Finally, the only way category definitions can be constructed correctly is to know what you are trying to achieve with the database and this requires an explicit statement of database objectives.

IMPLICATIONS FOR INFORMATION MODELING

The different metaphysical positions we have discussed lead to quite different approaches to information modeling and different results in the model produced. Class realism is often adopted by naïve information modelers and often implicit in books on information modeling that do not explicitly address the discovery problem. Unfortunately, class realism is not supportable under any circumstances. If the class realist develops the correct model it is either just luck, or the demands of the application have been defined after the fact as those information needs that the database can support.

Class conceptualsim is a far better foundation for the practice. This, however, suggests some fairly radical changes for the practice of information modeling. Currently, we focus on diagramming techniques and automated tools to support diagramming. If class conceptualism holds, which appears to be the case, then we should be focusing on the question of how classes are constructed to meet various information needs. Further, we can no longer validate an information model by comparing it to the real world (since that assumes class realism). We have to define objectives for the model and evaluate constructs according to how well they meet those objectives.

Attribute realism is, at least, slightly suspect. Entities in the real world do have physical characteristics. However, the purpose of a database and the purpose of a scientific taxonomy are likely to be quite different. Scientific taxonomies do not consider functional or artificial attributes in their classification. Yet information models do. Assuming that entities have a limited (and small) number of physical attributes that can be used to group them into classes is hard to justify in practice. Entities have lots of attributes (physical and artificial), some that they share in common with other entities some that they do not. Attribute realism does not allow for functional or artificial attributes. Limited attribute realism does not allow for the fact that entities may not have uniform properties. Hence, attribute realism does not provide an adequate foundation for the practice.

Attribute conceptualism seems to provide the richest foundation because it acknowledges the existence of nonphysical attributes. It also allows for the fact that we pick and choose attributes based upon (possibly implicit) objectives in the modeling process. It also allows for the fact that we may invent some of the attributes. This leaves the question of whether or not the attributes can be constructed from the linguistic usage.

If the model must represent usage and the usage is somewhat consistent, then it may be possible to construct an information model of the domain in question. If the model must represent usage but usage is not consistent then it will not be possible to construct a coherent model. Finally, if the model does not have to reflect usage, it can be constructed to meet information objectives. If the objectives are consistent, then the model can be constructed, otherwise not. Yet the resulting model may not be consistent with the users concept of what the various constructs mean.

CONCLUSION

The Problem of Universals provides both a metaphysical foundation for information modeling and substantial insight into the nature of the process. Information modeling research should focus less on representational techniques and more on the problem of what is to be represented. Since class and attribute conceptualism provides a much firmer philosophical foundation, then the work of researchers in information modeling is to determine how to define modeling objectives and how to compare competing models with respect to those objectives. A secondary area of research interest should be in understanding how cognitive factors and individual differences between information modelers affect the models they produce.

REFERENCES

Aaron, R. I. (1967). *The Theory of Universals.* (2nd. ed.) Oxford: Clarendon Press.

Aaron, R. I. (1933). Locke's Theory of Universals. *Proceedings of the Aristotelian Society,* 33, 171-202.

Aaron, R. I. (1942). Hume's Theory of Universals. *Proceedings of the Aristotelian Society.* 42, 117-140.

Armstrong, D. M. (1989). *Universals: An Opinionated Introduction.* Boulder, CO: Westview Press.

Artz, J. M. (2007). Philosophical Foundations of Information Modeling. *International Journal of Intelligent Information Technologies, 3*(3).

Artz, J. (2006). Conflicting Ontological Assumptions in Information Modeling. *Encyclopedia of Database Technologies and Applications.* Information Science Publishing.

Artz, J. (2001). A Teleological Approach to Information Systems Development. in *Managing Information Technology in a Global Economy.* Mehdi Khosrow-pour (ed.) Idea Group Publishing.

Artz, J. (1999). An Analysis of Ontological Assumptions in Information Modeling. In Managing Information *Technology Resources in Organizations in the Next Millennium.* Mehdi Khosrow-pour (ed.) Idea Group Publishing.

Artz, J. (1998). Information Modeling and the Problem of Universals: A Preliminary Analysis of Metaphysical Assumptions. *Proceedings of the Association for Information Systems 1998 Americas Conference.*

Artz, J. (1997). A Crash Course in Metaphysics for the Database Designer. *Journal of Database Management,* 8(4).

Bacon, F. (2000). *The New Organon.* Jardine, L. and Silverthorne, M. (eds.) Cambridge Texts in the History of Philosophy. Cambridge University Press.

Bambrough, R. (1961). Universals and Family Resemblances. *Proceedings of the Aristotelian Society, 61,* 207 - 222.

Benbasat, I., & Zmud, R. (2003). The Identity Crisis Within the IS Discipline: Defining and Communicating the Discipline's Core Properties. *MIS Quarterly.* 27(2),183-194.

Burrell, G., & Morgan, G. (1979). *Sociological Paradigms and Organizational Analysis.* Heinemann, London.

Carr, N. (2003). IT doesn't matter. *HBR at Large.* May, 41-49.

Checkland, P. B. (1989). Soft Systems Methodology. *Human Systems Management, 8*(4), 271-289.

Chen, P. (1976). The Entity Relationship Model: Towards a Unified View of Data. *Association of Computing Machinery Transactions on Database Systems,* 1(1).

Codd, E. F. (1970, June). A Relational Model of Data for Large Shared Data Banks. *Communications of the ACM,* 377-387.

Culnan, M. (1986). The Intellectual Development of Management Information Systems, 1972-1982: A Co-citation Analysis. *Management Science.* 32(2),156-172.

Farhoomand, A., & Drury, D. (2001). Diversity and Scientific Progress in the Information Systems Discipline. *Communications of the AIS, 5*(12).

Flavin, M. (1981) *Fundamental Concepts of Information Modeling.* Yourdon Press.

Gottlieb, A. (2002). *The Dream of Reason.* W.W. Norton & Company.

Gray, P. (2003). Editorial: Introduction to the Debate on the Core of the Information Systems Field. *Communications of AIS.* 12(42).

Hirsch, E. (1982). *The Concept of Identity.* Oxford University Press.

Hirsch, E. (1993). *Dividing Reality.* Oxford University Press.

Hirschheim, R., Klein, H. K., & Lyytinen, K. (1995). *Information Systems Development and Data Modeling: Conceptual and Philosophical Foundations.* Cambridge University Press.

Hirschheim, R., & Klein, H. K. (1989). Four Paradigms of Information Systems Development. *Communications of the ACM.,* 32(32), 1199-1216.

Keen, P. (1980). MIS Research: Reference Disciplines and a Cumulative Tradition. *Proceedings of the 1st International Conference on Information Systems.* pp. 9-18.

Kent, W. (1978). *Data and Reality: Basic Assumptions in Data Processing Reconsidered.* North-Holland.

Kent, W. (1979). Limitations of Record-Based Information Models. *ACM Transactions on Database Systems,* 1(4),107-131.

Klein, H. K., & Hirschheim, R. A. (1987). A Comparative Framework of Data Modelling Paradigms and Approaches. *The Computer Journal,* 1(30), 8-15.

Lakoff, G. (1987). *Women, Fire, and Dangerous Things: What Categories Reveal about the Mind.* Chicago: University of Chicago Press.

Lakoff, G. (1988). Cognitive Semantics. In Eco, U., Santambrogio, M. and Violi, P. (Eds.) *Meaning and Mental Representations.* Bloomington: Indiana University Press, pp. 119-154.

Losee, J. (1993). *A Historical Introduction to the Philosophy of Science.* Oxford University Press.

Luria, A. R. (1976). *Cognitive Development: Its Cultural and Social Foundations.* Cambridge, MA. Harvard University Press.

Nijssen, G. M., & Halpin, T. A.(1989). *Conceptual Schema and Relational Database Design: A fact oriented approach.* New York:Prentice Hall.

Orlikowski, W., & Iacono, C. (2001). Research Commentary: Desperately Seeking the "IT" in IT Research – A Call to Theorizing the IT Artifact. *Information Systems Research*, 12(2), 121-134.

Pirsig, R. (1992) *Lila: An Inquiry into Morals.* Bantam.

Plato. (1992). *The Republic.* Translated by Grube, G. M. and Reeve, C. D. Harvard University Press.

Prior, A. N. (1967). Correspondence Theory of Truth. In *Encyclopedia of Philosophy.* Paul Edwards (ed). Macmillan Publishing, New York. 1, 223-232.

Robey, D. (2003). Identity, Legitimacy and the Dominant Research Paradigm: An Alternative Prescription for the IS Discipline. *Journal of the Association for Information Systems*, 4(7), 352-359.

Roochnik, D. (2002). *An Introduction to Greek Philosophy.* The Teaching Company.

Rosch, E., & Lloyd, B. B. (Eds.) (1978A). *Cognition and Categorization.* New Jersey: Lawrence Erlbaum Assoc. Publishers.

Rosch, E. (1978B). Principles of Categorization. In Rosch, E. and Lloyd, B.B. (Eds.) *Cognition and Categorization.* New Jersey: Lawrence Erlbaum Assoc. Publishers.

Schoedinger, A. B. (Ed.) (1992). *The Problem of Universals.* New Jersey: Humanities Press.

Shlaer, S., & Mellor, S. J. (1988) *Object-Oriented Systems Analysis: Modeling the World in Data.* Englewood Cliffs, New Jersey: Yourdon Press, 1988.

Smith, E., & Medin, D. (1981) *Categories and Concepts.* Cognitive Science Series, 4, University Microfilms International.

Stroll, A. (1967). Identity. In *Encyclopedia of Philosophy.* Paul Edwards (ed). Macmillan Publishing, New York. 4. pp. 121-124.

Teorey, T. J. (1990). *Database Modeling and Design: The Entity-Relationship Approach.* San Mateo, CA: Morgan Kaufman Publishers, Inc.

Twain, M. (2000). *Diary of Adam and Eve.* Prometheus Books.

Veryard, R. (1992). *Information Modeling.* New York: Prentice-Hall, Inc.

Veryard, R. (1984). *Pragmatic Data Analysis.* Oxford: Blackwell Scientific Publications.

Weber, R. (1987). Toward a Theory of Artifacts: A Paradigmatic Base For Information Systems Research. *Journal of Information Systems.* Spring, pp 3-19.

Weber, R. (2003). Still Desperately Seeking for the IT Artifact (editor's comments). *MIS Quarterly*, (27) 2. pp. iii-xi.

White, A. R. (1967). Coherence Theory of Truth. *Encyclopedia of Philosophy.* Paul Edwards (ed). Macmillan Publishing, New York. Vol. 1. Pp. 130-133.

Woozley, A. D. (1949). *Theory of Knowledge.* Hutchinson's University Library.

Woozley, A. D. (1967). Universals. In Edwards, P. (ed.) *Encyclopedia of Philosophy*, 8, 194-206.

Chapter XVI
Empirical Inference of Numerical Information into Causal Strategy Models by Means of Artificial Intelligence

Christian Hillbrand
University of Liechtenstein, Principality of Liechtenstein

ABSTRACT

The motivation for this chapter is the observation that many companies build their strategy upon poorly validated hypotheses about cause and effect of certain business variables. However, the soundness of these cause-and-effect-relations as well as the knowledge of the approximate shape of the functional dependencies underlying these associations turns out to be the biggest issue for the quality of the results of decision supporting procedures. Since it is sufficiently clear that mere correlation of time series is not suitable to prove the causality of two business concepts, there seems to be a rather dogmatic perception of the inadmissibility of empirical validation mechanisms for causal models within the field of strategic management as well as management science. However, one can find proven causality techniques in other sciences like econometrics, mechanics, neuroscience, or philosophy. Therefore this chapter presents an approach which applies a combination of well-established statistical causal proofing methods to strategy models in order to validate them. These validated causal strategy models are then used as the basis for approximating the functional form of causal dependencies by the means of Artificial Neural Networks. This in turn can be employed to build an approximate simulation or forecasting model of the strategic system.

INTRODUCTION

Planning and implementing corporate strategy very often requires substantial efforts in gathering relevant data and information underlying the decisions to be met. Hence, the decision makers face at least two elementary issues: First, the planner has to be supplied with appropriate data about the underlying relevant key figures and business drivers as well as environmental information related to the market or competitors. This first function of data support as outlined before is the main focus of so-called management information systems (MIS). These tools usually employ powerful techniques to gather the necessary figures as a basis for strategic planning efforts.

Second, this raw data has to be arranged within decision models in order to reduce the variety and complexity coming with it: One characteristic of a complex strategic decision is that it is influenced by an immense set of business variables which have to be analyzed in this context. As a consequence data supporting tools do not provide appropriate aids for this type of entrepreneurial function: It is to reduce the complexity emerging from this amount of data which becomes the principal task of decision support systems (DSS). Hence it can be observed that the architecture of any arbitrary DSS is highly dependent of the managerial approach it is designed to support. It necessarily incorporates the notion of a mental model underlying the respective decision theory as well as techniques to derive decisions from these assumptions. Sprague & Carlson (1982) specify these two core components of a DSS as model base and method base, respectively. The former defines the structure of the decision model which arranges the raw data provided by a data support component, whereas the latter encompasses decision theoretic methods specifically designed to operate on the given decision model. According to the type of the model base, analytic techniques like optimization as well as statistical methods or stochastic approaches like simulation are used to draw decisions from the raw data organized in the decision model.

The rest of the chapter is organized as follows: The following section provides review of the appropriate literature within the field of causal strategy planning techniques as well as of causality concepts. Consequently, specific causality criteria are defined on this basis. This definition is employed in the subsequent section in order to establish an approach for the automated proof of nomothetic cause-and-effect hypotheses. Since every single of these proven causal relations are characterized by an arbitrary unknown cause-and-effect function, this function has to be approximated in order to build a quantitative model base for DSSs. Therefore this chapter discusses appropriate approximation techniques and proposes a nonparametric approach for the universal approximation of arbitrary cause-and-effect functions by the means of ANNs. This chapter is concluded by the presentation of experimental results.

LITERATURE REVIEW

Causal Strategy Planning Approaches

A considerable number of recent approaches within the domain of strategic decision making proposes to organize business indicators in the form of causal models. The main task of these models is to visualize the cause-and-effect relations which the decision maker assumes to exist between the given variables and/or goals (Hillbrand & Karagiannis, 2002a).

One well-known example for this type of strategic decision methodologies is the Balanced Scorecard approach (Kaplan & Norton, 1992): The main idea behind this concept is that short term goals of financial nature like the improvement of profitability measures are usually influenced by long term objectives of non-financial type. Therefore Kaplan and Norton (1992) postulate a balanced selection of strategic goals out of (at least) four distinct dimensions: Financial, customer-, process- and, development-specific perspectives should be included in the strategic process. Between the goals and measures of these dimensions the decision maker has to make hypotheses about the underlying cause-and-effect relations. Subsequently they can be used to disaggregate main strategic goals into tactical objectives and measures.

Similar principles are encompassed by the French Tableau de Board methodology (Mendoza et al., 2002) as well as by cybernetic management principles as proposed for example by Vester (1988) in his Biocybernetic Approach whose main concepts are reused in the St. Gallen Management Model (Gomez & Probst, 1999; Schwaninger, 2001; Spickers, 2003).

Although these managerial approaches for strategic decision support provide some practical approaches for the reduction of complexity coming with a sense-making process the implementations of these ideas in the form of DSS are rather weak: It can be observed that software tools supporting such approaches are focused on techniques out of the method base in order to draw conclusions from a hypothetically assumed cause-and-effect model as outlined before (Hillbrand & Karagiannis, 2002a, p. 368). Therefore most DSS of this type provide simulation techniques as well as how-to-achieve- and what-if-analyses. However, the model base usually remains unproven with respect to the empirical evidence of the hypothetically assumed cause-and-effect relations between the business variables. As a logical consequence, the overall quality of the decision support provided by such a system is directly related to the completeness and soundness of the underlying causal hypotheses. Moreover these techniques are not able to provide quantitative forecasts for future impacts of an analyzed strategic scenario. The reason for this lack of approaches for causal proof and quantitative techniques for managerial cause-and-effect models can be traced back to a proposition of Kaplan and Norton (1996): In their book they recommend "correlational studies" in order to infer causal knowledge from time series of business variables in the course of double loop learning. This postulate caused an intense discussion about the admissibility of such techniques with respect to the purpose as mentioned before: As for example Weber and Schäffer (2000) conjecture, the "basic problem of an analytic derivation of the `correct` cause-and-effect relations cannot be solved in this way" (p. 8). Horvàth & Partner (2001) come to a similar conclusion:

Cause-and-effect relations [...] do not describe arithmetical logics e.g. in the form of the known ROI-scheme [...]. The goals and for this reason also the measures are causally associated in a logical but not in a calculative sense. If the value of one goal changes, the impacts on another variable of the same system cannot be predicted exactly. (p. 44f.)

Other authors only refer to the need for further research in this area (Probst, 2001, p. 81). However, this discussion and its limitation to the construct of correlation leads to a rather dogmatic conception that managerial cause-and-effect models must not be evaluated in a quantitative way which is typical for the relevant managerial literature. According to Schneiderman (1999) this is one of the major reasons for the failure of Balanced Scorecard projects:

We all know that correlation does not mean causality. But try explaining these data to someone who has been only reluctantly convinced that the non-financial scorecard metrics are a leading indicator of future financial success. (p. 10)

However, if we abandon the restriction to correlation as a concept for the proof of causality and a measure of association, it seems to be possible to infer further causal knowledge from empirical data and therefore improve the quality of the model base significantly. Hence, this chapter proposes an approach to automatically prove managerial cause-and-effect relations and to approximate the unknown causal function underlying these associations.

Causality Concepts

Since one main objective of this chapter is to provide an approach to proof hypothetically assumed cause-and-effect relations between managerial variables, it is necessary to define necessary and sufficient conditions for the concept of causality in this environment. As it has been outlined in the introduction, the mere correlation of two variables seems to be insufficient for this purpose. Moreover, causality per se cannot be observed or tested by objective means. According to Kant it is a synthetic judgment a priori (Schnell et al., 1999, p. 56). Causality must therefore be regarded as an assumption about the connection between cause and effect made by the human mind and based on a variety of experiences rather than some kind of natural phenomenon which can be observed in an objective manner.

As a consequence of the lack of observability of causal relations as outlined above, there has been a broad scientific dispute within the philosophy of science about the concept of causality. The beginning of this discussion can be traced back to the Humean regularity theory (Sondhauss, 1998): This notion of causality is founded mainly on the two concepts of contiguity and temporal succession (Hume 1748), i.e. two events always have to occur within temporal and/or spacial limits and the effect *must* follow the cause in time. Although this theory does not seem to be fully sufficient to explain the concept of causality[1], it introduces an important property which is part of almost every causality theory: Causal relations are usually regarded as asymmetric associations of two events.

However, there are (at least) two objections regarding this basic theory of causation:

Firstly, representatives of probabilistic causality theories bring forward the argument that the deterministic association between cause and effect as an integral part of the regulatory theory represents a too rigorous characteristic. According to their notion, the occurrence of a cause only raises the probability of an effect but does not necessarily imply it.

Secondly, the Humean regulatory theory is criticized because of temporal precedence being the only characteristic to establish the necessary asymmetric property of a causal relation as for example Brady (2002) explains:

The Humean theory does even less well with the asymmetrical feature of the causal relationship because it provides no way to determine asymmetry except temporal precedence. [...] Causes not only typically precede their effects, but they also can be used to explain effects or to manipulate effects while effects cannot be used to explain causes or to manipulate them. (p. 18)

Approaches to overcome these shortcomings lead to the notion of causality as it is proposed by interventionistic theories. The central ideas of these theories are driven by human action as the definition of Gasking (1955) shows:

The notion of causation is essentially connected with our manipulative techniques for producing results. (p. 483)

According to this perception, a causal relation can only be verified in experimental settings where a response can be observed after a cause has been manipulated and the system can be isolated from other (unknown) influences. This is necessary because there exist situations where the mere observation of cause and effect misleadingly suggest causality between two events where there is none. For example the influence of an exogenous third variable U on two endogenous variables C and E can lead to correlation as well as to a temporal precedence relation between C and E although they are not causing each other. This example demonstrates the inability of mere temporal precedence to explain the asymmetry in causal relations quite graphically.

The restriction of interventionistic approaches to analyze the concept of causality only experimentally is the main reason for their failure to explain many real-life problems as it is also the case for managerial cause-and-effect relations: In an enterprise there is hardly any situation where an experiment-like situation can be created because the trial-and-error manner of these settings usually would inflict losses for the business and the response time of basic cause-and-effect relations can be rather long. As a consequence it seems to be too costly to prove causality in this way.

There has been a broad discussion of causal theories in economics – as in many other sciences. In the first half of the 20th century economists mostly neglected causal concepts as described above. The standard solution was to identify additional determinants which discriminate between otherwise simultaneous relationships (Hoover 2008, p. 6). One important momentum for the discussion of causality in economics was the conception of the Cowles Commission in the 1950s (Koopmans 1950). According to this, the solution for finding causal relationships was the a priori knowledge from economic models. This implies that – according to this notion of causality – causal structures cannot be inferred merely by empirical data but have to be built upon well-known hypotheses which can only be falsified.

One major critique of this approach comes from the work of Lucas (1976) who argues that a change in economic policy renders the parameters of the causal structures unstable. Lucas' critique led to the postulate of invariance (i.e. the independence of policy changes) of economic causal structures and therefore was the most important reason why the discussion shifted more towards so-called inferential approaches (cf. Granger 2003, p. 70). These techniques infer causal structure only form empirical observations without the need for a priori knowledge. One of the most important contributions in this area originates from the works of Granger who proposed a generic definition of inferential causality. He argued that "a (time series) variable A causes B, if the probability of B conditional on its own past history and the past history of A (besides the set Ω of the available information) does not equal the probability of B conditional on its own past history alone." (Granger 1980, p. 330; cited after Moneta, 2004, p. 1). The asymmetry of cause and effect in this concept known as Granger causality is secured by the requirement that A occurs before B in time (Hoover 2008, p. 12). This notion of causality led to numerous applications within the field of economics and was awarded the 2003 Nobel Prize in economics.

Newer inferential approaches employ graphical models in order to describe the causal structures which are then tested by conditional causality concepts. These graph-theoretic approaches were mostly developed in other scientific areas like computer science (Pearl 2000) or psychology (Glymour 2001). However, they were then transferred to economic issues (cf. e.g. Hoover 2001; Hoover 2008). The logic behind these techniques is rather simple: It is possible to depict a simple causal relation between two variables as a directed edge between two nodes representing the dependent and the independent variables. By combining more causal edges it becomes possible to model more complex causal structures as for example shielded colliders which is a common term for two causes for one indicator variable. By analyzing the conditional correlations between these variables it is possible to introduce undirected edges into the structural model. By analyzing the conditional behavior and the graphical model it becomes possible to direct some or all of these edges. The most common of these causal search algorithms—the PC-algorithm—has first been proposed by Pearl and Verma (1991). Spirtes et al. (2000) used these principles for their causal proving software application TETRAD. Within this chapter, this technique is employed to rule out third variable effects and is therefore explained in more detail in the respective section.

A SYNTHETIC CONCEPT OF CAUSALITY BETWEEN BUSINESS VARIABLES

Applied to managerial cause-and-effect relations, an appropriate concept of causality must restrict itself to observational studies in terms of empirical data as a consequence. Therefore we can summarize the above disquisition of definitions for causality as follows: A cause should provide information which can be used to (partly) explain its effects. In case of linear cause-and-effect relations this property of informational redundancy is also known as correlation or covariance. However, as it has been shown in the introduction these concepts do not succeed to fully explain causality. According to Hume, there has to be a temporal precedence relation between a cause and its effects additionally to informational redundancy as for example Pearl and Verma (1991) state:

Temporal precedence is normally assumed essential for defining causation, and it is undoubtedly one of the most important clues that people use to distinguish causal from other types of associations. (p. 442)

Regardless of the ability of these two necessary properties to fully explain many causal relations there still remains the problem of an exogenous common cause to induce spurious associations between presumably causal variables. Therefore the definition of causality has to be enhanced by the postulate to control for this type of association. This leads to a notion similar to the one of Suppes (1970):

X and Y must covary, X must precede Y, and other causes of Y must be controlled.

Based on these foundations the following definition of an appropriate concept of causality to analyze associations between managerial variables can be derived:

Theorem 1 (managerial causal relation): A causal relation between variables of a managerial system exists if and only if there exist appropriate nomothetic (i.e. unproven) cause-and-effect hypotheses based on causal a priori knowledge where the following conditions are fulfilled:

- The empirical observations of a potential cause provide informational redundancy regarding its potential effect.
- The variation within the time series of the potential cause must always precede the response of this variation within the time series of the potential effect.
- The three causality properties as defined above (causal a priori knowledge, informational redundancy and temporal precedence) must not originate from the influence of a known or unknown cause, common to the potential cause and the potential effect.

As it is obvious from the above theorem, the underlying notion of causality follows the logic of logical empirism which regards a hypothesis as true as long as it cannot be falsified. Therefore it is the task of a causality proof to rule out non-causal associations according to the above criteria from a given strategy model consisting of nomothetic cause-and-effect hypotheses. The next section develops an appropriate approach for the automated proof of causality.

AN EMPIRICAL VALIDATION APPROACH FOR CAUSAL STRATEGY MODELS

As the previous section provides a homogeneous notion of causality it remains to identify an approach to apply this definition to the causal knowledge of an enterprise in order to distinguish between genuine and spurious cause-and-effect relations. The conceptual basis for the construction of proven causal models for strategic decision support is therefore represented by the necessary and sufficient properties of causality as defined above.

Modeling Nomologic Cause-and-Effect Hypotheses

The starting point for this approach is the compilation of causal knowledge in the form of implicit mental models or corresponding data into an explicit model of nomologic cause-and-effect hypotheses. The latter are contained in a rudimentary cause-and-effect model which has to be given by strategic decision makers and represents the first necessary causal property of a priori knowledge.

One possible approach to model causal strategy maps has been proposed by Hillbrand and Karagiannis (2002b, p. 53): The meta-model of their modeling framework consists of indicators which can be of crisp or fuzzy type and two types of associations which connect a pair of indicators:

- Defined influence relations represent causal associations between variables which can be fully explained by decision makers. Usually the target variable of this type of relation is some kind of synthetic ratio which has been axiomatically devised by a formula consisting of several input parameters. A well-established example for influence relations are profitability measures like ROI, ROCE, etc. As a consequence defined influences can only be modeled between crisp indicators where the values of the result variable can be fully explained by some algebraic function of input indicators.

- All remaining potentially causal associations between either crisp or fuzzy variables which do not fulfill both conditions for a defined influence relation are called undefined. For this type of relation it is not possible to assume causality a priori as in the preceding case. Rather the decision makers are forced to rely on nomothetic cause-and-effect hypotheses. However, the empirical knowledge of past time-series enables managers to scrutinize the causal content of the interjacent potential cause-and-effect relation.

Consequently it is the focus of this section to provide appropriate methods in order to analyze the hypothetically defined model base of a strategic DSS with respect to its causal validity. This task of the proposed approach is to detect so-called α-errors[2] of nomothetic cause-and-effect hypotheses between variables. Therefore the starting point for the reconstruction of a proven causal model is a rather over-defined rudimentary model as described above.

Identification of Temporally Lagged Informational Redundancy

The second necessary condition for causality—as defined in the previous section—is informational redundancy between a potential cause and its potential effect. As a consequence the time series of the dependent variable as the output of an unknown causal function associated with the respective relation must also reflect patterns or variations of independent time series. Very often these patterns are transformed by the underlying causal function and superposed by the influences of other exogenous or endogenous variables. Therefore they cannot always be detected a prima facie. If the causal function which transforms the values of a set of independent variables into the value of a dependent value is of linear type, the concept of correlation can be used as a measure for informational redundancy. In all other cases one has to find other techniques to analyze whether two time-series are informationally redundant or not. For the purpose of this approach it seems to be suitable to restrict to the linear case because the causality proof per se does not build the model base but is used to select variables for the following approximation of a nonlinear causal function. Therefore it is not necessary to rule out all possibilities of α-errors because the ANNs—assigned to perform the causal approximation task—are supposed to detect the non existing influence of marginally spurious associations. The admissibility of this theory for different types of causal functions has been shown by Hillbrand (2003, pp. 299ff.).

When considering the third necessary condition for causality of temporal precedence of cause and effect the inadequacy of the concept of correlation alone to prove cause-and-effect relations becomes obvious: The correlation of two time series would show that the variations of a independent and a dependent variable are similar and that they take place contemporaneously.

As this is mutually contradictory to the notion of causality as defined in the previous section, the concept of correlation has to be adopted to measure temporally lagged responses of the variation of an independent factor within the time series of the dependent variable. Therefore cross correlation $\rho_{X,Y}(\Delta t)$ implies a time lag Δt between a cause X and an effect Y in the following form:

$$\rho_{X,Y}(\Delta t) = \frac{\frac{\sum_{t=1}^{T}(y_t - \bar{Y})(x_{t-\Delta t} - \bar{X})}{T}}{\sigma_X \cdot \sigma_Y}$$

Where y_t and x_t stand for the values of the variables Y and X at time t, $\bar{X}$ and $\bar{Y}$ stand for the average values and σ_x as well as σ_y for the standard deviation of the respective time series. As it is evident from the above expression, the upper part of the fraction is derived from the construct of covariance.

As a consequence, this approach employs this concept to identify the two causality conditions of informational redundancy and temporal precedence: By calculating the cross correlations for varying time lags it is possible to identify a window of impact between an independent and a dependent variable. This window of impact is characterized by a minimum time lag and a number of subsequent effects (i.e. the length of the window of impact). For this purpose it is necessary to identify the significance of a cross correlation at a given time lag. Therefore this approach uses Bartlett's significance test (Bartlett, 1955) following the suggestions of the appropriate literature in this area (Makridakis & Wheelwright, 1978; Levich & Rizzo, 1997): The null hypothesis of this test is formed by the assumption that two given time series at a certain time lag are independent if their cross correlation shows a value of zero. This hypothesis has to be accepted if the cross correlation lies within the boundaries which are given by the standard deviation of the cross correlation. If it exceeds this critical value, the null hypothesis is rejected and it is said to be significant. Since the standard deviation of the cross correlation is usually not known a priori the critical test value is replaced by the following estimate (Bartlett, 1955):

$$\sigma_{\rho_{x,y}(\Delta t)} = \frac{1}{\sqrt{n - |\Delta t|}}$$

Where n stands for the number of samples in the time series of X and Y, respectively.

By increasing the time lag Δt by discrete steps beginning at a lag of zero time periods, it is possible to identify the minimum time lag by recording the first significant cross correlation between the time series.

This approach is illustrated in Figure 1 for the following synthetically generated time series:

$$x_t = \varepsilon_{U(0;1)}$$

$$y_t = 0.2 y_{t-1} + 0.5 x_{t-2} + 0.2 x_{t-3} \varepsilon_{U(0;1)}$$

Where $\varepsilon_{U(0;1)}$ is a random variable uniformly distributed between zero and one.

As it is obvious from the above equations, the time series y_t of the independent variable Y incorporates past values of the time series x_t with a time lag of two and three time periods, respectively. Therefore the correct window of impact is [2,3].

Figure 1 shows the cross correlations computed from the artificial time series x_t and y_t for the time lags $\Delta t = 0,...,9$ as well as the bandwidth of their standard deviation which lies between the dotted lines. The clear consequence which can be drawn from this correlogram is that the first significant correlation

Figure 1. Correlogram between two time series

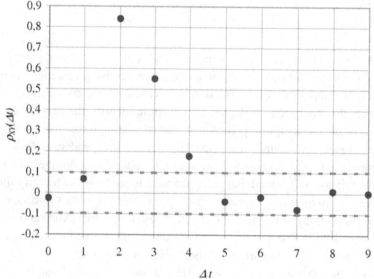

starting from zero occurs at a time lag of $\Delta t = 2$ which corresponds exactly to the generating function of y_t as stated above. Therefore the minimum time lag for this potentially causal relation is $b = 2$ time periods. This means that the variation of the independent variable X is first repeated within the time series of the dependent variable Y after two time periods.

The first attempt to determine the appropriate length of the window of impact using the correlogram in Figure 1 yields time lags between $\Delta t = 2$ and $\Delta t = 4$ because the last significant cross correlation occurs with a time lag of four time periods. As this is not correct with respect to the generating function above, one has to take the autocorrelation of the two variables into account. It can be shown that significant autocorrelation of the independent time series leads to the so-called echo effect (Hillbrand 2004, p. 181) which describes the indirect effects of independent values prior to the window of impact through an autocorrelated dependent time series. In the example of Figure 1 this effect becomes evident when scrutinizing the generating function of the time series y_t. This function includes the term "... $0.2y_{t-1}$ ..." which means that the actual value of the variable Y reflects also a fraction the preceding value y_{t-1}. As this in turn is influenced by the independent values x_{t-3} and x_{t-4} it becomes evident that the latter is reflected in y_t with the weight $0.2 \cdot 0.2 = 0.04$ (cf. Figure 2). As the autocorrelation of the dependent variable can be regarded as an infinite series, it can lead to putative random patterns for the echo effect.

Therefore it is crucial for a correct identification of the impact window to eliminate any autocorrelation within the time series to be analyzed. This preprocessing of the time series is known as prewhitening in the appropriate literature (Makridakis & Wheelwright, 1978; pp. 382f.). As a prerequisite for this task, the order of autocorrelation for independent and dependent variables has to be determined by the use of the autocorrelation coefficient[3]. Thus this approach analyzes the autocorrelation coefficients for ascending orders which exceed the critical value of the Bartlett test (for details see above) and consequently are denoted as significant. This approach comes to reliable results for the analysis of independent time series. However, it does not perform well for result variables as a further disturbance effect can be observed in this context: Influences with a significant number of subsequent effects (i.e. the window of impact is larger than one time period) tend to induce an autocorrelation-like pattern in the dependent time series although there is no significant autocorrelation from the generating process of y_t. As a consequence it seems to be necessary to identify the appropriate window of impact before analyzing the autocorrelation of the dependent time series. Therefore a circular dilemma occurs because the autocorrelation of the dependent variable is a prerequisite for the prewhitening process which is in turn necessary to avoid echo effects and to identify the appropriate size of the window of impact consequently.

Figure 2. Echo effect

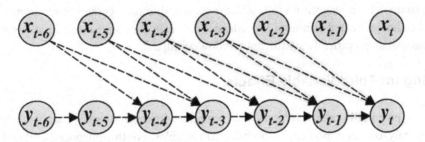

Approaches for this dilemma include the solution of separated autoregressive generating processes for each time series as well as iterative approximation techniques. The separated generating processes as mentioned above are characterized by partial autocorrelation coefficients. The combination of partial autocorrelations of dependent and independent time series as well as the cross correlation between the two of them result in the specific cross correlation pattern observable in the correlogram (cf. Figure 1). Since the relevant literature knows solutions for this problem which are far from trivial, this chapter employs an approach which is based on an iterative approximation of an appropriate length for the window of impact:

1. Prewhitening of independent variables:
    a. Determine orders of significant autocorrelation within the time series of every independent variable X_t.
    b. For every order o of significant autocorrelation for every independent variable X_t determine the respective autoregression coefficient $\beta_{X,o}$.
    c. For every value $x_{i,t}$ of an autocorrelated independent variable X_t subtract past values of the same time series weighted by the appropriate autoregression coefficient in the following form:
        $$x'_{i,t} = x_{i,t} - \sum_{\forall o} \left(\beta_{X_{i,o}} \cdot x_{i,t-o} \right).$$
2. Determine significant cross correlations between every prewhitened independent time series $x'_{i,t}$ and the dependent time series y_t for different time lags Δt.
3. Identify the windows of impact – determined by the minimum time lag b_i and the following effects s_i – from the the correlograms between every prewhitened independent variable X'_i and the dependent variable Y.
4. Determine the regression coefficients $\beta_{X'_{i,\Delta t}}$ between any independent variable X'_i and the dependent element Y for time lags Δt with a significant cross correlation.
5. Eliminate all impacts of independent variables on the dependent variable by subtracting the respective past values of the independent time series $x'_{i,t-\Delta t}$ weighted by the appropriate regression coefficient $\beta_{X'_{i,\Delta t}}$ according to the prewhitening procedure as described in step 1c.
6. The isolated dependent time series y_t^* resulting from the previous step is tested for significant autocorrelation.
    a. If no significant autocorrelation can be identified within the time series of y_t^*, the procedure terminates. Therefore the windows of impact for each independent variable X_i are given as determined in step 3.
    b. If the time series y_t^* is significantly autocorrelated, the the raw time series y_t is prewhitened according to steps 1b and 1c. The procedure resumes with a new iteration at step 2 using the prewhitened dependent time series y_t^*.

Having an appropriate algorithm to test the second and third necessary condition of causality (informational redundancy and temporal precedence) non-causal or spurious relations can be identified by the absence of an empirically significant window of impact.

Controlling for Third Variable Effects

The remaining potentially causal relations which comply with the first three causality criteria are subject to a further analysis of common causation by third variables. For this purpose Pearl and Verma (1991) propose an approach (PC-algorithm) to distinguish spurious associations induced by a common cause from genuine causation:

Theorem 2 (Controlling for third variables): One can assume a relation $X \rightarrow Y$ to be causal if and only if the time series of the potential effect Y incorporates not only patterns of its potential cause X but also those of the predecessors P (i.e. causes) of X in the cause-and-effect model. If X and Y as well as P and X are informationally redundant but P and Y are not, an unknown third variable U rather than a causal relation must be assumed to induce the informational redundancy between X and Y.

As a consequence the patterns of P are reflected within the time series of X but they are not passed on to Y due to the absence of a genuine cause-and-effect relation $X \rightarrow Y$.

A basic tool for the analysis of these assumptions within causal graphs is the concept of conditional independence: Two variables A and B are conditionally independent given a set of variables S_{AB} – written as $(A \perp B \mid S_{AB})$ – if A and B are informationally redundant but if the impacts of S_{AB} on B are eliminated, this property vanishes. Therefore S_{AB} is said to "block" the causal path between A and B.

Applying this concept to the above theory, spurious associations between a potential cause X and a potential effect Y can be ruled out by the following observations:

- There exists a minimal set of blocking variables S_{PY} causing conditional independence between any predecessor P of X and the effect Y, denoted as $(P \perp Y \mid S_{PY})$.
- X is part of the set S_{PY}.

The theory to detect third variable effects as outlined in this chapter is implemented by the IC^4 or PC-algorithm. For reasons of lucidity, this chapter dispenses with a detailed discussion of these procedures but refers to the appropriate literature (Pearl & Verma, 1991; Hillbrand, 2003, p. 198).

Summarizing this approach, the mapping of nomothetic cause-and-effect hypotheses by decision makers represents a prerequisite for their proof as well as the first causality criterion. The second and third condition for causality – informational redundancy and temporal sequence – are tested by analyzing the cross correlations between the prewhitened time series of the respective variables connected by a cause-and-effect hypothesis. To rule out a third variable inducing informational redundancy between two lagged variables, this analysis is completed by the application of the IC-Algorithm as outlined above. Only relations which pass all these tests satisfy the necessary causality conditions and are therefore said to be genuinely causal.

APPROXIMATION OF UNKNOWN CAUSAL FUNCTIONS

The proof of causality as proposed in the previous section is the main prerequisite for the approximation of the unknown causal function affecting the values of any arbitrary business variable within a cause-and-effect structure. This provides the necessary numeric properties for the causal model base of a DSS to run simulations as well as how-to-achieve or what-if analyses. One crucial issue of this task is that the form of these cause-and-effect functions cannot be assessed a priori. Therefore three alternative approaches are to be considered in this context:

- First, the base functions for the approximated associations have to be predetermined (e.g.: linear, logarithmic, logistic, exponential, etc.). With this assumption it is possible to approximate the unknown function by estimating the parameters of an appropriate regression model.
- Second, a function can be locally approximated by developing an appropriate polynomial. This principle is used for the Taylor or Fourier series expansion. A disadvantage of these techniques is that their approximation is only accurate within local limits of the function.
- Third, unknown functions can also be reconstructed without prior knowledge of their shape by so-called universal approximators (Tikk et al., 2001). Hence these techniques are able to learn a function from mere empirical observations without the need to narrow down some base function. This characteristic becomes increasingly important whenever the unknown function to be approximated is of nonlinear type. As it can be shown by numerous examples, microeconomic functions which usually underly strategic reasoning are almost never of linear type (Hillbrand, 2003, pp. 201ff.). The reasons for this observation are manifold: Saturation as well as scale effects or resource limitations are only a few causes for the nonlinearity of relations between business variables. One well known example is the association between the market price and the customer demand for a certain product: Raising prices will not linearly result in an increasing demand. Rather it is likely that there is some maximum price level the customer is willing to pay, which therefore provides a limit for the demand. As an example Allen (1964) supposes demand functions to follow some S-shaped—also known as sigmoidal or logistic—pattern.

For these reasons it is essential to abandon all restrictions regarding a priori assumptions about the unknown function underlying a cause-and-effect relation. This postulate leads to the necessity to employ universal function approximators in order to identify the functional form of the causally proven associations. Therefore this approach studies the potential and limitations of artificial neural networks (ANNs) for universal causal function approximation. The theoretic foundations of this property of ANNs is the result of the endeavors to approximate an unknown mapping by the combination of known functions. The central theory in this area has been proposed by Kolmogorov (1957) who argued that any arbitrary unknown function f can be approximated by two nested known functions $\emptyset$ and ψ. This theory is usually regarded as the central concept for universal function approximation in the relevant literature (Tikk et al., 2001, p. 2):

Theorem 3 (Kolmogorov's superposition theorem): For all $n \geq 2$, and for any continuous real function f of n variables on the domain [0, 1], f: $[0,1]^n \to \mathbb{R}$, there exist n(2n+1) continuous, monotone increasing univariate functions on [0, 1], by which f can be reconstructed according to the following equation

$$f\left(x_1, \ldots x_n\right) = \sum_{q=1}^{2n} \varphi_q \left(\sum_{p=1}^{n} \psi_{pq} \left(x_p\right) \right)$$

Further enhancements of Kolmogorov's superposition theory are developed by several authors which lead to the notion of ANNs as universal function approximators (De Figueiredo, 1980; Hecht-Nielsen, 1987). Since the inner function of Kolmogorv's theorem can be highly nonsmooth it has to be weighted with a factor λ in order to use specific continuous functions (squashing functions) for this purpose. Therefore the resulting function can be represented by a multi layer perceptron (MLP).

Separating Causal Function Kernels from Causal Strategy Models

Since the universal approximation property has been proved for numerous of types of ANNs, this approach focuses on the construction of MLPs out of empirically proven cause-and-effect hypotheses. Therefore the causal strategy model has to be separated into causal function kernels (CFK). The latter describes a set of variables and interjacent cause-and-effect relations, each of which consists of a dependent element and its direct predecessors. Therefore the number of CFKs derived from a causal strategy model corresponds to the number of contained variables which show an empirically significant influence by other elements. Following the theory underlying this approach, the total cause-and-effect relations within a causal function kernel represent the unknown causal function determining the values of the dependent variable. Taking the above discussion into account, this function can be approximated sufficiently accurate by an MLP with the appropriate time series of the independent variables as input and those of the dependent element as output node.

Due to the possible existence of indirect associations between independent and dependent variables within a CFK it is likely that the overall effect between such two elements has to be separated in order to obtain the direct share of influence. This effect is called multicollinearity in the appropriate statistical literature and perturbs the approximation quality if it remains unsolved. Hence it is necessary to extend the causal function kernels for cause-and-effect relations which directly and/or indirectly link two independent variables $X_1 \rightarrow X_2$ and consequently induce an indirect effect between X_1 and the dependent variable Y. These auxiliary cause-and-effect relations accounting for multicollinearity can be discovered by analyzing the transitive closure[5] of each independent variable within the global causal system: For every pair of independent variables X_i and X_j within a causal function kernel $\mathcal{K}_Y$ there exists an auxiliary cause-and-effect relation $X_i \dashrightarrow X_j$ if and only if X_j is contained in the transitive closure of X_i according to the global model $\mathcal{G}$. The procedure to construct extended causal function kernels (eCFK) from a causally proven global strategy model $\mathcal{G}$ is shown in Figure 3.

Figure 3. Separation of (extended) causal function kernels

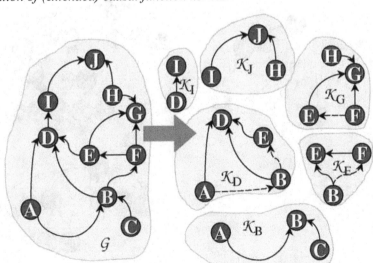

Temporal Disaggregation of Causal Function Kernels

Since an unknown causal function to be approximated does not exist between variables but rather between their lagged time series, the eCFKs have to be temporally disaggregated. Therefore this approach uses the window of impact as identified by the causal proof procedure: While the dependent variable Y is represented by its instantaneous time series y_t as an output node, each independent variable leads to a number of input nodes corresponding to the length of the appropriate window of impact. These input nodes each represent one lagged independent time series within the window of impact. As far as eCFKs are concerned, it is necessary to introduce a second input layer which accounts for auxiliary cause-and-effect relations: The time series of the second layer are derived by the same procedure as described above taking the influenced indirect time series of the auxiliary association as output node and the influencing element as input node. Second input layer elements which affect first layer time series and the output node directly are of specific interest because they combine direct and indirect influence as it is shown in Figure 4 for the extended causal function kernel $\mathcal{K}_D$. All other second layer input elements where this overlap does not exist can be eliminated from the temporally disaggregated causal function kernel (dCFK) since they are already encompassed by another (d)CFK.

As temporal disaggregation delivers the appropriate input and output nodes for a neural function approximator in the form of temporally lagged time series there remains the issue to complete the model selection of the ANN. This includes an adequate dimensioning of the hidden layer(s) as well as the selection of input and transfer functions for all ANN-nodes.

Since the universal approximation property postulates a limitation of the inner function of Kolmogorov's theorem, it is necessary to use transfer functions which map the input values to a certain output interval. This class of so-called squashing functions encompasses sigmoid as well as logistic sine or

Figure 4. Temporal disaggregation of (e)CFKs

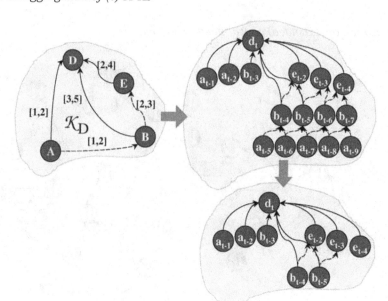

Figure 5. Neural function approximator for (e)CFKs

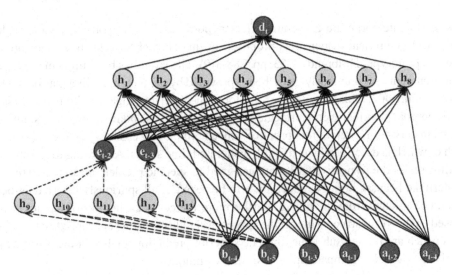

heaviside functions (Hillbrand, 2003, p. 214). For practical reasons the use of an additive input function for hidden and output neurons is recommended.

The selection of an appropriate number of hidden neurons is directly related to the generalization ability of the ANN (i.e. to learn a certain function instead of memorizing input-output mappings). As this specific model selection task depends on a variety of influences which cannot be fully assessed a priori, it is necessary to rely on heuristics (for details see Hillbrand, 2003, pp. 226 – 230) and validate the prediction accuracy of the ANN by using a validation data set[6].

As it follows from the temporal disaggregation of eCFKs as discussed above, the resulting auxiliary cause-and-effect relations between second-level and first-level time series have to be incorporated into the neural function approximator in order to account for indirect effects. Therefore auxiliary sub-MLPs are introduced as symbolized by dotted connectors in the example of Figure 5.

Before the training of the overall causal function approximator it is necessary to learn these correcting functions each of which has one first-level time series (e.g.: e_{t-2} and e_{t-3}) as output node and one or more second-level time series as input nodes. The hidden layer of a correcting ANN is dimensioned by the same heuristics like the main function approximator. After the training of all correcting ANNs, their weights are kept fixed and included in the main neuron model. For the overall training of the causal function approximator it is necessary to equip first-level nodes with a specific input function since they are input and hidden nodes in the same way. Consequently the input function of a first level node calculates the weighted output sum of all preceding nodes plus the respective input value of the node itself[7]. The ratio between these two shares of cumulative input is needed for training purposes when employing an error backpropagating algorithm: The same portion by which the overall input for a first-level node consists values from a lower network layer is used to distribute the output error – backpropagated from higher network levels (e.g.: $h_1 - h_8$) – among lower level neurons (e.g.: $h_9 - h_{13}$).

Since all further characteristics regarding layout and training of neural causal function approximators correspond with those of MLPs they are not discussed in further detail but referred to the relevant literature (e.g. Hillbrand, 2003).

EXPERIMENTAL RESULTS AND PROOF OF CONCEPT

The concepts to validate corporate cause-and-effect hypotheses and to approximate the underlying causal function from empirical evidence as proposed in this chapter have been implemented in the form of a research prototype (Hillbrand, 2003, pp. 288-319). The latter has been implemented based on a modeling environment—as previously described—provided by the metamodeling platform ADONIS (Karagiannis & Kühn, 2002). This provides the basis for an in-depth investigation about the admissibility of the proposed approach for real-world strategic scenarios as well as about its limitations with respect to several problem classes. Therefore this proof of concept employs a causal system consisting of five variables each of which is described by artificially generated time series. According to the characteristics of these time series the respective CFKs are assigned to specific problem classes. Starting from a completely interlinked causal strategy model it has to be tested, if all spuriously inserted associations are detected and eliminated from the model. Furthermore the correct windows of impact have to be identified. Based on this reconstructed model the approach should construct appropriate causal function approximators which are trained subsequently. The superior prediction quality of the trained function approximator is then tested in comparison with similar techniques.

A Generating Causal System for the Proof of Concept

The causal system in Figure 6 is implicitly represented by the following functional associations:

$$as_t = \varepsilon_{N(1;0.05)}$$

$$rm_t = \varepsilon_{N(1;0.05)}$$

$$sr_t = 0.95 + \frac{1}{30 \cdot as_{t-1} - 23.5} + \frac{1}{6.66 \cdot as_{t-2} - 5} - \frac{7 \cdot as_{t-1} - 6}{8} + \varepsilon_{U(-0.15,+0.15)}$$

$$cg_t = -2.5 + 0.25\left(4 - \sin\left(4 + 5sr_{t-1}\right)\right) + 0.2\left(4 - \sin\left(2 + 7sr_{t-2}\right)\right) + 1.1rm_{t-2} + 0.8rm_{t-3} + \varepsilon_{U(-0.3,+0.3)}$$

$$sp_t = \frac{\sum_{\Delta t=1}^{3} cg_{t-\Delta t}}{3} + \varepsilon_{U(-0.15,+0.15)}$$

Where as_t, rm_t, sr_t, cg_t and sp_t stand for the values of the variables *average salary, price of raw material, share of rejects, cost of goods manufactured* and *selling price* in period *t*, respectively. The term $\varepsilon_{U(-0.15,+0.15)}$ stands for uniformly distributed random number within the interval [-0.15,+0.15] and $\varepsilon_{N(1;0.05)}$ represents a normally distributed random number with expected value of 1 and a standard deviation of *0.05*.

Identification of Spuriously Inserted Cause-and-Effect Hypotheses

Since the generating system of causally related time series as defined above does not exist explicitly in real-world scenarios, it is the aim of this approach to reconstruct the structure of the causal model as shown in Figure 6, to identify the appropriate time lags and to approximate the functional dependencies. The basis for the application of this approach is a rudimentary causal strategy model which

Figure 6. Generating causal system

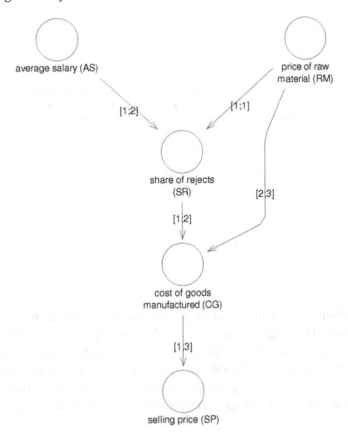

comprises the nomologic cause-and-effect hypotheses as assumed a priori by decision makers. For this purpose the functional proof of concept starts with a fully interlinked causal system consisting of the five variables already mentioned.

In order to rule out spurious associations according to the second and third causality criterion (informational redundancy and temporal precedence) the proposed approach analyzes the cross correlations for every link in the maximal strategic system model for different time lags. Since fourteen associations do not show a significant cross correlation at any Δt, they are marked as spurious. The remaining six potentially causal relations according to the second and third causality criterion yield cross correlation patterns as shown in Figure 7.

As it is obvious from this correlogram, the proposed proof of causality identifies the correct windows of impact of the five causal relations implicitly included in the generating system. However, this algorithm untruly identifies a sixth association ($SP \rightarrow CG$) to be potentially causal according to the second and third causality criterion because its cross correlation at a time lag of seven periods seems to be significant:

$$\rho_{SP,CG}(7) = 0.1458 > \sigma_{\rho_{SP,CG}(7)} = 0.1411.$$

Figure 7. Cross correlations resulting from the verification algorithm

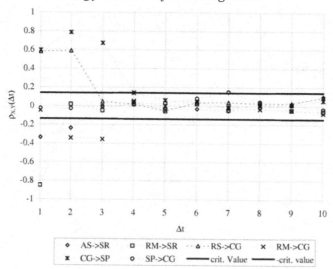

The test for exogenous third variables inducing a spurious correlation between two elements of the causal system is performed by the principles as proposed in this chapter. Since the variations of both, the variable *average salary* and *price of raw material* are not only reflected in the time series of their direct successor but also in those of the remaining elments it can be concluded that the potentially causal relations $SR \rightarrow CG$ as well as $CG \rightarrow SP$ are genuinely causal. As the latter proves that the direction of this relation is unambiguous, the potentially causal relation $SP \rightarrow CG$ is marked as spurious association.

Approximating Causal Functions

The next step according to the proposed approach is to approximate the unknown causal functions for each causal function kernel which consists of a positive number of proven causal relations. Therefore this approach derives three multi layer perceptrons (MLP) from the identified causal strategy model. For the $\mathcal{K}_{SR}$ this neural network consists of the output node sr_t as well as of an input layer consisting of as_{t-1}, as_{t-2} and rm_{t-1} and a four-element hidden layer being dimensioned using a heuristic proposed by Baum and Haussler (1988). Another MLP – approximating the causal function of $\mathcal{K}_{SP}$ – is established with the time series cg_{t-1}, cg_{t-2} and cg_{t-3} forming the input nodes and sp_t as an output node. The causal input and output nodes of the causal function approximator for $\mathcal{K}_{CG}$ are derived analogously: The time series sr_{t-1}, cg_{t-2}, rm_{t-2} and rm_{t-3} representing the input layer and cg_t as output node. However, since this CFK contains the influence relation $RM \rightarrow SR$ which causes multicollinearity, it is necessary to distinguish between first and second level input nodes and connect them with correcting function approximators. Therefore the temporal disaggregation algorithm introduces two correcting MLPs: One of them contains sr_{t-1} as output and rm_{t-2} as input node and the other receives input values from rm_{t-3} and has sr_{t-2} as output element. The resulting MLP is shown in Figure 8, where dashed arcs represent auxiliary correcting MLPs accounting for the relation $RM \rightarrow SR$ and solid links are part of the main function approximator.

After deriving the three neural function approximators as shown above, the latter have to be trained in order to inductively learn the unknown causal function from the empirical data: Therefore the time

Figure 8. Causal function approximator for K_{CG}

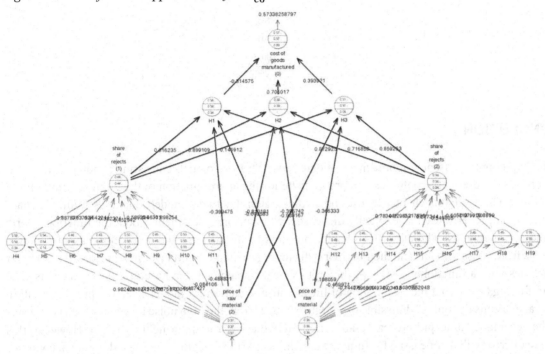

series associated with each input and output nodes are split into a training and a validation set. If an MLP incorporates correcting function approximators the latter have to be trained independently first. After reaching a global error minimum for these correcting ANNs, their weights are kept fixed and are included in the main function approximator as specified in this chapter including the special input functions for first level input nodes as well as its inverse function for error backpropagation purposes.

The training of these MLPs leads to an approximation of the causal function determining the values of the dependent variable of each causal function kernel. With the approximate knowledge of its functional dependencies in the form of the trained ANN, the causal strategy models can be enhanced by a prediction model which allows numerical analyses on future impacts of strategic scenarios. Since ANNs are known for their universal approximation properties in the relevant literature, they are expected to yield better approximation results than other techniques. A comparision with linear forecasting models like multiple linear regression analysis shows a predominantly clear picture:

As it is shown in Table 1, the proposed approach enables decision makers to approximate a more precise causal function compared to linear regression in all cases. As the latter does not account for nonlinear functions, indirect effects, autocorrelation or noisy time series, it yields significantly[8] higher mean squared errors (MSE) for the validation set than the connectionist approach especially for these problem classes. The only exception of this observation is CFK K_{SP}, which is not included in any of the problem classes: Only for these—strictly linear—functions, given the absence of other disturbances, it is not possible to achieve significantly better predictive results using the connectionist approach.

Table 1. Prediction quality of linear regression vs. connectionist approximator

CFK	$MSE_{lin.}$	MSE_{ANN}	significant
$\mathcal{K}_{SR}$	0.0048	0.0015	yes
$\mathcal{K}_{CG}$	0.0143	0.0056	yes
$\mathcal{K}_{SP}$	0.0022	0.0020	no

CONCLUSION

This chapter proposes a new approach to validate causal strategy models consisting of nomologic managerial cause-and-effect hypotheses as a prerequisite for the approximation of the unknown underlying functions: Therefore this chapter focuses on artificial neural network models due to their universal approximation properties which explicitly dispenses with a priori assessments about the functional form of these associations. Therefore this chapter presents techniques for the separation causal function kernels from causal models and their temporal disaggregation into multi layer perceptrons. The chapter concludes with a functional review of the prototypical implementation based on these concepts. The main findings show that the assumption of linear causal function for model selection purposes within the stage of causal proof is admissible to a large extent. Merely the high noise level of one variable leads to the acceptance of a spurious cause-and-effect hypothesis for an intermediary result. However, this source of error will be one issue for future research: As Bartlett's significance test does not account for the noise level of a dependent variable this technique has to be enhanced in order to provide improved significance boundaries which are sensitive with respect to the predictive uncertainty.

In order to integrate this approach into a DSS it seems to be necessary to extend this approach for analytic techniques based on this improved model base like simulation, what-if- or how-to-achieve-analyses. These applications allow the quantitative anticipation and prediction of future impacts of strategic scenarios.

Another field of interest is the transfer of the approach—as proposed here—to other scientific areas. Basically, these techniques could be employed for every decision theoretic problem based on causal networks such as economic theories, medical diagnostics, etc.

REFERENCES

Allen, R. (1964). *Mathematical analysis for economists*. New York: St. Martin's Press.

Bartlett, P. S. (1955). *Stochastic processes*. Cambridge, UK: Cambridge University Press.

Baum, E. B., & Haussler, D. (1988). What size net gives valid generalization? *Neural Computation, 1*, 151-160.

Brady, H. (2002, 16 July). *Models of causal inference: Going beyond the neyman-rubin-holland theory*. Seattle (WA).

De Figueiredo, R. J. P. (1980). Implications and applications of Kolmogorov's superposition theorem. *IEEE Transactions of Autom. Control*, 1227-1230.

Gasking, D. (1955, October). Causation and recipes. *Mind, New Series,* (256), 479-487.

Glymour, C. (2001). *The Mind's Arrows: Bayes Nets and Graphical Causal Models in Psychology.* Boston: MIT Press.

Granger, C. W. J. (1980). Testing for causality. A personal viewpoint. *Journal of Economic Dynamic and Control, 2*(4), 329-352.

Granger, C. W. J. (2003). Some aspects of causal relationships. *Journal of Econometrics, 112*(2003), 69-71.

Hecht-Nielsen, R. (1987). *Counter propagation networks.* New York.

Hillbrand, C. (2002). *Inferenz in betriebswirtschaftlichen Kausalmodellen auf der Basis von Ursache-Wirkungshypothesen* (Technical Report No. 02/2002). Vienna: University of Vienna. (in German)

Hillbrand, C. (2003). *Inference-based construction of managerial causal models supporting strategic enterprise planning.* PhD Thesis, Vienna: University of Vienna.

Hillbrand, C., & Karagiannis, D. (2002a). An approach to facilitate complex planning issues by means of machine learning techniques applied to cybernetic cause-and-effect models. In N. Callaos, A. Breda, and M. Fernandez, (eds.), *Proceedings of SCI 2002,* 2, 51-56, Orlando, FL.

Hillbrand, C. (2004). Building proven causal model bases for strategic decision support. In Seruca, I., Filipe, J. Hammoudi, S. and Cordeiro, J., editors. *Proceedings of ICEIS 2004 - the Sixth International Conference on Enterprise Information Systems,* 2, 178-183, Universidade Portucalense, Porto, Portugal.

Hillbrand, C., & Karagiannis, D. (2002b). Using artificial neural networks to prove hypothetic cause-and-effect relations: A metamodel-based approach to support strategic decisions. In Piattini, M., Filipe, J., and Braz, J., editors, *Proceedings of ICEIS 2002,* 1, 367-373, Ciudad Real, Spain.

Hoover, K. D. (2001). *Causality in macroeconomics.* Cambridge: Cambridge University Press.

Hoover, K. D. (2008). Causality in economics and econometrics. In Durlauf, S. and Blume, L., editors, *The New Palgrave Dictionary of Economics (2ⁿᵈ ed.),* London: MacMillan

Horvath & Partner. (2001). *Balanced Scorecard umsetzen* (2ⁿᵈ ed.). Stuttgart: Schäffer-Poeschel Verlag. (in German)

Hume, D. (1748). An enqiry concerning human understanding. In J. Fieser, editor, *The writings of David Hume,* [electronic version], Retreived 03/01/2008, from http://www.infomotions.com/etexts/philosophy/1700-1799/hume-enquiry-65.txt

Kaplan, R., & Norton, D. (1992). The balanced scorecard: Measures that drive performance. *Harvard Business Review, 70*(1), 71-79.

Kaplan, R., & Norton, D. (1996). *The balanced scorecard: Translating strategy into action.* Boston: Harvard Business School Press.

Karagiannis, D., & Kühn, H. (2002). *Metamodelling platforms – invited paper* (No. 2455). Berlin: Springer Verlag.

Kolmogorov, A. N. (1957). On the representation of continuous functions of many variables by superposition of continuous functions of one variable and addition. *Doklady Akademii Nauk SSSR, 114,* 953-956.

Koopmans, T. (1950). *Statistical Inference in Dynamic Economic Models.* Cowles Commission Monograph, 10. New York: Wiley.

Levich, R. M., & Rizzo, R. M. (1997). *Alternative tests for time series dependence based on autocorrelation coefficients.* New York.

Lucas, R. (1976). Econometric policy evaluation: A critique. In Brunner, K and Meltzer, A.H., editors. *The Phillips Curve and Labor Markets, Carnegie-Rochester Conference Series on Public Policy*, Amsterdam: North Holland: 161-168.

Makridakis, S., & Wheelwright, S. C. (1978). *Forecasting. methods and applications.* Santa Barbara, CA: John Wiley & Sons.

Mendoza, C., Delemond, M.-H., Giraud, F., & Loening, H. (2002). *Tableaux de bord et Balanced Scorecards.* Publications Fiduciaires. (in French).

Moneta, A. (2004). Causality and econometrics: some philosophical underpinnings, *Methods in Economics Seminar Series*, Pisa.

Pearl, J. (2000). *Causality. Models, reasoning and inference.* Cambridge: Cambridge University Press.

Pearl, J., & Verma, T. (1991). *A theory of inferred causation.* San Mateo, CA: Morgan Kaufmann Publishers.

Probst, H.-J. (2001). *Balanced Scorecard leicht gemacht. Warum sollten Sie mit weichen Faktoren hart rechnen?* Vienna: Ueberreuter Wirtschaft. (in German)

Schneiderman, A. (1999). Why balanced scorecards fail. *Journal of Strategic Performance Measurement,* 6 – 11.

Schnell, R., Hill, P. B., & Esser, E. (1999). *Methoden der empirischen Sozialforschung* (6th ed.). Munich et al.: Oldenbourg-Verlag. (in German)

Sondhauss, U. (1998). *Influence of philosophical concepts of causality on causal modelling in statistical research* (Technical Report No. 30/98). Dortmund: Department of Statistics, University of Dortmund.

Spirtes, P., Glymour C., & Scheines R. (2000). *Causation, Prediction, and Search (2nd ed.).* Boston: MIT Press.

Sprague, R., & Carlson, R. (1982). *Building effective decision support systems.* Englewood Cliffs, NJ: Prentice Hall.

Suppes, P. (1970). *A probabilistic theory of causality.* Amsterdam: North Holland.

Tikk, D., Kóczy, L. T., & Gedeon, T. D. (2001). *Universal approximation and its limits in soft computing techniques. An overview* (Research Working Paper No. RWP-IT-02-2001). Perth (W.A.): Murdoch University.

Vester, F. (1988). The biocybernetic approach as a basis for planning our environment. *Systems Practice*, *4*, 399-413.

Weber, J., & Schäffer, U. (2000). *Balanced Scorecard und Controlling. Implementierung – Nutzen für Manager und Controller – Erfahrungen in deutschen Unternehmen* (3rd ed.). Wiesbaden: Dr. Th. Gabler Verlag. (in German)

ENDNOTES

[1]   If the two Humean properties of causality would be sufficient to explain causal structures, a bad weather forecast would be the regarded as the cause for bad weather.

[2]   An α -error or type-1-error denotes a cause-and-effect relation between two variables in a causal strategy model although the corresponding time-series are not causal. On the contrary the term β- or type-2-error is used if there exists a causal relation in reality (i.e. between the time-series of two variables but it is not represented in the causal strategy model.

[3]   The computation of the autocorrelation of a variable X and a given order n corresponds to the one of the cross correlation $\rho_{X,X}(n)$. Hence it will be abbreviated by the symbol $\rho_X(n)$ for the rest of this chapter.

[4]   IC = Inductive Causation

[5]   The transitive closure is the set of all direct and indirect successors of a node within a directed graph (e.g. a causal strategy model).

[6]   A validation data set is a subset of the empirical data which is not used to train the ANN

[7]   e.g.: $net_{e_{t-2}} = in_{e_{t-2}} + \sum_{i=9}^{11} w_{h_i,e_{t-2}} \cdot out_{h_i}$

[8]   The statistical significance of this statement has been validated by testing the group average of the squared errors for both techniques using variance analysis.

Chapter XVII
Improving Mobile Web Navigation Using N–Grams Prediction Models

Yongjian Fu
Cleveland State University, USA

Hironmoy Paul
Cleveland State University, USA

Namita Shetty
Cleveland State University, USA

ABSTRACT

In this chapter, we propose to use N-gram models for improving Web navigation for mobile users. N-gram models are built from Web server logs to learn navigation patterns of mobile users. They are used as prediction models in an existing algorithm which improves mobile Web navigation by recommending shortcuts. Our experiments on two real data sets show that N-gram models are as effective as other more complex models in improving mobile Web navigation.

INTRODUCTION

Wireless users of the Web grow rapidly as more and more mobile devices such as PDAs, mobile phones and pagers are now equipped with browsing capabilities. Many current Web sites are optimized for desktop, broadband clients, and deliver content poorly for mobile devices due to display size and bandwidth. Moreover, the associated cost will prohibit maintaining two versions of a site, one for wired users and the other for mobile users. A viable solution is adaptive Web sites (Perkowitz & Etzioni, 1997). An adaptive Web site dynamically changes its contents or structure based on browsing activities.

Following the idea of adaptive Web sites, Anderson, Domingos, and Weld (2001) proposed shortcuts to improve mobile Web navigation. A shortcut is a dynamic link that provides a shorter path with fewer clicks for users to reach their desired pages. A shortcut to a destination page is dynamically created and inserted into the next page a user is going to browse. If that destination page is the one in which the user is interested, the user can access the page by following the shortcut. For example, assume a browsing session consists of A-B-C-D-E-F-G, where each letter represents a page. After browsing pages A and B, if a shortcut to G is created and inserted into page C, the user can follow the shortcut to reach G, without going through intermediate pages D, E, and F. The critical question is how to find shortcuts that are useful with only part of the session known. A shortcut C $\rightarrow$ H, for example, is useless in the previous example.

In order to provide useful shortcuts, Web usage mining techniques are employed. User browsing patterns are extracted from Web server logs. These patterns are built into prediction models that can be used to predict user browsing behaviors. Given a partial session, such prediction models will compute what other pages in which the user may be interested. These predictions are used to create and recommend shortcuts for mobile users.

A critical component in this approach is the prediction model. The model should be as accurate as possible with as little information about the session as possible. An accurate shortcut found earlier in a session is more worthwhile than one found close to the end of a session. Moreover, the prediction model should be easy to build and use. In their MINPATH algorithm, Anderson et al. (2001) used Markov models, which proved to be accurate (Anderson et al., 2001). However, those models require Web graphs. In this chapter, we propose to use a simpler prediction model, N-gram, for learning user browsing patterns.

N-grams are well known and are widely used in speech and text processing applications. Researchers have found that accuracy increases with N, the order of N-grams. For example, 4-grams are more accurate than 3-grams, which is turn is more accurate than 2-grams. Though accuracy increases with higher values of N, it requires a larger number of training sessions to have a well trained N-gram model.

An N-gram based prediction model for Web browsing patterns is proposed by Su et al. (2000). The N-gram model has several advantages over other prediction models. It is simple, robust, and easy to use. Besides, N-gram does not use a Web graph. In our study, the same N-gram model with a slightly different lookup operation is used. Moreover, its effectiveness in improving mobile Web navigation is examined.

In our approach, first, Web server logs are preprocessed to identify sessions. A session is conceptually a single visit. The sessions are then used to train an N-gram model. A revised version of MINPATH algorithm, MINCOST, is proposed to find shortcuts. MINCOST uses a different function in calculating the saving and ranking of shortcuts. Our approach has been implemented and evaluated against two real data sets from NASA and EPA Web servers. Our experiments show that the N-gram prediction model is as effective as more sophisticated models in recommending useful shortcuts.

The chapter is organized as follows. The second section discusses related work in Web usage mining, adaptive Web sites, and MINPATH algorithm. Our approach is presented in Section 3. Experimental results with two data sets are reported in the fourth section The fifth section concludes the chapter and gives some future research direction.

RELATED WORK

We briefly discuss Web usage mining techniques and its applications in adaptive Web sites and mobile Web navigation.

Web Usage Mining

Web usage mining refers to the mining of Web server logs to find interesting patterns in Web usage. Web server logs are preprocessed to find sessions. Conceptually, a session is a single visit to a Web site by a user. A session is represented by the pages browsed in that visit. From sessions, many Web usage patterns can be extracted, including associations, frequent paths, and clusters.

Association rules represent correlations among objects, which were first proposed to capture correlations among items in transactional data. If a session is viewed as a transaction, association rule mining algorithms can be employed to find associative relations among pages browsed (Mobasher, Cooley, & Srivastava, 1999a; Yang, Zhang, & Li, 2001). Using the same algorithms, we may find frequent paths traversed by many users (Frias-Martines & Karamcheti, 2002).

If each Web page represents a dimension, a session can be represented as a vector in the page space. Sessions can be clustered based on their similarity in the page space. In other words, sessions containing similar pages will be grouped into clusters (Fu, Sandhu, & Shih, 1999; Shahabi, Zarkesh, Adibi, & Shah, 1997).

Adaptive Web Sites

Perkowitz and Etzioni (1997) proposed adaptive Web site as a solution to the problem of Web navigation. An adaptive Web site is a Web site that automatically or semi-automatically adapts it structure based on user browsing. They proposed creating dynamic links using Web usage mining techniques. Koutri, Daskalaki, & Avouris, (2002) gives an overview of techniques for adaptive Web sites.

Anderson et al. (2001) argued that an adaptive Web site is especially interesting for mobile Web navigation. Due to limited display size, computing and storage capability, and network bandwidth, Web sites developed mainly for desktops deliver content poorly to mobile devices. To better serve the needs of mobile Web users, they proposed building Web site "personalizers" that observe the behavior of Web visitors and automatically customize and adapt Web sites for each mobile visitor. The MINPATH algorithm as described in Section 2.3 epitomizes their approach.

The MINPATH algorithm tries to improve the mobile Web user browsing experience by suggesting useful shortcuts. MINPATH finds shortcuts by using a learned model of user behavior to estimate the savings provided by shortcuts. The shortcuts are dynamically inserted into the page that the user will browse next. For example, after a user browsed pages A-B-C, MINPATH may provide a shortcut D->K in the next page D. It uses a prediction model that learns the user browsing behaviors to find the best shortcuts. If the user follows this shortcut, the user session becomes A-B-C-D-K. Assuming that without shortcut, the user session would contain pages A-B-C-D-E-F-G-H-I-J-K, the shortcut results in a saving of six pages or links.

MINPATH Algorithm

The MINCOST algorithm works as follows Anderson et al. (2001). Given a sequence of pages, called prefix, it uses prediction models to find the possible next pages and their probabilities. These pages and their savings are added to a shortcut list. For each page found by the prediction model, it is appended to the sequence, forming a suffix, which is used to find more shortcuts following the same procedure. This process continues recursively until the length of the suffix exceeds the depth bound or the probability of the predicted page becomes less than the probability threshold. Once the recursive part is over, the shortcuts found are sorted in descending order based on savings and the best shortcuts are returned. The number of shortcuts to be returned are user specified.

To estimate savings of a shortcut, MINPATH counts the number of links saved by following the shortcut. For example, if a prefix is A-B-C, and a suffix is A-B-C-D-E-F-G, the expected saving for a shortcut D-> G is two.

There are two threshold parameters, depth bound and probability threshold; used in the MINPATH algorithm to limit searches for shortcuts. Depth bound represents the maximum length of the suffix. Probability threshold represents the minimum value of page probability.

MINPATH algorithm uses Markov models (Deshpande & Karypis, 2000; Sarukkai, 2000). Though accurate these models are complex and require Web graphs as a part of their implementation. There is a need to find less complex prediction models with comparable accuracy. Besides, MINPATH does not consider page size in estimating saving.

THE PROPOSED APPROACH

There are three steps in our approach to improve navigation for mobile Web users. First, Web server logs are preprocessed to extract sessions. Second, an N-gram prediction model is built from these sessions. Third, an algorithm that extends MINPATH, called MINCOST, recommends shortcuts based on the N-gram model and the current browsing sequence.

Server Log Preprocessing

A record in a server log file contains raw browsing data, such as the IP address of the user, date and time of the request, URL of the page, the return code of the server, and the size of the page, if the request is successful. Since such records are in chronological order, they do not provide much meaningful information about user browsing. The Web server log files are transformed into a set of sessions. A session represents a single visit of a user. The following procedure is used to transform a server log file into sessions (Mobasher, Cooley, & Srivastava, 1999b).

1. Records about image files (.gif, .jpg, etc.) and unsuccessful requests (return code belonging to the 4XX series) are filtered out.
2. Requests from the same IP address are grouped into a session. A timeout of *max-idle* is used to decide the end of a session, i.e., if the same IP address does not occur within a period of *max-idle* seconds, the current session is closed. Subsequent requests from the same IP address will be treated as a new session.

In our experiments, we used a value of 1800 seconds for *max-idle,* which is very common in Web usage mining studies.

Prediction Model Learning

Once we are done with preprocessing of Web logs, the next step is to build prediction models to predict the navigation patterns of Web users. If P_1, P_2, P_3, . . ., P_i are the pages browsed by the user so far, the prediction models will try to predict the next page, P_{i+1}.

We use an N-gram based prediction model. An N-gram is a substring of N characters, each character from an alphabet. The order of an N-gram is defined as N, the number of characters in the N-gram. In the context of this work, the alphabet is the set of URLs of Web pages on the Web server. An N-gram is a sequence of URLs.

After Web server logs are preprocessed into a number of sessions, an N-gram prediction model can be built as follows:

1. Each session is decomposed into a set of overlapping, subsequent paths of length N.
2. These paths are entered into an N-gram table T as N-grams.
3. For each path in T, the next pages right after it and their occurrences, in all the sessions, are recorded.
4. The probabilities of the next pages for all paths are calculated from the occurrences of all possible next pages.

For example, given a log file consisting of the following sessions, a 3-gram model for prediction can be built as follows:

A, B, C, D, H
B, C, D, G

The first session is decomposed into two 3-grams: "A, B, C" and "B, C, D." The second session is decomposed into one 3-gram: "B, C, D." For 3-gram "A, B, C," the next page would be D, while for 3-gram "B, C, D," the next page may be G or H. The complete N-gram table, T, is given in Table 1.

The N-gram table T is used as our prediction model. Given an observed path, it is matched against N-grams in T. The predicted next pages and their corresponding probabilities of the matching entries in T are returned for shortcut recommendations.

The algorithm for constructing an N-gram model is given in Figure 1. It is modified from the algorithm from Su et al., (2000) such that it stores all possible next pages for an N-gram, rather than the most probable one only.

This algorithm has a time complexity of $O(|L| * |S|)$ where $|L|$ is the number of sessions and $|S|$ is the length of sessions. The time of the algorithm is dominated by the first for loop. Its outer loop runs $|L|$ times and its inner loop runs $|S|$ times, which gives the time complexity of $O(|L| * |S|)$.

An N-gram based prediction model is proposed in Su et al. (2000), which evaluates the model's accuracy without a specific application. In our study, the N-gram model is evaluated on its effectiveness in improving mobile Web navigation. To suit our application, the model is modified so that a lookup operation for an N-gram will return all predictions, instead of just the most probable one.

Table 1. A 3-gram prediction table

3-gram	Predicted next page	Probability of next page
A, B, C	D	1.0000
B, C, D	G	0.5000
B, C, D	H	0.5000

Figure 1. Algorithm for constructing N-gram models

Input:

L: sessions from Web server logs.

N: order of N-gram

Output:

T: N-gram prediction table

// for an N-gram P and a predicted next page C, cell T[P, C] stores the probability.

Procedure:

Begin

For i = 1 to |L| do   // for every session

S = L[i];   // the i-th session

For j =1 to |S| do   // |S| represents the number of pages in session S

If (|S| - j)> N // Find a sub-string of length N starting at j

P = sub-string (S, j, N);   // the j-th N-gram

//sub-string returns N consecutive pages in S,

                    // starting from j-th page,

                            C = sub-string(S, j+N, 1); // Find the next page

T [P, C] = T [P, C] + 1;   // increment count of (N-gram, next page) pair

End If

End For

    End For

For each [P, C] in T

                T [P, C]= T [P, C] / Σ_C(T[P, C]); // convert count into probability

End For

Return T;

End

Shortcut Recommendation

The MINPATH algorithm ranks shortcuts based on their expected savings. In computing expected savings, MINPATH considers only the number of links saved. We modified MINPATH to reflect expected saving in total cost.

Given a prefix $< P_0, P_1, P_2,....,P_i >$, of a session $< P_0, P_1, P_2,....,P_n >$, a shortcut to P_n, i.e. , $P_{i+1} \rightarrow P_n$, can be added to page P_{i+1}. In MINPATH, the expected saving of the shortcut is calculated as the product of the number of links saved by following that particular shortcut and the probability that P_n is the destination page. Instead, we compute the expected saving as a cost function of page size and page probability.

The cost of browsing a page P_k, cost(P_k), is composed of the times to download the page, to view the page, and to click the link for next page. In other words, if a page is skipped by following a shortcut, the times to download, view, and click the page, are saved. The time to view and click is constant, but the time to download depends on page size. A parameter, Δ, is introduced to represent the download cost, which can be thought as time for transmission a unit of data. By introducing Δ, download time is separated from view and click time. The value of Δ is determined by network bandwidth and congestion. Since the cost function is relative, i.e., only the ratio of download time to view and click time matters, the view and click time is normalized to 1 in the cost function and Δ is adjusted accordingly.

$$Cost(P_k) = \text{download time} + \text{view and click time} = Size(P_k) * \Delta + 1 \qquad (1)$$

where Size(P_k) is the size of page P_k in kilobytes.

The saving of a shortcut is the sum of the costs of pages skipped.

Expected savings $(P_{i+1} \rightarrow P_n) =$

$$P_s * \{ \sum_{k=i+2}^{N-1} Cost(P_k) \} =$$

$$P_s * \{ \sum_{k=i+2}^{N-1} [Size(Pk) * \Delta + 1] \} \qquad (2)$$

where P_s is the probability that page P_n is the destination page.

In our experiments, we found Δ has little effect on results, because pages have similar sizes. Its value is fixed at 0.5 assuming an effective bandwidth of 1 kbps and view and click time of 2 seconds. When pages have quite different sizes, Δ may have an impact on results.

To differentiate, we call the modified algorithm MINCOST since it takes into consideration cost for downloading. MINPATH considers only savings in view and click time, while MINCOST considers both view and click time and download time. It is easy to see that MINCOST is a generalization of MINPATH. When Δ is set to 0, the cost function in (2) degrades into the number of links saved which is used in MINPATH.

PERFORMANCE EVALUATION

The MINCOST algorithm is implemented in the C programming language and experiments are performed to evaluate the efficiency of our approach to improve mobile Web navigation with real datasets. The experiments are run on a PC with a 2.66 GHz Intel Pentium 4 processor, a memory of 512 MB, and running Windows XP professional.

Datasets

Two datasets are used in our experiments, the NASA dataset and the EPA dataset. The NASA dataset was collected from July 1, 1995 through July 31, 1995 for a total of one month's requests from the NASA server at Kennedy Space Center. The EPA dataset was collected from 23:53:25 August 29, 1995 through 23:53:07 August 30, 1995 for a total of 24 hours of requests from the EPA server at Research Triangle Park, NC.

The NASA and EPA datasets are converted into sessions as described in the third section. Table 2 gives a summary of the datasets.

Performance Measurements

The efficiency of the MINCOST algorithm is evaluated using average cost saved and percentage of average cost saved. The total cost of pages in the initial sessions and the total cost of pages in the final sessions after MINCOST are calculated using the definition in Equation 1. The difference between these two gives the total cost saved. The total cost saved is averaged over all sessions giving the average cost saved. The percentage of average cost saved is the average cost saved as a percentage of the average cost.

Total Cost Saved = Total Cost without MINCOST - Total Cost with MINCOST
Average Cost = Total Cost without MINCOST / Total Sessions
Average Cost Saved = Total Cost Saved/Total Sessions
Average Cost Saved (%) = (Average Cost Saved / Average Cost) * 100

Experimental Parameters

The average cost saved and the percentage of average cost saved are measured with respect to probability threshold, depth bound, number of shortcuts, and the order of the N-gram. In each experiment, we vary one parameter while keeping others to their default values. The results are reported from a 10 fold cross-validation. The entire dataset is divided into ten equal portions. Each portion is used as the

Table 2. NASA and EPA datasets summary

	NASA DATASET	EPA DATASET
Total Log Records	3,461,612	47,748
Total Sessions	132539	2074
Unique URLs	768	1821
Average Session Length (Number of Pages in a Session)	3.134	4.222
URL For Download	http://ita.ee.lbl.gov/html/ contrib/NASA-HTTP.html	http://ita.ee.lbl.gov/html/ contrib/EPA-HTTP.html

Table 3. Parameters and their default values

PARAMETER	DEFAULT VALUE	DESCRIPTION
Probability Threshold	0.006	Minimum probability of a shortcut
Depth Bound	5	Maximum length of suffix
Number of Shortcuts	3	Number of top shortcuts recommended
N	2	Order of N-gram model

testing set for MINCOST, while the remaining portions are used as training set for building the N-gram model as described in the third section. The results are averaged over these ten runs.

The parameters and their default values are given in Table 3.

The user behavior when provided with shortcuts is simulated by making two assumptions. First, it is assumed that when presented with one or more shortcuts that lead to destinations along the user's session, the user will select the shortcut that leads farthest along the session. Second, when no shortcuts lead to pages in the user's session, the user will follow the next link in the session.

Experimental Results from NASA Dataset

The results from experiments on NASA data set are presented in this section. Similar results are obtained from experiments on EPA data set, and are thus omitted.

Figures 2 and 3 show the average cost saved and percentage of average cost saved with respect to probability threshold, respectively. It is observed that both measures increase with decrease in probability threshold and stabilize around 0.0080. This is because there are not many shortcuts with significant savings after this value.

From Figures 2 and 3, it is obvious that the two performance measures, average cost saved and percentage of average cost saved, react similarly to changes in probability threshold. It is not a coincidence. Other experiments also reveal the high correlation of these two measures. In the rest of this section, only the results for percentage of average cost saved are presented.

As shown in Figure 4, the percentage of average cost saved is not affected by depth bound except when it increases from 1 to 2. Just like MINPATH, MINCOST is more sensitive to probability threshold than depth bound. Depth bound has a larger impact when the probability threshold is large. However, for most reasonable probability thresholds, depth bound's effect is overshadowed by that of probability threshold.

As expected, the percentage of average cost saved increases with the number of shortcuts recommended by MINCOST, as shown in Figure 5. The increase in percentage of average cost saved is especially significant when the number of shortcuts increases from 1 to 2 and 2 to 3. However, the increase is much smaller for larger numbers of shortcuts, for example, when the number of shortcuts increases

Figure 2. Average cost saved vs. probability threshold

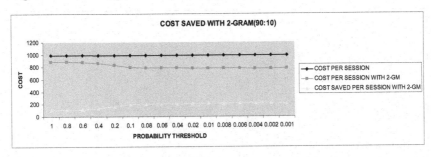

Figure 3. Percentage of average cost saved vs. probability threshold

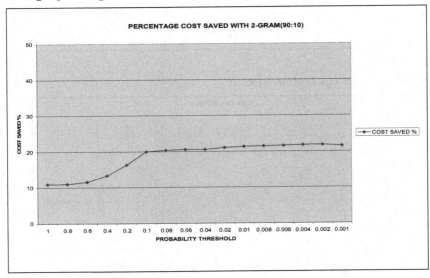

Figure 4. Percentage of average cost saved vs. depth bound

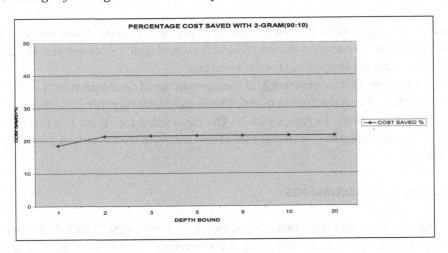

Figure 5. Percentage of average cost saved vs. number of shortcuts recommended

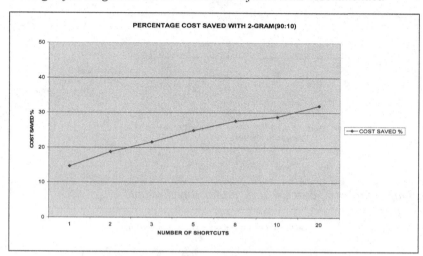

Figure 6. Percentage of average cost saved vs. N

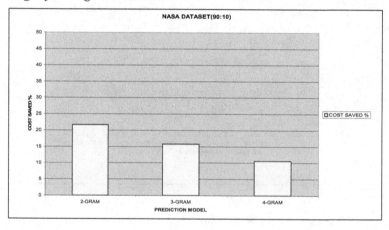

from 10 to 20. More importantly, it is not possible to display many shortcuts due to screen size limitations of mobile devices. We select a default value of 3 even though it does not provide the maximum savings. Besides, too many shortcuts may confuse users.

From Figure 6 we see that the percentage of average cost saved decreases with N. We conclude that best results are obtained with the 2-gram model. This is somewhat surprising. As discussed in Section 3.2, N-gram model's accuracy increases with N. The explanation for Figure 6 is that as N increases, N-grams become less applicable, i.e., fewer predictions are available for a given prefix, which results in fewer shortcuts.

Observations and Discussions

The percentage of average cost saved ranges from 19.4% to 23.0% for the NASA dataset and from 9.6% to 37.1% for the EPA dataset. The number of shortcuts recommended has the biggest impact among the parameters followed by the probability threshold, while depth bound has little impact. The best prediction model is the 2-gram model followed by 3-gram model and 4-gram model.

These results are comparable to results from the MINPATH algorithm with N-gram model. Moreover, the percentage of savings are comparable to these reported by Anderson et al., (2001), though a different data set was used. This demonstrates that N-gram models work as well as other models.

CONCLUSION AND FUTURE WORK

In this chapter, we proposed to use a simple prediction model, N-gram, for improving mobile Web navigation. Our approach is implemented and experimented with two real datasets. Experimental results show that N-gram is as effective as more complex models used in other research in predicting useful shortcuts. An interesting finding is that 2-gram works better than 3-gram and 4-gram in predicting useful shortcut. Higher order N-grams require more training and are less applicable.

In the future, we plan to use mixed N-gram models as a prediction model. Multiple N-gram models of various N used simultaneously for suggesting the best shortcuts.

It will also be interesting to mix Web content mining and Web usage mining techniques. For example, the destination page of a session is predicted by looking at current browsing sequence as well as its contents.

Another interesting research topic is to compare N-gram models with models that learn from their errors such as neural networks.

REFERENCES

Anderson, C. R., Domingos, P., & Weld, D. S. (2001). Adaptive web navigation for wireless devices. In *Proceedings of IJCAI-01 Workshop*. Seattle, WA.

Deshpande, M. & Karypis, G. (2000). *Selective markov models for predicting Web-page accesses*. (Tech. Rep. No. 00-056). University of Minnesota, IN.

Frias-Martinez, E., & Karamcheti, V. (2002). A prediction model for user access sequences, In *Proceedings of the Workshop on Web Mining for Usage Patterns and User Profiles*.

Fu, Y., Sandhu, K., & Shih, M. (1999). *Clustering of Web users based on access patterns*. International Workshop on Web Usage Analysis and User Profiling. San Diego, CA.

Koutri, M., Daskalaki, S., & Avouris N. (2002). Adaptive interaction with Web Sites: An overview of methods and techniques. In *Proceedings of the 4th International Workshop on Computer Science and Information Technologies*.Patras, Greece.

Mobasher, B., Cooley, R., & Srivastava, J. (1999a). Automatic personalization based on web usage mining. *Communications of the ACM, 43*(8), 142-151.

Mobasher, B., Cooley, R. & Srivastava, J. (1999b). Data preparation for mining world wide web browsing patterns. *Knowledge and Information Systems, 1*(1), 5-32.

Perkowitz, M., & Etzioni, O. (1997). Adaptive Web sites: An AI challenge. In *Proceedings of IJCAI-97 Workshop*. Nagoya, Japan.

Sarukkai, R. (2000). Link prediction and path analysis using markov chains. *Computer Networks, 33*(1-6), 377-386.

Shahabi, C., Zarkesh, A., Adibi, J. & Shah, V. (1997). *Knowledge discovery from users Web-page navigation*. In Workshop on Research Issues in Data Engineering, Birminghan, UK.

Su, Z., Yang, Q., Lu, Y. & Zhang, H. (2000). WhatNext: A prediction system for Web requests using n-gram sequence models. In *Proceedings of First International Conference on Web Information Systems and Engineering Conference*. Hong Kong, China.

Yang, Q., Zhang, H. H., & Li, T. (2001). Mining Web logs for prediction models in WWW caching and prefetching. In *Proceedings of KDD-01 Workshop*. San Francisco, CA.

This work was previously published in International Journal of Intelligent Information Technologies, Vol. 3, Issue 2, edited by V. Sugumaran, pp. 51-64, copyright 2007 by IGI Publishing, formerly known as Idea Group Publishing (an imprint of IGI Global).

Section IV
Supply Chain Management

Chapter XVIII
Forecasting Supply Chain Demand Using Machine Learning Algorithms

Réal Carbonneau
Department of Management Sciences, HEC Montréal, Canada

Rustam Vahidov
John Molson School of Business, Concorida University, Canada

Kevin Laframboise
John Molson School of Business, Concorida University, Canada

ABSTRACT

Managing supply chains in today's complex, dynamic, and uncertain environment is one of the key challenges affecting the success of the businesses. One of the crucial determinants of effective supply chain management is the ability to recognize customer demand patterns and react accordingly to the changes in face of intense competition. Thus the ability to adequately predict demand by the participants in a supply chain is vital to the survival of businesses. Demand prediction is aggravated by the fact that communication patterns between participants that emerge in a supply chain tend to distort the original consumer's demand and create high levels of noise. Distortion and noise negatively impact forecast quality of the participants. This work investigates the applicability of machine learning (ML) techniques and compares their performances with the more traditional methods in order to improve demand forecast accuracy in supply chains. To this end we used two data sets from particular companies (chocolate manufacturer and toner cartridge manufacturer), as well as data from the Statistics Canada manufacturing survey. A representative set of traditional and ML-based forecasting techniques have been applied to the demand data and the accuracy of the methods was compared. As a group, Machine

Learning techniques outperformed traditional techniques in terms of overall average, but not in terms of overall ranking. We also found that a support vector machine (SVM) trained on multiple demand series produced the most accurate forecasts.

INTRODUCTION

Supply chain integration looks to combine resources in order to provide value to the end consumer by improving the flow and quality of information being passed between the participants in the chain (Zhao, Xie, & Wei, 2002). Thus, in an idealized case, where all participants adopt the integration philosophy and make efforts to implement it fully, the entire chain would perform effectively and efficiently in responding to end customer demands. However, although integration and sharing information can potentially reduce forecast errors, in reality they are neither ubiquitous nor complete and demand forecast errors still abound.

This is due to the fact that the original demand signal becomes distorted as it travels through the extended supply chain (a holistic notion of supply chain (Tan, 2001) that requires collaborative relationships (Davis & Spekman, 2004)). Demand forecast quality can be improved if done cooperatively by the partners in the chain. Collaborative forecasting and replenishment (CFAR) permits a firm and its supplier-firm to coordinate decisions by exchanging complex decision-support models and strategies, thus facilitating integration of forecasting and production schedules (Raghunathan, 1999). In the absence of CFAR, firms are relegated to traditional forecasting and production scheduling, a challenging task due to what the well-known phenomenon of "bullwhip effect" (Lee, Padmanabhan, & Whang, 1997a).

The value of information sharing across the supply chain is widely recognized as the means of combating demand signal distortion (Lee, Padmanabhan, & Whang, 1997b). However, there is a gap between the ideal of integrated supply chains and reality (Gunasekaran & Ngai, 2004).

Researchers have identified several factors that could hinder such long-term stable collaborative efforts. Premkumar (2000) lists some required critical issues that must be addressed to permit successful supply chain collaboration, including: (i) alignment of business interests, (ii) long-term relationship management, (iii) reluctance to share information, (iv) complexity of large-scale supply chain management, (v) competence of personnel supporting supply chain management and (vi) performance measurement and incentive systems to support supply chain management. Although these are important issues, in many companies, these issues have not yet been addressed in attempts to enable effective extended supply chain collaboration (Davis & Spekman, 2004). Additionally, in many supply chains there are power regimes and power sub-regimes that can prevent supply chain optimization (Cox, Sanderson, & Watson, 2001). The introduction of inaccurate information into the system could also lead to demand distortion, e.g., double forecasting and ration gaming by the partners, ordering more quantities than needed, despite the presence of a collaborative system and an incentive towards its usage (Heikkila, 2002).

Furthermore, the globalization trends and the advance of E-business increase the tendency towards more "dynamic" (Vakharia, 2002) and "agile" (Gunasekaran & Ngai, 2004; Yusuf, Gunasekaran, Adeleye, & Sivayoganathan, 2004) supply chains. While this trend enables the supply chains to be more flexible and adaptive, it could discourage companies from investing in long-term collaborative relationships among each other due to the restrictive nature of such commitments. The over-emphasis on investing in extensive relationships among the partners could lead to a "lock-in" situation, thus seriously jeopardizing the flexibility of the supply chain (Gossain, Malhotra, & El Sawy, 2005). Gossain et al. (2005) argue that developing robust and reconfigurable links would promote the agility of the chain in terms of offering and partnering flexibilities. In their study they found that while the quality of the information sharing in a supply chain could promote flexibility, the breadth of information shared has a detrimental effect on it. The modularity and loose couplings between the partners have been identified as positive factors in this regard. Overall, we see many realities that effectively form information exchange collaboration barriers, which limit the possibilities of information exchange within the supply chain.

Effective demand forecasting is therefore still a serious hurdle for many businesses. The objective of this work is to study the feasibility of forecasting the distorted demand signals in the extended supply chain using the advanced machine learning techniques as opposed to the more traditional techniques at the upstream (manufacturer's) end of the supply chain. We are particularly interested in the upstream end, since that is where the distortion is at its worst, and the demand swings tend to be most erratic. In light of the above considerations, the problem of forecasting distorted demand is of significant importance to businesses, especially to those operating towards the upstream end of the extended supply chain.

In this work we investigate the potential value of applying advanced machine learning techniques, including artificial neural networks (ANN), recurrent neural networks (RNN), and support vector machines (SVM) to demand forecasting in supply chains. These learning techniques permit machines to identify patterns in data. The performances of these machine-learning (ML) methods are contrasted with baseline traditional approaches such as exponential smoothing, moving average, linear regression and the Theta model. To this end we have collected real industry data from three different sources. The first two data sets are from the enterprise systems of a chocolate manufacturer and a toner cartridge manufacturer. Both of these companies, by the nature of their position in the supply chain, are subject to considerable demand distortion. The third source of data comes from the Statistics Canada manufacturing survey. Inclusion of this survey in the study has the aim of increasing the validity and facilitating the possibility of replication of results by others.

In the sections that follow we provide the background, describe the data sources and the experimental setup and present the results of our experiments. The work concludes with the discussion of findings and directions for future research.

BACKGROUND

This section discusses the problems with demand distortion in supply chains, and reviews traditional and machine learning-based (ML-based) forecasting techniques.

Demand Distortion in Supply Chains

Companies need to consider the inter-relationships among demand forecast, perfect order, and inventory. Hofman (2007) indicates that there is a strong correlation between demand forecast accuracy and the perfect order and that companies that are better at demand forecasting have significantly lower inventories, stronger perfect order fulfillment, and shorter cash-to-cash cycle times. She argues that demand planning and forecasting methods and their supporting technologies enable or constrain a company's business performance metrics. Accordingly, as indicated by (Raghunathan, 1999), one of the major purposes of supply chain collaboration is improving the accuracy of forecasts.

However, full collaboration is not always possible and therefore it is important to investigate the feasibility of forecasting demand in the absence of extensive information from other partners. The source of the demand distortion in the extended supply chain is due to demand signal processing by the members in the supply chain (Forrester, 1961). According to Lee, Padmanabhan et al. (1997b), demand signal processing means that each party in the supply chain does some processing on the original demand signal, thus transforming it before passing it along to the next member. As the end-customer's demand signal moves up the supply chain, it becomes increasingly distorted. This occurs even if the demand signal processing function is identical in all parties of the extended supply chain. For example, even if all supply chain members use a 6-month trend to forecast demand, distortion will still occur. The phenomenon could be explained in terms of the chaos theory, where a small variation in the input could result in large, seemingly random behavior in the output of the chaotic system, which, in the context of the supply chain leads to the "bullwhip" effect. Figure 1 depicts a section of the supply chain with a collaboration barrier, i.e., the link at which no additional information sharing occurs between the partners, which results in distorted demand forecasting. Our objective is to forecast future demand based only on manufacturer's past and current orders. An increase in forecasting accuracy will result in lower costs because of reduced inventory as well as increased customer satisfaction and retention that will result from an increase in on-time deliveries (Stitt, 2004).

It has been shown that the use of simple techniques such as moving average or naïve forecasting will induce the bullwhip effect (Dejonckheere, Disney, Lambrecht, & Towill, 2003), while autoregressive linear forecasting could diminish it (Chandra & Grabis, 2005). Furthermore, a simulation based study has shown that genetic algorithm-based artificial agents can achieve lower overall costs in managing supply chain than human players can (Kimbrough, Wu, & Zhong, 2002). In this work we will evaluate the performance of advanced machine learning techniques to investigate their applicability and compare their performance with the more traditional forecasting methods.

Traditional Forecasting Techniques

Extensive research on forecasting has provided a large number of forecasting techniques and algorithms in mathematics, statistics, operations management and supply chain academic outlets. Forecasting competitions have consistently found that the simpler forecasting methods had better overall accuracy than more complex ones (Makridakis, Andersen, Carbone, & Fildes, 1982; Makridakis et al., 1993; Makridakis &

Figure 1. Distorted demand signal in an extended supply chain

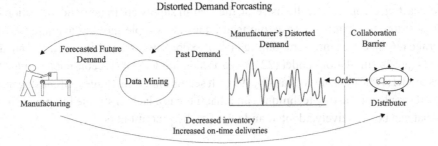

Hibon, 1979, 2000). The M3-Competition is a kind of a tournament set up to evaluate the performance of various forecasting techniques. It features various academic and commercial forecasting methods, including Naïve/simple, explicit trend models, decomposition, variations of the general ARMA (auto-regressive moving average) model, expert systems and neural networks. The results, even with a new and much enlarged set of data demonstrated, that simple methods developed by practicing forecasters do as well, or in many cases better, than more sophisticated ones (Makridakis & Hibon, 2000).

Even though there is an array of forecasting methods that perform well in certain situations and simple traditional forecasting techniques seem to outperform more complex ones, there is still no recommendation for the best forecasting technique to use that would result in the most accurate forecast.

Forecasting Methods Used by Practitioners

Jain (2004c) notes that in general there are three types of forecasting models commonly used in the industry, including: Time-Series (71%), Cause-and-Effect (19%), and Judgmental (10%) categories. Within the Time-Series category, the most common methods are Averages and Simple Trend (65%); Exponential-Smoothing (24%); Box-Jenkins (6%); and Decomposition methods (5%). The Cause-and-Effect modeling is most often executed with Regression analysis (74%), Econometric models (21%), and Neural Networks (5%). Furthermore, Jain (2004b) indicates that when these models are implemented using computer software; 63% of the forecasting market share is held by Microsoft Excel. Among the stand-alone forecasting software packages, John Gault has a large part of the market (46%) followed by SAS (28%). Regarding the integrated software solutions, SAP (23%) and Manugistics (16%) dominate market share. From these numbers we see that most forecasting is still done with time-series analysis in spreadsheet software and that a minority of businesses uses integrated solutions that include forecasting solutions. The average forecasting error across all industries for 1 month ahead is 26%, for 2 months and 1 quarter ahead is 29% and for 1 year ahead is 30% (Jain, 2004a). This indicates that there can be significant competitive advantages gained from improved forecast accuracy.

On the other hand, Wisner and Stanley (1994) reported that 39% of their respondents rarely or never used forecasts, which may indicate lack of data available for forecasting, lack of simple but effective forecasting techniques, or lack of skills and resources needed to perform forecasting. Additionally, 73% of respondents indicated that they have been using purchasing-forecasting for less then 10 years. With respect to actual forecasting, 67% indicated that they generated their forecasts manually and about half attempted to change the forecast parameters to increase forecast accuracy. Although this adjustment may lead to better forecasts, it is important to note that tuning forecasts may result in high accuracy on the known existing data set while decreasing the accuracy of future forecasts. These adjustments can potentially lead to over-fitting of the forecasting to past data, which can decrease forecasting accuracy. This is not only detrimental to the individual supply chain member, but also to other members since the increased forecasting errors drastically increase the overall supply chain demand distortion in a cascading fashion. The top quantitative forecasting techniques are simple moving average (62%), weighted moving average (46%), exponential smoothing (45%), exponential smoothing using trend and seasonal enhancements (39%), simulation model (22%), regression model (21%), econometric model (19%) and Box-Jenkins model (14%) (Wisner & Stanley, 1994). It seems that, on average, purchasing managers rely on manual and simple forecasting techniques and that there is a lack of simple but powerful forecasting techniques that can be effectively adopted and relied on by practitioners.

Machine Learning Techniques

With such as large number of forecasting techniques and parameters available for tuning them, it becomes more difficult to choose the appropriate one in a particular context. In addition, as the complexity of patterns present in the noisy data increases, such as demand at the end of supply chain, it becomes difficult to choose an appropriate model for forecasting purposes. One possible solution is to rely on a class of algorithms called "universal approximators", which can approximate any function to an arbitrary accuracy. Using such universal approximators, any function within the in the time series data can be learned. This effectively makes traditional forecasting techniques a subset of the functions that the universal approximators can learn. Machine learning (ML) techniques, such as artificial neural networks (ANN) and support vector machines (SVM) are examples of universal approximators.

Forecasting time-series such as those in supply chains involves a data domain that is very noisy. It is highly desirable only to learn true patterns in the data that will be repeated in the future and to ignore the noise (e.g. random error). The, ML-based techniques have two important features that are useful for supply chain forecasting problems in the presence of noise: (i) the ability to learn an arbitrary function and (ii) the ability to control the learning process itself.

Artificial neural networks (ANN) and recurrent neural networks (RNN) are frequently used to predict time series data (Dorffner, 1996; Giles, Lawrence, & Tsoi, 2001; Herbrich, Keilbach, Graepel, Bollmann-Sdorra, & Obermayer, 1999; Landt, 1997). For example, because manufacturer's demand in general can be a chaotic time-series, RNNs can be trained using so-called "backpropagation of error" through time, which permits them to learn patterns through to an arbitrary depth in time. Support vector machines (SVM), a more recent learning algorithm that has been developed from statistical learning theory (Vapnik, 1995; Vapnik, Golowich, & Smola, 1997), have a strong mathematical foundation and have been previously applied to time series analysis (Mukherjee, Osuna, & Girosi, 1997).

Neural Networks

Neural networks have been used successfully in the past for forecasting in complex business domains. Some examples of such applications include predicting foreign exchange rates (Walczak, 2001) and expert judgments in bankruptcy prediction (Kim & McLeod, 1999). The most commonly used artificial neural networks are the "feed-forward-error, backpropagation" type. In these networks, the individual elements ("neurons") are organized into layers in such a way that output signals from the neurons of a given layer are passed to all of the neurons of the next layer. Thus, the flow of neural activations goes in one direction only, layer-by-layer (feed-forward). Errors made by the neural network are then used to adjust all the network weights by moving back through the network (error backpropagation). The smallest number of layers is two, namely the input and output layers. More layers, called hidden layers, could be added between the input and the output layer and the non-linear transfer function of the hidden layers is to increase the computational power of the neural nets. ANNs have been proven to be universal approximators assuming that sufficient hidden layer neurons are provided and assuming that the activation function is bounded and non-constant (de Figueiredo, 1980).

Recurrent Neural Networks

Recurrent neural networks (RNN) are a type of ANN, which allow output signals of some of their neurons to flow back and serve as inputs for the neurons of the same layer or those of the previous layers. RNN serve as a powerful tool for many complex problems, in particular when time series data is involved. The training method called "backpropagation through time" can be applied to train a RNN on a given training set (Werbos, 1990). The Elman network implements backpropagation through time as a two-layer backpropagation neural network with a one step delayed feedback from the output of the hidden layer to its input (Elman, 1990). Figure 2 shows schematically the structure of RNN for the supply chain demand-forecasting problem. The arrows represent connections within the neural network with the thicker ones representing recurrent connection weights.

Support Vector Machines

Support vector machines (SVM) are a newer type of universal function approximators that are based on the structural risk minimization principle from statistical learning theory (Vapnik, 1995) as opposed to the empirical risk minimization principle on which ANN and Multiple Linear Regression (MLR) models, to name a few, are based. The objective of structural risk minimization is to reduce the true error on an unseen and randomly selected test example as opposed to ANN and MLR, which minimize the error for the currently seen examples.

Support vector machines project the data into a higher or lower dimensional space and maximize the margins between classes or minimize the error margin for regression using support vectors. Projecting into a higher or lower dimensional space permits identifying patterns that may not be clear in the input space, but which become better identifiable in a space with a different number of dimensions. Margins are "soft", meaning that a solution can be found even if there are contradicting examples in the training set. The problem is formulated as a convex optimization problem with no local minima, thus

Figure 2. Recurrent neural network for demand forecasting

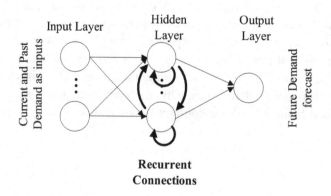

334

providing a unique solution (as opposed to backpropagation neural networks, which may have multiple local minima and, thus cannot guarantee that the global minimum error will be achieved by training). A complexity parameter permits the adjustment of the level of error versus the model complexity, and different "kernels", such as the radial basis function (RBF) kernel, can be used to permit non-linear mapping into the higher or lower dimensional space.

RESEARCH METHODOLOGY

Due to the inherent predictive power of universal approximators, it would seem that using ML-based techniques could provide a simple but powerful solution for forecasting chaotic, noisy and distorted customer demand at the end of a supply chain. Thus, in this work we set out to investigate whether ML algorithms, in general, perform better than traditional forecasting techniques. We formulate three hypotheses to probe our research question:

H1: Machine Learning-based techniques will have better average-performance than traditional techniques for manufacturer's forecasting of distorted customer demand
H2: Machine Learning-based techniques will have better rank-performance than traditional techniques for manufacturer's forecasting of distorted customer demand
H3: The best Machine Learning-based technique will out-perform the best traditional counter-part for manufacturer's forecasting of distorted customer demand

To answer our research question, we conducted an experiment to compare the accuracy of ML forecasting techniques with traditional forecasting techniques in the context of noisy supply chain demand as seen by the manufacturer. In our study, the traditional techniques were represented by the moving average, trend, exponential smoothing, and multiple linear regression. Additionally, based on the M3-Competition (Makridakis & Hibon, 2000), we included the Theta method (Assimakopoulos & Nikolpoulos, 2000). For completeness we also included the frequently used, ARMA (Auto-Regressive Moving Average) model, sometimes also referred to as the Box-Jenkins model (Box, Jenkins, & Reinsel, 1994). The ML- based forecasting techniques were limited to the 3 general classes mentioned previously: artificial neural networks (ANN), recurrent neural networks (RNN) and support vector machines (SVM).

Sample Size and Statistical Power

The following statistical power analysis is based on recommendations from Russell (2001) for determining sample size. Determining the required sample size is very difficult, since the variance of a forecasting technique on an unknown data set is difficult to estimate in advance. One can vaguely guess that the deviation of a forecast would be the same as the average forecast error. Since an average forecast error of 26% has been identified (Jain, 2004a), we will use this as the estimate average deviation. However, since we are concerned only with the manufacturer's end of the supply chain, who by the nature of their position in the supply chain experiences extremely noisy demand, this estimate is at the most conservative end of the spectrum.

The next issue to determine is the minimum size of the difference between the means that we want to detect. To determine this, we must identify what level of forecasting accuracy increase is useful, which depends of the potential cost savings. An in-depth survey of six companies has identified the inventory carrying costs to be between 14% and 43% (Lambert & Lalonde, 1976). A more recent survey by the Institutes of Management and Administration as reported by the Controller's Report (Anonymous, 2005) has also identified most inventory carrying costs to be between 10% and 40% and represents an average holding cost of around 21%.

It is also noteworthy that about 68% of the respondents to this survey were manufacturers, which means that these inventory carrying costs have a higher relevance for the current research. Using a conservative average inventory carrying cost of 20%, we can make some very rough calculations. For example, a company that has an inventory of 10 million dollars may have an inventory carrying cost of 2 million dollars a year and consequently, increasing forecasting accuracy by 1% would lead to a cost saving of about 20,000$ a year. We can also take a large manufacturer as an example, such as Proctor and Gamble that has 4.4 billion dollars of inventory (Proctor and Gamble, 2005). From this, we could estimate an approximate 880 million dollars of inventory carrying costs and thus a 1% increase in forecasting accuracy may result in a cost saving of 8.8 million dollars a year.

To detect a 1% change for a dataset that has an estimated minimum standard deviation of 26%, and to do so at a 0.05 significance level for a one-tailed test, would require a minimum of 1833. Rounding off, we targeted a sample size of over 2000 and as will be seen later on, for various reasons, most of the answers will come from a sample size of 2200 observations that come from two problem domain specific datasets. From this sample size and the above parameters, at a 1% change, we have a statistical power of 53%, at a 2% change, we have a statistical power of 96% and at a 3% change we have a statistical power of 99.98%.

Data Sources

We have included data from manufacturers that have integrated ERP systems, where every product or service that goes in and out of the system is controlled, as are all monetary transactions. There are two manufacturers who provided demand data as extracted from their ERP systems.

Chocolate Manufacturer

The first manufacturer produces chocolate starting from the cocoa beans, which must be roasted, converted into cacao and then combined with other ingredients according to a recipe. The geographic scope of the data set is North America. Since the inception of the ERP system and up to the time of the extraction of the data for this research, information was available for 47 months (October 2000-August 2004) of demand for a product.

Because of the number of forecasting models that must be processed and the complexity of some of the models, the number of time-series retained for the experiment must be limited. We considered the top hundred products with the most cumulative volume during this period, since these are the most important products for which the accuracy of forecasts is critical. Even though these products represent only 6% of the products sold by this manufacturer, they account for over 34% of the total sales volume. Example demand histories for the 10th and 50th products are shown in Figure 3 and Figure 4.

Figure 3. Demand for the 10th product

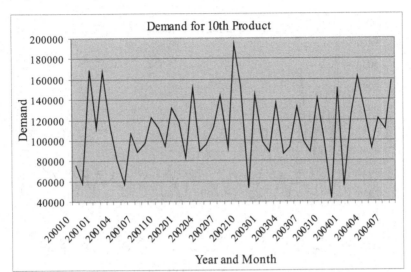

Figure 4. Demand for the 50th product

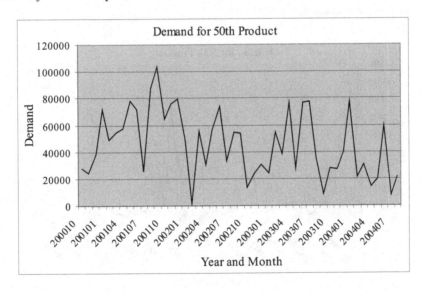

Toner Cartridge Manufacturer

The second manufacturer specializes in generic photocopier and laser printer toner cartridges and other related products. The geographic scope is of the data is North America. The demand data extracted from the ERP system represents a total of 65 periods of data. Again only the top hundred products were retained for the experiment since they are considered most important. Since the total number of active products in their system is 3369, these 100 products represent less than 3 percent of all products. How-

Figure 5. Demand for 10th product

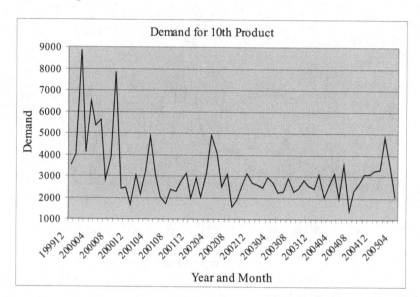

Figure 6. Demand for 50th product

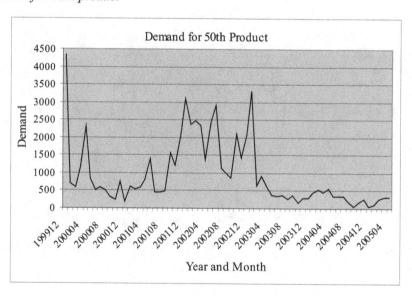

ever, these top products account for 38.35% of sales volume for the manufacturer. As depicted in Figure 5 and Figure 6, the time series seem quite chaotic with large variation and no clear seasonal patterns.

Statistics Canada Manufacturing

To add validity to the experiment and increase reproducibility, we included time series data about manufacturers demand as collected by Statistics Canada. This is publicly available historical data that cover a large part of the manufacturing sectors in the Canadian economy. Specifically, the data source

Figure 7. Demand for Sawmill and woodworking machinery man. cat

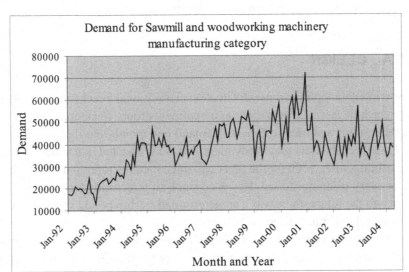

Figure 8. Demand for Urethane and other ... man. cat

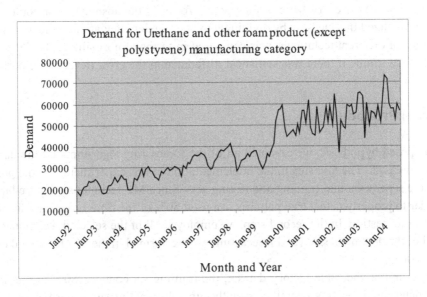

included the manufacturers' monthly new orders by North American Industry Classification System (NAICS) referred to as table 304-0014 (Statistics Canada, 2005). This dataset provided a good way to experiment on a variety of demand patterns across a large number of industries (214 industrial categories). We used the most recent "new order" observations representing 12 years and 4 months of data or 148 periods. To be consistent with the other two datasets we randomly selected one hundred categories (Appendix A). Two examples of the data series are presented in Figure 7 and Figure 8.

The patterns in the Statistics Canada data are different from those of the individual manufacturers because of their aggregate nature and lengthy data collection time span. Variability is much lower than that of the individual manufacturers because of the aggregation effect. In summary, the three data sources provided us with a total of 300 time series for our experiments.

EXPERIMENTAL DESIGN

We conducted experiments adopting a representative set of traditional forecasting techniques as a control group and a set of machine learning techniques as a treatment group. To compare the two groups, every technique from each group was used to forecast demand one month into the future for all of the 100 series for each of the three datasets previously identified. This resulted in a series of 4700 data points for the chocolate manufacturer, 6500 for the toner cartridge manufacturer and 14,800 for the Statistics Canada dataset for every technique tested. However, since all forecasting techniques require past data to make a forecast into the future, there was a predetermined startup period specific to each algorithm, which slightly reduces the number of forecast observations.

Additionally, the demand time series were formally separated into training sets and testing sets. This is particularly important for the ML techniques, where the training set was used for ML models to learn the demand patterns and the testing set used to estimate how well the forecasting capability could generalize in the future. The main performance measure that we used to test the hypotheses was the absolute error (AE) for every forecast data point. To make the absolute error comparable across products, we normalized this measure by dividing it by the standard deviation of the training set. Thus, the performance of different techniques was compared in terms of normalized absolute error (NAE) using a t-test to determine if there was statistical difference in the error (forecasting performance) of the techniques.

Experimental Procedure

To test the proposed hypothesis, we executed all of the forecasting algorithms on the demand series from the three datasets. The first step to the implementation of this experiment was the preparation of the data and the separation into training and testing sets. Since ML techniques require large amounts of data in order to properly detect true patterns, we used 80% of the time series data for training and 20% of the data for testing. In the second step, we employed all of the selected techniques to produce forecasts. All of the data processing and forecasting was performed in the MATLAB 7.0 environment (MathWorks, 2005c).

To illustrate, in the chocolate factory dataset, the training set contains 80% of the data, thus 38 months of demand and the testing set will contain the other 20% of the data that is 9 months of demand. This represents data from October 2000 to November 2003 for the training set and December 2003 to August 2004 for the testing set. The testing set contained the total of 900 forecast observations used for comparing performance of forecasting techniques.

Some forecasting algorithms, such as multiple linear regression, neural networks and support vector machines, require windowed data, i.e., past data that is used to predict future demand. For example a window size of 3 months could be defined, thus indicating that this current month's data and the data from the previous 2 months were used to predict next month's data. For some of the simpler forecasting techniques such as the moving average, trend, and exponential smoothing, we implemented two versions: ones with the pre-set parameter, and the "automatic" versions, whereby the parameters, which resulted in the most accurate forecasts on the training set were calculated.

Although, as mentioned previously, exponential smoothing performs well in many forecasting problems, the choice of the initial value may have a significant impact on the accuracy of forecasts. The exponential smoothing implementation in MATLAB Financial Toolbox (MathWorks, 2005a) and in Excel use the first value as the initial value, but, other implementations such as SPSS use the series average as the starting value. For this reason we implemented both approaches in our exponential smoothing and Theta models. The main purpose of the Multiple Linear Regression model is to provide a linear benchmark for all of the auto-regressive type models such as the neural networks and support vector machines.

ARMA

The ARMA model combines both Auto-Regressive forecast and a Moving Average forecast (Box et al., 1994). To minimize the error, we optimized the lag used in the auto-regression portion and the lag used in the moving average portion. This functionality is provided by the MATLAB GARCH Toolbox (MathWorks, 2005b). The ARMAX model is optimized to minimize the error using the Optimization Toolbox (MathWorks, 2005e). Only the ARMA part of the ARMAX model was used in the current experiments.

Theta Model

We have used the version of the Theta model (Assimakopoulos & Nikolpoulos, 2000) used in M3 forecasting competition. First, the linear trend was calculated, and then exponential smoothing performed on double the difference between the raw data and trend values to minimize the error on the training set. The two individual series, the linear trend and the optimized exponential smoothing on the decomposed series were recombined by an average of the two. As already mentioned, we implemented both versions of the Theta model, one with the first observation of the time series as the initialization value and the other with the average of the training set as the initialization value.

Neural Network Details

Neural networks, while being universal approximators may suffer from the "overfitting" problem: i.e. building complex non-linear mappings when different mappings are actually required. Overfitting leads to poor generalization and can be combated by adding more data to the training set or keeping the learning power (size) of the network low. Setting a window size of 5% of the training set data for the regular time series data models, results in a ratio of 1 input to 20 observations. Therefore, to provide appropriate level of non-linearity and additional modeling power, we created one hidden layer that contained 2 neurons with non-linear transfer functions. Even then, with the small datasets there is still a danger of overfitting the data. The total number of weights for a neural network with one hidden layer can be calculated as follows:

Total Weights $= p \cdot w \cdot h + b \cdot h + h \cdot o + b \cdot o$, where p is the number of periods in the data; w is the window ratio; h is the number of hidden layer neurons; b is the number of biases (one per computational element); and o is the number of outputs.

Therefore for the current implementation, the number of weights will always be:

$$\text{Total Weights} = p \cdot w \cdot 2 + 1 \cdot 2 + 2 \cdot 1 + 1 \cdot 1$$

And the Observations to Weights ratio is:

$$\text{Observations to Weights} = \frac{p \cdot (1 - w)}{(p \cdot w \cdot h + b \cdot h + h \cdot o + b \cdot o)}$$

Therefore, for the chocolate manufacturer dataset, Observations to Weights ratio is:

$$\text{Observations to Weights} = \frac{38 \cdot (1 - 0.05)}{(38 \cdot 0.05 \cdot 2 + 1 \cdot 2 + 2 \cdot 1 + 1 \cdot 1)} = 4.10$$

As with linear regression where at least 10 observations per variable are desirable, there should be a minimum of 10 observations for each weight. This estimation varies based on the expected complexity of the pattern being modeled. For example, the more complex the expected pattern or the more noise, the more observation per a weight is required. Thus an observations-to-weights ratio of 4.1 is somewhat low. However, because time series forecasting is a function of the past information, we determined that the window size must include 2 or more periods. For the current research project, since our smallest data set contains 47 periods, including 38 for the training set, a window size of 5% represents 2 past periods. For our largest dataset, there are 148 periods, 118 for the training set, thus representing a window of 6 periods.

The transfer function we used in the hidden layer is the tan-sigmoid function, which does non-linear scaling from an infinite range to values between -1 and 1, and the output layer transfer function is linear. Additionally, each neuron contains a bias input that has a constant of unity.

The relevant aspects of the supply chain demand modeling neural network are displayed in Figure 9. In this figure, the sum is represented sigma (Σ), the tan-sigmoid transfer function is represented by ($\digamma$), and the linear transfer function is represented by ($\digamma$). All of the inputs to the neural network, as well as the outputs are individually scaled between -1 and 1 to ensure that they are within the appropriate range for neural network training. The final results are then un-scaled to permit comprehensible analysis and usage.

The first implementation of neural networks is based on the traditional backpropagation algorithm. The structure of neural networks must be defined in advance by specifying such parameters as the number of hidden layers and the neurons within each hidden layer. Other settings that must be defined relate to the learning algorithm, e.g., the learning rate and the momentum.

Setting a constant learning rate for the training session is not desirable because the ideal learning rate may change based on the current progress of the networks learning. An adaptive variable learning rate training algorithm has been adopted, which adjusts the learning rate for the current learning error space (Hagan, Demuth, & Beale, 1996). This algorithm tries to maximize the learning rate subject to stable learning, thus adapting to the complexity of the local learning error space. For example, if the descent path to the lowest error is straight and simple, the learning rate will be high. If the descent path is variable, complicated and unclear, the learning rate will be very small to permit more stable learning

Figure 9. Supply chain demand modeling neural network design

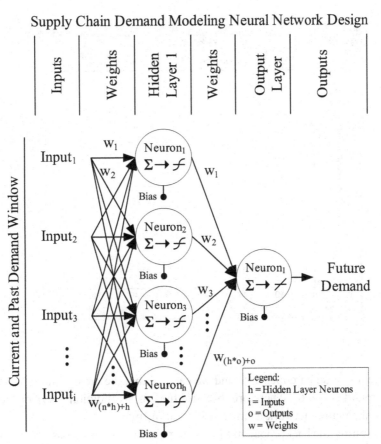

Supply Chain Demand Modeling Neural Network Design

and avoid oscillations in the learning space. In addition to the variable learning rate, our first neural network learning algorithm also included the momentum (Hagan et al., 1996).

To help the neural network stop training before it overfits the training set to the detriment of generalization, we use a cross-validation set for early stopping. This cross-validation set is an attempt to estimate the neural network's generalization performance. As previously presented, based on the amount of data available, we have defined the cross-validation (CV) set as the last 20% of the training set. This set is removed from the training set and is verified after every training epoch. An epoch is a single cycle over all of the training data. The error on the cross-validation set will decrease as the network starts to learn general patterns and then will increase as the network starts to memorize the training set. Thus, the weights that resulted in the lowest error rate on the cross-validation set are identified as the neural network model that provides the best generalization performance.

An example graph of the training and cross-validation set errors is presented in Figure 10 where we see the training set error as a dark shaded line and the cross-validation set error as a light shaded line. The y-axis represents the error and the x-axis represents the epochs, so Figure 10 presents a visual representation of the error minimization as the neural network learns through the epochs. The example

Figure 10. Example neural network training and cross-validation errors

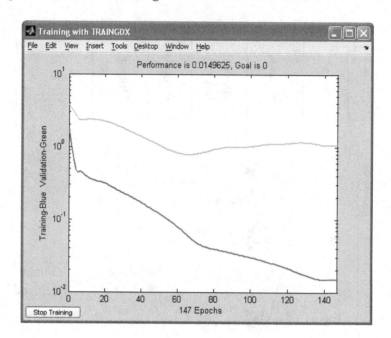

presented is currently at about epoch 145, and we can see that the cross-validation set error was at its lowest point at around epoch 65. Therefore, because the cross-validation set error increases after that, this suggests that the neural network is presumably overfitting.

In addition to testing the backpropagation-learning algorithm with cross-validation early stopping, we also used a faster training algorithms as well as an attempt to improve the generalization of the model. In particular, we used the Levenberg-Marquardt algorithm (Marquardt, 1963) as applied to Neural Networks (Hagan et al., 1996; Hagan & Menhaj, 1994). This algorithm is one of the fastest training algorithms available with training being 10-100 times faster than simple gradient descent backpropagation of error (Hagan & Menhaj, 1994).

The Levenberg-Marquardt neural network-training algorithm is further combined into a framework that permits estimation of the network's generalization by the use of a regularization parameter. Neural Network performance measures typically measure the error of the outputs of the network, such as the mean squared error (MSE). However, a regularization performance function which includes the sum of the weights and biases can be used instead, combined with a regularization parameter, which determines how much weight is given to the sum of weights and bias in the formula (MSEREG = γ MSE + $(1 - \gamma)$ MSW). This regularization parameter permits the control of the ratio of impact between reducing the error of the network and the number of weights or power of the network such that one can be less concerned with the size of the neural network and control the effective power of it directly by the use of this parameter.

The tuning of this regularization parameter is automated within the Bayesian framework (MacKay, 1992) and, when combined with the Levenberg-Marquardt training algorithm, results in high performance training combined with a preservation of generalization by avoiding overfitting of the training data

Figure 11. Example Levenberg-Marquardt Neural Network training details

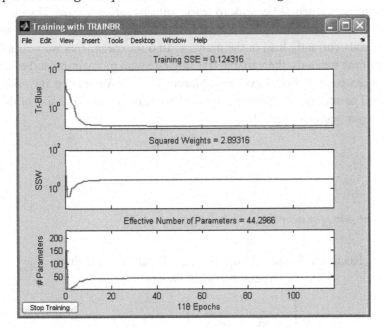

(Foresee & Hagan, 1997). Not only does this algorithm help eliminate overfitting of the target function, it also provides an estimate of how many weights and biases are being effectively used by the network. Larger networks should result in approximately the same performance since regularization results in a trade off between error and network parameters, which is relatively independent of network size.

All neural network modeling and training is performed in MATLAB 7.0 and MATLAB's Neural Network Toolbox (MathWorks, 2005d). An example of a Levenberg-Marquardt with Automated Bayesian Regularization training session is presented in Figure 11 where we can see that the algorithm is attempting to converge the network to a point of best generalization based on the current training set. Even though this particular network has 256 weights, the algorithm is controlling the power of the neural network at effective number of parameters of about 44. The network could further reduce the error on the training set (Sum of Squared Error: SSE) since it could use all 256 weights. However, it has determined that using more than the 44 weights will cause overfitting of the data and thus reduced generalization performance.

Compared to the early stopping based on a cross-validation set, the Levenberg-Marquardt with Automated Bayesian Regularization training algorithm is superior especially for small datasets since separating out a cross-validation set it not required.

Recurrent Neural Networks Details

The recurrent neural network architecture is the same as the above-described feed-forward architecture, except for one essential difference. There are recurrent network connections within the hidden layer as presented in the subset architecture in Figure 12. This architecture is known as an Elman Network

(Elman, 1990). The recurrent connections feed information from the past execution cycle back into the network. This permits a neural network to learn patterns through time. Thus the same recurrent networks with the same weights and given the same inputs may result in different outputs depending on the feedback signals currently held in the network. In our experiments we will use the two previously described training methods, the variable learning rate with momentum and early stopping based on cross-validation set error and the Levenberg-Marquardt with Automated Bayesian Regularization training algorithm. The addition of recurrent connections also increases the size of the network by the number of hidden layer neurons squared.

Figure 12. Recurrent subset of neural network design

Recurrent Subset of Supply Chain Demand Modeling
Neural Network Design

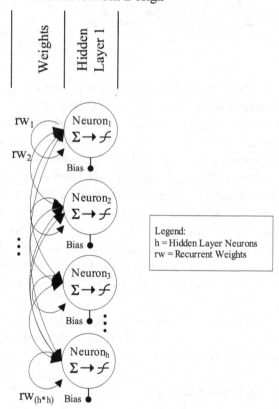

We can calculate the total number of weights as:

Total Weights $= p \cdot w \cdot h + b \cdot h + h \cdot h + h \cdot o + b \cdot o$

Therefore for the current implementation, the number of weights will always be:

Total Weights $= p \cdot w \cdot 2 + 1 \cdot 2 + 2 \cdot 2 + 2 \cdot 1 + 1 \cdot 1$

For example, for the chocolate manufacturer dataset, Observations to Weights ratio is:

$$\text{Observations to Weights} = \frac{38 \cdot (1 - 0.05)}{(38 \cdot 0.05 \cdot 2 + 1 \cdot 2 + 2 \cdot 2 + 2 \cdot 1 + 1 \cdot 1)} = 2.82$$

Naturally, the observations-to-weights ratio is even lower than the 4.1 previously identified for the neural network without the recurrent connections. However, the window size ratio and the number of hidden layer neurons should not be further reduced since they are already at their lowest meaningful levels.

Support Vector Machine Details

The support vector machine software implementation selected for the current experiment was mySVM (Rüping, 2005) which is based on the SVMLight optimization algorithm (Joachims, 1999). The inner product kernel was used and the complexity constant was automatically determined using cross-validation procedure.

Two cross-validation procedures were tested. The first one was a simple 10 fold cross-validation that ignores the time direction of the data. Thus, for 10 iterations, 9/10th of the data were used to build a model and the remaining 1/10th was used to test the accuracy. The second one simulated time ordered predictions, called windowed cross-validation. This cross-validation procedure split the training data set into 10 parts and the algorithm trained the model using 5 parts and tested on a 6th part. This 5-part window was moved along the data, which resulted in the procedure being repeated 5 times. For example blocks 1-5 were used to train and the model was tested on block 6, then blocks 2-6 were used to train the model and tested on block 7, and so on.

The errors of these five models were averaged and the complexity constant with the smallest cross-validation error was selected as the level of complexity that provided the best generalization. Increasing the complexity constant from a very small value, which does not model the data well, to a very large value, which overfits the data, results in an error curve which permits the minimization of the generalization error. An example error curve for the complexity constant search on a 10-fold cross-validation set with a 5 fold sliding window for the complexity constant range between 0.00000001 and 100 with a multiplicative step of 1.1, is presented in Figure 13.

We also present an example of the data underfitting the model with complexity constant 0.00000001, overfitting with 1000 and the optimal estimated generalization fit is with a complexity constant of 0.012154154 in Figure 14. In this diagram, we can see that the Support Vector Machine with a very low complexity constant just presents the average of the training set and thus does not offer much predictive power. The very high complexity constant memorizes the training set, as can be seen in the diagram where the high complexity forecast overlaps the actual demand in the training set (period 1

Figure 13. SVM cross-validation error for complexity constant

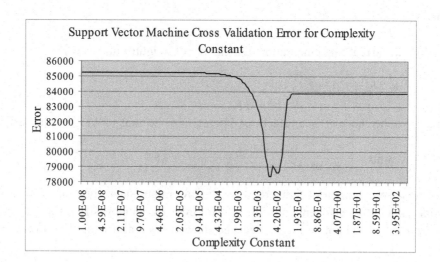

Figure 14. SVM forecasts with varying complexity constants

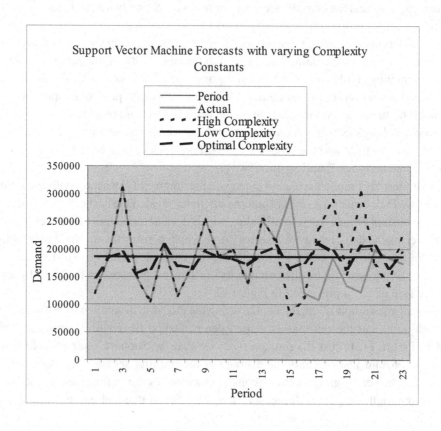

to 14); however, it generalizes very poorly during the testing set (period 15+). The optimal complexity constant of 0.012154154, as identified by the complexity constant optimization based on the windowed cross-validation procedure (as described in the previous paragraphs), provides a forecast that represents the level of patterns learning that seems to generalize best.

Super Wide Model

As indicated earlier by the observations-to-weights ratio, since the available time series are very short, there are not many examples for learning complex patterns. The separation of the data set into training, cross-validation and testing sets and the loss of periods due to the windowing all combined to further reduce the set of usable observations. Based on the assumption that several products of the same manufacturer probably have similar demand patterns, we introduced what we called a Super Wide Model. This method takes a wide selection of time-series from the same problem domain and combines them into one large model that effectively increases the number of training examples. This large number of training examples permits an increase in input dimensionality (e.g. larger window size) and model complexity.

For example, in this experiment, we consider 100 time series for each of the sources. With the Super Wide Model, we use the data from all of the 100 time series simultaneously to train the model. This provides a large number of training examples and permits us to greatly increase the window size so that the models can look deep into the past data. Additionally, it could also be used to look across various other information sources that may be correlated to the demand, such as category averages or complement or substitute product demand information.

For example, for the chocolate factory data set, there are 100 products and 47 periods of time series data. Once the training and testing set are separated, we have 38 periods of data. For this type of model, we choose a window size of 50%, which is a perfect balance between modeling the demand behavior as a function of the past 50% of the data and using 50% of the data as examples. Using this large window size of 50% with the traditional time series model would provide a training set of 19 examples for a window size of 19 that would not represent very much data to identify patterns that may be present in the future. However, with the Super Wide Model, we have 1900 examples for a window size of 19 that represent sufficient data to find the best forecasting patterns for the problem domain.

All of the models that learn from past demand, such as the multiple linear regression, neural networks and support vector machines will be tested also on the Super Wide Models. The only exception is the recurrent neural networks because the necessary tools are not yet available. Although training a recurrent neural network on a Super Wide Model is feasible in principle, it would require a reset of the recurrent connections for every product because time lagged signals between products would not make sense.

The neural network models were enlarged to 10 hidden layer neurons, which in combination with the very large window, results in large network sizes compared to the patterns to be detected. With a window size of 50% of the training data, we have a ratio of 1 input to 1 observation. We then multiplied the observations by 100 products (because of the Super Wide model format) to calculate the observations-to-weights ratio for the chocolate manufacturer dataset. We can calculate the total number of weights as:

$$\text{Total Weights} = p \cdot w \cdot h + b \cdot h + h \cdot o + b \cdot o$$

Therefore for the current implementation, the number of weights will always be:

Total Weights $= p \cdot w \cdot 10 + 1 \cdot 10 + 10 \cdot 1 + 1 \cdot 1$

And the Observations to Weights ratio is:

Observations to Weights $= \dfrac{n \cdot p \cdot (1 - w)}{(p \cdot w \cdot h + b \cdot h + h \cdot o + b \cdot o)}$

Therefore, for the chocolate manufacturer dataset, Observation to Weights ratio is:

Observation to Weights $= \dfrac{100 \cdot 38 \cdot (1 - 0.05)}{(38 \cdot 0.05 \cdot 10 + 1 \cdot 10 + 10 \cdot 1 + 1 \cdot 1)} = 90.25$

We can see that we now have a very high observations-to-weights ratio, which will help us achieve much better models, especially for very noisy data.

RESULTS

This section discusses the performance of the selected models on three data sets. Table 1 presents the mean absolute errors (MAE) of all the tested forecasting techniques as applied to the chocolate manufacturer's dataset in ascending order of testing set error with the best-performing techniques at the top of the list, and the worst at the bottom. The results are also provided in similar format for the Toner Cartridge manufacturer's dataset (Table 2) and the Statistics Canada manufacturing dataset (Table 3).

The results suggest that one of the ML approaches, the support vector machine (SVM) under the Super Wide modeling approach is at the top on all three data sets by providing consistently better performance. If we ignore the Super Wide models, we find that the results of previous research and the M3-Competition were, in essence reproduced. That is, simple techniques outperform the more complicated and sophisticated approaches. For example, in the two primary datasets of interests, the Chocolate (Table 1) and Toner Cartridge (Table 2) manufacturer, exponential smoothing has the best performance. They are at Rank 5 and Rank 3 respectively, immediately after the top Super Wide models. This is especially true in our experiments since the data we are concerned with are very noisy and the exponential smoothing (ES) approach outperformed all of the other approaches including the advanced ML ones, in some cases by considerable margins. Noticeably, the Toner Cartridge data set was so noisy or the patterns changed so much with time that even the exponential smoothing with a fixed parameter of 20% outperformed (Table 2 – Rank 3) the automated one (Table 2 – Rank 5), which optimized the parameter for the training set.

We observed the same problem with the Moving Average approach that was fixed to a window of 6 periods (Table 2 – Rank 4). The automatic versions likewise had overfitting problems and had lower performance (Table 2 – Rank 7) than setting a constant parameter value (Table 2 – Rank 4). The average error of the automatic exponential smoothing for the two manufacturer's dataset is 0.7516 and the average for the fixed exponential smoothing of 20% is 0.7501 and the difference has a significance of 0.4037. The moving average with a window of 6 periods has an average error of 0.7561 and a mean difference significance of 0.2273 with the average of the automatic exponential smoothing. Although we see this overfitting pattern repeats itself, the difference in means is statistically insignificant for the

Table 1. Performance of forecasting techniques for chocolate manufacturer's dataset

Rank	Method	Group	NMAE
1	SuperWide Support Vector Machine, Windowed Cross-Validation	Treatment	0.7693
2	SuperWide Support Vector Machine, Cross-Validation	Treatment	0.7717
3	SuperWide Multiple Linear Regression	Control	0.7776
4	SuperWide Neural Network, Cross-Validation	Treatment	0.7998
5	Exponential Smoothing, Automatic, Initialization=First	Control	0.8270
6	Exponential Smoothing, 20%	Control	0.8329
7	Theta, Exponential Smoothing Initialization=First	Control	0.8347
8	Moving Average, 6 Periods	Control	0.8381
9	Moving Average, Automatic	Control	0.8534
10	Exponential Smoothing, Automatic, Initialization=Average	Control	0.8613
11	Theta, Exponential Smoothing Initialization=Average	Control	0.8775
12	Multiple Linear Regression	Control	0.9047
13	SuperWide Neural Network, Levenberg-Marquardt, Bayesian Regularization	Treatment	0.9209
14	Recurrent Neural Network, Levenberg-Marquardt, Bayesian Regularization	Treatment	0.9307
15	Neural Network, Levenberg-Marquardt, Bayesian Regularization	Treatment	0.9331
16	Support Vector Machine, Cross-Validation	Treatment	0.9335
17	Support Vector Machine, Windowed Cross-Validation	Treatment	0.9427
18	Neural Network, Backpropagation, Cross-Validation	Treatment	0.9810
19	Recurrent Neural Network, Backpropagation, Cross-Validation	Treatment	0.9954
20	Auto Regressive Moving Average	Control	1.0151
21	Trend, Automatic	Control	1.6043
22	Trend, 6 Periods	Control	8.1978

Table 2. Performance of forecasting techniques for toner cartridge manufacturer's dataset

Rank	Method	Group	NMAE
1	SuperWide Support Vector Machine, Cross-Validation	Treatment	0.6777
2	SuperWide Support Vector Machine, Windowed Cross-Validation	Treatment	0.6781
3	Exponential Smoothing, 20%	Control	0.6928
4	Moving Average, 6 Periods	Control	0.6993
5	Exponential Smoothing, Automatic, Initialization=First	Control	0.6994
6	Support Vector Machine, Windowed Cross-Validation	Treatment	0.7003
7	Moving Average, Automatic	Control	0.7054
8	SuperWide Multiple Linear Regression	Control	0.7060
9	Support Vector Machine, Cross-Validation	Treatment	0.7221
10	Theta, Exponential Smoothing Initialization=First	Control	0.7244
11	Exponential Smoothing, Automatic, Initialization=Average	Control	0.7259

continued on following page

Table 2. continued

12	Theta, Exponential Smoothing Initialization=Average	Control	0.7358
13	Multiple Linear Regression	Control	0.7677
14	SuperWide Neural Network, Levenberg-Marquardt, Bayesian Regularization	Treatment	0.7781
15	Recurrent Neural Network, Backpropagation, Cross-Validation	Treatment	0.8090
16	Recurrent Neural Network, Levenberg-Marquardt, Bayesian Regularization	Treatment	0.8187
17	Neural Network, Levenberg-Marquardt, Bayesian Regularization	Treatment	0.8189
18	Neural Network, Backpropagation, Cross-Validation	Treatment	0.8498
19	SuperWide Neural Network, Cross-Validation	Treatment	0.8818
20	Auto Regressive Moving Average	Control	0.9319
21	Trend, Automatic	Control	1.6058
22	Trend, 6 Periods	Control	8.6140

Table 3. Performance of forecasting techniques for Statistics Canada manufacturing dataset

Rank	Method	Group	NMAE
1	SuperWide Support Vector Machine, Windowed Cross-Validation	Treatment	0.4478
2	SuperWide Support Vector Machine, Cross-Validation	Treatment	0.4547
3	Multiple Linear Regression	Control	0.4910
4	Support Vector Machine, Windowed Cross-Validation	Treatment	0.4914
5	Support Vector Machine, Cross-Validation	Treatment	0.4932
6	Theta, Exponential Smoothing Initialization=First	Control	0.5052
7	Exponential Smoothing, Automatic, Initialization=First	Control	0.5055
8	Exponential Smoothing, Automatic, Initialization=Average	Control	0.5086
9	Moving Average, Automatic	Control	0.5108
10	Theta, Exponential Smoothing Initialization=Average	Control	0.5137
11	SuperWide Multiple Linear Regression	Control	0.5327
12	Moving Average, 6 Periods	Control	0.5354
13	Recurrent Neural Network, Levenberg-Marquardt, Bayesian Regularization	Treatment	0.5355
14	Neural Network, Levenberg-Marquardt, Bayesian Regularization	Treatment	0.5374
15	Exponential Smoothing, 20%	Control	0.5483
16	SuperWide Neural Network, Cross-Validation	Treatment	0.5872
17	SuperWide Neural Network, Levenberg-Marquardt, Bayesian Regularization	Treatment	0.6453
18	Recurrent Neural Network, Backpropagation, Cross-Validation	Treatment	0.8060
19	Neural Network, Backpropagation, Cross-Validation	Treatment	0.8238
20	Auto Regressive Moving Average	Control	1.3662
21	Trend, Automatic	Control	1.9956
22	Trend, 6 Periods	Control	20.8977

manufacturers' data sets. Therefore, the automatic exponential smoothing, 20% exponential smoothing and the 6 period window moving average all provide about the same performance.

The difference when including the Statistics Canada manufacturing data was much larger since the patterns were stronger as a result of its aggregate nature and there were more data for the automatic version to achieve better performance. The average error of the automatic exponential smoothing for all three datasets is 0.6096 and the average for the fixed exponential smoothing of 20% is 0.6337 and the difference has a significance of 0.00000002159. The moving average with a window of 6 periods had an average error of 0.6288 and a significance of 0.0000005752 with the average of the automatic exponential smoothing. We are impartial about which method is best when testing with only the two manufacturer's data sets. However, when we included the Statistics Canada data set in the testing, there was a significant difference in favor of the automatic exponential smoothing and consequently we would identify this technique to be superior since there is added value at no loss.

In the case of the Statistics Canada dataset, the results were a little different; we found the MLR (Table 3 – Rank 3), SVM (Table 3 – Rank 4 and 5) and Theta (Table 3 – Rank 6) outperformed exponential smoothing (Table 3 – Rank 7). However, because these approaches had such poor performance on the chocolate and toner cartridge manufacturer datasets and because the performance gain by these over the ES method was very small, we did not consider these results convincing. They may be the result of the very large amount of data (12 years) and the aggregate nature of the data that was less noisy.

It is interesting to note that the trend approach (an informal way of planning by extrapolating that a certain trend will continue in the future) was by far the worst forecasting approach since it always ranked at the bottom of all three tables (Rank 21 and 22). Also, ARMA and most of the ML approaches other than SVM showed a relatively poor performance.

Support Vector Machines Using the Super Wide Model

The overall best performance was obtained using support vector machines in combination with the Super Wide model. Since we have previously identified that the best traditional technique was automatic exponential smoothing (it performed well on both manufacturers' data, as well as the aggregate manufacturing data), we can calculate the forecast error reduction provided by the best ML approach. For the chocolate manufacturer's dataset (Table 1 – Rank 2 and 5), we found a 6.70% ((0.8270 - 0.7717) / 0.8270) reduction in the overall forecasting error and for the toner cartridge manufacturer dataset (Table 2 – Rank 1 and 5) we found a 3.11% ((0.6994 - 0.6777) / 0.6994) reduction in the overall forecasting error. In the case of the Statistics Canada manufacturing dataset (Table 3 – Rank 2 and 7), we found a 10.00% ((0.5055 - 0.4547 / 0.5055) reduction in the forecasting error as compared to automatic exponential smoothing. This was an average of 4.90% for our two manufacturers' dataset and an average of 6.61% for all three as compared to automatic exponential smoothing. The performance of the Super Wide models has a potential to improve further, if more products are included beyond the limit of 100 used in our study. We will further examine in detail four major components of results; (1) cross- validation, (2) alternative methods, (3) t-tests and (4) sensitivity analysis.

Cross-Validation

We tested two different support vector machine cross-validation-based parameter optimization procedures: the windowed (time-oriented) approach and the standard approach. For the chocolate manufacturer and for the Statistics Canada datasets, the windowed cross-validation was superior and for the toner cartridge manufacturer the unordered approach was better. Accordingly, we are impartial regarding the cross-validation (CV) procedure. Since the standard cross-validation procedure is simpler to implement than the windowed counterpart and, since there can be more models tested while at the same time using more data for each CV model and, further, since the error curves seemed more stable (had lower variation and clearer concave shape), we recommend the standard CV procedure over the windowed one.

It is interesting to further examine how the cross-validation-based parameter selection behaves. It is this key feature in combination with the guaranteed optimality of the SVM that makes it possible to determine the best level of complexity. The cross-validation error curves for the range of complexity constants is presented in Figure 15 for the chocolate manufacturer's dataset, Figure 16 for the toner cartridge manufacturer's dataset and Figure 17 for Statistics Canada manufacturing dataset. In both Figure 15 and Figure 16 there is a clear concave pattern that indicates that a complexity constant that generalizes well, is identified without ambiguity. The optimal complexity is more difficult to identify in Figure 17 because as the complexity increases, the error stays relatively low and stable. This is probably a result of the larger amount of data and less noise and so there is a range of complexity that may generalize well. In all three figures, there is a clear distinction between complexity levels that generalize better than others thus permitting the selection of a complexity level. By contrast, if these figures presented error lines that randomly moved up and down as the complexity constant varied, this would indicate that the cross-validation (CV) procedure was not providing any value.

Alternatives

In the case of the chocolate manufacturer's dataset, we found that the next best performing algorithms that were better than exponential smoothing were the Super Wide multiple lnear regression (MLR) and the Super Wide artificial neural networks (ANN) with cross-validation based early stopping. In analyz-

Figure 15. Complexity optimization CV error on chocolate man dataset

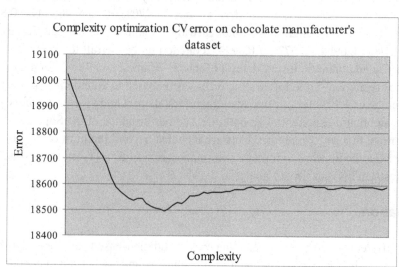

Figure 16. Complexity optimization CV error on tone cartridge man. dataset

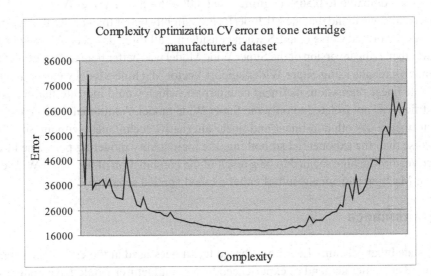

Figure 17. Complexity optimization CV error on Statistics Canada dataset

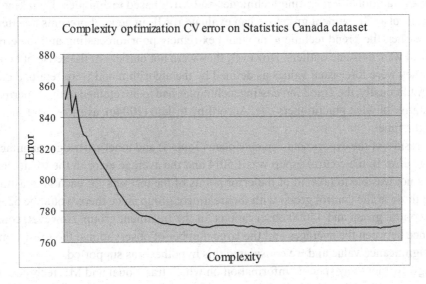

ing the ANN's performance, it turns out that even though its performance was strong on the chocolate manufacturer's dataset (Table 1 – Rank 4), it had extremely poor performance on both the toner cartridge manufacturer dataset (Table 2 – Rank 19) and on the Statistics Canada manufacturing dataset (Table 3 – Rank 16). As a result, the Super Wide artificial neural networks with cross-validation based early stopping method was disregarded as a potential alternative.

The Super Wide multiple linear regression (MLR) was much closer with an average error across the two manufacturer's dataset of 0.7353 compared to 0.7516 (significance 0.0274) for the automatic exponential smoothing (ES) and compared to 0.7154 (significance 0.0000) for the Super Wide SVM. The averages across all three datasets were 0.6184 for Super Wide MLR compared to 0.6096 (significance 0.1066) for ES and compared to 0.5651 (significance 0.0000) for Super Wide SVM.

From these results, we found that the MLR performed slightly better than ES for the two manufacturer's datasets, but performed worse than ES when considering all three datasets. Although we could not clearly state whether a linear version of the Super Wide Model was better than the traditional and simple ES, we did find that results using Super Wide Support Vector Machine Model were significantly better than the multiple linear regression, its linear counterpart, which would indicate that the performance increase identified was not isolated to only the Super Wide model. Additionally, since in almost all of the cases performance of both non-linear and linear alternative techniques (without Super Wide data) were much worse than the exponential smoothing, the high quality modeling performed by the Super Wide Support Vector Machine seemed to be a result of the combination of the Super Wide data and the Support Vector Machine and not a result of either method applied separately.

Average Performance

Hypothesis 1 stated that Machine Learning - based techniques used at the end of the supply chain to forecast distorted customer demand as experienced by a manufacturer would have better average performance than traditional techniques. To test this hypothesis, we examined the difference between the average error of traditional forecasting techniques and ML - based techniques. By taking the average error of the control and treatment group we can evaluate if ML in general presents a better solution.

As noted earlier, the Trend technique provided extremely poor forecasting and the error measurements produced were extreme outliers. However, they were not outliers in the sense of being measurement errors, they were forecasted values as defined by the algorithm and were retained in the average calculation. Additionally, the Trend forecasting techniques had to be retained in the experiment because it is representative of what practitioners use. According to Jain (2004c), averages and simple trend are used 65% of the time.

Using the results of the experiments on chocolate (Table 1) and toner cartridge manufacturer (Table 2), the average error in the control group was 1.5014 and the average error in the treatment group was 0.8356. It was not feasible to take all of the error points of the test sets for each forecasting technique and compare those of the control group with the treatment group since there would be 52800 observations for the control group and 44000 observations for the treatment group. However, considering the large difference between the averages and the large number of observations, the t-test would have had a very high significance value and we considered this hypothesis as supported.

Accordingly, without any specific information on which traditional and ML techniques are best or if there is a lack of experience and knowledge related to traditional and ML techniques, one would be more likely to be better off in choosing a random ML solution to induce the lower expected error.

Rank Performance

In hypothesis 2, we stated that ML - based techniques used at the end of the supply chain to forecast distorted customer demand as experienced by a manufacturer would have better ranked-performance than traditional techniques. By taking the average rank of the control and treatment group we evaluated if ML in general presents a better solution. Using the results of the experiments on chocolate (Table 1) and toner cartridge manufacturer (Table 2), the average rank in the control group was 11.25 and the average rank in the treatment group was 11.8. Therefore, on average, ML techniques ranked worse than the traditional ones. Thus, the hypothesis is rejected and a rigorous testing is not required as the difference is in the direction opposite to the expected one. If the Statistics Canada data are included, the averages rank of both the control and the treatment group were 11.5, which also implies rejection of the hypothesis.

Accordingly, without any specific information on which traditional and which ML techniques are best or if there is a lack of experience and knowledge related to traditional and ML techniques, one cannot just select any ML method and generally expect it to perform better (i.e. in terms of the "winning" method, not based on the magnitude of error) than a random traditional technique.

Comparison of the Best ML and Best Traditional Technique

Hypothesis 3 stated that the best ML - based technique used at the end of the supply chain to forecast distorted customer demand as experienced by a manufacturer will have better performance than the best traditional technique. To statistically compare the performance of the two we performed a t-test. The difference between the support vector machine error average of 0.7154 and the automatic exponential smoothing error average of 0.7516 had a p-value of 0.0000. Across the three datasets the support vector machine error average was 0.5651 and the automatic exponential smoothing error average was 0.6096, a statistically significant difference with p-value of 0.0000. Thus, we can conclude that the best ML approach has performed significantly better than the best traditional approach.

Sensitivity Analysis

Using the Super Wide data for the Support Vector Machine modeling permitted an analysis of much more data simultaneously and thus produced a very high historical window size while still having a very large dataset to learn from. As a result of this, we set the historical window size to 50% of the history. However, we investigated whether 50% was the correct setting and whether this setting had an impact on the performance of the model. Although a historical window size of 50% seemed normal,

Table 4. Sensitivity analysis of window size

Data set	Window	MAE
Chocolate	0.40	0.7806
Chocolate	0.50	0.7717
Chocolate	0.60	0.7703
Toner Cartridge	0.40	0.6770
Toner Cartridge	0.50	0.6777
Toner Cartridge	0.60	0.6846
Statistics Canada	0.40	0.3903
Statistics Canada	0.50	0.4547
Statistics Canada	0.60	0.4414

we re-executed the Super Wide Support Vector Machine models for a window size of 40% and one of 60% to evaluate the impact of this choice. The Mean Absolute Errors for the Super Wide Support Vector Machine with parameter optimization via standard cross-validation for a historical window size of 40%, 50% and 60% are presented in Table 4.

From these results we find that for the chocolate manufacturer's dataset the error decreased when the window size increased, however, for the toner cartridge dataset the error increased with window size increase. The Statistics Canada manufacturing dataset showed mixed results with no trend. Therefore, we did not see a trend that would indicate that a smaller or larger window size would have an impact on the performance. Additionally, the performance difference between such large window size change (10%) resulted in very small differences in performance and all of these performances remained better than the identified next contender which was exponential smoothing. Thus, we found that the Super Wide Support Vector Machine with parameter optimization via standard cross-validation was relatively insensitive to the window size and that a window size of 50% seemed to be a good choice.

CONCLUSION AND DISCUSSION

The purpose of this work has been to investigate the applicability and benefits of machine learning techniques in forecasting distorted demand signals with a high noise to pattern ratio in the context of supply chains. Although there are several forecasting algorithms available to practitioners, there are very few objective and reproducible guidelines regarding which method should be employed. In this research, we have shown empirically that the best traditional method for a manufacturer is the automatic exponential smoothing with the first value of the series as the initial value. We have also found that all of the more advanced machine learning techniques have relatively poor performance as a result of the noisy nature of data and the limited number of past time periods for any given product. None of the ML techniques can reliably outperform the best traditional counterpart (exponential smoothing) when learning and forecasting single time-series. Thus, they are not recommended as forecasting techniques for noisy demand at the manufacturer's end of the supply chain.

However, one important finding concerns the usefulness of combining the data from multiple products in what we called a Super Wide model in conjunction with a relatively new technique, the support vector machine. The domain-specific empirical results show that this approach is superior to the exponential smoothing. The error reduction found range from 3.11% to 10%, which can result in large financial savings for a company depending on the cost related to inventory errors. This assumes that the company is already using the best forecasting method available, or otherwise the performance gains would be even greater. We feel confident with regards to the generalizability of our findings, since the work used actual data from a large number of products from two North American manufacturers, with the additional verification against Statistics Canada manufacturing survey. We also feel that as the number of products added to the combined time series model (Super Wide approach) increases, the performance will also probably increase further since there will be more data to learn from. As any business decision, the use of the technology presented here should be based on a cost-benefit analysis of the benefits of implementing such technology weighed against its associated costs. If this approach is viable, in the long run it may be integrated into enterprise resource planning systems for automated and interaction free forecasting.

One important point to note is that support vector machines are computationally intensive and the cross-validation-based complexity parameter optimization procedure results in running a large amount of support vector machines depending on the precision of the complexity search. The longest running models in this research took over 3 days of processing on a modern computer. There are many optimization techniques that could be performed to reduce the processing time such as parallelization, which is trivial for a cross-validation procedure and reduction of the complexity term search precision. We hope that in time, further optimizations to the support vector machine algorithms and an increase in processing power would reduce the processing time significantly. Once the models have been completed, they can be used for forecasting with relatively little processing time. There is also research into hardware based support vector machine implementations. One such initiative is the Kerneltron project, which provides performance increases by a factor of 100 to 10,000 (Genov & Cauwenberghs, 2001, 2003; Genov, Chakrabartty, & Cauwenberghs, 2003), thus increasing the probability that such large SVM applications are feasible in the medium term future.

One important possibility for future research would be investigating the benefits of the ML techniques when using other sources of data and in the context of collaborative forecasting. This additional data may include economic indicators, market indicators, collaborative information sources, product group averages and other relevant information.

REFERENCES

Anonymous. (2005). Inventory carrying costs. *The Controller's Report*, (4), 5.

Assimakopoulos, V., & Nikolpoulos, K. (2000). The theta model: A decomposition approach to forecasting. *International Journal of Forecasting, 16*(4), 521.

Box, G., Jenkins, G. M., & Reinsel, G. (1994). *Time series analysis: Forecasting and control* (Third ed.). Englewood Cliffs: NJ: Prentice Hall.

Chandra, C., & Grabis, J. (2005). Application of multi-steps forecasting for restraining the bullwhip effect and improving inventory performance under autoregressive demand. *European Journal of Operational Research, 166*(2), 337.

Cox, A., Sanderson, J., & Watson, G. (2001). Supply chains and power regimes: Toward an analytic framework for managing extended networks of buyer and supplier relationships. *Journal of Supply Chain Management, 37*(2), 28.

Davis, E. W., & Spekman, R. E. (2004). *The extended enterprise: gaining competitive advantage through collaborative supply chains.* Upper Saddle River: NJ: FT Prentice Hall.

de Figueiredo, R. J. P. (1980). Implications and applications of Kolmogorov's superposition theorem. *IEEE Transactions on Automatic Control, 25*(6), 1227–1231.

Dejonckheere, J., Disney, S. M., Lambrecht, M. R., & Towill, D. R. (2003). Measuring and avoiding the bullwhip effect: A control theoretic approach. *European Journal of Operational Research, 147*(3), 567.

Dorffner, G. (1996). Neural networks for time series processing. *Neural Network World, 96*(4), 447-468.

Elman, J. L. (1990). Finding structure in time. *Cognitive Science, 14*(2), 179-211.

Foresee, F. D., & Hagan, M. T. (1997). Gauss-Newton approximation to Bayesian regularization. In *Proceedings of the 1997 International Joint Conference on Neural Networks*, 1930-1935.

Forrester, J. (1961). *Industrial dynamics.* Cambridge: MA: Productivity Press.

Genov, R., & Cauwenberghs, G. (2001). Charge-mode parallel architecture for matrix-vector multiplication. *IEEE Trans. Circuits and Systems II: Analog and Digital Signal Processing, 48*(10), 930-936.

Genov, R., & Cauwenberghs, G. (2003). Kerneltron: Support vector "machine" in Silicon. *IEEE Transactions on Neural Networks, 14*(5), 1426-1434.

Genov, R., Chakrabartty, S., & Cauwenberghs, G. (2003). Silicon support vector machine with on-line learning. *International Journal of Pattern Recognition and Artificial Intelligence, 17*(3), 385-404.

Giles, C. L., Lawrence, S., & Tsoi, A. C. (2001). Noisy time series prediction using recurrent neural networks and grammatical inference. *Machine Learning, 44,* 161-184.

Gossain, S., Malhotra, A., & El Sawy, O. A. (2005). Coordinating forflexibility in e-business supply chains. *Journal of Management Information Systems, 21*(3), 7-45.

Gunasekaran, A., & Ngai, E. W. T. (2004). Information systems in supply chain integration and management. *European Journal of Operational Research, 159*(2), 269.

Hagan, M. T., Demuth, H. B., & Beale, M. H. (1996). *Neural network design.* Boston: PWS Publishing.

Hagan, M. T., & Menhaj, M. (1994). Training feedforward networks with the Marquardt algorithm. *IEEE Transactions on Neural Networks, 5*(6), 989–993.

Heikkila, J. (2002). From supply to demand chain management: Efficiency and customer satisfaction. *Journal of Operations Management, 20*(6), 747.

Herbrich, R., Keilbach, M., Graepel, T., Bollmann-Sdorra, P., & Obermayer, K. (1999). *Neural networks in economics: Background, applications and new developments* (Vol. 11). Boston: Kluwer Academics.

Hofman, D. (2007). Supply chain measurement: Turning data into action. *Supply Chain Management Review, 11*(8), 20-26.

Jain, C. L. (2004a). Benchmarking forecasting error. *The Journal of Business Forecasting Methods & Systems, 23*(3), 8.

Jain, C. L. (2004b). Benchmarking forecasting software and systems. *The Journal of Business Forecasting Methods & Systems, 23*(3), 13.

Jain, C. L. (2004c). Business forecasting practices in 2003. *The Journal of Business Forecasting Methods & Systems, 23*(3), 2.

Joachims, T. (1999). Making large-scale SVM learning practical. Advances in Kernel Methods - Support Vector Learning.

Kim, C. N., & McLeod, R. J. (1999). Expert, linear models, and nonlinear models of expert decision making in bankruptcy prediction: A lens model analysis. *Journal of Management Information Systems, 16*(1), 189-206.

Kimbrough, S. O., Wu, D. J., & Zhong, F. (2002). Computers play the beer game: Can artificial agents manage supply chains? *Decision Support Systems, 33*(3), 323.

Lambert, D. M., & Lalonde, B. J. (1976). Inventory carrying costs. *Management Accounting, 58*(2), 31.

Landt, F. W. (1997). *Stock price prediction using neural networks*. Leiden University, Leiden, Netherlands.

Lee, H. L., Padmanabhan, V., & Whang, S. (1997a). The bullwhip effect in supply chains. *Sloan Management Review, 38*(3), 93.

Lee, H. L., Padmanabhan, V., & Whang, S. (1997b). Information distortion in a supply chain: The bullwhip effect. *Management Science, 43*(4), 546.

MacKay, D. J. C. (1992). Bayesian interpolation. *Neural Computation, 4*(3), 415-447.

Makridakis, S., Andersen, A., Carbone, R., & Fildes, R. (1982). The accuracy of extrapolation (time series) methods: Results of a forecasting competition. *Journal of Forecasting* (pre-1986), *1*(2), 111.

Makridakis, S., Chatfield, C., Hibon, M., Lawrence, M., Mills, T., Ord, K., et al. (1993). The M2-competition: A real-time judgmentally based forecasting study. *International Journal of Forecasting, 9*(1), 5.

Makridakis, S., & Hibon, M. (1979). Accuracy of forecasting: an empirical investigation (with discussion). *Journal of the Royal Statistical Society. Series A (General), 142*(2), 97-145.

Makridakis, S., & Hibon, M. (2000). The M3-competition: Results, conclusions and implications. *International Journal of Forecasting, 16*(4), 451.

Marquardt, D. W. (1963). An algorithm for least-squares estimation of nonlinear parameters. SIAM *Journal of Applied Mathematics, 11*, 431-441.

MathWorks, Inc. (2005a). *Financial time series toolbox for use with MATLAB*. Natick: MA: MathWorks Inc.

MathWorks, Inc. (2005b). *GARCH toolbox for use with MATLAB*. Natick: MA: MathWorks Inc.

MathWorks, Inc. (2005c). *Getting started with MATLAB*. Natick: MA: MathWorks Inc.

MathWorks, Inc. (2005d). *Neural network toolbox for use with MATLAB*. Natick: MA: MathWorks Inc.

MathWorks, Inc. (2005e). *Optimization toolbox for use with MATLAB*. Natick: MA: MathWorks Inc.

Mukherjee, S., Osuna, E., & Girosi, F. (1997). Nonlinear prediction of chaotic time series using support vector machines. Paper presented at the {IEEE} Workshop on Neural Networks for Signal Processing {VII}, Ameila Island, FL, USA.

Premkumar, G. P. (2000). Interorganization systems and supply chain management: An information processing perspective. *Information Systems Management, 17*(3), 56.

Proctor and Gamble, Co. (2005). *2004 annual report.* Cincinnati: Proctor and Gamble Co.

Raghunathan, S. (1999). Interorganizational collaborative forecasting and replenishment systems and supply chain implications. *Decision Sciences, 30*(4), 1053.

Rüping, S. (2005). *mySVM-Manual:* Universitat Dortmund, Lehrstuhl Informatik 8.

Russell, V. L. (2001). Some practical guidelines for effective sample size determination. *The American Statistician, 55*(3), 187.

Statistics Canada. (2005). Monthly survey of manufacturing (Code 2101) (Publication no. Table 304-0014). Retrieved April 2005, from Statistics Canada.

Stitt, B. (2004). Demand planning: Pushing the rest Of the company to drive results. *The Journal of Business Forecasting Methods & Systems, 23*(2), 2.

Tan, K. C. (2001). A framework of supply chain management literature. *European Journal of Purchasing & Supply Management, 7*(1), 39-48.

Vakharia, A. J. (2002). E-business and supply chain management. *Decision Sciences, 33*(4), 495.

Vapnik, V. N. (1995). The nature of statistical learning theory. New York: Springer-Verlag.

Vapnik, V. N. Golowich, S., & Smola, A. (1997). Support vector method for function approximation, regression estimation, and signal processing. *Advances in Neural Information Systems, 9,* 281-287.

Walczak, S. (2001). An empirical analysis of data requirements for financial forecasting with neural networks. *Journal of Management Information Systems, 17*(4), 203-222.

Werbos, P. J. (1990). Backpropagation through time: what it does and how to do it. *Proceedings of the IEEE, 78*(10), 1550-1560.

Wisner, J. D., & Stanley, L. L. (1994). Forecasting practices in purchasing. *International Journal of Purchasing and Materials Management, 30*(1), 22.

Yusuf, Y. Y., Gunasekaran, A., Adeleye, E. O., & Sivayoganathan, K. (2004). Agile supply chain capabilities: Determinants of competitive objectives. *European Journal of Operational Research, 159*(2), 379.

Zhao, X., Xie, J., & Wei, J. C. (2002). The impact of forecast errors on early order commitment in a supply chain. *Decision Sciences, 33*(2), 251.

APPENDIX A. SELECTED CATEGORIES FROM STATISTICS CANADA MANU-FACTURING SURVEY

Category
Men's and boys' cut and sew shirt manufacturing
Glass manufacturing
Narrow fabric mills and Schiffli machine embroidery
Metal window and door manufacturing
Fabric coating
Office furniture (including fixtures) manufacturing
Motor vehicle metal stamping
Resin and synthetic rubber manufacturing
Other women's and girls' cut and sew clothing manufacturing
Women's and girls' cut and sew blouse and shirt manufacturing
Cold-rolled steel shape manufacturing
Automobile and light-duty motor vehicle manufacturing
Prefabricated metal building and component manufacturing
Mattress manufacturing
Fertilizer manufacturing
Power boiler and heat exchanger manufacturing
Stationery product manufacturing
Paint and coating manufacturing
Other industrial machinery manufacturing
Rubber and plastic hose and belting manufacturing
Hosiery and sock mills
Commercial and service industry machinery manufacturing
Particle board and fibreboard mills
Non-ferrous metal foundries
All other converted paper product manufacturing
Wood window and door manufacturing
Boat building
Wineries
All other general-purpose machinery manufacturing
Pulp mills
Non-chocolate confectionery manufacturing
Plastic bottle manufacturing
Men's and boys' cut and sew trouser, slack and jean manufacturing
Copper rolling, drawing, extruding and alloying
Audio and video equipment manufacturing
Flour milling and malt manufacturing

continued on following page

APPENDIX A. CONTINUED

Dairy product manufacturing
Railroad rolling stock manufacturing
Forging and stamping
Institutional furniture manufacturing
Ready-mix concrete manufacturing
Support activities for printing
Industrial gas manufacturing
Household furniture (except wood and upholstered) manufacturing
Other concrete product manufacturing
Non-ferrous metal (except copper and aluminum) rolling, drawing, extruding and alloying
Motor vehicle transmission and power train parts manufacturing
Spring and wire product manufacturing
Synthetic dye and pigment manufacturing
Sawmill and woodworking machinery manufacturing
Textile and fabric finishing
Jewellery and silverware manufacturing
Motor and generator manufacturing
Concrete reinforcing bar manufacturing
Corrugated and solid fibre box manufacturing
Motor vehicle transmission and power train parts manufacturing
Pump and compressor manufacturing
Other men's and boys' cut and sew clothing manufacturing
Women's and girls' cut and sew lingerie, loungewear and nightwear manufacturing
Nonwoven fabric mills
Other paperboard container manufacturing
Carpet and rug mills
Aerospace product and parts manufacturing
Poultry processing
Explosives manufacturing
Cut and sew clothing contracting
Motor home, travel trailer and camper manufacturing
Folding paperboard box manufacturing
Pharmaceutical and medicine manufacturing
Office supplies (except paper) manufacturing
Battery manufacturing
Small electrical appliance manufacturing
Construction machinery manufacturing
Plastics pipe, pipe fitting, and unlaminated profile shape manufacturing

continued on following page

APPENDIX A. CONTINUED

Other transportation equipment manufacturing
Petroleum refineries
Motor vehicle gasoline engine and engine parts manufacturing
Starch and vegetable fat and oil manufacturing
Knit fabric mills
Heavy-duty truck manufacturing
Artificial and synthetic fibres and filaments manufacturing
Paper (except newsprint) mills
Women's and girls' cut and sew suit, coat, tailored jacket and skirt manufacturing
Radio and television broadcasting and wireless communications equipment manufacturing
Soap and cleaning compound manufacturing
Power, distribution and specialty transformers manufacturing
Shingle and shake mills
Adhesive manufacturing
Motor vehicle plastic parts manufacturing
Wood preservation
Toilet preparation manufacturing
Other basic inorganic chemical manufacturing
Wood kitchen cabinet and counter top manufacturing
Wiring device manufacturing
Sign manufacturing
Steel foundries
Non-ferrous metal (except aluminum) smelting and refining
Semiconductor and other electronic component manufacturing
Urethane and other foam product (except polystyrene) manufacturing
Sawmills (except shingle and shake mills)

Chapter XIX
Supporting Demand Supply Network Optimization with Petri Nets

Teemu Tynjala
Nokia Group, Finland

ABSTRACT

The present study implements a generic methodology for describing and analyzing demand supply networks (i.e. networks from a company's suppliers through to its customers). There can be many possible demand supply networks with different logistics costs for a product. Therefore, we introduced a Petri Net-based formalism, and a reachability analysis-based algorithm that finds the optimum demand supply network for a user-specified product structure. The method has been implemented and is currently in production use inside all Nokia business groups. It is used in demand supply planning of both network elements and handsets. An example of the method's application to a concrete Nokia product is included.

INTRODUCTION

Logistics refers to the flow of materials, information and money between the suppliers and customers. A *demand supply network* refers to the manner in which components flow from suppliers to the manufacturer's plants, and finally to the end customers. The logistics costs associated with a demand supply network include such costs as freight, warehousing, interest rate, duties and taxes.

A typical problem that logistics professionals face in a global corporation is to find the cheapest and most reliable way of producing a product and delivering it to customers. Often the product structures and supplier bases vary considerably during a product design phase. The logistics manager must decide the most economical component suppliers and the best-positioned assembly factories over the product's lifecycle. Typically there are hundreds or thousands of different demand supply network setup options for a given product. Therefore, manual analysis of demand supply networks is practically impossible.

Companies have considerable incentives to optimize their end-to-end demand supply chains. Firms approach this problem in two fronts: optimization of manufacturing functions on one hand and the demand supply chains on the other. As such, several methods for demand supply network analysis have been introduced in the literature. Most solutions use operations research paradigm—mixed integer programming—or discrete simulation to analyze demand supply networks (Simchi-Levi et al., 2003; Bramel & Simchi-Levi, 1997).

Recently, the industry has seen several examples of disasters brought up by broken demand supply networks (Norrmann & Jansson, 2004). A logistics manager must know all the demand supply network options available to reduce possible risks. This enumeration requires reachability analysis where each path (i.e. a possible demand supply network setup) is explored. Also, dynamic analysis of demand supply networks is required to explore whether a chosen network responds well to fluctuating customer demand. Mathematical optimization gives the optimal setup quickly via analytic or heuristic methods (Powers, 1989). However, optimization methods do not support the analysis of network dynamics. Discrete simulation, on the other hand, is excellent in dynamic analysis of a single demand supply network (Bowersox & Closs, 1989). Yet, it lacks the capability of choosing the best network structures, given by optimization. Thus, interplay of both techniques is required for a logistics professional to choose the best possible network (Riddalls, Bennett & Tipi, 2000). Simulation-optimization (Azadivar, 1999; Truong & Azadivar, 2003) has been developed to combine the advantages of optimization and simulation. However, the modelling languages used in optimization and simulation are very different from one another, and this creates a challenge for the co-use of the methods (Azadivar, 1999).

Petri Nets have been used successfully in modeling various kinds of systems, including telecommunication protocols and workflow systems (Jensen, 1996; van der Aalst, 1998). The hypothesis of this research was that reachability analysis is adaptable to solving small and medium size demand supply network optimization problems. As there are Petri net tools capable of dynamic simulation (van der Aalst, 1992; ExSpect, 1999), such addition would provide a single methodology amenable to both, static and dynamic analysis. Therefore, my research question became: **"How to apply reachability analysis in demand supply network analysis?"**

The result was a generic Petri Net model for describing arbitrary demand supply network options, and a reachability analysis algorithm that computes the network setups and costs from the Petri Net model. A Web-based analysis tool based on the methodology was constructed during 2004 and has been in production use since February 2005.

The rest of the chapter is organized as follows: the remainder of the introduction reviews the current approaches to demand supply network analysis. Section 2 gives the generic Petri Net model for demand supply networks through example and formal definitions. Section 3 presents the reachability analysis algorithm for the model. Section 4 presents a concrete Nokia case for the tool use. Section 5 concludes with discussion and future work.

Literature Review

The literature contains multiple methods for analyzing demand supply networks. Next, I describe Operations Research methods (Zeng & Rossetti, 2003; Thomas & Griffin, 1996; Vidal & Goetschalckx, 2001; Fandel & Stammen, 2004), Analytic Hierarchy Processes (Wang, Huang,& Dismukes, 2004; Dotoli et al., 2005), control theoretical methods (Ortega & Lin, 2004), discrete simulation methods (Persson & Olhager, 2002), simulation optimization (Azadivar, 1999; Truong & Azadivar, 2003), and Workflow net related methods (vad der Aalst, 1998a; van der Aalst, 1998b; van der Aalst & ter Hofstede, 2005; Desel & Erwin, 2000). Each of these methods fits into one of four categories: deterministic analytical, stochastic analytical, economic or simulation (Beamon, 1998). The six methods are briefly described along with their position in Beamon's categorization.

Operations research has been used to analyze demand supply network problems at least since the early 1970's (Zeng & Rossetti, 2003; Thomas & Griffin, 1996). These methods have been used primarily in plant and inventory location problems (Bowersox & Closs, 1989). Optimization methods were the first technique to be used in demand supply network analysis, where the focus was on cost reduction given a static customer service level (Bowersox & Closs, 1989; p. 139-40). The first mathematical programs had drawbacks, such as the possibility of analyzing only single transport modes, but the mixed integer programs have been developed to include multiple transport modes, transfer pricing (Vidal & Goetschalckx, 2001), development and recycling costs (Fandel & Stammen, 2004). Currently, mixed integer programs are the most powerful methods of finding the single best solution for very large problems. In finding the optimum, they converge to the result rather than enumerating the entire solution space. operations research methods are deterministic analytical, however, so they must be augmented with simulation to understand the dynamic behaviour of solutions (Riddalls, Bennett, & Tipi, 2000).

Analytic hierarchy processes (Wang, Huang, & Dismukes, 2004) can be employed in situations where each level in the product hierarchy has a large number of possible suppliers. Analytic hierarchy process uses balanced scorecard approach with set criteria to determine the best supplier choices (without regard to the complete product structure) for a single component. In the second stage of the analysis, the best supplier choices for each component are fed into preemptive goal programming for the entire product structure. This approach fits in situations where there are tens or hundreds of possible suppliers for each component, and a short list is needed first. However, it also requires expert knowledge to faithfully compare one supplier against another. Analytic Hierarchy Process is a deterministic analytical method.

Control theoretical methods for demand supply network analysis have recently surfaced as they provide an analytical method for estimating bullwhip effects in demand supply networks (Ortega & Lin, 2004). The demand supply networks are modeled in z-space, and z-transforms are used to arrive at Bode plots for dynamic behaviour. This method can analyze only one demand supply network setup at a time, but it has the benefit of estimating system dynamics without discrete simulation. However, the modeling of supply networks in Z-space requires expert knowledge, which may be a drawback in the business environment. Control theoretical methods of demand supply network analysis are stochastic analytical in nature.

Discrete simulation methods allows for dynamic analysis of a single demand supply network (Persson & Olhager, 2002). An arbitrary demand signal may be fed to the network, and simulation determines possible stockouts and order fulfillment lead time violations. The advantage of discrete simulation over control theoretical methods is the ease of specifying input signals, and the increasing processing power of computers keeps simulation runtimes reasonable. Discrete simulation is currently viewed as a de facto standard of analyzing dynamic behaviour of demand supply networks (Riddalls, Bennett, & Tipi, 2000). However, discrete simulation is incapable of network optimization – i.e. the user must specify the network structure to be simulated herself.

Recently, simulation optimization emerged as a way of combining the static analysis power of optimization and dynamic analysis power of simulation (Azadivar, 1999; Truong & Azadivar, 2003). This method is a combination of "what-if" and "how-to" questions (Azadivar, 1999). In answering "what-if" questions, a candidate demand supply network is simulated against a demand pattern to determine its agility. "How-to" questions use optimization to answer questions such as how many line operators should be used in each manufacturing line. There are theoretical methods of solving simulation optimization problems, such as simulated annealing and response surface methods (Azadivar, 1999) but these are computationally expensive. In practice, analyses iterate between optimization and simulation. Optimization proposes a demand supply network including e.g. the number of line operators, and the location and size of inventories. The proposed solution is then simulated N times to see if it fulfills network agility criteria. If it does not, the simulation proposes changes to the parameter to set to be used in optimization, and a new iteration begins. This "metaheuristic" for simulation optimization does not guarantee solution convergence, but it has other useful properties such as the ability to generate multiple alternative solutions (April et al., 2005; p.9). In Beamon's categorization simulation optimization covers deterministic analytical and simulation methods.

Workflow nets (van der Aalst, 1998a; van der Aalst 1998b; van der Aalst, 2000; van der Aalst & ter Hofstede, 2005) have been introduced in Petri Net community to analyze the dynamics of business processes. Workflow net is a stochastic analytical method for a single demand supply network. Each DSNnet setup (topic of the current chapter) may be refined to a workflow net for dynamic analysis. Process nets (Desel & Erwin, 2000) have also been used in Petri Net community to analyze business processes. In this technique, the user specifies demand supply network skeletons of interest, without any cost parameters. When the interesting skeletons are determined, actual cost parameters are inserted and analysis and simulation routines are run. This approach is useful when the number of possible demand supply network skeletons and suppliers is low. However, in situations where there are thousands of possibilities, the user involvement required may be too great. The DSNnet takes a different approach. The cost parameters are specified first for all possible suppliers of components, and the possible demand supply networks are determined via reachability analysis and are ordered by average cost.

Research Methodology

The current chapter uses constructive paradigm (Kasanen, Lukka, & Siitonen, 1993), where Petri Net theory is employed to solve a concrete business problem. The resulting solution is applied to solving demand supply network analysis problems in Nokia more efficiently than earlier spreadsheet methodologies. The present work gives all the applicable decision algorithms and discusses validation issues. The research is done in the spirit of pragmatism (McDermott, 1976), where a theory's practical evidence is tested in real life: if it works, it is true

.

DSN NET: NET FORMALISM FOR DEMAND SUPPLY NETWORKS

Introduction and Motivation

A demand supply network (DSNnet in the rest of this chapter) may be seen as a net whose topmost node is the combination of a product and its customer. All the nodes below contain the product's constituent modules (according to the product structure) and their alternative suppliers. Consider the simple product structure in Figure 1. The final product is called "End Product", and it consists of two child modules, "Module B" and "Module C".

Figure 1. Simple product structure

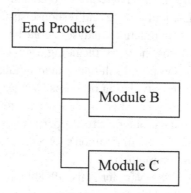

An example of a scenario which a logistics professional may consider could be described as follows:

- End Product will have one customer
- End Product will have only one supplier, "End Product Manufacturer". In this case the End Product is produced by the manufacturer itself, but the method also supports the analysis of contract manufacturers
- Module B can be sourced from two suppliers, and the sourcing options are:
  - Purchase all components from "Supplier 1 for Module B"
  - Buy 60% of the volume from "Supplier 1 for Module B" and 40% of the volume from "Supplier 2 for Module B"
- Module C has two suppliers and the sourcing options are:
  - Buy 100% of the volume from "Supplier 1 for Module C"
  - Buy 100% of the volume from "Supplier 2 for Module C"

Evidently the notion of choice and aggregation is vital in formalism for demand supply network options. Aggregation (AND logic) is needed for situations where a module has several parallel child modules. Choice (OR logic) is needed to describe alternative suppliers. Moreover, an OR may be immediately followed by an AND if two or more suppliers are simultaneously used to source a component in a given volume split.

The central idea of the DSNnet is to combine seamlessly the product structure and the associated demand supply network. The design of a product in parallel with its demand supply network renders a company's product design process more effective (Prasad, 1986). This mode of operation also requires specialized tool support. The logistics professional is looking for a tool where he can:

1. Choose the bill of materials for a product (key components)
2. Input the possible suppliers and associated costs for every component
3. Input the customers and their demand volumes

The logistics professional expects a computer to give all possible demand supply network combinations and associated costs for the input entered. The DSNnet instance in Figure 2 depicts the sourcing options for the product structure in Figure 1. Notice the inclusion of 'AND' nodes before single suppliers. Since volume splits between multiple suppliers are possible at every tier of the supply chain, the generic translation routine from product structure to DSNnet includes an AND-node after every OR-node. The AND node is really needed only in the 60/40 split of Suppliers 1 and 2 for Module B in Figure 2.

After the generation of DSNnet above, a reachability analysis algorithm is executed to determine the demand supply network options and costs for each. For this example, there were no costs specified but the possible demand supply networks are:

1.   End Product Manufacturer – 100% volume
        Supplier 1 for Module B – 100% volume
        Supplier 1 for Module C – 100% volume
2.   End Product Manufacturer – 100% volume
        Supplier 1 for Module B – 100% volume
        Supplier 2 for Module C – 100% volume
3.   End Product Manufacturer – 100% volume
        Supplier 1 for Module B – 60% volume
        Supplier 2 for Module B – 40% volume
        Supplier 1 for Module C – 100% volume

Figure 2. DSNnet describing sourcing options for the product in Figure 1

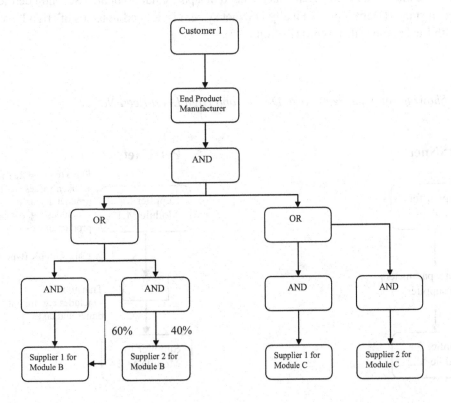

4.   End Product Manufacturer – 100% volume
       Supplier 1 for Module B – 60% volume
       Supplier 2 for Module B – 40% volume
       Supplier 2 for Module C – 100% volume

DSNnet does not resemble a Petri Net since the notion of transitions is missing as in Figure 2. However, between each pair of nodes a logistics network will incur e.g. freight and duty costs and these elements are included inside a transition. The transitions are not drawn in the figure for notational convenience, but Figure 3 shows an equivalent High Level Petri net interpretation of a DSNnet instance. As indicated, the color of each place is the real number type and each arc contains a variable for a single real number token. Petri Net interpretations of AND and OR nodes are presented in Figures 4 and 5, respectively. AND-OR logic for Petri Nets was first introduced in (Baer, 1973; Agerwala & Flynn, 1973).

The above formalism satisfies the modeling requirements for network alternatives but the issue of data has not yet been addressed. The cost elements pertinent to logistics change from industry to industry, and some cost elements such as obsolescence rate per annum are very different for if one is selling bricks (low obsolescence rate) or mobile phones (high obsolescence rate). To address this requirement it is vital to have "metadata" on the types of cost elements as well as their values related to particular industry or firm. This metadata approach is adopted in the formal definitions below.

Formal Definitions

The definition of DSNnet is divided into three parts. First, I define DSNnet_skeleton (Definition 1), which gives the metadata for cost elements included in a particular company. Second I define a particular DSNnet instance (Definition 2). Finally DSNnet system is defined in terms of High Level Petri Net system with Real number data types (Definition 3).

Figure 3. Showing equivalence between DSNnet and High Level Petri Net

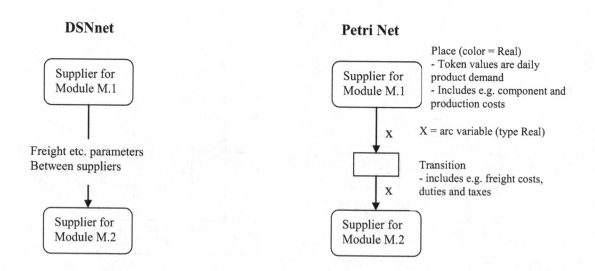

372

Figure 4. Semantics of DSNnet AND node

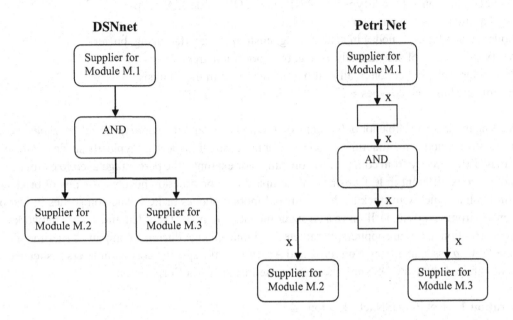

Figure 5. Semantics of DSNnet OR node

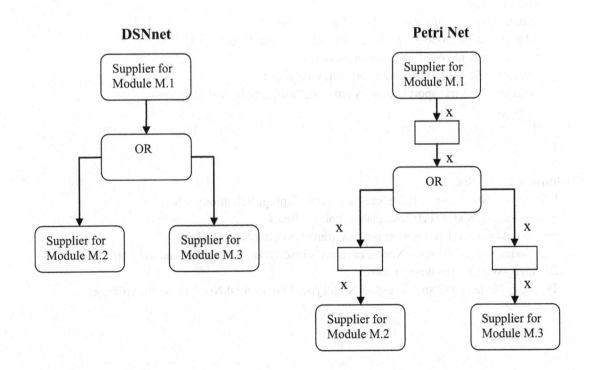

Definition 1

DSNnet_skeleton = { NodeTypes $\cup$ { AND_node, OR_node }, ArcTypes,
    ParameterPool, ParameterMap }, where

NodeTypes = types of nodes in analysis (e.g. customer, manufacturing, buffer)

ArcTypes = types of arcs in analysis (e.g. transportation arcs)

ParameterPool = collection of all cost parameters used in the analysis

ParameterMap $\subseteq$ NodeTypes $\times 2^{\text{ParameterPool}} \cup$ ArcTypes $\times 2^{\text{ParameterPool}}$

A company is responsible for defining its own DSNnet_skeleton. *NodeTypes* and *ArcTypes* are standard—customer node, manufacturing node, buffer node, and transport arc typically suffice. *ParameterPool* may differ greatly from company to company. For example, the percentage used to estimate stock obsolescence is different in ICT business as compared to construction business - value of bricks does not diminish as quickly in stock as that of unsold mobile phones or PCs. The companies in fast price erosion environments (e.g. Dell) have a stronger incentive to make their demand supply networks agile than construction material suppliers. ParameterPool may change during a company's lifetime. Finally, *ParameterMap* associates each NodeType and ArcType to the specific cost parameters associated with it. To illustrate, I show the DSNnet_skeleton in use inside Nokia Corporation.

Illustration 1 – Nokia's DSNnet_skeleton

{ NodeTypes = { Customer, Manufacturing, Buffer } $\cup$ { AND_node, OR_node},

ArcTypes = { DSNarc },

ParameterPool = { bill of materials cost, buffer inventory carrying cost,
    transport inventory carrying cost, freight cost, production cost,
    investment cost, duty cost, tax cost, manufacturing line verification cost,
    sales volume },

ParameterMap = { Customer node $\mapsto$ { sales volume },

    Manufacturing node $\mapsto$ { bill of materials cost, production cost,
        investment cost, line verification cost },

    Buffer node $\mapsto$ { buffer inventory carrying cost },

    DSNarc $\mapsto$ { transport inventory carrying cost, freight cost, duty cost,
     tax cost }

    }

}

Definition 2 – DSNnet

DSNnet = { Nodes, Arcs, F, DSNnet_skeleton, Typing, Valuation}, where

Nodes = set of Nodes (Petri Net places, color = Real)

Arcs = set of Arcs (Petri Net transitions, transition guards are TRUE)

F $\subseteq$ Nodes $\times$ Arcs $\cup$ Arcs $\times$ Nodes, each arc's inscription is X, a Real number variable

DSNnet_skeleton = as defined above

Typing $\subseteq$ Nodes $\times$ DSNnet_skeleton.NodeTypes $\cup$ Arcs $\times$ DSNnet_skeleton.ArcTypes

Valuation = **V**(Nodes, Arcs, Typing) – a function that assigns relevant parameter values to each node and arc according to its type (joint responsibility of tool user and the user interface in real world)

Definition 3 – DSNnet_system

DSNnet_system = { DSNnet, $Nodes_0$, M_0 : $Nodes_0 \mapsto Real$ }

A DSNnet_system has a valid DSNnet structure, a set of initial nodes (Customer nodes) $Nodes_0$, and initial marking M_0 that maps a single token of type Real to each initial node (this value represents a customer's average daily demand for a certain product). The firing rule for DSNnet_system is that of High Level Petri Nets.

REACHABILITY ANALYSIS OF DSN NET

The traditional Petri Net reachability analysis algorithm computes all reachable system states. In DSN-net formalism, reachability analysis differs in two important points:

1. The algorithm computes all possible paths of a system (valid DSNnet structures are directed and acyclic, guaranteeing the absence of infinite paths)
2. The algorithm allows for several initial states, and aggregates the separate reachability graphs to a single result

The result of the reachability analysis is a list of complete paths in the DSNnet, each associated with a cost. The optimum path is the one with the lowest cost. In DSNnet context, a reachability graph is an array of arrays (matrix) where each component array (matrix column) is one demand supply network setup with its cost.

The pseudocode for the algorithm is presented next. RG is used as a shorthand for "reachability graph", and arrays are indexed in C language style from 0 to array_size-1. The pseudocode uses four helper functions: *append_node*, *append_RG*, *aggregate_RG* and *add_per_item_costs*. *Append_node* appends a node (first argument) to all paths in the reachability graph (second argument). *Append_RG* joins two reachability graphs to form a single reachability graph – i.e. the appending of RG1 with 5 paths and RG2 with 3 paths results in a single RG with 8 paths. *Aggregate_RG* takes the Cartesian product of two reachability graphs, where each path in the resulting reachability graph has a cost equal to the sum of the two constituents. The Cartesian product of RG1 with 5 paths and RG2 with 3 paths has 15 paths. Finally, *add_per_item_costs* adds the costs of an arc or a node (the first argument) to each path in the reachability graph (the second argument). The preliminary version of the algorithm has been published in (Tynjälä, 2006).

Main DSNnet Analysis Routine

The main analysis routine is given in Algorithm 1. The investment costs are computed last because several customers can source their products from the same suppliers (manufacturing nodes). The total volumes for each supplier are known when the second for-loop has been executed. The second for loop – aggregation of individual customers' reachability graphs – is also the source of the algorithm's computational

Algorithm 1. Main Analysis Routine

```
RG_main(DSNnet_system – cf. Definition 3) returns all DSN setups with cost {
    RG[] = array of new Reachability Graphs;
    total_RG = new Reachability Graph;
    for each initial customer node do
        RG[i] = RG_1_customer(customer_node[i]);
    end
    for i = 0..number of customer nodes -1 do
        total_RG = aggregate_RG( total_RG, RG[i]);
    end
    for each path in total_RG do
        investment_cost = compute_investments(path);
        add investment_cost to the path's cost;
    end
    return total_RG;
}
```

complexity. For, assume that we have C customers and P is the maximum of the number of DSN setup options for a customer. Then the size of the state space (and computation time) grows exponentially as $O(P^C)$. Parallelizing this part of the algorithm is included in the topics for future research.

Reachability Analysis Routine for a Single Customer Node

The algorithm that computes the reachability graph for one customer is presented in Algorithm 2. It follows the traditional reachability analysis algorithm with the addition of AND and OR nodes.

This part of the algorithm computes investment costs that depend on production volume in a stepwise manner. For example, if a manufacturing line capacity for a particular phone is 7500 phones per day, this algorithm computes the number of needed manufacturing lines based on total volume throughput, and calculates the needed investments.

Algorithm Validation

The algorithm was validated in two steps. First, a series of tests with different product structures and customers was carried out to ensure that the paths were computed correctly. This step concentrated on the correct functioning of the AND and OR nodes which were our additions to the traditional reachability analysis algorithm. In the second phase, the cost figures obtained for a single setup were compared with those obtained from the previous spreadsheet-based tool. The second validation phase uncovered some errors in cost computation, which were corrected and revalidated.

Algorithm 2. Reachability analysis routine for a single customer

```
RG_1_customer(Start Node with volume marking, Start RG) returns RG {
    RG[] = array of empty Reachability Graphs;
    theChildNodes[] = Array for children of AND and OR nodes;
    theChildArcs[] = Array for arcs leading to theChildNodes;
    Add volume marking to Start Node's total volume;
    if Start Node has 0 children then
        append_node(Start RG, Start Node);
        Start RG = add_per_unit_costs(Start RG, Start Node, NULL);
        return Start RG;
    else if Start Node has 1 childNode then
        childArc = DSN Arc between Start Node and childNode;
        append_node(Start RG, Start Node);
        Add volume marking from Start Node to childNode and childArc;
        Start RG = RG_1_customer(childNode, Start RG);
        Start RG = add_per_unit_costs(Start RG, Start Node, childArc);
        return Start RG;
    else if Start Node is AND then
        total_RG = new Reachability Graph;
        append_node(Start RG, Start Node);
        Add the volume marking to theChildNodes[] and theChildArcs[];
        for each theChildNodes[i] do
            RG[i] = RG_1_customer(theChildNodes[i], RG[i]);
        end
        for i = 0..number of Child Nodes-1 do
            total_RG = aggregate_RG(total_RG, RG[i]);
        end
        total_RG = aggregate_RG(Start RG, total_RG);
        return total_RG;
    else if Start Node is OR then
        total_RG = new Reachability Graph;
        append_node(Start RG, Start Node);
        Add the volume marking to theChildNodes[] and theChildArcs[];
        for each theChildNodes[i] do
            RG[i] = RG_1_customer(theChildNodes[i], RG[i]);
        end
        for i = 0..number of Child Nodes-1 do
            total_RG = append_RG(total_RG, aggregate_RG(Start RG, RG[i]));
        end
        return total_RG;
}
```

Algorithm 3. Computation of investment costs

```
Computation of Investment Costs
    compute_investments(one DSN setup) returns InvestmentCost {
        for each manufacturing node in setup do
            determine total volume throughput;
            determine number of manufacturing lines;
            InvestmentCost = InvestmentCost + (no. of manuf. lines * investment per line);
            end
            return InvestmentCost;
}
```

NOKIA IMPLEMENTATION AND CASE STUDY

Tool Implementation Method

The tool based on above formalism was developed in Java2 language, and embedded in the Oracle environment hosting demand supply planning data repository. The tool's Web user interface lets the logistics managers specify product structures, and costs for alternate suppliers. Common data such as transportation costs between cities, duty and tax rates are centrally updated by few key users. The Web UI has "analyze" button associated which invokes the Java algorithm. The Java algorithm first reads the database tables for product and supplier information, constructs the corresponding DSNnet instance, and runs the reachability analysis on it. Final results are stored in database tables and displayed in Web browser. Permissions to view data are granted in such a way that a normal user may see only his work when using the tool. Key users for each business group have view of all programs in that business unit. Finally, the global logistics directors see all programs in every business unit. The next subsection contains a real example of an analysis case for a product that started shipping in the summer of 2006.

Analysis of a New Handset

The product structure for the new handset that started to ship in the summer of 2006 is shown in Figure 6.

As indicated in the diagram modules A, B and H had 2 supplier options, with the rest having a single decided supplier. For a single customer this product structure produces 8 (2*2*2) demand supply network setups. The analysis covered two customers, so the total number of demand supply networks came to 64 (8^2). Interestingly, the static costs for the alternative suppliers of modules A, B and H (e.g. production costs, investment costs) were not radically different. However, their global position was such that the buffering and transportation costs associated with the total demand supply network were significantly different from one solution to another. For this product, whose expected lifetime is one year, the demonstrated cost differences from the cheapest to the most expensive demand supply network were ca. 15 Million Euros. The analysis tool was able to compute these 64 solutions in approximately 10

Figure 6. Product structure of a recently released Nokia handset

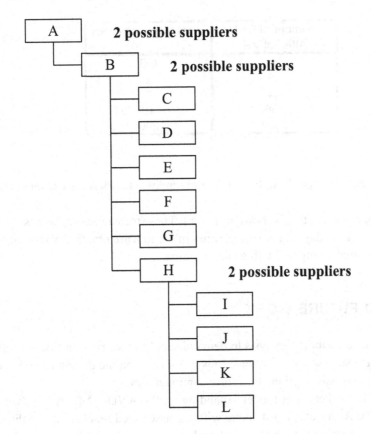

seconds, whereas the spreadsheet solution would have required several days (5 days with the optimistic target of 10 demand supply networks analyzed per day) to complete the job. The Nokia logistics team has established a target of one-week lead time for all demand supply network analyses (i.e. each week a new analysis report is generated based on the most current data). The spreadsheet method could not support this requirement because of time required for hand-generation of networks. With the new tool, this leadtime is feasible. The next subsection gives sample analysis times for problems of different complexity.

Usage and Performance Data in Nokia Environment

The tool has been actively used inside Nokia's business groups since February 10, 2005. The number of concrete product programs studied is over 300 at the end of January 2008. A product program represents a possible handset or network element under development that may or may not come to the market. The granularity of analyses is different in each business unit. The handset business units, where the volumes are large, consider few big customers, usually representing sales areas. The network business, where volumes are lower, relative logistics costs higher, and margins thinner, the granularity is more precise. The customers are modeled at least on a country level. A study where the method was applied

Table 1. Sample response times of Petri Net tool

Number of DSN Alternatives	Analysis time (sec)
4	0.5
16	2
64	7
256	40
1024	290

to determination of variant effect on the optimal demand supply network setup can be found in (Tynjälä & Eloranta, 2007).

The typical performance of the tool is shown in Table 1. These measurements were single data points taken during a typical working day. The response times of the tool are practically the same globally, as the transport delays are small compared to the analysis time.

DISCUSSION AND FUTURE WORK

Applying Petri Nets and reachability analysis to demand supply network optimization has the benefit of exploring the complete state space of options. In wake of risks on the demand supply network, it is vital to explore also the expensive options for future contingencies.

I developed a High Level Petri Net model expanding on the AND-AND, AND-XOR formalisms presented in (Baer, 1973; Agerwala, 1973), along with the associated reachability analysis algorithm. The Petri Net model is general and it may be employed in various types of businesses. In terms of expressive power, DSNnet stays within the normal Petri Net confines.

A tool based on the DSNnet methodology was developed during 2004 inside Nokia Corporation, and it has been in active use since February 2005. The tool has been used in all business units and the results are very positive. The users have especially thanked the possibility of designing the product structure together with its demand supply network, which was not possible with the former spreadsheet methods. The work relating to DSNnet tool inside Nokia is ongoing, and the second release of the tool became operational in October 2006. This release enhanced the tool with multimodal transport capabilities and improved duty and tax considerations. In the future, the tool is envisioned to become integrated to a data warehouse, which updates the cost and transport parameters automatically based on actual business transactions.

The current method may be used in aiding hierarchical "zoom-and-focus" analyses on demand supply networks. Simulation-optimization suffers from the fact that the modeling languages used in optimization and simulation are very different. This means that an off-the-shelf optimization engine is unable to directly export models to an arbitrary discrete simulation engine. Petri nets are a way of making transition from static to dynamic analysis realms straightforward (van der Aalst et al., 2000; Billington et al., 2003). An interface from ExSpect analysis tool to other Petri net simulation tools was easy to construct (van der Aalst et al., 2000; p.461). Moreover a Petri Net Markup Language (PNML) initiative has been formed to render the transfer of models between any Petri net tools possible (Billington et al.,

2003). Currently there are several tools that are able to import and export PNML specifications. The interval timed colored Petri net formalism invented by van der Aalst (van der Aalst, 1992) is the basis for the ExSpect analysis tool (ExSpect, 1999). This tool is able to model production systems hierarchically to more detailed levels and to perform stochastic analyses. Petri nets have also been recently used in designing shop floor scheduling (Artigues & Roubellat, 2001) and short-term batch plant scheduling (Ghaeli et al., 2005). An interesting avenue of future research would be the construction a PNML-based interface between the DSNnet tool of Nokia and ExSpect (and similar tools) which would allow the modeling and analysis of production systems from factory network level systematically down to manufacturing cell level.

REFERENCES

Agerwala, T., & Flynn, M. (1973). Comments on capabilities, limitations and "correctness" of Petri nets. *ACM Special Interest Group on Architectures (SIGARCH) Computer Architectures News, 2*(4), 81-86.

April, J., Better, M., Glover, F., Kelly, J. P., & Laguna, M. (2005). Enhancing business process management with simulation optimization. *BP Trends. January 2005.* Retrieved January 15, 2008, from http://www.bptrends.com/resources_publications.cfm?publicationtypeID=DFC61D66-1031-D522-3EBDAB1F65A451AA

Artigues, C., & Roubellat, F. (2001). A Petri net model and a general method for on and off-line multi-resource shop floor scheduling with setup times. *International Journal of Production Economics, 74,* 63-75.

Azadivar, F. (1999). Simulation Optimization Methodologies. In P.A. Farrington, H. B. Nembhard, D. T. Sturrock, and G. W. Evans,(Eds.), *Proceedings of the 1999 Winter Simulation Conference* (pp. 93-100). New York: ACM.

Baer, J. L. (1973). Modeling for parallel computation: A case study. In *Proceedings of the 1973 Sagamore Computer Conference on Parallel Processing* (pp. 13-22). IEEE catalog no. 73, CH0812-8.

Beamon, B. M. (1998). Supply chain design and analysis: Models and methods. *International Journal of Production Economics, 55,* 281-294.

Billington, J., Christensen, S., van Hee, K., Kindler, E., Kummer, O, Petrucci, L., Post, R., Stehno, C., & Weber, M. (2003). *The Petri Net markup language: Concepts, technology and tools.* (Lecture Notes in Computer Science, 2679, pp. 483-505).

Bowersox, D. J., & Closs, D. J. (1989). Simulation in logistics: A review of present practice and a look to the future. *Journal of Business Logistics, 10(1),* 133-48.

Bramel, J., & Simchi-Levi, D. (1997). *The Logic of logistics: Theory, algorithms and applications for logistics management.* New York: Springer.

Desel, J., & Erwin, T. (2000). *Modeling, simulation and analysis of business processes.* (Lecture Notes in Computer Science, 1806, pp. 129-141).

Dotoli, M., Fanti, M. P., Meloni, C., & Zhou, M. C. (2005). A multi-level approach for network design of integrated supply chains. *International Journal of Production Research, 43*(20), 4267-4287.

ExSpect (1999). *ExSpect 6.4 user manual.* Retrieved January 21, 2008, from www.exspect.com

Fandel, G., & Stammen, M. (2004). A general model for extended strategic supply chain management with emphasis on product life cycles including development and recycling. *International Journal of Production Economics, 89,* 293-308.

Ghaeli, M., Bahri, P. A., Lee, P., & Gu, T. (2005). Petri-net based formulation and algorithm for short-term scheduling of batch plants. *Computers and Chemical Engineering, 29,* 249-59.

Jensen, K. (1996). Coloured Petri Nets: Basic concepts, analysis methods and practical use. 2nd ed., Vol. 1, *EATCS Monographs on Theoretical Computer Science.* London: Springer.

Kasanen, E., Lukka, K., Siitonen, A. (1993). The constructive approach in management accounting research. *Journal of Management Accounting Research, 5*(3), 243-64.

Kindler, E., Martens, A., & Reisig, W. (2000). *Inter-operability of workflow applications: local criteria for local soundness.* (Lecture Notes in Computer Science, 1806, pp. 235-253).

McDermott, J. J. (Ed.) (1976). *The writings of William James: A comprehensive edition.* Chicago: The University of Chicago Press.

Norrmann, A., & Jansson, U. (2004). Ericsson's proactive supply chain risk management approach after a serious sub-supplier accident. *International Journal of Physical Distribution & Logistics Management. 34*(5), 434-456.

Ortega, M., & Lin, L. (2004). Control theory applications to the production-inventory problem: A review. *International Journal of Production Research, 42*(11), 2303-2322.

Persson, F., & Olhager, J. (2002). Performance simulation of supply chain designs. *International Journal of Production Economics, 77,* 231-245.

Powers, R. F. (1989). Optimization models for logistics decisions. *Journal of Business Logistics, 10*(1), 106-21.

Prasad, B. (1996). *Concurrent engineering fundamentals: Integrated product development.* Upper Saddle River, NJ: Prentice-Hall.

Riddalls, C. E., Bennett, S., & Tipi, N. S. (2000). Modelling the dynamics of supply chains. *International Journal of Systems Science, 31*(8), 969-976.

Simchi-Levi, D., Kaminsky, P., & Simchi-Levi, E. (2003). *Designing & managing the supply chain – Concepts, strategies & case studies,* 2nd edition. Burr Ridge, IL: McGraw-Hill.

Thomas, D. J., & Griffin, P.M. (1996). Co-ordinated supply chain management. *European Journal of Operations Research, 94,* 1-15.

Truong, T. H., & Azadivar, F. (2003). Simulation-based optimization for supply chain configuration design. In S. Chick, P.J. Sanchez, D. Ferrin, D., & D. J. Morrice, (Eds.) *Proceedings of 2003 Winter*

Simulation Conference (pp. 1268-75), IEEE.

Tynjälä, T. (2006). A formal, product structure driven design of optimized end-to-end demand supply chains. *Journal of Systemics, Cybernetics, and Informatics, 3*(1).Retrieved from www.iiisci.org/Journal/SCI/Past.asp

Tynjälä, T., & Eloranta, E. (2007). Investigating the effect of product variants, and demand distributions on the optimal demand supply network setup. *Production Planning & Control, 18*(7), 561-72.

Van der Aalst, W. M. P. (1992). *Timed coloured Petri nets and their application to logistics.* Unpublished doctoral dissertation. Eindhoven University of Technology, Eindhoven, The Netherlands.

Van der Aalst, W. M. P. (1998a). Modeling and analyzing interorganizational workflows. *Proceedings of Application of Concurrency to System Design* (pp. 262-272). Washington, DC: IEEE Computer Society.

Van der Aalst, W.M.P. (1998b). The application of Petri nets to workflow management. *Journal of Circuits, Systems and Computers, 8*(1), 21-66.

Van der Aalst, W.M.P. (2000). Loosely coupled interorganizational workflows: Modeling and analyzing workflows crossing organizational boundaries. *Information & Management, 37,* 67-75.

Van der Aalst, W. M. P., de Crom, P. J. N., Goverde, R. R. H., van Hee, K. M., Hofman, W. J., Reijers, H. A., & van der Toorn, R. A. (2000). *ExSpect 6.4: An executable specification tool for hierarchical colored Petri nets.* (Lecture Notes In Computer Science, 1825, pp. 455-464).

Van der Aalst, W. M. P., & ter Hofstede, A. H. M. (2005). YAWL: Yet another workflow language. *Information Systems, 30*(4), 245-275.

Vidal, C. J., & Goetschalckx, M. (2001). A global supply chain model with transfer pricing and transportation cost allocation. *European Journal of Operations Research, 129,* 134-158.

Wang, G., Huang, S. H. & Dismukes, J. P. (2004). Product-driven supply chain selection using integrated multi-criteria decision-making methodology. *International Journal of Production Economics, 91,* 1-15.

Zeng, A. Z., & Rossetti, C. (2003). Developing a framework for evaluating the logistics costs in global sourcing processes: An implementation and insights. *International Journal of Physical Distribution & Logistics Management, 33*(9), 785-803.

Compilation of References

Aaron, R. I. (1933). Locke's Theory of Universals. *Proceedings of the Aristotelian Society*, 33, 171-202.

Aaron, R. I. (1942). Hume's Theory of Universals. *Proceedings of the Aristotelian Society*. 42, 117-140.

Aaron, R. I. (1967). *The Theory of Universals*. (2nd. ed.) Oxford: Clarendon Press.

Aarts, C., et. al. (1992). *A relational theory of datatypes*. Technical report. The Netherlands: Utrecht University.

Adriaans, P., & Zantinge, D. (1996). *Data mining*. Harlow, UK: Addison-Wesley.

Agerwala, T., & Flynn, M. (1973). Comments on capabilities, limitations and "correctness" of Petri nets. *ACM Special Interest Group on Architectures (SIGARCH) Computer Architectures News, 2*(4), 81-86.

Agrawal, R., & Srikant, R. (1994). Fast algorithms for mining association rules. In *Proceedings of the 20th International Conference on Very Large Data Bases* (pp. 487-499).

Agrawal, R., & Srikant, R. (1995). Mining sequential patterns. In *Proceedings of the 11th International Conference on Data Engineering* (pp. 3-14).

Agrawal, R., Gehrke, J., Gunopulos, D., & Raghavan, P. (1998, June). Automatic subspace clustering for high dimensional data for data mining applications. In *Proceedings of the 1998 ACM SIGMOD Conference on Management of Data*, Seattle, WA.

Aguilera, M. K., Chen, W. & Toueg, S. (2000). Failure detection and consensus in the crash-recovery model. *Distributed Computing, 13*(2), 99-125.

Ahuja, N., & Rosefeld, A. (1978). A note on the use of second-order gray-level statistics for threshold selection. *IEEE Trans. Systems, Man, and Cybernatics, SMC (8)*, 895-898.

Akhter, F., Hobbs, D., & Maamar, Z. (2005). A fuzzy logic-based system for assessing the level of business-to-consumer (B2C) trust in electronic commerce. *Expert Systems with Applications, 28*,623–628.

Aknine, S., Pinson, S., & Shakun, M. F. (2004). A multi-agent coalition formation method based on preference models. *Group Decision and Negotiation, 13*, 513-538.

Albanese, M., Picariello, A., & Rinaldi A. (2004). A Semantic search engine for WEB information retrieval: An approach based on Dynamic Semantic Networks. *Semantic Web Workshop, ACM SIGIR 2004,* (pp. 25-29).

Allen, G. N., & March, S. T. (2003). Modeling temporal dynamics for business systems. *Journal of Database Management, 14*, 21-36.

Allen, G. N., & March, S. T. (2006). The effect of state-based and event-based data representations on user performance in query formulation tasks. *MIS Quarterly 30*, 269-290.

Allen, J., & Perrault, R. (1980). Analyzing intention in utterances. *Artificial Intelligence, 15(3)*, 11-18.

Allen, R. (1964). *Mathematical analysis for economists*. New York: St. Martin's Press.

AltaVista (2005). *AltaVista search engine*. Retrieved November, 2005, from http://www.altavista.com/

Alter, S. (2003). 18 reasons why IT-reliant work systems should replace 'The IT Artifact' as the core subject matter of the IS field. *Communications of the AIS, 12,* 365-394.

Alter, S. (2006). *The work system method: Connecting people, processes, and IT for business results.* Work System Press.

Amgoud, L., & Prade, H. (2003). A possibilistic logic modeling of autonomous agents negotiation. In *Epia* (p. 360-365).

Anderson, C. R., Domingos, P., & Weld, D. S. (2001). Adaptive web navigation for wireless devices. In *Proceedings of IJCAI-01 Workshop.* Seattle, WA.

Angluin, D. (1987). Queries and concept learning. *Machine Learning, 2*(4), 319-342.

Anklesaria, F., McCahill, M., Lindner, P., Johnson, D., Torrey, D., & Alberti, B. (1993). *The Internet Gopher Protocol (A distributed document search and retrieval protocol).* RFC 1436, University of Minnesota, March 1993.

Anonymous. (2005). Inventory carrying costs. *The Controller's Report,* (4), 5.

Antoniou, G., & van Harmelen, F. (2004). *A Semantic Web Primer.* Cambridge, MA: The MIT Press.

Anussornnitisarn, P., Nof, S. Y., & Etzion, O. (2005). Decentralized control of cooperative and autonomous agents for solving the distributed resource allocation problem. *International Journal of Production Economics, 98,* 114-128.

April, J., Better, M., Glover, F., Kelly, J. P., & Laguna, M. (2005). Enhancing business process management with simulation optimization. *BP Trends. January 2005.* Retrieved January 15, 2008, from http://www.bptrends. com/resources_publications.cfm?publicationtypeID=D FC61D66-1031-D522-3EBDAB1F65A451AA

Apte, C., & Weiss, S. (1997). Data mining with decision trees and decision rules. *Future Generation Computer Systems,* (13), 197-210.

Apté, C., Damerau, F., & Weiss, S. (1994). Towards language independent automated learning of text categorization models. In *Proceedings of the 17th ACM SIGIR Conference on Research and Development in Information Retrieval (SIGIR '94)* (pp. 23-30).

Araujo, I., & Araujo I. (2003). Developing trust in internet commerce. *In proceedings of the IBM conference of the Centre for Advanced Studies on Collaborative Research,* (pp. 1-15). Toronto, Canada.

Armstrong, D. M. (1989). *Universals: An Opinionated Introduction.* Boulder, CO: Westview Press.

Artigues, C., & Roubellat, F. (2001). A Petri net model and a general method for on and off-line multi-resource shop floor scheduling with setup times. *International Journal of Production Economics, 74,* 63-75.

Artz, J. (1997). A Crash Course in Metaphysics for the Database Designer. *Journal of Database Management,* 8(4).

Artz, J. (1998). Information Modeling and the Problem of Universals: A Preliminary Analysis of Metaphysical Assumptions. *Proceedings of the Association for Information Systems 1998 Americas Conference.*

Artz, J. (1999). An Analysis of Ontological Assumptions in Information Modeling. In Managing Information *Technology Resources in Organizations in the Next Millennium.* Mehdi Khosrow-pour (ed.) Idea Group Publishing.

Artz, J. (2001). A Teleological Approach to Information Systems Development. in *Managing Information Technology in a Global Economy.* Mehdi Khosrow-pour (ed.) Idea Group Publishing.

Artz, J. (2006). Conflicting Ontological Assumptions in Information Modeling. *Encyclopedia of Database Technologies and Applications.* Information Science Publishing.

Artz, J. M. (2007). Philosophical Foundations of Information Modeling. *International Journal of Intelligent Information Technologies, 3*(3).

Ashcraft, C., & Liu, J. (1998). Robust ordering of sparse matrices using Multisection. *SIAM Journal on Matrix Analysis and Applications, 19*(3), 816-832.

Ashish G., Saroj, K., Meher, & Uma, B. S. (2008). A novel fuzzy classifier based on product aggregation operator. *Pattern Recognition, 41*(3), 961-971.

Asoh, H., Motomura, Y., Hara, I., Akaho, S., Hayamizu, S., & Matsui, T. (1996). Acquiring a probabilistic map with dialogue-based learning. In H. Hexmoor and L. Meeden (Eds.), *ROBOLEARN '96: An International Workshop on Learning for Autonomous Robots,* (pp. 11-18).

Assimakopoulos, V., & Nikolpoulos, K. (2000). The theta model: A decomposition approach to forecasting. *International Journal of Forecasting, 16*(4), 521.

ATW (2008). *AlltheWeb search engine.* Retrieved March 1, 2008, from http://www.AlltheWeb.com/

Azadivar, F. (1999). Simulation Optimization Methodologies. In P.A. Farrington, H. B. Nembhard, D. T. Sturrock, and G. W. Evans,(Eds.), *Proceedings of the 1999 Winter Simulation Conference* (pp. 93-100). New York: ACM.

Ba, S., Lang, K. R., & Whinston, A. B. (1997). Enterprise decision support using Intranet technology. *Decision Support Systems, 2*(20), 99-134.

Baader, F., Calvanese, D., McGuinness, D., Nardi, D., & Patel-Schneider, P.F. (Eds.). (2003). *The description logic handbook: Theory, implementation and applications.* Cambridge: Cambridge University Press.

Baberwal, S., & Choi, B. (2004, November). Speeding up keyword search for search engines. *The 3rd IASTED International Conference on Communications, Internet, and Information Technology.* St.Thomas, VI.

Bacon, F. (2000). *The New Organon.* Jardine, L. and Silverthorne, M. (eds.) Cambridge Texts in the History of Philosophy. Cambridge University Press.

Baer, J. L. (1973). Modeling for parallel computation: A case study. In *Proceedings of the 1973 Sagamore Computer Conference on Parallel Processing* (pp. 13-22). IEEE catalog no. 73, CH0812-8.

Baeza-Yates, R., & Ribeiro-Neto, B. (1999). *Modern information retrieval.* Addison Wesley.

Baker, M. (1994). A model for negotiation in teaching-learning dialogues. *Journal of Artificial Intelligence in Education, 5*(2), 199-254.

Bambrough, R. (1961). Universals and Family Resemblances. *Proceedings of the Aristotelian Society, 61,* 207 - 222.

Banatre J.-P., & Le Metayer, D. (1993). Programming by multiset transformation. *CACM, 36*(1), 98-111.

Banatre, J.-P., & Le Metayer, D. (1990). The gamma model and its discipline of programming. *Science of Computer Programming, 15,* 55-77.

Banâtre, J.-P., Fradet, P., & Radenac, Y. (2004, July). Chemical specification of autonomic systems. In *Proceedings of the 13th International Conference on Intelligent and Adaptive Systems and Software Engineering (IASSE'04).*

Banâtre, J.-P., Fradet, P., & Radenac, Y. (2005). Higher-order chemical programming style. In *Proceedings of Unconventional Programming Paradigms.* (LNCS, 3566, 84-98). Springer-Verlag.

Banâtre, J.-P., Fradet, P., & Radenac, Y. (2005). Principles of chemical programming. In S. Abdennadher and C. Ringeissen (eds.), *Proceedings of the 5th International Workshop on Rule-Based Programming (RULE'04), 124,* ENTCS, (pp. 133-147).

Banko, M., Cafarella, M. J., Soderland, S., Broadhead, M., & Etzioni, O. (2007, January 6-12). Open information extraction from the Web. In *Proceedings of the 20th International Joint Conference on Artificial Intelligence (IJCAI 2007)*, Hyderabad, India.

Barbar'a, D., Chen, P., & Nazeri, Z. (2004). Self-similar mining of time association rules. In *8th Pacific Asia Conference on Knowledge Discovery and Data Mining,* (Lecture Notes in Artificial Intelligence, 3056, pp. 86-95).

Barroso, L. A., Dean, J., & Holzle, U. (2003). Web search for a planet: The Google cluster architecture. *IEEE Micro, 23*(2), 22-28.

Barry, C. L. (1998). Document representations and clues to document relevance. *Journal of the American Society for Information Science, 49*(14), 1293-1303.

Bartlett, P. S. (1955). *Stochastic processes.* Cambridge, UK: Cambridge University Press.

Basso, A., Goldberg, D., Greenspan, S., & Weimer, D. (2001). First impressions: Emotional and cognitive factors underlying judgments of trust E-Commerce. *In Proceedings of the 3rd ACM conference on Electronic Commerce,* (pp.137-143). Tampa, FL.

Bauer, F.L., et. al. (1985). *The Munich Project CIP, Vol. 1: The wide spectrum language.* CIP-L, (LNCS 183).

Baum, E. B., & Haussler, D. (1988). What size net gives valid generalization? *Neural Computation, 1,* 151-160.

Bayles, D. L. (2001). E-commerce logistics and fulfillment: Delivering the goods. New Jersey:Prentice Hall.

Bazan, J., Skowron, A., & Synak, P. (1994). Dynamic reducts as a tool for extracting laws from decision tables. In *Proceedings of the Symposium On Methodologies for Intelligent Systems* (pp. 346-355). Berlin: Springer-Verlag.

Beamon, B. M. (1998). Supply chain design and analysis: Models and methods. *International Journal of Production Economics, 55,* 281-294.

Benbasat, I., & Zmud, R. (2003). The Identity Crisis Within the IS Discipline: Defining and Communicating the Discipline's Core Properties. *MIS Quarterly.* 27(2),183-194.

Berkhin, P. (2002). *Survey of clustering data mining techniques.* (Tech. Rep.). San Jose, CA: Accrue Software.

Berners-Lee, T., Hendler, J., & Lassila, O. (2001). The Semantic Web. *Scientific American,* 36-43.

Berry, G., & Boudol, G. (1992). The chemical abstract machine. *Theoretical Computer Science, 96,* 217-248.

Berry, M. W., & Browne, M. (1999). Understanding Search Engines. Philadelphia: SIAM.

Bertsekas, D. P. (2000). *Dynamic programming and optimal control, 1.* Belmont, MA: Athena Scientific.

Beun, R.-J., & van Eijk, R. M. (2003). A cooperative dialogue game for resolving ontological discrepancies. In *Workshop on agent communication languages.* (Lecture notes in computer science, pp. 349-363).

Beun, R.-J., & van Eijk, R. M. (2005). Conceptual mismatches and repair in human-computer interaction. In *Proceedings of the Seventh Belgium-Netherlands Conference on Artificial Intelligence, BNAIC,* (pp. 315-316).

Billington, J., Christensen, S., van Hee, K., Kindler, E., Kummer, O, Petrucci, L., Post, R., Stehno, C., & Weber, M. (2003). *The Petri Net markup language: Concepts, technology and tools.* (Lecture Notes in Computer Science, 2679, pp. 483-505).

Binbasioglu, M. (1999). Problem structuring support for collaboration and problem solving. *Journal of Computer Information Systems, 40*(2), 54-63.

Bodart, F., Patel, A., Sim, M., & Weber, R. (2001). Should the optional property construct be used in conceptual modeling? A theory and three empirical tests. *Information Systems Research, 12,* 384-405.

Bolloju, N., Khalifa, M., & Turban, E. (2002). Integrating knowledge management into enterprise environments for the next generation decision support. *Decision Support Systems,* (33), 163-176.

Borlund, P., & Ingwersen, P. (1997). The development of a method for the evaluation of interactive information retrieval systems. *Journal of Documentation. 53*(3), 225-250.

Bowen, P. L., O'Farrell, R. A., & Rohde, F. H. (2004). How does your model grow? An empirical investigation of the effects of ontological clarity and application domain size on query performance. In *Proceedings of the International Conference on Information Systems,* Association for Information Systems, 77-90.

Bowersox, D. J., & Closs, D. J. (1989). Simulation in logistics: A review of present practice and a look to the future. *Journal of Business Logistics, 10(1),* 133-48.

Box, G., Jenkins, G. M., & Reinsel, G. (1994). *Time series analysis: Forecasting and control* (Third ed.). Englewood Cliffs: NJ: Prentice Hall.

Brachman, R., Khabaza, T., Kloesgen, W., Piatetsky-Shapiro, G., & Simoudis, E., (1996). Mining business databases. *Communications of ACM, 39*(11), 42-48.

Bradshaw, J. M., (1997). *Software agents.* Boston: MIT Press.

Brady, H. (2002, 16 July). *Models of causal inference: Going beyond the neyman-rubin-holland theory.* Seattle (WA).

Bramel, J., & Simchi-Levi, D. (1997). *The Logic of logistics: Theory, algorithms and applications for logistics management.* New York: Springer.

Brin, S., & Page, L. (1998). The anatomy of a large-scale hypertextual Web search engine. In *Proceedings of the Seventh World Wide Web Conference*, April 1998. Brisbane, Australia.

Brocklehurst, S., Littlewood, B., Olovsson, T., & Jonsson, E. (1994). On measurement of operational security. In *Proceedings of the Ninth Conference on Computer Assurance (COMPASS'94): Safety, Reliability, Fault Tolerance and Real Time, Security* (pp. 257-266).

Brooks Jr., F. P. (1987). No silver bullet: Essence and accidents of software engineering. *IEEE Computer, 20,* 10-19.

Budanitsky, A. (1999). *Lexical Semantic relatedness and its application in natural language processing.* (Technical report). Department of Computer Science, University of Toronto, Toronto, Canada.

Bunge, M. (1977). Ontology I: The furniture of the world, volume 3 of *Treatise on basic philosophy.* Boston: D. Reidel Publishing Company.

Burrell, G., & Morgan, G. (1979). *Sociological Paradigms and Organizational Analysis.* Heinemann, London.

Busse, S., Kutsche, R., Leser, U., & Weber, H. (1999). Federated information systems: Concepts, terminology, and architectures. *Federated information systems.* Retrieved from http://citeseer.ist.psu.edu/cache/papers/cs/8150/http:zSzzSzcis.cs.tu-berlin

Calinski, T., & Harabasz, J. (1974). A dendrite method for cluster analysis. *Communications in Statistics, 3*(1), 1-27.

Carr, N. (2003). IT doesn't matter. *HBR at Large.* May, 41-49.

Carson, C., Thomas, M., Belongie, S., Hellerstein, J. M., & Malik, J. (1999). Blobworld: A system for region-based image indexing and retrieval. *Third International Conference on Visual Information Systems*, Amsterdam, Netherland, pp. 509-516.

Casati, R., & Varzi, A. C. (1996). *Events.* Dartmouth Publishing Group (Ashgate).

Castelfranchi, C., & Pedone, R. (2003). *A review of trust in information technology.* The ALFEBIITE Project, http://alfebiite.ee.ic.ac.uk/docs/papers/D1/ab-d1-cas+ped-trust.pdf

Cazier, J. A., Shao, B. B. M., & Louis, R. D. St. (2006). E-business differentiation through value-based trust. *Information & Management, 43*(6), 718-727.

Center for the Digital Future (2004). *USC Annenberg School, The digital future report.* Retrieved from http://www.digitalcenter.org/downloads/DigitalFutureReport-Year4-2004.pdf

Cerri, S. A., & Jonquet, C. (2003). Apprentissage issu de la communication pour des agents cognitifs. *Technique et Science Informatiques, 22*(4), 83-87.

Chakrabarti, S., Dom, B. E., & Indyk, P. (1998). Enhanced hypertext categorization using hyperlinks. In L. M. Haas & A. Tiwary, (Eds.), *Proceedings of SIGMOD-98, ACM International Conference on Management of Data* (pp.307-318). New York: ACM Press,

Chan, H. W., Wong , K. M., & Lyu, R. (1993). Design ,implementation ,and experimentation on mobile agent security for electronic commerce application. In S. Mullender (Ed.), *Distributed systems* (2nd ed.) (pp. 199-216), Reading, MA: Addison-Wesley.

Chandra, C., & Grabis, J. (2005). Application of multisteps forecasting for restraining the bullwhip effect and improving inventory performance under autoregressive demand. *European Journal of Operational Research, 166*(2), 337.

Chang, Y. C., & Chen, S. M. (2006). A new query reweighting method for document retrieval based on genetic algorithms. *IEEE Transactions on Evolutionary Computation, 10*(5), 617-622.

Chang, Y. K., Cirillo, C., & Razon, J. (1971). Evaluation of feedback retrieval using modified freezing, residual collection & test and control groups. In G. Salton (Ed.), *The SMART retrieval system—experiments in automatic document processing,* (pp. 355-370).

Checkland, P. B. (1989). Soft Systems Methodology. *Human Systems Management, 8*(4), 271-289.

Chen, G., & Choi, B. (2008, March). Web page genre classification. *The 23rd Annual ACM Symposium on Applied Computing,* Ceará, Brazil.

Chen, P. (1976). The Entity Relationship Model: Towards a Unified View of Data. *Association of Computing Machinery Transactions on Database Systems*, 1(1).

Chen, P. P. S. (1976). The entity-relationship model-toward a unified view. *ACM Transactions on Database Systems, 1,* 9-36.

Chen, P. P. S., & Wong, L. (2005). A proposed preliminary framework for conceptual modeling of learning from surprises. *International Conference on Artificial Intelligence,* CSREA Press, 905-910.

Chen, S. Y. & Liu, X. (2005). Data mining from 1994 to 2004: An application-oriented review. *International Journal of Business Intelligence and Data Mining, 1*(1), 4-21.

Chen, Z., & Meng, X. (2002). MARS: Applying multiplicative adaptive user preference retrieval to Web

search. In *Proceedings of the International Conference on Internet Computing 2002,* (pp. 643-648).

Cheskin Research group (1999). *E-commerce study trust.* Retrieved from http://www.studioarchetype.com/cheskin/assets/images/etrust.pdf

Chess, D., Harrison, C. G., & Kershenbaum, A. (1998). Mobile agents: Are they a good idea? In G. Vigna (Ed.), *Mobile agents and security* (pp. 25-47). Springer-Verlag.

Cheung, C. & Lee, Matthew, K. O. (2000). Trust in Internet shopping: A proposed model and measurement instrument. In *Proceeding of the Americas Conference on Information System (AMCIS 2000),* Long Beach, California.

Choi, B. (2001, October). Making sense of search results by automatic webpage classifications. *WebNet 2001 World Conference on the WWW and Internet,* Orlando, FL.

Choi, B., & Dhawan, R. (2004, September). Agent space architecture for search engines. *The 2004 IEEE/WIC/ACM International Conference on Intelligent Agent Technology,* Beijing, China.

Choi, B., & Guo, Q. (2003). Applying semantic links for classifying web pages. *Developments in Applied Artificial Intelligence, IEA/AIE 2003, Lecture Notes in Artificial Intelligence,* 2718, pp.148-153.

Choi, B., & Peng, X. (2004). Dynamic and hierarchical classification of web pages. *Online Information Review, 28*(2), 139-147.

Choi, B., & Yao, Z. (2005). Web page classification. In W. Chu & T. Lin (Eds.), *Foundations and Advances in Data Mining* (pp. 221- 274). Springer-Verag.

Christophides, V. Karvounarakis, G., & Plexousakis, D. (2003). Optimizing taxanomic Semantic Web queries using labelling schemes. *Journal of Web Semantics, 1*(2), 207-228.

Cios, K., Pedrycz, W., & Swiniarski, R. (1998). *Data mining methods for knowledge discovery.* City: Norwell, MA, USA, Kluwer Academic Publishers.

Claude, I., Daire, J. L., & Sebag, G. (2004). Fetal brain MRI: Segmentation and biometric analysis of the posterior fossa. *IEEE Transactions on Biomedical Engineering, 51*(4), 617-626.

Cleverdon, C., Mills, J., & Keen, M. (1966). *Factors determining the performance of indexing systems.* (Technical report). ASLIB Cranfield Research Project, Cranfield.

Codd, E. F. (1970, June). A relational model of data for large shared data banks. *Communications of the ACM,* 377-387.

Cohan, P. S. (2000). E-profit: High-payoff strategies for capturing the e-commerce edge. New York: American Management Association.

Cohen, D., & Muylaert-Filho, J. (1996). Introducing a calculus for higher-order multiset programming. In *Coordination languages and models.* (LNCS 1061, 124-141).

Cohen, P., & Levesque, H. (1992). *Intentions in communication.* Bradford: Rational Interaction as the Basis for Communication. Bradford Books, MIT Press, seconde édition, chap. 12.

Cook, J. (2000, June). Cooperative problem-seeking dialogues in learning. In G. Gauthier, C. Frasson and K. VanLehn (Eds.), *Intelligent Tutoring Systems: 5th International Conference, ITS 2000 Montreal, Canada, 1839,* (pp. 615-624).

Cooper, W. S. (1968). Expected search length: A single measure of retrieval effectiveness based on weak ordering action of retrieval systems. *Journal of the American Society for Information Science, 19*(1), 30-41.

Corbitt B. J., Thanasankit T., & Yi H.(2003). Trust and e-commerce: A study of consumer perceptions. *Electronic Commerce Research and Applications,* (2), 203-215.

Cox, A., Sanderson, J., & Watson, G. (2001). Supply chains and power regimes: Toward an analytic framework for managing extended networks of buyer and supplier relationships. *Journal of Supply Chain Management, 37*(2), 28.

Creveuil, C. (1991). Implementation of gamma on the connection machine. In *Proceedings of the Workshop on Research Directions in High-Level Parallel Programming Languages,* Mont-Saint Michel, 1991. (LNCS 574, 219-230). Springer-Verlag.

Culnan, M. (1986). The Intellectual Development of Management Information Systems, 1972-1982: A Co-citation Analysis. *Management Science.* 32(2),156-172.

Cutler, M., Shih, Y., & Meng, W. (1997). Using the structure of HTML documents to improve retrieval. In *USENIX Symposium on Internet Technologies and Systems.*

Datta, R., Dhiraj, J., D., Li, J., & Wang, J. Z. (in press). Image retrieval: Ideas, influences, and trends of the New Age. *ACM Computing Surveys.*

Davidson, D. (1980). *Essays on actions and events.* Oxford University Press.

Davies, D., & Bouldin D. (1979). A cluster separation measure. *IEEE Transactions on Pattern Analysis and Machine Intelligence, 1*(4), 224-227.

Davis, E. W., & Spekman, R. E. (2004). *The extended enterprise: gaining competitive advantage through collaborative supply chains.* Upper Saddle River: NJ: FT Prentice Hall.

Davison, B. (2000). Topical locality in the Web. In *Research and Development in Information Retrieval (SIGIR)* (pp. 272-279).

de Figueiredo, R. J. P. (1980). Implications and applications of Kolmogorov's superposition theorem. *IEEE Transactions on Automatic Control, 25*(6), 1227–1231.

Defago, X., Schiper, A. & Sergent, N. (1998, October). Semi-passive replication. In *Proceedings of the 17th IEEE Symposium on Reliable Distributed System (SRDS'98)* (pp. 43-50).

Dejonckheere, J., Disney, S. M., Lambrecht, M. R., & Towill, D. R. (2003). Measuring and avoiding the bullwhip effect: A control theoretic approach. *European Journal of Operational Research, 147*(3), 567.

Desel, J., & Erwin, T. (2000). *Modeling, simulation and analysis of business processes.* (Lecture Notes in Computer Science, 1806, pp. 129-141).

Deshpande, M. & Karypis, G. (2000). *Selective markov models for predicting Web-page accesses.* (Tech. Rep. No. 00-056). University of Minnesota, IN.

Dhillon, I., Fan J., & Guan, Y. (2001). Efficient clustering of very large document collections. In R. Grossman, C. Kamath, P. Kegelmeyer, V. Kumar, & R. Namburu, (Eds.), *Data Mining for Scientific and Engineering Applications* (357-381). Kluwer Academic Publisher.

Djordjevic, D., & Izquierdo, E. (2007). An object- and user-driven system for Semantic-based image annotation and retrieval. *IEEE Transactions on Circuits and Systems for Video Technology, 17*(3), 313-323.

Dominik, S., Marcin, S., Szczuka & Jakub, W. (2004) Harnessing classifier networks: Towards hierarchical concept construction. *Rough Sets and Current Trends in Computing 2004,* (pp. 554-560).

Dorffner, G. (1996). Neural networks for time series processing. *Neural Network World, 96*(4), 447-468.

Dotoli, M., Fanti, M. P., Meloni, C., & Zhou, M. C. (2005). A multi-level approach for network design of integrated supply chains. *International Journal of Production Research, 43*(20), 4267-4287.

Draper, S., & Anderson, A. (1991). The significance of dialogue in learning and observing learning. *Computers and Education, 17*(1), 93-107.

Dretske, F. (1967). Can events move? *Mind, 76,* 479-92.

Dudoit, S., & Fridlyand, J. (2002). A prediction-based resampling method to estimate the number of clusters in a dataset. *Genome Biology, 3*(7), 1-21.

Ehrig, H., & Mahr, B. (1990). Fundamentals of algebraic specification. Brauer, W., Rozenberg, G., & Salomaa, A. (eds.), *EATCS Monographs on Theoretical Computer Science, 21,* Springer-Verlag.

Eirinaki, M. & Vazirgaiannis, M. (2003). Web mining for Web personalization. *ACM Transactions on Internet Technology, 3*(1), 1-27.

Elman, J. L. (1990). Finding structure in time. *Cognitive Science, 14*(2), 179-211.

Emtage, A., & Deutsch, P. (1992). Archie: An electronic directory service for the Internet. In *Proceedings of the USENIX Association Winter Conference,* (pp. 93-110). San Francisco.

Ester, M., Kriegel, H. P., Sander, J., & Xu, X. (1996). A density based algorithm for discovering clusters in large spatial database with noise. *International Conference on Knowledge Discovery in Databases and Data Mining,* Portland, OR.

Everitt, B. S., Landua, S., & Leese, M. (2001). *Cluster analysis.* London: Arnold.

ExSpect (1999). *ExSpect 6.4 user manual.* Retrieved January 21, 2008, from www.exspect.com

Fan, W., Lu, H., Madnick, S. E., & Cheung, D. (2002). DIRECT: A system for mining data value conversion rules from disparate data sources. *Decision Support Systems,* (34), 19-39.

Fandel, G., & Stammen, M. (2004). A general model for extended strategic supply chain management with emphasis on product life cycles including development and recycling. *International Journal of Production Economics, 89,* 293-308.

Farhoomand, A., & Drury, D. (2001). Diversity and Scientific Progress in the Information Systems Discipline. *Communications of the AIS, 5*(12).

Faulkner, S., & Kolp (Isys), M. (2002). *Towards an agent architectural description language for information systems.* School of Management, the Catholic University of Louvain (UCL), Technical Report, November 2002.

Fayyad, U. (2004). Data mining grand challenges. In *8th Pacific Asia Conference on Knowledge Discovery and Data Mining, LNAI, 3056* (p. 2).

Fayyad, U., Piatetsky-Shapiro, G., & Smyth, P. (1996). From data mining to knowledge discovery: an overview. In: U. Fayyad, G. Piatetsky-Shapiro, P. Smyth and R. Uthurusamy, (Eds.), *Advances in knowledge discovery and data mining*, (pp. 1-36). Cambridge, MA: AAAI/MIT Press.

Fensel, D., (2000). The Semantic Web and its languages. *IEEE Intelligent Systems*, Nov./Dec., 67.

Fiduccia, C. M., & Mattheyses, R. M. (1982, June). A Linear Time Heuristic for Improving Network Partitions. In *Proceedings 19th IEEE Design Automation Conference*. Las Vegas, NV.

FIPA2000 compliant agent development environment. (n.d.). Retrieved March 27, 2006, from http://jade.tilab.com

Fischer, M. J., Lynch, N. A. & Paterson, M. S. (1983, March). Impossibility of distributed consensus with one faulty process. In *Proceedings of the second ACM SIGACT-SIGMOD Symposium: Principles of Database System* (p. 17).

Flavin, M. (1981) *Fundamental Concepts of Information Modeling.* Yourdon Press.

Foresee, F. D., & Hagan, M. T. (1997). Gauss-Newton approximation to Bayesian regularization. In *Proceedings of the 1997 International Joint Conference on Neural Networks*, 1930-1935.

Forrester, J. (1961). *Industrial dynamics.* Cambridge: MA: Productivity Press.

Foundation for Intelligent Physical Agents (FIPA). (n.d.). Retrieved March 27, 2006, from http://www.fipa.org

Fox, M., *Barbuceanu, M.,* & Teigen, R. (2000). Agent-oriented supply chain management. *International Journal of Flexible Manufacturing Systems, 12*(2/3), 165-188.

Fradet, P., & Le Metayer, D. (1998). Structured gamma. *Science of Computer Programming, 31*(2-3), 263-289.

Frei, H. P., Meienberg, S., & Schauble, P. (1991). The perils of interpreting recall and precision values. In *Proceedings of GI/GMD-Workshop Information Retrieval*, (pp. 1-10).

Frias-Martinez, E., & Karamcheti, V. (2002). A prediction model for user access sequences, In *Proceedings of the Workshop on Web Mining for Usage Patterns and User Profiles*.

Fu, Y., Sandhu, K., & Shih, M. (1999). *Clustering of Web users based on access patterns.* International Workshop on Web Usage Analysis and User Profiling. San Diego, CA.

Garlan, D., Allen, R., & Ockerbloom, J. (1994, December). Exploiting style in architectural design environments. *In Proceedings of SIGSOFT'94: Foundations of Software Engineering*, New Orleans, Louisiana, (pp. 175-188).

Garlan, D., Monroe, R., & Wile, D. (1997, January). ACME: An architecture description interchange language. In *Proceedings of CASCON 97*, Toronto, (pp. 169-183).

Gasking, D. (1955, October). Causation and recipes. *Mind, New Series,* (256), 479-487.

Geerts, G. L., & McCarthy, W. E. (2002). An ontological analysis of the economic primitives of the extended-REA enterprise information architecture. *International Journal of Accounting Information Systems, 3*, March, 1-16.

Gemino, A. & Wand, Y. (2005). Complexity and clarity in conceptual modeling: Comparison of mandatory and optional properties. *Data and Knowledge Engineering, 55,* 301-326.

Genov, R., & Cauwenberghs, G. (2001). Charge-mode parallel architecture for matrix-vector multiplication. *IEEE Trans. Circuits and Systems II: Analog and Digital Signal Processing, 48*(10), 930-936.

Genov, R., & Cauwenberghs, G. (2003). Kerneltron: Support vector "machine" in Silicon. *IEEE Transactions on Neural Networks, 14*(5), 1426-1434.

Genov, R., Chakrabartty, S., & Cauwenberghs, G. (2003). Silicon support vector machine with on-line learning.

International Journal of Pattern Recognition and Artificial Intelligence, 17(3), 385-404.

Ghaeli, M., Bahri, P. A., Lee, P., & Gu, T. (2005). Petri-net based formulation and algorithm for short-term scheduling of batch plants. *Computers and Chemical Engineering, 29,* 249-59.

Ghemawat, S., Gobioff, H., & Leung, S.T., (1999). The Google file system. In *Proceedings of the 19th ACM Symposium on Operating Systems Principles*, vol. 400, (pp. 107-109).

Ghezzi, C. & Vigna, G. (1997, April). Mobile code paradigms and technologies: A case study. In K. Rothermet, R. Popescu-Zeletin (Eds.), *Mobile Agents, First International Workshop, MA'97, Proceedings, LNCS 1219* (pp. 39-49), Berlin, Germany. Springer.

Giles, C. L., Lawrence, S., & Tsoi, A. C. (2001). Noisy time series prediction using recurrent neural networks and grammatical inference. *Machine Learning, 44,* 161-184.

Gladitz, K., & Kuchen, H. (1996). Shared memory implementation of the gamma-operation. *Journal of Symbolic Computation 21,* 577-591.

Glymour, C. (2001). *The Mind's Arrows: Bayes Nets and Graphical Causal Models in Psychology.* Boston: MIT Press.

Goh, J. & Taniar, D. (2004). Mining frequency pattern from mobile users. *Knowledge-Based Intelligent Information & Engineering and Systems.* (Lecture Notes in Computer Science Part III, 3215, pp. 795-801).

Goh, J. & Taniar, D. (2004). Mobile user data mining by location dependencies. In *5th International Conference on Intelligent Data Engineering and Automated Learning,* (Lecture Notes in Computer Science, 3177, pp. 225-231).

Goh, J. & Taniar, D. (2005). Mining parallel pattern from mobile users. *International Journal of Business Data Communications and Networking, 1*(1), 50-76.

Google (2008). Google search engine: http://www.google.com/ last accessed March 1, 2008.

GoogleAPI (2008). Google Web APIs: http://www.google.com/apis/ last accessed March 1, 2008.

Gossain, S., Malhotra, A., & El Sawy, O. A. (2005). Coordinating for flexibility in e-business supply chains. *Journal of Management Information Systems, 21*(3), 7-45.

Gottlieb, A. (2002). *The Dream of Reason.* W.W. Norton & Company.

Goul, M., & Corral, K. (**2005**). Enterprise model management and next generation decision support *Decision Support Systems.* (**In Press**,) Corrected Proof, Available online 12 July 2005.

Gräfe, G. & Werner, L. (2004). Context-based information retrieval for improved information quality in decision-making processes. In K. Tochtermann & H. Maurer, (Eds.), *Proceedings of the 4ᵗʰ International Conference on Knowledge Management* (pp. 379-387). Graz, Austria.

Graham, M. E. (2004). Enhancing visual resources for searching and retrieval - Is content based image retrieval solution? *Literary and Linguistic Computing, 19*(3), 321-333.

Granger, C. W. J. (1980). Testing for causality. A personal viewpoint. *Journal of Economic Dynamic and Control, 2*(4), 329-352.

Granger, C. W. J. (2003). Some aspects of causal relationships. *Journal of Econometrics, 112*(2003), 69-71.

Grau, J. (2006). Retail e-commerce: Future trends. Retrieved from http://www.ecominfocenter.com/index.html?page=/infossources/websites/ststistics.html

Gray, P. (2003). Editorial: Introduction to the Debate on the Core of the Information Systems Field. *Communications of AIS.* 12(42).

Green, S. (2004). *Manager's guide to the Sarbanes-Oxley Act: Improving internal controls to prevent fraud.* Wiley Press.

Greenberg, M. S., Byington, J. C., & Harper, D. G. (1998). Mobile agents and security. *IEEE Communications Magazine, 367.*

Grigorova, A., De Natale, F. G. B., Dagli, C., & Huang, T. S. (2007). Content-based image retrieval by feature adaptation and relevance feedback. *IEEE Transactions on Multimedia, 9*(6), 1183-1192.

Griss M., & Pour, G. (2001). Accelerating development with agent components. *Computer, IEEE*, 37-43.

Gruber, T. R. (1993). A translation approach to portable ontology specifications. *Knowledge Acquisition, 5*(2), 199-220.

Grzymala-Busse, J., Pawlak, Z., Slowinski, R., & Ziarko, W. (1999). Rough Sets. *Communications of the ACM, 38*(11), 88-95.

Guha, S., Rastogi, R. & Shim, K. (1998, June). CURE: A Clustering Algorithm for Large Databases. In *Proceedings of the 1998 ACM SIGMOD Conference on Management of Data*. Seattle.

Guha, S., Rastogi, R. & Shim, K. (1999, March). ROCK: A Robust Clustering Algorithm for Categorical Attributes. In *Proceedings of the 15th International Conference on Data Engineering*, Sydney.

Gunasekaran, A., & Ngai, E. W. T. (2004). Information systems in supply chain integration and management. *European Journal of Operational Research, 159*(2), 269.

Guo, J., & Sun, C. (2004). Global electronic markets and global traditional darkets. *Electronic Markets 14*(1), 4-12.

Hacker, P. M. S. (1982). Events, ontology and grammar. *Philosophy, 57*, 477-486.

Hacker, P. M. S. (1982). Events and objects in space and time. *Mind, 91*, 1-19.

Hagan, M. T., & Menhaj, M. (1994). Training feedforward networks with the Marquardt algorithm. *IEEE Transactions on Neural Networks, 5*(6), 989–993.

Hagan, M. T., Demuth, H. B., & Beale, M. H. (1996). *Neural network design.* Boston: PWS Publishing.

Häkkilä, J. & Mäntyjärvi, J. (2005). Combining location-aware mobile phone applications and multimedia messaging. *Journal of Mobile Multimedia, 1*(1), 18-32.

Hamidi, H. & Mohammadi, K. (2005, March). Modeling and evaluation of fault tolerant mobile agents in distributed systems. In *Proceedings of the 2nd IEEE Conference on Wireless & Optical Communications Networks (WOCN2005)* (pp. 91-95).

Han, J. Dong, G., & Yin, Y. (1999). Efficient mining of partial periodic patterns in time series database. In *Proceedings of the International Conference on Data Engineering* (pp. 106-115).

Han, J., Gong, W., & Yin, Y. (1998). Mining segment-wise periodic patterns in time related databases. In *Proceedings of the 4th International Conference on Knowledge Discovery and Data Mining* (pp. 214-218).

Han, J., Pei, J., & Yin, Y. (2000). Mining frequent patterns without candidate generation. In *Proceedings of the International Conference on Special Interest Group of Management of Data* (pp. 1-12).

Han, K. S., & Noh, M. H. (1999). Critical failure factors that discourage the growth of electronic commerce. *International Journal of Electronic Commerce, 4*(2), 25-43.

Haralick, R. M. (1979). Statistical and structural approaches to texture. *Proceeding of the IEEE, 67*(5), 786-804.

Harman, D. (1992) Relevance feedback revisited. In *Proceedings of the 15th Annual International ACM SIGIR Conference on Research and Development in Information*, (pp. 1-10).

Harter, S. P. (1992). Psychological relevance and information science. *Journal of the American Society for Information Science, 43*(9), 602-615.

Hartigan, J. (1985). Statistical theory in clustering. *Journal of Classification, 2*, 63-76.

Hartley, J. (1986). Planning the typographical structure of instructional text. *Educational Psychologist, 21*(4), 315–332.

Hassanien, A. & Ajith, A. (in press). Rough morphology hybrid approach for mammography image classification and prediction. *International Journal of Computational Intelligence and Application.* \

Hassanien, A., & Ali, J. (2004). Enhanced rough sets rule reduction algorithm for classification digital mammography. *Intelligent System Journal, 13*(2), 117-151.

Hassanien, A., & Dominik, S. (2007). Rough neural intelligent approach for image classification: A case of patients with suspected breast cancer. *International Journal of Hybrid Intelligent Systems, 3*(4), 205-218.

Hasselbring, W., Heuvel, W., & Roantree, M. (2000). Research and practice in federated information systems: Report of the EFIS 2000 International Workshop. *SIGMOD Record, 29*(4), 16-18.

Hecht-Nielsen, R. (1987). *Counter propagation networks.* New York.

Heikkila, J. (2002). From supply to demand chain management: Efficiency and customer satisfaction. *Journal of Operations Management, 20*(6), 747.

Hendrickson, B., & Leland, R. (1993). *A multilevel algorithm for partitioning graphs.* (Tech. Rep. No. SAND93-1301). California: Sandia National Laboratories.

Herbrich, R., Keilbach, M., Graepel, T., Bollmann-Sdorra, P., & Obermayer, K. (1999). *Neural networks in economics: Background, applications and new developments* (Vol. 11). Boston: Kluwer Academics.

Hevner, A., March, S. T., Park, J., & Ram, S. (2004). Design science research in information systems. *MIS Quarterly, 28,* 75-105.

Hill, J. C., Johnson, F. R., Archibald, J. K., Frost, R. L., & Stirling, W. C. (2005). A cooperative multi-agent approach to free flight. In *Proceedings of the Fourth International Joint Conference on Autonomous Agents and Multiagent Systems AAMAS '05,* (pp. 1083-1090).

Hillbrand, C. (2002). *Inferenz in betriebswirtschaftlichen Kausalmodellen auf der Basis von Ursache-Wirkungshypothesen* (Technical Report No. 02/2002). Vienna: University of Vienna. (in German)

Hillbrand, C. (2003). *Inference-based construction of managerial causal models supporting strategic enterprise planning.* PhD Thesis, Vienna: University of Vienna.

Hillbrand, C. (2004). Building proven causal model bases for strategic decision support. In Seruca, I., Filipe, J. Hammoudi, S. and Cordeiro, J., editors. *Proceedings of ICEIS 2004 - the Sixth International Conference on Enterprise Information Systems, 2,* 178-183, Universidade Portucalense, Porto, Portugal.

Hillbrand, C., & Karagiannis, D. (2002). An approach to facilitate complex planning issues by means of machine learning techniques applied to cybernetic cause-and-effect models. In N. Callaos, A. Breda, and M. Fernandez, (eds.), *Proceedings of SCI 2002, 2,* 51-56, Orlando, FL.

Hillbrand, C., & Karagiannis, D. (2002). Using artificial neural networks to prove hypothetic cause-and-effect relations: A metamodel-based approach to support strategic decisions. In Piattini, M., Filipe, J., and Braz, J., editors, *Proceedings of ICEIS 2002, 1,* 367-373, Ciudad Real, Spain.

Hinneburg, A., & Keim, D. (1999, September). An optimal gridclustering: Towards breaking the curse of dimensionality in high-dimensional clustering. In *Proceedings of 25th International Conference on Very Large Data Bases.* Scotland, UK.

Hirsch, E. (1982). *The Concept of Identity.* Oxford University Press.

Hirsch, E. (1993). *Dividing Reality.* Oxford University Press.

Hirschheim, R., & Klein, H. K. (1989). Four Paradigms of Information Systems Development. *Communications of the ACM., 32*(32), 1199-1216.

Hirschheim, R., Klein, H. K., & Lyytinen, K. (1995). *Information Systems Development and Data Modeling: Conceptual and Philosophical Foundations.* Cambridge University Press.

Hirschheim, R., Klein, H. K., & Lyytinen, K. (1996). Exploring the intellectual structures of information systems development: A social action theoretic analysis. *Accounting, Management and Information Technologies, 6,* 1-64.

Hoffman, D. L., Novak, T. P., & Chatterjee, P. (1995). Commercial scenario for the Web: Opportunities and challenges. *Journal of Computer-Mediated Communication, Special Issues on Electronic Commerce, 1*(3). [Electronic version available online at http://jcmc.indiana.edu/vol1/issue3/hoffman.html].

Hoffman, D. L., Novak, T. P., & Peralta, M. (1999). Building consumer trust online. *CACM, 42*(4), 80-85.

Hofman, D. (2007). Supply chain measurement: Turning data into action. *Supply Chain Management Review, 11*(8), 20-26.

Hohl, F. (1998) Time limited Blackbox security: Protecting mobile agents from malicious hosts. In G. Vigna (Ed.), *Mobile agents and security, LNCS 1419* (pp. 92-113). Springer.

Hohl, F. (1998). A model of attacks of malicious hosts against mobile agents. In *Fourth Workshop on Mobile Object Systems (MOS'98): Secure Internet Mobile Computations.* Retrieved from http://cuiwww.unige.ch/~ecoopws/ws98/papers/hohl.ps

Holland, J., Holyoak, K., Nisbett, R., & Thagard, P. (1989). *Induction: Processes of inference, learning, and discovery.* Cambridge, MA: The MIT Press.

Holsapple, C., & Singh, M., (2000, July/September). Toward a unified view of electronic commerce, electronic business, and collaborative commerce: A knowledge management approach. *Knowledge and Process Management, 7*(3), 159.

Hoover, K. D. (2001). *Causality in macroeconomics.* Cambridge: Cambridge University Press.

Hoover, K. D. (2008). Causality in economics and econometrics. In Durlauf, S. and Blume, L., editors, *The New Palgrave Dictionary of Economics (2nd ed.),* London: MacMillan

Horvath & Partner. (2001). *Balanced Scorecard umsetzen* (2nd ed.). Stuttgart: Schäffer-Poeschel Verlag. (in German)

Hu, J., Shima, K., Oehlmann, R., Zhao, J., Takemura, Y., & Matsumoto, K. (2004). An empirical study of audience impressions of B2C Web pages in Japan, China and the UK. *Electronic Commerce Research and Applications,* (3), 176-189.

Huang, W., Tan, C. L., & Loew, W. K. (2003). Model-based chart image recognition. In *Proceedings of the International Workshop on Graphics Recognition (GREC),* (pp. 87-99).

Hui, S., & Jha, G. (2000). Data mining for customer service support. *Information and Management, 38*(1), 1-14.

Hume, D. (1748). An enqiry concerning human understanding. In J. Fieser, editor, *The writings of David Hume,* [electronic version], Retreived 03/01/2008, from http://www.infomotions.com/etexts/philosophy/1700-1799/hume-enquiry-65.txt

Izatt, M., Chan, P., & Brecht, T. (1999, June). Agents: Towards an environment for parallel, distributed and mobile Java applications. In *Proceedings of the 1999 ACM Conference on Java Grande* (pp. 15-24).

JADE Project. (n.d.). *Jade white paper.* Retrieved March 27, 2006, from http://jade.cselt.it/

Jafar, M. A. (2007). Content-based image classification and retrieval: A rule-based system using rough sets framework. *International Journal of Intelligent Information Technologies, 3*(3), 41-58.

Jain, A. K., & Dubes, R. C. (1988). *Algorithms for clustering data.* Englewood Cliffs, NJ: Prentice- Hall.

Jain, A., Murty, M., & Flynn, P. (1999). Data clustering: A review. *ACM Computing Surveys, 31*(3), 255- 323.

Jain, C. L. (2004). Benchmarking forecasting error. *The Journal of Business Forecasting Methods & Systems, 23*(3), 8.

Jain, C. L. (2004). Benchmarking forecasting software and systems. *The Journal of Business Forecasting Methods & Systems, 23*(3), 13.

Jain, C. L. (2004). Business forecasting practices in 2003. *The Journal of Business Forecasting Methods & Systems, 23*(3), 2.

Jarke, M., Jeusfeld, M., Quix, C., & Vassiliadis, P. (1999). Architecture and quality in data warehouses: An extended repository approach. *Information Systems, 24*(3), 229-253.

Jarvenpaa, S. L, Tranctinsky, N., & Vitale, M. (2000). Consumer trust in an Internet store. *Information Technology and Management Journal, 1*(1-2), 45-71.

Jennings, N. R., & Wooldridge, M. (1998). *Agent technology: Foundations, applications, and markets*. London: Springer.

Jennings, N., Sycara, K., & Wooldridge, M. (1998). A roadmap of agent research and development. *International Journal of Autonomous Agents and Multi-Agent Systems, 1*(1), 7-38.

Jensen, K. (1996). Coloured Petri Nets: Basic concepts, analysis methods and practical use. 2nd ed., Vol. 1, *EATCS Monographs on Theoretical Computer Science*. London: Springer.

Joachims, T. (1999). Making large-scale SVM learning practical. Advances in Kernel Methods - Support Vector Learning.

Jonsson, E. (1997). A quantitative model of the security intrusion process based on attacker behavior. *IEEE Transactions on Software Engineering, 23*(4).

Jøsang, A. (1998). Modelling trust in information society. Unpublished doctoral thesis, Department of Telematics, Norwegian University of Science and Technology, Trondheim, Norway.

Josephson, J., & Josephson, S. (1994). *Abductive inference, computation, philosophy, technology*. New York: Cambridge University Press.

Kahle, B., & Medlar. A. (1991). An information system for corporate users: Wide area information servers. *ConneXions—The Interoperability Report, 5*(11), 2-9.

Kaldewaij, A., & Schoenmakers, B. (1990). Searching by elimination. *SCP, 14*, 243-254.

Kantor, P., Boros, E., Melamed, B., Menkov, V., Shapira, B., & Neu, D. (2000). Capturing human intelligence in the Net. *Communications of the ACM, 43*(8), 112-115.

Kaplan, R., & Norton, D. (1992). The balanced scorecard: Measures that drive performance. *Harvard Business Review, 70*(1), 71-79.

Kaplan, R., & Norton, D. (1996). *The balanced scorecard: Translating strategy into action*. Boston: Harvard Business School Press.

Karagiannis, D., & Kühn, H. (2002). *Metamodelling platforms – invited paper* (No. 2455). Berlin: Springer Verlag.

Karypis, G., & Kumar, V. (1999). A fast and high quality multilevel scheme for partitioning rrregular graphs. *SIAM Journal of Scientific Computing, 20*(1), 359-392.

Karypis, G., Han, E.-H., & Kumar, V. (1999). CHAMELEON: A hierarchical clustering algorithm using dynamic modeling. *IEEE Computer, 32*(8), 68-75.

Kasanen, E., Lukka, K., Siitonen, A. (1993). The constructive approach in management accounting research. *Journal of Management Accounting Research, 5*(3), 243-64.

Kasiran, M. K., & Meziane, F. (2002). An information framework for a merchant trust agent in electronic commerce. In H. Yin, N. Allinson, R. Freeman, J. Keane, & Hubbard S. (Eds), *Intelligent data engineering and automated learning*, (pp. 243-248). Springer.

Kasiran, M. K., & Meziane, F. (2004). The usage of third party endorsement in ecommerce websites. *In proceedings of the 7th International Conference on Work with Computing Systems (WWCS2004)*, (pp.794-798). Kuala Lumpur, Malaysia.

Kaufman, L., & Rousseeuw, P. J. (1990). *Finding groups in data: An introduction to cluster analysis*. New York: Wiley.

Keen, P. (1980). MIS Research: Reference Disciplines and a Cumulative Tradition. *Proceedings of the 1ˢᵗ International Conference on Information Systems*. pp. 9-18.

Keen, P., Balance, C., Chan, S., & Schrump, S. (2000). Electronic commerce relationship: Trust by design. New Jearsey: Prentice Hall.

Kent, R. E. (1994). Rough concept analysis, rough sets, fuzzy sets knowledge discovery. In W. P. Ziarko (Ed.), *Proceedings of the International Workshop on Rough Sets, Knowledge, Discovery* (pp. 248-255). Banff, AB, Canada: Springer-Verlag.

Kent, W. (1978). *Data and Reality: Basic Assumptions in Data Processing Reconsidered*. North-Holland.

Kent, W. (1979). Limitations of Record-Based Information Models. *ACM Transactions on Database Systems*, 1(4),107-131.

Kherfi, M. L., Ziou, D., & Bernardi, A. (2004). Image retrieval from the World Wide Web: Issues, techniques, and systems. *ACM Computing Survey*, 36(1), 35-67.

Kiang, M. Y. (2003, July). A comparative assessment of classification methods. *Decision Support Systems*, 35(4), 441-454.

Kim, C. N., Chung, H. M., & Paradice, D. B. (1997). Inductive modeling of expert decision making in loan evaluation: A decision strategy perspective. *Decision Support Systems*, 21(2), 83-98.

Kim, C. N., & McLeod, R. J. (1999). Expert, linear models, and nonlinear models of expert decision making in bankruptcy prediction: A lens model analysis. *Journal of Management Information Systems, 16*(1), 189-206.

Kim, J., Oard, D., & Romanik, K. (2000). *Using implicit feedback for user modelling in Internet and Intranet searching*. (Technical Report). College of Library and In- formation Services, University of Maryland at College Park, MD

Kim, S. & Zhang, B.-T. (2000). Web-document retrieval by genetic learning of importance factors for HTML tags. In *PRICAI Workshop on Text and Web Mining* (pp. 13-23).

Kimbrough, S. O., Wu, D. J., & Zhong, F. (2002). Computers play the beer game: Can artificial agents manage supply chains? *Decision Support Systems, 33*(3), 323.

Kindler, E., Martens, A., & Reisig, W. (2000). *Interoperability of workflow applications: local criteria for local soundness*. (Lecture Notes in Computer Science, 1806, pp. 235-253).

Klang, M. (2001). Who do you trust: Beyond encryption, secure e-business. *Decision Support System, 31*(3), 293-301.

Klein, H. K., & Hirschheim, R. A. (1987). A Comparative Framework of Data Modelling Paradigms and Approaches. *The Computer Journal*, 1(30), 8-15.

Klop, J. W. (1990). Term rewriting systems. In: Abramsky, S., Gabbay, D., & Maibaum, T. (eds.), *Handbook of logic in computer science, 1*. Oxford University Press.

Kokar, M. M., Baclawski, K., & Eracar, Y. (1999). Control theory-based foundations of self-controlling software. *IEEE Intelligent Systems*, May/June, 37-45.

Kolmogorov, A. N. (1957). On the representation of continuous functions of many variables by superposition of continuous functions of one variable and addition. *Doklady Akademii Nauk SSSR, 114*, 953-956.

Konrad, K., Fuchs, G., & Barthel, J. (1999). Trust and electronic commerce – More than a technical problem. In *Proceeding of the 18th IEEE Symposium on Reliable Distributed Systems,* (pp 360-365). Lausanne, Switzerland.

Koopmans, T. (1950). *Statistical Inference in Dynamic Economic Models*. Cowles Commission Monograph, 10. New York: Wiley.

Koperski, K. & Han, J. (1995). Discovery of spatial association rules in geographical information databases. In *Proceedings of the 4th International Symposium on Advances in Spatial Databases* (pp. 47-66).

Korfhage, R. R. (1997). *Information storage and retrieval*. New York: John Wiley & Sons.

Kosakaya, J., & Yamaoka, K. (2001). Cooperative multi-agent intelligent field terminals. In *Proceedings of the Fifth International Conference on Autonomous Agents,* (pp. 348-354).

Koskela, M., Laaksonen, J., & Oja, E. (2004). Entropy-based measures for clustering and SOM topology preservation applied to content-based image indexing and retrieval. In *Proceedings of 17th International Conference on Pattern Recognition (ICPR 2004),* (pp. 1005-1009).

Koutri, M., Daskalaki, S., & Avouris N. (2002). Adaptive interaction with Web Sites: An overview of methods and techniques. In *Proceedings of the 4th International Workshop on Computer Science and Information Technologies.*Patras, Greece.

Kryszkiewicz, M., & Rybinski, H. (1994). Finding reducts in composed information systems, rough sets, fuzzy sets knowledge discovery. In W. P. Ziarko (Ed.), *Proceedings of the International Workshop on Rough Sets, Knowledge* (pp. 261-273). Banff, AB, Canada: Springer-Verlag.

Krzanowski, W., & Lai, Y. (1985). A criterion for determining the number of groups in a dataset using sum of squares clustering. *Biometrics, 44,* 23-34.

Kudoh, Y., Haraguchi, M., & Okubo, Y. (2003, January 27). Data abstractions for decision tree induction. *Theoretical Computer Science, 292*(2), 387-416.

Kundu, A., & Chen, J. L. (1992). Texture classification using QMF Bank-based subband decomposition. *CVGIP: Graphical Models and Image Processing, 54,* 369-384.

Kwon, O.-W. & Lee, J.-H. (2000). Web page classification based on k-nearest neighbor approach. In *IRAL '00: Proceedings of the fifth international workshop on Information retrieval with Asian languages* (pp. 9-15). New York: ACM Press.

Labrou, Y., & Finin, T. (1997). Semantics and conversations for an agent communication language. In *Readings in agents* (pp. 235-242). Morgan Kaufmann Publishers Inc.

Lad, A., & Yang, Y. (2007). Generalizing from relevance feedback using named entity wildcards. In *Proceedings of the Sixteenth ACM Conference on Conference on information and Knowledge Management - CIKM '07,* (pp. 721-730).

Lakoff, G. (1987). *Women, fire and dangerous things: What categories reveal about the mind.* Chicago: University of Chicago Press.

Lakoff, G. (1987). *Women, Fire, and Dangerous Things: What Categories Reveal about the Mind.* Chicago: University of Chicago Press.

Lakoff, G. (1988). Cognitive Semantics. In Eco, U., Santambrogio, M. and Violi, P. (Eds.) *Meaning and Mental Representations.* Bloomington: Indiana University Press, pp. 119-154.

Lambert, D. M., & Lalonde, B. J. (1976). Inventory carrying costs. *Management Accounting, 58*(2), 31.

Landt, F. W. (1997). *Stock price prediction using neural networks.* Leiden University, Leiden, Netherlands.

Larsen, B., & Aone, C. (1999, August). Fast and effective text mining using linear-time document clustering. In *Proceedings of the 5th ACM SIGKDD International Conference on Knowledge Discovery and Data Mining.* San Diego.

Laudon, K. C., & Laudon, J. P. (2006). *Management information system: Managing the digital FIRM* (9th ed.). New Jersey, Prentice Hall.

Le Metayer, D. (1994). Higher-order multiset processing. *DIMACS Series in Discrete Mathematics and Theoretical Computer Science, 18,* 179-200.

Lee, D. L., Xu, J., Zheng, B., & Lee, W. C. (2002). Data management in location-dependent information services. *Pervasive Computing, IEEE, 1*(3), 65-72.

Lee, H. L., Padmanabhan, V., & Whang, S. (1997). The bullwhip effect in supply chains. *Sloan Management Review, 38*(3), 93.

Lee, H. L., Padmanabhan, V., & Whang, S. (1997). Information distortion in a supply chain: The bullwhip effect. *Management Science, 43*(4), 546.

Levich, R. M., & Rizzo, R. M. (1997). *Alternative tests for time series dependence based on autocorrelation coefficients*. New York.

Lewicki, R. J., & Bunker, B. B. (1996). Developing and maintaining trust in working relationships. In R.M. Kramer & T. Tyler (Eds.), *Trust in organizations*, (pp.114–139). Thousand Oaks, CA: Sage.

Lewis, D. (1992). An evaluation of phrasal and clustered representations on a text categorization task. In *SIGIR '92: Proceedings of the 15th annual international ACM SIGIR conference on Research and development in information retrieval* (pp. 37-50). ACM Press.

Li, H., Kuo, C., & Russell, M. G. (1999, December). The impact of perceived channel utilities, shopping orientation, and demographics on the consumer's online buying behaviour. *Journal of Computer-Mediated Communication, 5*(2).

Li, J., Gray, R. M., & Olshen, R. A. (2000). Multiresolution image classification by hierarchical modeling with two-dimensional hidden Markov models. *IEEE Trans. on Information Theory, 46*(5), 1826-1841.

Li, J., Tang, B., & Cercone, N. (2004). Applying association rules for interesting recommendations using rule templates. In *8th Pacific-Asia Conference on Knowledge Discovery and Data Mining 2004*, (Lecture Notes in Artificial Intelligence, 3056, pp. 166-170).

Li, Y., Bandar Z. A., & Mclean, D. (2003). An approach for measuring Semantic similarity between words using multiple information sources. *IEEE Transactions on Knowledge and Data Engineering, 15*(4), 871-882.

Lienhart, R., & Hartmann, A. (2002). Classifying images on the Web automatically. *Journal of Electronic Imaging, 11*, 31-40.

Lim, E. P., Wang, Y., Ong, K. L., et al. (2003). Search of knowledge about mobile users. *ERCIM News, 1*(54), 10.

Lin F., Norrie D. H., Flores, R. A., & Kremer R.C. (2000, June 3-7). Incorporating conversation managers into multi-agent systems. In M. Greaves, F. Dignum, J. Bradshaw & B. Chaib-draa (Eds.), *Proceedings of the Workshop on Agent Communication and Languages, 4th Inter. Conf. on Autonomous Agents (Agents 2000)*, Barcelona, Spain, (pp. 1-9).

Lin, F. O., Lin, H., & Holt, P. (2003, May 18-23). A method for implementing distributed learning environments. *Proceedings of 2003 Information Resources Management Association International Conference*, Philadelphia, Pennsylvania, (pp. 484-487).

Lin, H. (2004). A language for specifying agent systems in e-learning environments. In F.O. Lin (ed.), *Designing distributed learning environments with intelligent software agents*, 242-272.

Lin, H., & Chen, G. (1998). Program construction by verifying specification. *Journal of Computer Science and Technology, 13*(6), 597-607.

Lin, H., & Yang, C. (2006). Specifying distributed multi-agent systems in chemical reaction metaphor. *The International Journal of Artificial Intelligence, Neural Networks, and Complex Problem-Solving Technologies, 24*(2), 155-168. Springer-Verlag

Lin, H., Chen, G., & Wang, M. (1997). Program transformation between unity and gamma. *Neural, Parallel & Scientific Computations, 5*(4), 511-534. Atlanta,GA: Dynamic Publishers.

Linoff, G.S., & Berry, M.J.A. (2001). *Mining the Web*. New York: Wiley Computer Publishing.

Live (2008). *Microsoft Live search engine*. Retrieved March 1, 2008, from http://www.live.com/

Losee, J. (1993). *A Historical Introduction to the Philosophy of Science*. Oxford University Press.

Losee, R. M. (1998). *Text retrieval and filtering: Analytic models of performance*. Boston:Kluwer Publisher.

Losee, R. M. (1999). Measuring search engine quality and query difficulty: Ranking with target and freestyle. *Journal of the American Society for Information Science, 50*(10), 882-889.

Losee, R. M. (2000). When information retrieval measures agree about the relative quality of document rankings. *Journal of the American Society for Information Science, 51*(9), 834-840.

Lucas, R. (1976). Econometric policy evaluation: A critique. In Brunner, K and Meltzer, A.H., editors. *The Phillips Curve and Labor Markets, Carnegie-Rochester Conference Series on Public Policy*, Amsterdam: North Holland: 161-168.

Luckham, D. C., Kenney, J. J., Augustin, L. M., Vera, J., Bryan, D., & Mann, W. (1995). Specification and analysis of system architecture using Rapide. *IEEE Trans. on Software Engineering*, April, 336-355.

Luhn, H. (1958). The automatic creation of literature abstracts. *IBM Journal of Research and Development, 2*,159–165.

Luo, X. (2002). Trust production and privacy concerns on the Internet: A framework based on relationship marketing and social exchange theory. *Industrial Marketing Management, 31*(2), 111-118.

Luria, A. R. (1976). *Cognitive Development: Its Cultural and Social Foundations.* Cambridge, MA. Harvard University Press.

Lycan, W. (1999). *Mind and cognition: An anthology.* Madden, MA: Blackwell Publishers, Inc.

Ma, W. Y., & Manjunath, B. S. (1999). NeTra: A toolbox for navigating large image databases. *Multimedia Systems, 7*(3), 184-198.

MacKay, D. J. C. (1992). Bayesian interpolation. *Neural Computation, 4*(3), 415-447.

MadKit Project. (n.d.). *MadKit documentation.* Retrieved March 27, 2006 from http://www.madkit.org/madkit/doc/index.php3

Magee, J., & Kramer, J. (1996, October). Dynamic structure in software architectures. In *Proceedings of the 4th Symposium on the Foundations of Software Engineering (FSE4)*, San Francisco, CA, (pp.3-14).

Makridakis, S., & Hibon, M. (1979). Accuracy of forecasting: an empirical investigation (with discussion). *Journal of the Royal Statistical Society. Series A (General), 142*(2), 97-145.

Makridakis, S., & Hibon, M. (2000). The M3-competition: Results, conclusions and implications. *International Journal of Forecasting, 16*(4), 451.

Makridakis, S., & Wheelwright, S. C. (1978). *Forecasting. methods and applications.* Santa Barbara, CA: John Wiley & Sons.

Makridakis, S., Andersen, A., Carbone, R., & Fildes, R. (1982). The accuracy of extrapolation (time series) methods: Results of a forecasting competition. *Journal of Forecasting* (pre-1986), *1*(2), 111.

Makridakis, S., Chatfield, C., Hibon, M., Lawrence, M., Mills, T., Ord, K., et al. (1993). The M2-competition: A real-time judgmentally based forecasting study. *International Journal of Forecasting, 9*(1), 5.

Mamdani, E. (1994). Application of fuzzy algorithms of simple dynamic plants. In *Proceedings of IEEE, 121*, (pp. 585-588).

Manchala, D. W. (2000). E-commerce trust metrics and models. *IEEE Internet Computing, March-April*, 36-44.

Manna, Z. (1974). *Mathematical theory of computation.* International Student Edition. McGraw Hill Computer Science Series.

Manna, Z., & Waldinger, R. (1992). Fundamentals of deductive program synthesis. *IEEE Trans. On Software Engineering, 18*(8), 674-704.

Mao, J., & Benbasat, I. (2000, Fall). The use of explanations in knowledge-based systems: Cognitive perspectives and a process-tracing analysis. *Journal of Management Information Systems, 17*(2), 153-179.

March, S. T. and Smith, G. F. (1995). Design and natural science research on information technology. *Decision Support Systems, 15*, 251-266.

March, S. T., & Allen, G. N. (2007, June 3-6). Challenges in requirements engineering: A research agenda for conceptual modeling. *NSF Science of Design – Design Requirements Workshop*, Cleveland, OH.

March, S. T., & Allen, G. N. (2007). Ontological foundations for active information systems. *International Journal of Intelligent Information Technologies, 3*, 1-13.

Mardia, K.V., Kent, J. T., & Bibby, J. M. (1979). *Multivariate analysis*. New York: Academic Press.

Mari, P., Bogdan, C., Moncef, G., & Ari, V. (2002, October). *Rock texture retrieval using gray level co-occurrence matrix*. Paper presented at the NORSIG-2002, 5th NORDIC Signal Processing Symposium, Hurtigruten from Tromsø to Trondheim, Norway.

Marquardt, D. W. (1963). An algorithm for least-squares estimation of nonlinear parameters. SIAM *Journal of Applied Mathematics, 11*, 431-441.

Martin, D., Burstein, M., Lassila, O., Paolucci, M., Payne, T., & McIlraith, S. (2003). Retrieved from http://www.daml.org/services/owl-s/1.0/owl-s-wsdl.html

Martin-Lof, P. (1980). Intuitionistic type theory. *Notes by Giovanni Sambin of a series of lectures given in Padua, Bibliopolis*.

Mataric, M. (1997). Using communication to reduce locality in multi-robot learning. In *AAAI-97* (pp. 643-648). Menlo Park: CA: AAAI Press.

MathWorks, Inc. (2005). *Financial time series toolbox for use with MATLAB*. Natick: MA: MathWorks Inc.

MathWorks, Inc. (2005). *GARCH toolbox for use with MATLAB*. Natick: MA: MathWorks Inc.

MathWorks, Inc. (2005). *Getting started with MATLAB*. Natick: MA: MathWorks Inc.

MathWorks, Inc. (2005). *Neural network toolbox for use with MATLAB*. Natick: MA: MathWorks Inc.

MathWorks, Inc. (2005). *Optimization toolbox for use with MATLAB*. Natick: MA: MathWorks Inc.

Matthew, K. O., & Turban, E. (2001). A trust model for consumer internet shopping. *International Journal of Electronic Commerce, 6*(1), 75-91.

Mayer, R. C., Davis, J. H., & Schoorman, F. D. (1995). An integrative model of organizational trust. *Academy of Management Review, 20*(3), 709-734.

McCarthy, W. E. (1982). The REA accounting model: A general framework for accounting systems in a shared data environment. *The Accounting Review, 57*, 554-578.

McCullagh, A. (1998, November 7). The establishment of trust in the electronic commerce environment. *Proceedings of The 1998 Information Industry Outlook Conference*. Retrieved from http://www.acs.org.au/president/1998/past/io98/mccullgh.htm

McDermott, J. J. (Ed.) (1976). *The writings of William James: A comprehensive edition*. Chicago: The University of Chicago Press.

McIlraith, S., Son, T. C., & Zeng, H. (2001). Semantic Web Services. *IEEE Intelligent Systems*, March/April, 46-53.

Mehta, M., Agrawal, R., & Rissanen, J. (1996). SLIQ: A fast scalable classifier for data mining. In *Proceedings of the 5th International Conference on Extending Database Technology*, Avignon, France

Mellor, D. H. (1980). Things and causes in spacetime. *British Journal for the Philosophy of Science, 31*, 282-88.

Mena, J. (1999). *Data Mining Your Website*. Boston: Digital Press.

Mendoza, C., Delemond, M.-H., Giraud, F., & Loening, H. (2002). *Tableaux de bord et Balanced Scorecards*. Publications Fiduciaires. (in French).

Meng, X. & Chen, Z. (2004, June 21-24). On user-oriented measurements of effectiveness of Web information retrieval systems. In *Proceedings of the 2004 International Conference on Internet Computing*, Las Vegas, NV, (pp. 527-533).

Meng, X. (2006, April 10-12). A Comparative Study of Performance Measures for Information Retrieval Systems. Poster presentation, in the *Proceedings of the Third International Conference on Information Technology: New Generations*, Las Vegas, NV, (pp. 578-579).

Meng, X., & Chen, Z. (2005). *On single-value performance measures of search engines from users' perspective*. Manuscript, submitted for publication. September 2005.

Meng, X., & Clark, T. (2005, April 4-6). An empirical user rating of popular search engines using *RankPower*. In *Proceedings of the 2005 International Conference on Information Technology*, Las Vegas, (pp. 521-525).

Merrilees, B. & Fry, M. (2003). E-Trust: The influence of perceived interactivity on e-tailing users. *Marketing Intelligence and Planning, 21*(2),123-128.

Meseguer, J. (1992). Conditional rewriting logic as a unified model of concurrency. *Theoretical Computer Science, 96*, 73-155.

Meseguer, J., & Winkler, T. (1991). Parallel programming in Maude. In Banatre, J.P., & Le Metayer, D. (eds.), *Proceedings of the Workshop on Research Directions in High-Level Parallel programming Languages*, Mont Saint-Michel, France, (pp. 253-293). Springer-Verlag.

Meziane, F., & Kasiran, M. K. (2003). Extracting unstructured information from the WWW to support merchant existence in e-commerce. In A. Dusterhoft & B. Thalheim (Eds.), *Lecture Notes in Informatics, Natural Language Processing and Information Systems*, GI-Edition (pp.175-185). Bonn, Germany.

Meziane, F., & Kasiran, M. K. (2005, June). Strategizing consumer logistic requirements in e-commerce transactions: Evaluation of current implementations. In *Proceedings of the 3rd European Conference on Intelligent Management Systems in Operations*, (pp.116-125). Salford, Manchester, UK: The Operational Research Society.

Meziane, F., & Kasiran, M. K. (2008). Evaluating trust in electronic commerce: A study based on the information provided on merchants' Web sites. *Journal of the Operational Research Society, 59*(4), 464-472.

Miller, G. (1995). WordNet: A lexical database for English. *Communication of the ACM, 38*(11), 39-41.

Milligan, G., & Cooper, M. (1985). An examination of procedures for determining the number of clusters in a data set. *Psychometrika, 50*, 159-179.

Mitchell, T. M. (1997). *Machine learning*. McGraw-Hill.

Mitra, S., Pal, S. K., & Mitra, P. (2002). Data mining in soft computing framework: A survey. *IEEE Trans. Neural Networks, 13*(1), 3-14.

Miyahara, T. Suzuki, Y., Shoudai, T. Uchida, T. Takahashi, K., & Uedal, H. (2004). Discovery of maximally frequent tag tree patterns with contractible variables from semistructured documents. In *8th Pacific-Asia Conference on Knowledge Discovery and Data Mining 2004,* (Lecture Notes in Artificial Intelligence, 3056, 133-144).

Mobasher, B., Cooley, R. & Srivastava, J. (1999). Data preparation for mining world wide web browsing patterns. *Knowledge and Information Systems, 1*(1), 5-32.

Mobasher, B., Cooley, R., & Srivastava, J. (1999). Automatic personalization based on web usage mining. *Communications of the ACM, 43*(8), 142-151.

Mohanty, B. K., & Bhasker, B. (2005), Product classification in the Internet business: A fuzzy approach. *Journal of Decision Support Systems, 38*, 611-619.

Molinier, M., Laaksonen, J., Ahola, J., & Häme, T. (2005, October 5-7). Self-organizing map application for retrieval of man-made structures in remote sensing data. In *Proceedings of ESA-EUSC 2005: Image Information Mining - Theory and Application to Earth Observation*, ESRIN, Frascati ,Italy.

Moneta, A. (2004). Causality and econometrics: some philosophical underpinnings, *Methods in Economics Seminar Series*, Pisa.

MSE (2005). *Microsoft Search Engine, Beta.* Retrieved January 23, 2005, from http://beta.search.msn.com

Muansuwan, N., Sirinaovakul, B., & Thepruangchai, P. (2004). Intelligent tutoring and knowledge base creation for the subject of computer programming. In *Proceedings of tencon 2004* (p. 353-356). IEEE.

Mukherjee, S., Osuna, E., & Girosi, F. (1997). Nonlinear prediction of chaotic time series using support vector machines. Paper presented at the {IEEE} Workshop on Neural Networks for Signal Processing {VII}, Ameila Island, FL, USA.

Nag, B. (2007). A Blackboard agent community architecture in a supply chain environment. *Design Principles and Practices, 1*(1), 91-104.

Nah, F., & Davis, S. (2002). HCI research issues in e-commerce. *Journal of Electronic Commerce Research, 3*(3), 98-113.

Naraine, R. (2003). B2C e-commerce market will reach $90 billion in 2003. Retrieved from http://gcis.ca/cdne-497-apr-26-2003.html

National Fraud InformationCentre (no date). *Fraud information centre.* Retrieved from http://www.fraud.org/2002intstats.htm

Neches, R., Fikes R., Finin, T., Gruber, T., Patil, R., Senator, T., & Swartout, W. R. (1991). Enabling technology for knowledge sharing. *AI Magazine, 12*(3), 36-56.

Nefti, S. (2002, October 6-9). New algorithm for simplification of rule base generated by automated fuzzy modeling. *IEEE International Conference on Systems, Man and Cybernetics, 2*, 190-195.

Nefti, S., & Djouani, K. (2002, October). Fuzzy modeling of MIMO non linear system: Complexity reduction. *IEEE International Conference on Systems, Man and Cybernetics, 2*, 185-189.

Nelson, K. (1996). *Language in cognitive development: Emergence of the mediated mind.* Cambridge University Press.

Ng, R., & Han, J. (1994). Efficient and effective clustering methods for spatial data mining. In *Proceedings of the 20th International Conference on Very Large Data Bases.* Santiago, Chile.

Ngai, E. W. T., & Wat, F. K. T. (2002). A literature review and classification of electronic commerce research. *Information & Management,* (39), 415-429.

Nigam, K., McCallum, A. K., Thrun, S., and Mitchell, T. M. (1998). Learning to classify text from labeled and unlabeled documents. In *Proceedings of AAAI-98, 15th Conference of the American Association for Artificial Intelligence* (pp.792-799). Madison: AAAI Press.

Nijssen, G. M., & Halpin, T. A.(1989). *Conceptual Schema and Relational Database Design: A fact oriented approach.* New York:Prentice Hall.

Nodine, M., Bohrer, W., & Ngu, A. (1999). Semantic brokering over dynamic heterogeneous data sources in InfoSleuth. *15th International Conference on Data Engineering,* 358-365.

Norrmann, A., & Jansson, U. (2004). Ericsson's proactive supply chain risk management approach after a serious sub-supplier accident. *International Journal of Physical Distribution & Logistics Management. 34*(5), 434-456.

Oliveira, S. R. M., Zaiane, O. R., & Saygin, Y. (2004). Secure association rule sharing. In *8th Pacific-Asia Conference on Knowledge Discovery and Data Mining 2004,* (Lecture Notes in Artificial Intelligence, 3056, pp. 74-85).

Open Financial Exchange (OFX). (2006). *Open Financial Exchange home page.* Retrieved from March 27, 2006, from http://www.ofx.net/ofx/default.asp

Orlikowski, W., & Iacono, C. (2001). Research Commentary: Desperately Seeking the "IT" in IT Research – A Call to Theorizing the IT Artifact. *Information Systems Research, 12*(2), 121-134.

Ortega, M., & Lin, L. (2004). Control theory applications to the production-inventory problem: A review. *International Journal of Production Research, 42*(11), 2303-2322.

Oussalah, S., Nefti, S., & Eltigani, A. (2007) Personalized information retrieval system in the framework of fuzzy logic. *Expert systems with applications.* Elsevier.

OWL-S. (n.d.). Retrieved March 10, 2006, from http://www.daml.org/services/owl-s/1.0/

Padmanabhan, B., & Tuzhilin A. (1999). Unexpectedness as a measure of interestingness in knowledge discovery. *Decision Support Systems, (27),* 303-318.

Pagnucco, M. (1996). *The role of abductive reasoning within the process of belief revision.* Unpublished doctoral dissertation, University of Sydney.

Paige, R., Reif, J., & Watcher, R. (eds.) (1993). Parallel aorithm derivation and program transformation. *The Kluwer International Series in Engineering and Computer Science.* Kluwer Academic Publishers.

Parekh, R. Yang, J., & Honavar, V. (2000). Constructive neural network learning algorithms for pattern classification. *IEEE Trans. Neural Networks, 11*(2), 436-451.

Park, T. (1993).The nature of relevance in information retrieval: An empirical study. *Library Quarterly, 63,* 318-351.

Park, T., Byun, I., Kim, H. & Yeom, H. Y. (2002). The performance of checkpointing and replication schemes for fault tolerant mobile agent systems. In *Proceedings of the 21st IEEE Symposium on Reliable Distributed Systems.*

Parsons, J., & Wand, Y. (2000). Emancipating instances from the tyranny of classes in information modeling. *ACM Transactions on Database Systems, 25,* 228-268.

Parsons, S., Sierra, C., & Jennings, N. (1998). Agents that reason and negotiate by arguing. *Journal of Logic and Computation, 8*(3), 261-292.

Patton, M. A., & Jøsang, A. (2004). Technologies for trust in electronic commerce. *Electronic Commerce Research,* (4), 9-21.

Pawlak, Z. (1982). Rough sets. *International Journal of Computer and Information Science, 11,* 341-356.

Pawlak, Z. (1991). *Rough sets-theoretical aspect of reasoning about data.* Norwell, MA, Kluwer Academic Publishers.

Pawlak, Z., Grzymala-Busse, J., Slowinski, R., & Ziarko, W. (1995). Rough sets. *Communications of the ACM, 38*(11), 89-95.

Pearl, J. (2000). *Causality. Models, reasoning and inference.* Cambridge: Cambridge University Press.

Pearl, J., & Verma, T. (1991). *A theory of inferred causation.* San Mateo, CA: Morgan Kaufmann Publishers.

Pedersen, H. (2002). *Speech acts and agents: A semantic analysis.* Unpublished master's thesis, Informatics and Mathematical Modelling, Technical University of Denmark, DTU.

Peng, X. & Choi, B. (2005). Document Classifications Based On Word Semantic Hierarchies. *The IASTED International Conference on Artificial Intelligence and Applications,* pp.362-367, Innsbruck, Austria.

Peng, X. (2002). *Automatic Web page classification in a dynamic and hierarchical way.* Master thesis, Louisiana Tech University.

Perkowitz, M., & Etzioni, O. (1997). Adaptive Web sites: An AI challenge. In *Proceedings of IJCAI-97 Workshop.* Nagoya, Japan.

Persson, F., & Olhager, J. (2002). Performance simulation of supply chain designs. *International Journal of Production Economics, 77,* 231-245.

Pillemer, D. B. (1998). *Momentous events, Vivid memories.* Cambridge, MA: Harvard University Press.

Pirsig, R. (1992) *Lila: An Inquiry into Morals.* Bantam.

Plato. (1992). *The Republic.* Translated by Grube, G. M. and Reeve, C. D. Harvard University Press.

Pleisch, S. & Schiper, A. (2000). Modeling fault: Tolerant mobile agent execution as a sequence of agree problems. In *Proceedings of the 19th IEEE Symposium on Reliable Distributed Systems* (pp. 11-20).

Pleisch, S. & Schiper, A. (2001, July). FATOMAS — A Fault-Tolerant Mobile Agent System based on the agent-dependent approach. In *Proceedings of the 2001 International Conference on Dependable Systems and Networks* (pp. 215-224).

Pleisch, S. & Schiper, A. (2003). Fault-tolerant mobile agent execution. *IEEE Transactions on Computers, 52*(2).

Pollack, M. E. (1998, July). Plan generation, plan management, and the design of computational agents. In *Proceedings of the 3rd International Conference on Multi-Agent Systems* (pp. 643-648). Paris, France.

Porter, M. (1980). An algorithm for suffix stripping. *Program, 14*(3),130-137.

Powers, R. F. (1989). Optimization models for logistics decisions. *Journal of Business Logistics, 10*(1), 106-21.

Prasad, B. (1996). *Concurrent engineering fundamentals: Integrated product development.* Upper Saddle River, NJ: Prentice-Hall.

Premkumar, G. P. (2000). Interorganization systems and supply chain management: An information processing perspective. *Information Systems Management, 17*(3), 56.

Prince, V. (1996). *Vers une informatique cognitive dans les organisations, le role central du langage.* Paris: Editions Masson.

Prince, V. (2006). Modelling and managing knowledge through dialogue: A model of communication-based knowledge management. In *ICSOFT 2006, First International Conference on Software and Data Technologies* (p. 266-271).

Prior, A. N. (1967). Correspondence Theory of Truth. In *Encyclopedia of Philosophy.* Paul Edwards (ed). Macmillan Publishing, New York. 1, 223-232.

Probst, H.-J. (2001). *Balanced Scorecard leicht gemacht. Warum sollten Sie mit weichen Faktoren hart rechnen?* Vienna: Ueberreuter Wirtschaft. (in German)

Proctor and Gamble, Co. (2005). *2004 annual report.* Cincinnati: Proctor and Gamble Co.

Puschmann, T., & Alt, R. (2005). Successful Use of E-procurement in Supply Chains. *Supply Chain Management: An International Journal, 10*(2), 122-133.

Quine, W. V. O. (1960). *Word and object.* Cambridge (MA): MIT Press.

Quine, W. V. O. (1970). *Philosophy of logic.* Englewood Cliffs, NJ: Prentice-Hall.

Quinlan, J. R. (1996). Improved use of continuous attributes in C4.5. *Journal of Artificial Intelligence Research,* (4) 77-90.

Quinlan, J. R. (1996). Learning first-order definitions of functions. *Journal of Artificial Intelligence Research,* (5) 139-161.

Quinton, A. (1979). Objects and events. *Mind, 88,* 197-214.

Raghunathan, S. (1999). Interorganizational collaborative forecasting and replenishment systems and supply chain implications. *Decision Sciences, 30*(4), 1053.

Rajaraman, K., & Pan, H. (2000). Document clustering using 3-tuples. *Pacific Rim International Conference on Artificial Intelligence Workshop on Text and Web Mining,* Melbourne.

Ramesh, V., & Browne, G. (1999). Expressing casual relationships in conceptual database schema. *The Journal of Systems and Software, 45,* 225-232.

Ranganathan, C., & Ganapathy, S. (2002). Key dimension of business-to- consumer Web sites. *Journal of Information & Management, 39,* 457-465.

Ravenscroft, A., & Pilkington, R. (2000). Investigation by design: Developing dialogue models to support reasoning and conceptual change. *International Journal of Artificial Intelligence in Education, 11*(1), 273-298.

Resnick, P., Iacovou, N., Suchak, M., Bergstrom, P., & Riedl, J. (1994). GroupLens: An open architecture for collaborative filtering of net- news. In *Proceedings* of the 1994 ACM Conference on Computer Supported Cooperative Work, (pp. 175-186).

Riboni, D. (2002). Feature selection for web page classification. In *Proceedings of the Workshop of EURASIA-ICT*. Austrian Computer Society.

Richstein, J. (2001). Verifying the Goldbach conjecture up to $4·10^{14}$. *Math. Comp., 70*(236), 1745-1749.

Riddalls, C. E., Bennett, S., & Tipi, N. S. (2000). Modelling the dynamics of supply chains. *International Journal of Systems Science, 31*(8), 969-976.

Riegelsberger, J., & Sasse, M. A. (2001). Trustbuilders and trustbusters: The role of trust cues in interfaces to e-commerce applications. In *Proceedings of the 1st IFIP Conference on E-Commerce, E-Business, E-Government*, (pp. 17-30). Kluwer.

Rijsbergen, C. J. (1979). *Information retrieval*. London: Butterworths. Salton, G., & Buckley, C. (1988). Term weighting approaches in automatic text retrieval. *Information Processing and Management, 24*, 513-523.

Rijsbergen, van C. (1974). Foundation of evaluation. *Journal of Documentation, 30*(4), 365-373.

Robey, D. (2003). Identity, Legitimacy and the Dominant Research Paradigm: An Alternative Prescription for the IS Discipline. *Journal of the Association for Information Systems, 4*(7), 352-359.

Robinson, J. A., & Hawpe, L. (1986). Narrative thinking as a heuristic process. In T. R. Sarvin (ed.) *Narrative psychology: The storied nature of human conduct*. New York: Prager Publishers.

Rocchio, J. (1971). Relevance feedback in information retrieval. *The SMART Retrieval System*, (pp. 313–323).

Romano, J., Nicholas C., & Fjermestad, J. (2003). Electronic commerce customer relationship management: A research agenda. *Information Technology and Management, 4*(2-3), 233-258.

Roochnik, D. (2002). *An Introduction to Greek Philosophy*. The Teaching Company.

Rosaci, D., Terracina, G., & Ursino, D. (2004). A framework for abstracting data sources having heterogeneous representation formats. *Data & Knowledge Engineering, 48*(1), 1-38.

Rosch, E. (1978). Principles of Categorization. In Rosch, E. and Lloyd, B.B. (Eds.) *Cognition and Categorization*. New Jersey: Lawrence Erlbaum Assoc. Publishers.

Rosch, E., & Lloyd, B. B. (Eds.) (1978). *Cognition and Categorization*. New Jersey: Lawrence Erlbaum Assoc. Publishers.

Roy, D., Anciaux, D., Monteiro, T., & Ouzizi, L. (2004). Multi-agent architecture for supply chain management. *Journal of Manufacturing Technology Management, 15*(8), 745-755.

Rüping, S. (2005). *mySVM-Manual*: Universitat Dortmund, Lehrstuhl Informatik 8.

Russ, G., Bottcher, M., & Kruse, R. (2007). Relevance feedback for association rules using fuzzy score aggregation. In *Proceedings of the Annual Meeting of the North American Fuzzy Information Processing Society-NAFIPS'07*, (pp. 54-59).

Russell, V. L. (2001). Some practical guidelines for effective sample size determination. *The American Statistician, 55*(3), 187.

Ruthven, I., & Lalmas, M. (2003). A survey on the use of relevance feedback for information access systems. *Knowledge Engineering Review, 18*(2), 95-145.

Sabah, G., Ferret, O., Prince, V., Vilnat, A., Vosniadou, S., Dimitrakopoulo, A., (1998). What dialogue analysis can tell about teacher strategies related to representational change. In *Modelling changes in understanding: Case studies in physical reasoning*. Oxford: Cambridge University Press.

Saber, E., & Tekalp, A. M. (1998). Integration of color, edge, shape and texture features for automatic region-based image annotation and retrieval. *Electronic Imaging, 7*, 684-700.

Salton, G., & Buckley, C. (1990). Improving retrieval performance by relevance feedback. *Journal of the American Society for Information Science, 41*(4), 288-97.

Salton, S. (1989). *Automatic text processing.* Addison Wesley.

Sander, J., Ester, M., Kriegel, H. P., & Xu X., (1998). Density-based clustering in spatial databases: The algorithm GDBSCAN and its applications. *Data Mining and Knowledge Discovery 2*(2), 169-194.

Sander, T. & Tschudin, C. F. (1998). Protecting mobile agents against malicious hosts. In G. Vigna (Ed.), *Mobile agents and security, LNCS 1419* (pp. 44-60). Springer.

Saracevic, T. (1975). Relevance: A review of and framework for the thinking n the notion in information science. *Journal of the American Society for Information Science, 26*(6), 321-343.

Saracevic, T. (1996). Relevance reconsidered. In *Proceedings of the Second Conference on Conceptions of Library and Information Science (CoLIS 2),* (pp. 201-218).

Sarukkai, R. (2000). Link prediction and path analysis using markov chains. *Computer Networks, 33*(1-6), 377-386.

Satchidananda D.i, Patnaik, S., Ashish G. & Rajib M. (2008) Application of elitist multi-objective genetic algorithm for classification rule generation. *Appl. Soft Comput. 8*(1), 477-487.

Schmid, H. (1994). Probabilistic part-of-speech tagging using decision trees. In *International Conference on New Methods in Language Processing,* Manchester, UK.

Schmitz, S.W., & Latzerb, M. (2000). Competition in B2C e-commerce: Analytical issues and empirical evidence. *Electronic Markets, 12*(3), 163-174.

Schneiderman, A. (1999). Why balanced scorecards fail. *Journal of Strategic Performance Measurement,* 6 – 11.

Schneier, B. (1996). *Applied cryptography.* Wiley.

Schnell, R., Hill, P. B., & Esser, E. (1999). *Methoden der empirischen Sozialforschung* (6*th* ed.). Munich et al.: Oldenbourg-Verlag. (in German)

Schoedinger, A. B. (Ed.) (1992). *The Problem of Universals.* New Jersey: Humanities Press.

Scime, A., & Sugumaran, V., (Eds.) (2007, April). Special Issue on Web Mining, *International Journal of Intelligent Information Technologies.*

Searle, J. (1969). *Speech acts: An essay in the philosophy of language.* Cambridge: Cambridge University Press.

Searle, J. R. (1995). *The construction of social reality.* New York: Free Press.

Searle, J. R. (2006). Social ontology: Some basic principles. *Anthropological Theory, 6* 12-29.

Service Component Architecture (SCA). (2005). *Service component architecture and service data objects.* Retrieved March 27, 2006, from http://www.128.ibm.com/developerworks/webservices/library/specification/ws-scasdosumm/

Shahabi, C., Zarkesh, A., Adibi, J. & Shah, V. (1997). *Knowledge discovery from users Web-page navigation.* In Workshop on Research Issues in Data Engineering, Birminghan, UK.

Shanks, G., Tansley, E., & Weber, R. (2003). Using ontology to validate conceptual models. *Communications of the ACM, 46,* 85-89.

Shapiro, D., Sheppard, B. H., & Cheraskin, L. (1992, October). Business on a handshake. *The Negotiation Journal,* 365-378.

Shapiro, E. Y. (1981). Inductive inference of theories from facts. (Report 192). Department of Computer Science, Yale University.

Shaw Jr., W. M. (1986). On the foundation of evaluation. *Journal of the American Society for Information Science, 37*(5), 346-348.

Shaw, M., DeLine, R., Klein, D. V., Ross, T. L., Young, D. M., & Zelesnik, G. (1995). Abstractions for software architecture and tools to support them. *IEEE Trans. On Software Engineering*, April, 314-335.

Shepard, R. N. (1987). Towards a universal law of generalisation for psychological science. *Science, 237*, 1317-1323.

Sherman, C. (2005). *Microsoft unveils its new search engine—At last.* SearchEngineWatch.com, published November 11, 2004, quoted January 20, 2005, http://searchenginewatch.com/searchday/article.php/3434261

Sheth, A. P., & Larson, J. A. (1990). Federated database systems for managing distributed, heterogeneous, and autonomous databases. *ACM Computing Surveys, 22*(3), 183-236.

Shim, J. P., Warkentin, M., Courtney, J. F., Power, D. J., Sharda, R., & Carlsson, C. (2002). Past, present, and future of decision support technology. *Decision Support Systems,* (33) 111-126.

Shiraishi, M., Enokido, T. & Takizawa, M. (2003). Fault-tolerant mobile agents in distributed objects systems. In *Proceedings of the Ninth IEEE Workshop on Future Trends of Distributed Computer Systems (FTDCS, 03)* (pp. 11-20).

Shlaer, S., & Mellor, S. J. (1988) *Object-Oriented Systems Analysis: Modeling the World in Data.* Englewood Cliffs, New Jersey: Yourdon Press, 1988.

Shoham, Y. (1993). Agent oriented programming. *Journal of Artificial Intelligence, 1*(60), 51-92.

Silberschatz, A., & Korth, H. F. (1996). Data models. *ACM Computing Surveys, 28*, 105-108.

Silva, L. Batista, V., & Silva, L.G. (2000). Fault-tolerant execution of mobile agents. In *Proceedings of the International Conference on Dependable Systems and IIIenvorks.*

Simchi-Levi, D., Kaminsky, P., & Simchi-Levi, E. (2003). *Designing & managing the supply chain – Concepts, strategies & case studies*, 2nd edition. Burr Ridge, IL: McGraw-Hill.

Simon, H. A. (1996). The sciences of the artificial, 3rd Edition. Cambridge, MA: MIT Press.

Singh, R. (2007). A multi-agent decision support architecture for knowledge representation and exchange. *International Journal of Intelligent Information Technologies, 3*(1), 37-59,

Slowinski, R. (1995). Rough set approach to decision analysis. *AI Expert Magazine, 10*(3), 18-25.

Smeulders, A., Worring, M., Santini, S., Gupta, A., & Jain, R. (2000). Content-based image retrieval at the end of the early years. *IEEE Transactions on Pattern Analysis and Machine Intelligence, 22*, 1349-1380.

Smith, D. R., & Lowry, M. R. (1990). Algorithm theories and design tactics. *SCP, 14*, 305-321.

Smith, D.R. (1990). KIDS: A semi-automatic program development system. *IEEE Trans. on Software Engineering, 16*(9), 1024-1043.

Smith, E., & Medin, D. (1981) *Categories and Concepts.* Cognitive Science Series, 4, University Microfilms International.

Smith, I. A., & Cohen, P. R. (1996). Toward a semantics for an agent communication language based on speech acts. In H. Shrobe & T. Senator (Eds.), *Proceedings of the Thirteenth National Conference on Artificial Intelligence and the Eighth Innovative Applications of Artificial Intelligence Conference,* vol. 2, (pp. 24-31). Menlo Park, California: AAAI Press.

Smith, J. R. (1998, June 21). Image retrieval evaluation. In *Proceedings Of IEEE Workshop on Content-based Access of Images and Video Libraries,* (pp. 112-113). Santa Barbara, California.

Snodgrass, R. (2000). *Developing time-oriented database applications in SQL.* San Francisco: Morgan Kaufmann,.

Sondhauss, U. (1998). *Influence of philosophical concepts of causality on causal modelling in statistical research* (Technical Report No. 30/98). Dortmund: Department of Statistics, University of Dortmund.

Sowa, J. F. (1999). *Knowledge representation: Logical, philosophical, and computational foundations.* Pacific Grove, CA: Brooks/Cole Publishing.

Spink, A., & Losee, R. (1996). Feedback in information retrieval. *Review of Information Science and Technology, 31*, 33-78.

Spink, A., Wolfram, D., Jansen, B. J., & Saracevic, T. (2001). Searching the Web: The public and their queries. *Journal of the American Society for Information Science and Technology, 52*(3), 226-234.

Spirtes, P., Glymour C., & Scheines R. (2000). *Causation, Prediction, and Search (2nd ed.).* Boston: MIT Press.

Sprague, R., & Carlson, R. (1982). *Building effective decision support systems.* Englewood Cliffs, NJ: Prentice Hall.

Stallings, W. (1999). *Cryptography and network security, principles and practice.* Prentice Hall.

Starzyk, J. A., Dale, N., & Sturtz, K. (2000). A mathematical foundation for improved reduct generation in information systems. *Knowledge and Information Systems Journal, 2,* 131-147.

Statistics Canada. (2005). Monthly survey of manufacturing (Code 2101) (Publication no. Table 304-0014). Retrieved April 2005, from Statistics Canada.

Stefanowski, J. (1993). Classification support based on the rough sets. *Foundations of Computing and Decision Sciences, 18*, 371-380.

Steinauer, D. D., Wakid, S. A., & Rasberry, S. (1999, September). Trust and traceability in electronic commerce. Retrieved from http://nii.nist. gov/pubs/trust-1.html

Stitt, B. (2004). Demand planning: Pushing the rest Of the company to drive results. *The Journal of Business Forecasting Methods & Systems, 23*(2), 2.

Strasser, M. & Rothermel, K. (2000). System mechanism for partial rollback of mobile agent execution. In *Proceedings of the 20th International Conference on Distributed Computing Systems.*

Strehl, A. (2002). *Relationship-based clustering and cluster ensembles for high-dimensional data mining.* Dissertation, The University of Texas at Austin.

Strehl, A. Ghosh, J., & Mooney, R. (2000, July). Impact of similarity measures on Web-page clustering. *AAAI-2000: Workshop of Artificial Intelligence for Web Search,* Austin, TX.

Stroll, A. (1967). Identity. In *Encyclopedia of Philosophy.* Paul Edwards (ed). Macmillan Publishing, New York. 4. pp. 121-124.

Stylianou, A. C. Madey, G. R., & Smith, R. D. (1992). Selection criteria for expert systems shells: A socio-technical framework. *Communications of the ACM, 10*(35), 30-48.

Su, Z., Yang, Q., Lu, Y. & Zhang, H. (2000). WhatNext: A prediction system for Web requests using n-gram sequence models. In *Proceedings of First International Conference on Web Information Systems and Engineering Conference.* Hong Kong, China.

Sung, T., Chang, N., & Lee, G. (1999). Dynamics of modeling in data mining: Interpretive approach to bankruptcy prediction. *Journal of Management Information Systems, 16*(1), Summer, 63-85.

Suppes, P. (1970). *A probabilistic theory of causality.* Amsterdam: North Holland.

Swanson, D. (1986). Subjective versus objective relevance in bibliographic retrieval systems. *Library Quarterly, 56*(4), 389-398

Swets, D., & Weng, J. (1999). Hierarchical discriminant analysis for image retrieval. *IEEE Trans. PAMI, 21*(5), 386-401.

Takimoto, E., & Maruoka, A. (2003). Top-Down decision tree learning as information based booting. *Theoretical Computer Science, 292*(2), 447-464.

Tan, B., Velivelli, A., Fang, H., & Zhai, C. (2007). Term feedback for information retrieval with language models. In *Proceedings of the 30th Annual international ACM SIGIR Conference on Research and Development in information Retrieval,* (pp. 263-270).

Tan, K. C. (2001). A framework of supply chain management literature. *European Journal of Purchasing & Supply Management, 7*(1), 39-48.

Tang, J., Chen, Z., Fu, A. W., & Cheung, D. W. (2007). Capabilities of outlier detection schemes in large databases, framework and methodologies. *Knowledge and Information Systems. 11*(1), 45-84. New York: Springer.

Tantrum, J., Murua, A., & Stuetzle, W. (2002, July). Hierarchical model-based clustering of large datasets through fractionation and refractionation. *The 8th ACM SIGKDD International Conference on Knowledge and Discovery and Data Mining Location.* Edmonton, Canada.

Tao-Huan, T., & Theon, W. (2001). Towards a generic model of trust in electronic commerce. *International Journal of Electronic Commerce, 5*(2), 61-74.

Teorey, T. J. (1990). *Database Modeling and Design: The Entity-Relationship Approach.* San Mateo, CA: Morgan Kaufman Publishers, Inc.

Thiruvady, D. R. & Webb, G. I. (2004). Mining negative rules using GRD. In *8th Pacific-Asia Conference on Knowledge Discovery and Data Mining 2004.* (Lecture Notes in Artificial Intelligence, 3056, pp. 161-165).

Thomas, D. J., & Griffin, P.M. (1996). Co-ordinated supply chain management. *European Journal of Operations Research, 94,* 1-15.

Thomas, M., Redmond, R., Yoon, V., & Singh, R. (2005). A semantic approach to monitor business process performance. *Communications of the ACM, 48,* 55-59.

Tibshirani R., Walther, G., & Hastie, T. (2000). *Estimating the number of clusters in a dataset via the gap statistic.* (Tech. Rep.) Palo Alto, California: Stanford University, Department of Bio-statistics.

Tikk, D., Kóczy, L. T., & Gedeon, T. D. (2001). *Universal approximation and its limits in soft computing techniques. An overview* (Research Working Paper No. RWP-IT-02-2001). Perth (W.A.): Murdoch University.

Tjioe, H. C., & Taniar, D. (2005). Mining association rules in data warehouses. *International Journal of Data Warehousing and Mining, 1*(3), 28-62.

Traugott, J. (1989). Deductive synthesis of sorting programs. *Journal of Symbolic Computation, 7,* 533-572.

Treu, S. (1967). Testing and evaluation— Literature review. In A. Kent, O.E. Taulbee, J. Belzer, & G.D. Goldstein (Eds.), *Electronic handling of information: Testing and evaluation* (pp. 71-88). Washington, D.C.: Thompson Book Co.

Truong, T. H., & Azadivar, F. (2003). Simulation-based optimization for supply chain configuration design. In S. Chick, P.J. Sanchez, D. Ferrin, D., & D. J. Morrice, (Eds.) *Proceedings of 2003 Winter Simulation Conference* (pp. 1268-75), IEEE.

Tschudin, C. F. (1999). Mobile agent security. In M. Klusch (Ed.), *Intelligent information agents* [Forthcoming LNCS]. Retrieved from http://www.docs.uu.se/~tschudin/pub/cft-1999-iia.ps.gz

Tse, P. K. C., Lam, W. K., Ng, K. W., & Chan, C. (2005). An implementation of location-aware multimedia information download to mobile system. *Journal of Mobile Multimedia, 1*(1), 33-46.

Tsechansky, M., Pliskin, N., Rabinowitz, G., & Porath, A. (1999). Mining relational patterns from multiple relational tables. *Decision Support Systems, 27*(1999), 177-195.

Tulving, E. (1983). *Elements of episodic memory.* New York: Oxford University Press.

Twain, M. (2000). *Diary of Adam and Eve.* Prometheus Books.

Tynjälä, T. (2006). A formal, product structure driven design of optimized end-to-end demand supply chains. *Journal of Systemics, Cybernetics, and Informatics, 3*(1). Retrieved from www.iiisci.org/Journal/SCI/Past.asp

Tynjälä, T., & Eloranta, E. (2007). Investigating the effect of product variants, and demand distributions on the optimal demand supply network setup. *Production Planning & Control, 18*(7), 561-72.

Tyrone, W. A., Grandison (2003). *Trust management for Internet applications.* Unpublished doctoral thesis, Imperial College of Science, Technology and Medicine University of London, Department of Computing.

Uma, B. Shankar, S. K., Meher, A. G. (2007). Neuro-wavelet classifier for remote sensing image classification. *ICCTA 2007*, (pp. 711-715).

Vakharia, A. J. (2002). E-business and supply chain management. *Decision Sciences, 33*(4), 495.

Vakkari, P., & Hakala, N. (2000). Changes in relevance criteria and problem stages in task performance. *Journal of Documentation, 56*(5), 540-562.

Van der Aalst, W. M. P. (1992). *Timed coloured Petri nets and their application to logistics.* Unpublished doctoral dissertation. Eindhoven University of Technology, Eindhoven, The Netherlands.

Van der Aalst, W. M. P. (1998). Modeling and analyzing interorganizational workflows. *Proceedings of Application of Concurrency to System Design* (pp. 262-272). Washington, DC: IEEE Computer Society.

Van der Aalst, W. M. P., & ter Hofstede, A. H. M. (2005). YAWL: Yet another workflow language. *Information Systems, 30*(4), 245-275.

Van der Aalst, W. M. P., de Crom, P. J. N., Goverde, R. R. H., van Hee, K. M., Hofman, W. J., Reijers, H. A., & van der Toorn, R. A. (2000). *ExSpect 6.4: An executable specification tool for hierarchical colored Petri nets.* (Lecture Notes In Computer Science, 1825, pp. 455-464).

Van der Aalst, W.M.P. (1998). The application of Petri nets to workflow management. *Journal of Circuits, Systems and Computers, 8*(1), 21-66.

Van der Aalst, W.M.P. (2000). Loosely coupled interorganizational workflows: Modeling and analyzing workflows crossing organizational boundaries. *Information & Management, 37,* 67-75.

VanLehn, K., Siler, S., & C.Murray. (1998). What makes a tutorial event effective? In *Proceedings of the Twenty-Frst Annual Conference of the Cognitive Science Society.*

VanRijsbergen, C. J. (1979). Information retrieval. Newton, MA: Butterworth-Heinemann.

Vapnik, V. N. (1995). The nature of statistical learning theory. New York: Springer-Verlag.

Vapnik, V. N. Golowich, S., & Smola, A. (1997). Support vector method for function approximation, regression estimation, and signal processing. *Advances in Neural Information Systems, 9,* 281-287.

Varelas, G., Voutsakis, E., Raftopoulou, P., Petrakis, E. G., & Milios, E. E. (2005). Semantic similarity methods in WordNet and their application to information retrieval on the web. In *Proceedings of the 7th Annual ACM international Workshop on Web information and Data Management - WIDM'05,* (pp. 10-16).

Veryard, R. (1984). *Pragmatic Data Analysis.* Oxford: Blackwell Scientific Publications.

Veryard, R. (1992). *Information Modeling.* New York: Prentice-Hall, Inc.

Vester, F. (1988). The biocybernetic approach as a basis for planning our environment. *Systems Practice, 4,* 399-413.

Vidal, C. J., & Goetschalckx, M. (2001). A global supply chain model with transfer pricing and transportation cost allocation. *European Journal of Operations Research, 129,* 134-158.

Viitaniemi, V., & Laaksonen, J. (2006). Techniques for still image scene classification and object detection. In *Proceedings of 16th International Conference on Artificial Neural Networks* (ICANN 2006).

Vivisimo (2008). *Vivisimo search engine.* Retrieved March 1, 2008, from http://www.vivisimo.com/

Walczak, S. (2001). An empirical analysis of data requirements for financial forecasting with neural networks. *Journal of Management Information Systems, 17*(4), 203-222.

Wand, Y., & Weber, R. (1990). Towards a theory of the deep structure of information systems. *International Conference on Information Systems,* Association For Information Systems, 61-71.

Wand, Y., & Weber, R. (1995). On the deep structure of information systems. *Information Systems Journal, 5,* 203-233.

Wand, Y., & Weber, R. (2002). Research commentary: Information systems and conceptual modeling — A research agenda. *Information Systems Research, 13,* 363-376.

Wand, Y., Storey, V. C., & Weber, R. (1999). An ontological analysis of the relationship construct in conceptual modeling. *ACM Transactions on Database Systems, 24,* 494-528.

Wang, G., Huang, S. H. & Dismukes, J. P. (2004). Product-driven supply chain selection using integrated multi-criteria decision-making methodology. *International Journal of Production Economics, 91,* 1-15.

Wang, J. Z. , Li, J., & Wiederhold, G. (2001). SIMPLIcity: Semantics-sensitive integrated matching for picture libraries. *IEEE Transactions on Pattern Analysis and Machine Intelligence, 23,* 947-963.

Wang, Y., Lim, E. P., & Hwang, S. Y. (2003). On mining group patterns of mobile users. In *Database and Expert System Applications.* (Lecture Notes in Computer Science, 2736, pp. 287-296).

Weber, J., & Schäffer, U. (2000). *Balanced Scorecard und Controlling. Implementierung – Nutzen für Manager und Controller – Erfahrungen in deutschen Unternehmen* (3rd ed.). Wiesbaden: Dr. Th. Gabler Verlag. (in German)

Weber, R. (1987). Toward a Theory of Artifacts: A Paradigmatic Base For Information Systems Research. *Journal of Information Systems.* Spring, pp 3-19.

Weber, R. (2003). Still Desperately Seeking for the IT Artifact (editor's comments). *MIS Quarterly,* (27) 2. pp. iii-xi.

Weber, R. O., & Aha, D. W. (2003). Intelligent delivery of military lessons learned. *Decision Support Systems, 3*(34), 287-304.

Weiss, R., Vélez, B., & Sheldon, M. A. (1996). HyPursuit: A hierarchical network search engine that exploits content-link hypertext clustering. In *Proceedings of the Seventh ACM Conference on Hypertext,* (pp. 180-193).

Weiss, S. & Kulikowski, C. A. (1991). *Computer systems that learn: classification and prediction methods from statistics, neural nets, machine learning, and expert systems.* San Francisco: Morgan Kaufmann Publishers Inc.

Werbos, P. J. (1990). Backpropagation through time: what it does and how to do it. *Proceedings of the IEEE, 78*(10), 1550-1560.

Werner, L., Böttcher, S., & Beckmann, R. (2005). Enhanced information retrieval by using HTML tags. In H. R. Arabnia & A. Scime (Eds.), *Proceedings of the 2005 International Conference on Data Mining,* (pp. 24-29). CSREA Press.

Whinston, A. B. (1997). Intelligent agents as a basis for decision support systems. *Decision Support Systems, 20*(1).

White, A. R. (1967). Coherence Theory of Truth. *Encyclopedia of Philosophy.* Paul Edwards (ed). Macmillan Publishing, New York. Vol. 1. Pp. 130-133.

White, R. W., Ruthven, I., & Jose, J. M. (2002). The use of implicit evidence for relevance feedback in web retrieval. In *Proceedings of 24th BCS-IRSG European Colloquium on IR Research. Lecture notes in Computer Science 2291,* (pp. 93-109).

Williams, A. B. (2004). Learning to share meaning in a multi-agent system. *Autonomous Agents and Multi-Agent Systems, 8*(2), 165-193.

Wilson, M. & Matthews, B. (2004). The future of the World Wide Web? In *21st Annual British National Conference on Databases 2004.* (Lecture Notes in Computer Science, 3112, pp. 4-15).

Wisner, J. D., & Stanley, L. L. (1994). Forecasting practices in purchasing. *International Journal of Purchasing and Materials Management, 30*(1), 22.

Wooldridge, M., & Parsons, S. (2000). Languages for negotiation. In *Proceedings of ECAI2000* (pp. 393-400).

413

Woozley, A. D. (1949). *Theory of Knowledge*. Hutchinson's University Library.

Woozley, A. D. (1967). Universals. In Edwards, P. (ed.) *Encyclopedia of Philosophy*, 8, 194-206.

Wu, Q. T., & Huang T. (2000). Discriminant algorithm with application to image retrieval. In *Proceedings to the IEEE Conference on Computer Vision and Pattern Recognition, 1*, (pp. 222-227).

Xiao, Y., Yao, J. F., & Yang, G. (2005). Discovering frequent embedded subtree patterns from large databases of unordered labelled trees. *International Journal of Data Warehousing and Mining, 1*(2), 70-92.

Yahoo (2008). *Yahoo! search engine*. Retrieved March 1, 2008, from http://www.yahoo.com/

Yan, T., & Garcia-Molina, H. (1995). SIFT—A tool for wide-area information dissemination. In *Proceedings of USENIX Winter 1995 Technical Conference*, (pp. 177-186)

Yang , C. C., Prasher, S. O., Enright P., Madramootoo C., Burgess M. Goel, Pradeep K. & Callum I. (2003, June) Application of decision tree technology for image classification using remote sensing data. *Agricultural Systems, 76*(3), 1101-1117.

Yang, Q., Zhang, H. H., & Li, T. (2001). Mining Web logs for prediction models in WWW caching and prefetching. In *Proceedings of KDD-01 Workshop*. San Francisco, CA.

Yang, Y. & Pedersen, J. O. (1997). A comparative study on feature selection in text categorization. In D. H. Fisher (Ed), *Proceedings of ICML-97, 14th International Conference on Machine Learning*, Nashville (pp. 412-420). San Francisco: Morgan Kaufmann Publishers.

Yang, Y., & Pedersen, J.(1997, July). A Comparative study on feature selection in text categorization. In *Proceedings of the 14th International Conference on Machine Learning*. Nashville, TN.

Yang, Z., & Laaksonen, J. (2005). Partial relevance in interactive facial image retrieval. In *Proceedings of*

3rd *International Conference on Advances in Pattern Recognition (ICAPR 2005)*, (pp. 216-225).

Yao Y., & Karypis, G. (2001). *Criterion functions for document clustering: Experiments and analysis* (Tech. Rep.) Minneapolis, MN: University of Minnesota, Department of Computer Science.

Yao, Z. (2004). *Bidirectional hierarchical clustering for Web browsing*. Master thesis, Louisiana Tech University, Ruston.

Yao, Z., & Choi, B. (2003, October). Bidirectional hierarchical clustering for Web mining. *IEEE/WIC International Conference on Web Intelligence*. Halifax, Canada.

Yao, Z., & Choi, B. (2005, June). Automatically discovering the number of clusters in Web page datasets. *The 2005 International Conference on Data Mining*, Las Vegas, NV.

Yao, Z., & Choi, B. (2007, April). Clustering Web Pages into Hierarchical Categories. *International Journal of Intelligent Information Technologies*, 3(2), 17-35.

Ye, L. R., & Johnson, P. E. (1995). The impact of explanation facilities on user acceptance of expert systems advice. *MIS Quarterly*, 2(19), 157-172.

Yining, D., & Manjuncth, B. S. (1999). An efficient low-dimensional color indexing scheme for region-based image retrieval. In *Proceedgins Of IEEE International. Conference on Acoustics, Speech, and Signal Processing (ICASSP)*, (pp. 3017-3020).

Yip, A. M., Wu, E. H., Ng, M. K., & Chan, T. F. (2004). An efficient algorithm for dense regions discovery from large-scale data streams. In *8th Pacific-Asia Conference on Knowledge Discovery and Data Mining 2004, Lecture Notes in Artificial Intelligence, 3056* (pp. 116-120).

Yousfi-Monod, M., & Prince, V. (2005). Knowledge acquisition modeling through dialogue between cognitive agents. In *ICEIS 2005, Proceedings of the Seventh International Conference on Enterprise Information Systems*, (pp. 201-206).

Yousfi-Monod, M., & Prince, V. (2007). Knowledge acquisition modeling through dialogue between cognitive agents. *International Journal of Intelligent Information Technologies, 3,* 60-78.

Yusuf, Y. Y., Gunasekaran, A., Adeleye, E. O., & Sivayoganathan, K. (2004). Agile supply chain capabilities: Determinants of competitive objectives. *European Journal of Operational Research, 159*(2), 379.

Zadeh, L. (1965). Fuzzy sets. *Information and Control, 8,* 338-353.

Zeng, A. Z., & Rossetti, C. (2003). Developing a framework for evaluating the logistics costs in global sourcing processes: An implementation and insights. *International Journal of Physical Distribution & Logistics Management, 33(9),* 785-803.

Zhang, C., Chai, J. Y., & Jin, R. (200%). User term feedback in interactive text-based image retrieval. In *Proceedings of the 28th Annual international ACM SIGIR Conference on Research and Development in information Retrieval,* (pp. 51-58).

Zhang, D., Foo, N., Meyer, T., & Kwok, R. (2004). Negotiation as mutual belief revision. In *Proceedings of AAAI 2004.*

Zhang, H., Gong, Y., Low, C. Y., & Smoliar, S. W. (1995). Image retrieval based on color feature: An evaluation study. In *Proceedings Of SPIE, 2606,* (pp. 212-220).

Zhang, T., Ramakrishnan, R., & Linvy, M. (1996, May). BIRCH: An efficient data clustering method for very large databases. In *Proceedings of the ACM SIGMOD Conference on Management of Data.* Montreal.

Zhao, G., Deng, J., & Shen, W. (2001). CLOVER: An agent-based approach to systems interoperability in cooperative design systems. *Computers in Industry, 45,* 261-276.

Zhao, X., Xie, J., & Wei, J. C. (2002). The impact of forecast errors on early order commitment in a supply chain. *Decision Sciences, 33*(2), 251.

Zhao, Y., & Karypis, G. (1999). Evaluation of hierarchical clustering algorithm for document datasets. *Computing Surveys, 31*(3), 264-323.

Zho, S. C., Ramirez-Serrano, A., & Brennan, R. W. (2006). Cooperative multi-agent reconfigurable manufacturing environments. *International Journal of Manufacturing Technology and Management, 8,* 283-303.

Zhong, N., & Skowron, A. (2000). Rough sets in KDD: Tutorial notes. *Bulletin of International Rough Set Society, 4*(1/2), 9-30.

Zhou, Z. H., Jiang, Y., & Chen, S. F. (2000). A general neural framework for classification rule mining. *International Journal of Computers, Systems, and Signals, 1*(2), 154-168.

Zimmermann, O., Krogdahl, P., & Gee, C. (2004). *Elements of service-oriented analysis and design.* Retrieved from http://www-128.ibm.com/developerworks/webservices/library/ws-soad1/

Zou, Y., Finin, T., Ding, L., Chen, H., & Pan, R. (2003). Using semantic Web technology in multi-agent systems: A case study in the TAGA trading agent environment. *Proceedings of the 5th International Conference on Electronic Commerce* (pp. 95-101).

About the Contributors

Vijayan Sugumaran is professor of Management Information Systems in the department of Decision and Information Sciences at Oakland University, Rochester, Michigan, USA. His research interests are in the areas of Ontologies and Semantic Web, Intelligent Agent and Multi-Agent Systems, Component Based Software Development, Knowledge-Based Systems, and Data & Information Modeling. He has published over 100 peer-reviewed articles in Journals, Conferences, and Books. He has edited five books and serves on the Editorial Boards of eight journals. His most recent publications have appeared in *Information systems Research*, *ACM Transactions on Database Systems*, *IEEE Transactions on Engineering Management*, *Communications of the ACM*, *Healthcare Management Science*, *Data and Knowledge Engineering*, *The DATABASE for Advances in Information Systems*, and *Information Systems Journal*. Dr. Sugumaran is the editor-in-chief of the *International Journal of Intelligent Information Technologies*. He was the Chair of Intelligent Information Systems track for the Information Resources Management Association International Conference (IRMA 2001 – 2002 and 2005 - 2007) and the Intelligent Agent and Multi-Agent Systems in Business mini-track for Americas Conference on Information Systems (AMCIS 1999 - 2008). Dr. Sugumaran served as Chair of the E-Commerce track for Decision Science Institute's Annual Conference, 2004. He is the Information Technology Coordinator for the Decision Sciences Institute. Recently, he served as the program co-chair for the 13th International Conference on Applications of Natural Language to Information Systems (NLDB 2008). He also regularly serves as a program committee member for numerous national and international conferences.

* * *

Jafar Ali is an associate professor of Management Information Systems at Kuwait University. He holds a PhD from Illinois Institute of Technology. His research interest includes end user computing, e-learning, and business application of artificial intelligence. His research has been published in several local and international journals and presented at various regional and national conferences

Gove N. Allen is currently an assistant professor of information systems at Brigham Young University's Marriott School of Management in Provo, Utah. Dr. Allen received his PhD from the University of Minnesota in 2001. Dr. Allen has consulted for many corporations in the areas of conceptual modeling and database implementation including, AT&T, Sprint, Hewlett Packard, Micron, Intel, and American Express. More recently, he developed and continues to support WebSQL.org, a site for teaching database management that allows dynamic execution of Structured Query Language against Oracle and Microsoft SQL Server databases through a simple web interface. Dr. Allen's research has appeared in such journals as *MIS Quarterly*, the *Journal of Database Management, Information Systems Frontiers* and others. He serves on the editorial boards of several journals and is an Associate Editor of *Electronic Commerce Research and Application.*

John M. Artz is an associate professor of Information Systems in the School of Business at the George Washington University in Washington, D.C. He teaches courses in relational databases, data warehousing, Web based systems development, and philosophy of science for business and management research. His research interests are in philosophical foundations of information systems, philosophical issues in relational database and data warehouse design and philosophy of science as it applies to information systems research. Dr. Artz has also written many articles on the role of stories in computer ethics and is currently working on *How to Write a Story to Explore an Ethical Dilemma.*

Réal Carbonneau is a PhD candidate at HEC Montréal, Canada and has spent nine years implementing enterprise systems. His main research interests include investigating novel approaches to using machine learning in enterprise systems for solving various commerce problems characterized by partial and noisy information. Some of his more specific research interests are genetic algorithms, neural networks, support vector machines and software agents as well as enterprise systems and data warehouses as information sources and transactional target points. Réal has published paper in the *International Journal of Intelligent Information Technologies, European Journal of Operational Research* and *Expert Systems with Applications.*

Ben Choi, PhD & pilot, is an associate professor in Computer Science at Louisiana Tech University and is a pilot of airplanes and helicopters. He has worked in the computer industry as a system performance engineer at Lucent Technologies (Bell Labs Innovations) and as a computer consultant. He received his bachelor's, master's, and PhD degrees from The Ohio State University. His areas are electrical engineering, computer engineering, and computer science. His works included associative memory, parallel computing, and machine learning. His research interests include developing software and hardware methods for building intelligent machines and abstracting the universe as a computer.

Aboul Ella Hassanien received his BSc with honours in 1986 and MSc degree in 1993, both from Ain Shams University, Faculty of Science, Pure Mathematics and Computer Science Department, Cairo, Egypt. On September 1998, he received his doctoral degree from the Department of Computer Science, Graduate School of Science & Engineering, Tokyo Institute of Technology, Japan. He is an associated professor at Cairo University, Faculty of Computer and Information, IT Department. Currently, he is a visiting professor at Kuwait University, College of Business Administration, Quantitative and Information System Department. He has authored/coauthored over 80 research publications in peer-reviewed reputed journals and conference proceedings. He has served as the program committee member of various international conferences and reviewer for various international journals. Since 2004, he is actively involved as technical committee in the International Association of Science and Technology for Development (IASTED) for Image Processing and Signal Processing. He has received the excellence younger researcher award from Kuwait University for the academic year 2003/2004. He has guest edited many special issues for international scientific journals. He has directed many funded research projects. Dr. Abo was a member of the Interim Advisory Board committee of the International Rough Set Society. He is the editor and co-editor for more than nine books in the area of rough computing, computational intelligence, and e-commerce. His research interests include, rough set theory, wavelet theory, X-ray mammogram analysis, medical image analysis, computational intelligence, fuzzy image processing and multimedia data mining.

Christian Hillbrand currently holds a position as lecturer of entrepreneurship and innovation at the Liechtenstein University of Applied Sciences. He is also affiliated with V-Research, a competence centre industrial research and development in Dornbirn, Austria. He holds teaching positions at the Aargau University of Applied Sciences and the Haute Ecole de Gestion, Fribourg, both in Switzerland. He earned an MSc degree in business information systems from the University of Vienna in 1997, where he also received his PhD in 2004. The topic of his doctoral dissertation was the inference-based construction of managerial causal models supporting strategic enterprise planning. Prior to his research career Dr. Hillbrand co-founded the Vienna-based software and consulting company BOC in 1995 where he designed and implemented strategic decision support systems.

Sungchul Hong is an assistant professor in the Department of Computer & Information Sciences at Towson University, Maryland, USA. He received his BS in computer science from the Soongsil University in South Korea and a MS in computer science from the University of Texas at Dallas. He received his PhD in management science from the University of Texas at Dallas. His major research interests are e-commerce related technologies, including automated algorithms in various markets, XML related applications, and intelligent agent systems. He has published in journals such as *INFORMS Journal on Computing* and *Journal of Information Systems Education*.

Kevin Laframboise has been a recognized and successful teacher for several decades often cited for his passion for both student and subject. He has taught at Concordia University and at the IÉSEG School of Management in Lille France. A long-time member of the American Society for Quality, he was awarded a MSc and a PhD in quality management from Concordia University in Montreal. His course in France forms the basis for a chapter on quality management in the *Global Business Handbook*. His recent research focus has been on the effect of enterprise systems on supply chain management. Kevin has presented at many highly rated international business conferences. As well, he has authored or co-authored articles in several business publications including the *European Journal of Operational Research, International Journal of Intelligent Information Technologies, International Journal of Enterprise Information Systems, International Journal of Knowledge Management, International Journal of Information and Operations Management Education, The Journal of Supply Chain Management,* and *Leadership Quarterly*.

Hong Lin is currently an associate professor in computer science at the University of Houston-Downtown. He earned his doctoral degree from the University of Science and Technology of China in 1994. His research interests include parallel/distributed computing, multi-agent systems, and formal methods.

Salvatore T. March is the David K. Wilson professor of management at the Owen Graduate School of Management, Vanderbilt University. His research on the design and evaluation of information systems artifacts has appeared in journals such as *ACM Computing Surveys, ACM Transactions on Database Systems, Communications of the ACM, Decision Sciences Journal, Decision Support Systems, IEEE*

Transactions on Knowledge and Data Engineering, Information Systems Research, Journal of MIS, Journal of Database Management, and *MIS Quarterly.* He has served as the Editor-in-Chief of *ACM Computing Surveys,* as an Associate Editor for *MIS Quarterly,* and as a Senior Editor for *Information Systems Research.* He is currently an Associate Editor for *Communications of the AIS, Decision Sciences Journal, Journal of Database Management, Information Systems and e-Business Management, The International Journal of Intelligent Information Technologies,* and *Information Systems Frontiers.*

Xiannong Meng received his PhD in computer science from Worcester Polytechnic Institute in May 1990. He is currently a professor in the Department of Computer Science of Bucknell University. He also taught and worked at University of Texas – Pan American, Worcester Polytechnic Institute, and Nanjing Institute of Technology (now Southeast University). His research interests include intelligent Web search, information retrieval, distributed computer systems, computer networks and operating systems. He has taught a wide range of computer science courses, and published over 50 papers in journals, conference proceedings, and contributed book chapters.

Farid Meziane is a reader in computer science in the School of Computing, Science and Engineering at the University of Salford, UK. He received the Ingénieur d'état degree in computer science with distinction from the National Institute for Computer Science and a PhD in computer science from the University of Salford in 1994. His research interests are in the area of software engineering with particular emphasis on the integration of formal methods in the software development process and electronic commerce. His research is published in journals that include *Annals of Software Engineering, the Computer Journal. The requirements Engineering Journal* and the *Journal of the Operational Research Society.* He was awarded the highly commended award from the literati club in 2001 for a paper published in the *Integrated Manufacturing Systems Journal* on the use of AI in manufacturing systems. He is in the programme committee of many international conferences, in the editorial board of the *International Journal of Information Technology and Web Engineering* and *the International Journal of Information Technology Research.* He was the editor of a special issue of the *Data and Knowledge Engineering Journal on the application of Natural Language to Information Systems* and the the programme chair of the 9th International Conference on the Application of Natural Language to Information Systems (NLDB04).

Barin N. Nag is a professor of management at Towson University, Maryland, USA. He has a BTech and a MTech in electrical engineering from the Institute of Radio Physics & Electronics, University of Calcutta, India. He has a PhD in business management (management science), in association with computer science, from the University of Maryland at College Park. He has diverse research interests in routing and scheduling, decision support systems, autonomous agents, and most recently in supply chain management. He has worked with NASA and the World Bank. He has published in many journals, such as *European Journal of Operational Research, Decision Support Systems, Decision Sciences, Annals of Operations Research,* and *Journal of Management Information Systems.*

Samia Nefti is a senior lecturer at the School of Computing, Science and Engineering (CSE), University of Salford,UK and the director of the Salford Robotics and Automation centre. She has received the MS degree in automatic control and her PhD in robotics and artificial intelligence from University of Paris XII France in 1995-1999 respectively. She spent 2000-2002 as postdoctoral fellow at Computer

Science, Liverpool University. She has been involved in several European and EPSRC projects where her main work was concerned with model-based predictive control, modelling and fuzzy decision making. She is an active researcher in the field of autonomous robotics, cognitive behaviour, hybrid reasoning systems, machine learning, data mining, pattern recognition and integrating AI into complex systems and she has published extensively in the above areas. She is a full member of Informatics Research Institute, (IRIS), a chartered member of the British Computer Society, and active member of the European Network for Advancement of Artificial Cognition Systems. She is a member of several conference IPC's and reviewer for several journals such as *IEEE transaction on Fuzzy System*, *Data Knowledge &Engineering*, etc.

Antonio Picariello received the Laurea degree in electronics engineering from the University of Napoli, Italy, in 1991. In 1993 he joined Istituto Ricerca Sui Sistemi Informatici Paralleli, The National Research Council, Napoli, Italy. He received a PhD degree in computer science and engineering in 1998 from the University of Naples Federico II. In 1999, he joined the Dipartimento di Informatica e Sistemistica, University of Napoli "Federico II", Italy, and is currently an associate professor of computer science and engineering. He has been active in the field of computer vision, medical image processing and pattern recognition, object-oriented models for image processing, multimedia data base and information retrieval. His current research interests lie in knowledge extraction and management, multimedia integration, image and video databases and multimedia mobile database. He is a member of the IAPR - Italian Chapter.

Violaine Prince is professor at the University of Montpellier (southern France), in computer science, since 2000. Previously, she was professor at the University of Paris 8,from 1994 to 2000, where she contributed to the foundation of the Artificial Cognition Laboratory. Her field of research ranges from artificial intelligence and cognitive sciences to natural language processing. After a PhD at the University Denis Diderot (Paris 7) in 1986, she moved to the University of Orsay where she rejoined LIMSI, a laboratory of the French National Research Center (CNRS), specialized in artificial intelligence and human-machine interaction. In 1992, she defended her 'habilitation' thesis (mandatory for full professor positions) on language and cognition in artificial systems. Since her arrival at Montpellier, she has helped constituting the natural language processing (NLP) team (12 members) at LIRMM, the local CNRS laboratory (330 members), and presently is head of this team since 2003. She teaches natural language and artificial cognition at the graduate level, is member of the IEEE Computer Society French chapter board, has co-organized the first ACM conference in Europe about European curricula in computer science, and actively pursues researches in syntax, semantics, machine translation and artificial cognition.

Antonio M. Rinaldi graduated in computer engineering at the University of Naples Federico II, in 2002 with a thesis on the use of geographic information systems for electromagnetic risk management. He received a PhD degree in computer science and systems in 2005 from the same university, with a dissertation on the use of ontologies and Semantic relatedness for information retrieval on the Web. In the last years, he has been involved in several research and industrial projects related to multimedia data base integration and geographic information systems. His fields of interest are: Semantic information retrieval, topic detection, Semantic annotation, multimedia database and GIS.

Rahul Singh is an associate professor in the Department of Information Systems and Operations Management, Bryan School of Business and Economics at The University of North Carolina at Greensboro. He obtained his PhD in business from Virginia Commonwealth University. His research interests include Semantic e-business, security of systems, secure business process design, knowledge management, intelligent agents, data mining and machine learning. His research work has been published in leading IS Journals including *IEEE Transactions on Systems, Man and Cybernetics, Communications of the ACM, Information Systems Management, eService Journal, International Journal of Semantic Web and Information Systems, International Journal of Intelligent Information Technologies, Information Resources Management Journal, International Journal of Production Engineering Socio-Economic Planning Sciences*. Singh is the editor-in-chief for the *Journal of Information Science and Technology* (JIST). Singh is a member of the editorial board for the *International Journal of Semantic Web and Information Systems*, the *International Journal for Intelligent Information Technologies*, the *Journal of Information Technology Theory and Applications*, and the *International Journal of Information Security and Privacy*. Singh regularly teaches undergraduate and graduate course in systems development, systems analysis and design, object-oriented programming, and information assurance and systems security. Singh teaches doctoral seminars in systems design and development and in information ssurance and systems security.

Teemu Tynjala is a doctoral candidate in the Department of Industrial Engineering and Management at Helsinki University of Technology. His research interests include applied formal methods and supply chain management, especially Petri Nets, process algebras and decision support systems. Prior to joining Nokia Corporation, he worked in the Theoretical Computer Science department at Helsinki University of Technology. There he applied Petri Nets to communication protocol analysis. He holds MSc and Licentiate of Technology degrees from the same department. In 2002 Tynjala joined Nokia Research Center with the task of applying formal methods to GSM and UMTS mobile communication protocol analysis. In late 2003, he started the work on application of Petri Net theory to demand supply network optimization. In early 2007, he joined Nokia Markets with the task of developing the architecture for Nokia's product delivery processes. As part of his current tasks, he develops interactions between demand supply planning and demand fulfillment processes under various outbound delivery models, for instance, vendor managed inventory and consumer direct model

Rustam Vahidov is an associate professor of MIS at the Department of Decision Sciences and MIS, John Molson School of Business, Concordia University (Montreal, Canada). He received his PhD and MBA from Georgia State University. Dr. Vahidov has published papers in a number of academic journals, including *Journal of MIS, Decision Support Systems, Information and Management, European Journal of Operational Research, IEEE Transactions on Systems, Man and Cybernetics, Fuzzy Sets and Systems*, and several others. His primary research interests include: decision support systems, supply chain management, e-commerce systems, distributed artificial intelligence and multi-agent systems, negotiation software agents, and soft computing.

Song Xing received his BS and MS degrees in electrical engineering from Southeast University, China, in 1985 and 1990, respectively, and his PhD degree in electrical and computer engineering from George Mason University, Virginia, in 2003. From 1985 to 1995, he was a lecturer in the Radio Engineering Department at Southeast University, China and also a researcher at the National Mobile

Communications Research Laboratory, China, from 1990 to 1995. He was a visiting researcher in the electrical and computer engineering departments at the University of Michigan-Dearborn from February 1995 to April 1995 and at Boston University from May 1995 to August 1996, respectively. In 2003, Dr. Xing joined California State University, Los Angeles where he is currently an assistant professor in the Information Systems Department. His research interests include Internet traffic and performance measurement, communication networks and digital systems, importance sampling simulations of stochastic systems, and speech/image processing.

Mehdi Yousfi-Monod is doctor of the University of Montpellier (southern France), in Computer Science, since Nov. 2007. Previously, he was PhD student in the same University, from 2003 to 2007, where he worked on natural language processing and more specifically on automatic summarization through syntactico-Semantic sentence compression, and taught in computer science fields at the graduate level. In 2002, he did a Master of Science in computer science where he worked on artificial cognitive agents and learning by dialog. Between 2000 and 2002, he worked on automatic nucleotide sequences alignment at the Human Genetic Institute of Montpellier. He published several papers and developped computer tools and/or prototypes for each of the three mentionned domains.

Dong-Qing Yao is an associate professor at Towson University, Maryland, USA. He received his BS in industrial engineering from Suzhou University, and a MS in systems engineering from Shanghai Jiao Tong University in China. He received his PhD in management science from the University of Wisconsin-Milwaukee. His research interests are in the areas of global operation management, and Internet-based supply chain management. He has published in journals such as *IIE Transactions, European Journal of Operational Research, International Society of Production Economics,* and *OMEGA.*

Zhongmei Yao is currently a PhD student in the Department of Computer Science at Texas A&M University, College Station, TX. She received the MS degree in computer science from Louisiana Tech University, Ruston, Louisiana, in 2004 and the BEng degree from Donghua University, Shanghai, China, in 1997. Her current research interests include peer-to-peer systems, Markov chains, stochastic network modeling, and Internet measurements.

Index